COMPLETE GUIDE TO LIFE IN FLORIDA

— 1995-96 EDITION —

Barbara Brumm LaFreniere & Edward N. LaFreniere

Pineapple Press, Inc.
Sarasota, Florida

DEDICATION

To our wonderful son, Christopher John.
With special thanks to the rest of our family for patience and understanding during this project.

ACKNOWLEDGMENTS

We would like to thank literally hundreds of people who helped us in our research, many of whom are quoted in this book. We would especially like to thank the scores of agencies of the State of Florida for information received and telephone calls returned. And we would like to thank the 200 or so chambers of commerce for their patience in providing statistics and literature on what to see and do in each area of the state.

Inquiries should be addressed to:
Pineapple Press, Inc.
P.O. Drawer 16008
Southside Station
Sarasota, Florida 34239

CATALOGING IN PUBLICATION DATA

LaFreniere, Ed, 1951–
    Complete guide to life in Florida / by Edward N. LaFreniere and
Barbara Brumm LaFreniere. — 95–96 ed.
        p. cm.
    Rev. ed. of: Complete guide to life in Florida / by Barbara Brumm
LaFreniere & Edward N. LaFreniere. 2nd ed. 1993.
    Includes index.
    ISBN 1-56164-066-2
    1. Florida—Guidebooks. 2. Florida—Handbooks, manuals, etc.
3. Florida—Directories. I. LaFreniere, Barbara Brumm, 1952–
II. LaFreniere, Barbara Brumm, 1952– Complete guide to life in
Florida. III. Title.
F309.3.L25 1995
917.5904'63—dc20   94–42574
                CIP

Third Edition
10 9 8 7 6 5 4 3 2

Design by Joan Lange Kresek
Typography by E.T. Lowe, Nashville, Tennessee
Printed and bound by Edwards Brothers, Lillington, North Carolina

CONTENTS

SECTION ONE: Everyday Life in Florida 9

continued

SECTION TWO: A Look at Florida, County by County 200

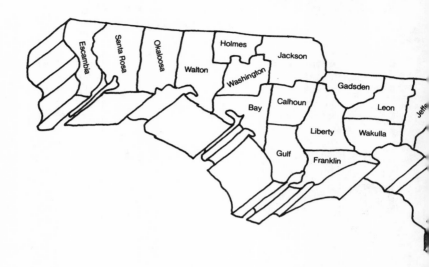

Opportunities for fishing, boating and other activities have lured millions of people to
Florida. In some of the popular areas, such as Palm Beach County (seen in this aerial view),
the population density has skyrocketed.

THE PEOPLE OF FLORIDA

AN OVERVIEW OF LIFE IN THE SUNSHINE STATE

It's 8 o'clock on a Sunday morning in March. A tall, lanky, 38-year-old real estate broker is brewing his coffee and wondering whether this afternoon's open house will finally entice a buyer. The house — 2 bedrooms, 2 baths on an 80-by-50-foot lot for $79,900 — has been on the market for a month. Sales up north were extremely slow in the early 1990s, and that means business around here was slow, too; if they couldn't sell their old homes up there, they couldn't buy new ones in Florida. Then business slowed when interest rates plummeted and retirees' incomes from investments dropped. But lately the market has seemed to have picked up.

The man is looking through the porch window at a foursome on the fifth green in his backyard. Their average age is about 72, and the agent marvels at their spryness — they don't look particularly distressed after four hours of waltzing and jigging during the neighborhood association's St. Patrick's Day dance the night before. He himself spent half the night dancing with more than a dozen women, many of them retired but still doing a respectable imitation of Ginger Rogers. He bends over to retrieve a cup from the dishwasher and discovers how sore his back muscles are. Here he is, half their age but feeling twice as old. He chuckles.

Across the street, a 31-year-old Midwestern transplant is leaving for work. He has a full-time job and two part-time jobs so that he can keep up the mortgage payments. When he moved down here in the late 1980s, he knew it was a boom time and saw opportunity everywhere. He fell in love with the area and moved without fully anticipating the strains that Florida's ubiquitous low wages — not to mention a severe recession — would have on his family. It was a good thing that he at least had set aside some down-payment money; otherwise these houses, which many Northerners consider inexpensive, would have been out of reach. Were he not working all these jobs, he'd be among hundreds of thousands of Floridians wishing for affordable housing. Today, he will freely concede that his quality of life up north was better. He saw more of his family. Now he questions whether he made the right move, and his wife wonders how long he can maintain this pace. She worries that he's drinking too much.

Next door to them, a recently retired couple sporting Izod shirts, Ralph Lauren jeans and boat shoes is packing the new Lincoln for a four-day trip to Disney World. That's about an hour and a half away from this neighborhood in the Tampa Bay area, on Florida's west coast. This couple is always doing something — sports activities, bridge clubs, garden clubs, travel. Theirs is the quintessential Florida retirement.

The palm trees sway gently in the 10-knot breeze in this community, which was built in the early 1970s. At that time, the 1,800-square-foot model sold for the princely sum of $13,000 — if you ordered the 30-foot porch and a garage. Now they go for $60,000 to $90,000. Within a mile, you can find smaller properties in the $40,000 range; mobile homes for as little as $15,000; new state-of-the-art four-bedroom houses with pools and sunken rooms for $400,000; waterfront manors for $1 million or more.

The real estate man sips his black coffee. Perhaps another young couple will buy that house this afternoon. After all, only 18.4 percent of the year-round population is over the age of 65. It is becoming more of a young person's state; the median age was 36.4 years in 1990. Maybe the buyer will be a young professional, someone who can afford to enjoy Florida's myriad outdoor and cultural amenities, someone who will love the state — someone who will provide a sales commission that will enable the agent to take his wife, a homesick native Bostonian, back to New England for the family reunion that she's dreamed about for three years.

The temperature is 68 degrees. Once again, it is sunny. Today the high is expected to be 78, quite a contrast from the day-in, day-out 90-plus degrees of late May until October, when the year-rounders shun outdoor chores after 9 a.m.; when the humidity usually tops 60 percent and often goes up near 100 percent; when you can don sunglasses in your air-conditioned living room, go outside in ultra-high humidity and find the glasses so fogged up that you have to remove them; when the Lincoln and its counterparts have long since fled north to cooler climes.

The real estate man watches as the foursome prepares to tee up on the next hole. One of them is smirking to himself. He just birdied the last hole, and is well on his way to winning a free breakfast from the other three. The agent smiles. He thinks about the Lincoln owner, whose trademark greeting is to feign a yawn and harrumph: "Ho-hum. Another lousy day in paradise."

For many of the state's 13,608,627 year-round residents, for hundreds of thousands of Snowbirds (retirees who spend several months in the state during the winter), and for millions of tourists, Florida certainly can be paradise. Its 58,664 square miles contain almost 10,000 miles of shoreline, if you include offshore islands, sounds, bays, rivers and creeks, and 4,500 square miles of inland water. About 700,000 boats are registered in the state, and many of them also ply the waters of the Intracoastal Waterway on both coasts. There are about 1,100 golf courses, hundreds of theme parks and other attractions, innumerable fairs and festivals, and beaches that are as appealing as any. Professional sports — baseball, golf, football, basketball, auto racing, pari-mutuel racing, even hockey — abound. Some counties have enough cultural events to keep you busy throughout the year. You'll rarely be in any area where you'll be more than a few miles from a fishing spot. You'll be able to visit any of the 100 or so state parks, museums, gardens or historical sites. And you'll discover that some big metropolitan regions, where 30 years ago some of today's major thoroughfares were dirt roads, have quickly transformed themselves into Major League cities.

The state had the nation's 19th-highest per-capita income in 1991: $18,992, a 1.9 percent increase over the previous year and $100 lower than the national average. You'll find that the cost of living is lower than in many northern states. You might be able to get yourself a three-bedroom or even a four-bedroom home for about $100,000 in many areas, and perhaps that will include a swimming pool. You might find that dinner for two even at some of the more popular restaurants will cost the same as breakfast for two in some Northeastern urban areas. If you're looking for conveniences, the most densely populated counties — mainly those along the shore from the center of the state down to the Keys — will offer you dozens, if not hundreds, of local places to shop and eat.

You'll soon learn that people tend to spend more time in leisure pursuits, and less time concentrating on their careers. You won't be stuck in six months of bone-chilling cold with nothing to do but work, watch TV, shovel snow and dream about next winter's trip south. You'll encounter more of a festive atmosphere here. People are in Florida to enjoy the winter, or to enjoy their two weeks in the warm weather. They're away from the approaching blizzard and love to snicker while reading local newspapers' stories about the weather back home.

Paradise indeed. But Florida's phenomenal growth has caused a variety of problems. While few will argue that the state is in imminent peril of an environmental Armageddon, serious problems exist. Many rivers and lakes have become polluted. Some drinking water supplies are in danger of being contaminated. More than half of Florida residents breathe air that violates clean-air standards for ground-level ozone.

And the dilemmas go way beyond ecology. In 1991, 15.4 percent of the population was below the poverty level ($13,924 for a family of four and $6,932 for an individual). The total across the country was 14.2 percent. And, as in the many parts of the nation, health care is at a crisis stage — 2.2 million Floridians lacked adequate insurance in 1990. In April 1993, the legislature voted to overhaul the health-care system, aimed at enabling everyone eventually to get care. It created 11 regional cooperatives that would negotiate the best rates for employers.

Solutions to many of the state's problems have been elusive, largely because of the expense. Many people are here to avoid things — cold weather and high taxes, largely — and politicians have been reluctant to risk vengeance from the electorate, including retirees who bring lots of money into the state and who don't have to worry about an income tax or estate taxes here. Nevertheless, Florida is at the point where some people believe that the growth is enkindling an age-old paradox: So many people are moving here to enjoy the good life that they're destroying the state.

Take the region where the real estate agent lives, for example. It is among the most densely populated parts of Florida, yet its features are not unlike those found along the coasts in central and southern Florida. Unlike the northern part of the state, which has four seasons, relatively few Snowbirds, and a tourist season that peaks in the summer, this area, with its sub-tropical climate and massive services industry, is geared to year-round tourism. With that comes an array of problems.

But the state's population is largely transient and thus political movements don't crystallize easily. Many people do not think of Florida as "home." They often stay here for a season, or plan to move out of the state at some point, and frequently don't feel a need to work toward making "my state" better. Only about a third of residents in recent years have been native Floridians. Florida Trend magazine's 1989 Economic Yearbook referred to the state's "pass-the-buck" culture and a "weak sense of community." Dr. Leslie G. Brewer, a Largo psychiatrist (see Psychology chapter), puts it another way: A lot of people are here to take what they can get out of Florida, not to give what they have.

Here are some of the problems you will likely encounter in the more populated parts of Florida:

Overdevelopment

Nature lovers would be aghast. An ad in the Miami Herald touted a 1.32-acre tract that it said was suitable for a 10-house subdivision. Uncommon? Not in many areas. For example, in Dade, Broward and Palm Beach counties in Southeast Florida and in some sections of Tampa-St. Petersburg and environs, quarter-acre lots are considered very large, and half-acre tracts are described — only somewhat facetiously — as near-mini-estate-sized. Granted, this is not the case throughout the state. One-acre lots are the norm in many parts of North Florida and in many inland areas. But land is at a real premium in other parts of the state. These places have become congested with frustrated, white-knuckled motorists who wait endlessly in traffic, with houses so close together that you can barely walk between them, with huge shopping malls, with major state and county roads that are cluttered with strip mall after strip mall, and with enough fast-food places to give you unheard-of cholesterol levels. High-rise condominium and hotel complexes line many beaches, making public access more difficult.

Simply put, some counties became over-built, and the state decided that it was time to impose strict regulations in the face of an almost uncontrolled surge in development. Between 1979 and 1987, according to the federal Bureau of Labor Statistics, Florida had been No. 1 in the nation in employment growth. Between 1987 and 1989, however, the state had dropped to No. 7, with an 8.4 percent growth rate. Office vacancy rates started to skyrocket. Overly optimistic developers had assumed incorrectly that the boom would continue. For example, in the fourth quarter of 1989, office vacancy rates in Boca Raton, in Palm Beach County, were 32.2 percent, the highest among major American cities surveyed by Cushman & Wakefield, a real estate and market research firm. Other areas with high rates — between 16 percent and 26 percent — were Fort Lauderdale, Miami, Orlando, Tampa and West Palm Beach.

In 1985 came Florida's Growth Management Act. A key part of it is known as concurrency, under which road, water, sewer, drainage and other utility services must be in place before the impact of a new development can occur. Some counties have been charging local impact fees on residential construction as well — as much as $5,000 or more per house in some of the more developed areas. The reasoning is that the rest of the taxpayers shouldn't have to pay for services needed in a new development. The law gives local governments a way to help schools, roads and utility services catch up with the population increase. It's an effort that's so serious that the state legislature in 1990 rejected a proposal that would have eased the burden on developers, who, along with big business interests, are a powerful lobby.

Under the Growth Management Act, which took effect fully in 1990, a total of 459 reports — from counties and municipalities — were submitted to the state for approval. An example of what the act is intended to do: A county might reject a plan for a small shopping center because the site is too close to a major thoroughfare, which would exacerbate traffic congestion.

The overall intent of the law is to maintain or improve the quality of life. Among the goals: protecting water resources; dealing with drainage in parking lots and on streets by controlling stormwater runoff; forcing local governments to develop land-use regulations and decide where housing and commercial developments are appropriate; forcing communities to preserve agricultural land and other natural resources.

Another major intent is to prevent leapfrog developments, under which developers buy huge tracts of cheap rural land away from the cities and put the cities in a position where they have to run sewer, water and other utility lines out to the development. The problem is that many municipalities got behind in paying for such improvements, state officials said.

But the law is not designed to prevent growth — most plans allow for about 20 years' growth in residential and commercial development anyway. The purpose is to direct the growth away from environmentally sensitive areas and to ensure that each locality has adequate public facilities. While some officials claim that growth has slowed, the state community affairs department said in 1993 that no authoritative study had been done and that the recession had caused such a slowdown that the question largely was moot.

Traffic

Many thoroughfares — interstates, county and state roads — are so crowded that traffic often crawls, at best. When a road was being repaired near Clearwater a few years ago, one man, expressing more than just humor, tried to make money serving coffee and juice, on the road, to morning rush-hour commuters. Along parts of the coast, as many as 100,000 motorists — even more in some parts of Southeast Florida — will use a single road each day. In the worst areas — notably around Miami, Fort Lauderdale, West Palm Beach, St. Petersburg, Clearwater, Tampa and Orlando — there is a great deal of frustration. Try I-95 around Miami and you'll find motorists darting from lane to lane, hoping to reach their destination a few seconds early, and you'll start wondering whether some drivers are transplanted New York City cabbies who were exiled from Manhattan for unbridled rudeness. It would take billions of dollars to solve all of the road problems, money that the state does not want to have to spend.

Heavy traffic usually means that shopping centers and restaurants are seldom more than a few blocks away. But that spawns a mindset that you'll have to adjust to: If, for instance, you have a hankering for Mexican food and the nearest Mexican restaurant is 10 miles away, that is considered "out of the area" and you'll have to "take a trip" to get there.

There's another side to this: waiting in lines in the big tourist communities. Getting to the shopping center or to the restaurant is one thing; getting inside the building is another. In the more congested regions, it may take a while to find a parking spot at the local shopping center during the day or on weekends. At many restaurants, particularly those on the water, you may have to wait an hour or two to get a table during the winter — even if you have a reservation. In fact, a lot of places don't accept reservations. With the influx of tourists, they don't have to. Some advice? Ask neighbors about the best times to eat at various restaurants. Some may be less crowded (and less expensive) during "early-bird" specials, for example. And you may discover that you'll have to schedule tee-off time a week or more in advance at the more popular local golf courses.

The Weather

It's a Sunday afternoon in mid-October at Tampa Stadium. The Tampa Bay Buccaneers' quarterback drops back for a pass, finds his target and fires the ball. He misses. There is a roar of applause from the crowd, though it has nothing to do with the on-field activities. The sun finally has dipped behind a large cloud, and it looks as if there will be about 10 minutes' respite from the 90-degree heat. You'll find similar reactions at other outdoor functions.

The heat and the humidity can be brutal during the hot months, roughly from May to October in central and southern Florida. Ask year-rounders about the weather, and most will tell you that it never gets above 95 degrees, that heat waves up north are worse because the temperature can rise above 100. They'll often say that the heat doesn't bother them in Florida; they're used to it, and as long as the air conditioner is working, they're comfortable. For roughly half the year, the weather in most of Florida is beautiful — daytime temperatures in the 60s, 70s and low 80s, nighttime temperatures usually in the 50s and 60s. But come summer, Floridians deal with the heat the way northerners deal with the cold — they wait it out. Humidity levels of 60, 70, 80 percent and even higher, combined with 95-degree heat, day after day, for months, will, at the very least, slow you down considerably. Once you move into the hotter areas of the state, it may take you several years to get your old energy level back (see Psychology chapter).

Education

Florida's public school system compares poorly with other states', according to comparative studies by the U.S. Department of Education. U.S. education reports in recent years have listed Florida's dropout rate as among the nation's highest, though state officials dispute the figures and say that the federal comparison ignores factors that otherwise would show a better rate. In addition, the federal reports show that Scholastic Aptitude Test scores have been declining here since 1972.

Some critics suggest that overall, Florida's education system lags way behind other states'. But many educators say that the quality of education is hard to quantify. If you're moving into an area and want to figure out how good the local schools are, you can check a variety of statistics: What are the average SAT scores? How high is the dropout rate? How high are teacher salaries compared with those in other counties? What percentage of high school graduates continue their education after high school? How much money does the local system spend on each pupil?

These statistics are available, though they are rarely ballyhooed by local officials or in chamber of commerce brochures. But statistics are not likely to tell you everything. Dr. William Snyder, an education consultant and professor of education leadership at Florida State University, says that parents can visit schools and ask the following questions:

— How good is the leadership at the school principal level? Does the principal provide strong instructional leadership? This usually is a key indicator.

— Is there an atmosphere of caring for students and a perception of a family-oriented school community? You can often tell just by walking into a school.

— Are student progress and performance tracked well and frequently? Beyond report cards every six weeks, how will a student know, day by day, week by week, how well he or she is doing?

— Is there evidence of individualized learning and teaching strategies? For example, is the curriculum designed to allow for individual differences? Does everyone sit in a line and do the same things at the same time, or are students allowed to move at their own rates and master the content if given adequate time and proper instruction?

— Is the school rewarding all good performance? For instance, Snyder says, not only the class valedictorian should be recognized — efforts from a variety of students should also be rewarded.

Crime

Florida's standard crime rate was the highest in the nation (except for Washington, D.C.) from 1983 into the 1990s. The reasons are varied. A spokesman for the Florida Department of Law Enforcement said, "There's not a sheriff or a police chief who won't say that drugs are at least one of the causes." In recent years South Florida has led the nation in the seizure of cocaine. South Florida has such a reputation for drug trafficking that visiting foreign journalists have told federal drug agents that they are disappointed when they don't see cocaine lining the streets.

The state also developed a reputation — and a dramatic loss in European tour business — after 10 foreign tourists were killed between October 1992 and April 1994.

There are other reasons for the state's high crime rate: 1. The climate. Criminals are less likely to be out if the temperature is below freezing. This is borne out in the statistics. In 1989, Texas, Arizona, New Mexico, California and Georgia had crimes rates that were higher than such populous, urban states as New York, New Jersey, Illinois and Michigan. 2. The transient population. Nearly 40 million people visit Florida in a single year. This obviously increases the population density, and makes it more likely that someone either will commit a crime or be victimized by one. Most areas of the state with the highest crime rates are among the most densely populated, and those with the lowest rates are among the least densely populated.

The standard crime rate, which is the basis for national comparisons, consists of these crimes: murder, forcible sex offenses; robbery; aggravated assault; burglary/breaking and entering; larceny/theft (pickpocketing, purse-snatching, shoplifting, thefts from buildings, thefts from coin-operated machines, thefts from motor vehicles, all other larceny); and thefts of motor vehicles. The rates are calculated by the number of offenses per 100,000 residents. Florida's rate in 1993 was 8,204 offenses per 100,000 population, down by about 400 offenses since 1989. The worst county, with 13,268 offenses per 100,000 population, was the Miami area, followed by the Tallahassee, Gainesville, Tampa, Jacksonville, Fort Lauderdale, Florida Keys, Orlando and Palm Beach areas. The lowest rates were in counties in the northern part of the state.

Bugs

An engineer who is a native Floridian remembers occasional childhood visits to an aunt in Southeast Florida during the 1940s.

"The mosquitoes were so bad," he says, "that she would spray the screen before opening the door, continuously spray the gap as she opened the door, walk out, close the door, and then reverse the process as she let us in. Say what you will about the development boom, but to us natives the main benefit has been that we don't have to worry about the mosquitoes to that extent."

Indeed, in densely populated parts of the state where yesterday's wetlands are today's monuments to the cement-block industry, mosquitoes are of much less concern now. But they are still a problem in most parts of the state, as are other pests that have left many Floridians — particularly the uninitiated — scratching their heads wondering why they're putting themselves through this.

Says Dr. John P. Smith, a medical entomologist with the Florida Department of Health and Rehabilitative Services: "People here have to develop a higher tolerance for bugs; otherwise, they'll either go crazy or spend half their income trying to get rid of them." Residents have to accept the fact that there are more insects here, or else "it's like moving to the coast and complaining about hurricanes," says Smith.

Some facts about mosquitoes: There are about 70 kinds of mosquitoes in Florida, Smith says, and almost 20 of those can be banes to humans: Some bite, some can transmit diseases, and some do both. They are found throughout the state and their numbers depend in part on rainfall, though you'll usually find them around wetlands regardless of the amount of rain. The one common denominator is water, however; mosquitoes cannot exist without it. Generally, if there's no rain, this means that fewer habitats will exist to support them.

Some mosquitoes can be dangerous. Every couple of years, Eastern Equine Encephalitis, a mosquito-borne disease, kills one or two people in Florida, typically those living near swamps in rural areas in northern Florida. However, the disease has been known to strike in other areas of the state as well, Smith says.

And about every 15 years, cases of the St. Louis strain of encephalitis, another mosquito-borne disease, develop. The last outbreak was in 1990; by November of that year, 87 people in 23 counties from Ocala to Miami had contracted it and another 47 were presumed to have contracted it. Five people had died. Symptoms vary, and in less serious cases people may simply feel as if they have a flu. In more serious cases, victims may have convulsions or become comatose. The mosquitoes that carry this disease actively feed at dusk and dawn. People should wear protective clothing, such as long-sleeved shirts, use insect repellant liberally, and curtail nighttime activities during these outbreaks.

There are freshwater mosquitoes and salt-marsh mosquitoes. The extent of the annoyance depends on where you live. If you're near the Everglades or near other marshes or wetlands, the probability of encountering the problem will be much greater than if you live in a highly developed county. Inland, you'll have to pay attention to water-holding containers — old tires, for example, as well as vases, metal cans and anything else that can hold stagnant water. The trick is to dispose of these items and, in such things as wading pools, change or circulate the water. Some experts believe that a square foot of water can result in as many as 100,000 mosquitoes. In temperatures of 85 to 90 degrees, it can take only about half a week for mosquitoes to develop from the egg to adulthood.

Smith says that most Florida counties provide mosquito-control programs. There are about 50 programs, he says, and, of those, 15 to 20 are well-funded and well-rounded. Some counties spend millions of dollars on equipment, people and research. They monitor and eliminate mosquito sources by spraying and by introducing mosquito-eating fish into ponds and fish pools. Beyond these top-notch pest-management programs, Smith says, are some of varying quality, right down to the guy who goes around in a truck and sprays at night. But in about a quarter of Florida's counties, he says, there are no programs.

Other bugs: Mosquitoes aren't the only pests in Florida. Among the others:

— Biting gnats and biting midges (or, as they're known in South Florida, sand flies) are the same insects that go by different names. Here, too, there are freshwater and saltwater varieties, but the season is shorter than that for mosquitoes. The saltwater flies peak in the summer, but are found throughout the year in South Florida; the freshwater seasons are in the spring and in the fall.

— Deer (or yellow) flies. These are the worst biters in the state, Smith says. The bites are very painful and the lesions that they cause persist for a couple of weeks. It is possible that the flies transmit some disease, but the evidence is far from conclusive, Smith says. These pests are at their worst in March or April and in August.

— Fleas. They come out in force in April and May and build up during the summer. If you have a pet that goes outdoors, you'll have to deal with this problem, but you'll find that fleas in Florida are immune to some insecticides. Smith says entomologists don't believe that flea collars will help much; the animal will have to be treated with a special shampoo when needed and you'll have to spray the pet's bedding area, maybe the carpet, and, if the problem is real bad, your yard. Throughout the state, you'll have to re-treat these areas with pesticides every three weeks or so, Smith says.

— Blind mosquitoes (or midges). These are more of a nuisance than a health problem, and they are found around the Orlando-Winter Haven-Lakeland region. They don't bite. They breed in local lakes, come out in the summer in huge numbers and can blanket the side of a house, leaving specks on the house and on your car. A pet can't walk across the lawn without finding these things packed in its nostrils and mouth. Problem times: June through August.

— Love bugs. These insects mate in the air, and come out for a few weeks usually in May and in September. The problems with these are similar to those with the blind mosquitoes, though the love bugs affect more people — they're prevalent in the central and northern parts of the state. They're hard to get out of your hair, literally, and that's why you'll see special plastic shields on car grills. Drive across the state at these times of year and it will look as if someone has taken a huge brush full of white paint and flicked it at your windshield. These pests can dissolve the paint right off the car.

— Cockroaches. There are more species of these here than in most any other state, Smith says. There are numerous outdoor species, including the palmetto bug (otherwise known as the Florida woodland roach). People panic when they see these creatures, which grow to more than an inch in length and look like miniaturized prehistoric killer ants that made Hollywood horror films famous. They don't breed indoors, but they'll find their way into homes when it rains a lot. Another common type of roach is the German cockroach. It's about half an inch long and breeds indoors. It is the most widespread indoor pest next to the flea, Smith says, and can be a frequent problem in apartment buildings.

— Spiders. These are found throughout the state, but are most common around wetlands and in heavily wooded areas — subtropical-jungle-type sites, Smith says. They can surround the exterior of a house and they often get inside. You'll find that you just can't get rid of them altogether. Every couple of weeks during the summer, you'll end up sweeping them down or spraying insecticide on the outside of the house. Rain washes off the insecticide, so after a downpour you have to start all over again.

If You've Decided to Make the Move

You and your spouse and your 25-year-old daughter spent another March vacation in the beautiful Sunshine State. You've just gotten back up north. Your hometown, with its long-dormant mill buildings, snow-covered golf courses, $175,000 "starter homes" and grumpy neighbors, is a mighty depressing sight. You're going to retire in January, and you've decided to put the old homestead on the market and head to Florida. As for your daughter, she's tired of paying $700 a month for a small apartment, quite a chunk on a $450-a-week salary. She'll never be able to buy a place in town. So she decides that she'll join you and buy her own house.

It happens often. It develops quickly. Florida Fever. Year-round residents will tell you that the best prescription — a dose of reality — should include a visit in July. That's when a lot of state residents buy houses. The market generally is slower because the winter residents have left, and you often can get a better deal at this time of year; properties may well have been on the market since the winter tourist season. A Snowbird who has had a Florida property on the market for six months and has been firm about the price may well have just returned from a successful day on the links and be more inclined to accept a few thousand dollars less. The same goes for estate properties; heirs may not want to have to carry the tax burden and often let a house go for a bargain price.

But perhaps even more importantly, you'll get a very good idea of what a hot and muggy Florida summer is like. The next time you're in a heat wave up north, imagine what it would be like if it lasted five months. Another common summertime problem: You may find that many of your future neighbors will continue to spend their summers up north, and that the heavily populated winter community thins considerably in the summer. You may get lonely.

Some other suggestions:

— Try it out for a year. If you own a house in another state now, you might want to rent it out so it's there if you choose to return to it. If you're lucky enough to have a nest egg, use the interest to rent a place here so that you don't invest your life savings in a property that you may want to get rid of in six months. If you plan to be a Snowbird and want to buy a house here that you can rent out during the summer, you may find occasional frustrations in being a landlord. Many tenants — including retirees — are set in their ways, and things have to be just so. Someone may not want the cable TV outlet in the Florida room; it's too hot out there in the summer and too cool in the winter. A tenant might demand that you change a lot of things that never would have bothered you.

— If you're going to buy, beware of strictures placed on homes in some retirement communities and condominium associations. Some people are pretty persnickety about any types of changes. You'll find associations run by various committees, and you may resent complaints — your placement of a new shrub, for example — that may leave you wondering if this really is a free country. Check the regulations and talk to neighborhood residents about how restrictive the community regulations — and leaders — are.

— If you have your heart set on a house, hire a contractor, architect, engineer or other independent expert to study the construction work very, very carefully to make sure that building codes have been met. Don't assume anything. South Florida had a reputation for tough building-code standards, but Hurricane Andrew proved that shoddy workmanship and outright violations of the code — many roofs were improperly braced or not even entirely nailed down, for example — were rampant. Even shortly after the hurricane, a grand jury reported that in the rush to rebuild, the same shoddy workmanship and code violations were evident. It's probably a good idea to hire someone outside the county building inspector's office; you don't want to end up with someone who did the original inspections.

— Find out about the quality of the water. Ask the local office of the state Department of Environmental Regulation if there are any problems with it. If you find out that the water is fine, as you likely will in most areas, bring along a paper cup on your house-hunting trip. Chemicals, such as chlorine, are added to the water in many systems around the state. In some counties, you get county water, or city water, or water from another source. Two miles away, that other house that may still be on your list might have water that tastes immeasurably better. If you fall in love with a house, but the tap water tastes as if it's coming directly from the swimming pool, find out about water filters. You might want to get a charcoal or other type of filter for drinking water and for water to make your coffee palatable. You can install a filter under the kitchen sink, for example.

— Shop around for the best deal. Housing prices vary markedly throughout the state. Find out what area best suits you economically, culturally and in terms of population (check the county-by-county listings in this book). You'll find that a new 2,200-square-foot house may cost $250,000 on a quarter-acre lot in a more densely populated city where little buildable land is available, and $90,000 on an acre in another, less urbanized community. Make sure that the price is consistent with what the county says it's worth. A major Florida housing contractor was convicted in 1992 on 40 counts of defrauding homebuyers in a scam said to involve 10,000 overpriced homes.

— Spend more than a few hours in the county where you think you want to live. Find out how bad the traffic is, how long it will take you to get to work, whether you'll have to arrange tee times on the local golf course a week ahead of time, how long the lines will be at the grocery store and at local restaurants, whether there is a sizable population in your age group and whether there is a hospital nearby. Live in town for a week in the summer and for a week during the winter tourist season. Find out whether you are likely to enjoy — or, at the very least, to be able to tolerate — the things that will affect your everyday life.

Do as much research as you can. Ask questions everywhere you go.

Know what you're in for, so that you don't end up disillusioned. If you've planned properly, you'll find plenty here to enjoy.

THE PSYCHOLOGY OF LIFE IN FLORIDA

Strong gale-force winds had damaged trees in a retirement community outside St. Petersburg. The next day, a woman in her mid-60s was in her back yard cleaning up some brush.

After summoning the courage, she introduced herself shyly to new neighbors and invited them into her house, which was spotless except for a dish on the kitchen counter that contained the remnants of a can of Franco-American spaghetti. All the blinds were drawn, and only one small fan had been turned on.

"We'll probably have to get the neighborhood association to help take down that big tree," she said nervously. She paused for several seconds and then covered her face with her hands. Tears streamed down her face.

"I don't know what to do," she said. "I'm all alone now. I lost my husband six months ago. I'm very sorry. But I'm glad you came over. I don't talk to anyone and I don't know how to handle this."

The woman is among thousands of Floridians who have lost loved ones and who don't know how to cope. Other people — including younger residents — encounter other problems. Many may have visited the state during vacations, been enticed by the state's climate and natural beauty, and made a move unprepared for new challenges. Some, lured by slick, colorful brochures, have decided after little research to move to a part of the state where they may not fit in.

What types of things should a would-be Floridian consider when deciding whether to relocate here? Which geographic areas might best be suited to him or her? What types of plans should people of all ages make to avoid loneliness? How can someone plan for retirement so that he or she can derive the full benefit of it? What kinds of precautions should be taken to become comfortably acclimated in new surroundings without the extended family? What can happen psychologically if someone loses a loved one and how can he or she deal with that loss?

Three Florida psychiatrists — Dr. Elliott Stein of Miami Beach, Dr. E. Michael Gutman of Orlando and Dr. Leslie G. Brewer of Largo — were asked these questions, and here they offer insight into life in the Sunshine State. Dr. Stein, who has a private practice in Miami Beach, was the president of the American Association for Geriatric Psychiatry from 1985 to 1987. Dr. Gutman was president of the Florida Psychiatric Society in 1988-1989 and is in private practice in Orlando. He also has been chief psychiatrist of Mental Health Services of Orange County. Dr. Brewer is in private practice and specializes in addiction treatment at the Center for Problem Resolution in Largo.

For the Young People of Florida

You're a carpenter in the Northeast. It's the middle of February. You're standing in your driveway, knee-deep in snow, about to shovel the drifts so that your in-laws and half a dozen friends will have a place to park at the party that you and your wife are throwing tonight.

You're telling yourself that you've had it with the harsh winters, with staying indoors, with spending half the year anticipating the warm weather and outdoor jobs. A week ago, you were in Florida. That sure was wonderful. The beaches, the palm trees, all that sunshine. And what a boom state! It would be so easy to find a construction job down there. Well, why not try? You decide to talk it over with your wife. After all, darn it, life is to enjoy.

Such scenarios are not uncommon. Thousands of people — more than 1,000 per day in the late 1980s — move to Florida. Some think everything through, decide that the benefits by far outweigh the disadvantages and make a smooth transition. On the other hand, some people don't figure on certain things. They end up feeling disenchanted and resentful. Some leave (though no statistics are kept on their numbers). What types of plans should you make so that you can adjust well and enjoy life in Florida? Dr. Brewer makes several suggestions:

Behind the facetiousness of this bumper sticker is an element of truth: Youth and the elderly often have difficulty relating to each other. However, many Floridians will attest that grand-parenting can be one of life's finest pleasures.

1. Pay attention to your relationships. You may be leaving an area where you have family, where you have roots. Try to make friends in Florida before you arrive. Relationships here, in general, tend to be more tenuous. Many Floridians have no long-term roots here. Snowbirds, for instance, are gone during the summer. It's a transient state, with many people coming and going. People may end up feeling lonely and, as a result, some may find themselves turning to alcohol or drugs. (According to the Florida Alcohol and Drug Abuse Association, a survey showed that 70 percent of Floridians who entered treatment programs in 1988 were in the 18-to-34-year-old category, and 65 percent of all those admitted were seeking treatment for cocaine addiction).

2. Move to an area where you have a better chance of making friends in your own age group, and join clubs. Look at the makeup of the local population (see the county-by-county listings for population breakdown by age groups). If you're considering the Tampa Bay area, for example, you'll find that 12.4 percent of the population of Hillsborough County (Tampa and environs) is 65 years of age or older. Across the bay in Pinellas County (the St. Petersburg-Cleawater area), that percentage rises to 25.8. Brewer suggests getting into active groups — watersports clubs, for instance — where you'll have more opportunities to make lasting friendships. Don't assume that the social structure you want will exist here. Part of the problem is that young people tend to get frustrated with old people, and vice versa, he says. Some elderly people may not hear as well, may misunderstand things, may well prefer the Big-Band sound to pop rock. The quality of education may be a young parent's top concern, but a retiree whose children are already grown may argue against tax increases that would improve the local schools; schools may no longer affect that retiree. There can be a mutual anger between the two groups, and the frustration often comes to a head in supermarket lines and in traffic. The bottom line: People often lack identification with others who aren't in the same age group.

3. If you have school-age children, get as much information as you can about the quality of the local school system. Brewer says that some recently transplanted northerners have chosen to send their children to private schools and discovered even then that their children were way ahead of their classmates. Traditionally there has been a difference between Florida and some other states over the standards of education, though there is an increasing commitment toward quality education here now, he says. Politically it's bad to have substandard education, and politicians realize that and are trying to do what they can, he says. One of the problems, he says, is that they're fighting an old perception that there was less need here for education. For years many Florida conservatives didn't demand better education; they didn't believe that schools were worth raising taxes over; they were afraid that retirees would balk at paying higher taxes, and they didn't want to risk the cash that retirees brought to the state.

4. Prepare youself for a slower, more relaxed pace. It gets hot and humid in most parts of Florida, and people have to slow down — it's not a question of laziness. The heat can drain your acuteness and awareness, says Brewer, who moved to Florida from Detroit in 1980. People usually think better in crisper weather because the nervous system gets more stimulated. The heat can act as an anesthetic and slow the transmitters to the brain, and it takes several years of adjusting to get your energy levels back up. But there's a flip side to that. Many people enjoy the more relaxed atmosphere of Florida, though it may take a while to change some old habits. For example, in most businesses the open-collar shirt is just fine here. It may seem anathema at first, but after a short while you'll likely yield to local custom and shed the vest, and then the coat, and, finally, the tie. And you'll wonder why you ever had to invest so much money in career outfits.

5. Be realistic about career opportunities in Florida. Innumerable high-tech companies have moved to the state, and other big industries are defense, aerospace, finance, insurance and real estate, but Florida is largely a tourism state, and that means low wages. As a whole, Brewer says, people are less career-oriented in Florida. Work is not all-encompassing, as it can be in northern climates where there are few opportunities for outdoor activities in the winter. However, Florida offers many such opportunities year-round, and people take time to enjoy them. Nevertheless, in densely populated areas of Florida, a high percentage of people work for restaurants, hotels, departments stores and small shops. Often those jobs pay the minimum wage. If you're doing well up north to the point where you can go out and get waited on, you may find that waiting on tourists in Florida will make you regret that you made the move. And if you're in other industries, you'll likely find smaller paychecks here. For example, you may get $25 an hour doing carpentry work up north. Here, you may be able to get little more than $10 an hour. If you're in real-estate sales and sell $250,000 homes up north, prepare yourself for

the smaller commissions that come from selling houses for an average of $100,000, and many for considerably less. Brewer suggests that you accept the reality that you may have to make career sacrifices if you move here.

6. Be realistic about leisure pursuits. You may get up on Saturday morning, pick up the dry cleaning, get stuck in all the traffic, do some banking, get home, load up the car, head for the beach, and discover that the tourists have already beaten you there. Or you may love watersports, but, having come from the Midwest, discover that the headaches of owning a boat in saltwater have negated one of the goals that brought you here. Or you may enjoy scuba diving, settle on the Gulf Coast and realize that you'd be facing level sand and virtually no natural coral unless you drive several hours across the state. Originally your intention in moving was to be near the water. You may end up wondering whether it was worth it.

Choosing the Area That's Right for You

Are you more interested in the Atlantic Coast or in the Gulf Coast? There may be good psychological reasons for choosing one over the other.

On the Gulf Coast (the western part of Florida), the ocean is calmer. It's easier to swim and wade in the water. Boating is less dangerous, housing generally is cheaper, and you'll probably find that golfing and other activities are less expensive as well. The traffic, while heavy in some urban areas, is lighter overall. This side of the state is less congested. This is smaller-town Florida.

The East Coast generally is more glamorous and faster-paced, though still slow compared with some northern states. It has the hubbub of the Miami and Fort Lauderdale metropolitan areas, as well as Cape Canaveral and the Daytona Speedway, for example. There are more storms in this part of Florida and the ocean waters are rougher. This is larger-city Florida.

What does this mean? Psychologically, says Gutman, this may mean that the Gulf Coast connotes safety. People there don't have to fight as much traffic, and many elderly people tend not to tolerate frustration very well. The East Coast, on the other hand, is more animated and faster-moving. If you want safety and more isolation, you may feel safer on the Gulf side. If you want more glamor, more expensive dining, you may prefer the Atlantic Coast; there's more affluence there —

it's been developed longer, and is more monied.

And, generally, north of Orlando, it's cooler in the winter. Farther south, you'll be able to find more year-round outdoor activities.

Other Factors To Consider

When looking for an area in which to settle, Gutman suggests that people — particularly the elderly — use this checklist:

1. Find a place that's close to a hospital, doctors and good medical services. This represents the safety factor. Call the county medical society to find out where the doctors and hospitals are. Some areas have many hospitals, but others, particularly some Panhandle counties that are not tourist-oriented, do not. And look for good police, fire and ambulance services.

2. If you're a member of the Elks, the American Legion, the VFW or some other fraternal organization, set up some contacts at the post in the town you plan to move to. This will provide you with more security — a home away from home.

3. If you're looking for a retirement atmosphere, make sure that you do plenty of research. Learn where the retirement communities are. If you've heard about a new development, ask the local chamber of commerce for specifics and go LOOK at it. Try to settle in a place that's popular among other people in your age group. And check out the association's common facilities, such as a clubhouse or a pool, to see whether they offer opportunities for socializing and activities that you enjoy. In addition, you may want to live in an ethnic community. For example, Canadians, ever proud of their heritage, tend to stay in groups, Gutman says (the Hollywood area, in southeast Florida, is a popular area). Many motels even fly the Canadian flag. These visitors, psychologically, are sojourners in a strange land, and together they can create closer, more charitable residential communities. You won't find armed-camp mentalities here as you might in larger cities.

Coexistence in the Sunshine State

Florida has been a tourist-oriented boom state for years. How resentful are native Floridians toward Snowbirds and other visitors? In Gutman's view, there's not much of an obstructionist attitude about economic expansion, aside from concerns about the environment. It's simple economics; tourists bring in the dollars that keep Floridians in business. Natives may complain about tourists and raise questions about their driving abilities, for instance, but overall, he says, there's no serious resentment. Disney World is one example: It is geared toward children and has a cheery atmosphere. That tends to blunt some criticism and allow for more tolerance in the Orlando area, Gutman says. The word "Snowbird" has a slightly negative connotation among year-rounders, but most year-rounders do not sneer at the Snowbirds, according to Gutman. The winter guests provide a common ground for identification and for discussion. Many year-rounders may complain that the Snowbirds use the state's services and don't pay taxes unless they own property (although even short-term visitors pay sales taxes and help keep businesses going). And, of course, visitors do put a strain on the highway system. But you won't find much snobbishness or direct, go-to-hell comments, Gutman says. Indeed, many year-rounders have a lot of friends who are part-time Florida residents and who they miss during the off-season. Brewer puts it this way: Many year-rounders were once Snowbirds or tourists themselves, and it may take years for them to feel like bonafide Floridians who can feel comfortable complaining about part-time residents.

Youth and the Elderly: American Social Values

How do young people generally relate to the elderly?

Generally they don't spend a lot of time thinking about them, Gutman says. Unless young people have a reason for dealing with the elderly — for example, if a person is in a fraternal organization or in a business that deals with older customers — they won't have much interest in older people. Younger folks are forging ahead. Theirs is a world of innovation, of computers, of a futuristic society, and they don't look upon the elderly as being on the leading edge of development. Youth is interested in youth and beauty, not in wrinkles or false teeth, Gutman says.

As a society, we do not respect elders in the way that the Japanese do, Gutman says. Japanese families live together and revere the elders. But in the United States, a young person does not believe that an elderly person is as vibrant or as refreshing as youth. The elderly person may be described as a has-been, as an old fogey, as a fragile person. "What does HE know?" the young person may ask. It

is only when a young person starts a family, thinks of church and begins to develop roots that the age groups start to merge, Gutman says.

The elderly tend to perceive teen-agers as careless and reckless, as people who drive too fast and who are too rough. An elderly person might assume that if he's walking down the road, teenage drivers might run into him. The elderly do not like hubbub or stress. Too many things at once are disquieting. They might view kids at a mall as a pack of thugs and be afraid of getting bumped or harassed. As the elderly person goes by them, he may think, "Look at them. They're making lots of noise." One of the main threats to an older person is getting knocked off his feet as he watches kids running or walking fast.

What does all this mean? The elderly should stick together, Gutman says. They should form their own networks — groups, clubs and other organizations. That way they have common interests and more clout (look at the lobbying power of AARP), and they can rely on each other in a friendlier atmosphere.

One unfortunate thing is that the elderly generally don't see themselves as reliable because they're not as honed or as sharp as they once were. They take longer to get going. But if you look at an office filled with older workers, you'll find an office that is more efficient, less cliquish, more productive and less gossipy, Gutman says. The older person tends to be more reliable and trustworthy, to revere institutional rules and authority. His word is his bond.

How will the young person of the 1990s behave once he or she reaches the golden years? Probably the same way as the elderly person of today, Gutman says. These are general morals, and as a person grows up and matures, he or she becomes seasoned and more responsible.

For Older Floridians

Preparing for Retirement

You're 64 years old. You've been a car salesman up north for 42 years. Since that first vacation to Florida 15 years ago, you've spent a lot of time dreaming about the day when you will turn in that last set of keys, shake the boss's hand, pack up the old buggy, and drive south to the land of warm weather, palm trees, and more golf courses than you'll be able to count.

A dream? Indeed, but it will be stressful and can turn into a nightmare of loneliness if you don't plan properly, says Dr. Stein.

Work does four major things, he says.

— It fills time.

— It provides income.

— It provides an identity ("I am a car salesman," for example).

— It provides relationships by giving you an opportunity to make friends.

But what happens when you retire? First, you will have lots of time on your hands. You probably will not have nearly as much income. You will have lost your identity as that car salesman, which can be shocking because many people define themselves by their jobs and, in retirement, struggle with this question: "Who or what am I now?" And you will be out of the daily environment in which close professional relationships can develop.

Once you retire, you've lost those four important aspects of your life. You need to try to replace them with other activities, and work at finding new things to do, Stein says. Otherwise, your life, which may have offered plenty of satisfaction when you were working, can change quickly and leave you feeling alone and isolated.

Those who retire and do well, Stein says, are people who are involved in other activities of importance and interest. These include hobbies — playing sports or following teams, traveling, watching the stock market, gardening, enjoying cultural activities, shopping, joining clubs, doing charity work. These hobbies fill time, stimulate the mind, provide a new identity ("I am a golfer, or a charity volunteer, or a sports nut," for instance) and offer an opportunity to meet people and develop relationships.

In addition, those who make a smooth transition into retirement have planned their finances well. Though your income may have dropped precipitously, you may think that it will be adequate, but many people eventually find that it is not. Many have not planned for unanticipated expenses. Housing costs, taxes and grocery prices may rise significantly in another year, and you may have forgotten to set aside air fare money for the kids' visit next Christmas. The best advice? Make sure that your income will exceed anticipated needs, just in case, Stein suggests.

And to prevent yourself from feeling isolated as your retirement begins, set up a network of contacts in your new area so that when you arrive, you will know where to find the local supermarket and the church. Many people retire with only minimal information about a new area; they may simply have visited it on vacations. They do not know anyone and are unfamiliar with the territory. You should carefully research the area, and make contacts early. Ask for referrals in your hometown, to start. Ask friends and relatives. Make contacts in

your new church. Try to make social contacts. Find out where your local branch of the American Legion, or other organization, is located. If you move and have no contacts, you may feel lonely and have difficulty making friends, Stein says. Brewer says that some retirees will develop chemical dependencies, sitting in front of the TV set all day drinking. And for those who drank heavily before retirement, the problem can worsen here because people no longer have work to occupy part of the day. At some liquor stores what you're likely to find is elderly people loading up their carts, he says.

You also should plan ahead regarding the family. Some people move to Florida to be near their children. Others, however, move away from their families, and this can cause problems, Stein says. When you were living down the street from your children, you may have had a lot of face-to-face contact. When there were problems, you'd all be there to help each other. You may have babysat for your children, gone out to dinner with them, and shared other enjoyable activities. You watched your grandchildren grow, and you felt needed. But now, you're a thousand miles away. You no longer see your family frequently. You may be more reluctant to call them for help or advice, and they may be, too. Now you may feel isolated. How can you all cope? Stein suggests that you anticipate all these things. Talk to family and friends and plan visits in advance. Plan trips during spring break or during the holidays. Work out routines for telephone calls and letter-writing. Stay in touch frequently.

Gutman says he has noticed that few people return to their old homes, but most who do have a need to restore the family ties. They do not like the breaking up of the family support system, and the ones who return usually find their dependence on their children is too strong, and they cannot make the break. The yearnings to reunite are usually very strong and, at the very least, cause many people to return to the north for at least part of the year, he says.

What Will I Do with All This Time Off?

Having all this time off can be stressful, and it may show up first in your marriage. For years, you and your spouse saw each other in the mornings, on some evenings and on weekends. Now, you may be together 24 hours a day, 7 days a week. You're not used to this. How will you adapt?

Assuming that the husband worked and the wife was the homemaker, the retired man now may feel out of place in the house — an intruder in another person's bailiwick. He may feel subservient to his wife's instructions, feel pushed around, and have a hard time adjusting day to day. If both spouses shared chores before, it will not be quite so difficult, but if not, some adjustment may be necessary. In addition, there will be problems, though less serious, in a family in which both spouses had careers outside the home. Given typical societal roles, it will still be easier for the retired wife; previously she had done double duty — having a job and taking care of the house — and will have an easier time adjusting.

What can you do to ease such friction? First, be aware it's a problem and talk about it, Stein says. You might divide up the chores, for example. Second, consider spending time apart in outside activities. And choose more than one activity. For instance, you may look forward to a garden club meeting once a week, but what about the other six days? Similarly, it's a fantasy to believe that you'll play golf every day. It's best to get involved in as many things as you feel comfortable with.

Once you broach the subject of outside activities, one spouse may feel hurt and take it personally. Stein's advice? Don't feel bad about it, and don't take it personally. It's based on an individual's needs, and new activities offer the same opportunities for enrichment that work did before.

What types of activities do Florida retirees get into? Some may decide to go back to school full-time, or to just a class or two. Some may work as volunteers. Yet others may want to start new careers. There are some caveats here, though. First, starting a new career may be de rigueur in the future, as more people retire earlier and fewer younger people are available to join the work force. But for now, Florida has hundreds of thousands of retirees and in parts of the state there is intense competition for jobs. In the Miami Beach area, for example, people who want to work as volunteers, say, in a hospital, are sometimes put on waiting lists, Stein says. It may be very difficult, if not impossible, to find such jobs in some areas today. So again, try to find out what is available.

Why People Should Stay Active

Thousands of people move to Florida with the idea of retiring. They see it as the land of milk and honey, and as a place for relaxation, warmth, sleep and safety. But for physical — and sometimes financial — reasons, many develop a need to be active. If people are idle, they tend to develop physical problems, dwell on those problems, and then allow those problems to become emotional ones. Some people may get aches and pains and complain constantly about them.

Dr. Gutman uses the example of an old sewing machine. It's old, but it does the job. If the shop closes down for a while and the machine is not in use, its operator may return and find that the machine doesn't work. It's not in shape. It's been in disuse. The same goes for a person. After having been idle for a while, a person can develop disabilities. When the body and mind are active, there's a sense of vitality. But otherwise a person may lose his sense of mission and get stale. Restlessness and sleeping disorders can develop. How can this be prevented? Physical exercise is one of the most essential things that an elderly person can do, Gutman says. Even light sports and walks on the beach are helpful.

Elderly people tend to get cranky, and that has to do with the nervous system. The body is less adaptable and less pliant. People often feel more threatened. They can get agitated, restless, irritable. Quite simply, the body is wearing out and doesn't handle change as well. Reflexes are not as good. People don't respond to things as quickly as they once did. Eyesight deteriorates. Distance-judging can be more difficult. All of these things make productive activity more difficult.

And sometimes a problem known as the Sundown Syndrome can occur. During the day you have light, sunshine, heat and general activity. The sights and sounds of daytime abound. Trucks go by. The mail gets delivered. You pick up groceries. The neighbor mows the lawn. These are positive influences and help keep the brain active. But as the sun goes down, some elderly people can become confused, less lucid and drowsy because these influences are not there to stimulate the nervous system.

People generally are happier in a sunny environment, but they also need to get the right flow of stimulation in the nervous system. If too much or too little activity is going on around them, they can become irritable, disruptive and even violent, Gutman says. The extent varies, but can be more pronounced among patients in nursing homes. In general, if you hear a sound during the day, you say, "So what?" But if you hear that same sound at night, you may get easily disturbed. You also can face the danger of falling. Emotionally and physically you're not as quick on your feet. You can become agitated and restless. The sooner the sun goes down (as in the winter), the sooner the disquieting symptoms can erupt.

You need the proper balance of stimulation. Too much — such as fast driving, too much noise, too much hustle and bustle — can be threatening. A lot of change and movement can connote danger to your well-being. But on the other hand, if you get too little stimulation, the brain's sensory receptors won't activate the nervous system. The system shuts down because it's not being used, and your capacities can become marginal. Spread your activities around; don't do too much, and don't do too little.

Preparing for the Inevitable

Planning Ahead

Death. It will happen to all of us, yet many people are so superstitious about the word that they will not plan ahead, instead leaving loved ones to make quick decisions in a moment of intense grief. How can you prevent this from happening? Stein suggests that you consider three options:

— Make sure you have a will and that it is current and legally acceptable in Florida. Update it regularly, at least every three to five years. Many people simply never get around to drawing up a will, which can lead to an enormous amount of anxiety for survivors.

— Even before you get sick, look into the possibility of a living will. This is a written statement that says how people should care for you in case life support or other heroic measures become the only option. Would you want to be on life support even if there is no hope?

— Consider a "durable family power of attorney." This allows someone to take over your affairs if you are unable to do so. That person can sign for surgery, for example, or sign to admit you to a hospital, pay your rent or take care of other bills. Some people hesitate to do this because they may not trust someone. Stein suggests that you find a relative — a spouse, a son or a daughter, for instance — in whom you have implicit faith, and entrust him or her with such powers.

Other experts also suggest that spouses communicate with each other about the family finances. Here's an example of what can happen: A woman who had just become a widow sold her car and put her small retirement ranch on the market because she wanted the money to pay bills on her house in the Midwest. The real estate agent became concerned after finding several dozen pieces of mail in the woman's mailbox. The agent called the woman's daughter, who lived nearby. The daughter went to look through the envelopes, did some research and called her mother.

"Mom, you're not in bad financial shape," she said.

"Do I have enough money to buy a car?" the mother asked.

"Mom, these are dividend checks. For God's sake, you're a millionaire. Didn't Dad ever tell you?"

That example had a happy ending. Others don't, and survivors may be left confused, uninformed and insecure.

When Illness Strikes

It is very difficult to adjust to increased incapacity. When people become ill, many become afraid of dying. This is more of a problem for the "younger old" — people in their 50s, 60s and some in their 70s, Stein says. People suddenly have to face the reality of their own mortality, or that of a spouse or parent, and this is a shocking realization. For older people, those in their 70s and 80s, one of the most anxiety-producing things is a chronic illness. Those in the older group are less frightened of dying but more frightened of being incapacitated. They worry about losing their independence, about caring for themselves or about becoming a burden to others. They worry about financial resources and support systems — spouses, children, other relatives. Sometimes the person they are concerned about burdening is even a next-door neighbor, someone who will help with the shopping or take them to the doctor.

Those feelings are normal, Stein says, and there are ways to ease the fears of imposing on people. But these are not things that most people ordinarily think of. For example, he suggests that you plan for your own funeral. Get your own cemetery plot and decide what kind of funeral arrangements you will want. And, morbid as this may seem, he suggests that you write your own obituary. Why? So that your survivors, in the midst of grief, won't have to do it. This is a very difficult, but sensible, thing to do, he says. Too often people will think, "If I'm dead, I won't care what happens." As a result, the funeral industry makes a fortune, Stein says, and some morticians may sell your survivors a "bill of goods" that may be frivolous. For instance, your grieving spouse might be tempted to buy the gold-plated, lead-lined casket and sign for a funeral that costs thousands of dollars. Is this what you would want? Or would you rather set aside the extra money for your grandchildren's education? These are difficult things to plan for, but if you ignore them, someone else will have to suffer through these decisions at a terrible time, Stein says.

The Grieving Process

Five years ago, you and your spouse retired and moved to Florida. Now your spouse has died. You are alone. You miss your long-time companion and helper. Your income may drop. You're no longer part of a couple. Even the new friends that you've made may be lost because couples tend to socialize with couples. You feel out of place. Worst of all, you are still grieving for your spouse.

The amount of time that the grieving process takes varies, depending on the nature and length of the relationship, the support system, and the nature of the final illness, Stein says. If death is abrupt (if the person has been sick no longer than a year or two), the reaction to it will be much different than if it occurs after years of burdensome suffering. In the first case, people will be shocked, surprised and traumatized. In the latter case, people may be relieved. And the number of possible reactions between those extremes is infinite.

Normal mourning lasts a few months to a couple of years, Stein says. In the beginning, people will be upset and shocked. They may not be able to function well at first, and feel lonely, lethargic and sad. They may cry and will miss the person. But over time, they will start doing things, take better care of themselves and look forward to other activities. There is an important distinction between normal mourning and serious depression. And normal mourning will vary; different cultures, religious and social groups have different processes for socially appropriate bereavement. But in general, normal grief is not the same thing as an abnormal depression. In normal grief, people may feel sad and depressed, and not sleep or eat well. They may imagine seeing or hearing the person who has died, or wake up thinking that the person is close by. They also may feel guilty about things that were done or not done, may think of their own death, and may wish they had died in place of the loved one. But over time, these feelings will be less intense.

On the other hand, some people may become severely depressed. They can't function, may feel guilty about other, unrelated things, may blame themselves constantly, and may be morbidly and excessively preoccupied with feelings of worthlessness. They may stop eating, not sleep for extended periods of time, not bother to bathe or change clothes, or even not eat food that is brought to them. Once these things happen, people need professional counseling, Stein says. After a few days, people who are grieving normally will eat, and otherwise begin life anew. But if someone loses more than a couple of pounds, if he isolates himself, even when others try to draw him out, or if he is preoccupied with the loss and other things for a while, he will need help.

Grieving is a gradual process, Stein says. But eventually, people will start going out, visiting friends or relatives, resuming usual activities and feeling that life is different and even enjoyable.

Should You Decide To Remarry

A decision to remarry can lead to complications. Many arguments may ensue and jealousies arise. Family members will want to know who will inherit what. The children may have the most difficult time adjusting.

The best way to cope, Stein says, is to talk about it and try to develop an understanding. Try to come to an agreement, and hope that everyone — child and parent alike — will accept it. You may need help in doing this, either through individual counseling or family therapy. Or you may choose to hire a lawyer to write a nuptial agreement that clearly delineates the inheritance.

There may be no easy solution to all of these problems. The new spouse or the children may be upset and feel left out. A parent may feel caught in the middle. The problem can be further complicated if both spouses have children who don't get along.

Seeking Help

In many Florida towns, support groups have been set up to help surviving spouses adjust. Local religious groups also are active throughout the state. And people with any type of problem can call county medical associations for a referral to a qualified therapist.

As of 1993, Florida was the sixth most densely populated state, with 252 people per square mile. contrasted here are high-rises in southeast Florida and a cattle ranch in the central part of the state.

THE POPULATION OF FLORIDA

In early 1970, the Orlando area consisted of little more than orange groves and cattle herds. Disney World was nearly two years from completion. Some of today's coastal resort areas had not even been conceived. In many areas of the state, the phrase "traffic congestion" meant a 30-second wait at a two-lane intersection. Florida's population was 6.2 million.

Today that figure has more than doubled. Estimates by the Bureau of Economic and Business Research at the University of Florida put the number of permanent state residents at 13,608,627 as of April 1, 1993, nearly a 40 percent increase since 1980. During the boom years of the late 1980s, as many as 1,000 people moved into the state each day. At one point, the U.S. Commerce Department reported that of the fastest-growing metropolitan areas of the country, 8 of the 10 were in Florida. In order they were: 1. **Naples**, 2. **Ocala**, 3. **Fort Pierce**, 4. **Fort Myers-Cape Coral**, 5. **Melbourne-Titusville-Palm Bay**, 6. **West Palm Beach-Boca Raton-Delray Beach**, 7. **Austin, Texas**, 8. **Orlando**, 9. **Fort Walton Beach**, and 10. **Las Cruces, N.M.**

Florida remains one of the fastest-growing states, though the rate slowed after 1990 amid the recession. Nevertheless, the increase from 1990 to 1993 was estimated at 670,556, or 5.2 percent.

In the national context, Florida passed Ohio, Illinois and Pennsylvania since 1984 to become the fourth most populous state, behind California, New York and Texas. The population increase between federal censuses in 1980 and 1990 was the biggest ever in Florida — 3.2 million people — and the second largest in the United States, behind California. And the rate of increase during the decade — 32.7 percent — was the fourth highest, behind Nevada, Alaska and Arizona.

Florida, of course, is a haven for retirees, though the stereotype might suggest that the vast majority of state residents are elderly. In fact, the median age in 1990 was 36.4 years, meaning that half were younger and half were older. As of 1993, those 65 and over made up 18.4 percent of the population — about 2.5 million people. That's up from 18.2 percent in 1990, 17.3 percent in 1980 and 14.5 percent in 1970. Florida's percentage is still by far the highest among Sunbelt states (in the latest comparison, Arkansas was second, at 14.9 percent, followed by Oklahoma at 13.5 and Arizona at 13.4), and higher than the other most populous states (Pennsylvania, 15.7; Massachusetts, 13.9; New Jersey, 13.6; Ohio, 13.2; New York, 13.1; Indiana, 12.7; Illinois, 12.6, and Michigan, 12.2). Nationwide, the percentage was 12.7.

In addition, Florida's elderly population soars during the winter, raising the percentage. No one keeps figures on the number of Snowbirds — including thousands of Canadians — who spend at least several months in the state each year. But Stanley K. Smith, director of the population program for the University of Florida, estimates the number at one million people, at least. Added to the 2.5 million year-rounders who are 65 and older, this would mean that during the winter, older residents and Snowbirds would account for more than one person out of every four.

But the majority of Florida residents — specifically, 61.4 percent — were younger than 45 as of 1992, according to the university. Those 14 years old or younger made up 19.1 percent of the population — higher than the year-round 65-plus population. The predominant age group consisted of those 15 to 44 — 42.3 percent of the overall population. And people 45 to 64 accounted for 20.2 percent, making them the second-largest group.

Retirees

During a 1990 episode of television's "The Golden Girls," Estelle Getty was trying to persuade Beatrice Arthur to join her in a mother-daughter beauty pageant in the Miami area.

"At my age, how many challenges do I have left in life? Trying to get halfway across the street before the don't-walk sign comes on?" she asked facetiously. "Trying to stay awake on the john...Realizing it IS the john?"

The situation comedy, employing humor to examine issues confronting the elderly, widows and divorcees, had made another point. Some elderly are frail, hopeless and poor; others are optimistic and are enjoying their golden years.

Such is the case in Florida. A 1988 report conducted for the state found that 12 percent of Florida's elderly population had very low or low incomes and "live in deplorable housing conditions." Another study found that more than 29 percent of the public-subsidized housing units in the state serve the elderly. (See the Cost of Living chapter for more information about these studies.)

On the other hand, well-to-do Snowbirds flock to the state each year, buy retirement dream homes, drive Cadillacs or Lincolns, play golf several times a week, go out to dinner frequently and join enough clubs and plan enough events to keep them busy until they're 95. It is this type of life that the chambers of commerce are touting, and they are luring people by the thousands each year.

Regardless of income (and no statistics are available to show exactly how much the average retiree earns), there are many thresholds for enjoying retirement. For one person, a 100-foot yacht might provide the diversion. A person who is on a fixed income might get a lot of pleasure out of buying that 25-cent cup of coffee once a week at the senior club's meeting. And another person might be able to afford two rounds of golf a week, go out to breakfast and dinner once or twice a week, catch the 99-cent special at the local movie theater, own a $65,000 home in a retirement community and be able to help the kids and the grandchildren finance their trip south for the holidays. There are sharp contrasts throughout this state.

But the elderly feel particularly comfortable in some areas. In terms of absolute numbers, Dade (Miami), Broward (the Fort Lauderdale area), Palm Beach and Pinellas (St. Petersburg-Clearwater) typically have had large numbers of residents 65 or older. But among the 10 counties with the highest percentages of residents 65 and older, the population ranged from 33,544 in Flagler County to 293,966 in Pasco. This suggests, as noted in the Psychology chapter, that elderly people generally like to be with other elderly people. Many also prefer the slower-paced life of an area that is small enough to make them feel secure yet large enough to offer many social events.

Of the 10 counties with the lowest percentages of residents 65 and older, eight were in the northern part of the state, where the climate is considerably cooler.

Counties with the highest percentages of residents 65 and older (1992)	Counties with the lowest percentages of residents 65 and older (1992)
1. **Charlotte** (southwest), 34.5	1. **Union** (northeast), 7.5
2. **Highlands** (central), 33.4	2. **Baker** (northeast), 8.2
3. **Pasco** (central west), 32.3	3. **Leon** (northwest), 8.4
4-5. **Sarasota** (southwest), 32.0	4-5. **Alachua** (northeast), 9.5
4-5. **Hernando** (central west), 32.0	4-5. **Okaloosa** (northwest), 9.5
6. **Citrus** (central west) 31.6	6. **Santa Rosa** (northwest), 9.9
7. **Lake** (central), 28	7. **Nassau** (northeast), 10.2
8. **Manatee** (central west), 27.9	8. **Seminole** (central), 10.6
9. **Flagler** (northeast), 27.6	9-10. **Hendry** (southwest), 10.9
10. **Martin** (central east), 27.4	9-10. **Duval** (northeast), 10.9

Source: 1993 Florida Estimates of Population, Bureau of Economic and Business Research, University of Florida

**Counties with the highest
percentages of residents
44 years old and younger**

1. **Union** (northeast), 75.7
2. **Leon** (northwest), 75.4
3. **Alachua** (northeast), 75.3
4. **Baker** (northeast), 73.7
5. **Clay** (northeast), 71.2
6. **Duval** (northeast), 71.0
7-8. **Okaloosa** (northwest), 70.9
7-8. **Hamilton** (northeast), 70.9
9-10. **Hendry** (southwest), 70.7
9-10. **Orange** (central), 70.7

**Counties with the lowest
percentages of residents
44 years old and younger**

1. **Charlotte** (southwest), 41.6
2. **Citrus** (central west), 43.8
3. **Hernando** (central west), 44.7
4. **Highlands** (central), 45.2
5. **Sarasota** (southwest), 45.6
6. **Pasco** (central west), 46.3
7. **Flagler** (northeast), 47.8
8. **Lake** (central), 50.1
9. **Indian River** (central east), 50.9
10. **Martin** (central east), 51.1

Source: 1993 Florida Estimates of Population

Population Density

Florida is among the most densely populated states. As of April 1, 1993, the estimate was 252 people per square mile of land area — roughly one person for every 2.53 acres. In 1992, the last year for which comparative statistics were available, the state was sixth in this category, behind New Jersey (1,050), Massachusetts (765), New York (384), Ohio (269) and Pennsylvania (268). Nationwide, the figure was 72.

In computing the people-per-square-mile data, the University of Florida figures in the total land area in the counties, which is not adjusted for land that can't be developed, such as government parks, or is uninhabitable, such as swamps and marshes. And no one can say just how much of each county is residential, how much is commercial, how much is industrial and how much is agricultural. However, there is no county where all of the land is residential. Because of this, you can assume that in residential areas there are likely to be more people per square mile than the total county figures would indicate.

As of April 1, 1993, the 10 most densely populated counties — and the number of people per square mile, the key cities in each, and the areas of the state in which they are located — were:

The most densely populated counties
(in people per square mile), 1993

1. **Pinellas** (the St. Petersburg-Clearwater area, central west), 3,087
2. **Broward** (the Fort Lauderdale area, southeast), 1,090
3. **Seminole** (the county just north of Orlando, central), 1,009
4. **Dade** (the Miami area, southeast), 1,003
5. **Duval** (the Jacksonville area, northeast), 907
6. **Hillsborough** (the Tampa area, central west), 824
7. **Orange** (the Orlando area, central), 802
8. **Sarasota** (Sarasota, southwest), 508
9. **Palm Beach** (West Palm Beach, southeast), 465
10. **Lee** (the Fort Myers area, southwest), 445

The least densely populated counties
(in people per square mile), 1993

1. **Liberty** (northwest), 7
2. **Lafayette** (northwest), 10
3. **Glades** (southeast), 11
4-5. **Taylor** (northwest), 17
4-5. **Dixie** (northwest), 17
6. **Franklin** (northwest), 18
7. **Calhoun** (northwest), 20
8-9. **Jefferson** (northwest), 22
8-9. **Gulf** (northwest), 22
10. **Hamilton** (northeast), 23

Population by County

Every county in the state gained population between 1990 and 1993. Two — Hardee, in southwest Florida, and Gadsden, in the northwest — lost population between 1980 and 1990; otherwise the boom, while not even across the state, has been phenomenal in many counties.

Between 1990 and 1993, Broward County gained the most, in terms of absolute numbers — adding 61,981 residents. Next were Palm Beach (54,720), Orange (50,289), and Hillsborough (32,080).

Dade, which had the largest numerical increase from 1990 to 1992, lost population between 1992 and 1993 because of Hurricane Andrew. Still, over those three years — 1990 to 1993 — the county had a net increase, of 13,922.

The 10 fastest-growing counties from 1990-1993 (in percentages)

1. **Union** (northeast), 17.4%
2. **Flagler** (northeast), 16.9%
3. **Osceola** (central), 16.7%
4. **Jefferson** (northwest), 15.0%
5. **Collier** (southwest), 14.8%
6. **Hardee** (southwest), 13.0%
7. **Dixie** (northwest), 11.6%
8. **Gilchrist** (northwest), 10.9%
9. **Santa Rosa** (northwest), 10.6%
10. **Hernando** (central west), 10.5%

The 10 slowest-growing counties from 1990-1993 (in percentages)

1. **Lafayette** (northwest), 0.4%
2. **Dade** (southeast), 0.7%
3. **Taylor** (northwest), 1.5%
4. **Pinellas** (central west), 1.6%
5. **Liberty** (northwest), 2.7%
6-8. **Holmes** (northwest), 3.5%
6-8. **Escambia** (northwest), 3.5%
6-8. **Bradford** (northeast), 3.5%
9-10. **Washington** (northwest), 3.8%
9-10. **Hillsborough** (central west), 3.8%

As of 1993, the counties with the largest population were Dade (Miami), Broward (Fort Lauderdale), Palm Beach, Pinellas (St. Petersburg-Clearwater) and Hillsborough (Tampa).

The April 1, 1993, figures below are estimates from the University of Florida; the April 1, 1990, counts are based on the federal census.

Largest numerical population gains, 1990 to 1993

1. **Broward** (Fort Lauderdale area, southeast), 61,981
2. **Palm Beach** (West Palm Beach area, southeast), 54,720
3. **Orange** (Orlando area, central), 50,289
4. **Hillsborough** (Tampa area, central west), 32,080
5. **Duval** (Jacksonville, northeast), 28,637
6. **Brevard** (Melbourne-Titusville area, central east), 28,057
7. **Polk** (Lakeland-Winter Haven area, central), 24,561
8. **Seminole** (Sanford-Altamonte Springs area, central), 23,369
9. **Collier** (Naples area, southwest), 22,565
10. **Lee** (Fort Myers area, southwest), 22,437

	April 1, 1993 (Estimated)	April 1, 1990 (Census)	% change 1990-1993	% change 1980-1990
FLORIDA	13,608,627	12,938,071	5.2%	32.7%
COUNTY				
Alachua	190,655	181,596	5.0%	20.0%
Baker	19,527	18,486	5.6%	20.9%
Bay	134,059	126,994	5.6%	29.9%
Bradford	23,312	22,515	3.5%	12.4%
Brevard	427,035	398,978	7.0%	46.2%
Broward	1,317,512	1,255,531	4.9%	23.3%
Calhoun	11,479	11,011	4.3%	18.5%

	April 1, 1993 (Estimated)	April 1, 1990 (Census)	% change 1990-1993	% change 1980-1990
FLORIDA	**13,608,627**	**12,938,071**	**5.2%**	**32.7%**
COUNTY				
Charlotte	121,695	110,975	9.7%	89.8%
Citrus	100,829	93,513	7.8%	70.9%
Clay	114,918	105,986	8.4%	58.1%
Collier	174,664	152,099	14.8%	76.9%
Columbia	46,430	42,613	9.0%	20.4%
Dade	1,951,116	1,937,194	0.7%	19.2%
De Soto	25,461	23,865	6.7%	25.3%
Dixie	11,810	10,585	11.6%	36.6%
Duval	701,608	672,971	4.3%	17.9%
Escambia	272,083	262,798	3.5%	12.4%
Flagler	33,544	28,701	16.9%	163.0%
Franklin	9,775	8,967	9.0%	17.0%
Gadsden	43,239	41,116	5.2%	-1.3%
Gilchrist	10,722	9,667	10.9%	67.6%
Glades	8,269	7,591	8.9%	26.7%
Gulf	12,393	11,504	7.7%	7.9%
Hamilton	11,604	10,930	6.2%	24.8%
Hardee	22,035	19,499	13.0%	-4.2%
Hendry	28,061	25,773	8.9%	38.6%
Hernando	111,695	101,115	10.5%	127.4%
Highlands	73,203	68,432	7.0%	44.0%
Hillsborough	866,134	834,054	3.8%	28.9%
Holmes	16,331	15,778	3.5%	7.2%
Indian River	95,641	90,208	6.0%	50.6%
Jackson	44,386	41,375	7.3%	5.7%
Jefferson	12,988	11,296	15.0%	5.5%
Lafayette	5,603	5,578	0.4%	38.2%
Lake	167,167	152,104	9.9%	45.0%
Lee	357,550	335,113	6.7%	63.3%
Leon	206,302	192,493	7.2%	29.5%
Levy	28,236	25,912	9.0%	30.4%
Liberty	5,720	5,569	2.7%	30.7%
Madison	17,316	16,569	4.5%	11.2%
Manatee	223,508	211,707	5.6%	42.6%
Marion	212,025	194,835	8.8%	59.1%
Martin	106,780	100,900	5.8%	57.6%
Monroe	81,766	78,024	4.8%	23.5%
Nassau	46,450	43,941	5.7%	33.6%
Okaloosa	154,512	143,777	7.5%	30.8%
Okeechobee	31,758	29,627	7.2%	46.2%
Orange	727,780	677,491	7.4%	43.9%
Osceola	125,675	107,728	16.7%	118.6%
Palm Beach	918,223	863,503	6.3%	49.7%
Pasco	293,966	281,131	4.6%	45.2%
Pinellas	864,953	851,659	1.6%	16.9%
Polk	429,943	405,382	6.1%	26.0%
Putnam	67,625	65,070	3.9%	28.7%
St. Johns	91,197	83,829	8.8%	63.4%
St. Lucie	163,192	150,171	8.7%	72.3%
Santa Rosa	90,259	81,608	10.6%	45.8%
Sarasota	290,612	277,776	4.6%	37.3%
Seminole	310,890	287,521	8.1%	60.0%
Sumter	33,814	32,577	7.1%	30.1%

	April 1, 1993 (Estimated)	April 1, 1990 (Census)	% change 1990-1993	% change 1980-1990
FLORIDA	**13,608,627**	**12,938,071**	**5.2%**	**32.7%**
COUNTY				
Suwannee	28,598	26,780	6.8%	20.2%
Taylor	17,374	17,111	1.5%	3.5%
Union	12,031	10,252	17.4%	0.8%
Volusia	390,066	370,737	5.2%	43.3%
Wakulla	15,401	14,202	8.4%	30.4%
Walton	30,568	27,759	10.1%	30.3%
Washington	17,554	16,919	3.8%	16.6%

Source: 1993 Florida Estimates of Population

Florida's Largest Cities

As of April 1, 1993, the largest cities in the state, the counties in which they are located, and their populations were:

1. **Jacksonville** (Duval County, northeast), 661,243
2. **Miami** (Dade, southeast), 364,679
3. **Tampa** (Hillsborough, central west), 282,848
4. **St. Petersburg** (Pinellas, central west), 239,701
5. **Hialeah** (Dade, southeast), 199,923
6. **Orlando** (Orange, central), 172,019
7. **Fort Lauderdale** (Broward, southeast), 148,743
8. **Tallahassee** (Leon, northwest), 131,683
9. **Hollywood** (Broward, southeast), 123,956
10. **Clearwater** (Pinellas, central west), 100,768
11. **Miami Beach** (Dade, southeast), 95,160
12. **Gainesville** (Alachua, northeast), 93,091
13. **Coral Springs** (Broward, southeast), 88,944
14. **Cape Coral** (Lee, southwest), 81,339
15. **Pembroke Pines** (Broward, southeast), 75,014
16. **Pompano Beach** (Broward, southeast), 73,219
17. **Lakeland** (Polk, central), 73,121
18. **Plantation** (Broward, southeast), 72,655
19. **Sunrise** (Broward, southeast), 71,542
20. **Palm Bay** (Brevard, central east), 69,197

Source: 1993 Florida Estimates of Population

The following cities were among the fastest-growing, in terms of percentages, between 1990 and 1993. Also noted are the counties in which they are located, the population as of 1990 and 1993, and the percentage increases. Omitted from the list are communities with populations of less than 1,000.

1. **Malone** (Jackson, northwest): 765; 1,583; 106.9%
2. **Parkland** (Broward, southeast): 3,773; 7,383; 95.7%
3. **Oviedo** (Seminole, central): 11,114; 15,722; 41.5%
4. **Lady Lake** (Lake County, central): 8,071; 11,117; 37.7%
5. **Hypoluxo** (Palm Beach, southeast): 807; 1,106; 37%
6. **Ocoee** (Orange, central): 12,778; 16,418; 28.5%
7. **Dania** (Broward, southeast): 13,183; 16,905; 28.2%
8. **Hialeah Gardens** (Dade, southeast): 7,727; 9,828; 27.2%

9. **Palm Beach Gardens** (Palm Beach, southeast): 22,990; 28,635; 24.6%
10. **Windermere** (Orange, central): 1,371; 1,667; 21.6%
11. **Casselberry** (Seminole, central): 18,849; 22,816; 21%
12. **Greenacres City** (Palm Beach, southeast): 18,683; 22,385; 19.8%
13. **Apopka** (Orange, central): 13,611; 16,307; 19.8%
14. **Cooper City** (Broward, southeast): 21,335; 25,539; 19.7%
15. **Sebastian** (Indian River, central east): 10,248; 12,154; 18.6%
16. **Winter Garden** (Orange, central): 9,863; 11,685; 18.5%
17. **Montverde** (Lake, central): 890; 1,051; 18.1%
18. **Port St. Lucie** (St. Lucie, central east): 55,761; 65,722; 17.9%
19. **Minneola** (Lake, central): 1,515; 1,783; 17.7%
20. **Ponce Inlet** (Volusia, central east): 1,704; 1,994; 17%

Where Do New Residents Come From?

No one can say exactly where all new Florida residents have moved from. And besides new year-round residents, some Snowbirds register their cars here but still go back up north for the summer. Others keep their registrations from northern states but spend a good part of the year here. But to give a general idea, the state motor vehicles division keeps statistics on the number of out-of-state vehicles registered in Florida according to the state of previous registration. From 1988 through 1992, there were nearly 2 million such vehicles. Overall, the states of origin were:

New York, 10.6 percent
Georgia, 8.8 percent
New Jersey, 6.4 percent
Alabama, 4.9 percent
Ohio, 4.8 percent
Michigan, 4.7 percent
Pennsylvania, 4.5 percent
Virginia, 4.1 percent
North Carolina, 4 percent
California, 4 percent
Texas, 3.9 percent
Massachusetts, 3.8 percent

Illinois, 3.7 percent
Tennessee, 3.2 percent
South Carolina, 2.6 percent
Connecticut, 2.6 percent
Maryland, 2.5 percent
Indiana, 2.2 percent
Louisiana, 1.3 percent
Kentucky, 1.3 percent
Missouri, 1.2 percent
Wisconsin, 1.1 percent
New Hampshire, 1.0 percent

States from which the percentages were less than 1 percent, in order, were: **Mississippi, Colorado, Maine, Minnesota, Arizona, Rhode Island, West Virginia, Oklahoma, Iowa, Arkansas, Washington and Kansas.**

Some Florida Population Trivia

— Between 1980 and 1990, there were 1.61 million births in Florida and 1.19 million deaths. The total natural increase in population as a result of the births and deaths was 420,867.

— On a percentage basis, Florida's population in 1990 was 83.1 percent white; 13.6 percent black; 1.2 percent Asian or Pacific Islander; .3 percent American Indian, Eskimo or Aleut; and 1.8 other. People of Hispanic origin, who can be of any race, accounted for 12.2 percent of the population.

— As of 1990, when Florida's population was 12.93 million, there were 6.26 million males and 6.67 million females.

— Average household size in the United States has declined since 1940, when the average was 3.67 people. It was 2.76 in 1980 and 2.63 in 1990. The reasons? According to the University of Florida, "This decline has been caused by declining birth rates, rising divorce rates, a rising average age at first marriage, a growing tendency for older persons to maintain their own households at higher ages, and the large number of young adults forming one- or two-person households during recent decades. In Florida an additional factor has been the high rate of immigration of older persons." The household sizes in Florida — all below the national averages — were 2.90 in 1970; 2.55 in 1980, and 2.46 in 1990.

— The total state population figure for 1993 included 63,295 prison inmates.

— In 1990, 90.8 percent of Floridians lived in metropolitan areas, behind New Jersey (100 percent), California (95.7) and New York (91.1) but ahead of Massachusetts (90.4), Pennsylvania (84.8) and Illinois (82.7), according to the Census Bureau. For the U.S. as a whole, the number was 77.5. A metropolitan area is defined as having a population of at least 100,000, which includes a city or "urbanized area" of at least 50,000.

A mobile home park in the St. Petersburg area contains a few of the more than 762,000 mobile homes in the state.

New cement tiles are stacked on the roof of a house in a typical retirement community. Such roofs can cost $4,000 to $7,000 but are durable and should last a generation.

THE COST OF LIVING IN FLORIDA

There are lists of median incomes, per-capita incomes, household incomes and household buying power.

There are consumer price indexes, producer price indexes and price level indexes.

You can look at charts showing costs of electricity per kilowatt-hour, and natural gas per therm. And you can read the total millage rates for local property taxes in all 67 counties.

But don't expect to make sense out of a lot of these statistics. A few are valuable. But many are outdated. Many are misleading. Many do not encompass the whole state. Some have data from very limited time periods. And trying to figure out how one relates to another is like comparing limes and tangerines.

But a couple of general statements can be made. The cost of living generally is below average in Florida. The New York Times in August 1994 cited an index showing that with a national average of 100, Florida's cost of living was 92.4.

And insofar as housing is concerned, the most appropriate thing to say is that Florida has such a wide array of lifestyle options that you can find just about any kind of housing in every imaginable price range in most areas.

You can buy a mobile home — used — for as little as $6,000. You can buy an oceanfront mansion for millions. In a county where the average house price may be $100,000, you can buy a well-cared-for two-bedroom, two-bath house in a retirement community for $60,000. And you can find another house a few streets over for many times that. As for building lots, you can get some for $7,000 and others for several hundred thousand dollars.

According to the federal government, if you bought the average Florida house in 1993 you paid $117,500 for it. The term of your mortgage is an average of 27.1 years and the interest rate is an average of 6.78 percent.

For mobile homes, precise Florida figures are hard to come by, but the average price nationally in recent years has been around $24,000. Typically you'll finance it for 15 years and, unless you own the land, pay an interest rate roughly 2.5 percentage points higher than that for site-built homes.

Apartment renters can expect to pay an average of $300 to $650 a month for a one-year lease, depending on area.

On top of the housing payments, the typical monthly Florida electric bill is around $80. Other typical monthly costs: Natural gas will cost you about $18; house insurance will run roughly from $15 to $30 (and up to $54 in southeast Florida), and local property taxes on an average house will vary widely — anywhere from $70 to $170 a month.

Here are the details.

Site-Built Houses

They're available in many styles. Queen Anne, Spanish Mission, Victorian, Mediterranean, and ranches — lots of ranches — are just a few. They're made out of cement, wood or brick.

History-conscious suburbanites in such areas as New York, Connecticut and Massachusetts might look at the vast majority of them as lacking in architectural charm. "There's nothing much older than 40 years down there," a recent visitor from Springfield, Mass., said. "I didn't see one wood-shingled saltbox like mine anywhere. And most of them are just one-floor ranches. The architectural style is Mid-20th-Century Cinder Block Splattered With Cement."

While such folks may not find that Florida communities exude the Old New England charm, they do find the prices enchanting. Instead of paying several hundred thousand dollars for a home outside New York City or Boston, they can buy a single-family house in Florida for a fraction of that.

To be specific, the average price of a Florida house — detached single-family or one of the state's million or so condominium units — was $117,500 in 1993, according to the Federal Housing Finance Board (formerly the Federal Home Loan Bank Board), which bases its figures on mortgage loan statistics from the last five working days of each month (until the late 1980s it was the first five days of the month).

True, chances are the house won't be listed on the National Register of Historic Places, it won't have wood-pegged, wideboard floors, and it won't be pictured on a White-Christmas postcard. But while the size may vary by area, chances are that it will have three bedrooms, two tiled baths, a living room, a dining room, probably a Florida room, a garage and, yes, maybe even a swimming pool and palm trees. In some areas, it might have frontage on a golf course, too.

In the late 80s and early 90s, the federal government says, 176,000 to 183,300 existing homes, apartments, condominiums and co-ops were sold each year. And as many as 100,000 new homes also are sold each year, according to the Florida Association of Realtors. The association keeps price statistics for some Metropolitan Statistical Areas, but further breakdowns are elusive: Many local associations, particularly in northwest Florida, do not have Multiple Listing Services that keep track of all sales ("What do you think this is, Miami? This is the sticks, son," said one Realtor).

Nevertheless, prices generally have increased over the years, but don't expect to buy a house here as a get-rich-quick scheme. In some parts of the country, into the late 80s, prices rose dramatically — as much as 20 percent, year after year, and even more. This was not the case in Florida.

As shown in the following chart, since 1974 the average price of a home in the Sunshine State has gone up annually anywhere from .8 percent to 20 percent. In three years, 1983, 1991 and 1992, the price actually went down. On average, the price has risen 6.7 percent each year since 1973, using the federal figures.

Year	Mortgage Interest Rate	Term to Maturity (In years)	Average Purchase Price	Percentage Increase In price
1973	8.15	22.3	$32,000	—
1974	9.31	23.3	$35,400	11%
1975	9.18	24.9	$40,600	15%
1976	9.01	24.8	$42,400	4%
1977	8.93	26.0	$44,600	5%
1978	9.48	26.6	$48,000	8%
1979	11.10	28.1	$55,800	16%
1980	13.45	27.4	$66,800	20%
1981	15.48	28.2	$78,100	17%
1982	15.83	26.7	$85,000	9%
1983	12.86	27.9	$78,100	- 8%
1984	12.21	28.6	$80,200	3%
1985	11.12	28.0	$84,600	5%
1986	10.03	27.1	$93,300	10%
1987	9.40	27.4	$100,400	8%
1988	8.96	28.7	$101,200	8%
1989	9.69	28.1	$106,400	5%
1990	9.67	28.0	$119,900	13%
1991	8.93	27.6	$114,600	-4%
1992	7.35	26.3	$112,400	-2%
1993	6.78	27.1	$117,500	5%

Source: Federal Housing Finance Board (formerly the Federal Home Loan Bank Board), based on loans closed by major lenders.

One of the factors that influences housing prices is local wages. Average prices in many areas of northwest Florida run roughly from $40,000 to about $60,000. Realtors will often say that that these prices are consistent with what workers are able to pay. Chamber of commerce brochures in that part of the state, some of which are aimed at luring new businesses, sometimes will tout "a favorable economic climate," "a willing work force" and low wages. But that's not the only factor. Prices in some coastal counties in central and southern Florida are much higher than many local workers can afford. Palm Beach County, for example, depends heavily on the tourist trade; this means that the service and retail industries, with their low wages, dominate the local economy, yet the average price of a house has topped $125,000 in recent years. Part of the reason: nearly a quarter of local residents are 65 years of age or older. That's another major factor in determining prices: retiree wealth. In the Palm Beach area, and in Naples on the Gulf coast, for example, prices are largely driven by the retirees. The local economy is geared to serving these residents, and many local workers are priced out of the market.

Common Types of House Construction in Florida

If you enjoy the warmth of wood, with all its esthetic values, you can have enough of it trucked into central and south Florida to build dream homes for every member of your family.

But if your pocketbook is more limited, chances are that you will surround yourself with concrete blocks.

Although it's also a matter of personal preference, economics plays a big role in the selection of house-construction materials in Florida. If you live in the central and southern parts of the state — generally from Ocala on down — you'll find that concrete block construction is prevalent, although there's a mix, according to the Florida Home Builders Association.

The reason? South Florida was timbered off years ago when the building boom began, and wood has to be trucked in from north Florida or Georgia. That's expensive. It's cheaper to build with concrete blocks, and they're big business in the state. The blocks — made with Portland cement, sand, water and some type of aggregate, usually gravel — are manufactured in just about every metropolitan area: Miami, Orlando, Tampa and West Palm Beach, for instance. You can buy them in light, medium and heavy grades. Some are insulated.

In the northern part of the state, on the other hand, wood-frame construction, or brick veneer over wood frame (brick and stick, as it is known), is dominant, again because of the availability and cost of the materials. Personal preference plays a role here, too, because you'll still find a lot of concrete-block homes in north Florida, just as you will wood-frame houses in the south.

Each type of construction has its advantages. Although some concrete-block homes are as architecturally pleasing as any other, many people prefer wood to the hardness of concrete. Wood affords an architect or a contractor more flexibility and versatility in design. You can do more with wood because it weighs less and is easier to handle, says the Florida Home Builders Association.

Concrete blocks, however, are less susceptible to fire damage. They also are less prone to termite damage, although termites usually have to work their way around pressure-treated lumber — to such things as untreated pine studs — to munch on much of a wood-frame house.

Many people believe that concrete-block homes are stronger and more resistant to hurricane damage, yet the oldest houses in the state are made of wood. A Miami Herald investigation in 1992, based on analyses of damage to 60,000 houses after Hurricane Andrew, showed that many wood-frame homes were destroyed. The Country Walk area of mostly wood-frame houses sustained the second greatest amount of damage in South Dade (despite relatively weak winds in the storm), but inadequate bracing may have been a leading cause, The Herald reported. One startling conclusion was that older houses generally fared better in the storm. The percentage of homes that were uninhabitable after the storm ranged from 15 percent of those built in the 60s to 59 percent of those built in the 90s. "The pattern was repeated throughout South Dade. Damage followed the rigid lines of subdivisions, not the whimsy of wind. Construction quality and design largely determined the degree of hurricane damage," The Herald said.

Most concrete-block homes have roofs made out of heavy cement or clay tiles. They're more expensive than other types of roofing materials, but they're also more durable and they don't absorb the heat as much as shingle roofs can. They cost more because the understructure has to be stronger to support them. Furthermore, they look better atop concrete-block homes: They simply blend in better. Cement-tile roofs normally should last about 30 years. For a 2,000-square-foot area, such a roof can cost anywhere from $4,000 to $7,500, contractors say.

Another idiosyncracy of Florida construction is that most homes have no basement, and there's a very good reason for that: groundwater. Dig down a few feet in some parts of the state and you've hit the water table. It'd be like building a basement in a swimming pool.

Caveat Emptor

Some guidelines for home buyers:
Under Florida law, counties must set up

systems for the inspection of new homes. Most follow standard building codes. Some, for example, require separate inspections for plumbing, mechanical, electrical and structural systems. Some cities within the counties have their own requirements.

Inspections usually begin once a building permit has been issued and continue until a certificate of occupancy is granted.

But on an existing home — whether it's a detached, single-family house or a condominium — mortgage lenders don't always require structural surveys. A lender frequently will order a property survey to determine boundaries and probably will require a termite inspection.

But buyers also should hire a contractor, an engineer, an architect or another independent expert to go over every inch of the house to make sure that the construction — including the roof substructure — is sound. Keep in mind that Hurricane Andrew proved that even relatively strict building codes are easily circumvented, especially in areas of high growth where the number of inspectors has not kept pace with the population increases. And don't hire a building inspector who does this type of structural study on the side in the county in which he or she works — you might end up hiring the same inspector who granted the original certificate of occupancy for an unsound structure.

Property Taxes

The state Department of Revenue puts out a comparative chart showing total millage rates for local annual property taxes in each county. Basic county millage rates — showing the number of dollars charged for each $1,000 in property value — ranged from $12.18 to $22.82 in 1993, but most were in the $15 to $18 range.

But put the calculator away.

The system is so complex and so variable that the only way of figuring out a bill is to ask the tax collector in whatever area of whatever town you want to live in.

Counties have taxes for county government, county schools, and special services. Some have fire districts, water districts, sewer districts, transit districts, street lighting and paving. And some cities within counties have their own taxes for some of these services. Conversely, some municipalities do not provide some of these services and consequently don't tax them. Roughly half of Florida's residents live in unincorporated communities. Some of these areas are very rural, but many have no special tax districts — meaning that

residents pay the county millage rates but little extra.

Pinellas County (the St. Petersburg-Clearwater area), for example, has millage rates that range from $16 to $26, depending on where you live. But the county tax collector's office says that there are 50 different millage codes — in other words, the rate you pay will be different from rates paid by people in 49 other areas of the county.

Under Florida law, local officials have to assess property at 100 percent of market value, meaning that you'd expect a $100,000 house to show up on the tax rolls assessed at $100,000.

Don't bet on it, though. By law, local officials can take up to 15 percent off the total assessment without having to justify it to the state. You might find the assessment lowered, for example, because the house really is worth $6,000 less since the seller just paid a commission to the real estate agent. And it might be lowered further because of deed costs associated with the purchase.

The total assessment also will be lowered if you qualify for the state's homestead exemption (a $25,000 break on the total assessment for bona-fide Florida residents). And if you're a widow, blind or disabled, you're entitled to further exemptions.

Example: You paid $100,000 for a house last year. You're a full-time Florida resident, so you qualify for the $25,000 homestead exemption. The local assessor takes off another $10,000 for costs related to the purchase.

Your total assessment now is $100,000 minus $35,000, or $65,000. If your tax rate is 15 mills, including all county, municipal and special-service taxes, you'll pay $15 for each thousand of the $65,000. Your total annual tax bill will be $975, or $81.25 a month.

House Insurance

Insurance rates vary, too, depending on the area of the state, but there is a general rule: You'll usually pay more to insure a wood-frame home than you will a masonry home, such as one built out of concrete blocks. The reason is that fire is the most frequent cause of house damage in Florida, and frame houses are more susceptible to fire damage.

And, of course, you can expect to pay higher rates if you live close to a beach area that is susceptible to wind damage from major storms.

Rates usually reflect an insurer's experience in an area.

The Florida Department of Insurance, which must approve all rates, keeps general statistics on insurance premiums. The rates differ by company, by policy and by area. One company, for example, may have the lowest rate in one area of the state and the highest in another.

The department figures rates based on $75,000 policies, with $100,000 liability coverage and a $250 deductible. The figures are from 1992 brochures and show annual premiums. The department today no longer publishes these brochures, but instead has an insurance HELP line for those wishing rate information. The in-state phone number for this HELP line is 800-342-5762 or out of state, 904-922-3132.

Area	Masonry Homes (Rates, low to high)	Frame Homes (Rates, low to high)
Daytona Beach	$188-$283	$235-$342
Fort Lauderdale	$201-$531	$201-$658
Fort Myers	$169-$280	$203-$336
Gainesville	$165-$251	$165-$310
Jacksonville	$165-$290	$165-$360
Miami	$321-$531	$321-$658
Orlando	$165-$251	$165-$310
Pensacola	$253-$419	$303-$483
St. Petersburg	$166-$327	$199-$327
Tallahassee	$158-$290	$158-$360
Tampa	$210-$340	$252-$391
West Palm Beach	$226-$331	$226-$394

Mobile Homes

If true immortality does lie in architecture, then some snobbish wags might view mobile homes as living nightmares.

While that may hold for some structures, the options for style, shape and size of today's mobile homes — manufactured homes, in industry parlance — are virtually unlimited. Some top-of-the-line models are nearly indistinguishable, both inside and out, from conventional houses. There is no doubt, however, that structurally they are not as sound as many site-built homes. Mobile homes were decimated during Hurricane Andrew and a state task force concluded that regular building standards should apply to them.

And their popularity continues to grow. In 1990, there were 762,855 of them in Florida — 12.5 percent of the state's total housing units, according to census figures. The Federation of Mobile Home Owners of Florida says that mobile homes are more than a $2-billion-a-year industry in Florida. The state leads the nation in the sale of them.

According to federal figures, prices for new ones range from $8,400 to $37,000 for a single-section model and from $15,000 to $100,000 for a multi-section model. Average prices in 1990, according to the federation, were about $18,500 for the single-section and $32,500 for the multi-section. Lots in Florida — for those who choose to buy instead of rent — generally go for $7,000 to $35,000.

The number of mobile homes sold in Florida has declined in recent years. In 1985, about 30,000 of them were sold. In 1988, the number had dropped to slightly more than 23,000. By 1989, the figure was 22,800, according to federation figures. Some mobile-home dealers say that part of the reason for the decline is a glut in some parts of the state — many parks are filled. But Fred Yonteck, executive director of the federation, said the primary reason why demand is down is because rental parks "are getting a reputation for a lack of financial soundness." People may pay $30,000 to $50,000 for nicer, more modern mobile homes and pay $200 to $250 per month in rent. After five years, the park has been fully developed and the owner raises the rent, cuts back on amenities or sells to someone who may do the same thing. Then the residents are stuck — they have to pay what the owners demand because the courts generally hold that the property owner has the rights, Yonteck said.

Some parks have increased overall monthly fees dramatically, he said. One raised them from $103 to $200, and another went from $150 to $280. Florida law, until October 1990, barred "unconscionable" rent increases, but proving that in court was difficult, said Yonteck. The law was changed and the word "unconscionable" was changed to "unreasonable," which many legislators believed will make legal challenges easier.

Pervasive rent increases "could destroy retirement and financial planning" for members of the federation, about 90 percent of whom are retirees, Yonteck said. Huge increases also can affect the resale value of a home. That's not so much a problem in the northern part of the state, where single-section homes that are not permanently tied down are more prevalent. "If they don't like a rent increase, they can move down the street," Yonteck said. But from Gainesville south, mobility is more of a misnomer because a lot of homes have carports or room additions that are permanently attached to the ground and these residents are at the mercy of the park owners.

The best form of rent control is for residents to buy their parks, Yonteck said. About 200 of the state's 5,400 parks are resident-owned and their numbers have been growing slowly.

One of the biggest selling points for mobile homes is price — generally half to two-thirds the cost of a comparably sized, site-built home.

You can finance mobile homes in many areas with conventional mortgages that require 10 percent to 25 percent down payments, though if you buy one without the land, you'll pay a rate that's 2 to 3 percentage points higher than the rate for a conventional fixed-rate mortgage on a site-built home. And you can pay for them over 20, and in some cases, 30 years. Even federal mortgage programs are available for permanently attached homes. However, generally you'll be able to finance for a term of more than 15 years only if you own the land.

Many people buy mobile homes not only because they're less expensive, but because parks offer enjoyable lifestyles. Some parks are on the water. Some are on golf courses. Many have their own swimming pools, club houses, member associations, organized social activities and security systems. And if you don't like one park and your home is truly "mobile," then you can always go somewhere else.

Monthly rental park charges vary from about $130 to more than $400. These usually will include water and sewer service and garbage pickup. And under Florida law, the owners of the parks can pass along a portion of property tax bills to the renters by pro-rating the land tax. That tax frequently is part of the monthly fee, too.

Some parks also charge pet fees, extra-person fees, golf course fees and late-payment fees.

Other expenses: You'll have to pay the state's sales tax if you don't own the land when you buy a mobile home, and you'll have to get a license tag, which will cost you roughly $25 to more than $80 per year, depending on the size of the home. About half the mobile homes in the state have been subject to the sales tax; others are more permanently attached and considered real property.

And, of course, you'll have to insure your home. The state Insurance Department says that mobile homes are insured either through homeowners' policies or as motor vehicles. Because mobile homes are often considered more hazardous properties than site-built homes, you may pay more for each thousand dollars worth of value to insure them.

Several guides to Florida mobile home parks are published. Further information is available from the Federation of Mobile Home Owners of Florida, P.O. Box 5350, Largo, Fla. 34649.

Some tips when shopping for a mobile home:

— Check with the local Chamber of Commerce about dealers.

— Take a pad and pen when you visit the dealer's lot.

— Note the features of each home you see. It's easy to forget, after seeing half a dozen of them, which one offered which amenities.

— Ask for a copy of the floor plans.

— Find out if the price includes set-up on the site where you'll be living. Does the price include removal of wheels and axles? Will it include hookup to utility lines? Does it include the tying down of steel straps that insurance companies require to prevent wind damage to the home?

— When you decide which one to buy, put everything in writing. Get a copy of the contract and make sure that all details are spelled out.

Apartments and Condominiums

Renting is big business in Florida and is getting bigger each year. This is especially noticeable in the number of apartments and condominiums for rent. For example, in fiscal year 1991-92, there were more than 1.157 million licensed public lodging units in the state. Of this number, there were 743,097 rental apartments, another 26,330 "transient" rental apartments (or those that rent for six months or less), and 44,403 rental condominiums. That's a jump from a few years earlier when in July 1988 those numbers stood at 608,484 apartments and 36,419 condominiums.

The Florida Department of Business Regulation, Division of Hotels and Restaurants, which keeps tabs on rentals, is responsible for licensing, inspecting and regulating all public lodging establishments. Apartments, rooming houses, guest houses and any condominium, time-share or complex that is rented to transients or rented under a managerial contract is considered a public lodging establishment.

Inspections are required at least four times each year for lodging establishments that rent to transient guests and two times each year for those not renting to transient guests.

Apartment rents vary markedly, depending on what you're looking for and where you want to live. Generally, though, for a two-bedroom, one-bath apartment with a one-year lease, rents average $400 a month in St. Petersburg; $550 in the West Palm Beach area; $450 in Panama City; $525 in Orlando; and $425 in St. Augustine, according to local real estate agents' estimates. No one keeps precise figures because of concerns over potential antitrust violations, according to the Florida Apartment Association. But you can be sure that seasonal rates will be much higher than year-round rates.

As a rule, condominium rentals are not cheap, as many are aimed at the vacationer. For example, a two-bedroom, two-bathroom oceanfront condominium at Ormond Beach rents for around $500 a week in the winter and $325 a week in the summer. A Gulf-front condominium with two bedrooms and two baths at any of several St. Petersburg Beach resorts rents for about $990 a week in the winter and $790 a week in the summer.

In the Panhandle, the opposite is true. Winters are much colder there, and rents consequently are higher in the summer.

When looking, watch out for minimum stay requirements. Many condominiums in St. Petersburg Beach, for example, have three-month minimum stays. With this in mind, winter rates there range from $1,500 to $2,500 a month. In the summer, the rates range from $750 to $1,000 a month.

Business is not booming for everyone who decides to get into the rental business in Florida. For two rental categories — rooming houses and transient apartments — business has fallen off in recent years. In July 1988, there were 13,465 rooming house units and 39,742 transient apartments for rent in Florida. By 1992, there were 9,229 rooming house units and 26,330 transient apartments.

The overall rental business, though, is not hurting. With the increase in new apartment units, along with rising numbers of hotel and motel rooms for rent, any slack left by the decline in rooming houses and transient apartments has been taken up. The number of licensed hotel rooms keeps rising: from 113,120 in 1988 to 127,431 in fiscal 1991-92; ditto with

the number of licensed motel rooms: from 203,075 in 1988 to 207,450 in fiscal 1991-92.

Affordable Housing

Contrary to what you may read in travel or chamber of commerce brochures, there also is a dark side to the housing picture in the state.

A study, released in September 1988 and conducted for the Florida Housing Finance Agency, concluded that "the dream of home ownership has become tenuous for the lower-middle and middle income groups."

And for households with "very low" incomes, or incomes 50 percent below the median income level, "the goal of owning a home has become totally unreachable," said the researchers, Sunbelt Research Associates, Inc. of Jupiter. Followup studies have confirmed these findings.

In 1988, researchers found 950,238 households classified as "very low income" in the state. This comprised 19.2 percent of the total number of households in Florida (4,950,000 in 1988). In 1990, the number of very low income households increased to a little more than 1 million, which represented about 19.1 percent of all households in the state (5,228,000 in 1990).

Another study, conducted by The Affordable Housing Study Commission —composed mainly of people appointed by the governor — concluded that there are "only seven states that report a greater per capita need for low income rental housing units than Florida." The commission is responsible for coming up with plans to ease the housing problem.

The commission said that "Florida is experiencing a critical shortage of affordable housing," and called for changes in local land development regulations and for more state funding for the elderly.

And it found that the problem of affordable housing has "reached a crisis level for very low and low-income persons."

For housing to be affordable, the commonly accepted definition is that you should not spend more than 30 percent to 35 percent of your household income on it. Housing costs include mortgage or rental payments; taxes; insurance; and utilities.

Under state housing programs, people with "very low" incomes are defined as those having household incomes below 50 percent of the median income of the county in which they live. Those with "low" incomes have household incomes between 50 percent and 80 percent of the median; and those with "moderate" incomes have household incomes between 80 percent and 120 percent of the median.

Sunbelt Research Associates found there was a need for another 315,360 very low income rental units in the state. Of this number, there was a need for 219,316 multi-family rental units. A 1990 study found that the need for very low income rental units had declined somewhat to 258,791 such units. Still, only about 13.8 percent of all rental housing offered in Florida "is affordable to very low income households," the 1990 study concluded.

Among the counties most needing affordable rental units: Dade, Broward, Pinellas, Orange, Duval and Hillsborough.

The 1990 study found that 60.1 percent of the rental units needed to serve very low households were located in six of the state's 67 counties — Dade, Broward, Palm Beach, Pinellas, Hillsborough and Duval.

The dichotomy was most pronounced in Palm Beach County. Here's an area, the 1988 study noted, that is among the most affluent in the country and among the poorest. "The Town of Palm Beach, which has long been the winter home of the rich, is only minutes away from a concentration of poverty in the City of West Palm Beach."

The governor's commission found that "the affordable housing shortage is not, and will not be, an isolated problem. As the shortage grows, the economy of the state will be threatened as affordable housing units become more difficult to obtain by an increasingly larger segment of the state's work force."

One group hard hit by rising housing costs is the elderly. As of 1988, more than 29 percent of the public subsidized housing units in the state served the elderly. And, by 1995 it was projected that 71,277 more very low income multi-family rental units would be needed for the elderly.

Older people are among the groups that encounter the longest waiting periods for affordable housing. In most cases, the wait is 6 months to 2 years.

"Elderly applicants often have to wait for the person in the apartment to move to a nursing home or die before an apartment becomes available," the Sunbelt study concluded.

The governor's commission found a similarly bleak situation: 12 percent of Florida's elderly population have very low or low incomes and "live in deplorable housing conditions."

Utilities

Telephone Companies

There are 13 companies — from very small to large — providing local phone service to Florida.

The long-distance market is crowded with dozens of other phone companies; AT&T Communications stands out as the dominant carrier.

The largest local company by far is Southern Bell of Miami, which services about 58 percent of the state. GTE Florida, headquartered in Tampa, is the next largest, servicing about 22 percent of the state, followed by United Telephone Co. of Florida, based in Altamonte Springs, nearly 15 percent, and Central Telephone Co. of Florida, in Tallahassee, about 3.8 percent.

The remaining 9 companies are: ALLTEL Florida Inc., Live Oak; St. Joseph Telephone and Telegraph Co., Port St. Joe; Gulf Telephone Co., Perry; Northeast Florida Telephone Co., Macclenny; Vista-United Telecommunications, Lake Buena Vista; Southland Telephone Co., Atmore, Ala.; Indiantown Telephone System Inc., Indiantown; Florala Telephone Co., Florala, Ala., and Quincy Telephone Co. of Quincy.

The areas some of these companies serve are scattered across the state, and a few are localized in one area. Following is a general description of service areas:

Southern Bell: all of Florida's East Coast and the Florida Keys, Brooksville, Cedar Key, Gainesville, Jacksonville, Orlando, Palatka, Panama City, Pensacola, Sanford and Weeki Wachee areas.

GTE Florida: Bartow, Bradenton, Clearwater, Frostproof, Lakeland, Lake Wales, New Port Richey, Plant City, Sarasota, St. Petersburg, Tampa, Tarpon Springs, Venice, Winter Haven and Zephyrhills.

United Telephone: Southwest Florida, including Everglades City, Fort Myers, Immokalee, Marco Island, Naples and Punta Gorda, and areas east to Okeechobee; Arcadia, Avon Park, Sebring and Kissimmee-St. Cloud areas; and an area that includes Dade City, Leesburg, Ocala, Eustis, Homosassa Springs, Inverness and Winter Park.

Central Telephone: Tallahassee, Marianna, Starke, Fort Walton Beach, Destin, Crestview, Monticello, Santa Rosa Beach, Valparaiso, Baker, Bonifay, Crawfordville and De Funiak Springs areas.

ALLTEL: Live Oak, Alachua, Branford, Crescent City, Hilliard, Jasper, Jennings, and Orange Springs areas.

St. Joseph Telephone: Apalachicola, Blountstown, Carrabelle and Port St. Joe areas.

Gulf Telephone: Perry and Keaton Beach area.

Quincy Telephone Co. of Quincy: Quincy, Greensboro and Gretna area.

Northeast Florida Telephone: Macclenny and Sanderson area.

Vista-United: Lake Buena Vista area.

Southland Telephone: extreme Northwest corner of Florida including Molino and Walnut Hill.

Indiantown Telephone: Indiantown area.

Florala Telephone: Laurel Hill and Paxton.

Rates for short-distance calls vary according to area. But for long-distance callers, daytime rates can be within the same range when calling from one end of the state to another. For example, according to AT&T Communications' rate schedule, the cost of a 5-minute daytime, direct-dialed call from Miami to Pensacola is $1.19; from Jacksonville to Tallahassee, $1.17; from Orlando to Sarasota, $1.15; from Sarasota to Tampa, $1.13; from Tampa to Miami, $1.17; and from Tallahassee to Miami, $1.19.

Electric Companies

More than 75 percent of Florida's power comes to you courtesy of several investor-owned utility companies, and the rest is delivered through a host of municipal systems, rural electric cooperatives and federal systems.

By far, the largest electric company in the state is Florida Power & Light Co., based in Miami. The company had about 3.3 million customers in 1992. Florida Power Corp. was next with around 1.2 million customers; and Tampa Electric Co. had about 470,000.

A publicly owned utility, Jacksonville Electric, has edged out another investor-owned company in the number of customers it has had in recent years. Jacksonville served around 300,000 customers, a few thousand more than Gulf Power Co., which had 294,000.

The fuels used in the generation of Florida's electricity include coal, oil, nuclear and natural gas.

During the early 1990s, coal was the fuel most used and Public Service Commission figures show this trend continuing for years. By 1996, nearly 43 percent of Florida's electricity was expected to be generated with coal; 15.5 percent from fuel oil; 13.9 percent, nuclear; 14.6 percent, natural gas, and the rest from such sources as coal-oil mixes and cogeneration. This is quite a reversal from the early 1980s when most of the generation was supplied by fuel oil, (about 47 percent). Coal was next at 21 percent, followed by nuclear at 16 and gas at 15.7.

At Florida Power & Light, nuclear energy plays a key role. The company has four nuclear operating units — Turkey Point #3 and Turkey Point #4 in Dade County and St. Lucie #1 and St. Lucie #2 in St. Lucie County. Florida Power Corp. owns the state's only other nuclear plant — Crystal River #3 in Citrus County.

Among investor-owned companies, the cost of residential electric customer service (excluding local taxes) as of Dec. 31, 1991, based on 1,000 kilowatt-hours, was: Florida Power & Light, $76.36; Florida Power Corp., $70.52; Gulf Power, $63.88; Tampa Electric, $79.84; Florida Public Utilities' Fernandina Beach division, $80.83; and Florida Public Utilities' Marianna division, $67.02. Mininum bills or customer charges ranged from $5.32 at Florida Power Corp. to $8 at Gulf Power Co., according to the state Public Service Commission.

Service Areas

Florida Power & Light Co. services a wide area, mostly along the East Coast and southwestern Florida, including Alachua, Baker, Bradford, Brevard, Broward, Charlotte, Clay, Collier, Columbia, Dade, De Soto, Duval, Flagler, Glades, Hardee, Hendry, Highlands, Indian River, Lee, Manatee, Martin, Monroe, Nassau, Okeechobee, Osceola, Orange, Palm Beach, Putnam, St. Johns, St. Lucie, Sarasota, Seminole, Suwanee, Union and Volusia counties.

Florida Power Corp. serves all or parts of the following counties: Alachua, Bay, Brevard, Citrus, Columbia, Dixie, Flagler, Franklin, Gadsden, Gilchrist, Gulf, Hamilton, Hardee, Hernando, Highlands, Hillsborough, Jefferson, Lafayette, Lake, Leon, Levy, Liberty, Madison, Marion, Orange, Osceola, Pasco, Pinellas, Polk, Seminole, Sumter, Suwannee, Taylor, Volusia and Wakulla.

Tampa Electric Co. serves parts of Hillsborough, Pasco, Pinellas and Polk counties.

Gulf Power Co. serves all or parts of Bay, Escambia, Holmes, Jackson, Okaloosa, Santa Rosa, Walton and Washington counties.

Natural Gas Companies

There are at least nine investor-owned natural gas utilities in the state, and the largest is Peoples Gas System of Tampa. This gas is used primarily for cooking, clothes drying, water heating and other heating systems. Peoples says the average residential household consumes about 300 therms, or 30,000 cubic feet, of natural gas a year. Company rates are calcuated by cents per therm. One therm equals 100 cubic feet.

The price of gas fluctuates throughout the year, depending on the season and market prices. Example: Using the price list below, City Gas Co. in late 1992 charged customers 29.15 cents per therm as "direct pass-through charges," which are the costs the company passes on to its customers for the gas itself. Since an average residential customer uses 300 therms a year, the average household spent 29.15 cents for each of the 300 therms, or about $87.45.

But other costs are added. All natural gas companies also add onto your bill an energy charge, or an overhead operating charge; and customer charges, or the costs associated with billing and meter reading. At City Gas, the energy charge was 34.50 cents per therm. Based on what an average customer uses, 300 therms, the annual energy charge would be $103.50. The customer charge at City Gas was $6 each month. Adding these figures up — the direct pass-through charges, the energy charges and the customer charges — the average residential customer would have paid $262.95 for a year's worth of natural gas.

Following is a comparative list of prices companies charge for one therm, based on a price list that was in effect in 1991 and 1992:

Companies	Customer Charge (Dollars)	Energy Charge (Cents)	Pass-through Gas Charge (Cents)
Chesapeake Utilities Corp. Dover, Del.	$6.50	43.12	28.10
City Gas Co. of Florida, Elizabethtown, N.J.	$6	34.50	29.15
Florida Public Utilities, W. Palm Beach	$8	29.54	25.43
Indiantown Gas Co., Indiantown	$5	6.63	30.10
Peoples Gas System, Tampa	$7	32.59	24.22
Peoples Gas (Palm Beach Division)	$5	36.48	24.22
Sebring Gas System Sebring	$7	35.50	33.32
St. Joe Natural Gas Co., Port St. Joe	$3	1.97	34.65
S. Florida Natural Gas Co., New Smyrna Beach	$7	56.65	29.46
West Florida Natural Gas, Panama City	$6	26.48	23.04

Food

When it comes to food, Florida is not starving for profits or national recognition. Its cash receipts from the sale of crops in 1991 totaled nearly $5 billion; and when including livestock and products, cash receipts totaled more than $6 billion. The state was No. 8 in agricultural sales, behind California, Texas, Iowa, Nebraska, Illinois, Minnesota and Kansas, according to the U.S. Department of Agriculture.

Florida was the leading producer, based on the value of cash receipts, of oranges (whose receipts made up nearly 65 percent of the U.S. value); sugarcane (about 49 percent — Hawaii was a distant second at nearly 25 percent); grapefruit (nearly 80 percent); green peppers (74 percent); tangerines (60.5 percent); squash (about 100 percent); radishes (about 100 percent); and limes (nearly 100 percent, before Hurricane Andrew).

The state ranked second in cash receipts, behind California, for fruits and nuts, greenhouse and nursery products and vegetables. It ranked 11th in cash receipts for dairy products (Wisconsin was ranked No. 1); 16th for poultry and eggs (Arkansas was No. 1); and 27th for cattle and calves (Texas was No. 1).

"Despite the rapid urban development under way in this state, agricultural production does not appear to be threatened," according to a Florida Market Bulletin. "Through new technology, new crops and new techniques for developing virgin farmland, Florida farmers have proved they can produce higher crop yields on less acreage," the bulletin states. As of 1990, Florida had 62,662 farms, according to the U.S. Department of Agriculture. Taking a look at fish alone, about 100 species are sold commercially in the state.

The availability of home-grown products may be one reason why restaurant prices are considerably lower in some parts of the state than in other regions of the country. A recent study done by the Florida Restaurant Association showed that the average breakfast check for one person eating out in the state was less than $4 in nearly 56 percent of the restaurants surveyed; the average lunch check was under $4 in about 27 percent of the restaurants and between $5.01 and $10 in 35.2 percent of the restaurants; and the average dinner check was between $5.01 and $15 in 55 percent of the restaurants.

With all the seafood and beef products in the state, it's not surprising to find that most of the restaurants surveyed specialize in this type of cuisine. If you're looking for Cuban, French, Nouvelle or Oriental food, you won't find it at every street corner. The survey showed that 18 percent of the respondents served American regional cuisine; 17 percent, seafood; 12.4 percent, steak; 11.3 percent, hamburger; 9.5 percent, chicken; 6.4 percent, Italian; 5.7 percent, breakfast; 4.8 percent, other; 4.7 percent, Mexican; 3.8 percent, pizza; 2.1 percent, barbecue; 2 percent, German; .9 percent, Oriental; .7 percent, Nouvelle; .6 percent, French; and .1 percent, Cuban.

One of the best ways to get a feel for food costs and how they measure up is to look at the Florida Price Level Index, compiled by the revenue section of the Office of Planning and Budgeting in the Governor's Office. This index compares cost of living in each of the state's 67 counties with a state average. Using a "population-weighted" state average of 100, all counties fall either below or above this 100 level. For example, in 1991 Broward County had a 101.27 index. This means the county's food costs were 1.27 higher than the state average of 100.

A shopping list of 32 food items is the basis for the county comparisons. The items are Kellogg's Corn Flakes, ground chuck, hamburger lunch, beer, frying chicken, carrots, apples, lettuce, cheese, chocolate sandwich cookies, wine, bananas, white bread, pork chops, bologna, tuna fish, whole milk, evaporated milk, pork and beans, cooking oil, ground coffee, baby food, a cup of coffee, macaroni, sirloin steak, canned ham, eggs, frozen orange juice, sugar, cola drink, chicken noodle soup and soft drinks served in a cup.

Florida Price Level Index for Food in 1991

County	Index	County	Index	County	Index
Alachua	99.21	Hamilton	99.82	Okeechobee	98.46
Baker	94.25	Hardee	92.75	Orange	104.35
Bay	98.36	Hendry	100.89	Osceola	92.96
Bradford	95.94	Hernando	96.00	Palm Beach	100.99
Brevard	104.41	Highlands	96.18	Pasco	96.71
Broward	101.27	Hillsborough	103.43	Pinellas	97.22
Calhoun	99.90	Holmes	95.01	Polk	94.75
Charlotte	97.72	Indian River	101.97	Putnam	97.35
Citrus	96.01	Jackson	96.43	St. Johns	100.48
Clay	101.06	Jefferson	99.56	St. Lucie	101.14
Collier	98.48	Lafayette	99.42	Santa Rosa	94.12
Columbia	93.19	Lake	99.15	Sarasota	92.12
Dade	101.66	Lee	98.84	Seminole	102.10
De Soto	103.28	Leon	101.29	Sumter	98.51
Dixie	98.14	Levy	92.68	Suwannee	97.46
Duval	100.40	Liberty	101.50	Taylor	98.10
Escambia	96.40	Madison	95.85	Union	97.53
Flagler	100.89	Manatee	97.43	Volusia	99.28
Franklin	98.33	Marion	100.41	Wakulla	103.44
Gadsden	96.85	Martin	96.16	Walton	90.87
Gilchrist	99.14	Monroe	111.80	Washington	97.05
Glades	101.14	Nassau	94.45		
Gulf	99.61	Okaloosa	97.01		

THE FLORIDA MENU

(Foods native to the state)

Appetizers

Shrimp cocktail: Available just about everywhere.

Peanuts: Sometimes you may think you're hungry enough to eat every peanut in Florida, but don't bet the farm on it: The state produced 233,120,000 pounds of them in 1990. Most active harvest dates: Sept. 15 to Oct. 15.

Salads

Fresh tomatoes: Florida is the nation's No. 2 producer. Most active harvest dates: Nov. 15 to June 1.
Lettuce and Romaine: Dec. 1 to May 1.
Carrots: Dec. 15 to May 25.
Celery: Dec. 15 to June 1.
Cucumbers: Nov. 1 to Dec. 15, and April 20 to June 1.
Radishes: Nov. 15 to May 1.
Green peppers: Nov. 15 to June 15.

Entrees

Meats

Beef: Florida was 10th in the nation, in 1992, for its number of beef cows. As of Jan. 1, 1991, the state's total number of cattle and calves was 1.9 million head.
Chicken: More than 100 million broilers are raised in the state each year.

Fish

About 100 species of saltwater fish are sold commercially in the state. Some of the most popular food fish native to Florida are:

Snapper, grouper, sea trout, mullet, swordfish, mahi mahi, flounder, king and Spanish mackerel, pompano, shark, tile fish, tuna, hard clams, soft and hard blue crab, stone crab, spiny lobster, octopus, oysters, calico scallops and shrimp — pink, brown, red and royal red.
To garnish your entree:
Parsley: Nov. 15 to May 25.

Vegetables

Potatoes: Feb. 1 to June 1.
Pole and snap beans: Nov. 1 to May 1.
Squash: Nov. 15 to May 15 (and a small amount is marketed locally during July and August).
Cauliflower: Jan. 1 to March 15.
Sweet corn: Nov. 15 to June 15.
Eggplant: Nov. 15 to July 1.
Spinach: Feb. 1 to March 1.
Cabbage: Jan. 1 to April 15.

Desserts

Fresh fruits: Florida leads the nation in the production of oranges and grapefruits. Peak seasons:
Oranges: November through June.
Grapefruits: October through April.
Tangerines: October through April.
Strawberries: February through March.
Watermelons: May through June.

For the sweet tooth: Chances are that some sweet delights may be laced with Florida sugarcane — the state leads the nation in its production. Most active harvesting dates: Dec. 1 to March 1.
Key lime pie: Limes used to be plentiful year-round. They've been hard to get, though, since Hurricane Andrew in 1992.
Honey: The state was third in the nation in its production.

Source: Florida Department of Agriculture & Consumer Services, Florida Agricultural Statistics Service; Florida Market Bulletin.

Where to Live in Florida?

On the next page is a chart that will give you a basic idea of where you might be able to afford to live in Florida. Columns, from left, show the total number of households in each county, the median incomes of each county, and the percentage of residents who are classified as having "very low" incomes.

County	Total Households 1990	Median Income 1990	Percent of Housholds With Very Low Incomes
Northwest:			
Bay	53,379	$28,000	19.5
Calhoun	4,028	$22,600	20.0
Dixie	4,396	$19,700	21.0
Escambia	103,191	$30,100	21.2
Franklin	3,684	$20,200	19.5
Gadsden	13,530	$32,900	22.8
Gilchrist	3,165	$21,700	19.2
Gulf	5,018	$28,000	25.2
Holmes	6,147	$22,100	21.6
Jackson	14,973	$23,500	21.4
Jefferson	4,127	$21,600	22.2
Lafayette	1,806	$22,400	20.4
Leon	74,274	$32,900	22.8
Levy	9,908	$23,800	18.7
Liberty	1,635	$24,400	19.9
Madison	5,601	$21,400	25.6
Okaloosa	54,699	$31,800	18.5
Santa Rosa	30,005	$30,100	21.2
Taylor	6,656	$28,500	26.0
Wakulla	4,825	$25,800	19.2
Walton	13,874	$25,200	22.2
Washington	6,722	$22,300	21.0
Northeast:			
Alachua	73,882	$31,900	22.6
Baker	5,658	$30,200	18.2
Bradford	7,088	$31,900	22.6
Clay	35,996	$33,700	21.1
Columbia	16,038	$28,000	22.5
Duval	262,721	$33,700	21.1
Flagler	11,011	$29,100	18.9
Hamilton	3,608	$23,400	22.1
Nassau	15,510	$33,700	21.1
Putnam	24,960	$24,300	21.2
St. Johns	33,333	$33,700	21.1
Suwannee	10,372	$23,100	19.8
Union	2,763	$26,200	19.9
Central East:			
Brevard	165,032	$34,800	18.6
Indian River	37,636	$31,900	18.9
Martin	41,475	$32,400	16.2
Okeechobee	9,742	$25,900	18.2
St. Lucie	58,592	$32,400	16.2
Volusia	154,190	$28,700	17.6
Central:			
Highlands	29,452	$24,200	16.9
Lake	62,618	$27,300	17.2
Marion	77,761	$24,400	18.6
Orange	260,291	$37,500	18.9

County	Total Households 1990	Median Income 1990	Percent of Housholds With Very Low Incomes
Osceola	36,754	$37,500	18.9
Polk	158,237	$28,800	19.0
Seminole	109,108	$37,500	18.9
Sumter	11,904	$25,400	18.6
Central West:			
Citrus	39,350	$24,7001	6.6
Hernando	39,479	$31,400	18.0
Hillsborough	332,485	$31,400	18.0
Pasco	120,324	$31,400	18.0
Pinellas	388,265	$31,400	18.0
Southwest:			
Charlotte	48,276	$29,300	15.6
Collier	63,315	$36,700	20.3
De Soto	8,674	$24,300	19.0
Hardee	7,136	$25,200	20.2
Lee	140,576	$32,500	17.2
Manatee	85,924	$30,300	17.1
Sarasota	123,401	$34,100	16.6
Southeast:			
Broward	542,201	$38,800	18.2
Dade	710,633	$36,400	21.9
Glades	2,985	$22,100	30.0
Hendry	8,510	$31,600	23.1
Monroe	32,132	$32,500	24.3
Palm Beach	365,350	$40,000	18.7

Sources: Reinhold P. Wolff Economic Research Inc.; U.S. Department of Housing and Urban Development, Jacksonville office

MAJOR INDUSTRIES

If you are a petroleum engineer, a marine architect, a diamond worker or a nuclear technician, you're going to have a tough time finding a job in Florida for the next 10 years.

But if you are a secretary, a cashier, a retail salesperson, a groundskeeper or a gardener, you won't have any trouble.

The steady stream of new residents and tourists to the state has led to an increased demand for employees to cater to the masses and has brought about a phenomenal growth in the service and retail occupation sectors. For example, the number of employees in the service industry grew by nearly 98 percent from 1976 to 1986. This rise has propelled the industry — which includes such different categories as hotels, health services and even motion pictures — to be Florida's largest one today, with about 1.5 million workers. That figures is projected to grow to nearly 2.5 million by the year 2000. Even using the gross state product (the gross market value of the goods and services attributable to labor and property in the state) as a yardstick, the services sector is the leading money producer — about $49 billion in 1991.

Counting the number of employees, the next largest industries, in order, are retail trade; manufacturing; finance, insurance and real estate; construction; wholesale trade; transportation, communications and public utilities; agriculture (including the country's No. 1 citrus industry), forestry and fishing; and mining, according to the Florida Department of Labor and Employment Security.

Some of the major products and services you will find in the state include electronics, jet engines, aerospace services, avionics, aircraft modification, shipping, nylon fibers, fiber optics, luxury yachts, small boats, pulp and paper, phosphates, sugar processing, publishing and computers.

Here is a breakdown of Florida's major industries. The figures show average monthly employment in 1990 and during the second quarter 1991 by firms paying unemployment compensation. Some figures for 1991 are lower than those for 1990, in many cases because of the recession.

Florida's Major Industries

	Employees 1990	Employees Second Quarter 1991
TOTAL ALL INDUSTRIES	5,407,358	5,326,752
Private sector	4,571,908	4,458,179
Local government	531,195	562,971
State government	178,418	182,375
Federal government	125,033	122,423
International government	805	804
Private Sector Industry		
Services	1,487,101	1,497,844
Health	410,400	433,705
Business	300,841	296,143

Sightseers ride through Clearwater Beach during spring break. As many as 40 million people visit Florida each year.

Florida is the king of the citrus industry in the United States despite a number of freezes during the 1980s.

Among tourist attractions are boats that offer cruises on the Intracoastal Waterway along both the Atlantic and Gulf coasts.

	Employees 1990	Employees Second Quarter 1991
Hotels, rooming houses, camps and other lodging places	139,377	132,602
Engineering, accounting, research, management and related services	124.224	122,213
Amusement and recreation services	107,425	107,925
Social services	82,323	88,212
Personal services	62,523	62,744
Auto repair, services and parking	55,583	54,522
Legal	54,536	54,560
Membership organizations	47,591	45,404
Educational services	44,291	43,576
Miscellaneous repair services	24,403	21,657
Motion pictures	15,131	15,995
Private households	14,471	14,494
Museums, art galleries, botanical and zoological gardens	2,284	2,460
Retail Trade	1,154,958	1,112,023
Eating and drinking places	391,338	383,346
Food stores	206,394	208,925
Miscellaneous retail stores (drug stores, shopping goods stores)	139,853	130,311
General merchandise stores	134,055	124,144
Auto, RV, motorcycle and boat dealers, and gas stations	116,580	109,966
Apparel and accessory stores	64,256	63,092
Furniture and home furnishing stores	55,446	49,983
Building materials, hardware, garden supply, mobile home dealers	47,035	42,256
Manufacturing	519,999	492,045
Printing and publishing	66,001	64,023
Electronic and other electrical equipment and components, except computer equipment	60,178	57,726
Transportation equipment	61,692	56,644
Food and kindred products	47,309	45,186
Industrial machinery and equipment and computer equipment	42,678	41,430
Instruments and related products (search and navigation equipment; medical instruments and supplies; ophthalmic goods; photographic equipment; watches and clocks)	35,463	34,676
Apparel and other textile products	32,915	32,268
Fabricated metal products	32,618	30,000
Chemicals and allied products	23,042	22,290
Stone, clay, glass and concrete products	22,994	19,751
Lumber and wood products	22,428	19,241
Rubber and miscellaneous plastics products	21,414	20,214
Paper and allied products	14,085	13,471
Furniture and fixtures	13,552	12,110

	Employees 1990	Employees Second Quarter 1991
Miscellaneous manufacturing industries (Jewelry, musical instruments, toys and sporting goods)	8,989	9,499
Primary metals	5,553	5,307
Textile mill products	3,962	4,399
Leather products	2,484	2,256
Petroleum and coal products	1,582	1,677
Tobacco manufacturing	1,060	985
Finance, real estate and insurance	366,140	355,656
Depository institutions	113,923	108,270
Real estate	97,965	94,278
Insurance carriers	59,033	59,076
Insurance agents, brokers and service	39,245	39,309
Nondeposit credit institutions	25,852	26,528
Securities and commodities brokers and services	18,586	18,257
Holding and other investment offices	11,536	9,937
Construction	322,985	277,557
Wholesale Trade	292,633	286,601
Durable goods (those having a life expectancy of a more than a year, such as wood, steel, cars, machinery, electronics)	169,867	163,291
Non-durable goods (those having a life expectancy of less than a year, such as food, drugs, cigarettes, paper, clothing)	122,766	123,310
Transportation, Communications and Public Utilities	268,215	264,509
Communications	68,037	67,002
Trucking and warehousing	59,005	59,765
Air transportation	51,066	45,919
Electric, gas and sanitary services	39,702	39,658
Transportation services	21,583	21,614
Water transportation	17,378	18,546
Local and suburban transit and inter-urban passenger transportation	11,357	11,908
Agriculture, Forestry and Fishing	143,872	149,659
Agricultural services	70,790	75,325
Agriculture production — crops	63,674	65,172
Agriculture production — livestock	7,546	7,531
Fishing, hunting and trapping	982	771
Forestry	880	860
Mining	8,916	8,030

Unemployment

In the boom years of the late 1980s into 1990, Florida's unemployment rate generally was lower than the country as a whole and better than most other Sunbelt states. In recent years, though, Florida's rate has jumped higher.

In 1988, the average rate in the state was 5 percent, compared with a 5.4 percent national rate. But by August 1991, as the recession worsened, Florida's rate had jumped to 7.7 percent, higher than the national rate of 6.8 percent. And by mid-1994, Florida's seasonally adjusted rate had declined to 6.2 percent, was still higher than the national rate of 6 percent.

A closer look at Florida's rates for mid-1994 reveals that joblessness did not confine itself to just one section of the state. The highest unemployment rates were in agricultural areas: Hendry County (southwest), 20 percent, followed by St. Lucie (in central eastern Florida) at 14.5 percent; Glades (southeast) at 13.6 percent; Hardee (southwest) at 13.4 percent

and Indian River (central east) at 13.3 percent. On the other end of the scale, Franklin County (northwest) enjoyed the lowest rate — 2.7 percent. In second place was Monroe County (the Keys) at 3.6 percent, followed by Lafayette (northwest) at 3.9 percent, Alachua (northeast) at 4.0, and Flagler (northeast), Union (northeast) and Wakulla (northwest), all at 4.1 percent.

Among the state's 20 metropolitan statistical areas, the Gainesville area had the lowest jobless rate, at 4 percent, followed by Tallahassee at 4.7 percent; Sarasota at 4.9; Fort Walton Beach at 5.1; and Pensacola at 5.2. Those with the highest rates were the Fort Pierce area, 11.9 percent; Naples, 9.9; Lakeland-Winter Haven, 9.1; West Palm Beach-Boca Raton, 8.8, and Miami, 8.1.

Here are unemployment rates, by county. They are preliminary figures from June 1994 and are not seasonally adjusted. At that time, the overall statewide rate was 6.8 percent (the seasonally adjusted rate was 6.2 percent, but was not available by county).

Unemployment Rates

	Labor Force	Number Employed	Unemployment Rate
Alachua	97,803	93,872	4.0%
Baker	9,373	8,761	6.5%
Bay	68,794	63,755	7.3%
Bradford	9,603	9,065	5.6%
Brevard	209,652	194,675	7.1%
Broward	715,307	668,560	6.5%
Calhoun	4,388	4,053	7.6%
Charlotte	44,167	41,542	5.9%
Citrus	35,666	32,870	7.8%
Clay	57,416	54,974	4.3%
Collier	77,505	69,854	9.9%
Columbia	22,362	20,454	8.5%
Dade	1,057,616	971,520	8.1%
De Soto	9,421	8,769	6.9%
Dixie	4,121	3,814	7.4%
Duval	363,946	343,615	5.6%
Escambia	123,732	117,249	5.2%
Flagler	12,976	12,443	4.1%
Franklin	5,054	4,918	2.7%
Gadsden	18,795	17,670	6.0%
Gilchrist	4,242	4,016	5.3%
Glades	3,281	2,834	13.6%
Gulf	6,168	5,804	5.9%
Hamilton	3,563	3,211	9.9%
Hardee	10,466	9,061	13.4%
Hendry	15,138	12,117	20.0%
Hernando	39,084	36,009	7.9%
Highlands	26,395	23,775	9.9%

	Labor Force	Number Employed	Unemployment Rate
Hillsborough	473,506	446,742	5.7%
Holmes	6,850	6,379	6.9%
Indian River	38,281	33,190	13.3%
Jackson	21,260	19,260	9.4%
Jefferson	5,973	5,648	5.4%
Lafayette	2,524	2,425	3.9%
Lake	72,038	66,657	7.5%
Lee	165,567	156,350	5.6%
Leon	120,845	115,338	4.6%
Levy	12,024	11,273	6.2%
Liberty	2,385	2,261	5.2%
Madison	7,157	6,748	5.7%
Manatee	106,020	100,800	4.9%
Marion	89,224	82,525	7.5%
Martin	45,851	42,356	7.6%
Monroe	44,084	42,476	3.6%
Nassau	24,021	22,663	5.7%
Okaloosa	74,290	70,468	5.1%
Okeechobee	16,664	14,860	10.8%
Orange	426,418	401,581	5.8%
Osceola	66,788	62,988	5.7%
Palm Beach	442,963	403,864	8.8%
Pasco	111,708	103,952	6.9%
Pinellas	427,266	404,019	5.4%
Polk	197,450	179,435	9.1%
Putnam	33,293	31,112	6.6%
St. Johns	47,0654	4,387	5.7%
St. Lucie	76,419	65,344	14.5%
Santa Rosa	42,629	40,519	4.9%
Sarasota	137,230	130,445	4.9%
Seminole	187,502	176,861	5.7%
Sumter	12,320	11,465	6.9%
Suwannee	13,611	12,642	7.1%
Taylor	7,220	6,348	12.1%
Union	3,838	3,682	4.1%
Volusia	175,512	164,312	6.4%
Wakulla	9,518	9,126	4.1%
Walton	15,017	14,333	4.6%
Washington	8,338	7,805	6.4%

Source: Florida Department of Labor and Employment Security, Bureau of Labor Market Information, in cooperation with the U.S. Bureau of Labor Statistics.

Wages

A few days after Christmas, in a convenience store in St. Petersburg Beach, the young woman behind the counter at 11 p.m. looked tired.

"What's the matter? Long day?" asked a visitor.

"Long year," she said. "I wish they'd do something about the wages around here. I left New York because I was tired of needing a roommate to help pay the rent. Now I've got my own place, but I'm working one full-time job and two part-time jobs. It's too bad. I love this area. But I don't know how long I can survive these low wages."

Indeed, wages represent one category where Florida is noticeably lagging. The average annual pay in the state was $20,072 in 1989, compared with a $22,567 average for the United States as a whole.

Statistics compiled by the Florida Department of Labor and Employment Security show that for jobs listed with the Job Service of Florida during a sample period (July 1, 1991 through Dec. 31, 1991), the average wage offered for professional, technical or managerial jobs was $9.15 an hour; for clerical positions, $5.50; sales jobs, $5.54; services sector jobs, $4.93; agricultural, fishery, forestry and related jobs, $4.88; processing jobs, $4.71; machine trade jobs, $6.19; benchwork jobs, $5.02; structural work positions, $6.67, and for jobs not included in the other categories, $5.81.

- Counselor: $8.16
- Licensed practical nurse: $8.40
- Accountant: $9.65
- Employment interviewer: $8.03
- Administrative assistant: $8.47
- Retail store manager: $6.39
- Food service manager: $7.59
- Management trainee: $5.56
- Legal secretary: $7.03
- Secretary: $6.33
- Clerk-typist: $5.63
- Word processing machine operator: $6.64
- Survey worker: $5.72
- General clerk: $5.17
- Mail handler: $5.87
- Cashier-checker: $4.58
- Telephone operator: $5.30
- Receptionist: $5.36
- General merchandise salesperson: $4.88
- General house worker: $5.15
- Yard worker: $5.04
- Fast-foods worker: $4.32
- Waiter/waitress (informal restaurant): $4.78

During this period, the Job Service received 205,276 openings and filled 75,651 of them. Many of the openings were in the services and clerical sectors.

A sampling of average wages offered for some of the more popular job openings during this period:

- Waiter/waitress (formal restaurant): $4.85
- Cook: $5.26
- Kitchen helper: $4.57
- Nurse's aide: $5.22
- Nursery school attendant: $4.46
- Security guard: $4.97
- Janitor: $4.86
- Fruit harvest worker: $5.15
- Industrial-commercial groundskeeper: $5.19
- Landscape laborer: $4.92
- Machinist: $7.90
- Automobile mechanic: $7.12
- Production assembler: $4.76
- Electrician: $8.53
- Painter: $6.40
- Cement mason: $7.57
- Carpenter: $7.33
- Plumber: $8.04
- Roofer: $6.12
- Construction worker: $5.16
- Heavy-truck driver: $6.22
- Light-truck driver: $6.40
- Store laborer: $5.26

Jobs To Look For (And Look Out For)

If you're going to a job placement service between now and the year 2000, don't expect an overabundance of jobs that will put you in a new Mercedes and an ocean-front villa.

That's because most of the openings will be in the service and sales industries, according to state labor department projections.

Here are the number of average annual openings expected between now and then:

Best Job Opening Bets

The state expects that these occupations will be among those with the highest numbers of openings by the year 2000:

- Retail salespersons: 20,547 average annual openings until 2000
- General managers and top executives: 13,345
- General office clerks: 12,086
- Cashiers: 10,715
- Janitors and cleaners: 10,602
- Secretaries (excluding legal & medical): 10,096
- Gardeners and groundskeepers: 9,350
- Waiters and waitresses: 7,939
- Registered nurses: 7,880
- Food preparation, service, fast food occupations: 7,313

The state also projects job openings by percentage change. Following are the top 10 jobs, ranked by change from 1989 to 2000. The first number is the number of average annual openings that are expected; the second number is the percentage change.

— Home health aides: 1,611 average annual openings until 2000; 87%
— Paralegals: 703; 81%
— Radiologic technologists: 491; 79%
— Physical therapists: 385; 78%
— Physical, corrective therapy assistants: 297; 77%
— Radiologic technicians: 275; 75%
— Medical records technicians: 359; 75%
— Medical assistants: 805; 68%
— Taxi drivers and chauffeurs: 974; 67%
— Medical secretaries: 1,290; 63%

Some of the Worst Job Bets

— Telephone station installation and repair workers: minus 14
— Electrical, electronic assemblers: minus 6
— Photo engraving and lithographic photography workers: 0
— Mine machinery mechanics workers: 0
— Marine architects: 0
— Gem and diamond workers: 0
— Locomotive firers: 0
— Signal or track switch maintenance workers: 1
— Blasters and explosives workers: 1
— Petroleum engineers: 1
— Choke setters: 1
— Roustabouts: 1
— Quarry rock splitters: 2
— Log graders and scalers: 2
— Nuclear technicians, technologists: 2
— Elevator operators: 2
— Rail track laying equipment operators: 2
— U.S. marshals: 3
— Pipelaying fitters: 4
— Mathematicians, math scientists: 6
— Mining Engineers: 8

Labor Unions

Compared with many other states, union membership in Florida is relatively low. In the early 1980s, 9.6 percent of Florida's non-farm workers were union members. That compared with a national average of 21.9 percent.

Today, that percentage for Florida probably is still accurate for private-sector employees, but the figure rises to about 15 percent for state, county and municipal workers, according to the Center for Labor Research and Studies at Florida International University in Miami. A 1990 report by the Institute for Southern Studies ranked the state 40th in the nation in the percentage of manufacturing workers who belonged to unions in 1988. Florida's percentage was 8.9.

Two reasons are cited for the low membership:

1. Florida's service industry is huge, and that industry is difficult to organize. It has grown quickly and typically it takes time to organize a union. The industry is fluid and includes a lot of part-time workers.

2. Florida is one of about 20 states that have a right-to-work law — meaning that union membership cannot be a condition of employment. In some other states, people starting work in a unionized company must join the union, but Florida's constitution bars this requirement.

In Florida's private industry, unions generally are more prevalent for airline and building trades workers and longshoremen in the major ports of Jacksonville, Miami and Tampa.

In government, firemen, policemen and sanitation workers are organized in most major cities, and there are large bargaining units for state workers.

Other Prominent Industries

Tourism

Thanks to movies such as "Where The Boys Are," to the advent of air conditioning, and to such state attractions as Disney World, the Sunshine State has become one of the most popular havens for tourists in the country. During 1993, state officials estimated that more than 41 million people visited Florida, better than 1992's 40.5 million visitors.

But the industry, like many others, can be fickle. During the first half of 1994, for example, the number of visitors was down — attributed to crime scares and competition from other vacation spots.

The avalanche of tourists has been both good and bad news. The good news: tourists have brought money to the state — spending $26 billion in 1991, for example, ranking Florida second to California in tourism expenditures. Tourism-recreation sales-tax collections totaled $1.98 billion in 1993.

The bad news: millions of tourists are finding their stay in Florida so enjoyable that they opt to stay, much to the dismay of many long-time residents. For in staying, new residents have brought myriad problems — from overdevelopment to water shortages — that were not around before.

The Florida Department of Commerce estimated that more than 19.7 million air visitors and nearly 21.3 million auto visitors came to Florida in 1993.

And the numbers of international visitors to the state have been growing markedly in recent years. U.S. Travel and Tourism Administration figures for 1993 show that more than 2.2 million Canadians visited Florida; more than 60 percent of them came from Ontario province and nearly 26 percent from Quebec province. And more than 4.6 million visitors from other countries made Florida their intended first stop in the United States in 1993 — 2.2 million from Western Europe, 1.1 million from South America, 536,000 from the Caribbean and 245,000 from Central America. However, some declines in foreign tourism have been recorded in the wake of publicity over the murders of foreign tourists between 1992 and 1994.

In an effort to keep track of tourism trends, the state's Division of Tourism each year conducts person-to-person interviews with visitors who are getting ready to go back home. In 1993, about 9,000 of these interviews took place in airport departure lounges and at various points along highways near the Florida border. All individuals interviewed had to meet two criteria: they were not residents and they had been in the state for at least one night and for no more than 180 nights.

A total of 4,229 air travelers who were waiting for non-stop commercial flights were interviewed in a number of Florida's airports. And a total of 4,695 auto visitor surveys were conducted along Florida's major highways.

Among the findings:

Air Visitors

— More air visitors came from New York than from any other state. A total of 16.1 percent came from New York, followed by 7.3 percent from New Jersey, 6.9 percent from California, 5.5 percent from Pennsylvania, 5 percent from Massachusetts, 5 percent from Ohio, 4.7 percent from Illinois, 4.2 percent from Texas, 3.8 percent from Michigan and 3.7 percent from Georgia.

— The Orange-Osceola-Walt Disney World region was the most popular destination, followed by Broward, Dade, Palm Beach, Pinellas, Hillsborough, Volusia, Lee, Brevard and Duval counties.

— The main purpose of air visitors' trips in 1993 was to go on vacation. Business travel was the No. 2 reason and visiting friends or relatives was No. 3.

— Of the top activities enjoyed by air visitors, shopping/restaurants was ranked No. 1, followed by rest/relaxation. The beaches were the No. 3 reason, followed by the climate, pool activities, visiting the state's attractions and going on daily cruises.

— Nearly 33 percent visited at least one Florida attraction during their stay.

— EPCOT Center was the top attraction visited — by 14.5 percent of the survey respondents. Walt Disney World's Magic Kingdom attracted the second highest percentage, 14.2 percent; followed by Disney-MGM Studios, 11.5 percent; Universal Studios, 8.1 percent; Sea World in Orlando, 4.4 percent; the state's parks and preserves, 4.3 percent; Busch Gardens in Tampa, 4 percent; Spaceport USA in Brevard County, 2.4 percent; Typhoon Lagoon at Walt Disney World, 2.2 percent; and Lake Buena Vista Village near Orlando, 1.9 percent.

— Air visitors spent $96.72 per party per day while in Florida. Broken down, this amounted to $10.70 for transportation, $2 for gas, $5.91 for groceries, $22.41 for food in restaurants, $30.89 for lodging, $9.55 for entertainment, $8.18 for gifts and $7.08 for other items.

— Most of the air visitors were 26 to 65 years old.

— A total of 92.9 percent said they were repeat visitors and 97 percent said they will return to Florida.

Auto Visitors

— 15.8 percent of those driving to Florida came from Georgia, 6 percent from Ohio, 5.3 percent from Michigan, 5.2 percent from New York, 5.1 percent from Ontario, 4.5 percent from Tennessee, 4.2 percent from North Carolina, 4.1 percent from South Carolina, 4.1 percent from Alabama and 4 percent from Pennsylvania.

— Around 21 percent drove to the Orange-Osceola-Walt Disney World region, while Bay County was the destination for 12.8 percent; Volusia, 11.6 percent; Pinellas, 6.7 percent; Okaloosa, 6.3 percent; Brevard, 6 percent; Broward, 5.8 percent; Palm Beach, 5.5 percent; Duval, 5.5 percent; and Hillsborough, 4.7 percent.

— The main purpose of coming to Florida was going on vacation (59.5 percent), followed by visiting friends and relatives (27.8 percent).

— About 36 percent of those driving visited at least one or more of Florida's attractions.

— Walt Disney World's Magic Kingdom was visited by 12.9 percent of auto visitors, followed by EPCOT Center, 12.6 percent; Disney-MGM Studios, 12 percent; Universal Studios, 7.9 percent; Sea World, 6.1 percent; Busch Gardens, 4.3 percent; Spaceport USA, 2.9 percent; Florida's parks/preserves, 2.8 percent; Cypress Gardens, 2.3 percent; and Church Street Station in Orlando, 1.7 percent.

— More than a third of those drivers surveyed came to Florida either for rest and relaxation or for shopping and restaurants, followed by going to the beach, enjoying the climate and visiting the state's attractions and daily cruises.

— Auto visitors spent $53.45 per party per day while in Florida — 73 cents for transportation, $3.78 for gas, $6.48 for groceries, $10.97 for food in restaurants, $18.49 for lodging, $6.71 for entertainment, $3.47 or gifts and $2.82 for other items.

— The majority of drivers were in the 36-and-up age group.

— A total of 94.6 percent said they were repeat visitors and 97 percent said they will return to Florida.

Citrus Industry

In 1894-95, the Great Freeze struck.

Just before then, Florida citrus production had reached a record high of more than 5 million boxes, but the freeze that year almost destroyed the industry. Fifteen years later, Florida citrus farmers were picking away at record levels again.

Since then, production has increased to the tune of around 250 million boxes. And despite a number of freezes during the 1980s, including a devastating one in the 1989-90 season, Florida today remains the king of the citrus industry in the United States. The Florida Agricultural Statistics Service estimates Florida accounts for around 73 percent of the nation's citrus production.

The preliminary on-tree value of the state's citrus crop during the 1992-93 season, for example, was $695 million, versus $1.209 billion the year before. Total production of all varieties for the 1992-93 season was 251.4 million boxes.

Florida produces about 61 percent of the value of the nation's oranges. Its closest competitors are: California, which produces about 38 percent of the U.S. orange crop value; Arizona, 0.7 percent; and Texas, 0.4 percent. Florida has no close competitor when it comes to grapefruit production.

Among the money-making citrus crops the Sunshine State produces are oranges, valued at $497.3 million during the 1992-93 season; grapefruit, valued at $141.9 million; tangerines, $38.1 million; tangelos, $8.7 million; limes, $1 million, (down substantially from $14.5 million the year before because of Hurricane Andrew in 1992); and lemons, $1.5 million, also down because of Andrew.

The top citrus-producing counties in Florida are Polk, St. Lucie, Hendry, Indian River, Highlands, Desoto and Hardee. The top orange-producing counties: Polk and Hendry; the top grapefruit producers: St. Lucie and Indian River.

The Film Industry

Movie and television producers and directors have flocked to the state for years, using Florida as backdrops for many films and television shows. Scores of films and television shows — including an occasional box office hit or two — have been shot on location in Florida. Among some of the titles: "Cocoon II," "Let It Ride," "The Adventures of Superboy," and "Spring Break '88." Even Disney-MGM Studios and Universal Studios have theme parks in the state.

The presence of the industry in the Sunshine State has led to jobs and has helped pump money into state coffers. "Cocoon II," for example, which was shot in Miami, had a capital investment of $17.5 million and employed 1,600 people. "Let it Ride," also shot in Miami, had a capital investment of $20 million and employed 5,600 people.

And the Florida Department of Labor and Employment Security estimates that by the year 2000, projected employment in the motion picture industry in Florida will be 18,382.

Miami has been a star attraction, but other cities have also had their place in the sun, including: Gainesville, Cape Canaveral, Lauderhill, Fort Lauderdale, Homosassa, Crystal River, Miami Beach, Jacksonville, Gulf Breeze, Tampa, Mount Dora, Madison, Key West, Orlando, Palm Beach, St. Petersburg, Bartow, Winter Haven, St. Augustine and Sarasota.

Among movies and television series that have been shot in Florida (and their capital investment figures): the "New Leave it to Beaver Series," shot in Orlando, $3.2 million capital; "Ernest Saves Christmas," also shot in Orlando, $5.5 million; "Burt Reynolds" (6 two-hour movies), shot in the Palm Beach area, $24 million; "Caddy Shack II," shot in Fort Lauderdale, $2 million; and "America's Most Wanted," also shot in Fort Lauderdale, $1 million.

Florida's banks are fiercely competitive; many offer special services to attract customers.

THE ESSENTIALS: THINGS YOU NEED TO KNOW

TAXES

Just as clouds will hover over the Sunshine State, so, too, will the tax man loom over residents. But for many people, he will offer a silver lining.

Florida provides tax incentives that some non-residents might envy: While many states do not give tax breaks to homeowners, Florida does. While others impose an income tax, Florida does not. And while some states will sock you with an inheritance tax, Florida will not.

The homestead exemption offers a hefty tax break for homeowners. The catch: You must prove you are making your Florida home your permanent residence.

But some of the silver lining may get tarnished as Florida's growth dictates the need for tax law changes. Various groups in the state say that more money is needed for a lagging education system; that traffic congestion will take billions to fix; that people moving into the state are putting an enormous strain on public services. Some residents even suggest that a state income tax eventually will be needed. And there have been proposals that would make the homestead exemption less attractive. Here is a look at Florida's other taxes:

State Taxes

* The sales tax. Yes, there is one. It was raised to 6 percent as of Feb. 1, 1988. Coun-ties also have the option of increasing this rate a percentage point, up to 7 percent. There are some exemptions to the tax: groceries, medicines, legal and accounting services and any other service that does not involve the sale of a tangible item. From July 1, 1987 to Jan. 1, 1988, there also was a sales tax on professional services. An outcry against this law led to its repeal.

* The intangible tax. This is due to the state on an individual or corporation's assets. These assets —such as stocks, bonds, mutual funds and money market funds — are taxed as of Jan. 1 and are payable no later than June 30 of the same year. Individuals are taxed on the market value of these investments. Cash is not included; certificates of deposit, Individual Retirement Accounts — anything convertible to cash — is exempt. Also exempt are federal government holdings, such as Treasury bonds, and Florida state, municipal and county bonds. However, taxes must be paid on similar bonds held in other states.

Of taxable assets, the first $20,000 per individual or $40,000 for couples filing joint tax returns is exempt. Above that, the tax is $1 for every $1,000 of fair market value. And as of 1993, on assets above $100,000 per individual or $200,000 for couples, there is another $1 per $1,000 that has been added to the tax. Here's an example: If a married couple has a total market value of $300,000 in intangible assets, they would pay no tax on the the first $40,000. After that, they would pay $1 for each $1,000 in assets on the remaining $260,000, or $260. In addition, they would pay $1 for each $1,000 in assets above the $200,000 exemption (or the remaining $100,000 in assets). This would amount to another $100. The couple's total tax would be $360. Assets are calculated for value as of Jan. 1. If you file by February, you get a 4 percent discount; by March, a 3 percent discount; by April, a 2 percent discount; by May, a 1 percent discount. If the total tax due is less than $5, you don't have to file.

* A state documentary tax. This is applied to mortgages, promissory notes, installment loans or any written obligation to pay money. The tax rate is 35 cents per $100. Real estate deeds are taxed at a higher rate — 70 cents per $100.

Local and County Taxes

* Local property taxes. The lien is attached on Jan. 1 of the tax year. Homeowners, though, do not receive their bill until more than 10 months later, usually by Nov. 1. Discounts

apply for prompt payment. You get a 4 percent discount if you pay in November, a 3 percent discount if you pay in December, a 2 percent discount if you pay in January, and a 1 percent discount if you pay in February. Taxes are due by April 1.

* The homestead exemption. On local property taxes, this exempts Florida residents from the first $25,000 of the assessed value on their home. Example: If you own a $75,000 house and the local property tax on the house otherwise would be $1,000, you'll pay tax based on a $50,000 assessment — or $667.

To get this break, you must prove that you own the property, are a Florida resident and are using this property as your permanent residence. You must file for this benefit at the county property appraiser's office between Jan. 1 and March 1. If you miss the deadline, you lose the exemption for the year. Initial filings must be made in person. At the option of each county, renewals can be automatic.

The important factor is whether you intend to make Florida your permanent residence. The property appraiser makes this determination by asking a number of questions. He or she may ask you where you work; where you're registered to vote; where your driver's license or license tags on any motor vehicle you own were issued; the address on your federal income tax return; whether you have filed Florida intangible tax returns; and where you lived previously and the date your non-Florida residency ended.

Widows, widowers, blind people and the totally and permanently disabled are allowed additional exemptions.

Giving false information subjects you to a fine of up to $2,500 and payment of back taxes with interest.

* The tangible tax. This is a county tax and must be paid by April 1. The tax is on business assets, such as equipment and other machinery — on all goods of value needed to run a business. Inventory and the building itself, which is subject to the real estate property tax, are exempt. If you have residential rental property, you must pay a tangible tax on the furniture and other items of value, such as appliances. Finally, attachments to mobile homes that are on rented land are subject to this tax. The rate varies, depending on the millage of each county. See the tax test at the end of this chapter.

* Gas taxes. All gasoline is taxed at 4 cents per gallon and is subject to a 7.8-cents-per-gallon sales tax. In addition to this tax of 11.8 cents per gallon, counties also can impose additional taxes — up to 11.3 more cents per gallon, for a total tax as high as 23.1 cents per gallon.

Tax Calendar

Nov. 1: Around this time, local property tax and tangible tax bills are sent out. Pay this month and get 4 percent discounts.

Dec. 1-31: Pay local property taxes and tangible taxes and get 3 percent discounts.

Jan. 1: Calculate value of stocks, bonds, mutual funds, money market funds for the state's intangible tax.

Jan. 1-31: Pay local property taxes and tangible taxes and get 2 percent discounts.

Feb. 1-28: Pay intangible tax and get a 4 percent discount.

Pay local property taxes and tangible taxes and get 1 percent discounts.

March 1: Deadline to apply for the homestead exemption.

March 1-31: Pay intangible tax and get a 3 percent discount.

April 1: Local property taxes and tangible taxes must be paid.

April 1-30: Pay intangible tax and get a 2 percent discount.

April 15: Federal income taxes due.

May 1-31: Pay intangible tax and get a 1 percent discount.

June 30: Intangible tax due.

Establishing Legal Residence

To become a resident, you must establish a home or a permanent dwelling place and demonstrate your intent to make Florida your permanent legal residence. No fixed waiting period is required before becoming a resident.

Newcomers, though, are urged to produce proof of intent to establish residence by filing a sworn statement with the clerk of circuit court in the county where your new home is located. There is a $6 charge for recording this affidavit and a Florida driver's license is required. The document makes it easier for you to become eligible for such things as voting, serving on juries and the waiving of tuition fees because waiting periods are computed from the date this statement is filed with the circuit court clerk.

Establishing legal residence in Florida does not make a person a citizen of the United States, although it is not necessary to be a U.S. citizen to be a state resident. It is necessary to contact the U.S. Immigration and Naturalization Service (with offices in Miami) for information on obtaining U.S. citizenship, entry visas and work permits. U.S. citizenship is required to be eligible to vote, to serve on a jury or to hold public office in Florida.

Legal residence is important in qualifying for tax breaks, such as the homestead exemption, and in a number of other areas:

1. Seeking state or county government jobs. While there are no residency requirements, preference may be given to Florida residents.

2. Voting and serving on a jury. As a permanent resident, you may register with the supervisor of elections in the county where you wish to qualify to vote. Registration books are closed 30 days before an election and re-opened after the election. People selected for jury duty are chosen from the roll of registered voters. All voters must be U.S. citizens and at least 18 years old.

3. Waiving of school tuition fees: Non-residents may be charged a $50 tuition fee for a student in kindergarten through grade 12. Pupils of parents or guardians who are non-residents of Florida should have a written Agreement of Transfer of Schools. The tuition may be waived if a parent or guardian has lived in Florida for more than one year, has bought a home in Florida that he or she occupies as his or her residence before the child is enrolled, or has filed an affidavit of domicile in the county where the school is located. Fees may be waived for certain categories, such as military personnel. To qualify for in-state tuition fees at the state's public universities and community colleges, a student (or parent if the student is a dependent) must have lived in the state for 12 consecutive months before enrolling.

4. Applying for noncommercial fishing and hunting licenses. To qualify for less expensive resident statewide or county licenses, you must have lived in Florida continuously for six months. Armed services personnel stationed in Florida and students enrolled in colleges and universities in the state are considered residents.

5. Getting a divorce. One of the parties to the marriage must live in Florida for six months before filing a petition.

6. Candidacy for public office. All candidates must be U.S. citizens and registered voters in Florida. Candidates for governor, lieutenant governor and the Florida cabinet must be at least 30 years old and have been a Florida resident for the preceding seven years; candidates for the Floirda legislature must be at least 21 years old and a resident of the district he or she wishes to represent; a candidate for local office must be a resident of the appropriate district.

Driver's Licenses

Florida's driver's license requirements are nothing to take lightly. The testing is more intensive than in some states, and renewals are not automatic. The laws against driving under the influence of alcohol or controlled substances are among the toughest in the nation.

You must get a Florida driver's license if you:

* Live in Florida and want to drive a motor vehicle.

* Move to Florida and become a resident. You become a resident if you enroll your children in public school, register to vote, file for a homestead exemption, accept employment or reside in Florida for more than six consecutive months. If you have a valid license from another state, you must get a Florida license within 30 days of becoming a resident.

Conversely, you do not need to get a Florida license if you:

* Are a non-resident.

* Work for the U.S. government and drive a U.S. government motor vehicle on official business.

* Are a non-resident working for a firm on a contract for the U.S. government (this exemption applies for only 60 days).

* Are a non-resident attending college in Florida.

* Are a member of the armed forces stationed in Florida. Dependents are also exempt. However, service members or their dependents who take a civilian job or apply for a homestead exemption must obtain a license.

* Are a migrant farm worker.

* Live in another state and travel regularly between your home and work in Florida.

Written, vision and road tests are required to get a license. A full examination includes five sections: a road sign test, a vision test, a road rules test, a vehicle inspection and a driving test.

The road sign test consists of looking at road signs and telling what they mean; the vision test requires passing a standard eye test; and the road rules test involves knowledge of Florida's traffic laws.

A complete written exam includes 20 questions on road signs and 20 questions on road rules. To pass, you must choose the right answer for at least 15 road signs and 15 road rules questions.

Some sample questions: If your name has been legally changed, how would you go about getting it changed on your driver's license? What would happen to the license of a driver who was involved in an accident and did not stop to help persons who were injured? Are you allowed to drive on the highways with a flat tire? When are you driving too slowly? When may you drive in a left lane on a road with four or more lanes with two-way traffic? When passing a vehicle you must return to the right side of the road before coming within how many feet of an oncoming vehicle?

During the vehicle inspection, your car is checked to make sure it is in good working order. And during the driving test, you may be asked to do the following: Turn your car around in a 40-foot space; back up for 50 feet at a slow speed without using the rear-view mirror by looking to the rear instead; stop quickly when driving at 20 miles an hour.

Driver's license offices are located in more than 120 cities and towns throughout the state. Express service for license renewals is also available by going to selected Eckerd Drugs stores throughout the state.

An appointment is advised in heavily populated areas as waits can be as long as four hours. Waits may be minimal in rural areas. For walk-ins, early mornings are a good time to avoid lines.

When applying for a license, you must bring your out-of-state driver's license and a Social Security card or another document with your name on it.

A Florida license is good for either four or six years. If you get a ticket that shows up on state computers before your license expires, you must renew in four years; ticket-free individuals don't renew for six. The fee is $19 for the initial license and $15 for renewals. Eye tests are required for all renewals.

The Department of Highway Safety and Motor Vehicles administers the driving tests and issues a "Florida Driver's Handbook," available at driver's license offices around the state. The booklet contains information on license requirements, study questions on road laws and sample test questions.

For example, did you know that under Florida law, you may not pass another vehicle within 100 feet of a bridge, viaduct, railroad crossing or tunnel? That pedestrians and drivers must yield the right-of-way to funeral processions? That parking is not allowed within 30 feet of a rural mail box on a state highway between 8 a.m. and 6 p.m.? That a pennant-shaped road sign denotes a no-passing zone? That it takes an average freight train traveling at 30 miles per hour more than a half mile to stop? That you may not have a television in your vehicle that the driver can see?

Inspection stickers are not required. But because of air pollution, auto-emissions testing began in 1991 in Florida's six most populated counties — Dade, Broward, Palm Beach, Hillsborough, Pinellas and Duval. Inspections cost $10 per vehicle and must be done within 90 days before the expiration of your tag. Waivers may be granted on an individual basis if required repairs are costly. A minimum of $100 for a vehicle built between 1975 and 1979, or a minimum of $200 for those built in 1980 or later, must be paid before a waiver can be granted.

Penalties for driving violations are strict. Under the state's "point system," if you accumulate 12 points within a 12-month period, your license is suspended for 30 days; 18 points within an 18-month period, the suspension is three months; and 24 points within a 36-month period, the suspension is one year.

You can accumulate 6 points for leaving the scene of an accident resulting in property damage of more than $50 and for unlawful speed resulting in an accident; 4 points for reckless driving, any moving violation resulting in an accident, passing a stopped school bus, or driving 16 miles per hour or more over the speed limit; 3 points for driving 15 miles per hour or less over the speed limit and all other moving violations including parking on the highway outside the limits of municipalities; and 2 points for an improper-equipment violation, such as brakes, lights or steering.

The state's laws against driving under the influence of alcohol or controlled substances are among the toughest in the nation. Penalties include:

* License revocation: at least 6 months for the first conviction; at least 5 years, if within 5 years of the first conviction, for the second offense; and at least 10 years, if within 10 years of the first conviction, for the third offense.

* Fines: minimums of $250 for the first conviction, $500 for the second, and $1,000 for the third.

* Imprisonment: First conviction: up to 6 months. Second conviction: up to 9 months, and at least 10 days if within three years of the first conviction. Third conviction: up to a year, and at least 30 days if within 5 years of the first conviction.

* Probation: At least one year after the first conviction.

* Community service: At least 50 hours after the first conviction.

* School: Must complete a substance abuse course for each conviction and pay for it. The school can require further treatment, if necessary, without court approval.

Insurance

At least $10,000 in property damage liability insurance is required for motor vehicles plus $10,000 in personal injury insurance. Failure to get the proper coverage can result in the loss of your license, registration and tags. In addition, all insurance companies are required to report lapses in insurance coverage to the state. The fee for reinstating your insurance is anywhere from $150 to $500 if the state discovers your insurance has lapsed.

You will need to have proof of insurance before you can get your license plate and registration certificate. Those who cannot get motor vehicle liability insurance must prove their financial responsibility in other ways, such as using a surety bond, a certificate of self-insurance or a certificate of deposit of cash or securities.

On Jan. 1, 1989, motor vehicle insurance discounts became available for those 55 years of age or older who pass a motor vehicle accident prevention course.

Registration, License Plates and Titles

Anyone who accepts employment or works in Florida, registers to vote, files for the homestead exemption or enrolls children in a public school in Florida must obtain a Florida license plate and a registration certificate within 10 days after beginning employment or enrollment. You also must have a Florida Certificate of Title for your vehicle, unless an out-of-state financial institution holds the title and will not release it to Florida.

And on top of obtaining these items in Florida, if you are just moving into the state, you will find that you'd better have your checkbook handy with several hundred dollars in your account. As of 1990, the legislature imposed a $295 impact fee on new residents who own autos and light trucks on which no state sales and use tax is paid. It also increased the new-wheels-on-the-road tax from $30 to $100.

Anyone would pay a 6 percent sales and use tax if: 1. he bought a vehicle in Florida; or 2. he is seeking a Florida title and owns a vehicle that was registered or titled in his name in another state for less than six months. If a sales tax lower than Florida's 6 percent tax has been paid in another state, the difference in the amount paid is due in Florida. For example, if you bought a $10,000 car in another state and paid a 4 percent — $400 — sales tax on it, you would owe Florida another 2 percent, or $200.

You are not subject to the tax if you paid more than 6 percent in another state or if you moved to Florida and own a motor vehicle that was registered or titled in your name in another state for six months or longer. But it is here that the law has been changed. Now people owning a vehicle more than six months in another state will pay a flat $295.

The new-wheels tax will also apply to people moving into Florida, or to anyone living in the state who buys a new car without trading in another. The tax is meant to cover the cost of a new vehicle on Florida's roadways.

So, many new residents are going to find themselves paying out $395 before they even start buying their registration, title and car tag.

Before you can get your license plate and registration certificate, you must prove you own your vehicle and have insurance. You do this by presenting your certificate of title. You apply for your title, license plates and registration at any tax collector's office in the state. The title fee is $8.75 for each auto title certificate. A transfer of a certificate of title or application for a duplicate title is also $8.75.

The cost of the plate depends on the type and weight of the vehicle. For private-use automobiles, the fee ranges from $31 to $49.

License plates and registrations must be renewed each year. Renewals can be by mail, as long as you prove that you have the required insurance. Renewals are due on or before the birthday of the first person listed on the title. There are exceptions: Mobile homes are renewed yearly by Jan. 31; truck-tractors and semi-trailers by Dec. 31, and vehicles owned by companies and corporations by June 30.

The Lemon Law

A number of consumer-related laws have taken effect in recent years. Among them is a revised lemon law, which allows consumers several avenues of recourse if they have a defective automobile. The law applies only to cars bought or leased after Jan. 1, 1989.

If the manufacturer or authorized service agent is unable to fix a defect after three attempts, or if the car has been out of service because of a defect for more than 20 calendar days, the manufacturer will have one last chance to make the repair. The consumer first must notify the manufacturer in writing (either by certified or express mail) of the circumstances and the need for repair.

If the manufacturer still cannot fix the defect, he must replace the car with one that is acceptable to the consumer, or repurchase it at the full price, plus expenses, less a reasonable charge for use.

The manufacturer, though, can institute a

"certified informal dispute settlement procedure." The consumer then would have to resort to relief under this procedure before making a claim for replacement or repurchase.

If no such procedure is instituted, a consumer may apply directly to the Division of Consumer Services to have the dispute submitted to the Florida New Motor Vehicle Arbitration Board in the Attorney General's office.

Warranty problems reported during the first 18 months of new car ownership, or 24,000 miles, whichever occurs first, are covered under this law. During 1991, for example, the arbitration board accepted 1,696 cases for review; 72 percent, or 1,216 or them, were decided in favor of the car owner.

A Look at Traffic Statistics

What advice do you have for people in Florida?

The woman didn't think long.

"Stay out of the right lane," she said. "And the middle lane and the left lane."

Mention traffic to a Floridian and you'll likely get such cynical responses, or, at least, a roll of the eyes, a raising of the eyebrows, or a loud, unmistakable grunt. Driving in Florida, especially during the peak winter months, is not exactly carefree in the more urban areas. Neither is it like the Saturday after Thanksgiving in New York, when Christmas shoppers turn Fifth Avenue into the world's longest parking lot. You may not see thousands of yellow taxis here, but you'll hear your share of horn-honking and swearing.

Despite such frustrations, the number of accidents decreased in Florida between 1990 and 1991, even as the population increased.

Some statistics from the state Department of Highway Safety & Motor Vehicles for 1991:

* Florida had 12,170,821 licensed drivers and 11,184,146 registered vehicles.

* Compared with 1990, there was a 9.7 percent decrease in traffic accidents — 195,312 accidents involving 297,329 drivers, an average of 535 accidents per day. This compares with 216,245 accidents in 1990 and 252,439 in 1989.

* Of the 1991 accidents, there were 195,122 non-fatal injuries and 2,523 deaths.

* 42.2 percent of traffic fatalities and 13.3 percent of all accidents were alcohol-related.

* 23.8 percent of those involved in accidents were not using safety equipment, such as seat belts or motorcycle helmets.

* Total property damage from accidents was estimated at $859,426,911, or $4,400 per accident.

* The highest number of accidents were reported in March. Next, in order, were May, August, April, July, June, January, October, December, November, February and September.

* By day of week, more accidents occurred on Fridays than on any other day. After Friday were, in order, Saturday, Thursday, Tuesday, Wednesday, Monday and Sunday.

* More traffic fatalities occurred during the Thanksgiving holiday period than during any other holiday period. Next were Labor Day, Independence Day, Memorial Day, New Year's, and Christmas.

* 62.2 percent of drivers involved in accidents were males; 37.8 percent were females.

* 19.92 percent of the Florida resident drivers involved in accidents were 25 to 29 years old; next were those 20 to 24 (17.83 percent); 30-34 (17.65 percent); 35-39 (13.02 percent). The rest in descending order were: 40-44 (8.44 percent); 15-19 (6.35 percent); 45-49 (5.36 percent); 50-54 (3.41 percent); 55-59 (2.42 percent); 60-64 (1.87 percent); 65-69 (1.52 percent); 70-74 (0.76 percent); 75-79 (0.37 percent); 80-84 (0.10 percent); 85 and over (0.09 percent); and under 15 years of age (0.09 percent). Ages were not stated in 0.81 percent of accidents.

* Of the 297,329 drivers involved in accidents, 280,384 were Florida residents.

* Circumstances contributing to accidents, were, in order: careless driving; failure to yield right of way; improper turn/lane change/backing; disregarding traffic controls; under the influence of alcohol or drugs; speeding; and following too closely. It should be noted that officers reported "no improper driving/action" for 44.2 percent of drivers in all accidents during 1991.

Help for Senior Citizens

The American Association of Retired Persons offers a "55 Alive/Mature Driving" program for older drivers. Anyone who is over age 50 is eligible to take the course. The program is conducted in two half-day sessions and consists of eight hours of classroom instruction that seeks to refine driving skills and develop defensive driving techniques.

Consumer Information

The state Division of Consumer Services is the official clearinghouse for consumer education and complaints. It provides educational materials, recommends legislation, helps consumers resolve business-related problems and keeps residents abreast of product safety, scams in the marketplace and recall information. The agency publishes a general-interest newsletter called "Consumer Interest," which is free on request. It also provides informal mediation and conciliation for consumers who have complaints against businesses, and deals with complaints about vacations; motor vehicles; mail orders; credit and banking; advertising; landlord-tenant disputes; and travel.

For a publications list write the Division of Consumer Services, Mayo Building, Tallahassee, Fla., 32399-0800.

Consumer Hotlines

For answers to questions and help with problems, Florida residents can dial toll-free from anywhere in the state. Here are some of those numbers.

Attorney's referral service	1-800-342-8011
Auto safety	1-800-424-9393
Banking and finance department	1-800-848-3792
Boat safety and recalls	1-800-368-5647
Bureau of condominiums	1-800-342-8081
Bureau of mobile homes	1-800-843-6106
Consumer Product Safety Commission	1-800-638-2772
Consumer services, division of	1-800-435-7352 (Complaints)
	1-800-321-5366 (Lemon Law)
Department of Commerce, Florida Business Line	1-800-342-0771
Education-career development	1-800-342-9271
Game and fish violations	1-800-342-1676
Health Care Cost Containment Board	1-800-342-0828
Highway Safety and Motor Vehicles	1-800-299-8247
Human Relations Commission job and housing discrimination	1-800-342-8170
Insurance department (complaints)	1-800-342-2762
Legislative information	1-800-342-1827 (during session only)
Lottery, player information	1-800-752-9352
Marine Patrol (24 hours)	1-800-342-5367
Professional regulation department	1-800-342-7940
Public Service Commission	1-800-342-3552
Social Security	1-800-772-1213
Taxpayers assistance	1-800-352-3671
U.S. Department of Veterans' Affairs	1-800-282-8821
Workers compensation	1-800-342-1741

A Few Laws To Be Aware of

* The Florida Litter Law: Anyone violating it is guilty of a second-degree misdemeanor, punishable by community service or picking up litter.

* The Obscene Bumper Sticker Law: Any person who knowingly has a sticker, decal or other device attached to a motor vehicle that contains obscene descriptions, photographs or depictions is guilty of a second-degree misdemeanor.

* The Open Containers Law: It prohibits open containers of alcoholic beverages in ve- hicles for both passengers and drivers. Exceptions: chauffered vehicles, buses and self-contained motor homes in excess of 21 feet. Drivers who violate the law are guilty of a non-criminal moving traffic offense. Passengers who violate it are guilty of a non-moving traffic violation.

Banking Services

Florida's banking industry is fiercely competitive. If you write to any of the state's 220-plus chambers of commerce looking for information, you ought to prepare yourself for the barrage of mail and phone calls that will follow. After you get an initial call touting a bank's services, you can expect to receive free packets of information containing community profiles, listings of what to see and do in an area, details about local utilities and services and, of course, reams of hype about the bank. You may also get a letter asking you to call the bank collect if you have any questions. The letters and the offers will keep coming. And when you think you've heard from the last bank, you'll get another phone call.

Naturally, many banks are trying to lure people 55 and older. A number offer special services for these residents, including checking with no fees and no minimum balances; discounts on brokerage service commissions; bank-by-mail service; free notary service; credit cards with no annual fees; $100,000 in free common carrier travel accidental death insurance; and free travelers' checks and cashier's checks.

In some of the more populated areas, you can find as many as half a dozen banks surrounding a major intersection. As of 1993, there were 248 state-chartered commercial bank and trust companies in the state.

Overall, according to the state Banking and Finance Department, Florida's banking industry is reasonably healthy. International banking has burgeoned, particularly in the Miami area. As of Dec. 31, 1993, there were 70 state-licensed international bank agencies, representative offices and administrative offices.

There are areas — South Florida and the Tampa Bay region, for instance — where banks in recent years have changed loan portfolios and tightened credit after having had bad luck with real estate loans, largely commercial ones. Generally, these problems stemmed from overdevelopment. Many developers failed in recent years. For example, office vacancy rates were very high in some major cities, especially in South Florida, yet developers continued to build, and many strip malls never made it. The banks ended up with loans that the developers could not pay back. In addition, some developers put up huge residential communities that they could not sell. Or they built golf courses across from golf courses.

As a result, many banks have had to change their strategies — getting out of commercial loans and into more residential mortgage loans, for instance. However, by and large, the state's banking industry is not in bad shape, according to the banking department.

Total assets for Florida's state commercial banks and trust companies totaled more than $51 billion in 1993, up from $41.5 billion in 1992. Deposits in the same period rose from $37.1 billion to $44.4 billion.

Another type of financial institution — savings and loan associations (there were 13 state-chartered ones in 1993 compared with more than 50 in 1989) — have not fared as well. The Resolution Trust Corp., which was established by the federal government to save failing thrift institutions, had taken over daily supervision of a number of S&Ls. According to the banking department, the S&L industry in Florida is not as healthy as the commercial banking industry. Once the industry was deregulated, some S&Ls in Florida got into commercial loans, which they had had no experience with (before, their portfolios had consisted mainly of home mortgages). And some others had big holdings in the risky junk-bond business, which declined dramatically. They ended up with worthless or devalued bonds, and some went belly up.

Total assets of Florida's state-chartered S&Ls as of Dec. 31, 1993, were slightly more than $4.5 billion, down from $35 billion in 1988. Total deposits were $3.23 billion in 1993, down from nearly $25 billion in 1988.

State-Chartered Banks and Trust Companies
Top 20 Banks as of Dec. 31, 1993
(All amounts are in thousands)

Name of Bank	Assets
1. Barnett Bank of Pinellas County, St. Petersburg	$3,265,817
2. Barnett Bank of Palm Beach County, West Palm Beach	$3,013,031
3. AmSouth Bank of Florida, Pensacola	$2,606,692
4. Barnett Bank of Tampa	$2,526,908
5. Barnett Bank of Southwest Florida, Sarasota	$2,017,533
6. Sun Bank of Tampa Bay, Tampa	$1,896,340
7. Sun Bank/Gulf Coast, Sarasota	$1,630,448
8. Barnett Bank of Volusia County, DeLand	$1,535,141
9. Capital Bank, Miami	$1,118,946
10. Barnett Bank of Pasco County, Holiday	$1,046,112

State-Chartered Banks and Trust Companies [*continued*]
Top 20 Banks as of Dec. 31, 1993
(All amounts are in thousands)

Name of Bank	Assets
11. Intercontinental Bank, Miami	$1,042,512
12. Sun Bank of Volusia County, Daytona Beach	$1,026,788
13. Barnett Bank of Polk County, Lakeland	$971,985
14. Ocean Bank, Miami	$880,393
15. Barnett Bank of Naples, Naples	$869,543
16. Barnett Bank of West Florida, Pensacola	$846,786
17. SouthTrust Bank of West Florida, St. Petersburg	$741,361
18. Barnett Bank of Tallahassee, Tallahassee	$662,950
19. Sun Bank and Trust Company, Brooksville	$661,444
20. Barnett Bank of the Treasure Coast, Port St. Lucie	$632,214

State-Chartered Banks and Trust Companies
Top 20 Independent Banks as of Dec. 31, 1993
(All amounts are in thousands)

Bank	Assets
1. Capital Bank, Miami	$1,118,946
2. Intercontinental Bank, Miami	$1,042,512
3. Ocean Bank, Miami	$880,393
4. Peoples Bank of Lakeland, Lakeland	$554,491
5. Republic Bank, Clearwater	$529,579
6. Regions Bank of Florida, Pensacola	$492,541
7. Bank of North America, Fort Lauderdale	$489,574
8. Orange Bank, Ocoee	$354,423
9. Jefferson Bank of Florida, Miami Beach	$324,772
10. Ready State Bank, Hialeah	$288,408
11. Community First Bank, Jacksonville	$281,296
12. Coconut Grove Bank, Miami	$267,982
13. Commercial Bank of Florida, Miami	$255,352
14. The Bank of Inverness, Inverness	$254,554
15. Espirito Santo Bank of Florida, Miami	$247,996
16. Community Bank of Homestead, Homestead	$228,265
17. Popular Bank of Florida, Hialeah	$221,670
18. Beach Bank of Vero Beach, Vero Beach	$218,208
19. American Bank of Hollywood, Hollywood	$216,373
20. Wauchula State Bank, Wauchula	$216,301

Liquor Laws

Like most other states, Florida requires that a person be 21 years of age to drink alcoholic beverages. The photo background on the state's driver'slicenses provides a clue to a person's age. If the background is yellow, the person was under 21 when the license was issued. If the background is blue, the holder was 21 or older.

State law allows the sale of alcoholic beverages from 7 a.m. to midnight, seven days a week. Hours of sale, though, may be changed by county or municipal ordinance. In some areas, for example, bars stay open until 2 a.m.

The state agency overseeing the compliance of beverage and tobacco laws and rules is the Division of Alcoholic Beverages and Tobacco, The Johns Building, 725 S. Bronough St., Tallahassee 32399-1020. Besides the Tallahassee office, there are a number of state district offices.

To sell alcoholic beverages or cigarettes in Florida, you must be licensed. The division requires that all alcoholic beverage licensees be at least 21 and not have been convicted of a felony in the past 15 years or of a beverage violation in the past five years. There is no law requiring the license holder either to be a resident of Florida or a United States citizen. However, aliens must certify that their involvement in the business would not conflict with federal immigration regulations. Out-of-state corporations must be registered to do business in Florida.

Test Your Knowledge of the Tangible Tax

Question: The tangible tax is due:
A. On Nov. 1.
B. On April 1.
C. On April 15.
D. Before Jan. 1.

Question: Items taxable under the tangible tax are:
A. Only business equipment, machinery, furniture — anything inside a business except the building itself. No residential property is included.
B. Only business equipment plus items such as furniture, washers, driers, and drapes inside a rental property, such as a condominium or a beach house.
C. Only business equipment, furniture in a rental property, and attachments to mobile homes, such as carports and porches.

Question: According to tax officials, the tax payment becomes delinquent on:
A. Feb. 1.
B. March 1.
C. April 1.

Question: To figure how much you owe in tangible taxes each year:
A. The county property appraiser pays a visit and sets the value.
B. The county property appraiser visits properties at least once every three years and updates the figures.
C. The county property appraiser figures how much the property is worth and assumes a value based on the square footage.
D. You, as the owner of a piece of property, have to declare the value of your possessions and send along the tax payment.
E. Each county has its own "way of discovery," such as computer records.

Question: A tangible tax is due on residential rental property if:
A. The property is rented out for more than six months a year.
B. The property is rented out for less than six months a year.

C. The property is rented out at any time, even for a week.
D. Residential property is not subject to the tangible tax.

No matter which answers you chose, you would be correct, depending on who you asked — state tax agents, other state tax department experts, county tax collectors and a private accountant. There was no agreement among more than a dozen experts we talked to.

In one case, a state agent said that the tax is payable in April, but that you'd be delinquent if you didn't pay it by February. Another state agent, when asked about the tangible tax, launched into a minute-long description of exemptions under the intangible tax, then said, "Now wait a minute. Were you asking about the tangible tax or the intangible tax? I guess I got mixed up there." An employee in a county tax collector's office, which is responsible for collecting the tax, referred us to state tax officials because, she said, they're the ones who set up the tax. Finally, another state agent referred us to county tax collectors because, he said, they're the ones who collect the tax.

Confusing?

According to a state Department of Revenue bureau chief for the Ad Valorem Division, here is how the tax works:

It is a county tax — not a state tax — and the county sends out the bills. The rates vary, depending on the millage rate of each county.

The tax applies to three types of personal property:

* Business equipment — machinery and furniture, anything needed to operate a business. Inventory excluded.

* Attachments to mobile homes that are on rented land. These include carports, porches, glass rooms and vinyl rooms. If you own the land, you're subject to the real estate property tax. If you don't own the land, you're subject to the tangible tax only on these attachments. Because mobile homes depreciate quickly, a glass room added on in 1975 would have a lower value than one added on in 1988.

* Items inside rental properties — beach houses and condominiums, for example — such as furniture, washers, dryers, stoves, refrigerators. The county appraiser is responsible for determining the value of these items. Some counties, based on computer records, send notices to anyone who does not have a homestead exemption. If you own a rental house but have no homestead exemption, you must send back the form indicating the value of the items. If you throw out the form or fail to return it, the county can assess a percentage

based on the real estate value of the property. In one county, for example, a condomimium would be billed at 4 percent of the real estate value; all other types of houses would be billed at 6 percent of the value. So, assuming a tangible tax mill rate of 1 percent on a $100,000 beach house, with $6,000 worth of furniture and appliances, your tangible tax would be $6. If you have a stove and refrigerator and some furniture, chances are you won't have to pay much more than $8 or $10 in many areas.

As for the amount of time a property is rented, this can — and does — vary by county. In one county, anything rented as of Jan. 1 is taxable (even if you sell the property by Jan. 15, you still have to pay). Other counties can tax properties based on the amount of time they are rented out.

The tax bills go out around Nov. 1. If you pay the tax in November, you get a 4 percent discount; in December, a 3 percent discount; in January, a 2 percent discount; and in February, a 1 percent discount. The tax technically is due in November when the bills go out, but, for practical purposes, they do not become delinquent until April 1. Essentially, you have to pay by April 1 to avoid delinquency fees.

An alligator roams through the Everglades. This unique region has such serious environmental problems that its life expectancy in 1990 was estimated at 5 to 10 years.

Many Floridians enjoy water sports, but the quality of some of the state's rivers and lakes has deteriorated.

Manatees play at the Homosassa Springs Wildlife Park in Citrus County, on the central west coast. As Florida's population has soared, habitats for some species, including the manatee, have been threatened.

THE ENVIRONMENT

In a state where the tourism ads beckon visitors to swim in seemingly crystal-clear waters, to watch the palm trees sway in a light breeze, and to soak up the sun on a half-mile-wide beach, you might not think that there is a dark side to Florida.

But there is. Such things as polluted air, waters filled with pesticides and contaminated fish, and drinking water shortages have become a fact of life in the Sunshine State. Gone are many of Florida's once pollution-free waters, many of the state's natural resources and many of the animals and birds that once lived here. For years you can expect more developments, more people, and more threats that will likely diminish the state's resources to an even greater extent.

Here are some facts you won't find in any tourism brochures:

—At least 81 percent of the shellfish beds in Florida were classified in 1990 as "harvest limited" because of pollution from sources that also put bathers at risk. And many of these beds were closed to all shellfishing — 20 percent of the Atlantic shellfish beds and 35 percent of the Gulf beds, according to a National Resources Defense Council report in mid-1992.

— More than 55 percent of Florida's population breathes air that failed to meet the clean air standard for ground-level ozone during 1989.

— A total of 2,118 miles of the state's rivers and 304,258 acres of its lakes were found to be polluted or unable to support the uses for which they have been designated, such as for drinking water supplies, for fishing or for swimming.

— 43 percent of the state's public water systems were found to have one or more violations of the Safe Drinking Water Act during fiscal 1987. And the federal Environmental Protection Agency found that 67 percent of Florida's population is served by public water supplies in counties where water is potentially contaminated by pesticides or agricultural chemicals.

— A number of beaches have needed to be closed on occasion because bacteria levels exceeded accepted standards. Among the closings in 1991 were: Maxima Beach in St. Petersburg; Oelsner Park in Pasco County; Boca Raton Beach in Palm Beach County; three beaches at Biscayne Bay at Reickenbacker; and Palm Beach in Palm Beach County. The National Resources Defense Council found that 25 Florida counties do not have regular water quality monitoring programs at their ocean and bay beaches. Among those that do: Broward, Dade, Escambia, Hillsborough, Pasco, Pinellas, Duval, Palm Beach, Hernando and Sarasota.

Furthermore, it has come to light that you'd better not eat that largemouth bass or warmouth you caught in some parts of the state — it may be contaminated with mercury and may be unfit for human consumption.

So when you ask the question how well is Florida doing in protecting its resources and in helping the environment, it shouldn't come as a shock to learn that according to some environmental watchdogs, the state is not doing so hot. Florida received only a below-average rating in an environmental health report issued by the Institute for Southern Studies in 1990.

The Sunshine State ranked No. 30 (out of the 50 states) overall. The top 10 states in order were Vermont, Massachusetts, Minnesota, Rhode Island, Connecticut, Wisconsin, Hawaii, New Hampshire, Oregon and Maine. The bottom 10 states — mostly in the south — were Kentucky, North Carolina, Indiana, Georgia, Arkansas, Tennessee, South Carolina, Louisiana, Mississippi and Alabama. Florida had the best rating of any southern state.

According to the institute, all states have a "good" and an "ugly" side. Florida's good: It had the third best score nationwide in its rating for managing growth and regulating land use. The ugly: The state had one of the highest concentrations of groundwater potentially contaminated by pesticides or agricultural chemicals.

The institute, based in Durham, N.C., is a research and education center that focuses on environmental, economic and social conditions. It issued its environmental findings in a report called the "1990 Green Index: A State-By-State Report Card on the Nation's Environment."

"Every state has something they can be proud of, but they also have areas that demand immediate attention," said Bob Hall, research director of the institute.

Nationwide, the three problem areas posing the biggest threat to the environment were industrial pollution, especially toxic chemicals; land-use practices that ruin wetlands, groundwater, neighborhoods and wildlife habitats; and the automobile. The car is "the most lethal weapon assaulting America's public health and environment," Hall said.

Even the top-rated states have serious problems. No. 1-ranked Vermont had more Superfund and other hazardous waste sites needing attention, ranked on a per-capita basis, than anywhere else in the country. And in No. 5-ranked Connecticut, 100 percent of the population breathes air violating carbon monoxide standards.

The institute issues ratings on four indexes that determine the states' overall ranking. The "Poisons Index" (measuring such things as how many pounds of pesticides are applied to the land and how many pounds of toxic chemicals are released into the air and in the water) ranked Florida 27th out of 50; the "Public Health Index" (measuring cancer incidences, premature deaths, public health spending, homes without complete plumbing and infant mortality rates) ranked Florida 21st; the "Worker Health Index" (measuring the number of occupational deaths and high-risk jobs, laws protecting workers and unemployment benefits and workers' compensation benefits) ranked Florida 30th; and the "Politics and Policies Index" (measuring state spending on environmental programs and ratings by the environmental group Renew America of state programs for drinking water protection, solid waste, recycling, land use and growth management) put Florida 22nd.

How does Florida fit in with the rest of the nation on specific environmental problems? Below is a sampling:

Poisons Index:
— Pounds per capita of pesticides applied: 1.3 (17th in nation).
— Percent of the accumulated U.S. radioactivity from low-level and high-level waste remaining in Florida: 6.1 (47th).
— Number of final and proposed Superfund sites and other hazardous waste sites identified by federal and state authorities as needing attention, ranked on a per capita basis: 868 (22nd).
— Pounds per capita of toxic chemicals released into the air: 4.2 (9th).
— Number of factories posing a high risk of cancer from chemicals released into the air: 7 (26th).
— Carbon emissions in pounds per capita (a way of measuring carbon dioxide releases from fossil fuel plants): 11,560 (28th).
— Percentage of Florida's population breathing air failing to meet Clean Air Standards of 1988: 51 (25th).
— Pounds per capita of toxics found in water: 12.2 (21st).
— Percent of publicly owned wastewater treatment systems in non-compliance: 19 (39th).
— Percent of public water systems with one or more violations of the Safe Drinking Water Act during fiscal year 1987: 43 (41st).
— Percent of Florida's population served by public water supplies in potentially contaminated counties (by pesticides or agricultural chemicals): 67 (45th).
— Total pounds per capita of toxic chemicals released by manufacturing facilities into the environment: 36.2 (15th).

Public Health Index:
— Number of cancer cases per 100,000 people (1989 estimate): 367 (16th).
— Number of premature deaths per 100,000 people who do not reach the age of 65 because of ill health or injury: 1,366 (33rd).
— Percent of year-round occupied housing units lacking complete plumbing (kitchen facilities, toilet and hot water): 1.1 (2nd).
— Rate of infant deaths per 1,000 live births between 1984 and 1986: 10.6 (38th).

Worker Health Index:
— Rate of traumatic deaths caused by work from 1980-85 (per 100,000 workers): 10.0 (29th).
— Percent of 1986 nonagricultural workforce in these occupations — mining; cotton weaving; manufacturing of other cotton products; chemicals and allied products; rubber and miscellaneous products; and leather tanning and manufacturing — with the higest rates of occupational diseases, particularly lung diseases from fumes or dust: 1.0 (8th).
— Grade given by the Southern Labor Institute for the number of laws enacted that protect workers' rights, safety, health and access to health information: 42 (out of a possible 100) (40th).
— Dollars of unemployment benefits paid in Florida, divided by the total number of work-

ers covered by these benefits in 1987: 65 (48th).

— Percent of manufacturing workers who belonged to unions in 1988: 8.9 (40th).

Politics and Policies Index:

— Percent of pro-environment votes cast by members of Florida's congressional delegation during five sessions in Congress, 1985 through 1989: 58 (21st).

— Percent of pro-environment votes cast by members of Florida's congressional delegation on nuclear power and nuclear safety issues during the 1986, 1987 and 1988 sessions of Congress: 34 (24th).

— Dollars per capita spent in Florida in fiscal 1986 for environment and natural resource protection, from wildlife programs and mining reclamation to hazardous waste cleanup: 14.65 (38th).

— Percentage of total state expenditures spent by Florida in fiscal 1986 for environment and natural resource protection: 0.98 (37th).

— Drinking water: State policies and programs for monitoring, regulating and protecting drinking water quality: 40 on a scale of 10 to 100 (27th).

— Solid waste: State policies and programs for solid waste reduction, waste management and recycling: 80 on a scale of 10 to 100 (3rd).

— Land use: State policies and programs to manage growth and regulate land use: 80 on a scale of 10 to 100 (3rd).

Other findings:

— Percent of all low-income residences that were weatherized from 1977 to 1987 under the U.S. Department of Energy's Weatherized Assistance Program: 0.9 (50th).

— Gallons of gasoline consumed in Florida per person: 499 (20th).

— Miles driven per gallon of gas in 1986: 13.7 (29th).

— Pounds per capita of toxic chemicals put in sewers in 1987: 3.3 (24th).

— Pounds per capita of toxic chemicals remaining on industrial sites in drums, empoundments, etc. in 1987: 15.9 (41st).

— Pounds per capita of toxic chemicals transferred to commercial landfills, incinerators, etc. in 1987: 1.4 (10th).

— Number of landfills and open dumps as of October 1988, ranked per capita: 170 (15th).

— Funds needed for adequate sewers to meet anticipated demand by 2008: $6,186,000,000 (45th).

— State and local funds spent on air pollution control for 1988: $6,241,000 (25th).

— Percent of Florida's population breathing air that failed to meet clean air standards for ground-level ozone during 1989: 55.1 (33rd).

— Percent of Florida's population breathing air that failed to meet clear air standards for carbon monoxide during 1989: 0.0 (tied for 1st with 19 other states).

— Acid rain level measured on a pH scale. (The lower the pH number, the more acid the rain): 5.1 (27th).

— Number of industrial plants releasing ozone-destroying chemicals into the air, ranked per capita: 65 (10th).

— Per capita pounds of toxic chemicals pumped into the ground: 245 (39th).

— Amount of solvents, oils and gasoline spilled in Florida's navigable waters during 1984, 1985 and 1986: 240,000 gallons (14th).

— Percent of shellfish waters capable of commercial harvesting that are restricted from fishing because of high levels of pollution: 68 (45th).

— Percent of inland and coastal wetlands lost in the past 200 years: 46 (24th).

— Number of fishing licenses issued in Florida for fiscal year 1988: 826,000 (42nd).

— Per capita state funds spent for parks during fiscal year 1988: $2.07 (42nd).

— Percent of cultivated and noncultivated cropland artificially irrigated in 1987: 54.6 (42nd).

— Percent of acres enrolled in programs to protect wetlands and other highly erodible lands. Rather than being farmed, the land is planted in trees or grasses for at least 10 years: 21.7 (26th).

— Average contribution of agriculture to Florida's total goods and services during 1963-1986: 2.6 percent (26th).

— Share of the gross state product from agriculture, timber, mining and energy industries from 1963-1986: 4.2 percent (33rd).

— Percent of Florida's land in forests for 1987: 48.4 (21st).

— Percent of forest land acreage owned by paper and pulp and wood products companies: 33 (49th).

— Percent of forest acreage gain between 1982 and 1987: 0.6 (25th).

Florida's Environmental Future

Concerns over the environment have been voiced by many groups for years in Florida. In the past few years, though, two groups' views have been particularly evident through state-sponsored studies. One of these reports, issued in March 1990 by the Commission on the Future of Florida's Environment to then-Gov. Bob Martinez, emphasized the need for increased spending to "avert even further damage and loss to Florida's environment." This view was shared by many Floridians (63 percent) who were interviewed in 1989 by state officials on their attitudes about environmental issues. In that report on Floridians' attitudes, 46 percent of those surveyed supported increased spending on the environment even if it meant higher taxes.

The governor's commission on the state's environment pointed to the state's "phenomenal growth" over the past 40 years. For example, in 1989 Florida hosted nearly 40 million tourists, compared with 20 million in 1980. This has resulted in "largescale problems" for the state's water quality, water supplies, ecological systems, fish and wildlife and other natural resources, the commission said. And population projections of 18 million by the year 2010 mean that "bold action" will be required.

In addition, "the environment has never received a fair, proportionate share of the state's revenues," the commission said. Over the past 10 years, funding of environmental programs averaged 2.5 percent of the state's budget. The funding for 1989: 2.9 percent.

The group listed seven "highest priority environmental needs":

1. Acquiring and managing environmentally sensitive lands. This is necessary to protect Florida's wetlands, rivers, lakes, streams and estuaries; to aid in the protection of the earth's ozone layer; to protect Florida's beaches and coastal and marine resources; and to reforest lands and restore waters that have lost biological productivity.

2. Establishing an "environmental ethos" through a widespread environmental education program and through television and radio public service announcements. "The attitude of Florida's residents and visitors needs to improve. This state and its environment deserves to be called home and treated accordingly," the commission said.

3. Conserving water, surface water and restoring wetlands. (Florida has lost 46 percent of its inland and coastal wetlands in the past 200 years, the Institute for Southern Studies estimated).

4. Protecting Florida's coastal and marine resources. Ninety percent of the saltwater fish species caught recreationally and commercially in Florida are believed to depend on estuaries during some phase of their life cycle.

5. Needing future direction for growth management. The commision found "little effective state guidance for establishing overall development patterns."

6. Needing more waste management. It is estimated that by the year 2000 Florida will be faced with about 30 million tons of garbage each year. The commission recommended, for example, that the legislature ban the use of styrofoam for any use other than building insulation. Styrofoam has been found to be destroying the ozone layer, which is protecting the Earth's inhabitants from large amounts of ultraviolet radiation.

7. Abating global warming, ozone depletion and acid rain. Some experts predict that global warming will cause sea levels to rise and inundate parts of Florida and that hurricanes will become stronger.

Overall, the governor's commission stressed that the "best means of protecting the state's environmental future is to substantially increase funding for acquisition, restoration and management of Florida's environmentally sensitive lands before they become unavailable."

It urged the state legislature to: authorize a bonding program to raise $300 million each year for 10 years to enable the state to purchase and restore land; ensure that environmental education be taught at all levels of the state's education system; restrict the location of marinas and require the licensing of boat operators; enact laws to protect manatees and environmentally sensitive vegetation and other coastal and marine resources; establish boat speed limits; implement a $5 million per year rural and urban reforestation program over the next 5 years (funded from a surcharge on nonrecyclable containers, packaging and paper products); require that 25 percent of all newsprint used in Florida be paper recycled from Florida; and develop mass transportation systems in metropolitan areas while discouraging the use of private motor vehicles through disincentives.

Meanwhile, 998 Floridians surveyed by the state Department of Environmental Regulation saw three environmental problem areas:

1. Water pollution, including drinking water, groundwater, rivers and lakes, Tampa Bay, and St. Andrews Bay. Residents of the southeastern portion of the state were more likely to mention water pollution than residents in the northern section of the state. In addition, 52 percent of those responding in north Florida said their drinking water was excellent or good but only 37 percent of those living in central Florida and 33 percent in the southeast gave such favorable ratings to their drinking water.

2. Loss of natural resources, such as marine life; loss of habitat; depletion of land resources; deterioration of wetlands; soil and coastal erosion; and water shortages.

3. Growth and development (lack of roads, damage to the environment from overcrowding and overbuilding).

The Floridians interviewed also agreed that increased spending on the environment — namely in the next two years — is needed. The favorite way to do this was by increasing impact fees on developers; the least popular method was the implementation of a state income tax.

They gave state government low marks in its handling of environmental issues. Many agreed that Florida officials have paid too little attention to the environment over the last five years; 88 percent said they would like to see Florida government give more attention to the environment. A total of 65 percent rated the job done by Florida government as fair or poor, but put Florida on a par with many other states — 55 percent said Florida was doing as good a job as other states.

College graduates and those earning more than $30,000 a year were harsher on Florida's handling of the environment than those earning under $15,000.

Many of those surveyed complained about Florida's natural resources: 40 percent said its beaches were polluted; 49 percent said the state's saltwater areas were only fair or poor; 65 percent rated its freshwater areas as only fair or poor; and 61 percent said their drinking water was only fair or poor.

Renew America

Florida came out with much better grades in a 1989 study of five environmentally sensitive areas — forest management; solid waste recycling; drinking water quality; food safety; and growth management and the environment — done by another environmental group, Renew America of Washington, D.C. The state still scored its lowest points in its drinking water quality but scored well in the solid waste and growth management categories — concluding the same thing that the Institute for Southern Studies discovered. Overall, Florida ranked No. 8 in the country, earning 32 points out of a possible 50. Top-rated California had 42 points, while Vermont, the top-rated state in the Institute for Southern Studies survey, was in a tie for 18th place.

Florida's high rating came because Renew America said it was one of eight states with the best programs to address the impact of growth on the environment. The state also earned high scores in its programs that promote solid waste recycling.

Some of the results of this study:

Forest Management:
Florida had 16,549,000 acres of forest land in 1987, covering 48 percent of its land area. About 10 percent of this land is owned by the federal government, 5 percent by the state, 33 percent by the timber industry and 50 percent is privately owned. The timber industry was the 6th largest employer in the state and was the 6th largest manufacturing industry in Florida as of 1985.

Solid Waste Recycling:
Florida was found to have 126 operating municipal solid waste landfills with a statewide average of 5 to 10 years of remaining capacity. About 65 percent of the municipal solid waste is currently in landfills, about 10 percent is recycled and 25 percent is incinerated. Florida has a solid waste management plan, has mandatory recycling, beverage container recycling, packaging restrictions and a state program on public education and promotion of recycling. The state also encourages used oil recycling and scrap tire recycling and promotes recycling and reduction of industrial nonhazardous waste, the study found. And there are a number of municipal solid waste mass burn incinerators. Florida state law sets a statewide goal of 30 percent reduction of solid waste going to landfills and waste-to-energy plants by the end of 1994 with an interim goal of 50 percent container recycling by 1992. The state was one of only eight that is either implementing or developing comprehensive recycling programs.

How are residents reacting to recycling? In the Florida Department of Environmental Regulation survey, about half (53 percent) of the residents interviewed said they do some kind of recycling at home, most of them recycling aluminum cans and newspapers. And most of those who do not currently recycle said they would separate glass, paper and aluminum if these things were picked up with the garbage, but some added that they would not do so if they had to take these items to a recycling center. This same survey found that only about 10 percent recycle their motor oil and only about 6 percent said they had ever taken chemicals such as paint thinners, solvents, aerosol cans, radiator antifreeze and oil-based paints to a recycling center for disposal. Most said they disposed of them in the garbage.

Drinking water:
The Renew America study found that Florida consumes 5,665,000 gallons of drinking water a day and has 4,722 public water systems. The state has 182 large water community systems (those serving more than

10,000 people year-round) for 78 percent of the population; 159 medium systems (those serving 3,301 to 10,000 people) for 8 percent; and 1,616 small systems (those serving 25 to 3,300 people) for 14 percent. It was estimated that 22 percent of Florida's population was affected by both community and non-community water system violations in fiscal 1987. A total of 4,373 Safe Drinking Water Act violations were recorded in fiscal 1987, but only 0.09 percent resulted in state enforcement action. Also, 93 systems were found to be in "significant noncompliance" with the Safe Drinking Water Act in fiscal 1987. No state enforcement actions were taken on these violations during that year.

Food Safety:

Florida's cash receipts from crops, livestock, poultry and livestock and poultry products amounted to $4,741,000,000 in 1986, with farm products making up 1.8 percent of the gross state product. The state did have meat and poultry inspection programs and its State Shellfish Sanitation Program was found to conform with the requirements of the National Shellfish Sanitation Program.

Growth and the Environment:

The state experienced a 245 percent increase in energy consumption from 1960 to 1986. In 1986, 26 percent of its total energy consumption was for residential uses; 21 percent for commercial; 15 percent for industrial; and 37 percent for transportation. Florida was rated as having "substantial building standards for energy efficiency." Fifty-one percent of the state's population was found to be living in counties that did not meet the EPA's clean air standards in June 1988. A total of 2,118 river miles, or 71 percent of the state's river miles that were assessed, and 304,258 acres, or 87 percent, of the state's lake acreage assessed, were found to be polluted, or not meeting EPA designated-use standards in 1986. There was a 197 percent growth rate in urban land area from 1960 to 1980.

Florida's Water Resources

In a state where there are huge bodies of water along its coasts, thousands of freshwater lakes and nearly 2,000 surface streams, it would seem ludicrous at first glance to question whether Florida has enough water to supply the public, agriculture, power generators and industry. When taking under consideration some nagging questions, though, the answer is not so obvious. If water is so plentiful, why has Florida had to become accustomed in recent years to water shortages and water restrictions — with residents at times allowed to water their lawns only twice a week, for example? Why is the water quality in central and southeastern Florida rated so poorly by residents who live there? And why are government leaders considering imposing a fee on all water users based on water used?

The fact is, while water supplies are seemingly abundant, they are not always readily drinkable or readily available. About 90 percent of Florida's drinking water comes from groundwater supplies in the state's aquifers, which are vulnerable to contamination. And when high levels of contaminants are found in water that could pose a risk to human health, these supplies are not used. Other water supplies do come from surface water — but these also are subject to contamination. A U.S. Geological Survey in 1985 found that about 10.3 million Floridians were served by groundwater sources and about 1.1 million by surface water sources.

Other studies show an alarming trend — that each Florida resident and visitor uses an average of 175 gallons of water per day, compared with the U.S. per-capita average of 110 gallons. Conversely, each resident and visitor creates 100 gallons of wastewater daily, amounting to 730 billion gallons of treated domestic and industrial wastewater discharged into the state's surface waters and onto upland areas each year. And water use in southern Florida has grown to such mammoth proportions that the continued existence of the Everglades National Park is in doubt. If the park is to survive, residents in South Florida are going to have to live with water restrictions, park spokesmen and environmentalists say.

Why is it that only 10 percent of Florida's population gets its water from surface-water sources when there are so many lakes and surface streams in the state? There are three major reasons:

— Most of the state's major streams and freshwater lakes are in central and northern Florida — away from the major population centers along both coasts and the southeast. To use this water, long aqueducts or canals would be needed. Consequently, much of northern Florida has a water surplus and the coastal areas of the state, where 80 percent of the state's population lives, have on occasion experienced inadequate supplies, such as during the drought years of 1989 and 1990.

— During droughts, many of these lakes and streams are low or dry. And the construction of reservoirs to collect water can take place only in a few areas because Florida's land is relatively low and flat. So, only a few reservoirs have been built in the state — such as Deer Point Lake near Panama City.

— All the state's large rivers (except the Kissimmee) empty into either the Gulf of Mexico or the Atlantic Ocean. During some periods — high tides, storms or when there is low freshwater discharge — salty water moves upstream in these rivers for many miles. State officials estimate that the St. Johns River in northeast Florida, for instance, contains salty water 60 to 80 miles upstream under some high tide and low-flow conditions.

Without its extensive freshwater groundwater supplies, Florida would be hurting for lower-priced water sources — desalinating saltwater from the ocean, for example, would be an expensive process.

The State of Florida's Drinking Water

How good is Florida's water? An EPA analysis of water quality in 1988 found that on the whole, there is "excellent ground-water quality, particularly in the Floridan aquifer which underlies all but the westernmost and southernmost parts of Florida." And most of Florida's surface waters are "of good quality," the agency said. But problem areas exist.

Contamination of groundwater supplies from underground storage tanks (mainly for gasoline), from agricultural activities, septic tanks, landfills, phosphate mining and hazardous waste sites is of concern, and water quality problems are "evident around the densely populated, major urban areas, including Jacksonville, Orlando, Tampa, the Cape Kennedy area and the southeastern Florida Coast," the EPA found. Another major area of concern: the discovery of the cancer-causing chemical, ethylene dibromide (EDB), in water supplies concentrated mostly in central Florida. But the northwestern and west central sections of the state have "very good water quality."

Among the major surface-water quality problems cited by the EPA: agricultural runoff, urban stormwater, domestic wastewater and pulp and paper mills. And one of the major causes of these problems: development.

The Florida Department of Environmental Regulation estimates that stormwater is responsible for:

— 80 percent to 95 percent of the heavy metals that enter Florida's surface waters.

— Almost all of the sediments. This can damage some communities of plants and animals.

Stormwater also is a major contributor to the overenrichment of Florida's lakes (by adding unwanted nutrients such as nitrogen and phosphorus) and has caused public swimming areas to close because of contamination by bacteria.

At one time or another, wells have had to be shut down in many parts of the state. In 1990 in Tallahassee, for example, six wells supplying water to the city had to be closed off because of the discovery of an unwanted chemical in the water. As a class, the most common contaminants found in groundwater supplies that bring about well shutdowns are volatile substances such as gas, benzenes and solvents, according to Kent Kimes, administrator of the drinking water section of the Bureau of Drinking Water and Groundwater Resources for the Department of Environmental Regulation. However, he said that overall, Florida's drinking water program is "more progressive" than other states' and that the state often has regulations in place ahead of EPA regulations.

Some people in central Florida have found that some of their drinking water supplies have high levels of EDB. The chemical, once used to kill nematodes and used in orange groves, today is banned in Florida. But its past use has caused present-day problems — the chemical was found to have seeped into the ground and entered water supplies. A June 1987 study of about 11,600 wells in Florida found that the chemical was present in 1,449 of them. The primary region affected: Lake, Polk, Highlands and Orange counties in central Florida. High concentrations of EDB have also been found in Jackson County in the Panhandle because the chemical was applied to such row crops as peanuts and soybeans, and some concentrations have been found in Madison County. Jackson County had been found to have the highest concentration of contaminated wells, Polk County the greatest number of contaminated wells.

While state officials say the problem had been contained, new land developments have caused new wells to be built and this has turned up new discoveries of high levels of EDB, which can remain in water supplies for years. For example, the last known application of EDB in Tampa was more than 20 years ago. Many years later, some wells were still turning up with high concentrations of the chemical. The state has an "EDB Remediation Program" that provides for regular testing of wells and for the delivery of bottled water to affected areas until the problem is solved. Solutions include putting carbon filters on affected wellheads, installing new water line connections and extending water distribution systems or drilling a new well.

And not long ago, there had been the discovery of another problem in central Florida: high levels of nitrates in drinking water supplies, which had been confined mainly to Highlands County.

The state required each of Florida's five water management districts to specify their water shortage areas by 1991. Among the areas of concern cited by some districts — because of either limited groundwater availability, salt water intrusion or other concerns — are the Panhandle coastal area from Pensacola to Appalachicola, Pinellas County, most of Hillsborough and Manatee counties and parts of Highlands, Polk, Sarasota and Pasco counties, and the Atlantic Ocean coastal region from Stuart south, including the Keys. One upbeat note: desalination today is becoming more of a cost-effective alternative, according to Kimes.

Groundwater Supplies

The state's groundwater comes from four aquifers: the Floridan Aquifer System, the Biscayne Aquifer, the Sand and Gravel Aquifer and the Unnamed Surficial and Intermediate Aquifers. Nearly all groundwater originates from precipitation. This water is found in underground aquifers and is drawn up to the surface for use by wells. There is a danger with most of the population dependent on these sources for their water — with so many cities along the coast using wells to get water from underlying aquifers, this is inviting salt water intrusion. And contamination of aquifers by other pollutants is not out of the question — the depth of groundwater supplies throughout the state is relatively shallow, most commonly 10 to 20 feet, and the ground above it for the most part is permeable.

Groundwater is an especially important commodity — it also is the principal source of fresh water for industrial, commercial and irrigation users in the state. And groundwater is important in maintaining the water level in most of the state's lakes and is the water source for the state's flow of spring water.

Floridan Aquifer:

This system extends across Florida, southern Georgia and small sections of Alabama and South Carolina. Its readily available resources extend from Wakulla County to Pasco County, in most of Holmes and Jackson counties and in a small part of Walton County. Elsewhere in Florida, it is buried to depths as much as 1,100 feet below sea level in southern Florida and 1,500 feet below sea level in the westernmost section of the Panhandle. Among the public supply systems tapping into this aquifer are those serving Jacksonville, Orlando, Clearwater, St. Petersburg and Tallahassee. Some agricultural runoff problems have been noted in parts of the state, and where the aquifer is at or near the surface, contamination from landfills and other waste disposal facilities is a concern. Increased development along coastal areas could result in saltwater in the aquifer. The water from this aquifer tends to be hard. A water's hardness or softness is determined by the levels of calcium and magnesium in it. If untreated, hard water will generally leave a scale on plumbing fixtures and cooking utensils.

Biscayne Aquifer:

Underlying all of Dade and Broward counties and parts of Palm Beach and Monroe counties, this system supplies the Miami-Palm Beach coastal area with nearly all of its water needs. It is the sole source of drinking water for more than 3 million people in southeast Florida. The aquifer has been contaminated by industrial discharges, landfill leachate and fuel spills. Most of the water here is classified as very hard.

Sand and Gravel Aquifer:

This is the major source of water supply in the western part of the Panhandle. Saltwater intrusion near the coast can occur. Industrial operations in and around Pensacola have caused local contamination of the water. This water is considered suitable for most uses, although safeguards against corrosion might be needed in some instances.

Unnamed Surficial and Intermediate Aquifers:

The unnamed surficial ones are used for public water supplies in an area southwest of Lake Okeechobee and in scattered towns along the East Coast from Palm Beach County north. They also have been contaminated with saltwater from uncontrolled flowing artesian wells that tap deeper aquifers. The intermediate aquifers, found between local surficial aquifer systems and the Floridan aquifer system, are sources of water for public supply in coastal southwestern Florida from Sarasota to Collier counties. These aquifers contain water too salty for human consumption in most of the area south of Lake Okeechobee. These systems also are prone to saltwater intrusion and upward movement of salty water from deeper aquifers. Surficial aquifer and intermediate aquifer waters are considered hard to very hard.

There have been a number of groundwater contamination cases (taken from information gathered from studies on drinking water supplies, hazardous and nonhazardous waste site monitoring and underground storage tanks) around the state. In many cases, the principal aquifer was not directly affected. The counties that have had the highest number of contamination cases include: Dade, Broward, Palm Beach, Highlands, Polk, Hillsborough, Orange, Seminole, Lake and Jackson.

Surface Water Sources

Some Florida communities need to use surface water as a source of supply for public water needs, principally because local groundwater is of poor quality. For example, along the coasts the groundwater may be salty. These cities include Tampa, Melbourne, West Palm Beach, Panama City, Bradenton and Belle Glade in Palm Beach County.

Florida submitted data to the EPA on the quality of its rivers, lakes, estuaries and ocean waters in both 1986 and 1987. About 63 percent of Florida's 12,659 miles of rivers were assessed or monitored for the EPA; about 45 percent of its 2,085,120 acres of lakes; and 62 percent of its 4,298 square miles of estuaries. The standard of measure used in determining whether water quality is good or bad is to look at whether these waters support the uses for which they have been designated by the state, such as for drinking water supplies, for fishing or for swimming. Among the findings:

— Of the 7,943 miles of rivers and streams in Florida that were either monitored or evaluated, 2,656 miles — 33 percent — were either only partially or not at all supporting their designated uses. The major pollution causes: nutrients (from such things as agricultural fertilizers) and organic enrichment (a cause closely linked to sewage treatment plants, feedlots and the growth of algae). The major sources of pollution were runoff from streets or other areas (carrying tars and oils from roadways and parking lots. This runoff enters sewers, pipes or ditches before discharge); agricultural runoff and wastes (from crop production, pastures, rangeland, feedlots) and discharges from septic tanks, landfills and hazardous waste disposal sites. It was found that 600 miles of rivers and streams should not be used for fishing and swimming.

— Of the 947,200 acres of lakes monitored or evaluated, 637,440 acres — 67 percent — were either partially or not at all supporting their designated uses. The major pollution causes: salinity, organic enrichment and siltation (the smothering of waters by sediments). The major sources of pollution were the same as for rivers and streams. It was found that

101,120 acres should not be used for fishing and swimming.

— Of the 2,655 square miles of estuaries monitored or evaluated, 1,106 square miles — 41 percent — were either partially or not at all supporing their designated uses. The major pollution causes: metals (such as lead, copper and mercury), siltation and unknown toxicity. The major sources: municipal discharges, discharges from septic tanks and other disposal sites, and agricultural runoff. A total of 291 square miles should not be used for fishing and swimming.

— Of the 835 ocean coastal miles monitored or evaluated, 74 miles — 8.8 percent — were found to be only partially supporting their designated uses. No miles were found not to be supporting their designated uses. All of these areas under study can be used for fishing and swimming.

— Florida also reported to the EPA that it monitored 2,695 miles of rivers for toxic contamination and found elevated levels in 510 miles; monitored 546,560 acres of lakes and found elevated levels in 50,560 miles; monitored 1,648 square miles of estuaries and found elevated levels in 938 square miles; and monitored 262 coastal miles of ocean waters and found elevated levels in 85 coastal miles.

— The state also reported there were 25 fish kills caused by pollution from 1986 to 1988 that affected an estimated 5.5 million fish.

Some specifics on water quality in the state's surface waters were provided by a task force — the Governor's Water Resource Commission — in a report in 1989 on the state's water supplies. Among its findings were:

Northwest region:

Lake Jackson's waters are polluted from stormwater runoff from Tallahassee; the Sopchoppy River has excellent water quality; stormwater runoff in urbanized areas along the coast causes problems.

Northeast region:

Alligator Lake is polluted by stormwater and wastewater from Lake City; some localized areas have poor water quality because of watewater treatment facilities and pulp and paper plants.

St. Johns River region:

This river originates in Indian River County and flows northward for almost 300 miles through Jacksonville. Pollution from nutrients has been found in Lake Washington in Brevard County, a public drinking water supply; water quality of the St. Johns River around Jacksonville is fair to poor because of leaching septic tanks, wastewater and industrial treatment plant discharges, and untreated stormwater; water quality of the river between Puzzle Lake and Lake Monroe goes down because of urban development around Orlando; Lake Apopka's water quality is very poor because of agricultural discharges and poor drainage activities.

Peace River and Tampa Bay region:

The Hillsborough River's quality in the Tampa Bay area (the river is collected and confined in Tampa for a drinking water supply reservoir) is poor because of stormwater runoff from urban and agricultural areas and food processing and wastewater discharges; water quality in the upper Peace River area in Polk County is poor because of discharges from phosphate mining and fertilizer manufacturing, and lakes in this area have some of the worst water quality in the state because of wastewater and stormwater discharges.

Southern Florida:

The Taylor Creek watershed, a tributary to Lake Okeechobee, has some of the poorest water quality in the state, primarily because of feedlot and pasture land runoff; Lake Okeechobee has fair water quality "with declining trends," says the commission; Big Cypress Swamp and the Caloosahatchee River, which serves as a public drinking water supply for Lee County in southwestern Florida, generally exhibit good water quality.

Meanwhile, the commission came up with its own list of what it considered the major threats to Florida's water quality:

Stormwater runoff. The commission said this causes more than half the surface water pollution in Florida and is a problem in both urban and rural areas. In cities, this runoff comes from construction, paved streets and parking lots, and residential lawns, which add silt, pesticides and fertilizers to surface water. In rural areas, this runoff — in the form of silt, pesticides and fertilizers — is from farm fields, feedlots and pastures. The Florida Department of Environmental Regulation points to this statistic: The state is second in the use of pesticides in the country, but 33rd in the amount of planted acreage.

Leaking Underground Storage Tanks. State estimates are that there are more than 9,000 sites of "known or suspected groundwater contamination" by petroleum products, mostly from leaking underground tanks. There are about 60,000 underground tanks in the state, 40,000 of them in service stations. State Department of Environmental Regulation officials say that one gallon of spilled gasoline can pollute up to one million gallons of water.

Domestic Wastewater. This is polluting both surface and groundwaters. About a billion gallons of domestic wastewater are generated in Florida each day. In surface waters, this can cause algae blooms and deplete the oxygen that aquatic life needs; in groundwaters, leakage from septic tanks can allow nitrate, bacterial and viral contamination.

Septic Tanks. About 60,000 septic tanks and other on-site sewage treatment systems are permitted each year. Many are found in some densely populated areas of the state and it's often impossible for the soil to treat the wastes before they reach groundwater supplies.

Landfills. Groundwater contamination is known or suspected at 76 active and inactive landfill sites.

Industrial Chemicals and Wastes. More than 1,900 permitted facilities discharge treated industrial wastes into the state's waterways, some found to contain toxic materials and heavy metals and nutrients.

Agricultural Chemicals and Wastes. Runoff has contributed to "major water quality problems in several areas," said the commission, including Lake Apopka, the Taylor Creek and Kissimmee River watershed and the Upper St. Johns River Basin.

Hazardous Wastes. It is estimated that more than 3 million tons of hazardous wastes are generated in Florida each year.

Mining Wastes. Water quality can be "significantly degraded" by mining, said the commission. For example, waste clays from phosphate mining can remain in the water for many years.

Domestic Sludge. This comes from wastewater treatment. When it is improperly applied over land areas, it can contaminate waterways.

Lake Excavations. Dredging and filling can kill fish and destroy wildlife habitats.

Sinkholes. They can lead a pathway into an underlying aquifer and possibly bring contamination into it. Sinkholes can occur in areas where there are both a shallow groundwater table and a thin layer of overburden (material overlying deposits of geological materials or bedrock).

Recommendations on Water for the Future

To ensure that Florida has enough water to supply future generations, the Governor's Water Resource Commission made a number of suggestions. Among these:

1. Integrate water and land-use planning in the state (from the water management district level to the municipal and county government level).

2. Require the water management districts in the state to complete their district water management plans by 1995.

3. Reuse water for such things as watering golf courses, lawns and gardens and for industrial uses, especially in areas where water supplies are low. For example, millions of gallons of water are reused in Orange County for irrigation of citrus groves. The city of St. Petersburg has hundreds of miles of pipe delivering reclaimed water to such users as golf courses, cemeteries, parks and apartment complexes.

4. Promote water conservation by restricting lawn irrigation during peak daylight hours throughout the state and using reclaimed water for lawns.

5. Require Public Service Commissions to set water rates that "will encourage water conservation."

6. Collect a fee from all users based on water used. Credits would be given for use of reclaimed water and other alternative technologies. These funds would be put into a Water Resource Trust Fund and used to promote such things as area-wide water reuse systems and the development of alternative water sources in critical water-supply problem areas.

7. Require the use of desalination and other technologies in critical problem areas instead of importing water.

Programs already in place to protect Florida's groundwater include a groundwater classification program; a permitting program to regulate underground injection of wastes; an underground storage tank program to monitor leakage and to provide cleanup procedures; a program to track pesticide use; a program to regulate hazardous waste storage, disposal and cleanup; and septic tank and landfill regulations.

The Everglades and Florida's Other Wetlands

Called the "Soul of the State," what's left of Florida's wetlands are considered important natural resources: They provide food and habitat for fish and wildlife (for many species wetlands are their primary habitats); offer flood protection (wetlands can be "natural sponges" that absorb flooding waters); provide for shoreline erosion control (since they often are located between rivers and high ground and can buffer shorelines against erosion); and can help improve the quality of the area's waterways (by removing and retaining nutrients and by processing chemical and organic wastes; and because wetlands are located between upland and deep water, they can intercept surface water runoff from land before it reaches open water).

The EPA further calls wetlands "the most productive natural ecosystems in the world (and) the farmlands of the aquatic environment since they produce great volumes of food in the form of plant material."

Today, about 33 percent of Florida's total land area is covered by wetlands — about 11.4 million acres. That's a far cry, though, from what the figure was about 60 years ago — well over 14 million acres. Wetlands are defined as "natural communities where the soil is saturated or covered with water for one or more months per year."

The largest and most well known of these wetlands is in the Everglades National Park, which also contains the largest freshwater marsh in North America. The park today covers more than 1.5 million acres and is a popular destination for visitors — more than 1.3 million visits were recorded in 1991. But because of severe water management problems, Florida may be on the verge of losing the Everglades, unless the trend is reversed. The problem has become so serious that the life expectancy of the park in 1990 was estimated at 5 to 10 years.

The reason the Everglades is on the path to extinction: the competition for water. Located in south Florida, near millions of people, the Everglades for years has been on the bottom rung of the ladder in getting enough usable fresh water to support its wildlife, park officials say. The park has three major concerns about water:

— The water the Everglades is getting is filled with nutrients (such as phosphorus and nitrogen, which destroy oxygen-producing aquatic plants) from sugar cane and other agricultural interests in the region.

— The water the park is supposed to receive is siphoned off for human consumption before getting to the park.

— The water the park does receive is sometimes dumped into the park at the wrong time of year, according to Park Superintendent Robert S. Chandler.

Today, "the Everglades National Park is probably the most seriously threatened unit in the national park system," Chandler said. The result of all this: Loss of wetland habitats, particularly in the east Everglades, which are critical feeding areas for park wildlife, park officials say; loss of more than 25,000 acres of native Everglades plant communities; the endangering and threatening of species that spend all or part of their time in the park (there are 14 such species, among them the Florida panther, whose numbers as of the early 1990s were down to between 30 and 50); decreases in the number of fish, snails and shrimp; a decline in the number of wading birds nesting in the area from about 265,000 birds to 18,500 (a 93 percent reduction since the 1930s. In addition, an aerial survey done in April and May of 1990 found the lowest number of birds on record); a decline in the population of the wood stork — from 6,000 nesting birds in the 1960s to 500 in 1989; the movement of many other wading species to areas outside the park's boundaries for nesting; the threatened loss of habitats for the American crocodiles and the West Indian manatees; and the drowning of alligator eggs in their nests when water is dumped into the park. (State wildlife officials estimate there still are 1 million alligators in the state).

Hurricane Andrew added to the worries of park officials. Following the hurricane, the most dramatic effect was seen in the structural damage to trees — virtually all of the park's large hammock trees were affected; nearly 25 percent of the park's royal palms and up to 40 percent of the pines were downed; some cypress stands were hit hard; and 90 percent of the known red-cockaded woodpecker nest trees were downed.

The news after the hurricane wasn't all bad — park officials noted that only 10 percent of the mangroves that were downed died and only 20 percent of the broken trees died; that many trees were starting to re-leaf; and that much of the wildlife apparently survived the storm. Park officials found that of the 160 wading bird rookeries in south Florida, only 16 were in the storm path. The coastal rookeries in the mangroves were "severely altered."

Everglades Park was closed for a time after the storm as repairs were made. Some buildings were severely damaged and had to be removed and rebuilt; fallen trees had to be cleared out; blocked trails had to be reopened and debris removed. The hardest hit of the park's facilities: Chekika, which had to be completely rebuilt.

Established in 1947, the park for years thrived on a natural water flow system that evolved from the area's six-month wet season and corresponding six-month dry season. The plants and animals inside the park had adapted to and become dependent upon this wet and dry cycle. Historically during the summer, floods would occur both in the Kissimmee River basin north of Lake Okeechobee and in the lake, and also in a large portion of the Everglades. This created a river, up to a few feet deep and 40 miles wide, that flowed south through the Everglades to Florida Bay and to the Gulf of Mexico. The summer rains then gave way to a six-month dry season.

But with development and agricultural interests this century, the cycle changed and the river was altered. A system of dikes, canals, levees, floodgates and pumps moved the water to agricultural lands, urban areas — and finally to the park. The continuous river flow through the park was curtailed as water was either held back or diverted. This change brought about a disruption in available food supplies and altered animal and plant habitats. The park became dependent on man for its water flow.

Even with its enormous man-made problems, no one is writing off the Everglades yet.

In 1994, Florida passed legislation aimed at getting sugar cane growers in the region to filter pollution out of water seeping toward the Everglades. Although the legislation was criticized as a sellout to farmers because this will not need to be done immediately, it has been looked on as a first step toward a long-term solution for saving the park. And in late 1994, plans were being formed on the federal level to further force a change in the region's farming practices.

Congress has also stepped in on occasion in behalf of the park. For example, it expanded the park's boundaries in December 1989. About 107,600 acres were added to the eastern boundary to provide a much-needed feeding area for wading birds. Specifically, the added acreage will help restore "natural conditions to the full width of Shark River Slough, the main watershed of the park," say park officials. "Federal ownership...should result in increased biological productivity of these wetlands. Only then can we expect the trend of declining wildlife populations in Everglades National Park to be reversed," a park brochure reads.

Toward this effort, in late 1991, Florida transferred 45,000 acres of state-owned land to the park, including its Chekika State Recreation Area, which has a beach, campground and a picnic area. This act "symbolizes a new sense of hope in the decades-long struggle to restore the Everglades ecosystem," say Everglades officials. To complete the expansion process of the eastern boundary acreage to the park, it is estimated that $40 million will be needed to buy 9,000 privately owned parcels. The state will provide 20 percent of the funding and the federal government the rest. It will take about five years to acquire all this property, a process that started at the end of 1990.

The National Park Service has also asked the U.S. Army Corps of Engineers and the South Florida Water Management District to ensure that the water supplies to the park will be based on "natural, actual rainfall occurrences and amounts within the normal drainage areas." Allowing water flows to be restored is another primary goal.

For the forseeable future, saving the park will be an uphill battle. Private interest groups don't want to be hurt: sugar cane growers generally have not wanted to take the responsibility for removing nutrients from their waste water and have been opposed to any alteration of their delivery schedules; landowners have opposed any devaluation of their property that would result if this land cannot be developed or is flooded; and hunters, fishermen and off-road-vehicle users support protection of the Everglades as long as it doesn't alter their customary use and enjoyment of the area.

Besides water-supply problems in the Everglades, there are a number of other threats to wetland areas in the state — dredging and fill activities, which can eliminate wetland areas or can "de-water" wetlands; construction projects; and pollution. Among the major sources of pollution: sewage and industrial waste. Rainwater can also carry tars and oils from roadways, fertilizers from home lawns and chemicals from agricultural projects into wetlands and waterways. Other human threats to wetlands include drainage, diking and damming, tilling for crop production, grazing by domestic animals and mining. Other natural threats include erosion, rising sea levels, droughts, hurricanes and other storms, and overgrazing by wildlife.

Florida carries two distinctions as far as wetlands are concerned — the state has the second largest acreage in the United States, behind Alaska, and its wetlands losses are among the most extensive in the country.

Florida has a wetlands protection act, which requires that a detailed record be kept of wetland acreage to control dredge and fill activities and to record the number of acres lost, disturbed, created, improved and preserved. Since 1979, the state also has purchased about a half million acres of land, much of it wetlands.

Restoration of Kissimmee River-Lake Okeechobee-Everglades System

At one time, the Kissimmee River was able to flow unimpeded from Lake Kissimmee 98 miles south to Lake Okeechobee. From there, when the seasonal rainfall came, Lake Okeechobee's banks overflowed and would spill into the Caloosahatchee River and into the Everglades. Man stopped this from continuing. In the 1960s, the river was transformed into a canal that functions as a drainage ditch for the lower Kissimmee Basin. The construction of this canal resulted in the drainage of almost 200,000 acres of river marsh and other wetlands and lowered groundwater levels in large areas of the basin. Meanwhile, Lake Okeechobee eventually was completely diked, and inflows and outflows were controlled by locks, spillways and pumps operated by the South Florida Water Management District.

Today, efforts are under way to restore sections of the original Kissimmee River channel. And besides efforts to save the Everglades, work is also being done to save Lake Okeechobee from choking on high levels of nutrients, which have greatly degraded water quality.

Lake Okeechobee, known for its bass, bream and crappie fishing, also is a lifeline for south Florida. In times of drought, for example, water from the lake is used to recharge the Biscayne Aquifer, a major water supply for southeastern Florida. Okeechobee, the largest freshwater lake in the United States south of the Great Lakes, was fed high levels of phosphorus from surrounding agriculture operations over the years. Studies found that the levels of phosphorus in the open waters of the lake more than doubled since the early 1970s and that something had to be done to prevent the lake from further deterioration. Today, efforts are ongoing to reduce the flow of phosphorus, partly by relocating cows from dairies near the lake, which were found to be polluting the waterway.

Mercury in Largemouth Bass

One health hazard that has come to light in recent years is the presence of high levels of mercury in largemouth bass and in several other species of fish, such as the mayan cichlid, warmouth, gar, bowfin, yellow bullhead catfish, spotted sunfish and oscar. The problem early on was most noticeable in the Everglades but since has spread across Florida. A state health department advisory urging people not to eat largemouth bass, bowfin or gar is in effect for the Shark River Drainage section of the Everglades National Park north and west of State Road 27 in Dade and Monroe counties and for water conservation areas 2a and 3 in Broward, Dade and Palm Beach counties. In addition, there are limited-consumption advisories affecting a number of fish in many areas of the state. Limited-consumption means adults should not eat these fish more than once a week, and children under age 15 and pregnant or lactating women should not more than once a month.

Among the health advisories that have been issued:

— Limited Consumption of Bowfin, Gar and Largemouth Bass:

Panhandle Area of Florida

Apalachicola River Drainage System including the upper Chipola River and Dead Lakes; Sweetwater Creek; Equaloxic Creek; Blackwater River; Choctawhatchee River; Crooked River; Deer Point Lake; Econfina Creek; Escambia River; Holmes Creek; Lake Iamonia; Lake Miccosukee; Ocheesee Pond; Ochlockonee River (including Lake Talquin); Perdido River; Sopchoppy River; Lower Suwannee River; and Yellow River.

Central Florida

Alapaha River; Anclote River; Brick Lake; Clermont Chain of Lakes: Louisa Lake; Crooked Lake; Crystal River; Dias Lake; Hillsborough River Drainage System; Kissimmee Chain of Lakes: Alligator Lake, Hatchineha, Lake Istokopoga, Lake Kissimmee, Lake Tohopekaliga and East Lake Tohopekaliga; Lake Annie, Lake Conway; Lake Down; Lake Hart; Lake Josephine; Lake Kerr; Lake Placid; Merritt Island National Wildlife Refuge; Mill Dam Lake; Ocala National Forest: Dorr Lake, Eaton Lake and Swim Pond; Oklawaha River; Peace River; St. Johns River and tributaries south of Lake Monroe: Econlockhatchee River, Lake Harney, Lake Hellen Blazes, Lake Sawgrass and Puzzle Lake; Tarpon Lake; Trout Lake and Withlacoochee River.

North Florida

Ocean Pond, Suwannee River Drainage System; Lake Altho, Santa Fe River, St. Mary's River and Waccasassa River.

Southeast Coast

Savannahs Marsh (south St. Lucie and north Martin counties.

South Florida

Big Cypress National Preserve: Turner River Canal and the L-28 Tieback; Black Creek Canal; Caloosa Park Fish Management Area; Honeyland Wildlife Management Area; Okeheelee Fish Management Area; Plantation Heritage Fish Management Area; Tropical Park and Turner River Canal.

— Limited Consumption of Largemouth Bass, Gar, Bowfin and Warmouth:
Everglades Water Conservation Area 1 (Loxahatchee National Wildlife Refuge).

— Limited Consumption of Spotted Sunfish, Oscar, Warmouth, Yellow Bullhead Catfish:
Everglades Water Conservation areas 2A and 3.

— Limited Consumption of Spotted Sunfish, Oscar, Warmouth, Mayan Cichlid and Yellow Bullhead Catfish:
Everglades National Park: north and west of SR 27 (the Shark River Drainage System).

— Limited Consumption of Spotted Sunfish, Mayan Cichlid, Largemouth Bass, Gar, Warmouth and Bowfin:
South and East of SR 27 (Taylor Slough).

The exact causes of the high mercury levels are still being studied. There are a number of theories — ranging from agricultural runoff to air pollution. Once mercury enters fish through their gills, it leaves the tissue of the fish at a very slow rate and consequently can build up to high levels in the fish. There is no known way to remove mercury from fish; cooking a mercury-infested fish does not reduce the mercury level. If ingested by humans, mercury poisoning can cause deafness, sight problems, numbness, trembling and loss of coordination. Children and the unborn are especially sensitive to mercury — cerebral palsy has been known to occur in an unborn baby if a pregnant woman eats too many contaminated fish.

And fish have not been the only ones affected — liver tissue from a dead Florida panther in 1989 showed high levels of mercury, and the animal was known to have fed almost exclusively on raccoon. In addition, alligator tissue analysis revealed high levels of contamination and led to the suspension of a public alligator hunt in Dade and Broward counties.

And "there are likely to be other environmental toxics problems in at least limited areas of Florida that are just as unknown today as mercury was a little over a year ago. No adequate system is in place to monitor for potential problems caused by pesticides or industrial chemicals," concluded a Mercury in Fish and Wildlife Task Force in 1990.

For more information on mercury health advisories, contact your local Department of Health and Rehabilitative Services' County Public Health office.

Beach Erosion

Florida is wrestling with another problem — beach erosion, which is threatening sea turtle nesting habitats, public and private property and recreational enjoyment.

A survey of the state's beaches along the Atlantic and Gulf coasts shows there are about 350 miles of problem erosion areas out of 823.5 miles of beaches. And the list is expected to expand, "given the long-term growth of development and recreation interests on the Florida coast," the Florida Department of Natural Resources' Division of Beaches and Shores said in a late 1991 report. A continuation of the rising sea level and the growing shortage of available sand to replenish the beaches during major coastal storms also will contribute to more erosion problems, the study said. Many of the beaches identified as problem areas also were labeled as "critical erosion areas," where substantial development or recreational interests are threatened by the erosion process. For example, many of the beaches along the south Atlantic Coast are of a "critical" nature. And, on the Gulf Coast, most of Pinellas County along with Manatee and Sarasota counties also fall under this category, as well as areas in Charlotte, Lee and Collier counties that have heavily developed coastal barriers.

Much of this erosion is blamed on the "stabilization, construction and development of barrier tidal inlets," said the beaches division. Among the erosion problem areas along the coasts:

Northeast:

Nassau County: Fort Clinch and Fernandina Beach (4.4 miles of erosion); South Amelia Island (3 miles).

Duval County: South end of Little Talbot Island (0.4 miles); St. Johns River to St. Johns County (10 miles).

St. Johns County: North of Vilano Beach (1.4 miles); Porpoise Point (0.1 miles); northern Anastasia Island (2.5 miles); Summer Haven (2.4 miles).

Flagler County: Marineland (0.6 miles); Flagler Beach (2.3 miles).

Volusia County: Daytona Beach Shores to Ponce Inlet (5.6 miles); Bethune Beach to Turtle Mound (3.7 miles).

Central East:

Brevard County: Canaveral National Seashore (8.7 miles); Cape Canaveral north shore (3.6 miles); Canaveral (2.0 miles); Cocoa Beach through Satellite Beach (12.3 miles); Indiatlantic and Melbourne Beach (2.1 miles).

Indian River County: Sebastian Inlet through Ambersand Beach (2.9 miles); Wabasso Beach (0.6 miles); Vero Beach (3.1 miles).

St. Lucie County: Fort Pierce Beach (1.1 miles); Hutchinson Island (3.0 miles).

Martin County: Jensen Beach through Tiger Shores (3.3 miles); Sailfish Point (1.0 miles); Jupiter Island (11.3 miles); south of Blowing Rocks (0.2 miles).

Southeast:

Palm Beach County: Southern Jupiter Island (1.0 miles); Jupiter and Juno Beach (4.6 miles); Singer Island (0.4 miles); Palm Beach (7.8 miles); South Palm Beach (0.7 miles); Ocean Ridge (1.7 miles); Delray Beach (3.0 miles); North Boca Raton (1.6 miles); South Boca Raton (1.0 miles).

Broward County: Hillsboro Beach (3.1 miles); Pompano Beach through Fort Lauderdale (8.0 miles); John U. Lloyd State Recreation Area (1.7 miles); Hollywood and Hallendale (5.4 miles).

Dade County: Broward County line to Baker's Haulover (5.1 miles); Miami Beach (9.4 miles); Fisher Island (0.5 miles); Virginia Key (0.4 miles); Key Biscayne (2.4 miles).

Monroe County: Long Key State Recreation area (0.6 miles); Coco Plum Beach (0.6 miles); Sombrero Beach, Vaca Key, (0.3 miles); Bahia Honda State Recreation Area (1.0 miles); Long Beach, Big Pine Key (1.0 miles); Sugarloaf Beach, Sugarloaf Key (0.6 miles); Boca Chica Key, (1.3 miles); Key West (2.8 miles); Fort Zachary Taylor State Historic Site (0.3 miles).

Northwest:

Escambia County: East Perdido Key (6.5 miles); Fort Pickens and Pensacola Beach (10.7 miles).

Santa Rosa County: Navarre Beach to Navarre Pass (1.9 miles).

Okaloosa County: East end of Santa Rosa Island (1.7 miles).

Walton County: None

Bay County: Phillips Inlet, Hollywood, Sunnyside (4.1 miles); Panama City Beach to St. Andrews Inlet (6.8 miles); Shell Island (6.1 miles); Dog Island (1.9 miles); Crooked Island (4.2 miles); Mexico Beach (2.8 miles).

Gulf County: St. Joseph Peninsula (14.3 miles); Indian Peninsula (2.6 miles).

Franklin County: St. Vincent Island (3.2 miles); west end of Little St. George Island (0.4 miles); Cape St. George (1.3 miles); western St. George Island (3.2 miles); St. George Plantation (3.3 miles); east end of St. George Island (0.5 miles); western Dog Island (2.4 miles); eastern Dog Island (0.7 miles); west end of Alligator Point (0.4 miles); Southwest Cape, Alligator Point (1.1 miles); Lighthouse Point (1.8 miles).

Wakulla County: Mashes Sands (1.0 miles); Shell Point (1.0 miles).

Central west:

Levy County: Seahorse Key (1.2 miles).

Pinellas County: Anclote Key (0.5 miles); Three Rooker Bar (unknown); Honeymoon Island (1.1 miles); Caladesi Island (0.5 miles); Clearwater Beach Island (0.8 miles); Clearwater Pass north shoreline (0.5 miles); Sand Key (11.0 miles); Treasure Island (3.5 miles); Long Key (3.6 miles); North Bunces Key (unknown); South Bunces Key (0.9 miles); Mullet Key (0.4 miles).

Hernando County: Pine Island (0.8 miles).

Hillsborough County: Egmont Key (2.1 miles).

Manatee County: North end of Anna Maria Island (0.4 miles); Holmes Beach, Anna Maria Island (1.3 miles); Holmes Beach and Bradenton Beach (2.9 miles); northern Longboat Key (1.4 miles); Longboat Key to Sarasota County (1.0 miles).

Pasco County: Hudson Beach (0.2 miles); Anclote Key (3.0 miles).

Sarasota County: Southern Longboat Key (4.6 miles); Lido Key (1.2 miles); north Siesta Key (1.2 miles); Point of Rocks to Midnight Pass (2.4 miles); Casey Key (2.9 miles); Venice to Caspersen Beach (5.1 miles); Manasota Key (1.7 miles).

Southwest:

Charlotte County: Manasota Key to Stump Pass (3.6 miles); Knight Island (1.4 miles); north Little Gasparilla Island (0.8 miles).

Lee County: Southern Gasparilla Island (3.7 miles); north end of Cayo Costa (1.3 miles); Cayo Costa (1.2 miles); south end of Cayo Costa (1.0 miles); north end of North Captiva Island (1.0 miles); southern North Captiva Island (2.0 miles); Captiva Island (5.1 miles); north end of Sanibel Island (1.7 miles); Estero Island (3.8 miles); south end of Estero Island (0.3 miles); north shoreline of Lover's Key (0.3 miles); Lover's Key (0.9 miles); Big Hickory Island and Bonita Beach (2.9 miles).

Collier County: Vanderbilt Beach (1.3 miles); Park Shore (1.1 miles); Naples (5.6 miles); northern Keewaydin Island (4.1 miles); Coconut Island (1.5 miles); north Marco Island (0.7 miles); central Marco Island (0.9 miles); south Marco Island (1.2 miles); Kice Island (2.5 miles); Morgan Island (1.7 miles). (The Ten Thousand Islands area was omitted from beach measurements because of a lack of available survey data).

Of the beaches listed in the survey as being eroded, 100.7 miles of Gulf beaches and 126.8 miles of Atlantic beaches (227.5 miles total) were classified as "Critically Eroding."

The county with the most Gulf beaches in the critical stage (where substantial development or recreational interests are threatened) was Pinellas (with 20.9 miles falling into this category); followed by Sarasota (19.1 miles) and Lee (16.9 miles). The worst problems on the Atlantic beaches are in Palm Beach (21.8 miles) followed by Broward (18.2 miles) and Dade (16.9 miles).

Red Tide

One pollution problem found periodically along Florida's West Coast in the Gulf of Mexico, predominantly in the area between Tampa Bay and Charlotte Harbor, is what is known as "red tide." This is caused by blooms of algae that can spur fish kills, can contaminate shellfishing areas and can cause respiratory irritation in humans (burning of the nose and throat, coughing, and choking) when the algae is blown ashore. The algae, called Ptychodiscus brevis, produces toxins that are released into the water when the cell membrane is ruptured. The waters turn a red-brown.

It is estimated that between 1975 and 1987, red tides most often occurred in the fall and winter and centered mostly in an area south of Tampa and north of Fort Myers. Between 1916 and 1980, there were 24 known red tides along the west coast of Florida. The known public health impact includes neurotoxic shellfish poisoning after people eat either raw or cooked contaminated shellfish. Among the symptoms are tingling of the face, throat and extremities, burning mucous membranes, reversal of hot and cold temperature sensations, loss of coordination, dizziness, headaches and convulsions. The ecological impact: Manatees feeding on seagrasses are affected by disorientation and other similar symptoms. The economic impact: fish kills resulting in money losses in the fishing and tourist industries. A 1971 red tide was estimated to have caused a $20 million tourism industry loss, and the 1973-74 red tide, a $15 million loss. A 1994 red tide wave killed thousands of fish in the Gulf of Mexico near Sarasota and Venice.

Research is under way in the hopes that one day scientists will be able to predict red tides and control them at the source.

The Air We Breathe

While Florida's air may be cleaner than the air Chicagoans or New Yorkers usually breathe, the state has its share of pollution problems — in its most populated areas. And the major source of its air pollution is motor vehicles, according to the Florida Department of Environmental Regulation.

"While traditional industrial sources, such as power plants and factories, are an important part of our concern for air quality, motor vehicles are the major source of air pollution in Florida's metropolitan areas," according to the department's winter 1990 newsletter.

Florida, consequently, is coming up with undesirable air quality ratings in a number of areas, particularly in Duval (Jacksonville), Hillsborough (Tampa), Pinellas (St. Petersburg-Clearwater), Dade (Miami), Broward (Fort Lauderdale), and Palm Beach counties.

In monitoring how safe it is to breathe the air, the EPA has established that the levels of six major pollutants should be measured:

"Particulate matter," or the dust, dirt, soot, smoke and liquid droplets emitted into the air by factories, power plants, cars, construction activity, fires and other sources.

Sulfur dioxide, which comes largely from coal and oil combustion (such as that generated by electric utilities — 93 percent comes from coal-fired power plants), refineries, pulp and paper mills and nonferrous smelters. The EPA estimates that 50 individual plants in 15 states account for one half of all power plant emissions.

Carbon monoxide, which is a colorless, odorless and poisonous gas produced by incomplete burning of carbon in fuels. The largest contributor to this pollutant is motor vehicles — automobiles and light trucks with gasoline-burning internal combustion engines. When this pollutant is inhaled, it enters the bloodstream and disrupts the delivery of oxygen to the body's organs and tissues. People with heart disease are most sensitive to this effect. Across the country, decreases in this pollutant in the air have been noted from 1979 to 1988 despite a 33 percent increase in vehicle miles traveled during the period.

Nitrogen dioxide, a yellowish-brown gas that forms when emitted from motor vehicles and fuel combustion sources, such as electric utilities and industrial boilers. Nitrogen oxides can irritate the lungs, cause bronchitis and pneumonia and lower resistance to respiratory infections. Los Angeles is the only urban area that has recorded too much of this gas in the last decade.

Ozone is a major component of smog. In the upper atmosphere, ozone shields the earth from harmful ultraviolet radiation from the sun — but at ground level, high concentrations of ozone are a major health concern. The highest ozone levels occur during the hot summer months. The main sources of this pollutant are automobiles, chemical manufacturing plants, dry cleaners, paint shops and other sources using solvents. Acute effects of ozone are inflammation of the lungs, impaired breathing, coughing, chest pains, nausea and throat irritations. There is evidence that ozone adversely affects vegetation and forests, reduces crop yields and is a contributor to the formation of acid gases and acid rain.

Lead, caused mostly from motor vehicles, mining and smelting operations. In 1975, unleaded gasoline was introduced for use in automobiles equipped with catalytic control devices, which reduce emissions of carbon monoxide and nitrogen oxides. By 1988, unleaded gasoline sales accounted for 82 percent of the total gasoline market. The result: these programs have "essentially eliminated violations of the lead standard in urban areas," said the EPA in its National Air Quality and Emissions Trends Report for 1988.

Florida's major trouble spot was ozone. Air-quality-monitoring data during 1986-88 showed that three major areas in Florida — the Jacksonville metropolitan area, the Tampa-St. Petersburg-Clearwater metropolitan area and the Miami consolidated metropolitan statistical area (which includes Dade, Broward and Palm Beach counties) — failed to meet the ozone standard. Around the country, there were 101 such areas — an increase of 37 percent over the 1985-87 period. The EPA said the increase "likely resulted from the hot, dry, stagnant conditions which dominated summer 1988 in the Eastern United States." 1988 was the third hottest summer in the country since 1931.

Orange County (the Orlando area) once made this list, but as of the late 1980s met the federal standard. State officials said, though, that conditions in Orange County and other areas of the state that are experiencing large population growth will continue to be monitored.

Estimates in Florida are that about 10 million cars and light-duty trucks registered in the state "contribute the largest share of ozone-forming emissions to its atmosphere," according to the state environmental regulation department. As a step to curb this problem, Florida enacted a Clean Outdoor Air Law. Under this law, any Floridian operating a 1975 or newer automobile or light-duty truck is prohibited from tampering with or removing emission-control equipment. The law also:

— Prohibits Floridians from operating gasoline or diesel-powered automobiles, trucks or buses that produce smoke from the tailpipe for more than five seconds at a time. (Diesel vehicles may produce smoke during engine acceleration, engine lugging or engine deceleration, but not when idling or traveling at a constant speed).

— Prohibits the sale or lease of motor vehicles whose emission control equipment has been tampered with or removed.

The law also requires that dealers and sellers certify to buyers that the vehicle has not been tampered with. And, annual emission inspections for motorists owning 1975 and newer vehicles in Duval, Pinellas, Hillsborough, Palm Beach, Broward and Dade counties have become mandatory. Under this first-in-Florida emissions inspections program, motorists must pay a $10 fee and must have inspections done once a year. If repairs are needed to a vehicle's emissions system, motorists are required to get these done and then are entitled to one free reinspection. Other counties will join the program if they become an "ozone nonattainment" area, or a county that does not meet ozone pollution standards.

The law is enforced mainly through random roadside inspections.

Statewide studies in 1987 also uncovered other pollution problem areas. For example, "particulate matter" pollutants were found to be on the increase in Florida. Monitors were kept at 135 stations in 33 counties in 1987, and 19 of those sites experienced a "statistically significant upward trend over the last six years." The worst problems were in Jacksonville and Tampa, largely because of grit blasting and construction activities.

Sulfur dioxide emissions also posed concerns in 1987 as high levels were recorded in Nassau County at the Fernandina Beach wastewater treatment plant. Upwind from this site is the ITT-Rayonier plant and a number of pulp and paper mills in Georgia. Also of concern was a site in Escambia County. But "substantial" year-to-year variations in sulfur dioxide levels are found and the future trend of these concentrations may be determined "by many factors, including possible acid rain legislation, changes in electrical demand, changes in industrial output and changes in the costs and availabilities of fuels," according to a state air quality report.

Also monitored continuously in nine Florida cities is the Air Quality Index — a way of advising the public daily of any possible adverse health effects because of air pollution. During 1987, the following cities recorded this number of "unhealthful" days: Clearwater: 0; Fort Lauderdale: 1; Jacksonville: 1; Miami: 3; Orlando: 0; Pensacola: 0; St. Petersburg: 1; Tampa: 3; and West Palm Beach: 0.

Around the country, the EPA noted that decreases have been shown since 1970 in most of the pollutants monitored. Lead decreases from 1970-1988 have totaled 96 percent; particulate matter, 63 percent; carbon monoxide, 40 percent; and sulfur oxides, 27 percent. Only nitrogen oxides did not show improvement during this period, with emissions estimated to have increased 7 percent — largely from motor vehicles, electric utilities and industrial boilers.

But, air pollution remains a serious problem, according to the EPA. "About 121 million people in the United States reside in counties which did not meet at least one air quality standard during 1988," it said in a March 1990 air quality report. The most common pollutant found across the country is ozone. There are 112 million people living in counties that exceeded the ozone standard in 1988 and this figure "is greater than the total for the other five pollutants," said the EPA.

It is important to note that when comparing different areas of the country in terms of air quality, these statistics unveil only one part of the picture, the EPA warns. Data on population characteristics, daily population mobility, transportation patterns, industrial composition, emission inventories, the location of the monitoring sites and meteorological factors are needed to complete the picture.

Toxic Chemicals

Florida was found to release more toxic chemicals than most states in the country in 1988, according to another EPA finding. The Sunshine State had the fourth highest total, releasing 226 million pounds of toxic chemicals into the air, water and land. The only other states surpassing Florida were Louisiana (716 million pounds), Texas (596 million pounds) and Ohio (229 million pounds).

Florida was found to have released 53 million pounds into the air, discharged 56 million pounds into rivers, lakes, streams and other bodies of water, injected 35 million pounds in underground wells, and released 83 million pounds in landfills. Another 8.8 million pounds were transferred to municipal wastewater treatment plants and another 14.8 million pounds were transferred to treatment and disposal facilities.

While the state is releasing large amounts of these chemicals, the EPA cautioned that these releases "are not an indicator of human or environmental exposure to these chemicals." The EPA figures show annual emissions of certain chemicals but do not show the rates at which these chemicals were released, what their concentrations in specific locations were or the extent of public exposure to these chemicals. "A very small release of a highly toxic chemical to the air near a town might be of much greater concern than an extremely large release of a lower-toxicity substance to a waterway in an unpopulated area," said the EPA.

But this does not lessen the importance or provide much comfort in knowing that so many chemicals are being released into the air and waters in Florida. "This information can be a first step towards determining risks from toxic releases in a given area," the EPA said.

Hurricane evacuation signs are a frequent sight along both coasts.

Black storm clouds are common, especially during the hot and muggy summers.

THE WEATHER

If you dream of moving to an area where the winters are mild and the summers are hot — if you've grown tired of digging out of foot-high snowfalls, coping with freezing temperatures for weeks on end and paying sky-high heating bills — this state may just be the place for you. That's not to say you can leave your sweaters and jackets behind in the frozen northland. Despite the adage in Florida — "You can bring your coats, but if the moths don't get them the Goodwill will" — there are days when the cold north wind finds its way into the state, when the temperatures drop below freezing and when you feel like hiding indoors. But the big difference between Florida and the northern section of the country is this: The winter winds usually don't stay around more than a few days and you can rest assured you won't see much, if any, snow on the ground. Snow is rare here, although traces of it have been recorded even in the southern part of the state.

Assuming you're not a downhill skier or an ice fisherman, those are the pluses. But you'll also find a few other things if you decide to take up residence in the Sunshine State — hot and humid summers, an occasional hurricane, (consider 1992's Hurricane Andrew), a summer rainy season, and, instead of high heating bills, high air-conditioning bills.

Even with the minuses, the weather is one of Florida's greatest natural resources. Air con-

ditioning has helped make the summers more bearable, and hurricanes don't occur all the time. For example, in the 16-year period from 1969 through 1984, three hurricanes struck the coast.

In many sections of the state, the climate is defined as "tropical" — one in which the average temperature of the coldest month is 64.4 degrees or above, according to weather service definitions. The climate along the east coast from Vero Beach south and along the west coast from Punta Gorda south fits the tropical definition.

Florida's land area is very flat — the elevation ranges mostly from 50 to 100 feet above sea level. The highest point in the state is 345 feet above sea level near Lakewood in Walton County in the northwestern part of the state. Soils are generally sandy and low in natural fertility, with the exception of the peat and muck soils in the Everglades.

The appealing climate is due largely to the southern latitude and the proximity to relatively warm ocean waters. The Gulf Stream flows around the western tip of Cuba, through the Straits of Florida and northward along the east coast, and it exerts a warming influence because its predominant wind is from the east. If you live on one of Florida's coasts, you'll find that average temperatures will be slightly warmer in the winter and cooler in the summer than if you're living inland at about the same latitude.

While much of the rest of the United States has four seasons, Florida mainly has two — the rainy season, from June through September, and the relatively dry season the rest of the year. Generally, more than half the precipitation for an average year falls during the rainy season. And if you live in the northwest section of the state, where it gets much colder in the winter, you'll probably find a secondary heavy rainfall, in February and in March.

Mean annual temperatures range from the upper 60s in the northern portions of the state to the middle 70s on the southern mainland, and rise to nearly 78 degrees at Key West. Summertime mean temperatures are between 81 and 82 degrees throughout the state. In the coolest months, temperatures average about 13 degrees lower in the northern sections of the state than in the south. As a rule of thumb, July and August are the warmest months in all areas, while December and January are the coolest in the northern and central portions. January and February, on average, are the coolest months in the extreme south and in the Keys.

Maximum temperatures during the warmest months average near 90 degrees along the coast and slightly above 90 degrees inland. During June, July and August, maximum temperatures exceed 90 degrees about two days in three in all interior areas; in May and September, 90 degrees or higher can be expected about one day in three in the northern interior and about one day in two in the southern interior. Temperatures of 100 degrees or higher are infrequent in northern Florida, are rare in central Florida and are "practically unknown" in southern Florida, according to National Climatic Center (NCC) data.

One way of cooling off during the summer is with the aid of what meteorologists call "nature's air conditioners" — thunderstorms. These are frequent in the afternoon or early evening in all areas of the state, occurring on about half the days in summer. They sometimes are accompanied by a rapid temperature drop of as much as 10 to 20 degrees. But sometimes there is no such drop, and you still feel as if you're in a steam bath. Another way nature helps to cool things off is with sea breezes, which are felt almost daily within several miles of the coast and occasionally 20 to 30 miles inland. These breezes "serve to mitigate further the oppressiveness that otherwise would accompany the prevailing summer temperature and humidity conditions," the NCC says. "Because most of the large-scale wind patterns affecting Florida have passed over water surfaces, hot drying winds seldom occur."

Average minimum temperatures during the coolest months range from the middle 40s in the northern section to the middle 50s in the south. "No place on the mainland is entirely safe from frost or freezing," the NCC says. But cold waves, except in rare instances, seldom last more than two or three days. It is extremely rare for temperatures to remain below freezing throughout the day at any place in the state. During the 20th century, some noteworthy cold spells included January 1905; December 1906; February 1947; the freezes of the 1957-58 winter season; December 1962; the early freeze of November 1970, the long freeze of January 1971, and a short freeze in late December 1989. "Winters with more than one severe cold wave, interspersed with periods of relative warmth, are especially distressing to the agricultural industry because the later freezes almost always find vegetation in a tender stage of growth and highly susceptible to additional cold damage," the NCC says.

It can be deceiving to look at wintertime minimum temperatures alone. For example, weather stations in northern Florida record 10 to 20 days a year with minimum temperatures of 32 degrees or below. But there have been only five days in 72 years at Jacksonville where the maximum temperature for the day failed to climb above freezing. "This means the coat you might wear at 7 a.m. will become heavy by 10 a.m., and, if you are driving, that you may well be in your shirt sleeves by noon," the NCC says.

The average maximum and average minimum temperatures in 1990 illustrate the generally mild winters, along with the hot summers, throughout the state. The first line under each of the following national weather station offices is the average maximum temperature for each month; the second line, the average minimum temperature; the third line, the amount of precipitation, in inches. NA means figures were not available.

Temperature Characteristics and Precipitation at National Weather Station Offices in 1990

	Jan.	Feb.	Mar.	Apr.	May	Jn.	Jly.	Aug.	Sep.	Oct.	Nov.	Dec.
Apalachicola												
Max.	67.3	69.6	72.3	76.8	84.1	90.1	90.5	91.8	88.2	81.2	74.0	69.6
Min.	48.1	53.5	53.7	57.7	65.4	72.2	74.3	74.7	69.9	62.3	51.5	51.0
Precp.	2.4	3.9	4.2	2.2	0.5	2.8	9.3	2.3	5.2	2.0	1.6	1.6
Pensacola												
Max.	65.0	68.5	73.2	76.3	83.4	90.9	92.0	94.5	90.1	80.5	73.8	67.3
Min.	45.3	50.9	52.6	56.0	65.0	72.5	74.1	73.5	69.6	58.7	50.2	48.1
Precp.	4.7	5.0	9.2	4.9	4.6	5.5	2.1	2.5	1.5	8.5	1.1	2.0
Tallahassee												
Max.	70.6	72.7	78.0	80.8	87.9	93.8	93.6	95.2	92.0	83.8	76.8	71.1
Min.	40.9	49.5	48.7	51.4	61.6	68.9	71.1	71.1	66.1	58.2	45.1	46.2
Precp.	3.1	7.3	3.4	3.4	1.9	4.0	3.4	6.8	4.9	2.5	0.6	4.5

	Jan.	Feb.	Mar.	Apr.	May	Jn.	Jly.	Aug.	Sep.	Oct.	Nov.	Dec.
Jacksonville												
Max.	71.2	73.9	77.7	79.2	87.5	92.3	93.4	93.6	91.0	83.5	76.7	72.8
Min.	45.4	52.2	52.5	54.3	63.1	69.4	73.5	71.9	67.9	61.8	50.1	48.7
Precp.	1.8	4.1	1.6	1.3	0.2	1.6	6.5	3.8	2.6	4.5	1.2	1.9
Daytona Beach												
Max.	74.0	76.5	77.4	79.6	86.3	90.4	90.6	91.4	88.9	84.0	77.8	77.0
Min.	51.4	58.4	55.3	59.6	68.2	70.9	73.1	72.3	72.0	67.9	56.9	53.2
Precp.	1.4	5.6	1.9	1.5	1.5	2.7	5.9	7.0	1.6	5.9	0.8	0.3
Orlando												
Max.	76.9	79.3	80.6	81.9	89.9	91.6	92.0	93.1	91.6	85.9	79.2	77.5
Min.	54.6	58.9	58.0	61.1	68.8	72.2	73.6	73.9	72.4	68.3	59.3	55.1
Precp.	0.2	4.1	1.9	1.7	0.6	6.2	6.7	3.8	2.5	2.1	1.1	0.8
Lakeland												
Max.	78.9	81.4	82.3	84.9	91.6	93.9	94.0	94.4	93.1	87.6	80.2	77.2
Min.	55.4	58.7	57.5	60.7	69.4	72.1	73.2	73.1	72.3	67.5	59.4	54.9
Precp.	0.4	4.3	1.2	1.2	4.4	7.2	7.7	6.4	3.3	2.2	0.9	0.4
Tampa												
Max.	76.6	78.8	80.8	82.7	90.0	91.7	91.3	92.7	92.4	87.2	81.5	78.1
Min.	55.5	59.5	58.5	61.4	71.0	73.7	73.7	75.0	73.1	68.0	58.9	55.6
Precp.	0.5	4.6	1.7	1.5	1.8	5.2	10.0	3.3	2.4	2.6	0.7	0.2
Fort Myers												
Max.	80.8	82.0	83.5	86.2	90.1	93.2	93.3	93.6	92.9	88.5	83.3	NA
Min.	58.4	60.7	60.1	62.5	70.7	72.9	73.9	74.5	73.9	70.3	62.0	NA
Precp.	0.5	3.4	0.9	0.4	3.7	9.0	6.5	15.0	7.4	2.3	0.0	NA
Miami												
Max.	81.1	80.8	80.6	82.6	86.8	90.3	91.2	91.5	89.9	84.1	81.7	80.1
Min.	66.0	67.1	66.7	67.8	73.7	75.6	75.7	75.8	76.3	75.4	67.0	65.6
Precp.	0.2	1.2	2.3	7.0	7.8	6.8	4.3	11.1	3.5	2.3	1.7	1.0
W. Palm Beach												
Max.	79.8	81.3	80.5	81.7	87.0	90.1	91.2	92.4	90.2	86.8	81.4	79.1
Min.	64.7	66.3	65.9	66.1	72.4	74.2	75.4	75.0	75.2	73.3	65.5	63.4
Precp.	1.2	1.4	1.9	2.8	6.7	6.7	10.2	6.6	11.7	3.5	1.2	1.9
Key West												
Max.	78.7	80.1	79.8	82.3	86.4	89.6	90.8	92.0	89.5	85.9	80.4	78.8
Min.	67.7	70.8	70.1	70.9	77.0	79.1	78.6	79.1	78.1	75.8	70.8	70.3
Precp.	Trace	1.1	0.8	1.4	5.5	0.9	4.1	8.0	5.3	5.1	2.9	1.3

Source: U.S. Department of Commerce, National Oceanic and Atmospheric Administration, Environmental Data Service, "Climatological Data: Florida, 1990" monthly reports.

Precipitation and Droughts

Rainfall amounts are distinctive in one way — they vary greatly from year to year. One year might produce twice the amount received during another year. Almost all weather stations have received less than 40 inches of rain in a calendar year, and maximum amounts have ranged from 80 to more than 100 inches. In general, the highest annual rainfall has been measured in the extreme northwestern counties and in the southern end of the state, excluding the Keys, where the annual averages are only about 40 inches.

Rainfall distribution during the year is uneven. In the summer rainy season, there is about a 50-50 chance that some rain will fall on any given day. During the rest of the year, some rain is likely to fall one or two days a week.

And this distribution varies, depending on where you live. In the northwest, rain is likely in the late winter and early spring and again during the summer; it is least likely in that section in October, April and May. In the rest of the state, rainfall is most likely from June through September. There also is a "rather abrupt start and end of the summer rainy season," the NCC says. In June, the average rainfall tends to be nearly double the amount that fell in May, while September's rainfall is about double the amount in October. There are exceptions to this: October is among the wettest months on the southeast coast and in the Keys.

Most of the summer rain is in the form of local showers or thunderstorms, and many Florida weather stations average more than 80 thunderstorms a year. This rain is often heavy and usually lasts one or two hours, generally near the hottest part of the day. Day-long summer rains are usually associated with tropical disturbances and are infrequent. "Even in the wet season, the rainfall duration is generally less than 10 percent of the time," the NCC says.

Winter usually brings low rainfall amounts to the state. "There are only rare occurrences of the overcast, drizzly days that are typical of winters in more northern latitudes," the NCC says.

There are years, though, when not enough rain falls, and the state experiences drought conditions. From July 1970 to June 1971, the 12-month rainfall was only 34.59 inches and the level of Lake Okeechobee dropped to 10.3 feet, only 0.16 of a foot above the record minimum of 10.14 feet. Drought conditions also existed in many areas of central and south Florida for long periods during 1989 and 1990. Overall, statewide droughts during the summer are rare. It is not unusual during a drought in one portion of the state for other portions to receive lots of rain.

Humidity and Other Factors

Just take a look at your car on a summer morning if you don't believe it gets humid here. Humid nights produce dew that shows up on cars unless they are put in a garage. On the average, humidities range from about 50 to 65 percent during the afternoon to about 85 to 95 percent during the night and early morning. If you're still a disbeliever, try exercising during that time. Weather forecasters use the Temperature-Humidity Index to determine humidity conditions. This index climbs to 79 in early June and stays between 79 and 81 during most of the afternoon until late September. If the index reaches 79, nearly all people will feel uncomfortable; as the index passes 80, discomfort becomes more pronounced. This is where air conditioning comes to the rescue.

Other weather notes:

— The windiest months are March and April.

— There are about 10 to 15 tornadoes, funnel clouds and waterspouts a year. Tornadoes occur in all seasons, but are most frequent in the spring and in connection with tropical storms.

— Heavy fogs are usually confined to the night and early morning in the late fall, winter and early spring. These fogs usually dissipate or thin soon after sunrise. Heavy daytime fog is seldom observed in the state.

— The sun shines about two-thirds of the possible sunlight hours during the year, ranging from slightly more than 60 percent of possible sunshine in December and January to more than 70 percent in April and May. In general, southern Florida has more sunshine hours than does northern Florida. And "in winter, when sunshine is highly valued, the sun can shine longer in Florida than in the more northern latitudes. In summer, the situation reverses itself with longer days returning to the north," according to the NCC.

— Sea-surface temperature averages on the Atlantic side of the state range from 74 degrees in February to 83 degrees in August. On the west coast, temperatures range from 70 degrees in February to 84 degrees in August. Remember that those are surface temperatures. Your nightly weather forecaster will report readings in the 50s and 60s in the winter.

The Hurricane

Besides its nickname, "The Sunshine State," Florida has earned another dubious weather-related nickname — "The Hurricane State." Hurricane Andrew's fury in August 1992 alone can attest to that. And over the years, more than twice as many hurricanes have hit Florida than any other state. From 1885 through 1985, for example, 86 of them struck the state's coastline. Texas was a distant second at 40. And of the 61 hurricanes classified by the National Hurricane Center as major that have affected the U.S. coastline since the turn of the century, more than a third, or 21, have hit Florida.

Before Hurricane Andrew there had been a dramatic drop in the number of hurricanes that had hit the coastline since the late 1960s. One big reason: The near absence of October hurricanes in the region. And until Andrew, the storms that had struck Florida had been of lesser intensity in recent years. This is especially important when considering the state's soaring population. "This minimal hurricane activity has occurred during a time period when the state's coastal county population has increased by three to four times that which it was in 1950," said hurricane specialists Gilbert B. Clark and Robert A. Case of the National Hurricane Center in a report titled, "Florida Hurricanes."

Hurricanes can be described as awesome, devastating, intriguing and deadly. No matter what the adjective, they are nothing to take lightly. For this reason, the Florida Department of Community Affairs' Division of Emergency Management has come up with a detailed plan on how Florida should respond to a hurricane and what steps need to be taken to recover from one. The state agency attempts to coordinate state assistance to local governments mainly by establishing such things as a centralized communication and warning network to help cut down rumors, helps coordinate evacuation and sheltering activities, and assists with damage assessment.

Here are some facts about hurricanes, as detailed by the National Hurricane Center and state experts:

— Before Hurricane Andrew, the last time a hurricane struck land in Florida was on Oct. 12, 1987, when Floyd hit the Keys. That hurricane did only minimal damage.

— Hurricanes are defined as tropical cyclones where winds reach speeds of 74 miles per hour or more. The winds blow in a large spiral around a relatively calm center — the eye of the hurricane. Tropical cyclones of the same type are called typhoons in the north Pacific and cyclones in the Indian Ocean.

— No section of Florida should be considered immune to hurricanes. History has shown, though, that more hurricanes have affected the extreme southern portion of the state than any other location.

— Hurricanes with 200-mile-per-hour winds are likely to occur only once every 100 or 200 years. The last one of this magnitude was in 1935 in the Keys. And how often can you expect a similarly violent storm of equal intensity in the same location? Less than once in 500 years.

— The hurricane season for Florida is a six-month period — from June 1 to Nov. 30.

— Winds in the eye of a hurricane diminish rapidly from extreme violence to 15 miles per hour or less, but only rarely to an absolute calm. As the eye moves over an area, rain ceases, the middle cloud deck vanishes, and low clouds often remain with occasional breaks through which the sun may shine briefly or stars may be seen. This lull in the wind might last a few minutes or half an hour or more. The average diameter of the eye is 14 miles. At the other side of the eye, the winds rise rapidly again to hurricane force and come from the opposite direction of those in the leading half of the storm.

— The most dangerous elements of a hurricane are the high tides and rough seas that churn up as the storm moves across a coastal area. "It is here that by far most of the death and destruction occur," Clark and Case said. Drowning is the greatest cause of hurricane deaths. The term to define what the hurricane is doing at this stage is called a "storm surge." The highest and most dangerous portion of the storm surge usually develops near the center of the storm and extends 20 to 50 miles in the direction of the on-shore hurricane winds. Seas gradually rise to above normal levels while the hurricane is still centered offshore, sometimes as much as 300 to 500 miles. As the center of the storm nears the coast, water levels rise until they reach a maximum about the time the eye moves inland, or when the barometer is at its lowest reading.

— Tornadoes are common with most of the recent tropical cyclones in Florida. In every case, they have occurred in the outer portion of the hurricane circulation and not near the center. The majority of these tornadoes, though, are of a much weaker variety than the vicious Midwestern types. In addition, recent studies have concluded that much of the wind damage attributed to tornadoes has really been associated with downbursts — extremely strong straight-line wind gusts that result from the outflow of heavy thunderstorm activity in the hurricane.

— Hurricanes sometimes drop many inches of rain. For example, 38.5 inches fell in a 24-hour period at Yankeetown, 20 miles southeast of Cedar Key, in September 1950.

— Hurricanes are given a scale number based on wind intensity and barometric pressure. The lowest scale number — 1 — means the hurricane's winds are the least intense for a hurricane (from 74 to 95 miles per hour) and a scale number of 5 means the hurricane's winds are at their strongest — 155 miles per hour or more.

— The frequency of Florida hurricanes has diminished considerably during the past several decades. From 1921 to 1950, 32 hurricanes affected the Florida coast; from 1951 to 1980, 15 hurricanes were produced.

— The average number of Florida hurricanes per year (based 101 years, from 1885 through 1985) is 0.85, or about 6 hurricanes every 7 years. However, in the 16-year period from 1969 through 1984, only three hurricanes struck the coast. The average here is less than 0.20 hurricanes per year, or one hurricane every 5 years.

— Jacksonville is the only port city from Cape Hatteras, N.C., to Brownsville, Texas, that from at least 1885 until 1964 never had sustained winds of full hurricane force.

— Most hurricanes hitting land on the west coast have originated in the Gulf of Mexico or the Caribbean. The Keys and the southeastern Florida coast are in the paths of storms originating in both the Atlantic and the Caribbean.

— Florida has been struck by the earliest-in-the-year hurricane ever to hit the U.S. coastline (June 9, 1966) as well as the latest (Nov. 30, 1925).

— Four of the five most intense hurricanes ever to strike the U.S. coast hit the south Florida area. Hurricane Andrew's gusts, for example, were recorded to be at least 164-miles-per-hour. Before Andrew, no storm with winds of more than 130 miles per hour had hit Florida since 1960, the year Donna struck.

Some records to note:

Worst winds: Sustained winds exceeding 200 miles per hour accompanied the Sept. 2, 1935, storm that hit Matecumbe Key. That hurricane luckily was only about 40 miles wide. Next worst winds: gusts to at least 164 miles per hour by Hurricane Andrew on Aug. 24, 1992.

Lowest pressure: In the 1935 Keys hurricane, a reading of 26.35 inches was reported at Craig, between Lower Matecumbe and Long Key. This is the lowest reported sea-level barometric pressure in the Western Hemisphere.

Heaviest rainfall: 38.5 inches fell in a 24-hour period at Yankeetown in the September 1950 storm. Next heaviest was 35 inches in a 48-hour period at Trenton, 30 miles west of Gainesville, in October 1941.

Worst storm surge: About 18 feet or more during the 1935 hurricane in the Keys. Next worst: 18 feet above mean sea level from hurricane Eloise in September 1975, 14 feet at Tampa Bay in 1848 and 13.2 feet at Dinner Key from the 1926 Miami hurricane.

Worst loss of life: 1,838 fatalities during the 1928 storm when water from Lake Okee-chobee was blown over the levee and flooded several communities.

Most destructive: By far, Hurricane Andrew. Estimated property and crop losses: $20 billion-plus. Next worst: $300 million (or $1 billion based on 1980 dollars) after Donna hit the state in September 1960. Most of the damage occurred in Monroe, Collier and Lee counties. **Next worst:** $75 million ($650 million in 1980 dollars) from the Miami hurricane of September 1926. The Oct. 18-19, 1944, hurricane that hit an area from Key West to Tampa caused $63 million worth of damage ($427 million in 1980 dollars), mostly to citrus and vegetable crops.

Earliest known hurricane: Sept. 19, 1559, when a hurricane struck the Pensacola area and caused severe damage.

Decade with most hurricanes since 1900: 1940s, when 13 struck.

Decade with least number of hurricanes since 1900: 1980s, when two hit.

Areas where many hurricanes strike: On the southeastern coast and the Keys, 33 hurricanes struck from 1885 through 1985; and in northwestern Florida, from Carrabelle to Pensacola, 29 hurricanes occurred in the same period.

Areas most free from hurricanes in western Florida: Tampa and St. Petersburg.

Deadliest hurricanes in U.S. history: Galveston, September 1900, when 6,000 people were killed; Florida Keys, September 1928, with 1,838 casualties; New England, September 1938, 600 killed; Hurricane Audrey, June 1957, 390 killed; Hurricane Camille, August 1969, 258 killed; and Hurricane Diane, August 1955, 184 killed.

Deadliest hurricane years in Florida since 1926: 1,838 killed in 1928; 405 in 1935; 243 in 1926; 41 in 1992; 18 in 1944; 17 in 1947; 15 in 1937; 13 in both 1960 and 1965; 11 in 1964; 9 in both 1966 and 1972; and 7 in 1936, 1956 and 1985.

Chances of hurricane-force winds in any given year (weighted averages based on available records from 1900-1985): Jacksonville: 1 in 28; Daytona Beach: 1 in 28; Melbourne-Vero Beach: 1 in 14; West Palm Beach: 1 in 11; Miami: 1 in 8; Key West: 1 in 6; Fort Myers: 1 in 22; Tampa-St. Petersburg: 1 in 28; Apalachicola-Panama City: 1 in 22; and Pensacola: 1 in 22.

Based on the scale shown on the next page, the worst Florida hurricanes from 1900 to 1985 were Sept. 2, 1935 at Matecumbe Key — a Category 5 hurricane; and these Category 4 hurricanes: Sept. 9-10, 1919 at Key West; Sept. 18, 1926 at Miami; Sept. 16-17, 1928 at Palm Beach and Lake Okeechobee; Sept. 17,

Hurricanes and Tropical Storms by Months for Florida (1885-1985)

	May	June	July	August	September	October	November
Hurricanes:	0	6	7	15	29	25	4
Tropical storms:	2	17	6	15	23	27	1
Total:	2	23	13	30	52	52	5

Hurricane Scale Ranges

Scale number	Winds (mph)	Storm surge (feet)	Damage
1	74-95	4-5	Minimal
2	96-110	6-8	Moderate
3	111-130	9-12	Extensive
4	131-155	13-18	Extreme
5	155 or more	18 and above	Catastrophic

1947 at Fort Lauderdale, and Sept. 10, 1960 at the Middle Keys, Naples and Fort Myers. (Hurricane Andrew in 1992 was also a Category 4 hurricane).

What To Do Before a Hurricane Approaches

Federal and state emergency preparedness officials have a checklist for people in areas vulnerable to hurricanes. Some of these safety guidelines are:

1. During the hurricane season, make sure you have a supply of boards, tools, batteries and nonperishable foods.

2. Check your homeowner's insurance policy to see what it covers in the event a hurricane strikes. National Flood Insurance is an option if your policy is found lacking in flood damage coverage.

3. After a hurricane warning is issued, meaning the storm is likely to hit your region, leave low-lying areas that may be swept by high tides or storm waves. Plan ahead to avoid last-minute hurry that might leave you marooned or unprepared.

4. Moor your boat securely before the storm arrives or put it in a designated safe area.

5. Board up windows or protect them with storm shutters or tape.

6. Secure outdoor objects that might be blown away or uprooted such as garbage cans, garden tools, toys, signs, porch furniture.

7. Store drinking water in clean bathtubs, jugs, bottles and cooking utensils as the water supply might be contaminated by flooding or damaged by hurricane floods.

8. Check your battery-powered equipment. Your radio may be your only link to the outside world. Emergency cooking facilities, lights and flashlights will be essential if utilities are interrupted.

9. If you live in a mobile home, leave it for more substantial shelter.

10. Keep your car fueled. Service stations might be inoperable for several days after the storm strikes.

11. If your home is on high ground, stay there. If not, move to a designated shelter.

During the Storm

1. Stay indoors. Do not try to travel.

2. Monitor the storm's position through National Weather Service advisories.

3. Beware of the eye of the hurricane. At the other side of the storm, winds rise rapidly to hurricane force again.

After the Storm

1. Seek medical care, if necessary, at Red Cross disaster stations or hospitals.

2. Stay out of disaster areas.

3. Avoid loose or dangling wires and report them to your power company or the nearest law enforcement officer.

4. Before entering buildings that may have been damaged by the disaster, use extreme caution. Buildings can collapse without warning.

5. Report broken sewer or water mains to the water department. Before flushing toilets, check to see that sewage lines are intact.

6. Check for leaking gas pipes in your home — by smell only. If you smell gas, imme-

diately open windows and doors, turn off the main gas valve, leave your house and go to another location and notify the gas company or the police or fire departments.

7. If any of your electrical appliances are wet, turn off the main power switch in your house and then unplug the wet appliances, dry them out and check for damage.

8. Use only battery-powered lanterns or flashlights to examine your home for damage; flammables may be inside.

9. Check food and water supplies before using them. Foods that require refrigeration may be spoiled if electric power has been off for some time. Don't eat fresh food that has come in contact with flood waters.

10. Notify your insurance agent or broker if your property was damaged.

Public Shelter Inventory

Would there be enough shelters for those needing them if a major hurricane struck Florida? Florida's Division of Emergency Management says no, if you happen to be in 19 of the state's 67 counties. As of 1988, the division found that these counties had more demand for shelter than shelter capacity, based on the assumption that a Category 3-5 hurricane struck its area: Charlotte, Collier, Lee, Sarasota, Glades, Hendry, Lake, Orange, St. Johns, Putnam, Monroe, Broward, Hillsborough, Pinellas, Pasco, Manatee, Franklin, DeSoto and Okeechobee. The remaining counties were found to have adequate shelter facilities.

Florida's Climate Compared with the Other 49

How does Florida's climate compare with the rest of the country? Nearly as well as Hawaii's — that is, if you find that little or no snow or ice accumulation and warm days are more desirable than cold and snowy ones.

This table helps detail the 50 states' weather during 1991. The first column lists the mean number of days that the minimum temperature was 32 degrees Fahrenheit or colder; the second column gives the normal daily mean temperature; and the third column has the number of inches of snow and ice pellets each state receives.

State (with city)	Mean Number of Days That Minimum Temperature Is 32 Degrees Or Colder	Normal Daily Mean Temperature	Inches of Snow, Ice Pellets
Alabama (Mobile)	23	67.5	0.4
Alaska (Juneau)	142	40.0	98.2
Arizona (Phoenix)	8	71.2	Trace
Arkansas (Little Rock)	61	61.9	5.5
California (Los Angeles)	Less than half day	62.9	Trace
(Sacramento)	16	60.6	Trace
(San Diego)	Less than half day	63.8	Trace
(San Francisco)	2	56.6	Trace
Colorado (Denver)	157	50.3	59.8
Connecticut (Hartford)	136	49.8	48.4
Delaware (Wilmington)	101	54.0	21.2
Florida (Jacksonville)	15	68.0	Trace
(Miami)	Less than half day	75.6	None
Georgia (Atlanta)	55	61.2	2.0
Hawaii (Honolulu)	None	77.0	None
Idaho (Boise)	124	51.1	21.1
Illinois (Chicago)	133	49.2	39.3
(Peoria)	129	50.4	25.3
Indiana (Indianapolis)	119	52.1	23.0
Iowa (Des Moines)	135	49.7	33.9
Kansas (Wichita)	112	56.4	16.8
Kentucky (Louisville)	90	56.2	16.6

State (with city)	Mean Number of Days That Minimum Temperature Is 32 Degrees Or Colder	Normal Daily Mean Temperature	Inches of Snow, Ice Pellets
Louisiana (New Orleans)	13	68.2	0.2
Maine (Portland)	158	45.0	70.7
Maryland (Baltimore)	98	55.1	21.7
Massachusetts (Boston)	99	51.5	40.8
Michigan (Detroit)	137	48.6	41.5
(Sault Ste. Marie)	181	39.7	116.4
Minnesota (Duluth)	185	38.2	77.1
(Minneapolis-St. Paul)	156	44.7	49.4
Mississippi (Jackson)	51	64.6	1.0
Missouri (Kansas City)	110	54.1	20.1
(St. Louis)	102	55.4	19.8
Montana (Great Falls)	157	44.7	59.7
Nebraska (Omaha)	141	51.1	30.1
Nevada (Reno)	175	49.4	24.6
New Hampshire (Concord)	174	45.3	63.8
New Jersey (Atlantic City)	110	53.1	17.0
New Mexico (Albuquerque)	119	56.2	10.9
New York (Albany)	150	47.3	64.3
(Buffalo)	133	47.6	91.7
(New York)	80	54.5	28.5
North Carolina (Charlotte)	68	60.0	5.9
(Raleigh)	80	59.0	7.5
North Dakota (Bismark)	186	41.3	41.2
Ohio (Cincinnati)	109	53.4	23.6
(Cleveland)	124	49.6	54.9
(Columbus)	119	51.7	28.2
Oklahoma (Oklahoma City)	78	59.9	9.5
Oregon (Portland)	43	53.0	6.7
Pennsylvania (Philadelphia)	98	54.3	21.6
(Pittsbugh)	124	50.3	43.4
Rhode Island (Providence)	119	50.3	36.0
South Carolina (Columbia)	62	63.3	1.9
South Dakota (Sioux Falls)	168	45.3	39.8
Tennessee (Memphis)	57	61.8	5.7
(Nashville)	77	59.2	10.9
Texas (Dallas-Fort Worth)	41	66.0	3.0
(El Paso)	65	63.4	5.7
(Houston)	22	68.3	0.4
Utah (Salt Lake City)	125	51.7	57.9
Vermont (Burlington)	156	44.1	77.1
Virginia (Norfolk)	55	59.5	8.0
(Richmond)	85	57.7	14.6
Washington (Seattle-Tocoma)	31	51.4	12.3
(Spokane)	139	47.2	50.7
West Virginia (Charleston)	100	54.8	32.5
Wisconsin (Milwaukee)	142	46.1	46.9
Wyoming (Cheyenne)	171	45.7	54.1

Source: U.S. Department of Commerce, Bureau of the Census, "Statistical Abstract of the United States, 1991."

Florida's Weather and Your Health

Is Florida's sunny weather good for you? Should you avoid moving to the state because of the hot, humid conditions that usually exist from June until September?

A top Florida expert says that weather alone is not a reason to avoid living in the state. With man's ability to control his environment, the hot summers should not deter people, says Dr. Charlton Prather, retired administrative director for the state health office.

Of course, precautions should be taken, especially by the elderly. People can suffer from sunstroke or get overheated in the summer. The warning signals if the sun is too much for you: You'll see spots before your eyes, feel very hot and notice that your heart rate is up. Dr. Prather's advice if you become overheated is to get in the shade, sit down and cool off. Another piece of advice: Stay inside during the hottest parts of the day and keep the breeze blowing, with the help of a fan or an air conditioner, and keep fluids in your body.

Another danger that has been brought to light in recent years is overexposure to the sun that can lead to skin cancer. Heading the awareness campaign is the American Cancer Society. Its warning to those who bask too much in the sun: "Fry now. Pay later."

The sun provides vitamin D and can help to relieve asthma, aching joints, acne and psoriasis. It also can give you prematurely aged skin — wrinkles and a tough, leathery look, the Cancer Society says. Although the society says it isn't necessary to give up the outdoors to reduce your chances of developing skin cancer, it does warn that repeated sunburns are "particularly risky." It estimates that more than 500,000 new cases of skin cancer are reported every year, making it the most common form of human cancer. Discovered early, this type of cancer is one of the most curable forms. But most of it is preventable.

About 90 percent of all skin cancer occurs on parts of the body that usually aren't covered by clothing, such as the face; tips of the ears; hands; forearms; shoulders, backs and chests of men; and the lower legs of women. This type of cancer rarely occurs in childhood; the average age for discovery of a first skin cancer is 50. But this age is decreasing as skin cancer becomes more common among younger people, the Cancer Society says. The warning signs are: a sore that does not heal; change in the size or color of a wart of a mole; development of any unusual pigmented area.

Those most prone to skin cancer are people who sunburn easily and have fair skin with red or blond hair. They lack sufficient quantities of melanin — the pigment that helps prevent burning. Also, the amount of time spent in the sun affects a person's risk of this type of cancer.

Luckily, the Cancer Society says, there are a number of prevention techniques:

— Cover up with a wide-brimmed hat and a bandanna for your neck.

— Wear long-sleeved shirts and pants that the sun cannot penetrate.

— Use suncreens, which also will guard against premature aging of your skin. A Sun Protective Factor rating of 15 or higher is recommended. Women also can get some added protection by using tinted opaque cosmetic foundation along with a sunscreen. Sunscreen should be applied at least an hour before going into the sun and again after swimming or perspiring a lot.

— Avoid indoor sunlamps, tanning parlors and tanning pills.

— Know when and where the sun's rays can do the most damage. A person can get burned on a cloudy day because 70 percent to 80 percent of the ultraviolet rays' burning power can penetrate clouds; the sun's rays can reach down into three feet of water; the sun's rays are the strongest between 11 a.m. and 2 p.m.; and the ultraviolet rays are more harmful in high altitudes where there's less atmosphere to filter these out.

— Don't think that you are fully protected in the shade of a beach umbrella, because the umbrella only partially deflects ultraviolet rays, which also can bounce at you from sand, water, a patio or a deck.

— A wet T-shirt can deceive you, too, because water droplets funnel at least half the ultraviolet power to the skin.

— Avoid sun reflectors because they expose delicate areas to the sun — the eyelids, the earlobes and under the chin.

— A moving target is more difficult for the rays to find than a motionless one. It's better to ride a bike or play golf than to lie on the beach.

EDUCATION

When you try to assess the quality of public education, you're taking a big risk. Some educators say it's impossible. Some say that certain comparative categories are unfair, or that they compare different things. Is Orlando's school system better than Tampa's? Will more seniors from one go to Ivy League schools than from the other? Will more be admitted to the public university system? How much does it matter where a student goes to college? Or if a student goes to college? What do standardized test scores show? How accurate are dropout rates?

Ask three educators, and you'll likely get three different answers. But ask the U.S. Department of Education or the Florida Chamber of Commerce, and you'll get an abundance of criticism about the state's education system. Evaluations by the education department for years and by the chamber in 1989 gave Florida's public school system overall grades of "needs major improvement." Two federal education reports — an annual dropout survey of students ages 16 through 19 and "the State Education Performance Chart" (commonly known as the U.S. Report Card) — detailed some major flaws in Florida's educational system: the dropout rate has been among the highest in the country (14.2 percent, according to the late 1992 survey); the high school graduation rate has been among the lowest in the country for years, bottoming out to last place in the 1988-89 school year; and the state's scores on the Scholastic Aptitude Test (SAT), a college entrance examination, have consistently been below the national average.

And the chamber study, called "Cornerstone, Foundations for Economic Leadership," concluded that math, science and engineering education needed to be expanded, that the vocational education and technical training system needed to be more responsive to industry needs, and that the high dropout rate is a "critical issue" that needs attention.

A U.S. education report in 1990 showed that the state ranked dead last among the 50 states and the District of Columbia in high school graduation rates. Florida's high school graduation rate for 1988, the year the 1990 education report was based on, was 58 percent. That was down from 1987's rate of 58.6 percent and 1986's rate of 62 percent. In fact, Florida's ranking in this area has been low for years, standing at 60.2 percent in 1982, when the state was 48th in the country.

Some Florida educators dispute the national figures. They say the state's graduation rate was much higher, standing at 71 percent in the 1988-89 school year and increasing since then. For the 1990-91 school year, the state calculated its graduation rate at 73.06 percent; for 1991-92, 78.31 percent and for 1992-93, 78.73 percent. Educators point to a number of reforms in the system. For example, the state requires minimum competency testing for graduation and enforces a law that says students can lose their driver's licenses if they drop out of school.

Why the disparity in figures? Officials who work for the state's dropout prevention program say the U.S. education survey looks simply at the number of students getting a regular diploma in Grade 12, compared with the number of students who had been enrolled in Grade 9 four years earlier. In doing this, they say, the survey fails to count students who take longer to get through school and eventually get a graduation equivalency diploma, or GED. State officials say a large migrant population is a big reason why so many GEDs are given out (however, during the 1990-91 school year, for example, 6,924 GED diplomas were awarded in the state). The U.S. Education Department also adds a growth-rate percentage, based on census projections, to the state's number of ninth grade students, without actually counting how many students entered ninth grade, state education officials say.

They add that students in Florida also must pass a state assessment test before they receive a diploma, and because not every state has such a requirement, this also brings down Florida's graduation rate (U.S. figures have shown that Florida is among 23 states that require minimum competency tests for graduation). Students who don't pass the test but

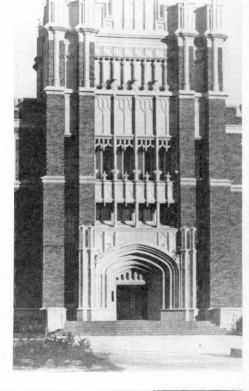

Sarasota High School was built in 1928. Paul Randolph designed the 1960 addition (below). Though each section is quite different from the other, both are renowned for their architecture.

complete other requirements for graduation simply receive a certificate of completion, which is not the same as a diploma and would not be counted in the national statistics. In the 1990-91 school year, just 447 certificates of completion were given out, though.

Florida can take some small consolation in one fact: It is not alone.

Former U.S. Education Secretary Lauro F. Cavazos sized up the U.S. education system in recent years this way: "We see our students performing minimally, lacking the advanced skills needed to succeed."

Many other states are also coping with low graduation rates.

In actual numbers, the U.S. education department says 600,000 to 700,000 students nationwide drop out of school each year, or 3,600 students per average school day. The role model: Minnesota, which led the nation in its graduation rate — 90.9 percent of its students who entered school four years earlier received high school diplomas in 1988.

While arguing that Florida's showing isn't as dismal as the U.S. Department of Education paints it, former Florida Education Commissioner Betty Castor said in 1989 that the state should aim for an 85 percent graduation rate by 1995. "In the face of daunting societal problems, we must raise our expectations. The consequences of inaction are too high: lost lives, and increasing costs in our welfare and criminal justice systems. We must believe we can graduate all of our students," she said in a newsletter published by the state education department. She also called on the state's school districts to become more accountable and announced plans to publish dropout rates for every district. Financial incentives were also to be awarded to school districts that lowered their dropout rates; $10 million was set aside for this purpose.

State figures show the state's dropout rate has been mainly declining in recent years. For the 1992-93 school year, the rate was 4.86 percent, compared with 5.6 percent for the 1990-91 school year and 6.55 percent for the 1989-90 school year. (State officials say you can't compare the graduation rate and the dropout rates because they are computed a different way. Graduation rates are counted from the time students enter Florida schools as ninth-graders until they graduate four years later. Dropout rates are computed for a single year, the officials say.)

The license/dropout law took effect Oct. 1, 1989. School districts give high school dropouts' names to the motor vehicles department. A student is urged to return and not lose his or her license and sign an "attendance con-tract" whereby he or she vows to go back to school and not miss an agreed-upon number of days. There are waivers to the law, such as family hardships.

Other incentives advanced to help lower the dropout rate in Florida included: increased funding for the dropout prevention program; programs aimed at keeping teenage parents in school, a group identified as contributing significantly to the dropout rate (every school district has access to this service and the teenagers' children are eligible for child care); a youth services program for those who have violated the law or who were abused or neglected (they are given educational instruction while they are in a Health and Rehabilitative Services facility, such as a community home); and the establishment of a pre-school program, where funding is provided for economically disadvantaged 3- and 4-year-old pupils to begin their education early.

In another area, the federal education survey found that Florida has been falling behind in some of its test scores for years. In 1994, for example, Florida's average SAT score was 879 out of a possible score of 1,600, below the national average of 902; five years before, in 1989, Florida's average SAT score was slightly higher at 887, but again below the national average of 903. Even more disturbing is the fact that state scores had been falling significantly since 1972, when the average stood at 941. Again, Florida is not alone, however; scores have fallen in recent years across the country.

The state was below average in terms of expenditures per pupil, the survey found. During 1988, it spent $4,092 (up nearly $300 from 1987), compared with a national average of $4,243. The state also was under the norm in teacher salaries. The average Florida salary, based on 10 months of employment, was estimated at $30,555 in 1990-91, compared with a national average of $33,000.

The budget for Florida's public school system for 1990-91, for example, was $5.2 billion. A total of $900 million came from the state's lottery, which was set up in large part to help finance education but which has drawn criticism for adding to its own bureaucracy at the expense of education. For the 1990-91 school year, lottery proceeds paid for 14 out of the 180 school days.

In terms of classroom teacher and student ratios, there was 1 teacher for every 17.2 Florida students in 1990-91. The ratio has been roughly the same as the national average in the past few years.

In 1990-91, of the 89,047 high school graduates, 53,341, or 59.9 percent, said they were planning to continue their education. The breakdown: 27,067 were heading to Florida's public community colleges; 570 to Florida's private junior colleges, 11,577 to Florida's public colleges and universities; 2,674 to Florida's private colleges and universities; 7,550 to out-of-state colleges and universities; 3,091 to in-state technical, trade or other schools; and 812 to out-of-state technical, trade or other schools.

Criticism from the Chamber

The Florida Chamber's "Cornerstone" study further underlined the need for improvements in the state's education system. The report, which outlined goals for the state in preparing for the 1990s, cited weaknesses in education as a roadblock to a stronger economic foundation in the state. According to the report, "Florida needs a skilled and flexible workforce to meet competitive challenges. A high-quality workforce is especially important for attracting and growing high-value-added industries. Currently, it ranks low in high school graduation rates and college attainment levels compared with both the nation and competitor states. Critical needs for industry include preparation of job graduates, enhancing technical training, and increasing math, science and engineering education."

The report gives the state a grade of C in its efforts to build skilled human resources, and a C- in its efforts toward new technology — the two areas where Florida has its "greatest current competitive weaknesses," the report says. Up until now, the report states, Florida industry has lacked the capability of gaining access to new technologies to be competitive. "Critical needs include both strengthening areas of technology excellence at the state's universities and developing a stronger university-industry cooperation in technology transfer," the report states. Among the suggestions for improvement: reducing the dropout rate; establishing an effective technical education and training system; including business needs in higher education planning; achieving research excellence in universities; and establishing partnerships for technology application.

"Florida was once able to compete effectively with other states by attracting domestic industry through its relatively low-cost environment. Today, the state faces both domestic and international competitors that can offer even lower costs to labor-intensive industries. As a result, the ingredients for economic health today have shifted from simply providing a low-cost environment to providing the necessary conditions for growing higher-value-added industries," the report says in its summary.

Included in the 24-page summary is a chart titled, "National rankings of key Florida business climate indicators," based on a 1988 study by Grant Thornton. The rankings show the state is: 4th in low taxes; 6th in low labor costs; 10th in state business incentives; 32nd in available workforce; 41st in transportation; and 46th in education.

Teaching Standards

Florida, like most states, requires that new teachers take a certification examination and provides temporary certification to those who teach while they complete the state requirements for teacher certification, such as additional course work and seminars.

One of the state's major requirements for a Florida teaching certificate is going through the Professional Orientation Program, intended to ensure that teachers seeking certification demonstrate the skills required by the State Board of Education. The program provides "support services for continuing professional development to individuals during the first year of employment as Florida teachers," according to the state board.

The program is mandatory for those applying for their first Florida 5-year professional teaching certificates. Participants must hold a valid temporary Florida teaching certificate while going through the program and must be employed at least four hours a day in a public or independent school that has an approved Professional Orientation Program plan.

There are exceptions to the mandatory requirement for experienced out-of-state teachers who: 1. hold a valid standard certificate issued by the state in which the most recent teaching experience was gained; 2. have five years of successful full-time teaching experience, including two continuous years during the five-year period preceding the application for a Florida certificate; and 3. are assigned to teach the subject or subjects shown on their out-of-state certificates.

Teachers must demonstrate a number of competencies during the orientation program. Among them: classroom instruction skills; the setting of short-term and long-term goals for given school subject areas; effective communication using verbal and nonverbal skills; the enhancement of students' feelings of dignity and self worth; an ability to recognize signs of severe emotional distress, alcohol and drug abuse, and child abuse and neglect; the setting of standards for student behavior in the classroom; the stimulation of student thinking and checking of comprehension through appropriate questioning techniques; the encouragement of student participation and academic focus; and the use of feedback.

Student Requirements

School attendance is required for anyone 6 to 16 years old. No child can be admitted to the first grade in any school without completing kindergarten in a public or nonpublic school.

While educational requirements are mapped out somewhat by the State Board of Education, it is up to each district school board to ensure that minimum performance standards approved by the state board are carried out. For example, state law dictates that each district school board establish a comprehensive program for progression of its pupils, based on an evaluation of each pupil's performance. In addition, each district determines and specifies the minimum number of hours of instruction in such areas as health education and alcohol and substance abuse prevention appropriate for each grade level, kindergarten through 12.

Florida, until 1992, did a lot of required testing of its students before they were promoted to the next grade level. Many of these tests have since been eliminated as requirements for graduation. Castor, the former education commissioner, said the state was testing too much; was testing basic skills rather than problem-solving skills; and was testing students at too young an age. One test still stands, though, as a prerequisite for graduation: an eleventh-grade High School Competency Test. This exam measures the application of basic skills to practical situations, with emphasis on mathematics and communication.

School districts continue testing students in some grade levels, but these tests are simply used as measures of a student's progress and for evaluation. Students' writing skills are tested in the fourth, eighth and 10th grades, while a reading comprehension and mathematics achievement test is also given to 10th graders.

By the time a student receives a diploma from a Florida high school, he or she must be able to master these standards:

Reading: demonstrate knowledge of basic vocabulary; determine word meaning from word parts; demonstrate comprehension skills; and demonstrate skills for obtaining information.

Writing: compose grammatically correct sentences; organize objects and information; write a paragraph; write to supply necessary information; write letters and messages; fill out common forms; spell correctly; punctuate correctly; capitalize correctly; and write legibly.

Mathematics: read and write numerals; round numbers; put numbers in order; determine equivalent fractions, decimals and percents; add whole numbers; subtract whole numbers; multiply whole numbers; divide whole numbers; add, subtract and multiply fractions; add and subtract decimals; multiply and divide decimals; find percentages; measure time, temperature, distance, capacity and mass/weight; identify geometric figures and shapes; determine information needed to solve a problem; estimate solutions by rounding; solve real-world problems involving whole numbers, fractions, decimals and percents; solve money problems; solve measurement problems; and interpret graphs, tables and maps.

High school students are required to complete a minimum of 24 academic credits in grades 9 through 12 before they can graduate. Among these are:

4 credits in English, with major concentration in composition and literature.

3 credits in mathematics.

3 credits in science, two of which must have a laboratory component. The only exception here is when a school district certifies that its laboratory facilities are inadequate, the State Board of Education may grant an annual waiver of the lab requirement, provided "the district submits a capital outlay plan to provide adequate facilities and makes the funding of this plan a priority of the school board."

1 credit in American history.

1 credit in world history, including a comparative study of the history, doctrines, and objectives of all major political systems.

1/2 credit in economics, including a comparative study of the history, doctrines and objectives of all major economic systems.

1/2 credit in American government.

1/2 credit in practical arts vocational education or exploratory vocational education.

1/2 credit in performing fine arts to be selected from music, dance, drama, painting or sculpture, speech and debate, or any art form that requires manual dexterity.

1/2 credit in life management skills, including consumer education, positive emotional development, nutrition, information and instruction on breast cancer detection and breast self-examination, cardiopulmonary resuscitation, drug education and the hazards of smoking.

1/2 credit in physical education to include assessment, improvement and maintenance of personal fitness.

9 elective credits.

In addition, individual Florida school districts might have minimum requirements that exceed these.

The State University System

For years, Florida's university system has been struggling to cast aside an image of low recognition on a national level. Although ranked as the fifth largest university system nationally, it has not been generally regarded as being among the top five systems. But things are improving.

For example, a late 1980s survey of 100 presidents of state universities in 44 states ranked the Florida system in the Top Ten — a national recognition that up to then was unprecedented. In 1994, U.S. News & World Report ranked the University of Florida in the second-tier category of national universities. It was among those ranked 26th to 57th out of 229, and was in the same category as Boston College, Brandeis, William and Mary, Lehigh, New York University and Tufts.

And state university system officials cite a few other trends that to them mean more growth and improvement in the coming years despite legislative spending restrictions. In 1991, the aggregate high school grade-point average was 3.3 out of a possible 4.0 for incoming freshmen; the average score on the American College Testing Program exam (ACT test) was 21.8 out of a possible 36 and on the Scholastic Aptitude Test (SAT) 1057 out of a possible 1600. In addition, the 1991 freshman class had 282 National Merit and National Achievement semi-finalists and finalists. Currently, the state university system reports test scores and grades by range, rather than by a numerical average.

More than 194,000 students are enrolled in the state's nine universities. By the year 2000, that number is expected to climb to 240,000. To help accommodate a little of this load, the opening of a 10th university in the Fort Myers area, to be named Florida Gulf Coast University, is planned for the fall of 1997.

In the 1993-94 academic year, 37,201 students applied for enrollment, of whom 14,811 enrolled. The system in 1992 awarded 29,340 bachelor's degrees, 7,529 master's degrees, 845 Ph.D degrees, and 949 professional degrees in medicine, law, pharmacy, dentistry and veterinary medicine.

In terms of tuition costs, Florida's universities have been very attractive, ranking among the lowest in the country. In 1993, Florida was 44th lowest among the 50 states. But this ranking might change. Tuition is expected to increase annually until students' contribution reaches 25 percent of the cost, instead of the 9.26 percent level in 1987, according to a policy adopted by the Board of Regents, the State Board of Education and the Florida Legislature.

Nevertheless, the budget office of the Board of Regents said that for the 1994-95 school year, the tuition for in-state undergraduates attending a Florida university and taking 30 credit hours for two semesters averaged $1,782.76.

In-state graduate school tuition, based on 24 credit hours for two semesters, was $2,677.94. Out-of-state tuition rates were much higher — $6,685.06 for undergraduates taking 30 credit hours for two semesters and $8,750.42 for graduates taking 24 credit hours for two semesters.

Average room and board cost throughout the university system for two semesters was $1,913 for room and $1,794 for board, based on the 1992-93 school year.

Here's a brief overview of the state's nine universities:

University of Florida, Gainesville. Founded 1853. This is the state's oldest, largest and most comprehensive university. It ranks as one of the three most diverse universities in the nation, in terms of academic program offerings. 1993 enrollment was 38,319, with 76.1 percent undergraduates and 23.9 percent graduates. Minority enrollment: 24.7 percent. About 80 percent of those attending were Florida residents; 8 percent international; and 12 percent out of state. The SAT range of 1993 freshman class: 1050-1230. The ACT range: 24-28. The grade point range of the 1993 freshman class: 3.3 - 3.9. The 1993 freshman class also included 149 National Merit and Achievement finalists, which placed it third highest in the nation among public universities.

Florida State University, Tallahassee. Founded 1857. 1993 enrollment was 28,853, with 80 percent undergraduates and 20 percent graduates. Minority enrollment was 18.7 percent. About 80 percent of those attending were Florida residents; 14 percent out of state; and 6 percent international. The SAT range: 990-1170. The ACT range: 23-27. The grade point range of 1993 freshman class: 3.1 - 3.9. In recent years, the university has been awarded grants in supercomputing, high-magnetic field research, superconductivity and structural biology.

Florida A&M University, Tallahassee. Founded 1887. Has achieved a number of firsts in its role as an institution for black students. Today is a leading recruiter of minority National Achievement Scholars. 1993 enrollment was 9,915 with 94 percent undergraduates and 6 percent graduates. Minority enrollment was 92 percent. About 76 percent of those attending were Florida residents; 23 percent out of state; and 1.5 percent international. The SAT range: 830-1040. The ACT range: 18-22. The grade point range of 1993 freshman class: 2.56 - 3.45. University is the first historically black college in the nation to have an accredited journalism program and is the only historically black university to offer a Ph.D in pharmacy — in 1991 awarded more Ph.D's to blacks at one time than all other institutions nationwide.

University of South Florida, Tampa. Founded 1956. Florida's second largest public university. Also has campuses in St. Petersburg, Sarasota, Fort Myers and Lakeland. Tampa campus is only one that offers full range of courses. Its New College branch in Sarasota, a liberal arts undergraduate school, has been listed among the top "Best College Buys" in the country by Money magazine. For both the 1993-94 and 1994-95 school years, the college has been ranked No. 1: for keeping its academic standards high and its tuition low. Among the factors the magazine considered in its ranking: entrance exam results, graduation rates, faculty resources and deployment and budgets for instruction and student services. The college also was named among the nation's 299 best educational buys by Barron's business magazine in 1994, which did not rank the colleges, but listed its picks alphabetically. Barron's evaluated 2,100 U.S. colleges and universities and compared tuition, the percentage of faculty with doctorate-level degrees, the percentage of graduates seeking advanced degrees, the school's libraries and the school's curriculum in coming up with its list. 95 percent of New College's professors have Ph.Ds.

1993 enrollment was 35,452, with 82 percent undergraduates and 18 percent graduates. Minority enrollment was 19 percent. About 91 percent of those attending were Florida residents; 7 percent out of state; and 2 percent international. The SAT range: 940-1140. The ACT range: 20-26. The grade point range of 1993 freshman class: 2.8 - 3.8. The university offers more than 100 master's and doctoral programs. Its Suncoast Area Teachers Training Program has been rated by the Educational Testing Service as one of the nation's five most innovative teaching programs.

Florida Atlantic University, Boca Raton. Founded 1961. Enrollment in 1993 was 16,257, with 86 percent undergraduates and 14 percent graduates. Minority enrollment was 25 percent. About 92 percent of those attending were Florida residents; 6 percent out of state; and 2 percent international. The SAT range: 910-1080. The ACT range: 20-25. The grade point range of 1993 freshman class: 2.75 - 3.56. Offers more than 41 master's and 14 Ph.D programs in nine colleges. Its ocean engineering program has ranked among the top three in the United States.

The University of West Florida, Pensacola. Founded 1963. Also has a Fort Walton Beach facility. 1993 enrollment was 7,746, with 85 percent undergraduates and 15 percent graduates. Minority enrollment was 13.6 percent. About 95 percent of those attending were Florida residents; 3.5 percent out of state; and 1.3 percent international. The SAT range: 850-1030. The ACT range: 19-25. The grade point range of 1993 freshman class: 2.82 - 3.72. University is located on a 1,000-acre nature preserve on the Escambia River. It offers bachelor's and master's degrees in such areas as business and finance, the social sciences, computer science, education, foreign languages, medical technology, nursing, life sciences, math and physical science.

University of Central Florida near Orlando. Founded 1963. Originally named Florida Technological University, it changed its name in 1978. 1993 enrollment was 23,972, with 86 percent undergraduates and 14 percent graduates. Minority enrollment was 21 percent. About 95 percent of those attending were Florida residents; 4 percent out of state; and 1 percent international. The SAT range: 900-1100. The ACT range: 22-26. The grade point range of 1993 freshman class: 2.9 - 3.7. Also has a campus at Daytona Beach. U.S. News & World Report has ranked the unversity among the top 12 regional universities in the South in its annual guide to the nation's best colleges and universities. Offers programs from computer programming and engineering to marketing research.

Florida International University, Miami. Founded 1965. Offers programs at University Park in southwest Miami, which has a School of Engineering, and North Miami, whose School of Hospitality Management has been nationally recognized. Two other centers are located in Broward County. For several years in a row, U.S. News & World Report included the university in its listing of the best regional universities in the South, based on its academic reputation, student selectivity, faculty resources, financial resources and student satisfaction. 1993 enrollment was 24,410, with 86 percent undergraduates and 14 percent graduates. Minority enrollment was 67.5 percent. About 94 percent of those attending were Florida residents; 3 percent out of state; and 3 percent international. The SAT range: 920-1080. The ACT range: 21-25. The grade point range of 1993 freshman class: 3.0 - 3.7. Offers more than 200 degree programs.

University of North Florida, Jacksonville. Founded 1972. 1993 enrollment was 9,484, with 85 percent undergraduates and 15 percent graduates. Minority enrollment was 17 percent. About 92 percent of those attending were Florida residents; 4 percent out of state; 4 percent international. The SAT range: 920-1110. The ACT range: 20-23. The grade point range of 1993 freshman class: 2.8 - 3.44. Offers programs in liberal arts, business, education in addition to health sciences. Also offers computer science and American music programs.

Community Colleges

Florida's community college system got its start in 1933 with the establishment of Palm Beach Junior College as a public two-year college. This college remained the state's only community college until 1947, when the status of St. Petersburg Junior College was changed from a private institution to a public college. A banner year for the system was 1957, when a master plan established a system of public community colleges within commuting distance of more than 99 percent of Florida's population. That year, the legislature appropriated funding for six new community colleges.

By 1972, the master plan was fully implemented and the state had 28 community colleges offering students the first two years of a baccalaureate degree, vocational education and adult continuing education programs. In addition, more than 2,000 other locations, such as churches, public schools and community centers, are used today for instruction.

Another master plan, in 1983, addressed a number of concerns that had arisen over that decade, including emphasis on the improvement of quality, the trend toward increased part-time enrollments, minority needs, women's needs and student financial aid needs. Another five-year plan, adopted in 1988, emphasized economic development, quality education and the quality of life.

During the 1993-94 school year, 802,796 students were enrolled in the community college system. Miami-Dade Community College had the largest enrollment at 102,546, followed by Florida Community College at Jacksonville, 86,710, St. Petersburg Junior College, 50,798, and Palm Beach Community College, 50,249. If a smaller college atmosphere is more suitable, you might try one of these: North Florida Junior College, with just 2,879 students; Florida Keys Community College, 5,549; or Lake-Sumter, 5,758.

The community college system offers community instructional services, citizenship, recreation and leisure programs, and other supplemental courses. Many vocational programs are also offered: accounting and bookkeeping, air conditioning, heating and refrigeration, airplane piloting and navigation, architectural design and construction technology, automotive mechanics, automotive body repair, business administration and management, commercial art, cosmetology, criminal justice administration, data processing, dental assisting, drafting and design technology, electronic technology, executive secretarial, fire control and safety technology, legal secretarial, machine tool operation, marketing management, medical laboratory technology, general nursing, trade and industrial supervision and management, and welding.

Florida's 28 community colleges and their main branch addresses are:

Brevard Community College, 1519 Clearlake Road, Cocoa, Fla., 32922; established in 1960;
Broward Community College, 225 E. Las Olas Blvd., Fort Lauderdale, Fla., 33301; 1960;
Central Florida Community College, P.O. Box 1388, Ocala, Fla., 32678; 1958;
Chipola Junior College, 309 Indian Circle, Marianna, Fla., 32446; established in 1947 as a private institution and became part of Florida's public system in 1948;
Daytona Beach Community College, P.O. Box 2811, Daytona Beach, Fla., 32120; 1958;
Edison Community College, P.O. Box 06210, S.W., Fort Myers, Fla., 33906; 1962;
Florida Community College at Jacksonville, 501 W. State St., Jacksonville, Fla. 32202; 1966;
Florida Keys Community College, 5901 W. Junior College Road, Key West, Fla., 33040; 1965;
Gulf Coast Community College, 5230 W. Highway 98, Panama City, Fla., 32401; 1957;
Hillsborough Community College, P.O. Box 31127, Tampa, Fla., 33631-3127; 1968;
Indian River Community College, 3209 Virginia Ave., Fort Pierce, Fla., 34981; 1960;

Lake City Community College, Route 3, Box 7, Lake City, Fla., 32055; 1962;

Lake-Sumter Community College, 9501 U.S. 441 S., Leesburg, Fla., 34788; 1962;

Manatee Community College, P.O. Box 1849, Bradenton, Fla. 34206; 1958;

Miami-Dade Community College, 300 N. E. Second Ave., Miami, Fla., 33132; 1960;

North Florida Junior College, 1000 Turner Davis Drive, Madison, Fla., 32340; 1958;

Okaloosa-Walton Community College, 100 College Blvd., Niceville, Fla., 32578; 1964;

Palm Beach Community College, 4200 Congress Ave., Lake Worth, Fla., 33461; 1933;

Pasco-Hernando Community College, 36727 Blanton Road, Dade City, Fla., 33525; 1972;

Pensacola Junior College, 1000 College Blvd., Pensacola, Fla., 32504; 1948;

Polk Community College, 999 Avenue H, N.E., Winter Haven, Fla., 33881; 1964;

St. Johns River Community College, 5001 St. Johns Ave., Palatka, Fla., 32177; 1958;

St. Petersburg Junior College, P.O. Box 13489, St. Petersburg, Fla., 33733; established in 1927 as a private institution and became part of Florida's public system in 1947;

Santa Fe Community College, P.O. Box 1530, Gainesville, Fla., 32602; 1966;

Seminole Community College, 100 Weldon Blvd., Sanford, Fla., 32771; 1966;

South Florida Community College, 600 W. College Drive, Avon Park, Fla., 33825; 1966;

Tallahassee Community College, 444 Appleyard Drive, Tallahassee, Fla., 32304; 1966;

Valencia Community College, P.O. Box 3028, Orlando, Fla., 32802; 1967.

Independent Colleges

There are more than 100 independent colleges in Florida. These institutions include those licensed by the state and those exempt from licensure by the State Board of Independent Colleges and Universities, a section of the Department of Education.

About half were licensed institutions, or those meeting the requirements for licensure under the state statutes. Under Florida law, institutions are granted either a temporary license, a provisional license or a regular license.

Many schools were exempt from licensure because they were accredited by a recognized accrediting agency, such as the American Association of Bible Colleges, American Bar Association, American Dental Association, Accrediting Commission for Independent Colleges and Schools, American Osteopathic Association, Association of Theological Schools, Middle States Association of Colleges and Schools, Accrediting Commission for Trade and Technical Schools, Northwest Association of Schools and Colleges, North Central Association of Colleges and Schools, New England Association of Schools and Colleges, New York Board of Regents, Southern Association of Colleges and Schools and the Western Association of Schools and Colleges.

Following is a listing of independent schools that had sizable enrollments:

Art Institute of Fort Lauderdale, 1799 S.E. 17th St., Ft. Lauderdale 33316; enrollment: 1,375 full time, 426 part time.

Barry University, 11300 N.E. 2nd Ave., Miami Shores 33161; enrollment: 2,592 full time, 4,181 part time. School also has branch campuses at South Dade County, 13701 N. Kendall Drive, Suite 304, Miami; Indian River Community College in Fort Pierce; Key West Professional Centre, 1342 Colonial Blvd., Suite 38-B, Fort Myers; 8177 W. Glades Road, Suite 217, Boca Raton; 4801 S. University Drive, Suite 4-S, Davie; Ames Plaza, 41 E. Merritt Ave., Merritt Island; and 9121 N. Military Trail, Suite 200, Palm Beach Gardens.

Bethune-Cookman College, 640 2nd Ave., Daytona Beach 32115; enrollment: 2,128 full time, 82 part time.

Caribbean Center for Advanced Studies, 8180 N.W. 36th St., 2nd Floor, Miami 33166; enrollment: 360 full time, 62 part time.

City College, 1401 N.W. 62nd St., Fort Lauderdale, 33309; enrollment: 398 full time, 44 part time.

Clearwater Christian College, 3400 Gulf-to-Bay Blvd., Clearwater 34619; enrollment: 408 full time, 43 part time.

College of Saint Francis Center, c/o Holmes Regional Medical Center, 3330 Spartina Ave., Merritt Island, 32953; enrollment: 397 part time. Home campus: 500 N. Wilcox St., Joliet, Ill., 60435.

Columbia College - Orlando Naval Training Center, NTC Building 2036, Orlando 32813; enrollment: 301 full time, 52 part time. Branch campus: P.O. Box 137 Building No. 8, Jacksonville NAS, Jacksonville, 32212.

Eckerd College, 4200 54th Ave. S., P.O. Box 12560, St. Petersburg 33733; enrollment: 1,574 full time, 749 part time. Branch campuses: North Pinellas Center, 1150 County Road 1, Palm Harbor, 34683; and 501 Bowman Court, Sarasota 34237.

Edward Waters College, 1658 Kings Road, Jacksonville 32209; enrollment: 585 full time, 40 part time.

Embry-Riddle Aeronautical University, 600 Clyde Morris Blvd., Daytona Beach 32114;

enrollment: 3,591 full time, 766 part time. Branch campuses: Fort Lauderdale Executive Airport Business Center, 1885 W. Commercial Blvd., Suite 120, Fort Lauderdale 33309; Building 26, Box 157, NAS Cecil Field, Jacksonville 32215; Naval Education & Training Support Center, Navy Campus Field Office, Building 718-A NAS, Key West 33040; MacDill Air Force Base, P.O. Box 6821, MacDill AFB 33608; and Education Services Office, 1140 School Ave., Patrick Air Force Base 32925.

Flagler College, P.O. Box 1027, St. Augustine 32085; enrollment: 1,345 full time, 44 part time.

Florida Baptist Theological College, 1306 College Drive, Graceville 32440; enrollment: 261 full time, 26 part time.

Florida Christian College, 1011 Bill Beck Blvd., Kissimmee, 34744; enrollment: 127 full time, 33 part time.

Florida College, 119 Glen Arven, Temple Terrace 33617; enrollment: 397 full time, 7 part time.

Florida Institute of Technology, 150 W. University Blvd., Melbourne 32901; enrollment: 2,292 full time, 1,323 part time. Branch campuses: F.I.T. Graduate Center, Suite 161, 3165 McCrory Place, Orlando 32803; F.I.T. Graduate Center, 9549 Cogar Blvd., Gadsden Building, Suite 109, St. Petersburg 33702; F.I.T. Graduate Center, 6770 A South U.S. 1, Spaceport, Titusville 32780; F.I.T. Graduate Center, Treasure Coast OCP, 3725 S.E. Ocean Blvd., Suite 104, Stuart 34966.

Florida Memorial College, 15800 N.W. 42nd Ave., Miami 33054; enrollment: 1,354 full time, 109 part time. Branch campuses: Hialeah Center, 6077 E. 7th Ave., Hialeah 33014; Little Havana Center, 4340 N.W. 3rd St., Miami 33126; Miami Palmetto Senior High School, 7460 S.W. 118th St., Miami; Richmond Heights Center, 15015 S.W. 103rd Ave., Miami 33176; and Library City Center, 1801 N.W. 60th St., Miami 33142.

Florida National College (formerly Florida International College) 4206 W. 12th Ave., Hialeah 33012; enrollment: 881 full time.

Florida Southern College, 111 Lake Hollingsworth Drive, Lakeland 33801; enrollment: 1,070 full time, 1,023 part time. Branch campuses: Florida Southern College at Orlando, 8578 Avenue C, Orlando 32812; and Florida Southern College at Port Charlotte, 1275 Sheri St., Lake Suzy 33821.

Florida Technical College, 1819 N. Semoran Blvd., Orlando 32807; enrollment: 177 full time, 9 part time.

Fort Lauderdale College, 1040 Bayview Drive, Ft. Lauderdale 33304; enrollment: 382 full time, 72 part time.

Hobe Sound Bible College, P.O. Box 1065, Hobe Sound, 33475; enrollment: 119 full time, 47 part time.

International Academy of Merchandising and Design, 5225 Memorial Highway, Tampa 33634; enrollment: 186 full time, 189 part time.

International College of Naples, 2654 E. Tamiami Trail, Naples 33962; enrollment: 257 full time, 290 part time; branch campus: Fort Myers Center, 8695 College Parkway, Fort Myers 33919.

International Fine Arts College, 1737 N. Bayshore Drive, Miami 33132; enrollment: 645 full time.

ITT Technical Institute, 4809 Memorial Highway, Tampa 33634; enrollment: 596.

ITT Technical Institute, 2600 Lake Lucien Drive, Suite, 140, Maitland, 32751; enrollment: 634 full time.

Jacksonville University, 2800 University Blvd. North, Jacksonville 32211; enrollment: 1,679 full time, 728 part time.

Johnson & Wales University, 1701 N.E. 127th St., North Miami, 33150; enrollment: 484. Home campus: 8 Abbott Park Place, Providence, R.I., 02903.

Jones College, 5353 Arlington Expressway, Jacksonville 32211; enrollment: 350 full time, 559 part time. Branch campus: 5975 Sunset Drive, S. Miami 33143.

Keiser College of Technology, 1500 N.W. 49th St., Fort Lauderdale 33309; enrollment: 1,075 full time. Branch campuses: 701 Babcock St., Melbourne 32901; 1605 E. Plaza Drive, Tallahassee, 32308.

Lynn University, (formerly College of Boca Raton), 3601 N. Military Trail, Boca Raton 33431; enrollment: 1,054 full time, 279 part time.

Martin College, 1901 N.W. 7th St., Miami 33125; enrollment: 607 full time.

National Education Center-Bauder College Campus, 4801 N. Dixie Highway, Fort Lauderdale 33334; enrollment: 604 full time; Home campus: National Education Corp., 1732 Reynolds St., Irvine, Calif., 92714. Branch campus: 7955 N.W. 12th St., Suite 300, Miami 33126.

National Education Center-Tampa Technical Institute Campus, 2410 E. Busch Blvd., Tampa 33612; enrollment: 1,042 full time.

National-Louis University (formerly National College of Education), 4890 W. Kennedy Blvd., Suite 145, Tampa 33609; enrollment: 237 full time. Branch campuses: locations in Orlando, Miami and Tampa Bay areas.

Northwood Institute-Florida Education Center, 2600 N. Military Trail, W. Palm Beach

33409; enrollment: 368 full time, 31 part time; Home campus: 3225 Cook Road, Midland, Mich., 48640.

Nova-Southeastern University, (formerly Nova University), 3301 College Ave., Ft. Lauderdale 33314; enrollment: 3,792 full time, 5,076 part time.

Orlando College, 5500 Diplomat Circle, Orlando 32810; enrollment: 1,597 full time. Branch campus: 2411 Sand Lake Road, Orlando 32809.

Palm Beach Atlantic College, P.O. Box 24708, West Palm Beach 33416; enrollment: 1,443 full time, 423 part time.

Pensacola Christian College, P.O. Box 18000, Pensacola 32523; enrollment: 3,046 full time, 193 part time.

Phillips Junior College of Florida, 2401 N. Harbor City Blvd., Melbourne 32935; enrollment: 781 full time. Branch campuses: 1479 S. Nova Road, Daytona Beach, 32114; 1040 Bayview Drive, Fort Lauderdale, 33404.

Ringling School of Art and Design, 2700 N. Tamiami Trail, Sarasota 34234; enrollment: 748 full time, 21 part time.

Rollins College, 1000 Holt Ave., Winter Park 32789; enrollment: 1,994 full time, 1,502 part time. Branch campus: Brevard campus, 1535 N. Cogswell St., Rockledge 32955.

St. Leo College, P.O. Box 2187, St. Leo 33574; enrollment: 1,331 full time, 1,314 part time. Branch campuses: Key West NAS, P.O. Box 9033, Key West 33040; Hurlburt/Eglin Resident Center, P.O. Box 9036, Hurlburt Field 32544; and MacDill Air Force Base, P.O. Box 6063, Tampa, 33608.

Saint Thomas University, 16400 N.W. 32nd Ave., Miami 33054; enrollment: 1,940 full time, 654 part time. Branch campuses: Villanueva Center, 4410 W. 16th Ave., Hialeah 33012; South Dade Center, 2950 S.W. 87th Ave., Miami 33165.

Schiller International University, 453 Edgewater Drive, Dunedin, 34968; enrollment: 124 full time. Home campus: Bergstrasse 106, 69121 Heidelberg, Germany.

South College - West Palm Beach Campus, 1760 N. Congress Ave., W. Palm Beach 33409; enrollment: 144 full time, 133 part time; Home campus: South College, 709 Mall Blvd., Savannah, Ga., 31406.

Southeastern College of the Assemblies of God, 1000 Longfellow Blvd., Lakeland 33801; enrollment: 1,078 full time, 66 part time.

Southern College, 5600 Lake Underhill Road, Orlando 32807; enrollment: 388 full time, 231 part time.

Southern Illinois University Center, P.O. Box 141, Cecil Field, Jacksonville 32215; enrollment: 227 full time, 67 part time; Home campus: Anthony Hall, Room 11, Carbondale, Ill., 62901. Branch campuses: Box 175, NAS, Mayport; Box 141, NAS Cecil Field, Jacksonville, 32215; Suite NCES, 1751 John Paul Jones Ave., NTC, Orlando; and P.O. Box 114, NAS Jacksonville, 32212.

Southwest Florida College of Business (formerly Florida Career Institute), 1685 Medical Lane, Fort Myers, 33907; enrollment: 269 full time, 130 part time.

Stetson University, 421 N. Woodland Blvd., DeLand 32720; enrollment: 2,663 full time, 292 part time. Branch campus: Stetson College of Law, 1401 61st St. S., St. Petersburg 33707; enrollment: 622.

Tampa College, 3319 W. Hillsborough Ave., Tampa 33614; enrollment: 2,017 full time. Branch campus: Tampa College/Brandon, 3925 Coconut Palm Drive, Tampa 33619.

Tampa College - Pinellas, 15064 U.S. Highway 19 N., Clearwater 34624; enrollment: 1,674 full time. Branch campus: 1200 U.S. Highway 98 South, Suite 45, Lakeland 33801; enrollment: 1,674 full time. Branch campus: 1200 U.S. Highway 98 S., Suite 45, Lakeland, 33801.

Trinity Baptist College, 426 S. McDuff Ave., Jacksonville 32205; enrollment: 235 full time, 57 part time.

Trinity College at Miami, 500 N.E. 1st Ave., Miami 33101; enrollment: 239 full time, 99 part time.

Troy State University - Florida Region, 81 Beach Parkway S.E., Fort Walton Beach, 32548; enrollment: 1,563 full time, 1,247 part time. Home campus: Troy State University System, Troy, Ala., 36082. Branch campuses: P.O. Box 9246, Hurlburt Field 32544; Troy State University, Building 718, P.O. Box 9033, Key West; Naby Campus Education Center, Naval Training Center, Building 2036, Orlando; Building 1416, NAS Whiting Field 32570; P.O. Box 33202, NAS Pensacola 32508-3202; P.O. Box 1955, Eglin Air Force Base 32542; Building 258, Room 301, MacDill Air Force Base, 33608; and Building 1230, Room 45A, Tyndall Air Force Base, 32403.

Union Institute, 16853 N.E. 2nd Ave., Suite 102, North Miami Beach, 33162; enrollment: 198 full time, 42 part time.

University of Miami, P.O. Box 248006, Coral Gables 33124; enrollment: 11,858 full time, 1,920 part time. Branch campuses: Broward Community College, Fort Lauderdale; Florida Keys Community College, Key West Campus, Key West; Miami Dade Community College, Miami Wolfson Campus, South Campus; Koubek Center, 2705 S.W. Third St., Miami 33135; James L. Knight Center, 400 S.E. Second Ave., Miami 33131; Naples Education Program, Naples; Miami Beach Center, Old City Hall, 11th St. and Washington Ave., Miami Beach; McDonald Douglas, 701 Columbia Blvd., Titusville 32780; and Naples Community Hospital, 350 7th St. N., Naples 33139.

University of Tampa, 401 W. Kennedy Blvd., Tampa 33606; enrollment: 1,545 full time, 832 part time.

Ward Stone College, 9020 S.W. 137th Ave., Miami, 33186; enrollment: 117 full time, 68 part time.

Warner Southern College, 5301 U.S. Highway 27 S., Lake Wales 33853; enrollment: 469 full time, 62 part time.

Webber College, 1201 Alternate Highway 27 South, P.O. Box 96, Babson Park, 33827; enrollment: 213 full time, 72 part time.

Webster College Center, 6551 Central Ave., St. Petersburg, 33710; enrollment: 916 total, all locations. Branch campuses: 2192 N. U.S. Highway 1, Fort Pierce, 34396; 5623 U.S. Highway 19, New Port Richey, 33652; 1530 S.W. Third Ave., Ocala, 32674; and 2002 N.W. 13th St., Gainesville, 32601.

Webster University, 151 Wymore Road, Suite 2000, Altamonte Springs, 32714; enrollment: 147 full time, 328 part time. Home campus, 470 E. Lockwood Ave., St. Louis, Mo., 63119. Branch campus: Jacksonville Metropolitan Campus, Conference Center at the Avenues, 6104 Gazebo Park Place South, Jacksonville, 32257.

West Virginia Career College Center. 1104 Beville Road, Suite J, Daytona Beach 32114; enrollment: 107 full time, 14 part time.

Florida's Prepaid College Program

For those interested in prepaying the cost of their child's college tuition and dormitory residence fees, Florida has a Prepaid College Program. All of Florida's nine state universities and 28 community colleges are covered under the plan, which guarantees payment of tuition and dorm housing at the time of enrollment.

Parents, grandparents, relatives or others can prepay a child's tuition. All children through the 11th grade, who have been Florida residents for 12 months at the time of the purchase of a contract, are eligible. Payment of tuition fees for either two or four years of college is available, either in a lump-sum amount or in installment payments for as long as 18 years. If a child decides to enroll in an out-of-state college or university, money paid into the plan is refunded. However, no interest will be paid because the plan is not like a traditional savings account — it is strictly a prepaid tuition

and dormitory expense fund. The only exceptions to this rule are if a beneficiary dies, becomes totally disabled or if the beneficiary receives a scholarship to a Florida college covering the same expenses as the prepaid college program. When this occurs, the purchaser of the program is entitled to a refund equaling the amount paid into the program plus interest at the rate of 5 percent, or the current interest rate at state postsecondary institutions, whichever is less. Contracts also may be transferred to an accredited, not-for-profit independent college or university in Florida.

First Union National Bank is the approved agent for the program. For example, if you had bought a contract for a four-year state university and your child was an infant in September 1992, a single payment of $5,169 could have been made. Or you could have chosen to make monthly payments, amounting to $44 a month. These payments would have started in April 1993 and would end in October of the projected enrollment year, 2010, meaning you would pay about $9,000 over the life of this contract. Under this same example for a two-year community college, single payments would amount to $1,192, or $11 a month; and for two years in a community college and two years in a state university, the single payment would be $3,757, or $32 a month.

Prepaid dormitory contracts are available only to those who also buy a four-year state university plan. Under the above example, a four-year prepaid dormitory contract could have been purchased for a $5,761 single payment or for $49 a month.

The program does not include books or cover health, athletics, laboratory, student activities and services fees. The dormitory contract covers the cost of a double occupancy air-conditioned room, but not meals. Graduate or professional schooling is not covered by the plan. All funds paid into the program are invested in a trust fund set up by the state. Payments are not tax-deductible and under 1988 Internal Revenue Service rulings, any tax liability is deferred until the student enters college. At that time, the difference between the amount paid into the plan and the value of the benefits received is taxable to the student over his college years. The purchase of a prepaid college contract does not guarantee a student admission to a state university — the student still must meet standard academic requirements.

More information about the program is available from the Florida Prepaid College Program, P.O. Box 6567, Tallahassee, 32314-6567 or phone toll-free in Florida at 1-800-552-4723.

HEALTH CARE

You have a history of medical problems, and have decided to move to Florida hoping for a cure that includes warm sunshine and relaxation. Up north, you needed frequent treatment, some of it in the emergency room of the local hospital. Now you want to make sure that adequate facilities are available near your new home. Where should you move?

In some of the more populated counties, you will find an abundance of health-care facilities. Look in newspapers, magazines, on radio and television, even on billboards, and you will find advertisements from local hospitals that are fighting for your business. Look in the yellow pages of the phone book and you will find hundreds or even thousands of physicians in the listings.

But in eight low-population counties in Florida, you will find nary a hospital. And in five counties you will find fewer than five doctors of medicine.

The situation with dentists is similar. They are easy to find in some areas. However, 16 Florida counties have fewer than five.

Availability of services varies greatly by area, but overall, Florida had 4.06 hospital beds per 1,000 population in 1990, down from 4.36 in 1989. In recent years the state has been about .3 above the national average.

Of great consequence has been lack of affordability, and the fact that as many as 2.5 million state residents in recent years have had no health insurance. With rising hospital costs, rising insurance premiums and cutbacks in some federal payment programs, the state, like others, has been dealing for years with a runaway economic monster.

But add to that other unusual demographics in Florida and the crisis becomes even more pointed: the high percentage of elderly residents, the huge numbers of immigrants, and the fact that the vast majority of people in the state work for small service-industry-type employers, many of which can't afford to insure their employees.

The problem has seemed intractable. But in April 1993, after a bitter fight among lawmakers and special-interest lobbies, the legislature gave Gov. Lawton Chiles a major victory — it voted for a massive overhaul of the state's health-care system. The move, seen nationally as bold and pioneering yet experimental, was aimed eventually at giving everyone in the state access to health care. The other major goal was to stem costs.

The legislation:

— Set up 11 regional purchasing alliances that would help individuals, families and companies get the best bargains on health care. The alliances would ask insurance companies, hospitals, HMOs, and other groups to submit proposals for members' coverage. The alliances then would offer members a selection of plans from which to choose. The state was authorized to participate in an alliance to buy health care for state workers.

— Created MedAccess, a state health insurance program open to all residents with incomes below 250 percent of the poverty level who have had no private health insurance for a year. The intent was to start improving access to basic health care quickly, without waiting for the extra state and federal funding that this broader coverage was likely to require.

— Revised some insurance requirements. It applied a "community rating" standard to small employers' policies, allowing for adjustments of premiums for age, gender, family composition, tobacco usage and geographic location. However, insurers and HMOs must issue all health benefit plans on a "guarantee-issue" basis to small employers, employees and dependents without regard to health status. This essentially means that premiums shouldn't be based on your medical condition.

Shortly after the legislation passed, it was unclear how much, if any, money this new system would save.

General Problems:

The state has a huge — and highly controversial — health department, called the Florida Department of Health and Rehabilitative Services, which offers many free health care services to those who are unable to pay. But the

In 1990, All Children's Hospital in St. Petersburg, which treats children from all over, underwent its biggest expansion in its history. Included in the expansion is the building of a Short Stay Surgery Unit and a larger surgery area.

agency, which gained notoriety in the late 1980s amid reports that dozens of children under its protection had died, faces massive dilemmas. Its 111-page "Strategic Plan for Results in the 1990s," published in October 1991, set scores of goals for improving health care in the state, but listed dozens of bleak statistics. Among the problems:

— The agency expects to spend more than $60 billion in the five years that began in 1991. Without change, projections show that the state Medicaid budget alone could rise from $4.3 billion to $20.3 billion in 1999.

— Florida is third nationally in the number of adults with AIDS and second in the number of children with AIDS. Some 2,196 cases were diagnosed in the state in 1993. The cumulative total from 1980 to 1993 was 30,839.

— About 20 percent of Florida's population is exposed to potentially unsafe drinking water. Only recently has the health department been allowed to monitor and test small public water systems (about 10,000 of these systems serve as many as 240,000 residents and tourists per year). In addition, the agency intends to increase from 37,500 to 100,000 the number of private wells it monitors for contamination.

— HRS, also accused in recent years of political favoritism and having loose controls, acknowledged in the report that it lacks credibility: "Neither the people served nor the taxpaying public feels confident that actions taken by the department and the programs it develops and funds will be effective...Few people are aware of the hundreds of little miracles and kind deeds that the deparment performs daily...The nature of the problems we deal with, the most difficult, complex and intractable human needs — poverty, disease, abuse, neglect, hunger, addiction and dysfunctions of all types — do not lend themselves to easy solutions. The department's inadequate performance in some cases and its huge size make it an easy target for criticism... Although the department is expected to be all things to all people, resources have not kept pace with need."

Children:

— More than 150,000 children under age 3 (28 percent) are "potentially at risk of reaching kindergarten unable to learn due to social, physical, emotional or medical problems...The at-risk group includes 42,700 children from unsafe homes and those who have been victims of abuse or neglect and 73,300 children from economically and socially disadvantaged families."

— In 1989-1990, there were 119,374 investigations of child neglect or abuse. The rate has been increasing about 12 percent a year. Physical abuse and inadequate supervision are the major categories. About 44 percent of those reported abused were 5 years old or younger. Overall, says the state, "Substance abuse plays a disproportionate role within families where child abuse occurs." A separate HRS fact sheet on child abuse cites these reasons for increases in abuse: 1. The population boom. 2. "Isolation, economic stress, lack of community roots and supports have taken their toll of families. At the same time, the social networks which at one time helped families in crisis, such as extended families and deep community or church ties, are not as common as they once were." 3. The rise in the use of crack cocaine and other drugs. 4. An increased public awareness of the problem.

— Since 1987, the average number of children in foster care has doubled, to 10,455. Case workers describe more than 25 percent of them as having "serious emotional or behavioral problems." The average foster care worker is estimated to have 35 cases; the nationally accepted standard, according to the agency, is 17. The average stay in foster or substitute care was 26.2 months in 1991; HRS's goal was 12 months by 1996.

— Almost 2,000 infants born in the state each year do not live until their first birthday, but the infant mortality rate dropped from 14.5 per 1,000 live births in 1980 to 9.8 in 1989.

— An estimated 11,000 infants (about 5.5 percent) born in 1989 tested positive for cocaine or other drugs.

— About 20,000 women do not have access to prenatal care, and many more get inadequate care. Says the report: "The ability of Florida's public health care system to provide adequate prenatal care services to all women in need is hampered by physician and registered nurse recruitment and retention problems, the lack of high risk obstetrical services in many parts of Florida, the shortage of trained case managers for at-home follow-up services, and the shortage of substance abuse treatment services for pregnant and post-partum women."

— The juvenile justice system has seen a 48 percent rise in delinquency cases in five years. The rate of cases related to drug offenses has increased 56 percent in four years, as has the severity — 21 percent were felony non-marijuana cases in 1983, compared with 63 percent in 1990. More than 60 percent of the juvenile offenders abuse alcohol and other drugs.

The elderly:

— Dozens of elderly and disabled residents have died in recent years because of abuse or neglect, in nursing and boarding facilities, their own homes, and in state institutions. The Miami Herald reported in a November 1992 series titled "A State of Neglect" that the abuse and neglect have gone unpunished for years. The state says there were nearly 23,000 cases of reported neglect, abuse or explotiation of disabled and elderly in the state in 1989-1990. The rate was up about 18 percent a year.

— There are 1,500 adult congregate living facilities in the state and 65,000 licensed beds. Two-thirds of residents are elderly. The number of complaints about the facilities has been rising. HRS has a goal of reducing the time it takes to process an administrative complaint to 218 days. As of 1991, it took 598 days.

— About 8.5 percent of elderly with severe impairments were getting community care services.

Health Insurance

If you're covered by an employer's group health insurance plan, your life will be simpler than if you have to shop for an individual plan. More than 450 companies sell health insurance in Florida, and their coverage plans and costs vary widely.

According to the state insurance department, half the problem is high costs. Another part of the problem is that certain companies won't write insurance for people in various risk groups. For example, one company might write insurance for entertainers, but another one might not because entertainers generally have histories of unemployment. For whatever reason, one company may decide not to insure lawyers, but another one will.

Yet another part of the problem is "uninsurability," meaning that insurance companies deem some people to be such high risks that they become unable to get insurance at any price. This category includes people with high blood pressure, epilepsy, diabetes or mental disability. For this group, the legislature in mid-1990 extended until the year 2000 the state's Comprehensive Health Plan, under which state residents who have been rejected for coverage by at least two insurance companies can get coverage through the State Comprehensive Health Association. Florida health insurers underwrite the association. More information is available in-state by calling 1-800-422-8559.

Most Floridians are insured through employer-sponsored plans. But for those not covered under group plans who have to buy individual plans, there are several types:

— Major medical policies. These protect against the huge costs of serious injuries or illness. They usually are the costliest of health plans, normally have a yearly deductible, and ordinarily pay at least 80 percent of major expenses. For example, if you have a policy with a $500 deductible and incur $10,000 in medical expenses, the plan would pay for 80 percent of $9,500, or $7,600.

— Basic medical policies. The hospital insurance part of this normally pays part of room and board. Medical/surgical insurance pays part of surgical expenses.

— Hospital confinement indemnity insurance pays a flat amount specified in the policy for each day, week or month you're in a hospital.

— Limited benefit policies. They cover stated expenses resulting from specific illnesses or injuries. Cancer policies are a common form. These policies pay for the treatment of the disease.

— Medicare supplement insurance. This helps provide coverage for expenses not covered by Medicare.

How can you figure out what insurance company is the right one for you? The state suggests two things: First, the Florida Department of Insurance in recent years has put out free consumer guides that provide the basics. One is on health insurance in general and the other is on Medicare supplement insurance. They are available by writing to the department at The Capitol, Lower Level 25, Tallahassee, 32399-0030. Telephone: 904-488-0030. Second, consumers can take a look at a life- and health-insurance rating book of A.M. Best, available at local libraries. It examines every health insurance carrier's assets, net worth, liabilities and, most important, each company's rating regarding performance toward policyholders.

Health Maintenance Organizations

More than 1.3 million Florida residents are members of health maintenance organizations (HMOs). HMOs differ from other health insurance plans in that they provide services at a set fee. They may even cover more services and often are much less expensive, but they also are more likely to have restrictions on choice of doctors and on areas of the state where services must be provided.

You'll usually pay a fixed premium, often

monthly, for preventive care, surgery and hospitalization. Coverage normally includes routine office visits, lab tests and X-rays. You may be able to get prescription drugs at lower costs. You use the HMO's doctors and facilities. If you don't get permission to use a "non-contracted" doctor, that doctor's services may not be covered. If you need specialized treatments, your HMO physician will refer you to a specialist. HMOs do not serve all Florida counties, and some HMOs require that you live in the county they serve. In addition, nurse practitioners or physicians' assistants normally staff HMOs under doctors' supervision and conduct examinations.

A booklet on HMOs is available from the Florida Department of Insurance (see address and phone number under health insurance section above).

Hospital Costs in Florida and in the U.S.

Studies by the Health Insurance Association of America have shown that average hospital costs generally have been higher in Florida compared with the national average.

Specifically, the average cost to a hospital for each inpatient day in 1990 was $769 for Florida and $687 nationally (up from $494 and $460 respectively in 1985). The average length of hospital stay in 1990 was 7 days, as opposed to 7.2 nationwide.

The average expense to the hospital in providing care for one inpatient stay in 1990 amounted to $5,312 in Florida vs. $4,947 nationally. Surveys further show that the number of hospital admissions is higher in Florida than in the United States as a whole, while the number of emergency room visits is lower in Florida.

The Florida Health Care Cost Containment Board publishes 11 brochures specifying what Florida's acute-care and regular hospitals charge for some of the most frequently occurring diagnoses.

The Jan. 1 through Dec. 31, 1990 survey shows that hospital rates generally are the highest in southeastern Florida and the lowest in northern Florida.

Below is a listing of these charges. The diagnoses were: normal childbirth (baby); normal childbirth (mother); cesarean section (mother); angina pectoris, the symptoms of which include severe pain and constriction about the heart, usually radiating to the left shoulder and down the left arm; heart failure and shock, which includes heart failure due to conditions characterized by inflammation and swelling, heart failure due to an excessive amount of blood or tissue fluid, and other heart failures; stroke, including brain hemorrhaging caused by the bursting of a blood vessel in the brain, cerebral blood clot and/or vessel blockage due to a traveling blood clot; chest pain, which is general nonspecific chest pain, upper chest pain and observation for suspected cardiovascular disease in patients with no significant complications or coexisting conditions; hysterectomy; digestive system problems; back problems, which include nonsurgical disc displacement, lumbago, sciatica, backache, fractures and dislocations of the vertebrae, sprains, curvature; and simple pneumonia and pleurisy, which includes only patients with no significant complications or coexisting conditions.

All figures below are average charges for hospital expenses only. Doctor bills, lab work and X-ray bills usually are separate. The costs below should be seen as simply a starting point for cost estimates. In addition, charges for the same or similar service might vary among hospitals because of area wage rates, length of stay, services offered and indigent care. Higher rates do not necessarily mean better care, the state says.

Asterisks indicate that the hospital reported 10 or fewer discharges for these diagnoses or had 10 or fewer discharges after excluding cases of unusually high cost.

AVERAGE CHARGE PER PATIENT BY HOSPITAL AND ILLNESS CATEGORY
Jan. 1, 1990 through Dec. 31, 1990

Normal birth: Baby	Normal birth: Mother	C-section: Mother	Angina Pectoris	Heart failure & Shock	Stroke	Chest pain	Hysterectomy	Digestive Problems	Back Problems	Pneumonia & pleurisy
AVERAGE FOR ALL OF FLORIDA:										
689	2289	5111	4036	7141	8595	3481	6171	4775	3850	4761
ALACHUA COUNTY										
Alachua General Hospital										
491	1959	4633	2906	5779	7631	2810	5457	3712	2713	3278
HCA North Florida Regional Medical Center										
417	1742	3652	2848	5405	6286	2295	5771	3942	2445	4920
Shands Teaching Hospital and Clinics										
344	1728	3870	3635	7372	9139	3432	5592	4784	2462	5262
BAKER COUNTY										
Ed Fraser Memorial Hospital										
——	——	——	3623	6479*	5564*	2298*	——	4225*	3048*	6693
BAY COUNTY										
Bay Medical Center										
541	1763	3724	2407	5868	10572	2636	4988	4205	4146	3521
HCA Gulf Coast Hospital										
544	1925	4334	2859	6762	9975	3026	5168	4841	3907	4064
BRADFORD COUNTY										
Bradford Hospital										
——	——	——	3143	5421	6873*	2930*	7355*	3095	3946	4246
BREVARD COUNTY										
Cape Canaveral Hospital										
577	1679	4142	2421	5384	6121	2122	5068	3241	3442	3322
James E. Holmes Regional Medical Center										
691	1783	3881	2440	5635	7102	2361	5623	3724	2988	3687
Jess Parrish Memorial Hospital										
722	1479	4212	3181	5710	7551	2905	5611	3504	3231	3432
Wuesthoff Memorial Hospital										
666	2086	5445	3740	8095	8660	3749	7015	5053	3534	4622
BROWARD COUNTY										
Broward General Medical Center										
696	2035	4900	3841	7868	9066	3464	5851	5027	4159	4853
Coral Springs Medical Center										
687	2820	5672	4233	10266	7843	3676	5813	4400	4802	5220
Doctor's Hospital of Hollywood										
——	——	——	4625	8093	8043	3751	9009*	6504	7163	6426
Florida Medical Center										
——	——	——	4227	8101	10072	4022	6284	5405	5034	6865
HCA Northwest Regional Hospital										
681	2215	4024	5334	9354	10035	4286	7704	6846	4206	6530
HCA University Hospital										
——	——	——	5582	9058	9693	4565	7215	5741	4574	6695

	Normal birth: Baby	Normal birth: Mother	C-section: Mother	Angina Pectoris	Heart failure & Shock	Stroke	Chest pain	Hyster-ectomy	Digestive Problems	Back Problems	Pneumonia & pleurisy
Hollywood Medical Center	—	—	—	5070	10283	9901	3993	7559	6692	5379	6058
Holy Cross Hospital	986	2565	5267	4212	7497	8251	3363	6676	4839	4467	4538
Humana Hospital Bennett	946	2472	4650	4216	8065	9851	3371	6886	5530	5850	5066
Humana Hospital Cypress	—	—	—	4426	7171	9582	4018	8844	5939	4320	6448
Humana Hospital Pembroke	789	2740	6255	4342	8154	12348	3948	7265	4755	5800	5893
Humana Hospital South Broward	1341	3447	7000	4845	9676	11337	3959	9160	5835	6659	6174
Imperial Point Medical Center	—	—	—	3853	8065	7291	3654	6149	5821	4561	6245
Memorial Hospital	799	2527	5241	3169	6389	8227	2868	5667	5544	3515	5021
North Beach Community Hospital	—	—	—	4316	7407	10630	3024	8098	4983	3661	5483*
North Broward Medical Center	1499*	912*	—	4217	9005	9887	3696	6293	5068	5077	5246
North Ridge Medical Center	—	—	—	4882	7881	9229	3835	6624	5993	6068	5988
Plantation General Hospital	854	2224	6549	4248	8724	10912	3923	7908	5080	6465	5554
Universal Medical Center	—	—	—	4936	9123	10135	2904	5426	5629	5362	5108

CALHOUN COUNTY

	Normal birth: Baby	Normal birth: Mother	C-section: Mother	Angina Pectoris	Heart failure & Shock	Stroke	Chest pain	Hyster-ectomy	Digestive Problems	Back Problems	Pneumonia & pleurisy
Calhoun General Hospital	—	—	—	1545*	2447	3441*	1148*	—	3363	—	3174

CHARLOTTE COUNTY

	Normal birth: Baby	Normal birth: Mother	C-section: Mother	Angina Pectoris	Heart failure & Shock	Stroke	Chest pain	Hyster-ectomy	Digestive Problems	Back Problems	Pneumonia & pleurisy
Fawcett Memorial Hospital	—	—	—	3562	7093	8102	3000	6564	5025	3475	5053
Medical Center Hospital	—	—	—	4609	8594	9463	4069	8187	6617	3651	6765
St. Joseph's Hospital	856	2385	5937	3479	6734	8123	3178	7520	3709	4034	5886

CITRUS COUNTY

	Normal birth: Baby	Normal birth: Mother	C-section: Mother	Angina Pectoris	Heart failure & Shock	Stroke	Chest pain	Hyster-ectomy	Digestive Problems	Back Problems	Pneumonia & pleurisy
Citrus Memorial Hospital	477	1520	3700	2902	4877	5558	2731	4373	4132	2428	2870
Seven Rivers Community Hospital	—	—	—	3901	6185	7822	3378	7241	5700	3059	4564

CLAY COUNTY

	Normal birth: Baby	Normal birth: Mother	C-section: Mother	Angina Pectoris	Heart failure & Shock	Stroke	Chest pain	Hyster-ectomy	Digestive Problems	Back Problems	Pneumonia & pleurisy
Clay Memorial Hospital	—	—	—	3307	5826	5525*	2675*	4822*	4042	2847*	3406
Humana Hospital Orange Park	573	2724	5579	2952	6318	9326	2790	6748	4494	3738	4351

COLLIER COUNTY

	Normal birth: Baby	Normal birth: Mother	C-section: Mother	Angina Pectoris	Heart failure & Shock	Stroke	Chest pain	Hyster-ectomy	Digestive Problems	Back Problems	Pneumonia & pleurisy
Naples Community Hospital	597	1918	5375	2844	6050	6609	2906	6067	4486	2051	3671

	Normal birth: Baby	Normal birth: Mother	C-section: Mother	Angina Pectoris	Heart failure & Shock	Stroke	Chest pain	Hyster-ectomy	Digestive Problems	Back Problems	Pneu-monia & pleurisy
COLUMBIA COUNTY											
Lake City Medical Center											
	——	——	——	3519	5684	6480	4246	7319	4650	3038	4414
Lake Shore Hospital											
	490	1695	5460	3284	4912	6675	3045	5724	3301	2882	3451
DADE COUNTY											
AMI Palmetto General Hospital											
	900	2922	6013	6265	11359	14028	5334	8407	5792	4784	7555
Anne Bates Leach Eye Hospital											
	——	——	——	——	——	——	——	——	——	4405*	——
Baptist Hospital of Miami											
	842	2678	4810	4487	8125	9857	3435	6408	4622	4453	4609
Cedars Medical Center											
	——	——	——	6145	11009	10764	5528	8764	7244	5561	9068
Coral Gables Hospital											
	1937*	——	——	4724	7392	9365	4324	7427	5107	4887	6265
Deering Hospital											
	——	——	——	4222	8124	9655	3842	7771	5671	4574	4122
Doctors Coral Gables											
	474	2641	5516	3685	7164	7610	3376	6202	4567	3694	5024
Golden Glades Regional Medical Center											
	——	——	——	5036	9907	9741	4046	7930	4588	4997	5514
Hialeah Hospital											
	853	3394	6587	6625	11664	15547	5703	7521	4940	5087	6768
Humana Hospital, Biscayne											
	——	——	——	5011	9429	12371	4479	10104	6012	5723	7620
Jackson Memorial Hospital											
	1172	2124	4977	3755	7368	11117	3340	8571	4835	4328	5030
James Archer Smith Hospital											
	695	2232	5598	4288	8208	15919	4073	6449	4925	4796	5138
Kendall Regional Medical Center											
	——	——	——	5571	9691	12785	4943	9819	6109	5067	7386
Larkin General Hospital											
	——	——	——	4824	8487	8011	3412	7551	5708	3482	7167
Mercy Hospital											
	960	3064	5714	4878	8170	11748	3899	8179	5929	5473	5931
Miami Children's Hospital											
	3964*	——	——	6877*	15109*	2581*	6234*	4475	2037	6624	
Miami Heart Institute											
	——	——	——	4877	8823	8503	3717	7739	5071	4629	7516
Mount Sinai Medical Center											
	838	3025	5805	6119	11282	12871	5088	6349	6054	6437	8303
North Gables Hospital											
	——	——	——	3988	7841	7957	2788	9031	6365	4373	7258
North Shore Medical Center											
	546	2241	4300	5655	9184	11015	4677	6866	4936	4565	6054
Palm Springs Hospital											
	——	——	——	5337	9804	9906	4813	7491	5641	5548	7207
Pan American Hospital											
	3220*	——	——	4859	8818	11525	3858	7704	5427	5372	6398
Parkway Regional Medical Center											
	826	2928	6032	4342	8596	10341	3501	9484	6334	6161	6097
South Miami Hospital											
	1045	3157	5536	4045	8511	9099	3458	7186	5340	4496	6510

	Normal birth: Baby	Normal birth: Mother	C-section: Mother	Angina Pectoris	Heart failure & Shock	Stroke	Chest pain	Hyster-ectomy	Digestive Problems	Back Problems	Pneu-monia & pleurisy
South Shore Hospital	—	—	—	4618	8352	7779	3584*	4865*	5519	8123	6466
St. Francis Hospital	615	3289	6201	5542	9371	11704	4330	6936	7534	5344	8476
University of Miami Hospitals and Clinics	—	—	—	11607*	3330*	—	—	6358	907*		4078*
Victoria Hospital	—	—	—	4216	8508	10685	2774	8248	6559	4801	5739
Westchester General Hospital	—	1950*	—	5108	11466	17319*	5943	7409	6434	5506	6174

DESOTO COUNTY

	Normal birth: Baby	Normal birth: Mother	C-section: Mother	Angina Pectoris	Heart failure & Shock	Stroke	Chest pain	Hyster-ectomy	Digestive Problems	Back Problems	Pneu-monia & pleurisy
DeSoto Memorial Hospital	844	1354	4278	3543	6125	6659	2893	4603	3270	2974	6130

DUVAL COUNTY

	Normal birth: Baby	Normal birth: Mother	C-section: Mother	Angina Pectoris	Heart failure & Shock	Stroke	Chest pain	Hyster-ectomy	Digestive Problems	Back Problems	Pneu-monia & pleurisy
Baptist Medical Center	644	2515	5381	3461	7163	9032	2985	5167	4111	2766	4046
Baptist Medical Center, Beaches	—	—	2621	5669	7577	2601	6015	4095	2894		3741*
Jacksonville Medical Center	—	—	—	3113*	6282	5523	2610	5049	4761	3460	6206
Memorial Medical Center of Jacksonville	691	2375	5213	3581	6864	7455	3563	5441	5233	3283	5127
Methodist Medical Center	—	2287*	—	5076	7876	9821	4887	5810	6389	4088	6105
Riverside Hospital	651	1905	3957	2819	6600	6895	2482	5407	3949	2993	3783*
St. Luke's Hospital	2041*	—	—	3587	7226	9025	3548	5310	5576	3490	4930
St. Vincent's Medical Center	609	2164	3941	3248	7369	8233	3432	4947	4808	3205	3261
University Medical Center of Jacksonville	477	2530	6278	3641	6855	10145	3638	7734	4677	2336	4348

ESCAMBIA COUNTY

	Normal birth: Baby	Normal birth: Mother	C-section: Mother	Angina Pectoris	Heart failure & Shock	Stroke	Chest pain	Hyster-ectomy	Digestive Problems	Back Problems	Pneu-monia & pleurisy
Baptist Hospital	555	2306	5343	2811	5318	7242	2370	6776	4312	3934	4858
HCA West Florida Regional Medical Center	429	2697	4658	2808	5506	6445	2494	5086	4615	2946	4729
Sacred Heart Hospital of Pensacola	506	2103	4132	2498	4718	7321	2362	5768	3791	3061	3202
University Hospital and Clinic	—	—	—	4242	5871	4616	2826*	5720	5197	3188*	4776*

FLAGLER COUNTY

	Normal birth: Baby	Normal birth: Mother	C-section: Mother	Angina Pectoris	Heart failure & Shock	Stroke	Chest pain	Hyster-ectomy	Digestive Problems	Back Problems	Pneu-monia & pleurisy
Memorial Hospital Flagler	—	—	—	2581	4505	6145	2388	3689*	3525	2968	2237

FRANKLIN COUNTY

	Normal birth: Baby	Normal birth: Mother	C-section: Mother	Angina Pectoris	Heart failure & Shock	Stroke	Chest pain	Hyster-ectomy	Digestive Problems	Back Problems	Pneu-monia & pleurisy
Emerald Coast Hospital	—	—	—	1098*	1952*	8298*	1448	5058*	1426	1304	2546*

Normal birth: Baby	Normal birth: Mother	C-section: Mother	Angina Pectoris	Heart failure & Shock	Stroke	Chest pain	Hyster-ectomy	Digestive Problems	Back Problems	Pneu-monia & pleurisy
				GADSDEN COUNTY						
Gadsden Memorial Hospital										
447	1992	4623	3544*	4789	6115	2637*	5888	3930	1685*	2989
				GULF COUNTY						
Gulf Pines Hospital										
——	——	——	2229*	3695	4326*	2135	6871*	2301	1514	4010
				HAMILTON COUNTY						
Hamilton County Memorial Hospital										
477	1619	2644*	2802*	5355*	2511*	2874*	4748*	1965	1502*	2529
				HARDEE COUNTY						
Hardee Memorial Hospital										
——	——	——	2856	5461	6386	2206*	——	3529	1966*	2664*
				HENDRY COUNTY						
Hendry General Hospital										
1964*	——	——	2364	4762	5898	2471	6941*	2908	2686	4869
				HERNANDO COUNTY						
Brooksville Regional Hospital										
643	2601	5481	3988	7606	8512	3375	7212	5200	3142	3515
HCA Oak Hill Community Hospital										
——	——	——	4372	7216	8287	3811	4494	5594	3755	5980
				HIGHLANDS COUNTY						
Highlands Regional Medical Center										
——	——	——	3149	6640	8251	2599	7761	4848	3751	3561
Walker Memorial Hospital										
655	1704	4690	3672	7860	8311	3406	6472	4484	3474	4661
				HILLSBOROUGH COUNTY						
AMI Memorial Hospital of Tampa										
——	——	——	2997	6699	9169	2601	6488	5414	4798	6636
AMI Town & Country Medical Center										
——	1388*	——	3001	6098	8619	2549	6871	4660	4557	4627
Centurion Hospital of Carrollwood										
——	——	——	3211	7522	6081	2917	6215	4859	4303	4692
Doctors' Hospital, Tampa										
——	——	——	3627	6921	9537	3906*	4744	5825	2715	6251
H. Lee Moffitt Cancer Center/Research Institute Inc.										
——	——	——	——	7670*	——	1967*	9213*	4204	——	7939*
Humana Hospital Brandon										
677	2274	4581	3198	6384	7878	2842	7549	4344	3699	4358
Humana Women's Hospital Tampa										
640	2087	4716	——	——	——	859*	5721	2826*	——	2714*
South Bay Hospital										
——	——	——	3350	6664	7283	3988*	7855*	4872	3681	4419*
South Florida Baptist Hospital										
674*	1042*	4345*	4156	7392	7409	4129	6851	3963	3483	3140
St. Joseph's Hospital, Tampa										
1037*	1684*	——	3980	7259	9597	3474	7216	4307	4060	4051

	Normal birth: Baby	Normal birth: Mother	C-section: Mother	Angina Pectoris	Heart failure & Shock	Stroke	Chest pain	Hyster-ectomy	Digestive Problems	Back Problems	Pneu-monia & pleurisy
Tampa General Hospital	664	2643	6255	3488	7000	10240	3319	6998	4888	4698	4014
University Community Hospital, Tampa	1650*	—	—	3247	6286	7978	2888	5465	3648	3171	3804
Vencor Hospital - Tampa	—	—	—	—	6516*	—	—	—	1594*	—	—
HOLMES COUNTY											
Doctors' Memorial Hospital	—	—	—	2654	5655	4569	1944*	4557*	3474	846	3579
INDIAN RIVER COUNTY											
Humana Hospital, Sebastian	668	2400	4845	4392	7104	11592	3076	7415	5153	4477	6011
Indian River Memorial Hospital	917	2609	6043	4037	7925	9438	3519	6025	4891	4082	4850
JACKSON COUNTY											
Campbellton-Graceville Hospital	—	—	—	2552	4312	5345*	—	—	3968	2555*	3658
Jackson Hospital	352	1218	3374	2451	4555	5235	1899	4522	2801	1922	2595
LAKE COUNTY											
Leesburg Regional Medical Center	348	2158	4989	3697	6936	9074	3352	5921	5258	2574	4369
South Lake Memorial Hospital	—	—	—	2486	5891	5363	2357	5039*	4358	3192	3824
Waterman Medical Center	675	2209	5920	2687	5670	7915	3136	7304	4938	3236	3484
LEE COUNTY											
Cape Coral Hospital	816	3050	5787	3934	7252	8279	3624	6056	5611	3102	4374*
East Pointe Hospital	—	—	—	3975	7534	9321	3790	7499*	5357	4050	6201
Lee Memorial Hospital	898	2570	5738	3508	6659	7277	3140	5721	4532	2441	4726
Southwest Florida Regional Medical Center	2395*	—	—	3463	6576	8123	3256	6712	4774	3717	4608
LEON COUNTY											
HCA Tallahassee Community Hospital	569	1912	3779	2380*	5101	8430	2173	5664	4651	2795	4240
Tallahassee Memorial Regional Medical Center	422	1713	4305	2542	5554	8897	2121	5334	4000	3028	2931
LEVY COUNTY											
Williston Memorial Hospital	—	—	—	3020	6197	5669	—	7367*	3282	1861*	4428
MADISON COUNTY											
Madison County Hospital	—	563*	—	2574	5386	6322	1781	—	2518	1399*	2826

Normal birth: Baby	Normal birth: Mother	C-section: Mother	Angina Pectoris	Heart failure & Shock	Stroke	Chest pain	Hyster-ectomy	Digestive Problems	Back Problems	Pneu-monia & pleurisy

MANATEE COUNTY

HCA L.W. Blake Memorial Hospital

| 407 | 1531 | 3067 | 3570 | 6832 | 8406 | 3511 | 5141 | 4988 | 3205 | 4669 |

Manatee Memorial Hospital

| 555 | 1957 | 4317 | 3938 | 7475 | 8786 | 4008 | 5695 | 5886 | 3906 | 5600 |

MARION COUNTY

HCA Marion Community Hospital

| —— | —— | —— | 3968 | 6941 | 7827 | 3673 | 5450 | 4408 | 1944 | 4977 |

Munroe Regional Medical Center

| 567 | 1870 | 4329 | 3807 | 6356 | 7044 | 3424 | 4925 | 3988 | 2957 | 3695 |

MARTIN COUNTY

Martin Memorial Hospital

| 531 | 1869 | 4869 | 4273 | 7289 | 9106 | 3975 | 6926 | 5157 | 2807 | 3617 |

MONROE COUNTY

Fishermen's Hospital

| —— | —— | —— | 2342 | 6264 | 6632 | 2386 | 7709 | 4128 | 3465 | 5996* |

Health System (formerly DePoo Hospital)

| 557 | 1756 | 3784 | 3287 | 5987 | 9357 | 2550 | 4242 | 3272 | 3413 | 3353 |

Mariners' Hospital

| —— | —— | —— | 3976 | 7164 | 7134 | 2796 | 11474* | 4253 | 2757 | 7924 |

NASSAU COUNTY

Nassau General Hospital

| 589 | 2614 | 4283 | 3953 | 4531* | 6788 | 2753 | 4156 | 3599 | 3201* | 4522 |

OKALOOSA COUNTY

HCA Twin Cities Hospital

| —— | —— | —— | 3416 | 5395 | 6826 | 3095* | 5743 | 3982 | 3919 | 4129 |

Humana Hospital, Fort Walton

| 709 | 2229 | 4702 | 3600 | 6269 | 7981 | 3234 | 5601 | 4775 | 4149 | 3001 |

North Okaloosa Medical Center

| —— | —— | —— | 2691 | 6077 | 7055 | 2292* | 2531* | 3736 | 4990 | 1381* |

OKEECHOBEE COUNTY

HCA H.H. Raulerson Hospital

| —— | —— | —— | 3727 | 6758 | 6750 | 2870* | 7456 | 5148 | 3180 | 4862 |

ORANGE COUNTY

AMI Medical Center

| 664 | 3238 | 8429 | 4973 | 7965 | 8751 | 3722 | 8050 | 4529 | 2939 | 4549 |

Florida Hospital

| 581 | 2555 | 5290 | 4307 | 8252 | 10323 | 4144 | 6146 | 4610 | 3225 | 4842 |

Humana Hospital, Lucerne

| 830 | 2569 | 5205 | 3847 | 6576 | 9750 | 3386 | 7014 | 4763 | 3184 | 4757 |

Orlando General Hospital

| 591 | 2023 | 5371 | 3416 | 9691 | 11487 | 3699 | 6064 | 5310 | 3905 | 5451 |

Orlando Regional Medical Center

| 572 | 2632 | 6593 | 3454 | 6686 | 9460 | 3410 | 6956 | 4393 | 4062 | 4544 |

West Orange Hospital

| 631 | 2330 | 6502 | 3727 | 7293 | 9304 | 3530 | 6301 | 4519 | 4070 | 3741 |

Winter Park Memorial Hospital

| 582 | 2054 | 4731 | 3720 | 6708 | 7899 | 3354 | 5630 | 3834 | 3109 | 3082 |

Normal birth: Baby	Normal birth: Mother	C-section: Mother	Angina Pectoris	Heart failure & Shock	Stroke	Chest pain	Hyster-ectomy	Digestive Problems	Back Problems	Pneumonia & pleurisy

OSCEOLA COUNTY

Humana Hospital Kissimmee

| 842 | 2236 | 4785 | 3847 | 8085 | 9784 | 3759 | 5656 | 4540 | 4038 | 4018 |

Kissimmee Memorial Hospital

| — | — | — | 4849 | 8029 | 9469 | 3926 | 6742 | 5883 | 3861 | 4566 |

St. Cloud Hospital

| — | — | — | 3633 | 6296 | 8641 | 3790 | 5869 | 4523 | 3445 | 3981 |

PALM BEACH COUNTY

AMI Palm Beach Gardens

| 697 | 2510 | 5353 | 4279 | 8045 | 9768 | 3848 | 6833 | 5029 | 3638 | 4897 |

Bethesda Memorial Hospital

| 718 | 2300 | 4864 | 3283 | 5498 | 6833 | 3090 | 5360 | 4121 | 2831 | 4277 |

Boca Raton Community Hospital

| — | — | — | 3476 | 6381 | 7167 | 3115 | 5090 | 4559 | 2793 | 5398 |

Delray Community Hospital

| — | — | — | 4495 | 7051 | 9477 | 4145 | 6309* | 5217 | 3297 | 5502 |

Everglades Memorial Hospital

| 784 | 2176 | 4816 | 3574 | 6157 | 7344 | 2333* | 5696 | 3621 | 3412 | 4691 |

Glades General Hospital

| — | — | — | 3487 | 5640 | 4410 | 2869 | 6710* | 3665 | 2428* | 3765 |

Good Samaritan Hospital

| 650 | 2307 | 4455 | 3935 | 7150 | 9556 | 4061 | 5863 | 4672 | 3399 | 5100 |

Humana Hospital, Palm Beaches

| — | — | — | 3054 | 5686 | 8084 | 2980 | 5633 | 4952 | 3023 | 5158 |

John F. Kennedy Medical Center

| — | — | — | 4125 | 8807 | 7639 | 3711 | 6664 | 5153 | 3138 | 4897 |

Jupiter Hospital

| — | — | — | 3361 | 6568 | 8277 | 2868 | 5533 | 5236 | 5110 | 5084 |

Palm Beach Regional Hospital

| — | — | — | 3198 | 6830 | 7380 | 2838 | 6321 | 4398 | 3688 | 4812 |

Palms West Hospital

| 822 | 3128 | 7352 | 4068 | 8096 | 8591 | 3676 | 7990 | 4172 | 3071 | 5738 |

St. Mary's Hospital

| 520 | 2584 | 5564 | 4769 | 7940 | 8731 | 4583 | 6617 | 5514 | 4271 | 5713 |

Wellington Regional Medical Center

| — | — | — | 4240 | 8558 | 10627 | 3369 | 6970 | 4161 | 4557 | 5551 |

West Boca Medical Center

| 786 | 2845 | 5646 | 4003 | 6944 | 8356 | 3319 | 8677 | 4073 | 4637 | 5056 |

PASCO COUNTY

East Pasco Medical Center

| 802 | 2060 | 6469 | 3803 | 6854 | 9247 | 3405 | 6407 | 4404 | 4407 | 5910 |

HCA Bayonet Point/Hudson Regional Medical Center

| — | — | — | 5808 | 9170 | 9270 | 5125 | 7359 | 6880 | 4601 | 5908 |

HCA New Port Richey Hospital

| — | — | — | 4234 | 7506 | 8055 | 3904 | 5062 | 5736 | 3399 | 5022 |

Humana Hospital Pasco

| 855 | 2398 | 5657 | 3964 | 7117 | 8854 | 3665 | 6665 | 5210 | 3853 | 4292 |

Riverside Hospital of Pasco County

| 492 | 2026 | 4868 | 4185 | 6821 | 8438 | 3708 | 5918 | 6037 | 3464 | 5621 |

PINELLAS COUNTY

All Children's Hospital

| 1906* | — | — | — | 8052* | — | 1827* | 5105* | 3817 | 2305* | 4288 |

Normal birth: Baby	Normal birth: Mother	C-section: Mother	Angina Pectoris	Heart failure & Shock	Stroke	Chest pain	Hyster-ectomy	Digestive Problems	Back Problems	Pneu-monia & pleurisy
AMI Clearwater Community Hospital										
—	—	—	3846	7229	7838	3149	7517	5750	3352	5308
Bayfront Medical Center										
914	2380	5135	3730	7998	9780	3406	5807	6025	2295	5576
Edward H. White Memorial Hospital										
—	—	—	4890	8656	10343	3536	6225	7133	4051	6559*
Florida Hospital of St. Petersburg										
—	—	—	—	—	—	—	—	—	2280*	—
HCA Medical Center Hospital - Largo										
—	—	—	4184	7904	7930	3635	5246	5584	3585	6345
Helen Ellis Hospital										
—	—	—	2885	5252	6845	2446	4681	3447	3123	3995
Humana Hospital Northside										
—	—	—	4060	7686	11492	3504	6102	5554	4598	4922
Humana Hospital St. Petersburg										
595	2166	4848	3928	7437	8700	3378	6638	5853	4067	4049*
Mease Hospital & Clinic										
754	2316	4522	3823	7373	8005	3799	6422	3816	2870	3546
Mease Hospital Countryside										
—	—	—	3067	5939	7351	2781	6217	4685	3111	6013
Metropolitan General Hospital										
—	—	—	4957	8134	7592	4312	6105	5797	3630	3977
Morton F. Plant Hospital										
912	2674	5008	3242	6341	7362	3023	5806	4835	3848	4523
Palms of Pasadena Hospital										
—	—	—	3690	6706	8254	3199	6792	6434	3589	6027
St. Anthony's Hospital										
709	2197	3750	4622	8104	11745	4335	6616	8003	5894	6236
Sun Bay Medical Center										
—	—	—	3139	7299	8851	2867*	5120*	5766	3474*	3086*
Sun Coast Hospital										
768	1901	4523	3989	6823	8608	3563	5045	4728	3238	4047
University General Hospital										
—	—	—	4335	7137	8548	3306	7803	6210	4012	3000
Womens' Medical Center										
1034	2702	6551	—	9460*	—	—	8087	7352*	—	10703*

POLK COUNTY

Normal birth: Baby	Normal birth: Mother	C-section: Mother	Angina Pectoris	Heart failure & Shock	Stroke	Chest pain	Hyster-ectomy	Digestive Problems	Back Problems	Pneu-monia & pleurisy
Bartow Memorial Hospital										
580	1468	4498	1946	5859	6262	1709*	5713	3382	1941*	3259
Lake Wales Hospital										
654	1612	4060	2678	4869	5145	3497	4437	3669	1975*	2411
Lakeland Regional Medical Center										
613	2285	4644	3282	5976	7996	3122	5021	4825	3152	4705
Mid-Florida Health Center										
—	360*	—	2566	3746	4865	2092	4873	2788	1964*	4868
Morrow Memorial Hospital										
—	—	—	—	1503*	—	—	4209	2405*	—	5674*
Polk General Hospital										
324	1154	2972	2718	4822	4534*	2240*	3345	1884	3583	3192
Winter Haven Hospital										
837	2132	3799	2776	5122	6882	2614	3851	3967	2557	4306

Normal birth: Baby	Normal birth: Mother	C-section: Mother	Angina Pectoris	Heart failure & Shock	Stroke	Chest pain	Hyster-ectomy	Digestive Problems	Back Problems	Pneu-monia & pleurisy
PUTNAM COUNTY										
HCA Putnam Community Hospital										
546	1620	5743	3079	6552	7308	2941	6322	4792	2527	4376
ST. JOHNS COUNTY										
Flagler Hospital										
573	1808	4207	3492	7314	6576	3091	5303	4475	2760	3117
St. Augustine General Hospital										
—	—	—	3384	6670	9449	3194	5690	5157	4380	4551
ST. LUCIE COUNTY										
HCA Lawnwood Regional Medical Center										
917	2704	7456	5072	9506	10593	4131	7483	5944	5366	6894
HCA Medical Center of Port St. Lucie										
—	—	—	4544	8385	9085	4112	8475	5444	3351	3296
SANTA ROSA COUNTY										
Gulf Breeze Hospital										
—	—	—	2874	5177	5514	2210	7171	3493	2685	4160*
Jay Hospital										
—	—	—	2761	4033	5828*	2593*	—	4113	3597	3927
Santa Rosa Medical Center										
567	2067	4329	3348	5241	7527	2384	4945	3138	2969	3046
SARASOTA COUNTY										
Doctors' Hospital of Sarasota										
—	—	—	2770	5691	6993	2816	5027	4111	3377	4414
Englewood Community Hospital										
—	—	—	3515	6659	7831	3178	7660	5266	3512	6006
Sarasota Memorial Hospital										
433	1982	3994	3250	5451	7529	3017	4571	4451	3482	3568
Venice Hospital										
—	—	—	3651	5967	6403	3492	7085	5166	3776	5947
SEMINOLE COUNTY										
Central Florida Regional Medical Center										
484	1422	5416	3826	6838	8440	3557	5609	4976	3221	4027
South Seminole Medical Center										
—	—	—	2508	5523	7579	2418	6812	4571	3474	3293*
SUWANNEE COUNTY										
Suwannee Hospital										
—	—	—	2318*	4887	7488*	1851*	5765*	3309	1877*	2778
TAYLOR COUNTY										
Doctors' Memorial Hospital										
552*	971*	—	2700	4222	4632*	2701	4791	3296	2400	3887
UNION COUNTY										
Ramadan Hand Surgery Center & Lake Butler Hospital										
—	—	—	2205*	3296*	—	2108	—	1588*	913*	3371
VOLUSIA COUNTY										
Fish Memorial Hospital										
—	916*	—	3653	6464	8295	3113	4473*	4652	1945*	4644

	Normal birth: Baby	Normal birth: Mother	C-section: Mother	Angina Pectoris	Heart failure & Shock	Stroke	Chest pain	Hyster-ectomy	Digestive Problems	Back Problems	Pneu-monia & pleurisy
Halifax Medical Center											
	584	1965	4069	3169	6102	9450	2397	4761	3433	2962	2505
Humana Hospital Daytona											
	—	—	—	3658	7229	8204	3554*	6655	5145	3584	4712*
Ormond Beach Memorial Hospital											
	—	—	—	3087	5908	8008	2364	4769	4325	3396	4711
Peninsula Medical Center											
	—	—	—	2769	6704	7684	2500	4335	4961	3213	3180
Southeast Volusia Hospital District											
	521	1013	3374	1863	4413	5316	2260	4050	2762	1106	2688
West Volusia Memorial Hospital											
	668	1432	4636	3466	5846	7562	3207	5402	4037	3575	3538

WALTON COUNTY

Walton Regional Hospital											
	—	—	—	2144	4002	4569	1936*	4495	3322	1556*	4532

WASHINGTON COUNTY

Northwest Florida Community Hospital											
	—	—	—	3369	4760	5573	1890	4439	4118	1465	3109

Source: Florida Health Care Cost Containment Board

Health Care Availability

Depending on where you live in Florida, there may or may not be a general medical and surgical hospital nearby.

Following is a county-by-county list showing the availability of dentists, physicians (doctors of medicine), general hospitals (plus general hospitals excluding obstetrics), hospital beds per 1,000 population, and nursing homes. The figures for dentists and physicians include all licensed persons, regardless of current status.

	Number of Dentists 1993	Doctors of Medicine 1993	Number of Hospitals 1990	Number of Hospital Beds 1990	Hosp. Beds Per 1,000 Pop. 1990	Nursing Homes (1992)
Alachua	223	1,319	6	1,279	6.85	6
Baker	6	19	2	25	1.29	2
Bay	51	210	3	438	3.23	6
Bradford	8	15	1	54	2.18	2
Brevard	223	694	8	1,166	2.89	15
Broward	865	3,028	29	6,031	4.85	33
Calhoun	5	6	1	36	3.19	1
Charlotte	49	207	3	622	6.27	6
Citrus	31	135	3	283	3.09	6
Clay	60	186	2	256	2.49	7
Collier	111	319	2	381	2.63	7
Columbia	16	80	2	203	4.66	1
Dade	1,468	6,742	39	9,305	4.97	55
De Soto	5	38	2	82	3.38	1
Dixie	3	2	0	0	0.00	0
Duval	394	1,842	14	2,635	3.84	30
Escambia	136	635	4	1,349	4.73	10

	Number of Dentists 1993	Doctors of Medicine 1993	Number of Hospitals 1990	Number of Hospital Beds 1990	Hosp. Beds Per 1,000 Pop. 1990	Nursing Homes (1992)
Flagler	11	28	1	81	3.39	1
Franklin	1	5	2	29	3.34	2
Gadsden	14	45	2	51	1.12	2
Gilchrist	0	3	0	0	0.00	1
Glades	0	3	0	0	0.00	0
Gulf	5	10	1	45	3.58	1
Hamilton	3	6	1	42	4.05	1
Hardee	3	13	1	50	2.20	1
Hendry	8	20	1	66	2.53	2
Hernando	36	124	3	262	2.89	4
Highlands	32	117	3	277	4.01	4
Hillsborough	438	2,332	19	3,366	4.00	30
Holmes	2	8	1	34	1.93	1
Indian River	57	242	3	410	4.49	6
Jackson	17	42	3	157	3.51	3
Jefferson	3	8	0	0	0.00	2
Lafayette	1	3	0	0	0.00	0
Lake	70	214	5	544	3.72	10
Lee	177	617	5	1,230	3.79	13
Leon	110	526	4	758	3.94	6
Levy	4	20	1	40	1.59	1
Liberty	1	3	0	0	0.00	2
Madison	6	11	1	42	2.55	0
Manatee	100	377	5	870	4.52	13
Marion	79	289	4	406	2.13	8
Martin	75	231	2	336	3.48	4
Monroe	40	150	4	224	2.84	3
Nassau	16	39	1	54	1.13	2
Okaloosa	80	229	5	434	2.76	6
Okeechobee	9	26	1	101	3.37	1
Orange	399	1,664	12	2,903	4.44	26
Osceola	31	143	4	373	3.82	6
Palm Beach	726	2,264	21	3,256	3.76	45
Pasco	73	373	6	875	3.21	14
Pinellas	579	1,942	23	4,329	5.06	81
Polk	140	639	8	1,785	4.34	22
Putnam	14	66	1	141	2.24	3
St. Johns	38	177	3	222	2.63	7
St. Lucie	66	218	3	425	2.97	6
Santa Rosa	27	92	4	268	3.86	3
Sarasota	230	753	6	1,294	4.90	23
Seminole	181	479	3	352	1.25	7
Sumter	4	9	0	0	0.00	1
Suwannee	4	10	1	60	2.17	3
Taylor	2	11	1	48	2.44	1
Union	0	17	2	180	17.19	0
Volusia	165	591	8	1,305	3.62	24
Wakulla	1	5	0	0	0.00	1
Walton	10	16	1	50	1.73	2
Washington	6	13	1	81	4.89	1

Source: Florida Department of Professional Regulation as of July 1992 for doctors and dentists; Florida Department of Health and Rehabilitative Services, Office of Licensure and Certification.

Florida's Nursing Shortage

One health concern making headlines in Florida in recent years has been a shortage of nurses. A 1990 Health Care Cost Containment Board report labeled the shortage as critical.

The rates aren't skyrocketing as the years pass, though, as the Center for the Promotion of Nursing, Florida Hospital Association, says Florida "is holding its ground in the fight to keep nurses," even with the shortages. Its survey of hospitals in 1989 showed a "slight increase" in the rate of vacant budgeted registered nursing positions in 1989 (16.3 percent) from 1988 (15.8 percent).

Reasons for serious concern remain. The cost containment board found that more than three-quarters of Florida's hospitals and nursing homes said they were experiencing an "overall shortage of staff registered nurses with a majority of hospitals (57.3 percent) indicating it was moderately severe." And a comparison of the vacancy rate for registered nurses in 1988 found that Florida's nearly 16 percent rate was higher than the national average of 11.3 percent. Nationwide, it has been estimated there will be a shortage of 600,000 nurses by the year 2000.

The demand for nurses was expected to "far exceed projected supply," said the cost containment board. A second reason: The state is importing more nurses into Florida to work than are being educated in the state — at a rate twice that of new graduates from Florida nursing education programs. And third, nursing salaries are "significantly higher" in northern parts of the country than in Florida, according to the health care board. Florida's situation is worsened by the fact that it has a higher percentage of an elderly population than other areas of the country and has a high proportion of special, high-risk populations such as migrants, refugees and those with AIDS.

The bulk of Florida's nurses work primarily in hospitals (65.3 percent in a recent survey), followed by home health agencies (5.9 percent), nursing homes (5.4 percent), physicians' offices (5.4 percent) and the remainder in government or industry.

Nursing Homes

A report in June 1990 by the U.S. Health Care Financing Administration found that more than a third of the country's skilled-care nursing homes did not meet the standards for clean food and that nearly one-fourth did not administer drugs properly.

No breakdown was available for Florida. The agency published a three-volume report on Florida's homes, but officials say there is no summary or comparative data. A copy of the report, which examines homes in 32 categories, is available for about $64. The agency's telephone number is 202-245-6762.

In addition, the state health department puts out a nursing home directory. It is available for about $10 from the Nursing Home Section, Department of Health and Rehabilitative Services, 2727 Mahan Drive, Tallahassee 32308.

In 1992, the number of nursing homes in Florida stood at 594, up from 518 in 1989. The number of beds rose from 59,497 to 69,917. The state in recent years has had the lowest number of nursing home beds per 1,000 population aged 65 and older. "Florida's elderly population is younger than elderly populations in other states and therefore does not have as a great a need for nursing home beds," HRS said in a 1991 report.

The Florida Department of Elder Affairs

Florida's Department of Elder Affairs has been organized to improve the quality of life for older Floridians — the active as well as the frail — by working to bring attention to issues of the aging as well as by working to improve long-term care. Since Jan. 1, 1992, the department has been coordinating four federally and state funded community programs:

— The Older Americans Act, which provides senior centers, nutrition and meals programs, transportation, education, legal services, adult day care and health promotion.

— Community Care for the Elderly, which offers services to frail, homebound residents 60 and older that enable people to stay in their homes as long as possible. Eligibility is based in part on whether residents can prepare meals, bathe or groom themselves. The program offers in-home services such as personal care, homemaker, chore, home health aid, meals and adult day care.

— Alzheimer's Disease Initiative, which provides money to research and to care for victims of the disease. Services include in-home respite, adult day care, support groups and training that helps caregivers and lengthens in-home care.

— Emergency Home Energy Assistance for Elderly and Handicapped, which helps people whose utilities are about to be shut off.

The department also has a special office of volunteers in its State Unit on Aging, the first state in the country to have such an office. A July 1992 survey showed that 24,000 volunteers — most of them older people — donated more than two million hours of service to older Floridians. Services included adult day care, companionship, counseling, homemakers, home repair, shopping help, meal delivery, and health promotion. Others serve on advisory councils and do bookkeeping, raise funds or plan programs.

The agency also is developing a statewide computerized information and referral directory so that residents using Elder Helpline Information and Referral Services in every county can get information over the phone about local services, issues of the aging, and referral help. The Aging Resources Center can be reached at 1-800-262-2243.

Finally, there is a State Long Term Care Ombudsman Council that receives and resolves complaints about nursing homes, adult congregate living facilities and adult foster homes; and a volunteer insurance counseling service for elders called Serving Health Insurance Needs of Elders, or SHINE.

Disciplinary Actions Against Physicians

Does Florida, like some states, look the other way when it receives complaints about incompetent or abusive doctors? Or is it aggressive in protecting the public from bad medical services? According to a 1990 report from the Public Citizen Health Research Group, a Washington-based organization founded by Ralph Nader, "Florida is the most active in medical discipline" among the largest states. The report, which ranks states by disciplinary actions taken against doctors per 1,000 practicing physicians, is controversial. Medical practitioners and health officials say the report may focus too much on just numbers.

Nevertheless, information about actions taken against doctors is not often publicized, and the report is regarded as one of the few barometers of how states compare in dealing with problem physicians. Florida in 1987 took 202 disciplinary actions against MDs. The rate was 7.3 per 1,000 doctors — 14th in the nation. Of those actions, 4.6 were "serious disciplinary actions" — also 14th in the nation.

The report said that Florida "has consistently disciplined large numbers of physicians for the past several years. In 1988, in the wake of a governor's commission report on medical malpractice problems, a special legislative session enacted a tort reform package that also added teeth and dollars to the state's medical quality regulation. The measure created a new Division of Medical Quality Assurance within the Department of Professional Regulation...It required hospitals and other health facilities to report disciplinary actions against physicians, and required hospitals to report malpractice actions against staff physicians as well. Doctors and nurses were both required to report physician misconduct."

Florida's Health Habits

As with everyone, Floridians have some bad habits — some drink too much and some smoke too much. But many Floridians also have some good habits, especially compared with the rest of the nation.

Results from a recent Behavioral Risk Factor Surveillance System were compiled by the U.S. Department of Health and Human Services. A total of 33 states and the District of Columbia participated in the survey, including 1,238 people — considered a representative sample of the adult population — in Florida.

Among the findings:

— **Current smokers.** Floridians as a whole smoked more than the national median (28 percent versus 25.2 percent). To qualify as a smoker, a person had to have smoked at least 100 cigarettes and must still smoke. The state reporting the lowest percentage was Utah, 15 percent, while Kentucky had the largest percentage of smokers, 32.3 percent.

— **Sedentary lifestyle.** About 59 percent of Florida's respondents said they spent less than 20 minutes in leisure-time physical activity three times a week. The national median was 59 percent. Montana had the lowest rate at 47.2 percent and New York the highest at 73.5 percent.

— **Binge drinking.** Of those who said they consumed at least 5 drinks on a single occasion in the last month, 15.3 percent of the Floridians said they had done so, the same as the national median. The state with the lowest rate was New Mexico, at 6.6 percent. Wisconsin had the highest rate, 29.4 percent.

— **Heavy drinking.** Those who said they consumed at least 60 drinks per month totaled 7 percent of the Florida respondents, compared with a 5.6 percent national median. The lowest rate: 3.7 percent in West Virginia; the highest: 10.3 percent in New Hampshire.

— **Drinking and driving.** Here Florida's ranking was the same as the national median. A total of 3.3 percent said they had driven after having had too much to drink at least once in the last month. The low state here was Kentucky, 1.3 percent, and the high state was Wisconsin, 8.3 percent.

— **Seatbelt nonuse.** This is one category Floridians did very well in. A total of 18 percent said they sometimes, seldom or never wore seatbelts, compared with a 42.1 percent national median. The state with the lowest rate was Hawaii, 7 percent, and the highest was South Dakota, 72.2 percent.

— **Cholesterol ever checked.** Again, Floridians did better than the national median, 50.9 percent versus 46.6 percent. The low state: New Mexico, 29.3 percent; the high state: Maryland, 56.8 percent.

— **Ever had a mammogram.** Those at least age 40 responded to this question. Floridians' rate was 45.8 percent, compared with a 44.2 percent national median. The lowest rate: New Mexico, 28.6 percent, and the highest, New Hampshire, 57.5 percent.

— **Influenza vaccine.** Those at least 65 years old were asked if they had an influenza vaccination in the preceding year. A total of 29.7 percent of the Floridians responded yes to this question, compared with a 34.3 percent national median. The lowest rate: Rhode Island, 24 percent, and the highest, Montana, 41.3 percent.

Resident Deaths

In 1992, resident deaths totaled 138,614 in the state. The leading cause of death was cardiovascular diseases, followed by cancer. Below is a listing of some of the leading causes of death that year with the estimated numbers of deaths:

Cause of Death	1992
All causes	138,614
Major cardiovascular diseases	59,033
Malignant neoplasm (cancer)	34,816
All other diseases	9,047
Chronic obstructive lung disease and allied conditions	6,506
Accidental injury and poisoning	4,834
Pneumonia and influenza	3,364
Human immunodeficiency virus (HIV) (AIDS)	3,098
Diabetes mellitus	3,058
Suicide	2,015
Chronic liver disease and cirrhosis	1,741
Symptoms, signs, ill-defined condition	1,679
Homicide	1,353
Nephritis (kidney infections), nephrosis, renal failure	835
Perinatal conditions	830
Septicemia (blood poisoning)	803
Congenital anomalies	680
Parkinson's disease	567
Pulmonary fibrosis and other alveolar pneumopathy	473
Alcohol psychosis, dependence, abuse	458
Ulcer of stomach, duodenum (part of small intestine)	396

Source: Department of Health and Rehabilitative Services

Medicaid Medically Needy Program

Beginning operation on July 1, 1986, this program was created by the legislature to help ensure that Florida's indigent citizens would not be denied health care because of an inability to pay. Government-run hospitals were bearing the greatest share of uncompensated indigent care costs and had "found themselves less able to compete financially with proprietary facilities, which were not absorbing a proportionate share of costs in treating the poor," a legislative review said. In addition, there was a lack of "meaningful price competition between providers."

The legislature responded to this growing problem by creating the Public Medical Assistance Act in 1984 under which every hospital in the state (except those run by HRS or the Department of Corrections) was assessed a fee that would go into a Public Medical Assistance Trust Fund. It was estimated that hospital assessments would total $110 million. In addition, $20 million from the state's General Revenue Fund was also appropriated. This fund was to help hospitals offset the inequity in indigent care. "By returning more of the funds to hospitals which provided greater amounts of indigent care through public assistance programs, it was anticipated that the fund would provide a means to shift the indigent care burden more fairly and equitably," the legislative review stated. And this is where the medically needy program came into the picture. This program would determine who would qualify for the state help.

Today, to qualify, participants basically must meet the income-limit requirements of such programs as the Aid to Families with Dependent Children program or the Supplemental Security Income program that serves mainly the elderly or the disabled. A person, though, can have higher income levels and still qualify for state money if he or she incurs medical bills that would force a person's income level to drop to AFDC or SSI levels if he or she paid for the medical bills.

For example, in July 1994, the number of eligible AFDC participants in the program totaled 16,638, with another 206,336 enrolled to become eligible when and if their medical bills forced them to require assistance. The number of eligible people served under the SSI portion of the program totaled 2,885.

The program ran into problems in its early years: The number of people who qualified was lower than expected. A study had estimated that around 178,000 people per month would participate and that first-year reimbursements to health-care providers would be nearly $105 million. But as the program reached its six-month stage, far fewer clients were qualifying. And in the first year, the monthly caseload never reached 12,000 people. This resulted in low rates of reimbursement to hospitals and the accumulation of a surplus in the trust fund. Because of these problems, the legislature reviewed the program.

The review said the program faced an uncertain future, yet called for its continuation, citing better performance after the first six months. The review said that "no other medical welfare assistance program in the state can claim that it potentially covers as many citizens in Florida."

But more needed to be done to assure the program's continuation, the review said, such as informing potential clients about the existence of the program. "No serious community education efforts...have been undertaken in an attempt to inform the citizens of this state about this program. Efforts to educate hospitals and their patients have been random and haphazard."

In future years, this program still might be eliminated if a comprehensive health security law is passed in Florida. Today, the program is administered by the Department of Insurance.

Department of Health and Rehabilitative Services

HRS administers services for young and old. Some have changed since the agency was reorganized in 1992; many remain. A lot of the health programs are offered free to those unable to pay, and some charge a fee based on ability to pay. Anyone wishing to receive any of them must apply at the agency's offices, which are located in all counties.

Among the services offered, according to an HRS booklet titled Community Services for Floridians and Their Families:

Aging and Adult Services: Aimed at people aged 60 or older and disabled adults 18 and older. Preference is given to those with the greatest social or financial need. A Home Care Program gives payments to a relative or friend caring for a disabled adult or elderly person at home, enabling people to stay in their own homes. The payments go toward housing, food and clothing, and medicine, medical and dental care for the person if he or she is not covered by Medicare, Medicaid or other types of insurance. In-home services such as health maintenance, housekeeping, home improvements, transportation and escort services enable disabled adults to stay out of nursing homes or other institutions.

Aging and Adult Services can offer information to people who don't want to live alone. Adult congregate living offers housing, food and personal services in state-licensed facilities. Adult foster homes offer income-eligible people an opportunity to live with "adopted families."

A displaced homemaker program helps adults older than 35 who have never worked outside the home. Counseling and education help such people become self-sustaining. A domestic violence program offers counseling and emergency shelter to victims and dependents. An adult protective services program investigates abuse and neglect of the elderly and disabled. A CARES program screens people applying for nursing home placement under Medicaid.

Alcohol, drug abuse and mental health programs: These services help people with emotional, marital or family problems related to alcohol and drug abuse. Services are found mainly in community-based programs and at community mental health centers. Counselors, who are available in many areas, also help clients find agencies to assist with vocational, economic and social needs. The state operates mental hospitals for those needing such treatment. Services include residential treatment, day care, outpatient care, methadone maintenance, and detoxification, aftercare and related services.

Children's medical services (CMS): Eligible for these services are children under 21 who have or face the risk of disabling conditions, high-risk pregnancies, or low birthweight newborns. Treatment is available in a local CMS clinic or at approved hospitals or referral centers. Clinics offer pediatrics and cardiac, orthopedic and spina bifida services. Other specialized care, through regional programs, offers treatment for renal disease, genetic disorders, pulmonary disorders, hematology/oncology, diabetes and other disorders. Statewide programs include developmental evaluation and intervention, infant screening, and child protection teams for abused and neglected children.

Children and families program: This is designed to help families work out problems that affect the well-being of their children. It assists children who have been abused or neglected or who are runaways, truants or ungovernable. The program works to improve parents' child-rearing skills and provides health and mental health services. If a child must be removed from a home, emergency shelters offer short-term placement and foster care is available for longer periods. If a child cannot return home because of neglect or abuse, permanent homes are found.

An adoption service is available for children age 8 or older, minority children, children with physical or mental handicaps and siblings who need to remain together in adoptive homes.

Low-income families that need help if a parent is ill can receive short-term services. And mental health services are available for emotionally disturbed children and their families and for teenage parents.

Developmental Services: These are available so that people with developmental disabilities such as mental retardation, cerebral palsy, epilepsy, autism and spina bifida can develop skills toward independence. The program helps find living arrangements for people who are mentally retarded; trains parents in ways to care for a handicapped child at home; provides special equipment for the home, such as lifts or ramps; and finds places for disabled people who cannot live with their own families, such as group or foster homes, cluster houses, residential "habilitation centers" and intermediate care facilities.

Economic Services: These provide financial and medical assistance, food stamps and supportive services to the needy. Financial assistance is available through Aid to Families with Dependent Children (AFDC), which provides money for food, clothing and shelter. Families qualifying for AFDC also are eligible for Medicaid.

Other forms of aid include a food stamp program, which provides coupons to increase the amount of food needy people can buy (offices are located in every county) and a Refugee Assistance program that gives cash assistance, medical help and other services.

Health programs: County health agencies provide personal health services such as education and evaluation for those unable to afford private medical care. A major aim is to help mothers and children and to assist in family planning and nutrition. Pregnant women, infants and young children are eligible for many such services.

One is the Healthy Start program, which began in 1991 and hoped to expand eligibility for health care to 18,000 more pregnant women and infants by raising the Medicaid eligibility rate to 185 percent of the poverty level. It creates partnerships among public agencies, doctors, hospitals and midwives. The aim is to expand prenatal and infant health care to more people. Community health professionals are supposed to educate potential clients about health services, how to get them, and the importance of early, preventative care. Next come home visits and counseling; childbirth and parenting education; more counseling, from social workers; and nutrition help.

Infants are screened at birth for health and environmental risks. Mothers then are referred as appropriate to further, voluntary services. A hotline — 1-800-451-BABY — offers basic information on prenatal health and how to get care.

Also available is the Women, Infants and Children program, which helps pregnant women and mothers on limited incomes buy food for themselves and their children. County public health agencies offer free immunizations required for entry into day care and school, and flu and pneumonia shots for adults.

Finally, an AIDS program offers testing, counseling and partner notification services through contracts with local AIDS networks around the state.

Abuse registry: Florida has a Protective Service System Abuse Registry, which receives reports of abuse or neglect of children, and abuse, neglect or exploitation of elderly or disabled persons. Reports are passed along to the HRS office responsible for investigating. The 24-hour, seven-day-a-week number is 1-800-962-2873.

State Health Care Referral Numbers

The toll-free numbers can be reached only within Florida.

Abuse registry: 1-800-962-2873 (For child and adult abuse, neglect and exploitation).

AIDS Hotline numbers: (For information and referrals) 1-800-FLA-AIDS (English); 1-800-545-SIDA (Spanish); 1-800-AIDS-101 (Haitian Creole); 1-800-AIDS-TTY (hearing impaired).

Adoption information and referrals:1-800-96-ADOPT.

Cancer information: 1-800-4CANCER.

Child care resource and referral network: 1-800-423-6786

Food stamp fraud and information: 1-800-342-9274.

Healthy Baby Hotline: 1-800-451-BABY.

Missing Children Information Clearinghouse: 1-800-342-0821

Client service complaints: 1-800-342-0825 (For HRS clients who complain about HRS services).

WIC (Women, Infants and Children program) information: 1-800-342-3556.

Traffic tieups, such as these near Clearwater, are legend in the heavily populated areas of Florida.

TRANSPORTA-TION

Roadways are meant for travel. But you may wonder about that on many of Florida's roads. In fact, gridlock is often the norm in major metropolitan areas, especially during rush hours. It's not uncommon to wait an hour or longer to travel a few miles. And many times, it would be faster to walk to your destination.

In recent years the *Miami Herald* ran a traffic feature titled "This Week's Nightmare" — incredible tales of gridlock wherein hapless residents often spent hours trying to get a few blocks down some South Florida road.

On the Gulf Coast, you may very well encounter other nightmares, though a few of them are being solved to a degree. Until recently, for instance, if you had wanted to cross from the St. Petersburg area into Tampa, you would have needed even more of a head start than you do today. Part of Interstate 275 was the old Howard Frankland bridge, a doozie of a causeway along which were signs warning you not to stop, even if you had a flat tire. All it took was one accident, and the backup would be tremendous, delaying commuters many a time. More than one unfortunate traveler who hadn't given himself or herself an extra hour or two would sit in a rental car on the causeway, staring at the pelicans atop the pilings of the parallel bridge under construction, and suddenly discover that the plane that had just taken off from Tampa International was missing a passenger.

That problem has eased. A new bridge over Tampa Bay has been constructed and the old bridge rehabilitated. Both bridges now carry a total of eight lanes of traffic.

On both coasts, be prepared for delays from drawbridges over the Intracoastal Waterway, which open often to allow large boats to pass, invariably when you're in a hurry.

Survival dictates that Floridians in densely populated areas develop the patience of Job, at the very least. Heavily traveled local thoroughfares usually sport traffic lights that may be just a few hundred yards apart but are rarely synchronized. So if you see a green light and gun it, you may be raising only the decibel level and your blood pressure. You'll seldom get through the next light without having to slam on the brakes.

There is one bright spot, though. Some cross-state roads carry little traffic and, at times, more interesting scenery. For example, if you're on Route 70 going from the Bradenton area to Fort Pierce, you'll see lots of trees, lots of cows, and a dandy little building called "Down Town Myakka City." It consists of one general store, two telephones, newspaper honor boxes, gasoline pumps, and an ice machine.

Nevertheless, the state's fantastic growth rate is blamed for much of the current mess on the major roads. Traffic is choking many of the state's most densely populated areas — from Orlando to Tampa to Miami. New lanes need to be added to existing roadways, new roadways urgently need to be built, and the backlog of road repairs and bridge replacements is mounting. Why are these problems becoming even greater than ever? For years, no great amounts of money have come to expand and build roads to meet the needs of a burgeoning population. And as the months go by, the problems get worse. For example, the state construction budget for fiscal 1989-90 was $70,758,961. Federal funds totaled $396,160,610. That's a far cry from what state studies indicate is necessary — one study said that $25 billion is needed over 10 years to bring transportation up to par. Efforts by the legislature to come up with a spending plan to help ease the problem fell by the wayside until June 1990.

In the waning hours of the 1990 legislative session, lawmakers approved a 4-cent increase in the state's gasoline tax, an increase in the state sales tax on gas, and a number of other taxes and surcharges on items such as rental cars to get state highway projects rolling. It is estimated that over five years, about $3.1 billion in extra revenue will be generated for state transportation needs.

The gas tax took effect Jan. 1, 1991 and subsequent increases have been enacted.

Other major fees, most of which took effect in 1990, included:

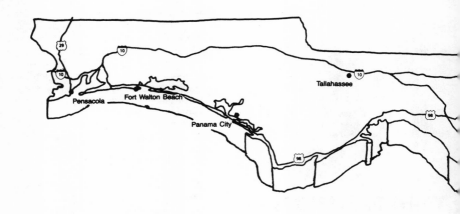

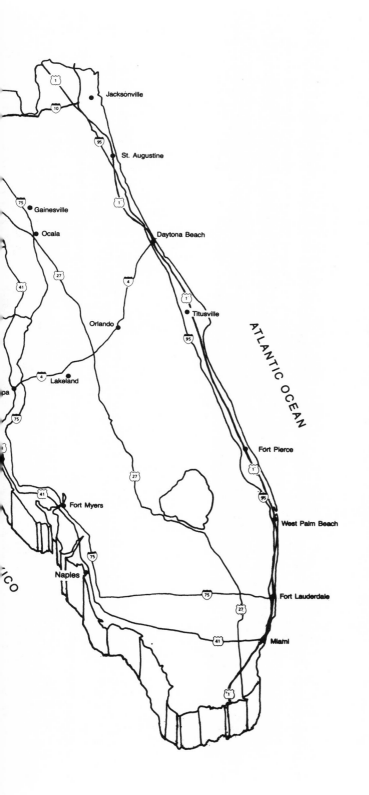

— Increasing the fee charged on vehicles registered in Florida for the first time from $30 to $100.

— Increasing the surcharge on rental cars from 50 cents a day to $2 a day. This surcharge has since been increased even more.

The state's major roads: For the newcomer, the interstates are **I-10**, which goes west to east from the western border of the state through Jacksonville; **I-75**, which enters the state near Jennings in Hamilton County, goes south to Naples and then crosses the state from the Naples area into Broward and Dade counties on the east coast; **I-95**, which enters the state from eastern Georgia and goes into Miami; and **I-4**, which goes from Tampa through Orlando and ends just south of Daytona Beach. Other major roadways include **U.S. Highway 1**, which runs the length of the state's east coast down to Key West; and two major highways along Florida's Gulf Coast: **U.S. Highway 19**, which begins northeast of Tallahassee and runs down through the St. Petersburg area; and **U.S. Highway 41**, which travelers can pick up south of Tampa Bay and which runs through Naples. Neither U.S. 19 nor 41 is the preferred route because of traffic jams along the heavily populated areas south of Hernando County. There also are innumerable traffic signals along these two routes and it may take an hour or more to travel through just one county. Another major Florida roadway is **Florida's Turnpike**, a toll road that drivers can take from Wildwood in Sumter County south to the Homestead-Florida City area in Dade County.

There are a lot of trouble spots for motorists. For example, in Broward County, transportation officials counted 154,615 cars traveling over the Interstate 95 and Northeast 48th Street interchange in just one day. On that same day, a total of 13,501 cars were counted in just a one-hour period.

Below is a listing of the major problem areas for motorists as projected by the State Department of Transportation. Some of the roadways listed were under construction and some will have to stay the way they are for the foreseeable future.

The Panhandle

This area consists of Escambia, Jefferson, Wakulla, Gadsden, Liberty, Franklin, Gulf, Calhoun, Jackson, Bay, Washington, Holmes, Walton, Okaloosa, Santa Rosa, and Leon counties.

Among the potential congested areas for motorists are:

— Capital Circle in Tallahassee. Several projects call for the widening of this roadway to four lanes. Sections are scheduled to be under construction for some time.

— There is continuing rehabilitation work on I-10 that restricts traffic to one lane at times.

— Other roads that are congested in Tallahassee include Thomasville Road, Monroe Street, Apalachee Parkway, U.S. 90, Pensacola Street and Tharpe Street.

North Central and Northeastern Florida

This section includes Alachua, Baker, Bradford, Clay, Columbia, Dixie, Duval, Gilchrist, Hamilton, Lafayette, Levy, Madison, Nassau, Putnam, St. Johns, Suwannee, Taylor and Union counties.

Several major areas are under construction to help relieve congestion problems, including some in the Jacksonville area.

— Interstate 95. The addition of lanes on I-95 south of Emerson Street to Interstate 295, a distance of 17 miles, was expected to begin in 1995-96. Design work is still under way on the Fuller Warren Bridge to replace the four-lane draw bridge. An eight-lane high-level span is planned. Sewage treatment plants also are being replaced at rest areas on this interstate in St. Johns County. Restrooms may be closed at times.

The welcome center at the Florida/Georgia line at I-95 is being demolished and replaced with a new facility and parking area. Work was to be onging until early 1996.

— Interstate 295. This interstate on the western side of Jacksonville is under construction and is being widened from four to six lanes from the Interstate 10 interchange to Interstate 95 South, a distance of about 20 miles. This work includes the widening of the Buckman Bridge from four to eight lanes. Roadway work was expected to be completed sometime in 1995 and the bridge is expected to be finished in 1997.

— Interstate 75. Large portions of this roadway are under construction from the Florida/Georgia line well into Sumter County. Projects were to be ongoing in 1995. In Alachua County, there is major construction to add two lanes in the median, expanding the roadway to six lanes. In Columbia County, this roadway is being expanded to six lanes for seven miles from U.S. 90 at Lake City north to Interstate 10. Two other segments are under construction starting at the Columbia/Alachua

County line and joining with the segment at U.S. 90, along with segments in Marion and Sumter counties. On top of all this work, the interstate is also being resurfaced and the bridges widened from State Road 6 to the Florida/Georgia line, a distance of 18.8 miles.

In addition, on I-75, sewage treatment plants are being replaced at rest areas along the interstate in Hamilton and Suwannee counties. Restrooms may be closed at times.

— U.S. 301 in Bradford and Alachua counties. Four bridges are being replaced — over the Olustee and Prevatt creeks in Bradford County and the Santa Fe River and Orange Creek in Alachua County. The four-lane highway is being reduced to two lanes in these areas and the speed limit is reduced. Work was expected to be ongoing into 1996.

— State Road 13 at the Duval/St. Johns County line and south into St. Johns County to Racetrack Road. The bridge over Julington Creek is being widened to four lanes, along with the roadway. Work will be ongoing well into 1996.

— The Vilano Bridge, a lift span over the Tolomato River north of St. Augustine in St. Johns County, is being replaced with a high-level span and was expected to be completed by 1996.

— U.S. 90 in Baker, Columbia and Nassau counties is being resurfaced and widened and work was to continue until 1996.

— Interstate 10 in Baker County is being resurfaced, a distance of about 26 miles. Work will be ongoing for some time. Also, sewage treatment plants are being replaced at rest areas along this interstate in Baker and Duval counties, and restrooms may be closed at times.

Central Florida

The counties in this region include Brevard, Volusia, Flagler, Orange, Osceola, Seminole, Lake, Marion, and Sumter.

There are two roads that are on the "try to avoid list" here:

— Interstate 4 going through Orlando during rush hour. This road was designed to accommodate about 80,000 vehicles a day and is now carrying about 150,000 through the downtown area. Widening of this roadway was scheduled in Seminole County in 1996.

— State Road 436. This roadway is described by transportation officials as heavily congested and one of the busiest in central Florida. Some sections are being widened from four lanes to six.

Other roadways that are heavily traveled

around Orlando and that may have construction delays over the next few years include:

— The section of U.S. 441 (Orange Blossom Trail) that goes through Orlando and lies east of Interstate 4 is very congested and is being expanded to six lanes.

— Goldenrod Road east of downtown Orlando is being expanded to four lanes. All sections of this road are being widened over three years.

Other congested roadways in other areas of this region include:

— State Road 5A (Nova Road), now a two-lane road, is a bypass of U.S. 1 in the Daytona Beach area and is scheduled to be expanded to four and six lanes in some sections.

— State Road 200 in Marion and Citrus counties. Development along the two-lane roadway prompted the need for expansion. A small part of the widening — to four lanes — is under way.

—U.S. Routes 17 and 92, north of Orlando in Seminole and Volusia counties, are congested but no widening is planned in the near future.

Central West Florida

This area of the state, encompassing Hillsborough, Pinellas, Hernando, Pasco and Citrus counties, is famous for its traffic. Clogged roadways are common, especially in Pinellas and Hillsborough and, to a lesser extent, in Pasco. Some construction projects are well under way; others will takes years to begin, much less complete.

Problem areas, because of construction or just too much traffic, include:

Hillsborough County:

— Interstate 4, from 14th Street in Tampa to the Hillsborough/Polk County line. Segments of Interstate 4 are scheduled to be expanded to six lanes, with construction taking place well into the late 1990s.

— U.S. Highway 41, from Fletcher Avenue to the Hillsborough/Pasco County line. Multi-lane construction on segments of U.S. Highway 41 is scheduled to be ongoing for several years.

— Interstate 275, from the Howard Frankland Bridge to the I-275 and Interstate 75 interchange, is scheduled to be expanded before the turn of the century.

— Hillsborough Avenue (State Road 580), from the Pinellas County line to east Double Branch Road, will be expanded to eight lanes; and from Eisenhower Boulevard to Florida Avenue, will be expanded to six lanes. This will include the rehabilitation of the Hillsborough

River Bridge and the building of a new three-lane bridge alongside the existing bridge. Construction is scheduled over the next five years.

— Dale Mabry Highway (State Road 597), from Cheval Trail to the Pasco-Hillsborough County line, will be expanded to four lanes; construction was scheduled to start in 1995.

— Martin Luther King Jr. Boulevard (State Road 574), from Interstate 4 to Pine Street, will be expanded to six lanes with construction ongoing over the next few years.

— Fowler Avenue (State Road 582), from U.S. Highway 41 to 22nd Street, is scheduled to be expanded to six lanes.

Pinellas County:

— East Bay and Roosevelt (State Road 686). Multi-lane construction from east of Belcher Road to 49th Street is scheduled.

— Ulmerton Road (State Road 688). Multi-lane construction is scheduled on segments of this road, from Gulf Boulevard to 113th Street and from west of Feather Sound to east of Feather Sound. Construction is set to begin within a few years.

— State Road 580. Multi-lane construction is scheduled from east of the Oldsmar Bridge to State Road 584 and from Race Track Road to east of Gim Gong Road in the near future.

— Tampa Road (State Road 584). Multi-lane construction is scheduled over the next few years.

— U.S. Highway 19, from State Road 60 to a railroad crossing, upgrading to a six-lane controlled access facility with frontage roads; and from Live Oak Street to the Pinellas and Pasco County line, upgrading to a six-lane road. Construction was scheduled for 1995 and 1996.

— Clearwater Pass Bridge on County Road 183, the bridge is being replaced with a 74-foot fixed bridge. Completion was expected in late 1996.

— Interstate 275 multi-lane construction from Big Island Gap to 4th Street. Construction to be ongoing through much of 1995, with the 4th Street interchange closed to traffic.

— South Skyway Bridge Fishing Pier renovation to allow vehicle access. Completion was set for early 1996.

Other upcoming projects:

— Blind Pass Bridge on Gulf Boulevard. Replacing the existing two-lane bridge with a four-lane, 12-foot fixed bridge.

— Clearwater Harbor Bridge rehabilitation.

Pasco County:

Upcoming projects:

— Interstate 75 resurfacing and repaving from the Hillsborough and Pasco County line to Overpass Road and interchange reconstruction at State Road 54.

— U.S. Highway 41, from Five Mile Creek to State Road 52, resurfacing is scheduled. In addition, from the Pasco/Hillsborough County line to Suydam Drive the highway is scheduled for multi-lane construction, beginning in 1996-97.

— State Road 54, from U.S. Highway 19 to County Road 581. This roadway will be expanded, with work on a segment from Rowan Road to the Mitchell Bypass scheduled to start in 1995-96 and other segments to be under construction for years to come.

— State Road 52, from Hicks Road to Moon Lake Road, expanding to a six-lane urban road. Construction scheduled for 1996-97.

— Dale Mabry, from the Hillsborough and Pasco County line to U.S. Highway 41, expanding to a four-lane roadway.

Hernando County:

— State Road 50, from County Road 41 to west of Lockhart Road; and from Cedar Lane Road to State Road 50 and 50A. Expanding to four lanes with construction in 1995. Other sections of the roadway are scheduled for construction in future years including a section from Colorado Street to U.S. Highway 98; from Rital-Croom to State Road 700; and from County Road 541 to Cedar Lane Road.

— U.S. Highway 19 is being expanded to six lanes from the Pasco County line to Toucan Trail and was scheduled to be completed in mid 1995. Further construction is set in 1998-1999 to expand a section from the Toucan Trail to State Road 50.

Citrus County:

Upcoming projects:

— State Road 44, from Loop Road to County Road 581, expanding to four lanes. Construction is planned in phases. Also planned in the future is expanding this roadway from U.S. Highway 41 to the Sumter County line.

— U.S. Highway 19 at State Road 44, construct southbound dual left-turn lanes at State Road 44 intersection. Construction was scheduled for 1995-96.

— U.S. Highway 19/98, construction of a second bridge across the barge canal north of the Crystal River. Construction is scheduled for 1998-99.

South-Central Florida

In south-central Florida, encompassing Sarasota, Manatee, Polk, Collier, Okeechobee, Hardee, De Soto, Glades, Hendry, Charlotte, Lee and Highlands counties, the most congested roadways (and the ones that will mean traffic delays) include:

— U.S. Highway 41 from Manatee County into Collier County. This roadway is almost always congested, especially during the winter. Some relief is in sight, but work will take at least another five years. The roadway is scheduled to be expanded to six lanes from Manatee County to Naples.

— Interstate 75. Reconstruction of this roadway is scheduled over the next five years in Sarasota and Manatee counties. Parts of the interstate will be closed at various times.

— U.S. 17 from State Road 655 in Eloise to Cypress Gardens Boulevard in Winter Haven. A new six-lane bridge is being constructed over the Chain of Lakes Canal (the bridge had been two lanes). The roadway is also being expanded from Eagle Lake to Cypress Gardens Boulevard.

— Construction work on State Road 80 through LaBelle will be ongoing.

— U.S. Highway 17, from north of Bowling Green to south of Fort Meade, was scheduled to be under construction in 1995.

— State Road 72 in south Sarasota will be expanded from U.S. Highway 41 to Interstate 75 until 1996. Traffic will be kept on the two-lane road while the multi-lane upgrade is under way.

— The replacement of the bridge on State Road 64 from Bradenton to Anna Maria Island and the rehabilitation of the Cortez Bridge in Manatee County will be ongoing for some time. Expect closures of the Cortez Bridge at some intervals.

Southeastern Florida

This area is made up of Broward, Palm Beach, Martin, St. Lucie and Indian River counties (see Dade and Monroe below).

Transportation efforts to relieve some of the congestion — which is particularly heavy in Broward and Palm Beach — have been centered in recent years on a major roadway — Interstate 95. The highway recently was widened from the Dade-Broward County line, through Broward County up to Linton Boulevard in south Palm Beach County (in the Boca Raton area), a distance of about 25 miles. In addition, shoulders along the interstate for about 15 miles in Dade County were widened. High-occupancy-vehicle lanes were added; Park & Ride lots with direct access ramps to and from the interstate at the Broward Boulevard interchange were constructed; and the Davie Boulevard interchange was reconstructed. Both the Broward and Davie boulevard interchanges go into downtown Fort Lauderdale. The result of this work: more numerous traffic tieups and backups even longer than before. But even misery has an ending, and nearly all of this work has come to an end.

Even while all this I-95 construction was going on, I-95 was still described as the fastest way to get from Fort Lauderdale to Miami. The other major north-south roadways, Routes 1 and A1A, are not suited to long-distance travel because they are in heavily populated urban areas and have a lot of traffic signals. The other major north-south roadway in the area, the Florida Turnpike, is a toll road and takes you away from Miami not long after you enter Dade County. A turnpike expansion project is under way to help alleviate this problem.

A point to remember: Interstate 95 in southeastern Florida is expanded as much as it probably will ever be, as there is no more room for widening, say transportation department officials. Officials will need to look at other alternatives, such as expanded commuter rail service. The Tri-County Commuter Rail Service has been in existence for five years; it runs parallel and adjacent to I-95 with 15 stations between West Palm Beach and Miami. The railway operates seven days a week and also runs during special events, such as Miami Dolphins' games and the Orange Bowl parade.

Other roadways in the area that at times are heavily conjested include:

South of Interstate 4, which is in central Florida, the only four-lane roadway across the state is the recently expanded Alligator Alley, which links up with I-75. Since the other roads leading out of the Atlantic Coast cities to the Gulf Coast are mainly two lanes, they are heavily traveled and some of these might have some traffic delays.

— State Road 70, from Fort Pierce to Manatee County, heavily used and nearly all of it two lanes wide. Long-range plans, though, call for four lanes on this roadway from Fort Pierce to Manatee County.

— State Road 60, from Vero Beach to Tampa, heavily used and mostly two lanes from Vero Beach to near Lake Wales. Long-range plans also call for four lanes from Vero Beach to Lake Wales.

— U.S. 41 (also known as the Tamiami Trail) connects Miami to Naples and is mostly two lanes.

Other potential trouble sites:

— U.S. 27 from the Broward/Palm Beach County line to the town of South Bay was being widened to four lanes in 1995.

— A number of moveable bridges over the Intracoastal Waterway linking the barrier islands with the mainland will be undergoing major renovation work. There will be some lane closures and temporary closures of these bridges over the next few years.

Dade and Monroe Counties

Within the Miami metropolitan area, which has a population of about two million people, it should be no surprise that there are a number of congested areas. Most of the city's major thoroughfares have very high traffic volume. In addition, construction projects either have been under way or will be for some of these expressways, which can produce even more delays. Here's a sampling of some of the major possible tie-ups:

— Interstate 95. The expressway's peak count is 200,000 vehicles a day. Construction work in the northern part of Dade County was scheduled to be finished by mid-1995 with the completion of a new Golden Glades HOV fly-over and the addition of new lanes. Informational signs alerting drivers to traffic conditions were to be in place in this area by late 1995.

— The Dolphin Expressway, or State Road 836, carries 120,000 vehicles a day on average. A proposed project calls for widening Dade County's only major east-west expressway. Construction may begin by 1996 and last into the next century.

— The Palmetto Expressway, or State Road 826, carries 175,000 vehicles a day on average. Expansion of Dade County's major north-south corridor has begun where the roadway meets Interstate 75, and will continue in increments south. This expressway is the most congested one in the county, and this 10-year, $500 million project will cause even more problems for commuters.

— State Road 112, the Airport Expressway, carries 80,000 vehicles a day on average.

— The Homestead Extension of the Florida Turnpike (also known as HEFT) carries 82,000 vehicles a day on average.

Another sore spot to people leaving Dade County and heading for the Keys is Route 1. There's been a cry to widen this roadway for years, but so far nothing has happened. Trying to move along this roadway on a Friday night is an experience you will not soon forget.

Some Traffic Statistics

To give an idea of traffic levels, the state counts vehicles at sites in about two-thirds of Florida's counties.

The figures below, except where noted, represent the 24-hour traffic "daycount" for Fri-day, Jan. 6, 1989. The count includes all vehicles and is measured with computers. We chose this date because it was one on which people were heading out for the weekend at one of the busiest times of the year. The second figure for each site is the highest hourly count for the year.

These numbers come from the state Department of Transportation's voluminous "Peak Hour Traffic Count Report," which contains figures from July 1988 through June 1989.

Alachua County: I-75, 2.2 miles north of Micanopy, Wacahoota Road: Daycount: 42,104; highest hourly count: 6,098.

Bay County: U.S. 98A, 100 yards east of SR79: Daycount: 7,614; highest hourly count: 2,052.

Bradford County: U.S. 301, 50 feet north of Santa Fe River Bridge: Daycount: 19,948; highest hourly count: 2,796.

Brevard County: SR 520, 0.5 miles east of Indian River Bridge: Daycount: 56,664; highest hourly count: 4,828.
U.S. 1, 0.2 miles south of SR 514 in Malabar: Daycount: 16,192; highest hourly count: 4,192.
I-95, 3.5 miles south of SR 514, Malabar: Daycount: 22,269; highest hourly count: 3,186.

Broward County: I-95 at Northeast 48th Street: Daycount: 154,615; highest hourly count: 13,501.

Calhoun County: SR 20, 0.6 miles east of SR 71: Daycount: not available for this date, but on other test days ranged from 6,839 to 9,744; highest hourly count: 3,373.

Charlotte County: U.S. 41, 4.8 miles north of Lee County line, north of Oilwell Road: Daycount: 12,798; highest hourly count: 2,465.
Citrus County: U.S. 19, 0.2 miles north of SR 480: Daycount: 13,873; highest hourly count: 2,164.

Collier County: U.S. 41, 0.3 miles south of C31A, south of Naples: Daycount: 43,198; highest hourly count: 4,378.

Columbia County: U.S. 90, 3.3 miles east of SR 137 (West Lake City): Daycount: not available for this date, but other figures for the month ranged from 2,695 to 4,962; highest hourly count: 1,938.

Dade County: A1A, MacArthur Causeway, 0.5 miles west of Palm Island Entrance, Miami: Daycount: 67,690; highest hourly count: 5,624.
I-95, 0.5 miles east of U.S. 1 in Miami: Daycount: 77,770; highest hourly count: 6,980.

De Soto County: U.S. 17, 1.4 miles north of SCL railroad overpass, north of Arcadia: Daycount: 6,459; highest hourly count: 698.

Duval County: I-10 at the SR 217 overpass,

south of Baldwin: Daycount: 30,908; highest hourly count: 6,354.

I-95, 2 miles south of I-295: Daycount: 37,873; highest hourly count: 5,190.

I-295, 3 miles north of I-10: Daycount: 43,496; highest hourly count: 4,323.

U.S. 90, west of White Avenue, Jacksonville: Daycount: 58,953; highest hourly count: 5,141.

Escambia County: I-10, 1.5 miles west of U.S. 90A: Daycount: 17,693; highest hourly count: 3,456.

U.S. 29, 0.8 miles north of U.S. 90A: Daycount: 27,851; highest hourly count: 2,422.

Franklin County: U.S. 98, 0.5 miles south of U.S. 319, northeast of Carrabelle: Daycount: not available for this date, but other figures for the month ranged from 1,771 to 2,331; highest hourly count: not available.

Gadsden County: SR 63/U.S. 27, Georgia/Florida line north of Hinson: Daycount: 5,752; highest hourly count: 1,213.

Hamilton County: I-75, south of the state line at Bellville Road: Daycount: 27,170; highest hourly count: 4,965.

Hendry County: U.S. 27, 0.54 miles east of Flag Hold Road, west of Clewiston: Daycount: not available for this date, but on other test days that month, figures ranged from 10,963 to 13,724; highest hourly count: 2,279.

Hillsborough County: I-4 at the Bethlehem Road overpass: Daycount: 65,529; highest hourly count: 6,192.

I-275, 1.3 miles east of the Howard Frankland Bridge: Daycount: 86,534; highest hourly count: 7,028.

I-275, at the south end of the Floribraska Avenue overpass: Daycount: 136,983; highest hourly count: 10,757.

Jackson County: U.S. 90, west of Russ Street, in Marianna: Daycount: 21,545; highest hourly count: 2,040.

Lake County: SR 44, 0.4 miles north of Silver Lake lake entrance: Daycount: 7,033; highest hourly count: 3,616.

Lafayette County: U.S. 27, .3 miles west of SR 349, west of Branford: Daycount: 2,636; highest hourly count: not available.

Leon County: U.S. 27 (Apalachee Parkway) at railroad overpass 0.4 miles east of Capitol: Daycount: 38,032; highest hourly count: 3,661.

Levy County: U.S. 19, 2 miles of SR 26: Daycount: 10,575; highest hourly count: 2,362.

Madison County: I-10, 0.5 miles west of U.S. 221, Greenville: Daycount: 28,538; highest hourly count: 3,259.

Manatee County: SR 64, 1 mile west of C675 South: Daycount: 2,965; highest hourly count: 389.

Marion County: U.S. 301, 0.2 miles north of

C326 West: Daycount: 21,961; highest hourly count: 3,014.

Monroe County: U.S. 1 at Key Largo before U.S. 1 turns to Miami Bridge: Daycount: 20,193; highest hourly count: 2,443.

U.S. 1 at Key West north of the city limits, Cow Key Bridge: Daycount: 38,426; highest hourly count: 3,698.

Nassau County: I-95, 2 miles south of the state line: Daycount: 39,144; highest hourly count: 5,418.

Okaloosa County: U.S. 98, 0.3 miles east of the Okaloosa County line: Daycount: 19,084; highest hourly count: 2,027.

Orange County: SR 50, 0.6 miles west of SR 535, 12 miles west of Orlando: Daycount: 27,819; highest hourly count: 2,309.

I-4, 0.8 miles south of SR 482: Daycount: 95,877; highest hourly count: 10,550.

SR 436, 1.4 miles north of SR 528: Daycount: 46,014; highest hourly count: 3,957.

Osceola County: SR 530 (U.S. 192) at Yates Road: Daycount: not available for this date, but on other test days ranged from 44,560 to 57,911; highest hourly count: 3,933.

Palm Beach County: U.S. 1, 4.5 miles south of SR 806, north of Newcastle Street, Boca Raton: Daycount: 36,181; highest hourly count: 3,304.

SR A1A at the east end of the bridge in Palm Beach: Daycount: 25,945; highest hourly count: 2,953.

Pasco County: U.S. 41, 0.4 miles north of Dale Mabry Highway: Daycount: 28,702; highest hourly count: 2,371.

U.S. 98/301, 0.5 miles south of U.S. 301 and U.S. 98 junction: Daycount: not available for this month, but figures for December 1988 ranged from 12,673 to 15,813; highest hourly count: 1,650.

Pinellas County: SR 699, north of 138th Avenue West in Redington Shores: Daycount: 17,079; highest hourly count: 2,182.

U.S. 92, 500 feet west of the Gandy Bridge: Daycount: not available for this month, but February figures range from 18,117 to 30,895; highest hourly count: 3,153.

Polk County: U.S. 27, 0.8 miles south of SR 60: Daycount: 23,677; highest hourly count: 6,675.

Putnam County: U.S. 17/SR 100, 2.75 miles south of SR 207: Daycount: 16,874; highest hourly count: 4,502.

St. Lucie County: SR 70, 0.3 miles west of C609, west of Fort Pierce: Daycount: 5,360; highest hourly count: 543.

Florida Turnpike, Becker Road overpass: Daycount: 25,771; highest hourly count: 4,446.

Seminole County: U.S. 17/92, 1.4 miles

south of SR 46, south of Sanford: Daycount: 49,243; highest hourly count: 6,036.

Sumter County: I-75, 3.5 miles south of the Florida Turnpike: Daycount: 30,311; highest hourly count: 4,219.

Volusia County: I-4, 1.2 miles west of the Deltona overpass, north of Sanford: Daycount: 41,756; highest hourly count: 4,886.

I-95, 2.7 miles north of SR 44 at the SR 40A overpass: Daycount: not available for this date, but on other test days of the same month, figures ranged from 19,940 to 25,395; highest hourly count: 3,277.

Walton County: U.S. 98, 1 mile east of the Okaloosa line: Daycount: 9,545; highest hourly count: 3,510.

Florida's Turnpike

To some state officials, the answer to some of Florida's traffic problems is clear-cut: expand Florida's Turnpike.

The adding on of more miles to the turnpike, these officials say, would help solve congestion problems on other roadways in the state, would reduce the time motorists spend on the state's highways and would even reduce traffic accidents.

But, approval of funding has come slowly. The turnpike carries on average 125.5 million vehicles a year and has served mainly the southeastern portion of the state. State planners, though, have been proposing for years to extend the roadway to other sections of Florida to relieve congestion on such highways as Interstate 95 and Interstate 4. The total cost: about $7.5 billion.

Among the projects that have been approved and that will affect traffic for months to come:

Dade County: Northbound and southbound motorists will face traffic shifts and periodic lane closures as a new interchange at Northwest 106th St. is being built. The interchange was scheduled for completion in the spring of 1996.

Construction of new toll plazas at the Coral Reef/Southwest 152nd Street interchange is under way. Toll plazas are being built on the southbound entrance ramp and the northbound exit ramp. Motorists using these ramps will experience traffic shifts and periodic lane closures. Construction completion date: late 1995.

Several interchanges on the Homestead Extension and new toll plazas at the Allapattah Road, Tallahassee Road, Biscayne Drive and Campbell Drive interchanges are being constructed. Motorists will experience traffic shifts

and periodic lane closures. Construction completion date: late 1995.

Broward County: The Cypress Creek mainline toll plaza has 14 existing toll lanes and will be expanded to 18 toll lanes. One of these new lanes will be constructed on the eastern end of the plaza and the other three lanes will be added to the western end. The plaza's toll booths will also be replaced. Completion: Summer 1995.

Other Southeastern projects: A $16 million renovation of the eight ticket- system toll plazas from Yeehaw Junction south to Lake Worth is under way. The existing toll-collection facilities, toll booths, administration buildings and parking lots of each of these plazas are being replaced and upgraded, and the number of toll lanes will be increased at five of the eight plazas. No significant traffic delays are expected.

Central Florida: A new 12-mile toll road, called the Seminole Expressway, which is connecting the Central Florida GreeneWay in southern Seminole County to U.S. Route 17/92 near Sanford, was opened in 1994. The roadway serves as an alternate route around Orlando.

The Southern Connector Extension, a 6.1-mile, four-lane limited-access toll facility connecting the Central Florida GreeneWay to Interstate 4 in Osceola County is under construction. Completion: late 1996. Interchanges will be constructed at Osceola Parkway, Celebration Boulevard (providing a link with U.S. Highway 192) and Interstate 4. Ramp toll plazas will be located at the Celebration Boulevard and Osceola Parkway interchanges for traffic to and from the north.

Central West Florida: The Veterans Expressay in Hillsborough County, a 15-mile, limited access, four-lane toll road, opened in October 1994. The expressway begins on Eisenhower Boulevard near the Courtney Campbell Causeway and goes north, crossing Van Dyke Road and then east to the Dale Mabry Highway near the Pasco County line. This $332-million project, which is part of Florida's Turnpike expansion program, is expected to relieve traffic congestion in the northwest Tampa area, especially on the Dale Mabry Highway, Anderson Road and Sheldon Road. The new roadway is an alternate route for drivers coming into the Tampa area from Pinellas and Pasco counties.

Other traffic delays: Construction is continuing to convert the northern turnpike from a ticket system to the coin system of toll collection. Toll plaza construction is under way at the Kissimmee interchange, Orlando South interchange, Orlando/I-4 interchange, Ocoee interchange, State Road 50/Clermont interchange and Leesburg interchange. Motorists should expect traffic shifts and delays during morning and afternoon rush hours.

Other projects on the drawing board: Seminole Expressway Project 2 is under design by the Seminole County Expressway Authority. A six-mile tolled expressway, this roadway will connect the new Seminole Expressway to Interstate 4 in southern Seminole County. Beginning: possibly in mid-1996.

In addition, right-of-way acquisition for the Polk Parkway is under way. The parkway is a 25-mile tolled highway that will form a partial western bypass around Lakeland.

Planners envision the turnpike one day as linking many of the state's urban areas. For years, the toll road has passed through just 11 counties — Dade, Broward, Palm Beach, Martin, St. Lucie, Indian River, Okeechobee, Osceola, Orange, Lake and Sumter.

A major portion of the roadway, or 266 miles, stretches from near Miami to Wildwood in Sumter County. In addition, there is an eight-mile extension in Orlando called the Bee Line Expressway that was opened in 1973 and a 47-mile extension to the Homestead-Florida City area in Dade County, opened in 1974. It is proposed that the turnpike one day will link Tampa to both Orlando and Jacksonville and the Tampa Bay area to the Fort Pierce and Stuart area. If backers get everything they request, 125 miles of new expressways will be added to the system throughout the state, along with 12 new interchanges.

The Train System

If you are going to ride the rails in Florida, most likely you will be riding an Amtrak train, unless you're on a monorail at Disney World or a commuter line in the Miami or West Palm Beach area.

Amtrak operates four long-distance passenger lines and an auto train that accommodates both passengers and their vehicles through Florida. Two of the four passenger lines, dubbed the Silver Star and the Silver Meteor, run from New York to Miami. Each train makes numerous stops along the way, and is popular; summer and holiday reservations should be made well in advance. Once in Florida, the lines split and passengers can take either the Tampa or Miami routes. One-way travel time from New York to Miami is between 26 and 28 hours. A third train, called the Palmetto, runs daily from New York to Jacksonville. And, in 1993, Amtrak started running

its first transcontinental train, called the Sunset Limited, which linked Los Angeles to Miami. The train makes the trip three days a week; the travel time from Los Angeles to Miami is around 70 hours. The trip takes passengers through eight states — California, Arizona, New Mexico, Texas, Louisiana, Mississippi, Alabama and Florida.

The auto train leaves daily from Lorton, Va. (near Washington, D.C.), and arrives in Sanford, Fla., about 30 miles from Disney World. There are no intermediate stops on this train and the travel time is 16.5 hours. The train is restricted to passengers with automobiles and has coaches, sleeping cars and food and lounge service. The busiest months are November and December.

Total Florida ridership aboard all Amtrak trains during fiscal 1993 was 1,226,224 passengers. Aside from the auto train stop at Sanford (220,744 passengers during the '93 fiscal year), the other most popular Florida destinations were Tampa, 149,722 riders; Orlando, 143,549; Jacksonville, 121,352; Miami, 96,843; West Palm Beach, 56,583; Winter Haven, 51,435; Fort Lauderdale, 51,306; Kissimmee, 44,425; Hollywood, 31,431; Deerfield Beach, 29,314; DeLand, 26,694; Winter Park, 26,219; and Ocala, 22,624.

High-speed Rail Service

The state's rapid development, combined with standoffs in the state legislature in recent years over how best to fund its highway system, have prompted Florida's leaders to become more interested in rail transportation. With projections that the state's population will continue to skyrocket, and with the cloud of highway construction funding delays, many people feel the time has come for Florida to look beyond highways to solve its transportation problems. The existing MetroRail and the MetroMover transport systems in Miami have been one attempt to alleviate congested highways and downtown traffic. Jacksonville also has a people-mover system downtown. But this is seen as only a start. And while statewide rail service expansion is under study, Amtrak would not be the principal carrier for passenger travel within Florida. The answer instead: the development of a high-speed rail service between the state's major growth areas.

If history is any clue, the state doesn't have a great track record with rail service experiments. Florida tried out local rail service between Miami and Tampa from November 1982 to April 1985 with its "Silver Palm" line. State funding was dropped when operating revenues did not meet expectations. And the state's West Palm Beach-Miami commuter line (Tri-Rail) service, started in 1989, has been struggling at times to attract enough riders to stay in business.

The idea for high-speed service has been around since the mid-1970s, when business, transportation, and government leaders began talking about the feasibility of this type of service in the state. A study committee was appointed in 1982, and in 1984 the state legislature passed the Florida High Speed Rail Transportation Act, calling for the development of a privately financed high-speed rail service — the first of its kind in the country. The service would link Miami, Orlando, and Tampa and parts of it would be operational by 1995. Trains would travel around 150 miles per hour, and the trip from Miami to Tampa would take between 2 hours and 40 minutes and 2 hours and 55 minutes; from Miami to Orlando, between 1 hour and 45 minutes and 2 hours; and from Orlando to Tampa, 41 to 49 minutes. The legislature also created a High Speed Rail Commission.

History soon repeated itself. A workable proposal for a fully privately funded system could not be found. The legislature eventually abolished the commission and instead shifted the responsibilities for overseeing high-speed rail service to the Department of Transportation.

But through all of its ups and downs, the proposal today is still alive. In 1992, the legislature allocated $1.2 million for the department to conduct more extensive ridership studies, this time using both private and public funding for high-speed rail service. These studies have been completed and proposals for this service are being sought. A new timetable called for a franchisee to be chosen by the end of 1995; for permits and certification to be obtained two years later; and for construction to take place after this. Trains are hoped to be operating by the turn of the century.

Another high-speed rail project looked like it would become a reality in the early 1990s, but financing snags put an end to this hope. Plans had called for 250-mile-per-hour train service from Orlando International Airport to International Drive, about three miles east of Disney World. It was anticipated that construction of the 13.5-mile-long track would begin by late 1993 or early 1994, with completion by 1996. But, by 1994, project sponsors could not put together a viable financing proposal and the Florida Department of Transportation was forced to recommend the termination of this project.

Airports

For those coming to Florida by air, you won't be alone. The U.S. Department of Transportation's Federal Aviation Administration reported that at least 34 million paying passengers used the state's major airports during 1990. And you'll have lots of airports to choose from: there are more than 130 public airports and scores of private airports in the state. Here is the FAA's listing of the number of paying air passengers for 1990 at the state's major airports:

All Florida: 34,081,249

1. Miami International: 9,226,103
2. Orlando International: 7,677,769
3. Tampa International: 4,781,020
4. Fort Lauderdale/Hollywood International: 3,875,357
5. Palm Beach International: 2,609,138
6. Southwest Florida Regional (Fort Myers): 1,712,679
7. Jacksonville International: 1,266,677
8. Sarasota/Bradenton: 989,935
9. Daytona Beach Regional: 490,336
10. Pensacola Regional: 394,222
11. Tallahassee Municipal: 381,840
12. Melbourne (Cape Kennedy Regional): 360,126
13. Gainesville Municipal: 166,264
14. Key West International: 80,203
15. Eglin Air Force Base (Valparaiso): 69,462

Regional Transit

While Greyhound basically is the state's sole commercial bus company, many of the state's urban and rural areas have bus service that is run by local transit authorities. A 1991 transportation department report, "Performance of Florida's Public Transit Sytems," showed there were 19 public transit systems in the state, with 17 systems having fixed-route bus services.

Among the largest of these services are the Metro-Dade County Transit Authority in Miami, which operates Metrobus/MetroRail/MetroMover systems; the Broward Transit Division; Jacksonville Transportation Authority; Pinellas Suncoast Transit Authority; Hillsborough Area Regional Transit; Space Coast Area Transit in the Brevard County area; and Tri-County Transit in the Orlando area.

Other systems operating public transportation include the Palm Beach County Transportation Authority; Regional Transit System of the Gainesville area; Tallahassee Transit Authority; Escambia County Transit System; East Volusia Transit Authority in the Daytona Beach area; Manatee County Transit; Sarasota County Area Transit; Lee County Transit Authority; Lakeland Area Mass Transit District; Smyrna Transit System of the New Smyrna Beach area; and the Pasco Area Transit System serving the Pasco County area. For rail commuters, there is the Tri-County Commuter Rail Authority, serving Palm Beach, Broward and Dade counties.

Transportation of the Disadvantaged

The need to provide transportation for those who are physically or mentally impaired, who cannot afford to buy their own cars, or who are too old to drive anymore is great in Florida. It has been estimated that about 4.2 million people need transportation to get to doctor's appointments, travel to work, go shopping, attend school, or just get somewhere. The number of handicapped persons needing this service is estimated at more than 1.5 million, while more than 1.4 million people 60 and older and nearly 1.1 million low-income persons need transportation.

Up until the 1970s, service for the disadvantaged was fragmented. There were believed to be about 800 social service agencies in the state that provided or purchased transportation services for their client groups. In 1979, the Florida legislature mandated that all these services be coordinated at the county level. The group put in charge of this was the Transportation Disadvantaged Commission, appointed by the governor.

There are three toll-free numbers to find out more about what is available: 1-800-983-2435 (for the transportation disadvantaged commission office); 1-800-342-5557 (for information about the share ride program) and 1-800-648-6084 (for the hearing impaired).

Port Activity

The export-import business has grown quickly in Florida. Gross and taxable sales reported to the Department of Revenue rose from $4.5 billion in 1988 to $5.4 billion in 1989 and $6.3 billion in 1990. Much of the importing and exporting is done through major ports around the state. Here is a listing of the number of short tons handled in those ports:

1. Tampa: 49,157,127 (fiscal 1991-92)
2. Everglades: 16,353,376 (fiscal 1991-92)
3. Manatee: 5,375,233 (fiscal 1991-92)
4. Jacksonville: 5,001,074 (fiscal 1991-92). This figure includes tonnage that passes only through facilities owned by the Jacksonville Port Authority. Other facilities in the port are excluded.
5. Miami: 4,596,481 (fiscal 1991-92)
6. Palm Beach: 3,788,805 (fiscal 1991-92)
7. Canaveral: 2,975,921 (fiscal 1991-92)
8. Pensacola: 1,372,879 (fiscal 1991-92)
9. Panama City: 565,302 (calendar 1992)
10. St. Lucie: 127,659 (calendar 1992)

There are about 1,100 golf courses in Florida.

THE WORST DAY DIVING
IS BETTER THAN
THE BEST DAY WORKING

Diving is popular along the southeast coast, particularly in the Keys.

Because waterfront land is at a premium, many marinas have taken to stacking boats on racks. Call ahead and a forklift will put your boat in the water.

LEISURE ACTIVITIES

As a newcomer, it won't take you long to discover this about Florida — you won't need to look far to find something to do in your spare time. Of course there's Disney World, as well as hundreds of other attractions across the state. But there are also hundreds of things to do close to home. Those things can be in the backyard or on a beach; at a Miami Dolphins football game or at a polo match; at a festival or at an arts and crafts show. Florida's warm climate can suddenly arouse an interest in gardening or can make that dream of a backyard swimming pool come true. The climate certainly will enable you to go to the beach more often than up north, and perhaps you'll find it more sensible to own a boat because you'll be able to use it year-round. Or you may become interested in one of the more than 100 state-run parks, recreational areas, museums and other sites.

Some of the things up north can also be found here: theaters, symphonies, operas and museums. There's also professional and college football (even though it's sometimes played in 90-degree weather here), professional basketball, football, baseball and hockey, tennis, jai alai, fishing, thoroughbred racing, greyhound racing and hunting. You'll find literally thousands of festivals and arts and crafts and sporting events every year. There are so many of them, in fact, that the Pinellas County Arts Council has a nearly 100-page

publication that lists just the state's arts and crafts festivals. On top of this, there is such a long list of tennis tournaments for the tennis buff, fishing tournaments for anglers, and fun runs, 5K runs and you-name-it runs for those who have the stamina, that it's best to check local newspapers each week to keep track of them.

And you'll also discover a number of things that you don't have up north: winter polo matches and baseball games, the Daytona 500 Speedway and the Orange Bowl, for instance.

Surveys of both state residents and tourists have shown that beach activities, outdoor pool use and golf are among the most popular forms of leisure activity in Florida. There are threats to the continued enjoyment of beach activities, though, as beach erosion and continuing beach development curtail the number of areas open to the public. Many areas along both the Gulf coast and the Atlantic coast have been eaten up by developers who have constructed high-rise condominiums, hotels and other buildings on what was once public beach property. It's not uncommon to have to drive for miles to find a small opening for public swimming between the buildings. And state planners warn that the situation will only worsen unless water access areas are acquired for public use.

Beginning with some of the most popular leisure activities, here is a look at what's in store for you in the Sunshine State.

Outside the Home

Golf

When it comes to golf, apparently some men find few things in life more rewarding. A recent Ann Landers column cited a survey that asked men to choose between sex or their favorite athletic activity. Among golfers who were asked this question, many said they'd rather experience the joy of golf than the joy of sex.

There can be no doubt that golf has become a much more popular sport in recent years, and not just among men. The number of golfers has more than doubled in the past two decades, and many golfers scramble to find places to play, line up tee-off times well in advance and at times play with three other players they don't know. All this for the sake of trying to get a white ball into a hole yards away in as few strokes as possible while trying to maintain a sense of humor and resisting the temptation to throw the clubs into the water hazard that claimed the last half dozen balls.

Florida may be the perfect place to fulfill

those fantasies of playing as much golf as possible. If, for example, your dream vacation is playing golf in warm weather during the winter or spending much of your retirement on the golf course, Florida can be tempting. The state leads the nation in the number of golf courses (it has about 1,100 of them) and also has become the most-sought-after place for golf vacations. And it offers such a variety of courses that you'll likely be able to find a greens fee that matches your wallet.

A market study done by the National Golf Foundation (NGF) of Jupiter, Fla., and Market Facts Inc. found that Florida was the No. 1 golfer vacation spot, followed by South Carolina and Arizona. And even more encouraging news for the state's tourism industry: Interest in U.S. golf keeps growing. A 1992 NGF survey showed that the number of golfers has grown substantially from 1970, when there were 11.2 million golfers. By the early 1990s, the number had swelled to 24.8 million. In an attempt to meet the growing demand, the number of golf facilities has risen each year since 1970 — from 10,188 in 1970 to 13,004 in 1991.

Who is the average U.S. golfer? The NGF does periodic surveys to find out. The most recent results: 77.8 percent of all U.S. golfers are male; 7.4 percent are 12-17 years old, 26.7 percent are 18-29 years, 26.1 percent 30-39 years, 17.5 percent 40-49 years, 9.1 percent 50-59 years, 4.2 percent 60-64 years and 9 percent 65 years and older.

Also, 77.6 percent of all golfers have household incomes of $30,000 and above, and 96.1 percent are from households where the head of the household is at least a high school graduate. Broken down by region, 5.5 percent of all golfers come from New England; 13.9 percent from the Middle Atlantic; 24.9 percent from the East North Central region; 10.1 percent from the West North Central region; 14.8 percent from the South Atlantic; 3.4 percent from the East South Central region; 7.5 percent from the West South Central region; 6.1 percent from the Mountain region; and 13.8 percent from the Pacific region.

In recent years, more women have taken to the game. In 1991, for example, women accounted for 41 percent of the 2.25 million individuals who entered the game during the year. Another trend: the sharp rise in the average household income among all golfers — from $49,900 in 1990 to $53,000 in 1991.

Florida has the highest percentage of golfers age 50 and over and has the highest average golfer age. Following is a table showing the total number of golfers in each state, the percentage of golfers aged 50 and above, the average golfer age, the mean golfer household income in thousands of dollars and the number of rounds each golfer plays annually:

	Total golfers	Percentage of golfers Age 50 +	Average golfer age	Mean golfer household income	Rounds played yearly
Ala.	213,332	33.6	40.9	40.5	29.4
Ariz.	324,753	36.7	42.6	39.2	26.8
Ark.	117,725	38.9	43.2	33.2	38.6
Calif.	2,364,909	33.4	41.0	51.6	25.1
Colo.	390,688	25.7	36.9	44.7	19.5
Conn.	334,403	29.0	39.1	53.3	21.9
Del.	51,259	37.2	41.0	46.1	26.6
D.C.	23,044	*	*	*	*
Fla.	1,171,635	42.6	45.6	37.7	36.0
Ga.	428,738	25.0	38.2	48.6	23.8
Idaho	123,728	14.0	34.5	36.3	15.4
Ill.	1,485,815	19.0	35.8	45.8	17.8
Ind.	655,824	20.7	37.0	42.5	19.0
Iowa	403,575	27.1	38.6	38.6	24.4
Kan.	313,144	25.4	37.0	38.2	17.9
Ky.	326,579	25.7	37.1	38.3	20.7
La.	250,545	19.9	34.4	40.8	24.5
Maine	98,561	35.4	42.5	38.9	24.9
Md.	377,325	24.9	37.8	55.1	19.7
Mass.	601,110	20.1	36.0	50.2	17.9
Mich.	1,279,734	23.7	36.7	48.8	17.7
Minn.	664,005	17.9	35.5	40.1	15.1

	Total golfers	Percentage of golfers Age 50 +	Average golfer age	Mean golfer household income	Rounds played yearly
Miss.	104,151	18.2	33.2	32.2	25.1
Mo.	417,787	13.7	35.2	40.4	13.5
Mont.	79,339	20.0	36.4	33.3	15.2
Neb.	171,462	16.0	35.0	35.4	18.3
Nev.	114,875	19.4	37.1	52.0	22.2
N.H.	89,733	10.6	34.7	42.9	20.2
N.J.	661,710	27.3	39.1	53.7	17.8
N.M.	170,629	23.6	36.9	46.1	29.8
N.Y.	1,660,393	28.1	39.8	44.7	20.8
N.C.	584,846	25.6	38.8	39.7	23.9
N.D.	95,922	23.5	34.5	30.6	11.4
Ohio	1,359,875	26.8	38.3	43.0	18.5
Okla.	263,533	19.4	36.7	41.0	24.2
Ore.	285,079	24.9	39.2	37.4	15.6
Pa.	897,000	25.1	37.2	40.7	17.2
R.I.	69,351	38.2	41.3	41.3	24.1
S.C.	286,008	32.3	40.1	38.7	32.0
S.D.	82,879	33.3	39.2	33.6	21.9
Tenn.	295,548	24.6	37.5	41.7	23.3
Texas	1,560,940	19.0	35.7	47.3	19.3
Utah	241,578	15.8	34.4	38.2	13.9
Vt.	49,793	14.9	33.9	45.2	16.4
Va.	451,024	26.8	38.3	49.7	18.7
Wash.	486,837	22.0	37.3	41.0	13.7
W.Va.	107,288	29.1	38.0	33.8	20.6
Wis.	748,207	26.1	39.8	38.9	17.5
Wyo.	63,778	27.3	38.5	44.6	27.2

* Insufficient data

These figures are excerpted from a report called, "Golf Participation in the United States," based on a U.S. survey conducted by Market Facts Inc. for the National Golf Foundation.

Golfers aged 60 and above comprise a sizable portion of all American golfers — 13.2 percent, or nearly 3.3 million golfers, as of 1991. Again, males accounted for most of the senior golf population, nearly 72 percent.

Other facts about senior golfers, according to the NGF:

— More than 55 percent of all senior golfers come from households with incomes less than $40,000.

— Males account for 71.8 percent of the senior golf population, compared with 77.8 percent of all golfers.

— Seniors appear to be from households where the head had less education than his or her counterparts who are younger — 62 percent of the seniors' heads of households had "some college" or were college graduates, compared with 71.4 percent for the total golf population.

— Senior golfers average 44.9 rounds of golf annually and account for more than 30 percent of all rounds of golf played in the United States.

Major Professional Golfers Association tournaments in Florida

Many professional golf tournaments are played in Florida during the year. Below are the months and places that PGA, Senior PGA, Ben Hogan and Ladies Professional Golf Association (LPGA) tournaments have been scheduled in the past. Some schedules change from year to year. For up-to-date information on the PGA and the Senior PGA, call 904-285-3700. For LPGA schedules, call 904-254-8800.

PGA tour

March: Doral Ryder Open, Miami; Honda Classic, Fort Lauderdale; Nestle Invitational, Orlando; THE PLAYERS Championship, Ponte Verde Beach.

October: Walt Disney World/Oldsmobile Classic, Orlando.
December: JCPenney Classic, Palm Harbor.

Senior PGA tour

Late January and Early February: Royal Caribbean Classic, Key Biscayne.
February: The IntelliNet Challenge, Naples; GTE Suncoast Classic, Tampa.
April: PGA Seniors Championship, Palm Beach Gardens.
Late October and Early November: Emerald Coast Classic, Pensacola.

LPGA tour

Late January and Early February: Oldsmobile LPGA Classic, Lake Worth.
February: The Phar-Mor at Inverrary, Lauderhill.
Late April and Early May: Centel Classic, Tallahassee.
December: JCPenney Classic, Tarpon Springs.

Boating

You're living on Cape Cod, and it's the middle of March.

December, January and February — the Dark Ages to all sensible sailors — have passed. You're in the boatyard, sanding the anti-fouling paint off the bottom of the old Clorox bottle and scraping barnacles off the propeller shaft. You're gazing through steamed-up goggles, and breathing through a surgical mask to avoid ingesting too much dust from the old paint. It's late afternoon and the temperature has dropped to 38 degrees. You wonder why more sane people aren't out there beside you scraping and sanding and looking like the Blob from Winter Past, covered with copper dust, wheezing, sneezing and wearing a smile as wide as Hyannis Harbor.

Ah, the sweet smell of spring! It's an annual rite. But after a few years of growing increasingly attached to the boat, you join others in asking yourself why on earth you put yourself through six months of abject deprivation while your most prized possession sits unattended on a slab of wood.

Welcome to Florida. It's a boater's paradise, offering the opportunity to indulge in your favorite pastime year-round on the ocean, the Intracoastal Waterway, rivers and lakes. Available to you are 8,426 statute miles of tidal shoreline and, according to the Marine Industries Association of South Florida in Fort Lauderdale, nearly 4,500 square miles of inland water. And you'll have plenty of company. About 700,000 boats were registered in Florida in 1992.

Any boat that is 16 feet or longer, or any boat that has a motor, must be registered with the state Department of Natural Resources. Any boat that is in Florida for more than 90 days also must be registered. The fees are paid to county tax collectors, who charge an extra $2.25 service fee and pass the money on to the state. Boats are registered for annual decals from June 1 to July 15. Here are the fees:

— For a boat up to 12 feet in length with a motor, $6.75.
— 12 to 16 feet, $13.75.
— 16 to 26 feet, $21.75.
— 26 to 40 feet, $53.75.
— 40 to 65 feet, $85.75.
— 65 to 110 feet, $101.75.
— 110 feet and over, $125.75.

Some counties impose extra fees as well, up to 50 percent of the state fee.

There are no property taxes on boats in Florida unless you live on a stationary house boat as your primary residence. So to keep your boat in Florida, you pay the annual fee and that's it. If you bought a $7.5 million 126-foot yacht from Broward Marine, resplendent with gold faucets, marble floors and sinks, silks, leather, suedes, and accommodations for eight plus five crew members, you'd still pay $125.75. But then there's the matter of dockage and, oh yes, $150,000 per year to pay for the crew, according to the manufacturer.

Florida in recent years has had the fourth-highest number of boats registered, behind Michigan, California and Minnesota, though registrations are not uniform among the states. If all boats in Florida were registered, including sailboards and small sailboats, the state's listed inventory would likely increase by another 150,000 boats.

Florida is Number One in the nation in sales. In recent years about 100 boats have been registered here every day. Twice as many are sold in Florida than in California. The Florida Department of Revenue says that sales of boats and other marine activity account for more than $2 billion a year.

Gross sales typically are highest in Broward County, followed by Dade, Pinellas and Palm Beach. Sales in these four counties have accounted for as much as half the state total. The high level of sales in southeast Florida is a result not only of population and tourism, but of a heavy concentration of boat brokers. There's a lot of big money in this part of the state; at major boat shows, sleek, modern, 100-footers abound.

The South Florida boat industry took quite a hit from Hurricane Andrew in 1992, however. Many boats in Dade County ended up aground

— either on shore or inland. A lot were smashed to smithereens. Soundings, the boating newspaper, reported boat-damage estimates as high as $500 million.

The average boat bought in the United States is roughly 16 feet long, but marine industry experts say the average is higher in Florida, largely because many buyers here are more affluent. Geography also is a factor. Broward, Dade and Palm Beach counties are the top sales area because the Bahamas are close. Some islands are only 50 miles off the Florida coast; an owner can hop on a large power boat and be there in just a few hours. This is also a reason why powerboats are much more popular than sailboats. That same trip to an island on a sailboat, depending on the direction and strength of the wind, ordinarily will take hours longer, or even a day or more. In addition, the waters around the islands are shallow, and most large sailboats need deeper water than powerboats.

Dockage fees vary greatly throughout the state. You will pay much more on the southeast coast than you will in the Panhandle. It's a supply-and-demand situation, and very little undeveloped waterfront property exists on the Gold Coast.

Here are some comparisons for a 30-foot powerboat.

In Fort Lauderdale, at one of the most expensive marinas, you will pay 95 cents per running foot (for each of the 30 feet) every day in the off-season, from May through September. In season, from October through April, the rate will more than double, to $2 per running foot each day. That's $28.50 per day in the off-season and $60 per day in season. That's $4,360.50 for the off-season and $12,720 for the high season. But if you keep the boat there year-round, you will get a 25 percent discount. That's $17,080.50 per year minus the 25 percent. Your total annual cost: $12,810.38.

If you keep the boat at a typical large marina on Tampa Bay, you will pay a flat rate of $184 per month. Your total annual cost: $2,208.

And if you want a wet slip at a marina in Panama City, you will pay $150 per month. But if you have an annual contract, you will pay for just 11 of the 12 months. Total annual cost: $1,650.

Many marinas also use dry-stack storage. A forklift puts the boat on racks, which may be up to a half dozen levels high. When you want the boat in the water, you call the marina office. Half an hour to 45 minutes later, the boat's off the rack, afloat and ready for you. Because waterfront land is at such a premium, this is the only way that many marinas have been able to expand. And some are able to lift and store speedboats as long as 40 feet.

Costs for this type of storage vary, too.

One popular marina in downtown Fort Lauderdale uses a sliding scale. For boats up to 20 feet in length, the monthly fee year-round is $110. For boats up to 40 feet in length, the monthly fee is $420.

In Panama City, monthly fees at a typical marina range from $80 to $120 per month for boats up to 30 feet in length. Those are stored on stacks in a barn, known as inside dry storage. Outdoor stack storage ranges up to $80 per month.

Speeding on the Waterways

Florida is a haven for boat racing. Aside from competitions such as the Southern Ocean Racing Conference — a popular offshore race involving some of the world's fastest and most colorful sailboats — grand-prix powerboat races abound. (Call the Marine Industries Association of South Florida at 305-524-2733 for up-to-date schedules of races.)

But there is a lot of other speeding on the waterways that has become very controversial. More than 100 people typically die in Florida boating accidents each year. Efforts to educate boaters and tighten restrictions have been pressed for years.

In addition, scores of manatees have been killed, many after being struck by propellers. In response, the state a few years ago ordered new boating speed limits in 13 counties that have manatee zones — Brevard, Broward, Citrus, Collier, Dade, Duval, Indian River, Lee, Martin, Palm Beach, Sarasota, St. Lucie and Volusia. State officials told the counties that unless they adopted their own rules, the speed limits would be set at 35 miles per hour in marked navigation channels during the daytime and 20 miles per hour at night.

As a result of these problems, the state and local officials have been setting speed limits in the other counties as well. They vary by county.

Also controversial has been the misuse of personal watercraft (trademark Jet Skis), which can best be described as motorcycles on water. They are fast, and some youths have taken to wake-jumping — riding behind bigger boats and jumping over their wakes. As many as a dozen youths have been killed on such craft in a year. Under legislation passed in 1989, lifejackets must be worn on such craft; you can't run them at night (30 minutes after sunset until 30 minutes before sunrise); and you have to be 14 or older to operate one. If you're 13 and you're caught, you'll have to pay a $35 fine by mail. If you're an adult and you lend your machine to a 13-year-old, you'll be arrested and be subject to a $500 fine and 60 days in jail.

Fishing

The popularity of fishing in the Sunshine State has spawned new regulations to protect a growing number of endangered species and to provide more funding for marine research and environmental programs. As fish are taken from Florida's waters each year, concern grows that there are not enough of every species to go around for everyone. Consequently, some of the newest regulations call for limiting the number and size of some catches. Both saltwater and freshwater fishermen are now required to be licensed and many have to pay a fee for this license. The fees help fund conservation and preservation efforts.

Saltwater fishing licenses: Both residents and nonresidents, with some exceptions, are required to get a license to take or possess any marine fish. These licenses are issued by the Department of Environmental Protection, through local tax collectors' offices and many bait and tackle shops. Residents can be issued either a 10-day license for $10 or an annual one for $12. Nonresidents have the option of a three-day license for $5, a seven-day license for $15 or an annual license for $30. In addition, a $1.50 tax collector's fee is added on to every saltwater fishing license, while another 50-cent "subagent's fee" is added on if one buys a license at bait and tackle shops. Among those exempt are: 1. any person under 16; 2. any Florida resident fishing in saltwater from land or a structure fixed to land; 3. any person fishing from a vessel issued a Vessel Saltwater Fishing License; 4. an individual aboard a vessel that has a valid Saltwater Products License. Only one individual can claim this exemption at any given time; 5. any person 65 or older; 6. any person accepted by the Department of Health and Rehabilitative Services for developmental services; 7. any resident who is a member of the armed forces, is home on leave for 30 days or less and has valid orders in his or her possession; 8. any person fishing from a licensed fishing pier; and 9. any resident who is certified as being totally and permanently disabled. This person is entitled to receive a permanent saltwater fishing license without charge from the county tax collector.

Any owner, operator or custodian of a charter fishing vessel also must be licensed. Fees range from $200 to $800 a year, depending on the number of customers the vessel is licensed to carry.

The fees collected are used for improving and restoring fish habitats, building artificial reefs, researching marine life and its habitats, tightening enforcement and educating the public about the state's natural resources.

Recreational bag limits: Daily bag limits, which are instituted to restrict the number of fish of one type a fisherman can keep so that no one gets a disproportionate number of fish and to ensure that various species are protected, have been in existence for a number of saltwater species. In addition, local regulations may exist. It is therefore advisable to contact the Florida Marine Patrol District Office nearest the location where you will be fishing.

The following restrictions apply for those taking fish for personal use and do not cover commercial harvesting. Among species with size limits and closed seasons, as of 1994, are: amberjack (28 inches fork); black drum (not less than 14 inches or more than 24 inches); sea bass (8 inches); billfish (sailfish, 57 inches; blue marlin, 86 inches; and white marlin, 62 inches); bluefish (12 inches fork); bonefish (18 inches); hard clams (1-inch thick); cobia (ling) (33 inches fork); blue crab (5 inches carapace); stone crab (2 3/4-inch claw and closed season between May 15 and Oct. 15); crawfish (more than a 3-inch carapace (the shield on the back of the crawfish) and closed season April 1 - Aug. 5); dolphin (20-inch size limit for sale); red drum (redfish) (not less than 18 inches or more than 27 inches and closed season March, April and May); flounder (11 inches); grouper (20 inches); king mackerel (20 inches fork); Spanish mackerel (12 inches); oysters (3 inches and closed season June, July and August in Dixie and Levy counties and July, August and September in all other areas); pompano (10 inches); scallops (closed season April 1-June 30); red snapper (14 inches on Gulf Coast and 20 inches on Atlantic Coast); schoolmaster, (10 inches); gray (mangrove) (10 inches); lane (8 inches); vermillion (8 inches on Gulf Coast and 10 inches on Atlantic Coast); mutton snapper, (16 inches); red porgy (12 inches on Atlantic Coast); hogfish (12 inches fork); all other snapper (12 inches); snook (not less than 24 inches or more than 34 inches and closed season Dec. 15 - Jan. 31, June, July and August); and spotted sea trout (spotted weakfish) (not less than 14 inches or more than 24 inches).

Where to find what: The Florida Marine Fisheries Commission constantly reviews and revises many marine fishery laws. For information on pending rules, contact the commission at 2540 Executive Center Circle West, 106

Douglas Building, Tallahassee, 32301. Also contact any of the 11 Florida Marine Patrol District offices — in Panama City Beach, Carrabelle, Homosassa Springs, Tampa, Fort Myers, Miami, Titusville, Jacksonville Beach, Marathon, Jupiter and Pensacola.

As a general rule, the warm Gulf Stream waters and associated currents provide subtropical environmental conditions along the east coast south of Cape Canaveral. Northern coastlines receive less of this current's moderating influence and are classified as "warm temperate." In addition, changing seasons affect the migration of Florida's saltwater fish. In the spring, for example, there is a migration of Spanish and king mackerel northward along both coasts of the state. During the winter, however, these fish are prominent from Fort Pierce to Boynton Beach in the Atlantic Ocean and off Naples and Fort Myers in the Gulf of Mexico.

Florida saltwater sportfishing areas: The following fish are found in these areas of the state at various times of the year:

Panhandle region

Spring: Amberjack, barracuda, cobia, bluefish, king mackerel, pompano, sea trout, sheepshead, red snapper, grouper and redfish.

Summer: Amberjack, marlin, bonito, sailfish, dolphin, barracuda, king mackerel, tarpon, cobia, flounder, sea trout, Spanish mackerel, grouper, red snapper and snapper.

Fall: Amberjack, marlin, sailfish, dolphin, barracuda, sea trout, sheepshead, Spanish mackerel, redfish, drum, grouper, snapper, cobia, flounder and bluefish.

Winter: Redfish, sheepshead, grouper, snapper, sea trout, drum and bluefish.

Upper northeast region

Spring: King mackerel, dolphin, cobia, pompano, sea trout, bluefish, redfish, mangrove snapper, sheepshead, Spanish mackerel, barracuda, tarpon, grouper and snapper.

Summer: Spanish mackerel, sea trout, cobia, flounder, redfish, tarpon, grouper, snapper, mangrove snapper and barracuda.

Fall: King mackerel, sea trout, flounder, bluefish, drum, grouper, snapper, tarpon, mangrove snapper and redfish.

Winter: Sheepshead, sea trout, grouper and snapper.

Central East Coast

Spring: Amberjack, bonito, dolphin, sailfish, wahoo, bonefish, cobia, flounder, sea trout, redfish, snook, tarpon, grouper, snapper, pompano, king mackerel, Spanish mackerel, barracuda, blackfin tuna and bluefish.

Summer: Amberjack, dolphin, sailfish, bonefish, sea trout, barracuda, tarpon, cero mackerel, Spanish mackerel, flounder, redfish, grouper, snapper, cobia, bonito, wahoo, bluefish and blackfin tuna.

Fall: Sailfish, dolphin, wahoo, marlin, bonefish, redfish, tarpon, snook, amberjack, sea trout, king mackerel, Spanish mackerel, grouper, snapper, cobia, mangrove snapper, flounder and sheepshead.

Winter: Sailfish, dolphin, wahoo, marlin, barracuda, redfish, tarpon, snook, cobia, mangrove snapper, bonefish, sea trout, grouper, snapper, blackfin tuna, cero mackerel, sheepshead and Spanish mackerel.

Gulf Coast

Spring: Sailfish, dolphin, wahoo, barracuda, bluefish, king mackerel, pompano, Spanish mackerel, redfish, tripletail, snook, sea trout, grouper, snapper and drum.

Summer: Sailfish, dolphin, amberjack, barracuda, Spanish mackerel, sea trout, whiting and pompano.

Fall: Sailfish, dolphin, wahoo, bluefish, king mackerel, sea trout, sheepshead, bluefish, redfish, snook, Spanish mackerel and whiting.

Winter: Sailfish, dolphin, wahoo, barracuda, blackfin tuna, sea trout, redfish, bonito, sheepshead and drum.

Southeast Atlantic Coast

Spring: Sailfish, bluefish, pompano, sheepshead, sea trout, grouper and snapper.

Summer: Sailfish, amberjack, bonito, dolphin, bluefish, king mackerel, Spanish mackerel, tarpon, grouper, snapper and flounder.

Fall: Sailfish, drum, flounder, king mackerel, Spanish mackerel, sheepshead, sea trout, redfish, snapper and grouper.

Winter: Sailfish, drum, flounder, bluefish, redfish, sheepshead, sea trout, grouper and snapper.

Freshwater fishing licenses: Again, residents and nonresidents are required to obtain these for fishing in the state's freshwater areas. The exemptions for this license are similar to the saltwater license exemptions. Resident fees are $12 a year. Nonresident fees are either $15 for a seven-consecutive-day license or $30 for an annual license. Residents also can obtain a combination freshwater fishing and hunting license for $22 a year. In addition, tax collectors can issue a $1 fee and their subagents a 50-cent fee on top of this.

Those not required to get a freshwater fishing license include: 1. Any person under 16; 2. Any person 65 or older. Senior citizens are required to carry a Senior Citizen Hunting and Fishing Certificate, which is available free of charge from county tax collectors; 3. Any person accepted by the Department of Health and Rehabilitative Services as a client for retardation services (with proof); 4. Any resident who is a member of the armed forces who is not stationed in Florida and is home on leave for 30 days or less may sport-fish without a license; 5. Any person possessing a resident/commerical fishing license is not required to purchase a resident fishing license; and 6. Anyone certified as being totally and permanently disabled. These residents can obtain a free certificate from county tax collectors.

No licenses are required to fish in private fishing ponds — man-made ponds of 20 acres or less, constructed for the primary purpose of fishing and entirely within the property lines of the owner. And, no license is required for a resident to fish in his county of residence with poles or hand lines that are not equipped with a reel. Meanwhile, a fishing license IS required to fish by any method in a state Fish Management Area.

Licenses can be purchased at many fish camps, bait dealers, sporting goods stores and hardware stores.

The fees collected here go into the State Game Trust Fund and are used to preserve and enhance the state's freshwater fish and wildlife resources.

Bag and length limit restrictions apply for the following freshwater species: black bass, including largemouth, Suwannee, redeye, spotted and shoal basses; striped bass, white bass and sunshine bass; chain pickerel; panfish, including bluegill, speckled perch, shellcracker, spotted sunfish, warmouth and redfin pickerel; and butterfly peacock bass. Fisher-

men are also required to release all speckled peacock bass. There are specific regulations for various lakes, ponds and other freshwater fishing areas of the state. Check with local Florida Game and Fresh Water Fish Commission officials for the latest regulations.

What to catch and where to catch it: Florida has more than 7,000 lakes of 10 or more acres and about 1,711 streams. There are public fishing camps and boat launching facilities in all 67 counties. The most popular freshwater game fish in the state is the largemouth bass. The bluegill is one of the most abundant game fish. The crappie is a favorite cold weather game fish. And sunshine bass is found in lakes and coastal rivers that produce an abundance of shad, their main food source.

All told, more than 24 gamefish species can be caught around the state.

Among some of the state's best freshwater fishing areas are:

Northwest region: Apalachicola River, Escambia River marsh, Blackwater River, Choctawhatchess River, Merritt's Mill Pond, Lake Talquin and Lake Jackson.Call 1-800-342-1676 for more information.

Northeast region: Orange Lake, Lochloosa Lake, Santa Fe River, Suwannee River and Newnans Lake. Call 1-800-342-8105.

Central region: Lake Poinsett, Lake Rousseau, Lake Butler, East Lake Tohopekaliga, Lake Kissimmee, Little Lake George, Lake Panasoffkee and Oklawaha River. Call 1-800-342-9620.

South region: Winter Haven Chain of Lakes, Lake Pierce, Lake Parker, Lake Tarpon, Lake Istokpoga and Lake Weohyakapka. Call 1-800-282-8002.

Everglades region: Lake Okeechobee, Everglades conservation areas, Lake Osborne, Lake Blue Cypress and Lake Trafford. Call 1-800-432-2046.

Record Freshwater Catches (As of March 1994)

Species	State Record
Largemouth bass	17.27 pounds (20.13 pounds*)
Redeye bass	7.83 pounds
Spotted bass	3.75 pounds
Suwannee bass	3.89 pounds
Striped bass	42.25 pounds
White bass	4.69 pounds
Sunshine bass	16.31 pounds
Butterfly peacock bass	9.08 pounds
Oscar	2.34 pounds
Black crappie	3.83 pounds

Flier	1.24 pounds
Bluegill	2.95 pounds
Redbreast sunfish	2.08 pounds
Redear sunfish	4.86 pounds
Spotted sunfish	0.83 pounds
Warmouth	2.44 pounds
Chain pickerel	8 pounds*
Redfin pickerel	1.05 pounds
Carp	40.56 pounds
Channel catfish	44.5 pounds
Flathead catfish	33.09 pounds
White catfish	18.88 pounds
Blue catfish	53 pounds
Brown bullhead	3.44 pounds
Bowfin	19 pounds
American shad	5.19 pounds
Alligator gar	122 pounds
Longnose gar	41 pounds
Florida gar	7 pounds

Most of these are certified state record fish that have been identified by a Florida Game and Fresh Water Fish Commission biologist and have been weighed on a certified scale. Records with an asterisk (*) are uncertified state records. These are believed to be accurate based on reliable witnesses and other evidence but are not certifiable or were caught by other than legal sport fishing methods.

For more information: Contact the Florida Game and Fresh Water Fish Commission, 620 S. Meridian St., Tallahassee, 32399-1600 (phone 904-488-1960). Also, call toll-free for information about obtaining fishing licenses, fishing locations, boat ramps and handicapped access, 1-800-ASKFISH.

Hunting

There are a number of areas across the state where hunting is permitted. Hunting of such game as deer, wild hog, turkey, black bear, quail, rabbit, raccoon, opossum, coyote, nutria, skunk, beaver and squirrel is allowed, with limited hunting seasons and bag limits for some game.

Among the regions of the state where hunting is permitted are Wildlife Management Areas and national wildlife refuges. Management areas of two types: Type I, or public hunting and recreation areas operated by the Florida Game and Fresh Water Fish Commission in cooperation with private, state and federal landowners. A $25 Wildlife Management Area Stamp is required to hunt here (except for those who are exempt). And Type II — areas operated by the landowner in cooperation with the commission. Fees and regulations vary among these regions. Regulation brochures are available from county tax collectors, the commission and private landowners. The commission, based in Tallahassee, also has five regional offices, including one in Panama City (phone number 904-265-3676), Lake City (904-758-0525), Ocala (904-732-1225), Lakeland (813-648-3203) and West Palm Beach (407-640-6100).

There are literally hundreds of thousands of acres set aside as public hunting and recreation areas in the state including areas that are federally and privately owned. Among the largest sites are in the Everglades (nearly 672,000 acres); Big Cypress (nearly 566,000 acres); and Apalachicola (558,000 acres).

To take game or fur-bearing animals in Florida, a valid hunting license, or a sportsman's license, is required. Fees are $11 for an annual resident hunting license; $150 for an annual nonresident hunting license, or $25 for a nonresident license for 10 consecutive days ($121 for Georgia residents); and $66 for a resident sportsman's license. A tax collector's fee and/or subagent's fee is also added to the cost of these licenses. A sportsman's license includes all resident licenses and stamps for fishing and hunting except the Federal Duck Stamp, the trapping license, other commercial license or saltwater fishing license.

There are a number of people who are exempt from having to buy a license or a stamp:

— People hunting in their county of residence on their homestead or the homestead of their spouse or minor child, or any minor child hunting on the homestead of his parents.

— Residents 65 or older who have a Resident Senior Citizen Hunting and Fishing Certificate. These can be obtained from county tax collectors.

— Those who are totally and permanently disabled and who have a Florida Resident Disabled Person Hunting and Fishing License. Disabled residents must present certification to the county tax collector from a licensed Florida physician or from the U.S. Veterans Administration, the U.S. Social Security Administration or from the U.S. Armed Services showing he or she is totally and permanently disabled.

— Those under 16 years old.

Baseball Fever

February signals baseball fever in Florida — 20 of the major league's 28 teams open their spring training camps in the state. By March, the schedule is in full swing as teams pare down their squads in time for opening day of the regular season in early April. The teams' stay is short and the games are only exhibitions, but this doesn't deter people — many of them retirees — who want to catch an early glimpse of their favorite team. It's often not easy finding a ticket for a game on the day of your choice — many games are sellouts. Consequently, early ticket purchases are suggested.

And, in 1993, Florida became host to a professional baseball team for the regular baseball season — The Florida Marlins, an expansion National League team playing at Joe Robbie Stadium in Miami.

Here's where the teams that come to Florida during the spring in recent years have been playing, along with addresses for ticket information and schedules. Spring training sites change on occasion, so it's best to check ahead of time:

Florida Marlins — Space Coast Stadium, 5800 Stadium Parkway, Melbourne, 32940.

Boston Red Sox — The City of Palms Park, 2201 Edison Ave., Fort Myers, 33901.

Houston Astros — Osceola County Stadium, 1000 Osceola Blvd., Kissimmee, 32743.

Toronto Blue Jays — Dunedin Stadium, 311 Douglas Ave., Dunedin, 34698.

Atlanta Braves — Municipal Stadium, 715 Hank Aaron Drive, P.O. Box 2619, West Palm Beach, 33402.

St. Louis Cardinals — Al Lang Stadium, 180 Second Ave. S.E., St. Petersburg, 33701.

Los Angeles Dodgers — Holman Stadium, Dodgertown, 4001 26th St., Vero Beach, 32960.

Montreal Expos — Municipal Stadium, 715 Hank Aaron Drive, West Palm Beach, 33402.

New York Mets — St. Lucie County Sports Complex, 525 N.W. Peacock Blvd., Port St. Lucie, 34986.

Baltimore Orioles — Al Lang Stadium, 180 Second Ave. S.E., St. Petersburg, 33701.

Philadelphia Phillies — Jack Russell Stadium, 800 Phillies Drive, Clearwater, 34617.

Pittsburg Pirates — McKechnie Field, 17th Avenue West and 9th St. West, Bradenton, 34205.

Texas Rangers — Charlotte County Stadium, 2300 El Jobean Road, Port Charlotte, 33948.

Cincinnati Reds — Plant City Stadium, P.O. Box 2275, Plant City, 33564.

Cleveland Indians — Chain O'Lakes Park, Cypress Gardens Boulevard, Winter Haven, 33880.

Kansas City Royals — Baseball City Stadium, 300 Stadium Way, Davenport, 33837.

Detroit Tigers — Joker Marchant Stadium, Lakeland Hills Blvd., Lakeland, 33801.

Minnesota Twins — Lee County Sports Complex, 14100 Six Mile Cypress Parkway, Fort Myers, 33912.

Chicago White Sox — Ed Smith Stadium Sports Complex, P.O. Box 1702, Sarasota, 34230.

New York Yankees — Fort Lauderdale Stadium, 5301 N.W. 12th Ave., Fort Lauderdale, 33309. (The team was expected to move to the Tampa area in 1996).

Other Major Sports

Football

Florida hosts three National Football League teams, and a number of college teams — some of which have been ranked by the Associated Press and other sportswriters among the top 10 in the country in recent years:

Miami Dolphins, Miami.
Tampa Bay Buccaneers, Tampa.
Jacksonville Jaguars, Jacksonville.

Major college teams:
University of Miami, Miami.
Florida State University, Tallahassee.
University of Florida, Gainesville.
Florida Agricultural & Mechanical University, Tallahassee.
University of Central Florida, Orlando.

In addition, five football bowl games are played in Florida:

Gator Bowl — Played in Jacksonville in late December.
Orange Bowl — Played in Miami at the Or-

ange Bowl on New Year's Day. (The last game at the Orange Bowl will be played on Jan. 1, 1996, after which the bowl game will be moved to Joe Robbie Stadium in Miami.)

Carquest Bowl — Played in Miami at Joe Robbie Stadium on New Year's Day.

Citrus Bowl — Played in Orlando on New Year's Day.

Hall of Fame Bowl — Played in Tampa on New Year's Day.

Hockey

Tampa Bay Lightning, Tampa.
Florida Panthers, Miami.

Basketball

Florida also is the home of two National Basketball Association teams:

Orlando Magic, Orlando.
Miami Heat, Miami.

Trying To Beat the Odds

Greyhound Racing

There are a number of tracks around the state:

Biscayne Kennel Club, Miami Shores; **Bonita-Fort Myers Greyhound Track,** Bonita Springs; **Sports Palace,** Melbourne; **North American Racing,** Key West; **Daytona Beach Kennel Club,** Daytona Beach; **Hollywood Kennel Club,** Hallandale; **Palm Beach Kennel Club,** West Palm Beach; **Jacksonville Kennel Club,** also known as **Triangle Kennel Club,** Jacksonville; **Jefferson County Kennel Club,** also known as **JCKC,** Monticello; **Orange Park Kennel Club,** Clay County; **Pensacola Greyhound Track,** Pensacola; **St. John's County Greyhound,** Jacksonville; **St. Petersburg Kennel Club,** St. Petersburg; **Sanford-Orlando Kennel Club,** Longwood; **Sarasota Kennel Club,** Sarasota; **Seminole Racing,** Casselberry; **Tampa Kennel Club,** Tampa; **Washington County Kennel Club,** also known as **Ebro Kennel Club,** Ebro; **Flagler Kennel Club,** Miami.

Jai Alai

Dania Jai Alai, Dania; **Florida Jai Alai,** Fern Park, also known as **Orlando Jai Alai; Fort Pierce Jai Alai,** Fort Pierce; **The Fronton,** West Palm Beach, also known as **Palm Beach Jai Alai; Miami Jai Alai,** Miami; **Ocala Jai Alai,** Orange Lake; **Tampa Jai Alai,** Tampa.

Thoroughbred Racing

Calder Race Course and Tropical Park, Miami; **Gulfstream Park,** Hallandale (this also was the site of the 1989 and 1992 Breeders'

Cup Race); **Hialeah Park,** Hialeah; **Tampa Bay Downs,** Oldsmar.

Harness Racing

Pompano Park, Pompano Beach

Polo

Palm Beach Polo and Country Club, West Palm Beach (this is the site of the U.S. Polo Association Rolex Gold Cup and the Cadillac World Cup in March and April); **Gulfstream Polo Club,** Lake Worth; **Royal Palm Polo & Sports Club,** Boca Raton; **Central Florida Polo Club,** Orlando; **Cheval Polo Club,** Lutz; **New York Polo Club,** Lake Worth; **North Florida Polo Club,** Baldwin; **Ocala Polo Club,** Ocala; **Orlando Polo Club,** Orlando; **Oxford Polo Club,** Oxford; **Ponte Vedra Polo Club,** Jacksonville; **Tampa Bay Polo Club at Walden Lake,** Plant City; and **Windsor Polo Club,** Vero Beach.

Motorsports

Below are when the major racing events at Daytona International Speedway are held each year.

January or February: Rolex 24 at Daytona, IMSA World Sports Car Championship, is always held two weekends before the Daytona 500 and is never held earlier than Jan. 30 and 31 and never later than Feb. 5 and 6.

February: Daytona 500 is always held the Sunday before the third Monday in February and never earlier than Feb. 14 and never later than Feb. 20.

March: Daytona 200 by Arai AMA Motorcycle Classic (the culmination of Camel Motorcycle Week) is always held the third Sunday after the Daytona 500 and is never earlier than March 7 and never later than March 13.

July: Pepsi 400 NASCAR Winston Cup Series is always held the first Saturday in July and never earlier than July 1 and never later than July 7.

October: Fall Cycle Scene AMA Championship Cup Series Motorcycle Road Races are always held the weekend before the time changes (which occur on the last Sunday in October) and are never held earlier than October 16-18 and never later than Oct. 22-24.

December: World Karting Association Enduro World Championships Kart Road Races are always held Dec. 27-30 at Daytona International Speedway, while the short-track races are always held Dec. 26 through Dec. 29 at Municipal Stadium.

Outdoor Recreation Resources and Facilities

Because of the state's climate, almost everywhere you look there is some sort of outdoor recreational opportunity at your fingertips.

No point in the state is more than 70 miles from either the Atantic Ocean or the Gulf coast. And there are 7,000 natural and man-made lakes larger than 10 acres.

But Florida may lose its distinction of being a land of plenty. With continued influxes of people to the state, natural resources are being threatened. By 1995, it is estimated that the number of residents and tourists will average nearly 14.3 million a day.

An in-depth look at Florida's outdoor resources by the Department of Natural Resources suggests that Florida for now is able to supply its residents and visitors with a variety of recreational opportunties. But problems are looming as the rapid rise in population presents state recreation planners with a dilemma: While the influx of new residents is leading to more of a demand for recreational facilities and services, planners say, the state is running out of land and shoreline areas to meet the need. "The opportunities for providing these facilties and services will become more and more limited as the state's fixed supply of land, water, shoreline areas and cultural resources that support outdoor recreation are committed to non-recreation purposes necessary for the support of an expanding population," planners say.

Their concerns are voiced in a report, "Outdoor Recreation in Florida — 1989," which is a guideline for state recreational planning until 1994. This report, viewed as the state's comprehensive outdoor recreation plan, underlines that "greater coordination and cooperation must be established among...public and private recreation suppliers in Florida to maximize the total outdoor recreation effort."

This won't be easy. The availability of recreation areas to meet future needs has been sharply reduced in recent years by several culprits, not the least of which are pollution, competing land uses and land speculation. "Lands that are available are expensive, often prohibitively so, and land values continue to be forced upward by the pressure of population growth and economic development," the report says.

Today, the areas of the state where recreation land is most urgently needed are the more heavily populated parts "where the real estate market is more active and the land prices are at a premium," planners said. In addition to the problem of high cost, once a prime ocean beach area is developed for hotels or high-rise apartments, "it is effectively lost forever as a possible public park or outdoor recreation site."

"This is a serious matter throughout most of the state: the selection of choice outdoor recreation areas is limited and grows more limited with each passing day."

As a result, the state is placing a high premium on buying or leasing land: "It is extremely important to realize that whatever Florida is going to do in the way of acquiring new outdoor recreation lands must be done within the relatively near future...The years immediately ahead may afford virtually the last opportunity to set aside and preserve land areas of exceptional natural or cultural quality for perpetual public enjoyment."

During the 1980s, state officials conducted surveys asking residents and tourists which recreational activities they participated in the most. The latest survey showed that saltwater beach activities were the most popular form of outdoor recreation in Florida — for more than 61 percent of the state's residents and half its tourists. Next in popularity were swimming pool use, bicycle riding, visiting archaeological and historical sites, picnicking, saltwater fishing by boat, and golf.

Based on surveys and past experience, state recreation officials focused on 14 "resource-based" outdoor recreational activities — those that are dependent on the state's natural resources: saltwater beach activities, bicycle riding, freshwater beach activities, picnicking, saltwater and freshwater fishing by boat, camping (recreational vehicle/trailer and tent), saltwater and freshwater fishing (non-boat), visiting archaeological and historical sites, saltwater and freshwater boat ramp use, hiking, nature study, horseback riding, canoeing and hunting.

Also included were eight "user-oriented" outdoor activities — those that can be located on any open site, space permitting: outdoor swimming pool use, golf, tennis, baseball/softball, outdoor basketball, football/soccer, outdoor handball/racquetball and shuffleboard.

While state planners see potential for growth in many of these activities, those listed here face complicated problems:

Saltwater Beach activities — Identified as the most popular form of resource-based outdoor recreation in Florida, planners predict this popularity will continue to increase. Problem areas: Seashore property is generally the most expensive in the state, especially in urban areas where demand is greatest. Also, beach erosion "is a serious problem in Florida," planners say. More than 140 miles of beach are "critically imperiled by coastal erosion," planners estimate. "The result has been that the availability of suitable beach resources has declined while demand has increased steadily."

Bicycle Riding — "Enormous needs for bicycle trails are projected for Florida in the future. Of all the outdoor recreation activities surveyed, bicycle riding displays the widest distribution of need in the state," planners said. Problem areas: High construction costs of bicycle trails, coupled with limited available funds. The cost of constructing an 8-foot-wide asphalt trail is estimated at more than $50,000 per mile for urban trails. Bicyclists, consequently, are forced to use existing public roads designed for automobile traffic only. In 1987, nearly 6,500 accidents involving bicyclists occurred in the state, with 81 deaths, which made Florida second in the nation in bicycle accidents and fatalities.

Canoeing — Problem area: There exists a need for an improved recreation program to supply canoeists with detailed maps showing where access points and camping and other points of interests are located. "One of the greatest problems for the continued expansion and popularity of this activity is the maintenance of an aestetically pleasing environment in which to canoe," note planners.

Hunting — Extensive land areas are needed to support sufficient game to meet the demand and to provide for the safety of the hunters. Urban growth has curtailed the number of available sites.

Outdoor swimming pools — The greatest need still exists in the central and southern portions of the state.

Outdoor handball/racquetball — Surveys show a need for more courts along the heavily populated coastal regions.

A look at the supply of outdoor recreation resources and facilities shows why Florida has attracted and keeps attracting millions of people. The following figures include only those outdoor recreation resources contained within designated recreation areas, sites and facilities. These 1987 figures do not include Florida's territorial coastal waters (which comprise a surface area of more than 66.4 million acres), the state's 12,000 miles of freshwater rivers, streams and canals, or the 2.25 million acres of freshwater lake surface in the state.

Outdoor Recreation Resources and Facilities

Type	Unit	Amount
Hunting Land	Acres	6,873,169
Picnic Tables	Tables	119,284
Camping Sites (RV/trailer and tent)	Sites	123,857
Bicycle Trails	Miles	1,959.3
Canoe Trails	Miles	1,408.0
Hiking Trails	Miles	1,744.0
Horseback Riding Trails	Miles	383.3
Multipurpose Trails	Miles	409.7
Nature Trails	Miles	527.8
Archaeological/Historical Sites	Sites	320
Saltwater Beach Length	Miles	459.0
Freshwater Beach Length	Miles	48.0
Saltwater Piers	Piers	88
Freshwater Piers	Piers	31
Saltwater Boat Ramps	Lanes	1,232
Freshwater Boat Ramps	Lanes	1,761
Saltwater Marinas	Sites	1,201
Freshwater Marinas	Sites	344
Swimming Pools	Pools	1,865
Basketball Goals	Goals	4,984
Handball/Racquetball Courts	Courts	1,573
Shuffleboard Courts	Courts	4,782
Tennis Courts	Courts	8,043

Type	Unit	Amount
Baseball/Softball Fields	Fields	3,686
Football/Soccer Fields	Fields	967
Golf Holes	Holes	13,446
Equipped Play Areas	Areas	3,091
Recreation Centers	Sites	2,526

Source: "Outdoor Recreation in Florida - 1989," State of Florida Department of Natural Resources, Division of Recreation and Parks.

State Parks and Other State-Run Sites

Florida's state park system encompasses more than 100 parks and recreation areas as well as museums, ornamental gardens and historical or archaeological sites. Many of them offer campsites, picnicking facilities, swimming, fishing, nature walks, hiking trails and boat ramps. Many also have distinctive features not readily found elsewhere in the state — you can catch a glimpse of a manatee, take a guided tour through caverns or snorkel in an underwater park. In addition, primitive overnight camping is available in a number of state parks to youth groups. This is referred to below as youth tent camping. Adults can use the sites on a first-come, first-served basis if youth groups aren't using the sites.

Visiting a state-run site is a popular leisure activity in Florida — during 1990-91, a total of 12.8 million people did so — according to the state Department of Natural Resources.

Below is a brief description of what is offered at these sites:

STATE PARKS:

These are defined by the state as parks of "regional or statewide significance established to preserve the natural setting, while permitting a full program of compatible recreational activities." Parks are intended to attract visitors from long distances.

Northwest Florida

Blackwater River. 15 miles northeast of Milton, off U.S. 90; 30 campsites, picnicking, swimming, canoeing, freshwater fishing, nature/hiking trails, boat ramp. Park lies on one of the cleanest rivers in the United States.

Florida Caverns. 3 miles north of Marianna on S.R. 167; interpretive center, 32 campsites, youth tent camping, picnicking, swimming, freshwater fishing, nature/hiking trails, guided one-hour tours, boat ramp. Park contains network of caverns. Formations include sodas-traws, stalactites, stalagmites, columns, rimstone and flowstone.

Manatee Springs. 6 miles west of Chiefland on S.R. 320; 100 campsites, youth tent camping, picnicking, swimming, freshwater fishing, nature/hiking trails, canoe rentals during the summer, boat ramp; summer concessions. Manatees make rare appearances near mouth of Manatee Springs, where 116.9 million gallons of crystal-clear water flows daily.

Ochlockonee River. 4 miles south of Sopchoppy on U.S. 319; 30 campsites, youth tent camping, picnicking, swimming, freshwater and saltwater fishing, nature/hiking trails, boat ramp, scenic drive, summer ranger-guided walks and campfire programs. Ochlockonee River runs through the park, which is a 392-acre site characteristic of north Florida's Gulf Coast.

St. George Island. 10 miles southeast of Eastpoint off U.S. 98 via toll bridge; 60 campsites, youth tent camping, picnicking, swimming, shelling, saltwater fishing, nature/hiking trails, boat ramp, observation platforms. The oyster industry thrives here near the mouth of the Apalachicola River. Has more than nine miles of undeveloped beaches and dunes.

St. Joseph Peninsula. Near Port St. Joe, off S.R. 30, west of U.S. 98; 119 campsites, vacation cabins, youth tent camping, picnicking, swimming, saltwater fishing, nature/hiking trails, boat ramp, seasonal campfire programs and guided walks. Best known for its white sand beaches and huge barrier dunes. Park also is a prime birding area, with sightings of 209 species recorded. In the fall, this is one of best sites in the eastern United States to observe migrating hawks.

Torreya. Between Bristol and Greensboro, via S.R. 12 to S.R. 271 north; interpretive center, 35 campsites, youth tent camping, picnicking, freshwater fishing, campfire programs, nature/hiking trails, guided tours. Area characterized by steep bluffs, some rising more than 150 feet above the Apalachicola River, and deep ravines. Surrounding hardwoods provide the best display of fall color in Florida. Area was occupied by Indians and in 1849 planter Jason Gregory built the Gregory House across the river at Ocheesee Landing. The plantation prospered until the beginning of the Civil War. His house today stands within park boundaries.

Wakulla Springs, Edward Ball. Wakulla County, south on U.S. 319 to S.R. 61; picnicking, swimming, nature/hiking trails, glass-bottom and wildlife observation boat tours, concessions, overnight accommodations. Contains one of the world's largest and deepest freshwater springs. From glass-bottom boats, visitors may see the entrance of a cavern 120 feet below. A 27-room Spanish-style lodge, built in 1937 and featuring marble floors, ornate ceilings and antique furniture, also is located here.

Northeast Florida

Big Talbot Island. 20 miles east of downtown Jacksonville on A1A North, immediately north of Little Talbot Island State Park; canoeing, fishing, swimming, hiking trails, bird watching.

Faver-Dykes. 15 miles south of St. Augustine, east of U.S. 1 on Faver-Dykes Road; 30 campsites, youth tent camping, picnicking, fishing, nature/hiking trails, boat ramp. Has 752 acres of pine and hardwood forests bordering the tidal marshes along Pellicer Creek.

Fort Clinch. Fernandina Beach, 2601 Atlantic Ave.; interpretive center, 62 campsites, youth tent camping, picnicking, swimming, saltwater fishing, nature/hiking trails, guided tours of fort; Civil War-era re-enactments; seasonal campfire programs; boat ramp. (See historical forts section later in this chapter.)

Gold Head Branch, Mike Roess. 6 miles northeast of Keystone Heights on S.R. 21; 74 campsites, vacation cabins, youth tent camping, picnicking, swimming, freshwater fishing, nature/hiking trails; canoe rentals; seasonal campfire programs and guided walks; park contains four lakes and a mill site that is thought to have been used to grind meal and gin cotton.

Guana River. St. Augustine, 12 miles north on S.R. AIA; swimming, saltwater fishing, boat ramp. One of the newest additions to the state park system.

Ichetucknee Springs. 4 miles northwest of Fort White, off S.R. 47 north and on C.R. 238; picnicking, swimming, nature/hiking trails, canoe ramp, tubing/snorkeling, concessions. Site characterized by at least nine springs. Average total flow of all springs is about 233 million gallons of water daily with the water temperature at a constant 73 degrees Fahrenheit.

Little Talbot Island. 17 miles northeast of Jacksonville on S.R. A1A; 40 campsites, youth tent camping, picnicking, swimming, surfing, saltwater fishing, observation deck, seasonal campfire programs and guided walks. Area has sand dunes, and sea turtles occasionally nest on the beach.

O'Leno. 20 miles south of Lake City on U.S. 441; 64 campsites, youth tent camping, group camp, picnicking, swimming, freshwater fishing, canoeing, horseback riding, seasonal campfire programs, guided walks, nature/hiking trails, suspension bridge. Features a "river sink" where a portion of the Santa Fe River disappears and flows underground for more than three miles before again becoming a surface stream. Alligators and turtles are often seen in the area.

Suwannee River. 13 miles west of Live Oak on U.S. 90; 31 campsites, youth tent camping, picnicking, freshwater fishing, nature/hiking trails, boat ramp, overlook view of Withlacoochee and Suwannee rivers. Site of former town of Columbus, which housed a railroad bridge, ferry landing, large sawmill and cemetery. Portion of route of old stage road, which ran from Pensacola to Jacksonville and was major travel route in the early 1800s, is also here.

Central East Florida

Blue Spring. Orange City, 2 miles west on French Avenue; interpretive center, 51 campsites, vacation cabins, picnicking, swimming, freshwater fishing, nature/hiking trails, ranger-guided canoe tour of St. Johns River, canoe rentals, boat ramp, concessions. Park is winter gathering place for manatees, seen here from an observation platform from November through April, especially when the weather is colder. There also is a guided tour of a restored 1850s-era home on the grounds.

Bulow Creek. North of Ormond Beach, 3351 Old Dixie Highway; freshwater fishing, two picnic tables and nature/hiking trails. 5,000-acre park, consisting of coastal hardwood forests and hammock and salt marsh. Attraction here is the Fairchild Oak Tree, believed to be more than 800 years old.

Hontoon Island. 6 miles west of DeLand, off S.R. 44; 24 campsites, primitive cabins, picnicking, nature/hiking trails. Area accessible only by private boat or a passenger ferry that operates free of charge from 9 a.m. until one hour before sundown. Park has 80-foot observation tower, a replica of large owl totem carved by the Indians more than 600 years ago, and a large Indian mound that contained the remnants of Indian life years ago.

Jonathan Dickinson. 13 miles south of Stuart on U.S. 1; 135 campsites, vacation cabins, youth tent camping, picnicking, swimming, freshwater fishing, nature/hiking trails, guided tours of site, guided boat tours of Loxahatchee River, canoe rentals, boat ramp, concessions; site of Trapper Nelson's cabin home and wildlife zoo.

Tomoka. 3 miles north of Ormond Beach on North Beach Street; interpretive center, 100 campsites, youth tent camping, picnicking, saltwater fishing, nature/hiking trails, guided tours, boat ramp, canoe rentals, concessions. Site where Indians once lived. Area in late 1700s became part of land-grant holdings of Richard Oswald, a wealthy English merchant and statesman who helped negotiate the treaty with England after the American Revolution.

Central Florida

Highlands Hammock. 6 miles west of Sebring on S.R. 634; interpretive center, 138 campsites, youth tent camping, picnicking, bicycling, horse trail, nature/hiking trails, guided tours, concessions, seasonal campfire programs. One of Florida's four original state parks; site was acquired after citizens became concerned about plans to turn the hardwood forests inside the park into farmland.

Lake Kissimmee. 15 miles east of Lake Wales on Camp Mack Road; 60 campsites, youth tent camping, picnicking, freshwater fishing, nature/hiking trails, guided tours, boat ramp; observation platform; re-enactments of life in a cow camp. (See historical forts section.)

Lake Louisa. 7 miles southwest of Clermont, off Lake Nellie Road; picnicking, swimming, freshwater fishing, canoeing. Park lies on 2 1/2 miles of the southern shore of Lake Louisa.

Wekiwa Springs. East of Apopka, 3 miles off S.R. 436 on Wekiwa Circle; 60 campsites, youth tent camping, picnicking, swimming, freshwater fishing, nature/hiking trails, canoe rentals, concessions, horse trail. 6,400-acre park includes Wekiwa Springs, formed by water flowing from beneath Florida's central ridge through limestone caverns.

Central West Florida

Caladesi Island. Dunedin Causeway to ferry at Honeymoon Island; picnicking, swimming, saltwater fishing, nature/hiking trails, concessions. One of the remaining few undisturbed barrier islands in the state. Has more than two miles of white sand beach frontage on the Gulf of Mexico.

Egmont Key. Access by private boat only, southwest of Fort DeSoto Beach at the mouth of Tampa Bay; swimming, boating, fishing. 440-acre island houses only manned light-house in the United States. Was a camp for captured Seminoles during the Third Seminole War and was a Union Navy base during the Civil War. Now is a wildlife refuge.

Fort Cooper. Inverness, off Old Floral City Road; youth tent camping; picnicking, swimming, freshwater fishing, nature/hiking trails, canoeing. Lake Holathlikaha is within the boundaries of this park, and is the site of a frontier fort that was occupied for 16 days in 1836 during the Second Seminole War.

Hillsborough River. 6 miles southwest of Zephyrhills on U.S. 301; 118 campsites, youth tent camping, picnicking, swimming, freshwater fishing, nature/hiking trails, guided tours of 1830s-era fort and role-playing soldiers, boat and canoe rentals, concessions, suspension bridge, rapids along river. (See Fort Foster under historical forts section.)

Homosassa Springs Wildlife Park. Homosassa Springs, west on Fish Bowl Road; interpretive center, guided tours, nature trail, boat ramp, concessions. A wildlife park on 150 acres of woodlands and wetlands surrounding a 55-foot-deep spring that is the headwater of the Homosassa River. Has floating observatory where visitors can go below water's surface to view fresh and saltwater fish and manatees. Also has jungle cruises, daily alligator and hippopotamus feeding programs, reptile shows and manatee educational programs. Black-and-white swans, flamingos, wild geese and turkeys, crocodiles, otters, monkeys, a black bear and caymans are also seen. Florida Nature Museum houses collection of artifacts and fossils found in the Central Florida region.

Southwest Florida

Cayo Costa. Offshore from Boca Grande, south of Placida, accessible by boat; primitive cabins, picnicking, saltwater fishing in waters adjacent to park and in Boca Grande Pass, swimming and nature/hiking trails; one of the largest undeveloped barrier islands with numerous Indian mounds. Park is known for displays of bird life; ospreys and bald eagles nest on the island, and frigate birds are a familiar sight. It houses one of the largest brown pelican rookeries in the state. Shelling is a popular activity, especially during the winter.

Collier-Seminole. 17 miles south of Naples, on U.S. 41; intrepretive center, 130 campsites; youth tent camping, picnicking, saltwater fishing, nature/hiking trails, observation platform, canoe rentals and boat ramp. One feature is a tropical hammock (hardwood forest) dominated by trees that are characteristic of coastal forests of the West Indies and the Yucatan. An extensive mangrove swamp occupies much of the 6,423-acre park. Some of the final campaigns of the Second Seminole War were conducted near here and a replica of a blockhouse used by U.S. forces and local defenders during that era is housed in the park. The area was named for Barron Collier, a pioneer developer in Collier County, and for the Seminole Indians who still live nearby. A monument to Collier also stands in the park.

Myakka River. 14 miles east of Sarasota on S.R. 72; interpretive center, 76 campsites, primitive cabins, youth tent camping, picnicking, freshwater fishing, nature/hiking trails, guided tours, boat and canoe rentals, boat ramp, summer concessions, seasonal campfire programs, concession boat tour of Upper Myakka Lake, seasonal tram tour of hardwood hammock and river floodplain, horse trails. Covering 28,875 acres, this is one of Florida's largest state parks. It is noted for its scenic panoramas of lakes, the Myakka River, marshes, hammocks and prairies. Deer, alligators and many species of wading birds are abundant, and ospreys, bald eagles and sandhill cranes are common.

Oscar Scherer. 2 miles south of Osprey on U.S. 41; 104 campsites, youth tent camping, picnicking, swimming, saltwater fishing, nature/hiking trails, canoe rentals. Exotic species found here include the cattle egret, rock dove, smooth-billed ani, European starling, house sparrow, Mediterranean gecko lizard, Indo-Pacific gecko lizard and brown anole lizard, nine-banded armadillo, black rat and the feral pig. Also home to the endangered Florida scrub jay.

Southeast Florida

Bahia Honda. Bahia Honda Key, 12 miles south of Marathon, mile marker 37; 76 campsites, vacation cabins, picnicking, swimming in Atlantic Ocean and Florida Bay, saltwater fishing, nature/hiking trails, boat ramp, concessions. Area contains a number of rare plant species, such as the satinwood tree, spiny catesbaea and dwarf morning glory, and a number of rare species of birdlife such as the white-crowned pigeon, great white heron, roseate spoonbill, reddish egret, osprey, brown pelican and least tern. Tarpon fishing among the best in the state.

John D. MacArthur Beach. N. Palm Beach on Singer Island, via S.R. 703; swimming, saltwater fishing, snorkeling, shell collecting, nature/hiking trails. One of the prime nesting beaches for sea turtles in the state. Popular snorkeling area.

John Pennekamp Coral Reef. Key Largo, off U.S. 1 at mile marker 102; interpretive center, 47 campsites, picnicking, swimming, saltwater fishing, nature/hiking trails, guided tours, snor-

keling, diving, boat and canoe rentals, boat ramp; concessions. First underwater state park in the United States. Along with the adjacent Key Largo Coral Reef National Marine Sanctuary, these areas cover about 178 nautical square miles of coral reefs, seagrass beds and mangrove swamps. Park contains only living coral reef in continental United States. Also abuts Key Largo National Marine Sanctuary, which has a 9-foot bronze statue, "Christ of the Deep," located in 20 feet of water in the Atlantic Ocean. This is one of the top diving and snorkeling areas in the state.

STATE RECREATION AREAS:

(These are defined by the state as "generally, any expanse of real estate, of no particular size, used for outdoor recreation.")

Northeast Florida

Amelia Island. 7 miles north of Little Talbot Island State Park on S.R. A1A, or 8 miles south of Fernandina Beach; swimming, horseback riding and fishing. A 200-acres area with salt marshes, beaches and coastal maritime forests.

Anastasia. Saint Augustine, 2 miles east on A1A via Bridge of Lions; 139 campsites, picnicking, swimming, saltwater fishing, nature/hiking trails, sailboard and paddle cruiser rentals and summer concessions. Features broad beach flanked by sand dunes and a lagoon. Many species of shorebirds, such as sandpipers, gulls, terns and pelicans, can be seen along beach areas.

Gamble Rogers Memorial at Flagler Beach. South of Flagler Beach on A1A; 34 campsites, picnicking, swimming, saltwater fishing, nature/hiking trails, boat ramp; sand dunes; ranger-guided walks; area extends across a barrier island south of Flagler Beach.

Peacock Springs. 16 miles southwest of Live Oak on S.R. 51; scuba diving for certified divers only; swimming; picnicking. Contains two major springs that are in near pristine condition. Has one of the longest underwater cave systems in the continental United States. About 28,000 feet of underwater passages has been explored and surveyed by cave divers.

Stephen Foster State Folk Culture Center. White Springs, off U.S. 41N, on the Suwannee River; interpretive center, picnicking, guided tours of a carillon tower and visitor center, boat tours. Honors memory of Stephen Foster and is a gathering place for those perpetuating the crafts, music and legends of early and contemporary Floridians. Houses a piano that the composer often played and a desk at which he arranged his composition, "Old Folks at Home."

Northwest Florida

Big Lagoon. 10 miles southwest of Pensacola, on S.R. 292; 104 campsites, picnicking, swimming, fishing, crabbing, nature/hiking trails, boat ramp. Has observation tower at the East Beach area providing panoramic view of park and 500-seat amphitheater.

Dead Lakes. 1 mile north of Wewahitchka, off S.R. 70; 29 campsites, picnicking, freshwater fishing, nature/hiking trails, boat ramp. Area's most interesting feature is the thousands of dead trees still standing in the waters of the lake. Levees on the Apalachicola River blocked the Chipola River and resulted in high water that killed the trees.

Falling Waters. 3 miles south of Chipley, off S.R. 77A; 24 campsites, youth tent camping, picnicking, swimming, nature/hiking trails, overlook platform to a waterfall and a sink, or a cylindrical, smooth-walled pit, 100 feet deep and 15 feet in diameter.

Grayton Beach. Grayton Beach on S.R. 30A south; 37 campsites, picnicking, swimming, saltwater fishing, nature/hiking trails, boat ramp, summer concessions, summer campfire programs. Park preserves some of the best examples of barrier sand dunes along the Gulf Coast. Sea turtles often nest here during the summer.

Henderson Beach. East of Destin, on U.S. 98 west; swimming, saltwater fishing, picnicking. A 208-acre habitat with dunes, southern magnolias, sand pines and scrub oaks. Boardwalks are provided for access to the beach.

Lake Talquin. 10 miles west of Tallahassee, off S.R. 20 on Vause Road; picnicking, freshwater fishing, nature/hiking trails. Area famous for sportfishing, especially largemouth bass and speckled perch.

Perdido Key. 15 miles southwest of Pensacola on S.R. 292; picnicking, swimming, saltwater fishing, nature trails. 247-acre site located near Pensacola containing dunes covered with sea oats.

Ponce de Leon Springs. Ponce de Leon Springs, off U.S. 90 on S.R. 181A; picnicking, swimming, nature/hiking trails; natural spring with two main boils that flow from a horizontal limestone cavity. The boils produce 14 million gallons of water daily at a year-round temperature of 68 degrees.

Rocky Bayou, Fred Gannon. 5 miles east of Niceville on S.R. 20; 42 campsites, picnicking, swimming, saltwater and freshwater fishing, nature/hiking trails, seasonal ranger-guided walks and campfire programs, boat ramp. Noted for its sand pine forest. Alligators may

be observed in the manmade Puddin Head Lake.

Saint Andrews. West of Panama City on U.S. 98, south on Thomas Drive; interpretive center, 176 campsites, youth tent camping, picnicking, swimming, saltwater fishing, seasonal campfire programs and guided walks, nature/hiking trails, boat ramp, rental boats during the summer, concessions. Park has white sand beaches, clear water, white sand dunes and a reconstructed turpentine still.

Three Rivers. 2 miles north of Sneads on S.R. 271; 65 campsites, youth tent camping, picnicking, freshwater fishing; nature/hiking trails, boat ramp; summer campfire programs; has four miles of shoreline on Lake Seminole at the Florida-Georgia border.

Central East Florida

De Leon Springs. De Leon Springs, off U.S. 17 north on Ponce de Leon Boulevard; picnicking, swimming, freshwater fishing, nature/hiking trails, canoe rentals, concessions, scuba diving. Area has a spring, once labeled as a fountain of youth, which flows out at 72 degrees Fahrenheit year-round.

Fort Pierce Inlet. 4 miles east of Fort Pierce via north causeway to Atlantic Beach Boulevard; youth tent camping, picnicking, swimming, surfing, saltwater fishing, nature/hiking trails, observation tower. Abundance of bird life found here.

Sebastian Inlet. Sebastian Inlet on A1A; interpretive center, 51 campsites, picnicking, swimming, surfing, skin and scuba diving, saltwater fishing and shrimping, boat ramp, concessions. Visitor center houses some of the treasure recovered from the wreckage of a Spanish fleet by a hurricane in 1715 while fleet was returning to Spain from Mexico and Peru.

Central Florida

Lake Griffin. Fruitland Park on U.S. 27-441; 40 campsites, picnicking, freshwater fishing, nature trail, boat ramp. A 427-acre park located in a live oak hammock on a sandhill terrain is typical of Florida's central ridge area.

Central West Florida

Honeymoon Island. Dunedin, S.R. 586 west from U.S. 19A; picnicking, swimming, saltwater fishing, nature/hiking trails, boat ramp. Site of a Florida virgin slash pine stand, which serves as important nesting site for the osprey. Island has more than 208 species of plants.

Lake Manatee. 14 miles east of Bradenton on S.R. 64; 60 campsites, picnicking, swimming, freshwater fishing, boat ramp. This 556-acre site extends along three miles of the south shore of Lake Manatee, a reservoir that provides drinking water for Manatee and Sarasota counties. The upland portions of the park are the home of the gopher tortoise and indigo snake, both threatened species.

Little Manatee River. 4 miles south of Sun City, off U.S. 301 on Lightfoot Road; 30 campsites, picnicking, freshwater fishing, horseback riding trails (riders must furnish own horses), nature trail, boat ramp. 1,638-acre site has a variety of plant and animal life.

Southwest Florida

Delnor-Wiggins Pass. 6 miles south of Bonita Springs, C.R. 901 off U.S. 41; picnicking, swimming, saltwater fishing, boat ramp. Area is noted for shell collecting. Best collecting times are at low tide, after a storm and during new or full moons that bring lower-than-usual tides.

Don Pedro Island. Offshore from Placida on S.R. 775, accessible by boat; swimming, saltwater fishing, nature/hiking trails. An undisturbed coastal dune area consisting of 132.9 acres.

Gasparilla Island. South of Placida on C.R. 775 at Boca Grande; interpretive center, picnicking, swimming, saltwater fishing. Fish and shellfish resources of the surrounding waters are among the richest in the state; commercial fishing has been an important pursuit here for more than 100 years. Area also is site of wooden lighthouse that was first put into use in 1890 as a mariners' guide to the entrance to Port Boca Grande and Charlotte Harbor.

Lovers Key. On C.R. 865 between Fort Myers Beach and Bonita Beach in Lee County; fishing, swimming and picnicking. Part of Black Island.

Southeast Florida

Cape Florida, Bill Baggs. Key Biscayne, Miami, off U.S. 1 via Rickenbacker Causeway; area heavily damaged by Hurricane Andrew; interpretive center, youth tent camping, picnicking, swimming, saltwater fishing, nature/hiking trails, guided tours of lighthouse area, concessions. Has Cape Florida Lighthouse, the oldest building in South Florida, constructed in 1825. Through the years, the lighthouse underwent an Indian siege, was rebuilt in 1846, was darkened during the Civil War, was repaired in 1866 and darkened again in 1878 when the Fowey Rock Light located two miles southeast of Key Biscayne went into operation. Area first explored by Ponce de Leon in 1513.

Hugh Taylor Birch. Fort Lauderdale, 3109 E. Sunrise Blvd.; youth tent camping, picnicking, swimming, saltwater fishing, nature/hiking trails, canoe rentals, concessions. A look at Fort Lauderdale before modern times.

John U. Lloyd Beach. Dania, off A1A; picnicking, swimming, saltwater fishing, nature/hiking trails, canoe rentals, boat ramp, concessions. Area has 244 acres of barrier island that protects Dania from storm waves. Natural environment made up of beaches, dunes, hammock and mangroves.

Long Key. Long Key on U.S. 1 at mile marker 68; 60 campsites, picnicking, swimming, saltwater fishing, nature/hiking trails, canoeing, campfire programs, guided walks, observation tower.

North Shore. N. Miami Beach, east of Collins Avenue at 83rd Street; picnicking, swimming, saltwater fishing, bicycling. Beach area surrounded on three sides by urban Miami Beach.

Oleta River. North Miami off U.S. 1 on Sunny Isles Boulevard (163rd Street); youth tent camping, picnicking, swimming, saltwater fishing, biking, canoeing, boating, boat ramp, concessions. Located in the middle of metropolitan Dade County, park was planned to bring the out-of-doors experience to the surrounding urban area.

STATE PRESERVES:

(Defined by the state as areas "set aside specifically for the protection and safekeeping of certain values within the area, such as game, wildlife, forest.")

Northeast Florida

Paynes Prairie. 1 mile north of Micanopy on U.S. 441; interpretive center, 57 campsites, picnicking, swimming, nature/hiking trails, freshwater fishing, guided tours, horse trail, observation tower, boat ramp. Area is largely a basin covered by a marsh and wet prairie vegetation with areas of open water. Indian artifacts found here have been dated to 10,000 B.C. During the late 1600s, the largest cattle ranch in Spanish Florida operated here.

San Felasco Hammock. Gainesville, north on U.S. 441, 6.5 miles west on S.R. 232; nature/hiking trails, seasonal guided hikes. Area is characterized by extremes in topography from pine forest and hardwood hammocks to steep sinkholes and brooks. Also has various prehistoric and historic Indian sites. A battle was fought here during the Second Seminole War.

Northwest Florida

Waccasassa Bay. Gulf Hammock, off U.S. 98-19, west on C.R. 326, accessible by boat only; saltwater fishing, primitive camping, nature study; 30,784-acre site in Levy County. Most of area is salt marsh with some wooded islands and tidal creeks. The marsh and creeks are breeding and nursery areas for saltwater fish, crabs and shellfish. Among the endangered and threatened wildlife sighted here are the Florida panther, manatee, bald eagle and black bear.

Central East Florida

St. Lucie Inlet. Port Salerno, accessible by boat, three-quarters of a mile south of inlet; picnicking, swimming, saltwater fishing, nature/hiking trails, 3/4-mile boardwalk to beach. Beach is important nesting area for sea turtles.

Central West Florida

Anclote Key. Three miles off Tarpon Springs, accessible only by private boat; lighthouse, primitive camping, swimming, boating, birdwatching (bald eagles and piping plovers have been seen here). Visitors must bring own water and supplies and carry litter out.

Southwest Florida

Fakahatchee Strand. 3 miles north of Carnestown, off S.R. 29 at Copeland; nature/hiking trails. This area, the major drainage slough of southwestern Big Cypress Swamp, is about 20 miles long and three to five miles wide and contains the largest stand of native royal palms and the largest concentration and variety of orchids in North America. Among the threatened or endangered species found here are the wood stork, Florida black bear, mangrove fox squirrel, Everglades mink and the Florida panther.

Southeast Florida

San Pedro Underwater Archeological Preserve. Located in 18 feet of water about 1.25 nautical miles south of Indian Key; scuba diving, swimming, boating, fishing. Site where a 287-ton Dutch-built ship called the San Pedro that sailed as part of the fleet of New Spain in 1733 sank. What remains today of the ship is a large pile of ballast stones covering an area 90 feet long and 30 feet wide.

STATE RESERVES:

(Defined by the state as areas managed to serve specific environmental purposes, such as preserving or restoring natural conditions and processes, preserving open space and cultural amenities, or influencing the type and direction of area growth and development.)

Northwest Florida

Cedar Key Scrub. Cedar Key, six miles north on S.R. 24. One of the newest additions to the state park system.

Central Florida

Lower Wekiva River. Sanford, 8300 West S.R. 46; freshwater fishing.
Rock Springs Run. Sorrento, S.R. 46 via S.R. 433; foot trails, canoeing, horseback riding, hunting, primitive camping. Area contains Indian mounds. A spring run/river system surrounds most of the reserve's perimeter. The Florida black bear, woodstork, sandhill crane and indigo snake are often seen here.
Tosohatchee. South of Christmas on Taylor Creek Road; freshwater fishing, hiking, primitive backpack camping, nature study, horseback riding and limited hunting. Reserve is 28,000 acres of woodlands and wetlands bordering 19 miles of the St. Johns River in east Orange County. Area contains one of the few remaining virgin cypress swamps left in the nation, a forest of virgin slash pine — the only known tract of its size in Florida — and Indian mounds.

STATE MUSEUMS:

Northwest Florida

Cedar Key. Cedar Key, off S.R. 24 on Museum Drive; interpretive center, guided tours of museum, which contains exhibits of history of Cedar Key area and a shell collection.
Constitution Convention. Port St. Joe, off U.S. 98; interpretive center, guided tours. Site recalls Florida's first State Constitution Convention and the once boom town of St. Joseph. The town later died after an outbreak of yellow fever in 1841 and after an 1844 hurricane that destroyed what remained of the area, with the exception of the cemetery. The area remained unpopulated until about 1900, when the new town of Port St. Joe was founded.
Forest Capital. South of Perry on U.S. 98-27A; interpretive center, picnicking, guided tours of museum, which interprets history of Florida's forest industry. Today this industry produces about $3.7 billion in income annually. Most unique exhibit: wooden map of state with each of the 67 counties shaped from a different species of native tree (Florida has 314 known species of trees growing in its boundaries). Also on the grounds is the Cracker Homestead, a log cabin that was typical of those found in north Florida at the turn of the century. The homestead is named for the Florida crackers, the early settlers so named because they cracked whips to drive their cattle and oxen.
John Gorrie. Apalachicola, one block south of U.S. 319-98 on 6th Street; interpretive center, guided tours; honors the inventor of the first ar-

tificial ice machine in 1851 that eventually led to air-conditioning and refrigeration. Has reproduction of the machine and displays on history of Apalachicola and exhibits of navigational instruments.

Central West Florida

Ybor City. Tampa, I-4 to Exit #1, south to 9th Avenue; interpretive center, historical site. Area became center of activities for the Cuban Revolution and once had thriving cigar industry. Today, museum depicts life in the late 1800s to early 1900s and houses the Ferlita Bakery and a worker's cottage, depicting where many cigar makers lived and raised their families.

ORNAMENTAL GARDENS:

Northeast Florida

Ravine. Palatka, south of S.R. 100 on Twigg Street; picnicking, nature/hiking trails, auditorium for meetings. Area is largely a steep ravine created by water flowing from beneath the sandy ridges flanking the west shore of the St. Johns River. Features extensive plantings of azaleas and camellias during peak blooming season in March and April.

Washington Oaks. 2 miles south of Marineland on A1A; interpretive center, picnicking, saltwater fishing, nature/hiking trails, ranger-guided walks. Formal gardens contain species of exotic plants. Gardens are well-known for their azaleas, camellias and roses.

Northwest Florida

Eden State Gardens. Point Washington, off U.S. 98 on S.R. 395; interpretive center, picnicking, guided tours of Wesley house, built in 1898; grounds and gardens contain moss-draped live oaks, camellias and azaleas.

Maclay, Alfred B. Tallahassee, on U.S. 319 north of I-10; interpretive center, picnicking, swimming, freshwater fishing, canoeing, nature/hiking trails, guided tours, pavilion, boat ramp. About 100 varieties of camellias and about 50 varieties of azaleas are found here, along with more than 160 other exotic species or varieties. Area also contains the Maclay house, open January through April.

ARCHAEOLOGICAL SITES:

Northwest Florida

Lake Jackson Mounds. Tallahassee, 2 miles north of I-10 off U.S. 27 on Crowder Road; picnicking, nature/hiking trails. Site contains Indian mounds from 1200 to 1500 A.D. Largest mound is 278 feet by 312 feet at the base and about 36 feet in height. Area was also location

of Col. Robert Butler's plantation in the early 1800s.

Northeast Florida

Fort George State Cultural Site. 16 miles east of downtown Jacksonville on S.R. A1A; bicycling, nature trails and hiking. Island has been occupied continuously by man for more than 5,000 years and traces remains of each occupation period. Mount Cornelia, at 65 feet, is the highest point along the Atlantic Coast south of Sandy Hook, N.J.

Central West Florida

Crystal River. northwest of Crystal River, off U.S. 19-98, west on State Park Street; interpretive center, guided tours. This site preserves an Indian mound complex that is one of the longest continuously occupied sites in Florida, from 200 B.C. to 1400 A.D. The complex consists of temple, burial and refuse mounds. More than 450 burials have been found at the site.

BOTANICAL SITE:

Southeast Florida

Lignumvitae Key. 1/2 mile off Lower Matecumbe near mile marker 79, accessible by boat; interpretive center, nature/hiking trails, guided tours, including a three-hour boat tour departing from Indian Key Fill on U.S. 1. Site of the Matheson House, built in 1919, and a virgin tropical forest containing mastic, strangler fig, poisonwood, pigeon plum and gumbo-limbo trees.

GEOLOGICAL SITE:

Northeast Florida

Devil's Millhopper. Gainesville, north on U.S. 441, west to 4732 NW 53rd Avenue; interpretive center, nature/hiking trails. Site of huge sinkhole that formed when a cavern roof collapsed. Today, streams tumble down steep slopes, disappearing through crevices in the floor of the sink. The collapse exposed rock layers that help tell the story of Florida's geological history.

STATE TRAIL:

Northwest Florida

Tallahassee-St. Marks Historic Railroad State Trail. 1022 DeSoto Park Drive, Tallahassee; bicycling, horseback riding, nature trail, concessions. A 16-mile trail that follows the abandoned railbed of the old Tallahassee-St. Marks Railroad. Bicycles are available for rent at the north end of the trail.

HISTORICAL SITES:

Northeast Florida

Bulow Plantation Ruins. 3 miles west of Flagler Beach on S.R. 100, south on C.R. 2001; interpretive center, picnicking, freshwater and saltwater fishing, nature/hiking trails, canoe rentals. Once thriving plantation in the early 1800s that today houses ruins of a sugar mill, several wells, a spring house and crumbling foundation of the mansion.

Marjorie Kinnan Rawlings. Cross Creek on C.R. 325; interpretive center, nature/hiking trails, guided tours of cracker house where this American writer, who authored such books as "The Yearling," lived during her most productive years.

Olustee Battlefield. 2 miles east of Olustee on U.S. 90; interpretive center, nature/hiking trails. Site commemorates major Civil War battle in Florida in 1864 that was a Confederate victory. Battle, which resulted in 1,861 Union and 946 Confederate casualties, is reenacted each February.

Northwest Florida

Natural Bridge Battlefield. 6 miles east of Woodville off S.R. 363; picnicking, freshwater fishing; Civil War battle re-enactment in early March. (See historical forts section).

San Marcos De Apalache. St. Marks, off S.R. 363; interpretive center, military cemetery, nature/hiking trails. Site of building and launching of first ships made by white men in the New World around 1528; a fort was later built here and was occupied at various times by the Spaniards and the English until it was turned over to the United States in 1821; from 1857-58, a federal marine hospital was built here to care for yellow fever victims. The fort was later occupied by the Confederates in 1861.

Central West Florida

Dade Battlefield. Bushnell, off S.R. 476W; interpretive center, picnicking, nature/hiking trails, guided tours; battle re-enactment in late December. (See historical forts section).

Gamble Plantation. Ellenton on U.S. 301; interpretive center, picnicking, guided tours of mansion, which was home of Major Robert Gamble and the headquarters of an extensive sugar plantation during the Civil War era. This is the only antebellum plantation house surviving in this part of Florida.

Yulee Sugar Mill Ruins. Old Homosassa on S.R. 490 west; picnicking. Site once was part of a thriving sugar plantation owned by David Levy Yulee in the mid-1800s. Today, mill has been partially restored and consists of large chimney, a 40-foot-long structure that houses the boiler and parts of the grinding machinery.

Southwest Florida

Koreshan. South of Estero on U.S. 41; interpretive center, 60 campsites, picnicking, saltwater fishing, nature/hiking trails, guided tours, boat ramp. Site of the Koreshan Unity Settlement, which endured from 1894 until 1977. The settlement had a member population of about 200 people at its peak in 1903. Among the structures found here are an art and music building, a bakery, and several residences.

Paynes Creek. 1/2 mile east of Bowling Green on S.R. 664A; interpretive center, picnicking, freshwater fishing, nature/hiking trails. Site of former trading post, frontier fort and blockhouse that guarded a bridge over the Peace River in the mid 1800s before the beginning of the third war with the Seminoles (1855-1858).

Southeast Florida

The Barnacle. Coconut Grove, 3485 Main Highway; interpretive center, guided tours of 1891 home of Commodore Ralph Munroe, who acquired a national reputation by designing seaworthy, shallow-draft boats that could navigate the shoals, bars and reefs along Florida's coast. The site suffered extensive damage from Hurricane Andrew and was being restored.

Fort Zachary Taylor. Key West, off Southard Street; interpretive center, picnicking, swimming, saltwater fishing, guided tours of fort, built in 1866. Excavations have uncovered a number of cannons and ammunition from Civil War times.

Indian Key. Off U.S. 1 near Islamorada at mile marker 79, accessible by boat; nature/hiking trails, guided three-hour boat tours to Indian Key depart Indian Key Fill on U.S. 1; observation tower, boat dock, shelter area. Site of 1830s era busy port with 60 to 70 permanent inhabitants. Area once housed a store, hotel, dwellings with cisterns, warehouses and wharves.

Historical Forts Come Alive, Major Battle Re-Enactments And a Cow Camp

Northeast Florida

Fort Clinch State Park: Fernandina Beach, 2601 Atlantic Ave. This mid-1800s fort was built by the U.S. government to protect shipping and the port of Fernandina and played a role in the Civil War. The Confederacy quietly took the fort in 1861 to secure the mouth of the

St. Mary's River, but Union troops pressured the Confederacy to withdraw its forces from Amelia Island in early 1862. Federal troops occupied the fort from 1862 until it was deactivated in 1867. Today, the life of the Union soldier in 1864 is recreated, with role-playing soldiers, bugle calls and drills.

Northwest Florida

Natural Bridge Battlefield State Historic Site Re-Enactment: 6 miles east of Woodville off S.R. 363. Recreates the March 6, 1865, battle between Union and Confederate troops in which Union forces attempted to land south of Tallahassee to disrupt Confederate sources of supplies. After 12 hours of skirmishes, the Union troops were forced to retreat and evacuate the area, leaving Tallahassee as the only uncaptured Confederate state capital east of the Mississippi River. Today, this battle is reenacted on the Sunday nearest March 6 each year.

Central Florida

Kissimmee Cow Camp: At Lake Kissimmee State Park, 15 miles east of Lake Wales on Camp Mack Road. A recreated 1876 camp along the route of a Florida cattle drive that today houses scrub cows, which are descendants of the Spanish Andalusian cows. In the late 1800s, these cows were rounded up in the spring by cow hunters and the cattle were driven to Punta Rassa near Fort Myers for shipment to Cuba. Florida consequently became the largest exporter of beef to the Spanish in Cuba. Today at the state park, role-playing cow hunters show how saddles were mended or how cow whips, used to round up the cattle, were used.

Central West Florida

Fort Foster: At Hillsborough River State Park, 6 miles southwest of Zephyrhills on U.S. 301. Named after Lt. Col. William S. Foster, the fort was built to help prevent Seminole Indian ambushes of U.S. troops during the Second Seminole War from 1836 to June 1837, when the fort was abandoned. It was reoccupied in October 1837 and was used as a supply depot until June 1838. Today, the fort has been reconstructed and there are role-playing rangers who recreate the presence of soldiers armed with muskets.

Dade Battlefield Re-Enactment: At Bushnell off U.S. 301. Recreates the battle between the Seminole Indians and the U.S. Army on Dec. 28, 1835 in which more than 100 Army officers and men were killed. The confrontation marks one of the most sweeping Indian victories over

the Army and was the start of the Second Seminole War. Today, the event is reenacted each year on the Saturday closest to Dec. 28.

OPEN LANDS:

(Defined by the state as properties that recently have been granted enhanced public access, but that generally do not have Florida Park Service staff assigned to these areas.)

Northwest Florida

Blackwater Heritage Trail: in Milton at the intersection of Highway 90 and Stewart.
Topsail: 10 miles east of Destin on Highway 98.
Econfina River: County Road 14, off Highway 98.

Northeast Florida

Big Shoals: 1 mile northeast of White Springs.
Fernandina Plaza State Historic Site: on Fernandina Beach, part of A1A.
Big Bend: 1.8 miles northeast of Horseshoe Beach off Dixie mainline.
River Rise State Preserve: one quarter mile along Santa Fe River on east side of Highway 41. All fees must be paid at O'Leno State Park.
DeSoto Site: DeSoto Park Drive in Tallahassee.
Haw Creek State Preserve: Accessible by boat only. Access point 8 miles west of Bunnell off County Road 318 through St. John Park.
North Peninsula State Recreation Area: U.S. A1A, about 6 miles south of Flagler Beach.

Central West Florida

Lake Rousseau State Recreation Area: north on U.S. 19, 6.5 miles to Basswood Road, right to Riverwood Road. Follow to dam site.
Withlacoochee State Trail: Trail begins at State Road 50 1 mile east of Interstate 75 and runs north to Citrus Springs.
Rainbow Springs State Park: 3 miles north of Dunnellon on U.S. 41.
Beker: 12 miles east of Parrish on State Road 62.
Madira Bickel Mound State Archaeological Site: On Terraceia Island, off Highway 19, about 1 mile on Bayshore Drive.

Central Florida

General James A. Van Fleet State Trail: trail begins under State Road 33 in Polk City and runs north to State Road 50 in Mabel.
Lake Arbuckle State Park: Off State Road 64, 10 miles east of Avon Park.

Catfish Creek State Preserve: off Hatcheneha Road, about 9 miles east of Dundee.

Central East Florida

Addison Blockhouse State Historic Site: in Tomoka State Park (accessible by boat only.)

Green Mound State Archaeological Site: south on A1A to S. Peninsula, on left 2-3 miles.

Spruce Creek: 4 miles west of New Smyrna Airport, off Martin Dairy Road.

Savannas State Reserve: 4842 S. U.S. 1, Fort Pierce.

Avalon State Recreation Area: on A1A, one mile north of Fort Pierce Inlet.

Seabranch: On A1A, south of Port Salerno.

Southwest Florida

Port Charlotte Beach State Recreation Area: south end of Manasota Key, end of Gulf Drive off State Road 775 out of Englewood, off Highway 41 to River Road, Port Charlotte.

Mount Key State Archaeological Site: At Koreshan State Historic Site.

Southeast Florida

Curry Hammock: Highway U.S. 1 north, east of Marathon to Vahalla Beach, Mile Marker 58 in the Florida Keys.

Windley Key Fossil Reef State Geological Site: Windley Key Mile Marker 85 1/2.

Key Largo Hammock Botanical Site: off State Road 905, upper Largo, between Mile Marker 106 and Ocean Reef four-way stop.

Park Fees

The fee schedule for Florida's state parks is broken down as follows:

Entrance fees

Per Vehicle (maximum 8 people)	$3.25
Pedestrians, bicyclists, extra passengers	$1
Children under 6 years of age	Free
Florida residents participating in Food Stamp program	One half entrance fee
Museum/visitor center fee	$1 - $2
Annual family entrance permit (maximum 8 people)	$60
Annual individual entrance permit	$30
Annual family special recreational use permit (for activities such as diving, boat launching, equestrian and after-hours use. Includes admission; maximum 4 people)	$80
Annual individual special recreational use permit	$40
Real Florida Vacation Pass, Family Entrance Permit (admits 8 persons in same vehicle and is valid for 15 days from date of purchase)	$20

Camping-Related fees

Campsite fees (Depending on time of year and camping area)	$8-$19/day
Waterfront site extra fee (Does not apply when campsite fee is at $8 minimum)	$2
Extra person camping	$2
Extra car overnight parking (for unoccupied vehicles)	$3
Electricity per unit	$2
Florida resident senior/disabled citizen	One half base camping fee
Primitive camping per person	$3 (adults) $2 (under 18)

National Parks

Among the national parks overseen by the National Park Service:

Canaveral National Seashore/Merritt Island National Wildlife Refuge. Located midway between Jacksonville and West Palm Beach, with New Smyrna Beach the northern access point on A1A and Titusville the southern access point on Fla. 402. Open for day use only, picnicking, swimming, boat ramps, nature/hiking trails, surfing, saltwater and freshwater fishing, crabbing, clamming, shrimping, canoeing, wildlife drives, Indian shell midden, restricted hunting; located beneath the Atlantic Flyway, a major migratory route for birds between their southern wintering grounds and northern breeding areas. Merritt Island is a key wintering area and supports a population of 50,000 to 70,000 ducks and more than 100,000 coots. Among the endangered and threatened wildlife species found on the island are the southern bald eagle, eastern brown pelican, peregrine falcon, eastern indigo snake, dusky seaside sparrow, Florida manatee, Atlantic salt marsh snake and several species of sea turtles.

De Soto National Memorial. On Tampa Bay, 5 miles west of Bradenton; nature trail, visitor center, De Soto monument, tabby house ruin (all that is left of one of the earliest American settlements in South Florida, dating back to the early 1800s); Commemorates Hernando De Soto's landing in Florida in May 1539. Park also provides insights into the way 16th-century man lived. From December through April, park employees in period dress demonstrate use of various weapons and show how food was prepared and preserved.

Everglades National Park. Suffered extensive facility damage in 1992 due to Hurricane Andrew. Main visitor center located 10.8 miles southwest of Homestead; park is huge (it consists of about 1.4 million acres and it's 92 miles from the main visitor center to the Gulf Coast Ranger Station); birdwatching, ranger-guided activities, hiking/nature trails, saltwater and freshwater fishing, boating, camping, canoeing, boat rentals, boat ramps, picnicking, marina, lodging and meals, gasoline. Park has been known for its birdlife, from great white herons to southern bald eagles. Other rare and endangered species that have been found in the park include the Florida panther, manatee, Everglades mink, green sea turtle, loggerhead turtle, Florida sandhill crane, snail kite, short-tailed hawk, peregrine falcon, Cape Sable sparrow and crocodile. The park also has provided protection for the alligator, reddish egret, spoonbill, Florida mangrove cuckoo, osprey, brown pelican and roundtail muskrat. Mosquitoes, sand flies and other biting insects call this home especially during the summer, so bring lots of insect repellent and wear long-sleeve shirts and long pants. (Also see environment chapter).

Biscayne National Park. Also suffered extensive storm damage to buildings in the park, but the underwater coral reefs survived the storm well. Principally a marine preserve, the park's headquarters and information station are located at Convoy Point, south of Miami off North Canal Drive or S.W. 328 Street. Convoy Point has a picnic area with tables, fire grills, restrooms and a short hiking trail that describes marine life and birds of the Biscayne Bay area. About 95 percent of the 181,500-acre park is water. Principal activities are boating, saltwater fishing, diving, snorkeling, scuba diving, glass-bottom-boat trips to coral reefs and canoe rentals. Offshore keys can be reached only by boat, with developed recreation areas and services limited to: Adams Key, which has a ranger station, free boat dock, restrooms, picnicking and a nature trail; Elliott Key, with a ranger station, restrooms, picnicking, nature trail, free boat docks and primitive camping; and Boca Chita Key, with restrooms, picnicking, free boat dock and primitive camping.

Gulf Islands National Seashore. Primarily beach areas on barrier islands, with access in Escambia, Santa Rosa and Okaloosa counties. Area characterized by sugar-white sand and dunes covered with sea oats. Has numerous picnic areas, freshwater showers, restrooms and open shelters. Park's boundaries stretch from West Ship Island in Mississippi to the far end of Santa Rosa Island in Florida. Lifeguards on duty in season at Johnson Beach in Perdido Key, and at the Santa Rosa Island and Fort Pickens swimming areas. Scuba diving also popular.

In addition, there are hundreds of sites listed on the National Register of Historic Places in more than 50 Florida counties.

Museums, Art Galleries and Art Centers

For the connoisseur of the fine arts, Florida has a lot to offer. Those yearning for a cultural diversion from the beaches, the sun and Disney World will find it. There is either a museum, an art gallery, an art center or a fine arts educational facility in a number of Florida's cities, as listed by the Florida Department of State, Division of Cultural Affairs:

An asterisk denotes accreditation by the American Association of Museums.

Avon Park: South Florida Junior College Art Department, 600 W. College Drive.

Belleair: Florida Gulf Coast Art Center, 222 Ponce de Leon Blvd.

Boca Raton: Boca Raton Museum of Art, 801 W. Palmetto Park Road; Florida Atlantic University, Ritter Art Gallery.

Bradenton: Manatee Junior College Department of Art, P.O. Box 1849.

Cape Coral: Cape Coral Art League, P.O. Box 707.

Cocoa: Brevard Community College Fine Arts Gallery, 1591 Clearlake Road.

Coral Gables: University of Miami, Lowe Art Museum *, 1301 Miller Drive; University of Miami, New Gallery, 1300 Camposano Drive.

Daytona Beach: Museum of Arts and Sciences *, 1040 Museum Blvd.; Daytona Beach Community College Fine Arts Gallery, 1200 Volusia Ave.

DeLand: Stetson University Sampson Art Gallery; DeLand Museum of Art, 449 E. New York Ave.

Delray Beach: Morikami Museum & Japanese Gardens, 4000 Morikami Park Road.

Dunedin: Dunedin Fine Arts and Cultural Center, 1143 Michigan Blvd.

Fort Lauderdale: Museum of Art *, 1 E. Las Olas Blvd.; Broward Community College Art Gallery, 3501 Southwest Davie Road; The Discovery Center, 231 Southwest 2nd Ave.

Fort Myers: Edison Community College Gallery of Fine Arts, College Parkway.

Fort Pierce: Indian River Community College Art Gallery, 3209 Virginia Ave.

Gainesville: University of Florida Samuel P. Harn Museum of Art; University of Florida University Gallery *; Santa Fe Community College Community Art Gallery, 3000 Northeast 83rd St.; and City of Gainesville Thomas Center Gallery, 302 Northeast Sixth Ave.

Hollywood: Broward Community College Art Lyceum Gallery, South Campus, Hollywood Blvd.; and The Art & Culture Center of Hollywood, 1301 S. Ocean Drive.

Jacksonville: Cummer Gallery of Art *, 829 Riverside Ave.; Jacksonville Art Museum*, 4160 Boulevard Center Drive; Florida Community College at Jacksonville, South Campus, South Gallery, 11901 Beach Blvd.; Jacksonville University Brest Gallery; Florida Community College at Jacksonville, Kent Gallery, Kent Campus, 3939 Roosevelt Blvd.; University of North Florida Art Gallery, 4567 St. John's Bluff Road; Jacksonville Museum of Science and History, 1025 Gulf Life Drive.

Key West: Florida Keys Community College, Tennessee Williams Fine Arts Center.

Lake City: Lake City Community College Art Department.

Lakeland: Florida Southern College Melvin Art Gallery, Ludd M. Spivey Fine Arts and Humanities Building; Polk Museum of Art*, 800 E. Palmetto.

Lake Worth: Palm Beach Junior College Art Gallery, 4200 Congress Ave.

Madison: North Florida Junior College Fine Arts Division, 1000 Turner Davis Drive.

Maitland: Maitland Art Center, 231 W. Packwood Ave.

Marianna: Chipola Junior College Music Department.

Melbourne: Brevard Art Center and Museum, 1463 Highland Ave.; and Brevard Community College Art Gallery, 3865 N. Wickham Road.

Miami area: Florida International University, The Art Museum, Tamiami Campus; Miami-Dade Community College Art Gallery, South Campus, 11011 Southwest 104th St.; Miami-Dade Community College Frances Wolfson Art Gallery, 300 Northeast 2nd Ave.; The Bakehouse Art Complex, 561 Northwest 32nd St.; Center for the Fine Arts *, 101 W. Flagler St.; Bass Museum of Art *, 2121 Park Ave., Miami Beach; South Florida Art Center, 924 Lincoln Road, Miami Beach; Barry College Department of Art, 11300 Northeast Second Ave., Miami Shores; and North Miami Museum and Art Center, 12340 Northeast 8th Ave., North Miami.

Mount Dora: Mount Dora Center for the Arts, 138 E. Fifth Ave.

New Port Richey: Pasco-Hernando Community College Art Gallery, West Campus, 7025 Moon Lake Road.

New Smyrna Beach: Atlantic Center for the Arts, 1414 Art Center Ave.

Niceville: Okaloosa-Walton Junior College Art Department, 100 College Blvd.

Ocala: Central Florida Community College Art Gallery, State Road 200 West; Appleton Museum of Art, 4333 E. Silver Springs Blvd.

Orlando: Orlando Museum of Art at Loch Haven *, 2416 N. Mills Ave.; Valencia Community College/East Campus Art Gallery; and University of Central Florida Art Gallery, 4000 Central Florida Blvd.

Ormond Beach: Ormond Memorial Art Museum, 78 E. Granada Blvd.

Palatka: Florida School of the Arts, Art Gallery, St. John's River Community College, 5001 St. Johns Ave.

Palm Beach: Henry Morrison Flagler Museum *, Whitehall Way; Society of the Four Arts *, Four Arts Plaza.

Panama City: Gulf Coast Community College Division of Fine Arts, 5230 W. Highway 98; Panama Art Association, P.O. Box 883; Visual Arts Center of Northwest Florida, 19 E. 4th St.

Pensacola: Pensacola Junior College Visual Arts Gallery, 1000 College Blvd.; Pensacola Museum of Art, 407 S. Jefferson St.; and University of West Florida University Art Gallery.

St. Augustine: Flagler College Visual Arts Department.

St. Petersburg: Museum of Fine Arts, 255 Beach Drive North; The Salvador Dali Museum, 1000 3rd St. S.; St. Petersburg Junior College Department of Humanities and Fine Arts; Eckerd College Elliot Gallery, 5401 34th St.

Sanford: Seminole Community College Art Gallery.

Sarasota: John and Mable Ringling Museum of Art *, 5401 Bayshore Road; Ringling School of Art and Design, Fine Arts Department, 1191-27th St.; and New College of the University of South Florida Humanities Division, 5700 N. Tamiami Trail.

Tallahassee: Florida State University University Gallery, Fine Arts Building; LeMoyne Art Foundation, 125 N. Gadsden St.; Florida A&M University Art Gallery, South Boulevard Street; and Tallahassee Community College Art Department.

Tampa: Museum of African American Art, 1308 Marion St.; Tampa Museum *, 601 Doyle Carlton Drive; University of South Florida University Galleries, College of Fine Arts, 4202 Fowler Ave.; Hillsborough Community College, Ybor City Campus; the University of Tampa Lee Scarfone Gallery, 401 W. Kennedy Blvd.; and Florida Center for Contemporary Art.

Vero Beach: Center for the Arts, 3001 Riverside Park Drive.

West Palm Beach: Norton Gallery and School of Art *, 1451 S. Olive Ave.; Armory School and Visual Arts Center, 1703 S. Lake Ave.

Winter Haven: Polk Community College Art Department, 999 Ave. H Northeast.

Winter Park: Rollins College * Cornell Fine Arts Center; Crealde Arts, 600 St. Andrews Blvd.

Among Florida's other major cultural institutions are:

Theaters: There are scores of these throughout the state. See county-by-county listings.

Orchestras and symphonies: The Florida Orchestra, **Tampa;** Music Orlando, **Orlando;** Philharmonic Orchestra of Florida, **Fort Lauderdale;** Florida Symphonic Pops of Boca Raton, **Boca Raton;** Brevard Symphony Orchestra, **Melbourne;** Broward Community College Youth Symphony, **Coconut Creek;** Central Florida Community College Aeolian Players, **Ocala;** Florida FestivalOrchestra, **Plantation;** Florida State University Symphony, **Tallahassee;** Florida Symphony Youth Orchestra, **Winter Park;** Florida West Coast Symphony Orchestra and Florida West Coast Youth Orchestra, **Sarasota;** Gainesville Chamber Orchestra, **Gainesville;** Greater Miami Youth Symphony, **Miami;** Greater Palm Beach Symphony, **Palm Beach;** Greater Pensacola Symphony Orchestra, **Pensacola;** Hillsborough Youth Orchestra, **Safety Harbor;** Imperial Symphony Orchestra, **Lakeland;** Jacksonville Symphony Orchestra, **Jacksonville;** Miami Chamber Symphony, **Miami;** The New World Symphony, **Miami Beach;** Pinellas Youth Symphony, **St. Petersburg;** Sarasota Community Orchestra, **Sarasota;** South Florida Youth Symphony, **Miami;** Southwest Florida Symphony Orchestra, **Fort Myers;** Stetson University Orchestra, **DeLand;** Tampa Bay Community Symphony, **St. Petersburg;** University of Central Florida Community Symphony, **Orlando;** University of Florida Symphony Orchestra, **Gainesville;** and Winter Haven Youth Symphony, **Winter Haven.**

Opera companies: Sarasota Opera, 61 N. Pineapple Ave., **Sarasota;** Greater Miami Opera, 1200 Coral Way, **Miami;** Florida Opera, 4902-B Creekside Drive, **Clearwater;** Gold Coast Opera, **Pompano Beach;** Monticello Opera House, **Monticello;** Opera Guild, 333 S.W. 2nd St., **Fort Lauderdale;** Orlando Opera, 1900 N. Mills Ave., Suite 4, **Orlando;** Palm Beach Opera, Paramount Center, 139 N. County Road, **Palm Beach;** Treasure Coast Opera Society, 1309 Indiana Ave., **Fort Pierce.**

Professional dance companies: Bad Dog Dance, **Miami;** Ballet Concerto Company, 3410 Coral Way, **Miami;** Ballet Flamenco La Rosa, 1008 Lincoln Road, **Miami Beach;** Ballet Florida, 4704 Broadway, **West Palm Beach;** Ballet Theatre of Miami, 1809 Ponce de Leon Blvd., **Coral Gables;** Body & Soul Dance Theatre, 2240 S.W. 70th Ave., **Davie;** Carrington Contemporary Dance, **Miami;** Case & Company, 333 Tressler Drive, **Stuart;** Dance Alive!, 1325 N.W. 2nd St., **Gainesville;** Dance Arts Foundation Inc., **Homestead;** Dance Theatre of Florida, **St. Petersburg;** Demetrius A. Klein & Dancers, **Lake Worth;** First City Dance Theatre, **Pensacola;** Florida Ballet, 123 E. Forsyth St., **Jacksonville;** Freddick Bratcher & Company, 5950 S.W. 74th St., No. 407, **Miami;** Gisela Solomayor Spanish Dance Co., 8501 N. 50th St., No. 1104, **Tampa;** Karen Peterson & Dancers, **Miami;** Key West Dance Theatre, 916 Ashe St., **Key West;** Kuumba Dancers & Drummers, **Tampa;** Mary Luft & Co., **Miami;** Mary Street Dance Theatre, **Miami;** Miami City Ballet, 905 Lincoln Road, **Miami Beach;** Miami Movement Dance Co., 8768 Sunset Drive, **Miami;** Miami Repertory Ballet Company, 8781 S.W. 134th St., **Miami;** Momentum Dance Company, **Miami;** New Moves Productions, 1507 N.E. 13th St., **Gainesville;** Northwest Florida Ballet, **Fort Walton Beach;** Oudansquerade, 3210 Holiday Springs Blvd., No. 307, **Margate;** Randy Warshaw Dance Company, 6555 S.W. 55th Lane, **Miami;** Sarasota Ballet of Florida, **Sarasota;** Southern Ballet Theatre, 976 Orange Ave., **Winter Park;** Tampa Ballet, 5010 W. Kennedy Blvd., No. 209, **Tampa;** and Troupe El Hiyat, Mid-Eastern Dance Association, 321 Bayside Road, **Palm Springs.**

Performing Arts Centers: There are dozens of these throughout the state. See county-by-county listings.

Arts and Crafts Festivals: There are hundreds of these festivals in Florida every year throughout the state. In an effort to give artists and the public an opportunity to plan, the Pinellas County Arts Council publishes a listing of arts and crafts shows, both large and small, juried and non-juried. The listing contains such information as the show's name, the show's location, contact person, entry fees, media eligibility and estimated attendance figures. For a copy of this guide, called "Florida Festivals, Who, What, When, Where," write to the Pinellas County Arts Council, 400 Pierce Blvd., Clearwater, 34616, or phone 813-464-3327. Cost of the publication was $12 by mail. Since information in this listing is published well before the festivals take place, it is strongly advisable to check local newspapers for updated schedules or to contact chambers of commerce in the cities or towns scheduled to hold the event.

Following is a partial listing of festivals that were scheduled to take place during 1994 and 1995, according to the Pinellas County Arts Council. Only festivals with an estimated attendance of 50,000 or more are listed here. Listings contain the show name, location and estimated attendance.

January:
Palm Beach Art on the Square, N. Palm Beach, 55,000.
Las Olas Art Fair, Fort Lauderdale, 165,000.
Downtown Delray Festival of the Arts, Delray Beach, 65,000.
Adventura Festival of the Arts, North Miami Beach, 75,000.
Boca Fest, Boca Raton, 145,000.

February:
Mount Dora Arts Festival, downtown Mount Dora, 240,000.
Las Olas Art Fair, Fort Lauderdale, 145,000.
Downtown West Palm Beach Art Festival, West Palm Beach, 65,000.
Vero Beach Art Festival, downtown Vero Beach, 65,000.
Miami Beach Festival of the Arts, Miami Beach, 300,000.
Sarasota Festival of the Arts, Sarasota, 85,000.
ArtiGras, Palm Beach Gardens, 55,000.
Coconut Grove Arts Festival, Coconut Grove, 750,000.
St. Stephen's Arts & Crafts Show, Coconut Grove, 500,000.
Boca Museum Festival, Crocker Center, Boca Raton, 50,000.
South Miami Craft Fest, Sunset Drive, Miami, 60,000.
Old Hyde Park Art Festival, Tampa, 55,000.
Downtown Stuart Art Festival, Stuart, 55,000.

March:
Medieval Fair, Ringling Museum of Art, Sarasota, 60,000.
Downtown Orlando Art Festival, Orlando, 105,000.
Gasparilla Festival of the Arts, downtown Tampa, 250,000.
Meet Me Downtown, Boca Raton, 150,000.
Naples 5th Avenue Festival of the Arts, Naples, 70,000.
Spring Craft Fair, Cocoa Village, 50,000.
Bay Area Renaissance Festival, Largo, 75,000.
SPIFFS International Folk Fair, Thunder-Dome, St. Petersburg, 60,000.
Winter Park Sidewalk Art Festival, Central Park, Winter Park, 350,000.
ArtFest By the Sea, Jupiter, 95,000.

April:

Santa Fe Community College Spring Arts Festival, downtown Gainesville, 80,000.

Ormond on the Halifax Art Festival, Ormond Beach, 50,000.

St. Augustine Arts & Crafts Festival, Old St. Augustine, 100,000.

Tarpon Springs Arts and Crafts Festival, Craig Park on Spring Bayou, Tarpon Springs, 55,000.

Sunshine Festival of States, St. Petersburg, 50,000.

Carrollwood Arts and Crafts Festival, Tampa, 55,000.

Downtown Fort Myers Street Art Festival, Fort Myers, 55,000.

Delray Affair, Delray Beach, 225,000.

Siesta Fiesta, Siesta Key, 85,000.

Melbourne Art Festival, downtown Melbourne, 50,000.

Pompano Beach Seafood Festival, Pompano Beach, 100,000.

May:

SunFest, downtown West Palm Beach, 335,000.

Mainsail Arts Festival, North Straub Park, St. Petersburg, 80,000.

Isle of Eight Flags Shrimp Festival Arts and Crafts Show, Fernandina Beach, 175,000.

Mayfaire-by-the-Lake, Lakeland, 65,000.

July:

America's Birthday Bash, Fourth of July Celebration, Bayfront Park, Miami, 175,000.

September:

Las Olas Labor Day Art Fair, Fort Lauderdale, 150,000.

Ponte Verde Art Festival at Sawgrass Village, Ponte Vedra Beach, Jacksonville, 55,000.

Arts Mania, Jacksonville Landing, 100,000.

October:

Destin Seafood Festival, Pelican Point, Destin, 60,000.

Old Hyde Park Village Art Festival, Tampa, 55,000.

Lake Mary-Heathrow Festival of the Arts, Lake Mary, 100,000.

Discovery of America Day (part of the Hispanic Heritage Festival), Bayfront Park, Miami, 75,000.

Our Town America Festival, Mullins Park, Coral Springs, 120,000.

Maitland Rotary Arts Festival, Maitland, 150,000.

Images in Art Show, Ocala City Government Complex, Ocala, 50,000.

Mount Dora Craft Fair, downtown Mount Dora, 100,000.

Festival of the Americas (part of the Hispanic Heritage Festival), Miami, 50,000.

John's Pass Seafood Festival Arts & Crafts Show, John's Pass Village, Madeira Beach, 120,000.

Cocoa Village Fall Judged Craft Fair, Cocoa Village, Cocoa, 60,000.

Downtown Boca Festival of the Arts, Boca Raton, 65,000.

November:

Great Gulfcoast Arts Festival, Seville Square, Pensacola, 150,000.

Fiesta in the Park, Lake Eola Park, Orlando, 200,000.

Venice Art Festival, Venice, 65,000.

Florida Heritage Festival, South Florida Fairgrounds, West Palm Beach, 95,000.

Festival of the Masters, Walt Disney World Village, Lake Buena Vista, 150,000.

Deerfest Community Festival, Deerfield Beach, 70,000.

Promenade in the Park, Holiday Park, Fort Lauderdale, 75,000.

Coral Gables International Festival of Craft Arts, Coral Gables, 85,000.

Carrollwood Arts & Crafts Festival, Tampa, 55,000.

Hyde Park Art Festival, Plant Park, Tampa, 50,000.

Downtown Festival & Art Show, Gainesville, 80,000.

Banyan Arts and Craft Festival, downtown Coconut Grove, 70,000.

Weston Art Festival, Weston, 65,000.

St. Augustine Fall Arts & Crafts Show, The Plaza, Old St. Augustine, 100,000.

Downtown Tarpon Springs Art Festival, Tarpon Springs, 55,000.

Space Coast Art Festival, downtown Cocoa Beach, 100,000.

December:

Cocoa Village Christmas Craft Fair, Cocoa Village, 50,000.

Marco Island Festival of the Arts, Marco Island, 50,000.

Schedule of Florida Fairs and Livestock Shows

January:

Charlotte County Fair in Port Charlotte; Collier County Fair in Naples; South Florida Fair/Palm Beach County Expo in West Palm Beach; and Manatee County Fair in Palmetto.

Late January/Early February:
Florida Citrus Festival/Polk County Fair in Winter Haven.

February:
Southwest Florida Fair and Lee County Fair in North Fort Myers; Florida State Fair in Tampa; Highlands County Fair in Sebring; Pasco County Fair in Dade City; Kissimmee Valley Fair and Livestock Show in Kissimmee; Monroe County Fair in Key West.

Late February/Early March:
Southeastern Youth Fair in Ocala; St. Lucie County Fair in Fort Pierce; Central Florida Fair in Orlando; and Florida Strawberry Festival in Plant City.

March:
Martin County Fair in Stuart; Sumter County Fair at Beville's Corner; Hardee County Fair in Wauchula; Sarasota County Agricultural Fair in Sarasota; Hendry County Fair and Livestock Show in Clewiston; Citrus County Fair in Inverness; Putnam County Fair in Palatka; Indian River County Fair in Vero Beach; DeSoto County Fair in Arcadia; and Pinellas County Fair in Pinellas Park.

March/Early April:
Dade County Youth Fair and Exposition in the Miami area; Clay County Agricultural Fair in Green Cove Springs.

April:
Hernando County Fair in Brooksville; Lake Agriculture and Youth Fair in Eustis; Bradford County Fair in Starke; Santa Rosa County Fair in Milton; and Flagler County Fair in Bunnell.

June:
Florida Blueberry Festival and County Fair in Ocala.

Fall:
Suwannee County Agricultural Fair in Live Oak.

October:
Bay County Fair in Panama City; Jackson County Fair in Marianna; Walton County Fair in DeFuniak Springs; Northeast Florida Fair in Callahan; Greater Okaloosa County Fair in Fort Walton Beach; Greater Holmes County Fair in Bonifay; Greater Jacksonville Agricultural Fair in Jacksonville; Hamilton County Fair; Marion County Fair in Ocala; and Pensacola Interstate Fair in Pensacola.

October or November:
Columbia County Fair in Lake City

Late October/Early November:
North Florida Fair in Tallahassee; and Volusia County Fair and Youth Show in DeLand.

November:
Baker County Fair in Macclenny; Alachua County Fair in Gainesville; Brevard County Fair in Cocoa; and Broward County Fair in Hallandale.

Things To Do Around the House

Backyard Swimming Pools

If you have a spare $15,000, you can pamper yourself and get yourself a good-sized, well-built backyard swimming pool with plenty of decking around it.

There are four types of materials used in pool construction. Two of them are concrete and have a plaster finish, and they are the most expensive: Gunite, which is a dry mix, and Shotcrete, which is a wet mix. The sizes and shapes of these pools are limited only by the imagination. Also becoming more popular in Florida is the vinyl-liner pool, which is prevalent in colder climates and which refugees from the north often prefer because they are familiar with it. Finally, the newest type of pool is made of fiberglass. It usually comes in a one-piece shell, or in rare cases in two pieces bolted together with rubber gaskets.

The type of pool that a homeowner chooses is largely a matter of taste. But the best advice from pool maintenance companies and the National Spa and Pool Institute in Sarasota is to make sure that you get a reputable, quality builder. Call the Better Business Bureau for names of reliable builders and get estimates from several of them. Make sure that they know what they're doing, because pool installations can be tricky in Florida.

Many areas have high water tables and sandy soil. According to Larry Bellinger of the National Spa and Pool Institute, water tables in some areas may even rise with the ocean tides. And in southeast Florida, a contractor often will have to dig out rock and coral.

These are not jobs for amateurs. In wet areas, the yard will have to be kept dry with pumps during installation. And it will have to remain dry until the pool is filled with enough water to prevent it from popping out of the ground.

Bellinger says that costs vary by area and by builder. He says that some people think they're getting a bargain if they order a pool for $7,000 and think that it will last forever.More likely, they'll be in for years of problems. Pools that win design awards typically cost $30,000 to $40,000, Bellinger says (though one recent winner was an 85-foot indoor pool at a private residence that went for $300,000).

Owners don't have to be slaves to their pools. There are automatic chlorinators, automatic timers, automatic cleaning devices, and automatic chemical testers. If you don't have all these amenities, you can get by if, three times a week, you use your test kit, which measures the chemical balance of the pool's water, Bellinger says. Checking the chemical balance is necessary to prevent algae growth. This balance is affected by rain, by sunshine, by the frequency of use and by the pool's circulation system. The sun breaks down the chlorine faster, and rain adds water and therefore dilutes the chemicals. No two pools are the same.

When you run the pump, it pulls water through the filter. Maintenance companies suggest that in general, the pool water should be turned over once in eight hours. You may need it up to 12 hours a day in the summer, but only six hours a day in the winter. Pumps are rated by horsepower, in gallons per minute. You size the pump to the pool, and the filter to the pump. Figure the number of gallons of water the pool has, divide it by the eight hours, and that should give you an idea of what size pump to get.

One other amenity common in Florida is the "cage," or screening that completely encloses the pool. Costs for these vary, too, but generally start around $5,000. Screens keep the bugs out, provide safety (no one can wander in and fall into the pool), enhance your privacy and keep the pool a little cooler because they screen out 20 percent of the sun's rays, Bellinger says.

Under a state law passed in October 1989, screens need to be stronger to prevent them from flying away in hurricanes. The law, Bellinger says, requires footers, steel reinforcement, and a heavier gauge aluminum.

Many pools are heated, allowing owners to enjoy them throughout the year. In the summer, the heat may make a swimmer feel as if he's in bath water. Water temperatures of 90 degrees are not unheard of. If you can afford a fountain that is part of the pool's pump system, you'll find that once run through the air, the water will be aerated and cooled. Some maintenance workers also suggest using the filter at night.

Gardening

Although, to some, this may not be as exciting as playing golf or watching a spring training baseball game, millions of Floridians love to till the soil. It's a rewarding pastime, and chances that a late Florida frost will ruin your newly planted springtime seedlings are much lower than farther north. Below is a planting guide compiled by the Florida Cooperative Extension Service at the University of Florida in Gainesville.

Planting Guide for Annual Flowers

	North Fla.		Central Fla.		South Fla.	
	Planting Date	Removal Date	Planting Date	Removal Date	Planting Date	Removal Date
Name of Flower						
Ageratum	March 1-15	Aug.	Feb. 15-March 15	July	Feb. 1-March 1	June
Alyssum	March 1-15	July	Feb. 15-March 15	July	Oct. 1-15 Feb. 1-Mar.1	March June
Amaranthus	Mar. 15-30	Sept.	Mar. 15-30	July	July-Aug. March 1-15	Frost July
Asters	Mar. 1-15	July	Feb. 15-28	June	Oct.-Feb.	June
Baby's Breath	Feb. 15-March 15	June	Feb.-March	June April	Aug.-Dec.	March-
Balsam	Mar. 15-30	Aug.	Mar. 1-30	July	Mar.1-30	June-July
Begonia (Nonstop)	March 1-15	June	Feb. 15-28	May	Nov.-March	May

Name of Flower	North Fla. Planting Date	North Fla. Removal Date	Central Fla. Planting Date	Central Fla. Removal Date	South Fla. Planting Date	South Fla. Removal Date
Begonia (Tuberous)	March 1-15	June	Feb. 15-28	May	Oct.-January	April
Begonia (Wax)	March 15-30	Sep.-Oct.	Feb.15-28	Sept.	Sept.-Nov.	Aug.
Browallia	March 1-15	Aug.	Feb. 15-28	Aug.	Oct.-Feb.	Aug.
Calendula	Feb.-March	June	Nov.-Feb.	June	Jan.-Mar.	May
Carnation (China Doll)	Nov.-Feb. 28	June	November-Feb. 28	May	October-Jan. 15	April
Celosia	March 15-July	Seed Set	Mar.-July	Seed Set	February-September	Seed Set
Coleus	April-August	Oct.	Apr.-Aug.	Oct.-Nov.	March-September	First Frost
Calliopsis	March-May	First Frost	March-May	First Frost	February-June	First Frost
Cosmos	March 15	Aug.	February	July	Nov.-Feb.	June
Crossandra	May-July	Oct.	Apr.-July	Oct.	Mar.-Aug.	Nov.
Dahlia	Mar. 15-30	Aug.	Mar. 1-15	Aug.	Sept.-Dec.	July
Dianthus	February	July-Aug.	February	July	October-February	June
Digitalis (Foxglove)	Sept.-Dec.	July	Sept.-Dec.	July	not recommended	
Dusty Miller	Feb.-April	Sept.	Feb.-April	Aug.	Oct.-March	Aug.
Exacum	Mar.-July	When overgrown	Mar.-July	When overgrown	Feb.-Oct.	When overgrown
Gaillardia	March-May	Aug.	Mar.-May	Aug.	Feb.-May	Aug.
Gazania	March-May	Nov.	Feb.15-May	Nov.	Nov.-May	Nov.
Geranium	Mar.-April	July	Feb.-Mar.	July	Oct.-March	June
Hollyhock (Althaea rosea)	Mar.15-June	First Frost	Feb. 15-July	First Frost	Aug.-Sept.	First Frost
Impatiens	Mar.15-July	First Frost	Mar.1-July	First Frost	Sept.-June	First Frost
Kalanchoe	May-July	First Frost	May-Sept.	First Frost	Sept.-Dec.	First Frost
Lobelia	March 15-April	Aug.	Feb.15-April	Aug.	Sept.-Feb.	July
Marguerite Daisy	Feb.15-April	June-July	Feb.-April	June-July	Oct.-Feb.	June
Marigold	March 15-May	3-4 months after planting	Mar.-Aug.	3-4 months after planting	Feb.-Dec.	3-4 months after planting
Nicotiana	March 15-July	Aug.-Sept.	March 1-July	Aug.-Sept.	Feb.-May	Jy/Aug
Ornamental Pepper	Mar.-July	Oct.	Mar.-July	Oct.	Mar.-Aug.	Nov.
Pansy	Oct.-Feb.	June	Oct.-Feb.	May	Oct.-Jan.	April
Pentas	Mar.-May	Leaf disease	Mar.-May	Leaf disease	All year	Leaf disease
Petunia	Oct.-Feb.	May-June	Oct.-Feb.	June	Sept.-Feb.	May
Phlox	Mar.-April	Aug.	Mar.-Apr.	Aug.	Feb.-March	July
Portulaca (Rose moss)	Apr.-July	First Frost	Apr.-July	First Frost	Mar.-August	First Frost
Rudbeckia	Mar.-April	Aug.	Mar.-April	Aug.	Feb.-March	July

Nicotiana South Fla. Removal Date: Ap/May

Name of Flower	North Fla. Planting Date	Removal Date	Central Fla. Planting Date	Removal Date	South Fla. Planting Date	Removal Date
Salvia	Mar.15-Aug.	When deteriorated	Mar.1-Aug.	When deteriorated	Feb.15-Dec.	When deteriorated
Shasta Daisy	Oct.-Dec.	July	Oct.-Dec.	July	Not recommended	
Snapdragon	Oct.-Feb.	June	Oct.-Feb.	May	Nov.-Feb.	April-May
Statice	Feb. 15	June	Dec.-Jan.	June	Sept.-Jan.	May
Strawflower	March 15	Aug.	Feb.	July	Nov.-Feb.	June
Streptocarpus	Mar.-April	June	Mar.-April	June	Feb.-Mar.	May
Sweet Williams	Mar.-April	Aug.	Mar.-April	Aug.	Feb.-Mar.	May
Thunbergia (alata)	Mar.-May	First frost	Mar.-May	First frost	Feb.-April	First frost
Torenia	Mar. 15-June	Leaf yellowing	Mar. 1-June	Leaf yellowing	Feb.-Oct.	Leaf yellowing
Verbena	Mar. 1-May	When undesired	Feb. 15-May	When undesired	Feb.-April Sept.-Nov.	When undesired
Vinca (Catharanthus) (periwinkle)	Mar.-July	When undesired	Feb. 15-July	When undesired	All year	When undesired
Zinnia	Mar.-June	Leaf disease	Mar.-June	Leaf disease	Feb.-Mar. Aug.-Sept.	Leaf disease

Choosing a lawn

Another popular activity in the state is taking care of the lawn. It's likely that whatever grass you planted up north probably won't last long here. Consequently, within Florida, a variety of turfgrasses are used in adapting to the year-round warm climate. While none of these grasses is perfect, as all don't adapt completely to all weather conditions, they'll likely fare a lot better than the grass you left behind. Among the most common types in Florida are St. Augustine and Bahia, according to the Co-operative Extension Service at the University of Florida in Gainesville.

St. Augustine is widely adapted to warm, humid regions, and in Florida is the most commonly planted turfgrass in the urban, coastal areas of the state, says the extension service. This turfgrass type can be grown in a wide variety of soils, but flourishes best in well-drained, fertile ground. Why is it so popular? First, it produces a dark green, dense turf that is well adapted to most soils and climatic regions around the state. Second, it generally tolerates shade better than other warm-season turfgrasses. But there are also some disadvantages: it has a coarse leaf texture that is objectionable to some people; it does not survive drought conditions without supplemental irrigation; some varieties are susceptible to cold damage; and most of its varieties are sus-

ceptible to pest problems, namely chinch bugs.

Bahia grass is widely planted along roadsides, on athletic fields and in urban landscapes. It is used most often in areas that will receive little maintenance — a definite advantage when one is looking for a low-maintenance grass. In fact, Bahia grass requires less maintenance than any other Florida turfgrass, says the extension service. It produces a light green turf and has excellent drought tolerance and, consequently, is the best turfgrass to plant where irrigation is limited or unavailable. In addition, only a few major pest problems exist for Bahai. But, there also are some disadvantages: it has low shoot density that makes it unsuitable in areas where high-quality turf is desired; it is difficult to mow because of its tough leaves and stems; and has a very poor salt tolerance and should not be planted on coastal sites.

Two other grasses are used statewide: bermuda and zoysia. Both can be planted in a wide range of soil conditions, both are rated by the extension service as having an excellent tolerance to drought and wear. Both have a less coarse turf texture than either St. Augustine or Bahia. But there are some problem areas: Bermuda grass has a "very poor" tolerance to shade, has "severe" pest problems and requires more maintenance than most other grasses in that it needs to be mowed every 3-7 days as opposed to 7-14 days for most other grasses. Zoysia's disadvantages also may outweigh any advantages: its tolerance to shade is poor and its pest problems are rated as "moderate-severe."

For more information on turfgrasses, plants, insects, shrubs, water conservation efforts and other gardening needs, contact the Florida Cooperative Extension Service at the University of Florida in Gainesville, or go to your nearest county extension office where copies of these publications are available free.

Other Activities

Shopping

If hell to you is shopping at a big mall, there are lots of places in Florida where you'll be miserable. But for the shop-till-you-drop types, some densely populated counties have more stores than you'll ever be able to visit. You'll find huge malls and strip malls everywhere. See the county-by-county listings for information about retail shopping.

There also are a couple of other types of shopping available in the state:

Antiques. Some communities in Florida have many shops and even antique districts. Among them:

Southeast Florida: Dania, Lake Worth, Palm Beach and West Palm Beach. In addition, the Original Miami Beach Antique Show is usually held in February at the Miami Beach Convention Center.

Southwest: Olde Naples, as well as shows in Naples and Charlotte County.

Central East: Cocoa Village.

Central: Mount Dora, Lakeland, Winter Park.

Central West: Tarpon Springs.

Northeast: Micanopy.

Northwest: Havana and Tallahassee.

Flea markets. Up north, you've probably been to flea markets, lawn sales, garage sales, tag sales and other types of sales. But flea markets in Florida can be huge — hundreds of yards, if not miles of aisles at some of them. No doubt you'll find a lot of junk, but you'll also find deals on personal items, clothing and arts and crafts. Some even sell Oriental rugs and furniture. Many people do their Christmas shopping at these markets. And some of the merchants earn their living by going to several markets a week. You'll find these flea markets in most heavily populated areas of the state.

The Lottery

One very popular form of entertainment in the Sunshine State is playing the lottery — residents and nonresidents have spent billions trying their luck.

The first lottery tickets where sold on Jan. 12, 1988. The game was almost an instant success, setting a national record in its first week of operation — selling $95 million in instant tickets, topping the previous record, held by California, of $80 million. The state also set a new North American record for first-month on-line computer sales — $52 million. This topped the old record of $29 million, again held by California.

The Florida Lottery was created by the state legislature in June 1987 after Floridians voted by a 2-1 margin in November 1986 to institute the game. A state agency, called the Department of the Lottery, was created to run the lottery as much as possible like a business. In creating the lottery, state officials also mandated that at least 35 percent of the lottery's gross revenue be set aside for educational enhancement. During its first year, the lottery generated more than $531 million for this purpose. By 1990-91, the figure was more than $833 million. The school-funding aspect of the lottery, though, has been controversial (see Education chapter).

Since 1988, the list of lottery winners has grown steadily, with $30 million, $50 million and even $100 million jackpots not unheard of. On Sept. 15, 1990, a $106,500,000 lotto prize was divided among six winning tickets (this prize is being paid in 20 annual installments of $887,500 to each of the six winners).

Some other lottery facts:

— First-year per capita sales in Florida were $128. States with the next highest first-year figures: California, $67; Washington, $45; Arizona, $36; Illinois, $13; and Pennsylvania, $10.

— A total of 50 percent of every lottery dollar spent goes into the lottery prize pool, 38 percent into the educational enhancement trust fund, 5.5 percent to lottery retailers, 4.15 percent to cover administrative costs and 2.35 percent to cover ticket-related costs.

— About three quarters of the lottery ticket sales have been handled by convenience and grocery stores.

— Among the games people can play are Lotto, where players pick six numbers from 1 through 49 and try to match them with the numbers drawn every Saturday at about 10:58 p.m. At the drawing, 49 ping-pong balls, numbered 1 through 49, are mixed in the Lotto drawing machine. Six of these numbers are drawn at random and the official winning numbers are announced. The grand prize winner must match six of the six numbers. Other prizes are given for those matching anywhere from three to five of the numbers. Since Lotto is a parimutuel game, you must be 18 years or older to play.

— The odds of picking 6 of 6 numbers are 1 in 13,983,816; 5 of 6 numbers are 1 in 54,200.84; 4 of 6 numbers are 1 in 1,032.4; and 3 of 6 numbers are 1 in 56.66.

— Prizes of up to $599 can be claimed at any Lotto retailer location; winners of more than $599 must validate their ticket at the Lotto retailer and then file a claim. Prizes of more than $599, except Grand Prize winners, are paid in full, less federal tax withholding. Grand Prize winners may be paid in 20 equal annual payments, or in a lump sum, at the discretion of the lottery.

— Other games include Fantasy 5, where players pick five numbers, from 1 through 39, with three drawings a week, on Mondays, Wednesdays and Fridays at around 11 p.m; Cash 3, where players choose any three numbers between 000 and 999. Players who have chosen all three winning numbers can win up to $500 for each $1 played. Drawings for this are held every night at 7:57 p.m.; and Play 4, where players choose any four-digit number of 0000 through 9999 and if that number matches the official winning number, the player can win up to $5,000. These numbers are also drawn daily at 7:57 p.m.

— The names of those winning more than $600 are matched against a list of people under court order by the Department of Health and Rehabilitative Services to pay child support. If names match, the child support money is taken out of the winnings.

— Among those who won lots and lots of money: Sheelah Ryan of Winter Springs, who won $55,160,000 on Sept. 3, 1988. Her winnings were being paid in 20 equal installments of $2,758,000. After she won, she established the Sheelah Ryan Foundation, which helps build low-cost housing in Seminole County for needy single mothers. Ryan, who had no immediate family, moved to Florida from the New York City area in 1975 and was a real estate agent. She chose her winning numbers by looking at the first six numbers she saw on the front page of the Aug. 3 edition of the Orlando Sentinel. She died in 1994.

— Other sizable single grand-prize winners include Gloria Mitchem of Bronson, who won $37,460,000; and Dennis Glover, 35, of Temple Terrace, $35,860,000.

— According to the state, the first recorded lottery with prize money was in Florence, Italy, in 1530. England established a lottery in 1569 and by the early 1600s lotteries had spread to America. The first American lottery raised money to help the Jamestown settlement, while George Washington authorized lotteries to raise money for the Revolutionary Army. Some Ivy League colleges later were funded by lottery proceeds.

— New Hampshire was the first state to operate a lottery, starting in 1964.

Metaphysical Florida

If people often say to you, "Good heavens, you've read my mind," you'll join scores of other Floridians, some of whom make their living with their sixth senses. Cassadaga, in central east Florida in Volusia County, is the home of the Southern Cassadaga Spiritualist Camp, a large contingent of mediums, clairvoyants and mind readers.

And on the southwest coast in Estero is the Koreshan Unity Settlement, a state historic site that is a former "religious utopia" that existed from 1894 until 1977. The state says that "by following the paths and roadways you will be able to visit the people of another time, whose beliefs brought them here to a life of strenuosity and sacrifice to establish a New Jerusalem in the Florida wilderness." Among the original settlers were seven women who made up the Planetary Chamber, the governing council of the Koreshan Unit. Each of the seven was called by the name of one of the seven planets.

Disney World, which includes EPCOT Center and its famous "Spaceship Earth" geosphere, is the state's top attraction.

Above: Sea World in Orlando, where kids can feed the dolphins, has had 4 million visitors in recent years.

Busch Gardens in Tampa houses more than 3,300 animals. It is both a zoo and a theme park and has a variety of rides, such as the "Congo River Rapids" ride.

MAJOR ATTRACTIONS

Disney World, EPCOT and MGM Studios

You're suffering from an aching back and sore leg muscles and can hardly get out of bed. You think about the day before and remember how much you walked — even raced — to as many rides and attractions as you could cram into 14 hours. You were at the gate before 9 a.m. and stayed at EPCOT Center until closing time, 11 p.m., because you wanted to see it all. Now you wish you hadn't stood in those long lines — some for more than an hour — just to experience a ride that lasted less than five minutes or a new thrill ride that gave you motion sickness. You wish you had eaten dinner instead of skipping it just so you could see most of the 260 acres of the park. And you wish you had delayed going to EPCOT until early May instead of seeing it in April with thousands of other people who were also on their spring vacation.

But, as with many people who visit the park, you probably would be willing to endure the aches and pains and long lines again and are already starting to make plans to come back again. You saw sights you probably won't see anywhere else and you already feel a desire to see them again. There aren't many places where you can see talking vegetables, ride in a "geosphere," see a 10 p.m. laser light show called "IllumiNations," or view a travel film about Canada or China on a 360-degree screen.

For the unsuspecting traveler to Disney World, which is 20 miles southwest of Orlando, there are some experiences, some great and some not so great, that await you. The best advice is to do your homework before you go to cut down on disappointments or unpleasant surprises. You might encounter traffic snarls, decide to visit at the wrong time of year, or be shocked at the entrance fees.

But there are many good things that likely will be in store for you. There's a reason why Disney World attracts millions of people each year — there's a lot to see in each of its three theme parks (the Magic Kingdom, EPCOT Center and Disney-MGM Studios):

MAGIC KINGDOM

This park covers 100 acres and has parking for more than 12,000 vehicles. Opened Oct. 1, 1971, today there are seven "lands" with about 45 shows and rides: **Main Street USA,** which has such rides as the Walt Disney Railroad and such attractions as the Walt Disney Story film and the penny arcade; **Mickey's Starland** with Mickey's House & Starland Show, Mickey's Hollywood Theatre and Grandma Duck's Farm; **Adventureland** with the Swiss Family Treehouse, the Jungle Cruise and the popular Pirates of the Caribbean ride; **Frontierland** with the Big Thunder Mountain Railroad ride, Tom Sawyer Island, the Country Bear Jamboree, a shooting arcade, a thrill ride called Splash Mountain and a live floor show called "The Diamond Horseshow Jamboree;" **Liberty Square** with The Hall of Presidents, Liberty Square Riverboat and the Haunted Mansion; **Fantasyland,** which contains a number of rides for youngsters, including Dumbo the Flying Elephant, Cinderella's Golden Carrousel, It's a Small World, Peter Pan's Flight, the Mad Tea Party, and a few rides that could be too intense for small children, including Mr. Toad's Wild Ride and Snow White's Adventures (and the Wicked Witch). One of the most popular rides here is 20,000 Leagues Under the Sea; and **Tomorrowland** with its Space Mountain rollercoaster ride, a Mission to Mars ride, the Carousel of Progress attraction, which shows how electricity has changed people's lives, Dreamflight and StarJets rides and the "American Journeys" film.

Of course, there is at least one restaurant and gift shop at every land you visit. Mickey Mouse and other Disney characters roam around the park during the day and pose for pictures, give out hugs and shake hands. And if you've dreamed of seeing Cinderella's castle, it's also here. To top off your stay, there are fireworks shows and parades. Times when the parks open and close vary according to the season.

EPCOT CENTER

There are two major areas to this park — Future World and the World Showcase. The parking area here also holds about 12,000 vehicles. EPCOT, which stands for Experimental Prototype Community of Tomorrow, opened Oct. 1, 1982.

Future World

You can't help but notice the entrance to Future World when you step through the admissions gates — an attraction called **Spaceship Earth.** This is a 180-foot-high "geosphere" where visitors can ride in slow-moving cars inside the globe, first up an incline and then down, for a view of an abbreviated, but excellent, history of communications, from cave men to satellites. A loudspeaker in each of the two-person cars carries the voice of Walter Cronkite, who narrates a commentary on what you are seeing. Also in this section of the park are a number of other attractions: the **Universe of Energy,** where you can see battling dinosaurs and a film, on a 210-foot-long screen, about energy sources; the **Wonders of Life** exhibit, where you can take a rocking-and-rolling ride called "Body Wars" through the human body (if you suffer from motion sickness, you'd better skip this one), or climb inside the head of a young boy or find out more about pregnancy and birth; the **Horizons** exhibit, where you view possible lifestyles of the 21st century such as floating cities and space colonies; the **World of Motion** exhibit, a comic look at the history of transportation and at a prototype of a 21st-century urban commuter car; the **Journey into Imagination** exhibit, where the depths of one's imagination are explored through animation and "talking" figures; **The Land** exhibit, which has a cruise through a tropical rain forest and a desert and offers a look at new ways crops are being grown today. Another section of the exhibit is on good nutrition through the use of "talking" vegetables; and **The Living Seas** exhibit, a huge aquarium that holds 5.7 million gallons of seawater and more than 80 species of fish and mammals.

Also opened in 1994 was an Innoventions Plaza within Future World. Here, visitors can test, feel and see products from dozens of companies, such as voice-controlled electric cars and advanced computer software.

World Showcase

Eleven countries offer views of their homelands through art exhibits, films, dance, rides or theatrical presentations. A common denominator is that all have at least one restaurant that gives visitors a taste of the native land and at least one shop filled with souvenir and gift items. Among the countries are **Mexico** (with its El Rio del Tiempo river ride); **Norway** (with its Maelstrom amusement ride); **China** (with its "Wonders of China" film presentation); **Germany** (with Oktoberfest entertainment at its Biergarten restaurant); **Italy** (with its L'Originale Alfredo di Roma Ristorante); **Canada** (with its "O Canada!" film); the **United Kingdom** (with its Rose & Crown Pub restaurant); **France** (with its "Impressions de France" motion picture); **Morocco** (with its live music and dance presentations); **Japan** (with its Bijutsu-kan Gallery); and the **United States** (with "The American Adventure" presentation).

DISNEY-MGM STUDIOS

Opened in 1989, this attraction seeks to give a behind-the-scenes look at how movies and television shows are produced. On the **Backstage Studio Tour,** which lasts under two hours, visitors spend some of their time on a tram and then take a hour-long walking tour. During the tram tour, visitors are taken to a working movie and television production center and get fleeting glimpses of the costuming department, a residential street (including the "house" — really just a building facade — seen on the "The Golden Girls"), the scenic shop, a New York street backlot with a simulated Empire State Building and Chrysler Building, a special-effects workshop and shooting stage, soundstages, the post-production editing and audio departments and a longer look at new movies that Disney is coming out with, at the Walt Disney Theater. During the tour, there's also a trip through **Catastrophe Canyon,** where visitors experience man-made disasters at close range, including an explosion, an earthquake, a fire and a flash flood (complete with a splash or two if you're sitting near the water). There's a stop at a water-effects tank (showing how miniature ships are used to simulate battle scenes in movies). There also are a couple of other tricks used by moviemakers that Disney reveals during the tour. Elsewhere in the theme park, there is a section called **Hollywood Boulevard,** with such attractions as **The Great Movie Ride** and a stage show featuring Disney characters. The movie ride tries to bring to life some scenes from such movie hits as "Casablanca," "The Wizard of Oz," "Alien" and "Indiana Jones." The Wicked

Witch of the West makes her appearance, as do Dorothy and Toto, Bogart and Bergman (who are standing outside that plane ready to take off in Casablanca) and Indiana Jones (who has found the Lost Ark). The restaurants in this section bear names such as "The Hollywood Brown Derby" and the "Hollywood & Vine" cafeteria. Other attractions in the park include **SuperStar Television** (where members of the audience can star alongside television personalities in clips from such shows as "I Love Lucy," the "Today Show," "The Tonight Show" and "General Hospital"; **The Chevy Chase and Martin Short in Monster Sound show,** where movie sound effects are explored (people are picked out of the audience to help create the sound effects for part of a movie starring Chevy Chase and Martin Short); **Star Tours,** a ride through the cosmos where visitors climb into flight simulators that turn and dive in conjunction with "Star Wars" film footage; and the **Indiana Jones Epic Stunt Spectacular** (with huge movable sets, lots of action, explosions, fires and stunts). Visitors also can take an **Animation Tour** and watch artists at work. With the help of a narration by Walter Cronkite and Robin Williams, visitors are taken through the stages of animation, from the story department (where characters and their situations are developed) to the editing stage (where scenes are joined and come out in a final movie form).

Other attractions include: a Beauty and the Beast stage presentation; Jim Henson's Muppet Vision 3D show; Twilight Zone Tower of Terror thrill ride, where visitors enter the "Holloywood Tower Hotel" and relive the journey of five elevator passengers who mysteriously disappeared on a stormy night in 1939; visitors face plunging from the 13th floor of the tower; Jim Henson's Muppets on Location; Voyage of The Little Mermaid show; and Aladdin's Royal Caravan and Teenage Mutant Ninja Turtles' appearances.

Disney Drawbacks

There are some not-so-great things about Disney World:

— Trying to make a reservation at a Disney World hotel the week before you have decided to visit. You've read that staying at a hotel on the grounds of Disney World is a great way to see the parks. You wouldn't have to rent a car because there are monorail trains, buses and boats to take you to the Magic Kingdom, EPCOT or Disney-MGM Studios. Even though there are nearly 20 Disney hotels, a campground, a vacation club and vacation villas (with about 20,500 rooms and growing yearly) you're looking at spring break week and you find out that no rooms will be available in the whole park. You're told you should have made reservations months ago. And you also find out the price of these rooms — many in the $200-a-night range.

— Snarled traffic. Having failed to get a room in the park, you finally are able to get a room elsewhere in the Orlando area, for they have well over 70,000 to choose from. But you may face another surprise. Especially for someone from a rural community, you may never have experienced anything like what you will see when you leave your hotel room near downtown Orlando and attempt to get on Interstate 4 to take you to Disney World. You may find yourself waiting in lines of traffic for more than an hour, and you'll spend much of your precious vacation time on the highway.

— Timing. Some times and days of the week are less crowded than others. Peak-attendance periods, according to Disney World officials, are in the summer and around Thanksgiving, Christmas, Easter and spring break. If you don't like standing in line, maybe you should plan your vacation in January, May or in the fall. Disney officials also say that Mondays, Tuesdays and Wednesdays are the busiest days of the week, Saturdays are only moderately busy, and Sundays, Thursdays and Fridays are lower-attendance days. Another rule of thumb: If you do go to the parks during peak attendance periods, arrive early — by 9 a.m. — to beat some of the crowds that come later in the morning. The parks also lengthen their hours of operation during peak tourist seasons and are open until 11 p.m. or midnight.

— Parking. You finally make it to Disney World and find out another surprise: You must pay for parking inside Disney World; $5 a car or $10 for campers.

— Entrance fees. Unless you do your homework beforehand, you may be shocked at the price of a ticket into the Magic Kingdom, EPCOT Center or Disney-MGM Studios. A one-day ticket was $38 (this includes tax) in 1994 (for children ages 3-9, the price was $30.60). This ticket entitles you to visit just one park that day (you can't spend half of your time at EPCOT and then decide at 1 p.m. you want to see the Magic Kingdom; that will cost you an additional $38).

There are four-day "hopper" tickets that allow you to go to any of the three theme parks any time of the day or night during ANY four days; these also save you money (about $10, based on buying a one-park, one-day adult ticket). The price in 1994: $134 plus tax (or $107 plus tax for children ages 3-9).

There is also a four-day "value-pass" ticket

that allows you to visit the Magic Kingdom for one day; EPCOT another day, MGM the third day and then any park of your choice the fourth day. This ticket is also good for ANY four days. The cost: $124 plus tax for adults and $97 for children ages 3-9.

And there are five-day "hopper" tickets allowing unlimited entrance for ANY five days into the three theme parks. And you can use these for a period of seven days, beginning with the first date stamped, to get into four other attractions — Typhoon Lagoon, Discovery Island, Pleasure Island and River Country ($179 plus tax or $143 plus tax for children 3-9 years old).

There are no two- and three-day packages that save you money. You pay the $38 each of the two or three days. Disney also offers annual passes (adults $205 plus tax and children $179 plus tax). These allow unlimited admission to the three parks for one year from the date of voucher redemption.

If you are a Florida resident, you can get what Disney calls a "Florida Four-Season Salute Pass" ($104.10 for adults and $93.65 for children) that allows unlimited visits to the parks during certain times of the year: from mid-August through September; from late November to just before Christmas; from January through early February; and from late April until early June.

— Food prices. If you're on a budget, plan ahead. The cost of a soft drink at some concession stands can be nearly $2, for example. Typical costs generally are higher — some sandwiches can go for several dollars more — than you would pay at off-site restaurants.

To the dismay of those who want Florida visitors to spend money in other parts of the Orlando area or the state, Disney World officials are working hard to keep Florida visitors only on their 28,000 acres. For example, Disney stresses that a rental car is usually unnecessary for guests who stay on their property. Once within its confines, you will find Disney hotels, eating places and places where you can swim. You also will discover other attractions: Typhoon Lagoon, a water park with man-made waves up to 6 feet high, a man-made 90-foot mountain, thrill rides and tube rides, a place for snorkeling and spots for the kids; River Country swimming and tubing area; a place called Pleasure Island, which contains nightclubs (dance, comedy and rock & roll); restaurants and shops including the Disney Village Marketplace; camping facilities, nature trails, golf courses, tennis courts, a marina, sailing, canoeing, fishing, horseback riding, a zoo (at Discovery Island), vacation villas, recreation and entertainment complexes and even convention facilities. Plans call for the possible creation of new theme parks, new residential areas, business and research centers and more resort facilities within the park.

Other Attractions

Consistently, nearly half of Florida's air and auto visitors who had visited an attraction and had been interviewed in state tourism studies said they went to a Disney theme park during their stay. But this hasn't deterred a number of other attractions from competing for tourists' money. Here are some other popular attractions.

UNIVERSAL STUDIOS

Opened officially in June 1990, this attraction is competing head-on with Disney's MGM studios theme park. There are some similarities: Both are located in the Orlando area, both contain working motion picture and television production facilities, both provide visitors with a behind-the-scenes look at how movie and television shows are produced, and both have movie-themed attractions. Each has its own cast of cartoon character stars — be it Mickey Mouse or Fred Flintstone. It'll be up to the visitor to decide which park does the better job.

The $650-million Universal complex claims to be the largest motion picture and television production facility outside of Hollywood. Universal is estimating that the park, located on 444 acres 10 miles southwest of Orlando, will lure 6 million visitors a year. It is owned by MCA Inc. and the London-based Rank Organisation. It has parking for 7,100 vehicles. The park offers many "interactive" attractions where visitors can relive action sequences and participate in set design, editing, sound effects and dubbing. For example, visitors can get behind-the-scenes looks at the television series "Murder, She Wrote Mystery Theatre" by participating in the post-production process. Visitors decide who committed the crime and who Angela Lansbury's guest star is for the show. Or they can learn how some horror scenes are shot by attending "The Gory, Gruesome & Grotesque Horror Make-Up Show." They can learn how razor blade cuts and gunshot wounds are made to look real and see how a person's neck can be sliced without leaving a scratch. "The Fly" also makes an appearance. For a look at how the shower scene in the movie "Psycho" was shot, the "Hitchcock's 3-D Movie Theatre" attraction will provide some answers. If you don't want to relive the shower scene, you'd better skip this one. An overview of some of Alfred Hitchcock's other movies is also seen, some through 3-D glasses.

Among the shows, some of which are interactive, are "Ghostbusters: A Live-Action Spooktacular," "Dynamite Nights Stunt Spectacular," "The Wild, Wild, WIld West Stunt Show," "Lucy: A Tribute," "American Tail: Fievel's Playland," "The Adventures of Rocky and Bullwinkle," and "Beetlejuice's Graveyard Revue."

Of course, Universal has a motion picture backlot, too — more than 40 set locations (from a New England village to its own version of New York City's Upper East Side) — that houses restaurants and shops and can be shot as film sets. On the Production Studio Tour, visitors can see the filming of some Nickelodeon Network shows, see sets under construction and learn about special effects, lighting and sound. Nickelodeon, a television network for kids, resides in the theme park. Kids can also audition to become part of televised shows either as guests or as contestants.

Long lines form around the movie-themed ride attractions including those featuring such movies as "Jaws," "Back to the Future," "Kongfrontation," "Earthquake: The Big One," and "E.T. Adventure" For example, in the E.T. attraction, visitors get on "starbound bicycles" and outrace the police and government agents who want to keep E.T. on Earth. Visitors then find themselves on the Green Planet, E.T.'s home. At the end of the ride, E.T. thanks guests by name (you turn in a name card as you get on this ride) for coming.

You won't find Mickey Mouse or Donald Duck walking around here, but a number of other animated characters and stars from both the cartoons and movies roam the park and pose for pictures with visitors. Among them are Woody Woodpecker, Frankenstein, Fred Flintstone, Yogi Bear, Scooby Doo, Charlie Chaplin, Marilyn Monroe, W.C. Fields and the Blues Brothers. Restaurants are plentiful here, too, and include Mel's Drive-In of "American Graffiti" fame and a Hard Rock Cafe. If you like to see animals performing on stage, you can see this here during the Animal Actors Show featuring working television and film animal stars. There's also an attraction called The Funtastic World of Hanna Barbera, where guests see the cartoon world of the Flintstones, the Jetsons, Yogi Bear and Scooby Doo in their animated lands. Guests also can try their own hand at animation. For those wanting to learn more about how to make their own record, there's an MCA Recording Studios in the park.

The motion picture and television production studios here opened in October 1988. Among the movies produced so far are "Parenthood" and "Psycho IV." A number of television shows also have been filmed here, including "The New Leave It to Beaver" and "Superboy" series.

Universal is open every day of the year. Daily operating hours vary by season. In 1994, a one-day studio pass for anyone 10 years and older was $38.16; for children ages 3-9, $30.74, and for those under age 3, free. Two-day passes for ages 10 and up were $58.30 and for children 3-9, $46.64. Annual passes were also available: ages 10 and up, $92.75; ages 3-9, $74.20, and under 3, free. Parking was $5 for cars and $7 for recreational vehicles and trailers.

SEA WORLD

Located about a 10-minute drive from Disney World in Orlando, this park draws a lot of people who want to see more than Mickey Mouse in Florida. While Sea World doesn't have the only aquarium in Florida, it has a lot of things no other place in the area has. For example, there's the legendary Shamu, the killer whale, who gets top billing here. There's also Baby Shamu, born Nov. 4, 1988, who stars in the popular killer whale show called **Shamu: New Visions,** performed in the 5,200-seat Shamu Stadium, which contains five million gallons of man-made seawater. A recent addition to the show is a video screen that gives guests up-close views of the whales and their trainers. Among the other shows are: a **Big Splash Bash** multimedia presentation in the Nautilus Theatre; **Shamu: Close Up!,** which allows visitors to get a closer view of the killer whale's habitat; **Mermaids, Myths & Monsters** fireworks and laser show; **Shamu: World Focus** killer whale presentation; **Mission: Bermuda Triangle,** which takes visitors on a submarine voyage; **Shamu's Happy Harbor,** a three-acre, four-story children's play area; an **Anheuser-Busch Hospitality Center** with a hospitality house and a Clydesdale hamlet; a **Terrors of the Deep** attraction that exposes visitors to such sea creatures as eels, barracuda and sharks. As a part of the show, visitors go down a moving walkway encased in a four-inch-thick clear acrylic tube where they are transported near the bottom of a huge aquarium; the **Whale and Dolphin Discovery** show that displays bottlenose dolphins and false killer whales; the **Gold Rush Ski Show** at the park's 17-acre Atlantis Lagoon where water skiers do long-distance jumping and acrobatic barefoot skiing; a comedy show called **Hotel Clyde and Seamore** that stars otters, walruses and sea lions; and a **Window to the Sea** show that gives visitors a behind-the-scenes look at Sea World, including a stop backstage at Shamu Stadium.

Two tours are available: an **Animal Lover's Adventure** 90-minute guided tour on marine conservation and animal habitats; and an **Animal Training Discoveries** 45-minute presentation exploring animal behavior and training techniques.

There also are a number of exhibits to explore, including a **Penguin Encounter** exhibit that houses hundreds of penguins and alcids (Arctic birds); a **Tropical Reef** display with more than 1,000 tropical fish in a 160,000-gallon man-made coral reef; a manatee exhibit; a **Pacific Point Preserve** setting that duplicates the northern Pacific coast; a **Caribbean Tide Pool** that allows visitors a close-up view of tropical fish and invertebrates such as sea urchins and starfish; **Community Pools** that allow visitors an opportunity to touch sting rays, dolphins and sea lions; and a **Hawaiian Village** performance where the "Hawaiian Rhythms" troupe performs songs and dances of the Polynesian isles.

Admission in 1994, including tax, was $34.95 for ages 10 and up; $29.95 for children ages 3-9 and free for children under age 3. Two-day passes were also available — $39.95 for adults and $34.95 for children 3-9. Discounts are avilable for AAA members, the handicapped, senior citizens and military personnel. The park is open generally from 9 a.m. to 7 p.m. year-round, with hours varying during the summer and holidays. Sea World says it takes about 8 hours to see all of its shows and attractions. Parking was $5 for cars and $7 for recreational vehicles and campers.

Sea World originally opened on Dec. 15, 1973, and was owned by Harcourt Brace Jovanovich, whose major business is book publishing, until 1989. Then it was purchased by the Busch Entertainment Corp., which owns Busch Gardens in Tampa.

BUSCH GARDENS, THE DARK CONTINENT

Using the theme of Africa as a backdrop, Busch Gardens houses more than 3,300 animals representing 330 species. Located on the west coast of Florida in Tampa, about an hour away from Disney World, this 300-acre attraction is both a zoo and a theme park with live entertainment, shops, restaurants and thrill rides. The park, which opened in 1959 as a hospitality center for the Anheuser-Busch brewery, draws millions of visitors. It is one of the most popular attractions in the state.

Here, come prepared to get wet on some of the rides. For example, the Tanganyika Tidal Wave sends riders down a 55-foot drop into a lake; the Congo River Rapids white water ride takes visitors on a white-water raft trip in which

lots of water will be sprayed and splashed into your craft (some people get completely soaked and others in the same raft manage to escape some of the drenching); and Stanley Falls sends visitors on a log flume ride. Raincoats are sold in the park. For thrill seekers, there are three roller coasters: the Kumba, the Python and the Scorpion.

For easier going, the park is divided into themed sections that are meant to "capture the spirit of turn-of-the-century Africa." The sections include one opened in 1992 called **Myombe Reserve: The Great Ape Domain** (has gorillas and chimpanzees in a misty and foggy environment); **Timbuktu** (housing the "Phoenix" boat swing ride, a 1,000-seat Das Festhaus dining and entertainment hall with German-style food — including a four-inch-square chocolate and cream cake about half a foot high — and music; the "Scorpion" roller coaster; Dolphin Theatre; "Carousel Caravan," a games arcade; a shopping area; a "Sandstorm" thrill ride, and African craftsmen at work); **Morocco** (housing Moroccan craft demonstrations; shopping, a Mystic Sheiks of Morocco marching band; and the 1,200-seat Moroccan Palace indoor theater, where an ice show is performed; **Serengeti Plain** (an 80-acre home to nearly 500 African animals such as hippos, giraffes, gazelles, Cape buffalo, zebras, rhinos and camels); **Nairobi** (housing an animal nursery, a petting zoo, reptile displays, the Nairobi train station, and Nocturnal Mountain — a place where visitors can observe species that are active at night); **Stanleyville** (housing the "Tanganyika Tidal Wave," a shopping bazaar, "Stanley Falls," and a theater); **The Congo** (housing the "Congo River Rapids" ride, the "Python," a 1,200-foot roller coaster with a 360-degree double spiral, the "Monstrous Mamba" and the "Kumba" rides and a white and yellow Bengal tiger display); **Bird Gardens** (housing 2,000 exotic birds, a koala exhibit, and a children's play area called Dwarf Village); and **Crown Colony** (housing the Questor ride and a full-service restaurant and hospitality center (where visitors can sample Anheuser-Busch products) with a Victorian atmosphere.

A train, a monorail and a skyride help visitors get around the park. In addition, it would be hard to go through an Anheuser-Busch park without seeing one of its trademarks — a Budweiser Clydesdale horse. Six of them are in the Crown Colony area of the park and you can get a closeup view of them. There's also a dolphin show here, which also features a 500-pound sea lion. The dolphins do a variety of tricks, such as catching a football and throwing it back and grabbing fish out of a trainer's mouth. There are a number of shows such as a "Stanleyville World Talent Showcase," with performances by such artists as jugglers, aerialists or acrobats; a "World of Birds" show; and a "Heart of the Country" music revue.

In 1994, admission was $32.95 for ages 10 and above, $26.55 for children ages 3-9; children under age 3 were admitted free. Annual passes were available: an adult pass was $79.95 and a children's pass for ages 3-9 was $49.95. Also available is a year-round combination ticket that serves as admission into Sea World, Busch Gardens and Cypress Gardens (another Anheuser-Busch attraction, near Winter Haven) for $119.95. Discounts are available for AAA members, groups and senior citizens. There was also a $3-per-car, $4-per-truck or camper and $2-per-motorcycle parking fee and 3,500 parking spaces. The park is open from 9:30 a.m. to 6 p.m. daily; hours are extended in the summer and on some holidays.

NASA KENNEDY SPACE CENTER'S SPACEPORT USA

Also drawing millions of visitors a year, this attraction has joined the ranks of major league tourist spots in the state. Located on the East Coast of Florida in Brevard County near Titusville, the center is less than an hour from Disney World (the point nearly all Florida attractions measure distances from). Even when no space shuttle missions were flown for more than 2 1/2 years, the visitors kept coming; in 1986 in the aftermath of the Challenger accident, 2.1 million people came to tour the space center; in 1992, the number was 2.8 million. Promoting itself as "Florida's Best Visitor Value," many of the exhibits and programs are free. The way to see everything during your tour (and perhaps even see a space shuttle sitting on a launch pad) is to pay $7 for adults or $4 for children ages 3-11 and take a bus tour. It's the best way to see or drive by the Vehicle Assembly building (where the space shuttle is assembled and readied for flight); the Crawler Transporters (which take the shuttle to the launch pad); the Communications Distribution and Switching Center (which serves as a link between the Kennedy Space Center and Mission Control in Houston and other NASA centers); the Central Instrumentation Facility (filled with computers that help analyze rocket and spacecraft performance of unmanned space vehicles); the Operations and Checkout Building (where the astronaut crews live before their missions); the Flight Crew Training Building (which houses a simulator firing room for an Apollo launch) and a view of some launch pads.

Not free are three films — "Destiny in Space," narrated by Leonard Nimoy, which is a 40-minute film that includes footage of the exterior views of the space shuttle in flight around the Earth and computer imaging sequences of Mars and Venus; "The Dream is Alive," narrated by Walter Cronkite, which is a 37-minute film that includes footage shot by astronauts while they were in space; and "Blue Planet," a 42-minute film that views Earth from 200 miles in space. The cost of the movies is $4 for adults and $2 for children ages 3-11. Among the freebies here are the Gallery of Manned Spaceflight Museum, housing such artifacts as a spacesuit worn by Astronaut David Scott, Gemini, Mercury and Apollo spacecraft and lunar rock samples; a "Satellites and You" exhibit with audio-animatronic characters that move, blink their eyes and talk about how satellites affect life on Earth, and simulated space station corridors and work stations (this exhibit takes about 45 minutes to walk through); an outdoor "rocket garden;" an art gallery; a full-sized replica of the space shuttle; an Astronauts Memorial near the Spaceport USA entrance, which honors the 15 U.S. astronauts who have died in the line of duty; and free parking. It will take about 5-6 hours to view this attraction and weekends are generally less busy than weekdays. The attraction is open from 9 a.m. until dusk every day except Christmas. The spaceport is also closed to the public on launch dates until the launch is completed. Visitors, though, can purchase a ticket to view an actual launch. The spaceport sells about 1,500 tickets to visitors to board buses to a viewing site about six miles away. Tickets are $7 for adults and $4 for children ages 3-11 and reservations should be made about one week before launch by calling 407-452-2121, extensions 260 or 261.

CYPRESS GARDENS

This park is located about 40 minutes from Disney World near Winter Haven and is Florida's oldest attraction, having opened in 1936. Cypress Gardens has been luring tourists for years for two major reasons: its water ski show and its botanical gardens. Today, Cypress Gardens still has world-class performers in daily waterskiing and more than 8,000 varieties of plants and flowers from 75 countries. Those revisiting the gardens, purchased by the Busch Entertainment Corp. in 1989, will find a few changes: several new attractions.

The ski show features barefoot skiing, ramp jumping and four-tier human pyramids. There is a seven-acre nursery complex needed to keep up the displays in the botanical gardens. More than 10,000 plants are produced each week, or more than 500,000 a year. For example, there are more than 500 American rose varieties in the All-American Rose Garden; there's a 40-foot-high bougainvillea and a floss silk tree. And there are four annual floral festivals: the Spring Flower Festival, with more than 75,000 bedding plants including an 18-foot high Easter bunny; the Victorian Garden Park during the summer with such topiary figures as a life-sized carousel, horse-drawn wagon and a town square; the Chrysanthemum Festival in November with more than 2 million multi-colored blooms; and a Christmastime Poinsettia Festival including a "Garden of Lights." Visitors walking through the gardens will notice something else — the presence of Southern Belles, dressed in gowns that were handmade in the Cypress Gardens wardrobe department. Each gown is made up of about 10 yards of fabric and 20 yards of lace or other trim. It is estimated that the belles are photographed 500 times a day.

Among the other sights are a butterfly conservatory; an Anheuser-Busch Hospitality Center; the Cypress Roots Museum, which houses a collection of cameras from the 1920s to 1970s, the water skis used in the original Cypress Gardens shows and photos of personalities who have visited the park; a display of radios from the 1920s through the 1950s; a "Feathered Follies" performance with macaws, cockatoos and parrots; the "Carousel Cove" children's play area with rides and games; an acrobatic circus performance; "Kodak's Island in the Sky" ride that takes visitors 153 feet in the air for a look at the park; and an exhibit called "Cypress Junction" — a model railroad that has more than 1,100 feet of track, about 400 buildings, 4,800 miniature figures and up to 20 trains moving at once; electric boat rides; and pontoon boat lake cruises (an additional charge.)

The park is open 365 days a year from 9:30 a.m. to 5:30 p.m., with extended hours during the Christmas season. Admission in 1994 was $26.45 for adults, $17.40 for children ages 3 through 9 and free for children under age 3. Parking was free. Annual passes were $49.95 plus tax for adults and $29.95 plus tax for children ages 3-9. Group, AAA and senior discounts were available.

SILVER SPRINGS

Home of glass-bottom-boat rides, the park has been chosen as a setting in about 200 films and television shows. It is located east of Ocala in the town of Silver Springs. The most popular attractions here are the boat rides in crystal-clear springs. Large glass viewing panels in the boats allow visitors to see underwater life and formations. A newer attraction, Jeep Safari, was added in 1990 (the first expansion at the park in 12 years). This attraction takes visitors on a 30-minute one-mile safari ride in Wrangler Jeeps. About 60 wildlife species can be viewed during the ride, along with a drive through an alligator pit. Also located in the vicinity of the rides is Doolittle's petting zoo. Visitors can pet and feed such baby animals as llamas, goats, sheep, deer and a giraffe. Among the other attractions are: a jungle cruise (a safari down the Fort King Waterway in electric boats where passengers can see emus, zebras, monkeys and ostriches); the Lost River Voyage, a 30-minute mile-long ride down the Silver River (during the trip, naturalists talk about the animals native to the area); and bird and animal shows including "Creature Feature," "Bird Talk," "The All American Medicine Show" and "Reptiles of the World." The park is owned by Florida Leisure Acquisition Corp., which also owns Weeki Wachee Spring in Weeki Wachee, Buccaneer Bay at Weeki Wachee Spring, and Wild Waters Family Water Playground next to Silver Springs.

Among the motion pictures filmed here are six original Tarzan movies, "The Yearling" and "Smokey and the Bandit." In addition, more than 100 episodes (the underwater sequences) of the television series "Sea Hunt" were produced here.

The park is open 365 days a year from 9 a.m. to 5:30 p.m., with extended hours during the summer, on holidays and for special events. Admission in 1994 was $26.45 for adults and $19.02 for children ages 3-10. Children under 3 were admitted free. Adult annual passes are $37.95 plus tax for adults and $27.95 plus tax for children. Discounts are available for senior citizens, the military, the handicapped and AAA members. Parking is free.

CHURCH STREET STATION: An entertainment, dining and shopping complex in downtown Orlando. Among the places here: Rosie O'Grady's Good Time Emporium, the Cheyenne Saloon & Opera House, Phineas Phogg's Balloon Works, the Orchid Garden Ballroom, Apple Annie's Courtyard and Commander Ragtime's. In 1994, there was one admission price for the live shows: $16.90 for adults and $10.55 for ages 4-12. Children under 4 were admitted free. Annual passes were also available: $29.95 plus tax for one person; $49.95 plus tax for two people and $79.95 plus tax for four people.

MIRACLE STRIP AMUSEMENT PARK: Located on Highway 98-A in Panama City Beach, this popular park has about 30 rides and attractions, including a roller coaster and the "Sea Dragon," a 54-foot-tall, 35-foot-long ship that sways back and forth. There are also concessions, gift shops, games and an arcade. Closed in the winter.

MIAMI METROZOO: Located southwest of Miami, the zoo is situated on more than 200 acres. There are no cages here, and animals such as white tigers, hippos and rhinos can be seen.

EDISON WINTER HOME: In Fort Myers, this home has tropical gardens, a museum and chemical laboratory. The gardens contain more than a thousand varieties of plants from around the world. The 7,500-square-foot museum contains memorabilia of Edison's life. A Model T Ford, given to him by friend and neighbor Henry Ford, is on display. The laboratory remains today as Edison left it when he experimented with the goldenrod weed as a source of rubber from 1925 to 1931.

ST. AUGUSTINE: Founded about 425 years ago and the oldest permanent European settlement in the continental United States, this is a city that prides itself on its Spanish heritage and has many points of interest and attractions — including an old fort, old homes of Spanish architecture, churches and museums.

And Yet Others

Most of the attractions listed below are popular among tourists. A few of them are just plain unusual.

Northeast Florida:

Marineland of Florida, on the Flagler County and St. Johns County line, has a porpoise show and two oceanariums that house sharks, barracuda, stingrays and sea turtles. This is the state's original marine life attraction. **Potters Wax Museum** in St. Augustine has more than 170 wax figures. **Ripley's Believe It or Not Museum** in St. Augustine has 750 exhibits collected by Robert Ripley. **St. Johns River** in northeast Florida has a reputation for some of the world's best bass fishing, is popular among water sports enthusiasts and is the site of colorful sailboat races. **Florida Sports Hall of Fame** in Columbia County covers state sports' highlights.

Northwest Florida:

Florida Capitol Complex in Tallahassee includes the Old Capitol, built in 1902, and the new 22-story Capitol. **Florida Caverns State Park,** three miles north of Marianna, contains a network of caverns and formations such as stalactites, stalagmites and columns. The largest caverns are lighted and open to the public for ranger-guided tours; **National Museum of Naval Aviation** in Pensacola has exhibits ranging from the early pioneers of Navy flight to Skylab.

Central Florida:

Bok Tower Gardens in Lake Wales is a carillon tower made up of 57 bronze bells and a mechanical keyboard where recitals are heard daily. Also on the grounds are gardens that encompass 128 acres and feature azaleas, camellias and magnolias. **Splendid China** in Kissimmee features more than 60 miniaturized replicas of China's most historic landmarks, including a half-mile-long Great Wall. **Spook Hill** near Bok Tower Gardens is a spot where you stop your car at the foot of a hill and discover that your car is backing slowly UP the hill. **Arabian Nights Dinner Attraction** in Kissimmee is a theater with nightly shows featuring Arabian dancing horses and chariot races. **Medieval Times** in Kissimmee is a spot where diners can have dinner in a European-style castle and watch knights competing in jousting matches and tournament games.

Central East Florida:

Daytona International Speedway has racing events throughout the year such as the Daytona 500 in February, supercross, vintage road racing and motorcycle road races in March and the Pepsi 400 NASCAR Winston Cup Series stock car race in July. **Merritt Island National Wildlife Refuge** shows how man co-exists with wildlife on Merritt Island in Brevard County. Visitors can see such wildlife as sea turtles, armadillos, porpoises, manatees, alligators, eagles, pelicans, wading birds and vultures and a number of endangered and threatened wildlife species, including the southern bald eagle, peregrine falcon, eastern indigo snake, Atlantic loggerhead sea turtle and the Atlantic salt marsh snake. **Canaveral National Seashore** next to the wildlife refuge is a protected beach area north of the Kennedy Space Center and is open to the public for day use only with picnicking, swimming, boat ramps, hiking, surfing, fishing, crabbing, clamming, shrimping, canoeing and restricted hunting. **Klassix Auto Museum,**

Daytona Beach, is a collection of Corvettes from each year since 1953.

Central West Florida:

Ybor City in Tampa is a revitalized Cuban cultural area where cigars are made by hand. It has Cuban architectural motifs, shops, museums, a renovated cigar worker's cottage and restaurants. **Homosassa Springs Wildlife Park** in Homosassa Springs is a spot where visitors can see manatees year-round. The area has floating underwater observatory, jungle cruises, alligator and hippopotamus feeding programs, nature museum, nature trail, boat ramp and concessions. **Tarpon Springs** has turn-of-the-century estates, Greek sponge divers, shrimp trawlers and antique shops. It also has sponge-diving exhibitions and educational cruises leaving from the Sponge Docks. **Sunken Gardens** in St. Petersburg has five acres of exotic flowers, trees and fruits, 500 tropical animals and birds, bird shows and a wax museum. **Weeki Wachee Spring** in Hernando County, about 45 miles north of Tampa, features an underwater mermaid show, a birds of prey show, a wilderness river cruise, a pelican preserve and a children's petting zoo.

Southeast Florida:

The Breakers in Palm Beach is a famous oceanfront resort in Palm Beach that describes itself as "a very Palm Beach tradition." It has a staff in the hundreds, is filled with bronze-and-crystal chandeliers, and was built in 1926, inspired by the Italian Renaissance, by the Henry Morrison Flagler family. It has ceilings hand-painted by 75 European artists and tapestries on walls. **Henry Morrison Flagler Museum** in Palm Beach is a mansion, called Whitehall, that was built in 1901 by the Standard Oil millionaire and stands much as it was during Flagler's lifetime. **Lion Country Safari,** West Palm Beach, where rhinos, elephants and lions roam over 650-acre African-style preserve, also is a theme amusement park and has a petting zoo. **The Everglades National Park** spans about 1.5 million acres and contains a variety of birdlife and animal life. Among the activities and services offered: ranger-guided activities, hiking, saltwater and freshwater fishing, boating, camping, canoeing, boat rentals, boat ramps, picnicking, marina facilities, lodging and meals and gasoline within the park boundaries. The park contains a number of rare and endangered species, including the Florida panther, Everglades mink, green sea turtle and manatee. On one of the **Dry Tortugas** islands, located 69 nautical miles from Key West, there is a large 19th-century fortress called **Fort Jefferson National Monument,** with 8-foot-thick walls that during the Civil War served as a Union prison. The area has snorkeling, sea turtles, sport fishing, docking facility and tours of the fort. **Ernest Hemingway Home and Museum** in Key West is where author resided from 1931 to 1961 and wrote 75 percent of his works. The furnishings are original; **John Pennekamp Coral Reef State Park** in Key Largo has an interpretive center, camping, picnicking, swimming, saltwater fishing, hiking, guided tours including a glass-bottom-boat tour, snorkeling, diving, boat and canoe rentals, boat ramp and concessions. The park contains the only living coral reef in the continental United States and was the first underwater state park in the country. **Key Largo National Marine Sanctuary** is located three miles offshore and is a protected area of coral reef, seagrass and sand beds and is where the best diving in the area is found. The area also has the Carysfort Lighthouse, built in 1852, and is the oldest functioning lighthouse of its kind in the country. The marine sanctuary is the site of shipwrecks and a 9-foot, 4,000-pound bronze statue called "Christ of the Deep," located in 25 feet of water in the Atlantic. **Bahia Honda State Park,** 12 miles south of Marathon in the Keys, has camping, vacation cabins, picnicking, swimming in the Atlantic Ocean and Florida Bay, saltwater fishing, hiking, boat ramp and concessions. Tarpon fishing is rated among the best in the state. A number of rare species of birdlife can be seen here such as the great white heron, reddish egret and the osprey. **Fairchild Tropical Gardens** in Coral Gables has tropical plants from around the world and boasts the largest tropical garden in the continental United States as well as tram rides. **Biscayne National Underwater Park,** nine miles east of Homestead, has glass-bottom-boat tours of the area, canoeing, scuba diving and snorkel trips. **Fred Hunter's Funeral Museum** in Hollywood has a collection of antique funeral equipment such as an all-glass casket, antique clothing and early-20th-century hearses. **Parrot Jungle** in Kendall has shows with trained birds and features macaws and cockatoos riding bicycles, roller skates and scooters. **Monkey Jungle** in Miami is for fanciers of monkeys, apes, gorillas and baboons; **Miccosukee Indian Village** in Dade County is an authentic tribal campsite with a culture center, museum, alligator wrestling and airboat rides through the Everglades. **Butterfly World** at Coconut Creek is a museum, laboratory, tropical rain forest and display that shows butterflies in all stages of life.

Southwest Florida:

Jungle Larry's Zoological Park at Caribbean Gardens in Naples contains 52 acres of tropical gardens, jungle animals, a wild animal show, a petting zoo, tropical birds and an animal training center. **Collier Automotive Museum** in Naples displays 75 racing cars. **John and Mable Ringling Museum of Art** in Sarasota is the state art museum and has more than 10,000 pieces, including Baroque and Italian works. Also on the grounds are the circus galleries, the Ringling residence and the **Asolo Theater,** Florida's state theater. Originally the theater was an 18th-century Italian castle. It was dismantled, moved and rebuilt in Sarasota in 1950.

II
Florida By County

FLORIDA BY COUNTY

You're planning to move to Florida, but you're not sure where to settle. You want a place near the ocean. You would prefer an area where the population is small enough so that it doesn't take you an hour to drive two miles to the beach. You can afford a house that costs about $90,000. You're Roman Catholic and want to make sure that a church is nearby. You also want to be near a big hospital. You don't want to move to a high-crime area, and you're looking for cultural amenities, a nice state park and lots of arts and crafts shows. You would like to be able to find a bank right around the corner, as well as restaurants and a municipal library. And, up north, your favorite department store has been JCPenney. You'd like to find one in your new neighborhood.

Where do you look?

This section of the book is intended to give you basic information about all of Florida's 67 counties. Here are the categories and the sources for this information:

POPULATION, LAND AREA and POPULATION DENSITY:

Florida Estimates of Population, April 1, 1993, published by the Bureau of Economic and Business Research, College of Business Administration, University of Florida. In municipal population statistics, you will notice high numbers of residents in unincorporated areas. Taxes generally are lower in many of these areas.

INTRODUCTION TO EACH COUNTY:

This information comes from numerous state and federal agencies, from private groups and associations, from personal observations, and from some chamber of commerce publications. It is intended just to provide a brief overview of the local economy as well as area attractions.

TOURISM:

The figures come mainly from chambers of commerce and tourism development councils. Even many of these officials, however, are cautious about the numbers. Some are simple estimates. Some are based on mathematical projections from small numbers of interviews with tourists. At least a dozen officials mentioned that precise figures are virtually impossible to pinpoint. One said, "I have no idea where that number comes from. I think they're just inflating the figures to make the area look good." This category is meant to give an idea of how congested a county might be.

HOUSING SALES:

For larger population centers in the state, the Florida Association of Realtors provided median sales prices for single-family existing homes in June 1994. The association no longer keeps annual or quarterly statistics — only monthly ones, and June 1994 was the latest month available before publication. For some counties, average prices came from Multiple Listing Service data on property that was sold in an area. In areas where there is no such service, local agents provided estimates.

NUMBER OF VACANT RESIDENTIAL LOTS, NUMBER OF SINGLE-FAMILY RESIDENCES, NUMBER OF MOBILE HOMES, AND NUMBER OF CONDOMINIUMS:

Florida Ad Valorem Valuations and Tax Data, December 1993. The figures are determined by the counties. Numbers for mobile homes may seem low in some localities. That's because these figures account for only about half of the mobile homes in the state — ones that in 1993 were taxed as real property. The rest were registered with the motor vehicles department and were not included in the ad valorem publication.

NUMBER OF SCHOOLS:

Florida Department of Education for the 1992-93 school year. Total figure includes elementary schools, middle schools, junior and senior high schools, schools for exceptional students, and other types of schools.

NUMBER OF STUDENTS ENROLLED:

Florida Department of Education, as of the fall of 1993. Figures include membership from pre-kindergarten through grade 12.

PERCENTAGE OF STUDENTS CONTINUING EDUCATION AFTER HIGH SCHOOL:

This is for the 1992-93 school year. The percentage includes graduates who go on to Florida public community colleges, Florida private junior colleges, public and private Florida colleges and universities, out-of-state colleges and universities, and technical and trade or other schools. The figures come from the state Department of Education.

TEACHER-TO-PUPIL RATIOS:
Profiles of Florida School Districts, 1992-93, Student and Staff Data, Florida Department of Education, Division of Public Schools.

AVERAGE TEACHER'S SALARY:
From the state education department statistical brief for 1993-94. The average teacher's salary in the state that year was $31,935.

COLLEGES, UNIVERSITIES, AND JUNIOR OR COMMUNITY COLLEGES SERVING THE AREA:
From the universities themselves, as well as from *Florida County Profiles*, 1993, published by the state Department of Commerce, Division of Economic Development.

TRADE AND TECHNICAL SCHOOLS SERVING THE AREA:
From *Florida County Profiles*, 1993, and from chamber of commerce literature, which, in brochures aimed at luring new businesses, usually lists technical training opportunities.

NUMBER OF GENERAL HOSPITALS:
This includes general hospitals and general hospitals that have no obstetrics services. *Florida County Profiles*, 1993. In a few counties, where updated information was available, numbers have been adjusted.

NUMBER OF HOSPITAL BEDS:
This pertains to general hospitals and to general hospitals that have no obstetrics services. *Florida County Profiles*, 1993. In a few counties, where updated information was available, numbers have been adjusted.

NUMBER OF PHYSICIANS:
1993 Florida Statistical Abstract. Figures are as of June, 1993. In a few counties, numbers have been adjusted based on updated information from counties.

TAXES:
Total county ad-valorem millage rate (1993): *Florida Ad Valorem Valuations & Tax Data,* December 1993. These are the basic millage rates that all county property owners have to pay. Most counties have municipalities that have millage rates above and beyond these for special services, such as utilities or education. Residents of a county with a total millage rate of 16, for example, may end up paying several mills more for other services provided in his or her neighborhood. There can be several dozen rates in just one county.

STANDARD CRIME RATE:
Florida Department of Law Enforcement report for 1993. The crimes counted in this rate are murder, forcible sex offenses (forcible rape, forcible sodomy, forcible fondling), robbery, aggravated assault, burglary/breaking and entering, larceny/theft (pick-pocketing, purse-snatching, shoplifting, thefts from buildings, thefts from coin-operated machines, thefts from motor vehicles, all other larceny), and thefts of motor vehicles. The rate consists of the number of offenses per 100,000 population. The standard crime rate for all of Florida in 1993 was 8,204.8 offenses per 100,000 residents.

LARGEST PRIVATE EMPLOYERS:
Florida County Profiles, 1993, and local chambers of commerce. The County Profiles show the largest private employers. In some cases, however, government employment far outweighs private employment, and the headings in those counties say simply, "Largest Employers." Information for those headings comes from local chambers of commerce, economic development agencies and, in some cases, the employers themselves. Overall, this category is designed to show the types of industries prominent in each area. However, the state commerce department suggests that its lists may not be completely updated; therefore, some of this information also comes from local sources that had more recent figures.

COMPANIES PROVIDING LOCAL UTILITIES:
Florida County Profiles, 1993; local chambers of commerce; state agencies.

POINTS OF INTEREST:
Local chambers of commerce and government agencies.

ANNUAL EVENTS:
Local chambers of commerce. **NOTE: From year to year, many annual events move from one month to another. These listings are based on the latest available information. But please check with chambers well in advance of a festival to make sure of the dates.**

SPORTS AND LEISURE ACTIVITIES:
Florida County Profiles, 1993; local chambers of commerce; *1993 Florida Statistical Abstract.*

SERVICES FOR RETIREES:
Local chambers of commerce.

NUMBER OF LOCAL BANKS:
Florida County Profiles, 1993.

NUMBER OF LOCAL SAVINGS AND LOAN ASSOCIATIONS:
Florida County Profiles, 1993.

LARGEST LOCAL NEWSPAPER:
Florida County Profiles, 1993.

CABLE TELEVISION:
Florida County Profiles, 1993.

MAJOR LOCAL RETAILERS:
Local chambers of commerce.

FOOD ESTABLISHMENTS:
Florida County Comparisons, 1993, published by the Florida Department of Commerce, Division of Economic Development.

NUMBER OF LOCAL LIBRARIES:
Florida County Profiles, 1993.

NUMBER OF LOCAL HOTELS/MOTELS:
Florida County Comparisons, 1993.

NUMBER OF CHURCHES:
Florida County Profiles, 1993.

TOURISM INQUIRIES:
These are the addresses and telephone numbers of most local chambers of commerce. Many people may think that local government agencies would provide information about a local area, but government offices almost always will refer you to the local chamber. It's a starting point.

SOUTHEAST FLORIDA

THE COUNTIES: Broward, Dade, Glades, Monroe and Palm Beach

MAJOR CITIES: Miami, Fort Lauderdale, West Palm Beach, Key West

TOP INDUSTRIES: Tourism, services, retail trade, health care, agriculture, high tech, and, in the wake of Hurricane Andrew in 1992, massive construction work.

MAJOR NEWSPAPERS: *The Miami Herald, Sun-Sentinel* in Fort Lauderdale, and *Palm Beach Post*

WEATHER:
On the first line is the average maximum temperature for each month; the second line, the average minimum temperature; the third line, the amount of precipitation, in inches, for 1990, from national weather stations.

Miami	Jan.	Feb.	Mar.	Apr.	May	June	July	Aug.	Sep.	Oct.	Nov.	Dec.
Max.	81.1	80.8	80.6	82.6	86.8	90.3	91.2	91.5	89.9	84.1	81.7	80.1
Min.	66.0	67.1	66.7	67.8	73.7	75.6	75.7	75.8	76.3	75.4	67.0	65.6
Precp.	0.2	1.2	2.3	7.0	7.8	6.8	4.3	11.1	3.5	2.3	1.7	1.0

West Palm Beach	Jan.	Feb.	Mar.	Apr.	May	June	July	Aug.	Sep.	Oct.	Nov.	Dec.
Max.	79.8	81.3	80.5	81.7	87.0	90.1	91.2	92.4	90.2	86.8	81.4	79.1
Min.	64.7	66.3	65.9	66.1	72.4	74.2	75.4	75.0	75.2	73.3	65.5	63.4
Precp.	1.2	1.4	1.9	2.8	6.7	6.7	10.2	6.6	11.7	3.5	1.2	1.9

Key West	Jan.	Feb.	Mar.	Apr.	May	June	July	Aug.	Sep.	Oct.	Nov.	Dec.
Max.	78.7	80.1	79.8	82.3	86.4	89.6	90.8	92.0	89.5	85.9	80.4	78.8
Min.	67.7	70.8	70.1	70.9	77.0	79.1	78.6	79.1	78.1	75.8	70.8	70.3
Precp.	Trace	1.1	0.8	1.4	5.5	0.9	4.1	8.0	5.3	5.1	2.9	1.3

BROWARD County
Southeast
County seat: Fort Lauderdale

POPULATION: 1990: 1,255,531
1993: 1,317,512
Increase: 4.9 percent

AGE DISTRIBUTION (1992) IN PERCENTAGES:
0-14 : 17.7
15-44: 42.3
45-64: 19.5
65+ : 20.5

Condominiums and hotels tower over the Intracoastal Waterway in Miami Beach.

Expensive cars line Worth Avenue in Palm Beach, one of Florida's most exclusive shopping districts.

Fort Lauderdale is known as the "Venice of America." Wealthy residents can walk into their back yards, hop on their yachts, and be in the Bahamas in a few hours.

MUNICIPAL POPULATION:
COCONUT CREEK: 1990: 27,269 1993: 31,626
COOPER CITY: 1990: 21,335; 1993: 25,539
CORAL SPRINGS: 1990: 78,864; 1993: 88,944
DANIA: 1990: 13,183; 1993: 16,905
DAVIE: 1990: 47,143; 1993: 52,332
DEERFIELD BEACH: 1990: 46,997; 1993: 47,639
FORT LAUDERDALE: 1990: 149,238; 1993: 148,743
HALLANDALE: 1990: 30,997; 1993: 31,217
HILLSBORO BEACH: 1990: 1,748; 1993: 1,747
HOLLYWOOD: 1990: 121,720; 1993: 123,956
LAUDERDALE-BY-THE-SEA: 1990: 2,990; 1993: 2,983
LAUDERDALE LAKES: 1990: 27,341; 1993: 27,691
LAUDERHILL: 1990: 49,015; 1993: 49,436
LAZY LAKE VILLAGE: 1990: 33; 1993: 40
LIGHTHOUSE POINT: 1990: 10,378; 1993: 10,386
MARGATE: 1990: 42,985; 1993: 45,274
MIRAMAR: 1990: 40,663; 1993: 42,282
NORTH LAUDERDALE: 1990: 26,473; 1993: 26,664
OAKLAND PARK: 1990: 26,326; 1993: 27,969
PARKLAND: 1990: 3,773; 1993: 7,383
PEMBROKE PARK: 1990: 4,933; 1993: 4,967
PEMBROKE PINES: 1990: 65,566; 1993: 75,014
PLANTATION: 1990: 66,814; 1993: 72,655
POMPANO BEACH: 1990: 72,411; 1993: 73,219
SEA RANCH LAKES: 1990: 619; 1993: 616
SUNRISE: 1990: 65,683; 1993: 71,542
TAMARAC: 1990: 44,822; 1993: 46,711
WILTON MANORS: 1990: 11,804; 1993: 11,757
UNINCORPORATED: 1990: 154,408; 1993: 152,275

LAND AREA: 1,209 square miles
POPULATION DENSITY: 1,090 people per square mile (2nd in the state)

For years, Fort Lauderdale's notoriety came in large part from the movie "Where the Boys Are" — as the spot to which hundreds of thousands of college students swarmed during their spring break. Things have changed. As the years passed, the noise and rowdiness got to be too much for local residents and city officials sent a message to the students: Go somewhere else. Today, the city is trying to rebuild its image as a place where families and older citizens can come. City officials are saying that a "new Fort Lauderdale" is arriving, minus many of the spring breakers and complete with a "new beach," a recently built Greater Fort Lauderdale/Broward County Convention Center, a Broward Center for the Performing Arts and a Museum of Discovery & Science. And there's more to come.

If you like lots of people around you, Broward County might be the perfect area. Although the county is the seventh largest in the state in land area (more than 1,200 square miles), most of its population has settled in the eastern half near the Atlantic Ocean. This means residential areas are packed, the highways are jammed and there's little chance of avoiding crowds. Broward is the second most densely populated county in the state (behind Pinellas). The western section of the county is virtually a ghost town compared with the east, and includes a couple of Indian reservations, the Miami Canal and part of Alligator Alley (the cross-Florida highway).

Fort Lauderdale, also the county seat, might find the task of luring older residents harder than expected. The percentage of county residents in this age group — those 65 and older — dropped from 23.5 percent in 1986 to 20.5 percent in 1992.

Nicknamed the Venice of America, the Fort Lauderdale area has about 165 miles of navigable inland canals and waterways. Restaurant-hopping by boat is commonplace here, either in a private craft or a water taxi. A large number of boats — about 42,000 — are berthed here, giving the area a second nickname: the yachting capital of the world. The county is home to one of the largest marinas in the world, the Bahia Mar Yachting Center. Some private yachts in the area look like the Queen Mary.

You'll be hard-pressed NOT to find something to do here: there are 12 major malls, 288 parks, more than 70 golf courses, 550 tennis courts, four pari-mutuel facilities, 18 major shipwrecks to explore, nearly 61,000 feet of nature trails and boardwalks, 15 museums, more than 100 night-clubs and 23 miles of beach.

And more is coming. A topic of conversation for many people in the area in 1994 was a planned development called the Blockbuster Sports and Entertainment Complex, locally dubbed "Wayne's World." Conceived by Blockbuster video magnate Wayne Huizenga, some are saying this could be the largest attraction to come to Florida since Walt Disney World. Plans call for a new domed baseball park for the Florida Marlins baseball team, a new hockey arena for the National Hockey League's Florida Panthers, a 150-acre theme park, a 50-acre water attraction and 36 holes of golf. But a lot of hurdles need to be cleared before any construction takes place; environmental concerns have been raised because the planned development would be built near the sensitive Everglades National Park and some residents are voicing concerns over the increased traffic and noise such a development would bring.

Other projects in the works include a new Fort Lauderdale Museum of History, which was expected to be completed in 1996; a recreation complex in downtown Fort Lauderdale called Brickell Station; and an international trade and fashion mart at Port Everglades.

Fort Lauderdale is by no means the only city in the county. There are dozens more, including:

Cooper City: This city has grown from 85 residents to more than 25,500 in little more than 30 years. It is mainly residential with upper-middle-class families and has a semi-rural atmosphere. It is estimated that 31.5 percent of local residents are under 18 years of age.

Davie: This town is home to the South Florida Education Center, which includes Nova-Southeastern University, a Broward Community College campus and the William T. McFatter Vocational-Technical training facility. Much of the city's land remains undeveloped. Citrus, ornamental horticulture and ranching are among the industries.

Deerfield Beach: Located in northern Broward on the Atlantic, it has a number of beaches and parks for the outdoor enthusiast and is home to many retirees. Among the beaches are North Beach, with surfing and volleyball areas; Middle Beach, with swimming, cabanas and umbrella rentals, and South Beach, with boardwalks and picnic areas. The northern boundary of the city is the Hillsboro Canal, which links up with Lake Okeechobee, 45 miles to the west.

Hallandale: The southernmost city in Broward, it is only 14 miles north of Miami. It is home to two pari-mutuel race tracks — Gulfstream Park, which is "The Home of the Florida Derby" and was host to the Breeders' Cup in 1989 and 1992, and the Hollywood Greyhound Track. The Broward County Fair, held at Gulfstream Park in November, attracts more than a half million people and has rides, food, entertainment and exhibitions. The Florida Derby Stakes has traditionally been a $500,000 thoroughbred race and is run in March.

Hollywood: The winter home of many French Canadians from Quebec, this city is wedged between Dania and Hallandale. Canadian newspapers are on sale here, people are often heard speaking French on the streets and even French language services are available at some local churches. City officials estimate that the number of winter residents is more than 50,000. The median age of the city's population is estimated at 43.2 years, with nearly 20 percent under 18.

Plantation: The major industries here are retailing, light industry and professional and general business. The city is located 10 minutes west of Fort Lauderdale.

Pompano Beach: It claims to be the swordfish capital of the world and has 3.5 miles of public beaches. The "Hillsboro Mile Millionaire's Row" is found here. The city is also home to Pompano Park, a harness racing track where summer quarter horse and Appaloosa racing has the South's richest stakes.

Countywide, diving is a popular pastime. There is a natural reef system in the area, along with a number of wrecks. Broward is also home to Port Everglades, the second largest cruise port in the world and the deepest Atlantic seaport south of Norfolk, Va. More than 2 million passengers go through this port each year; there are 28 cruise ships based here. During fiscal 1991-92, 16.3 million short tons of cargo were handled at the port.

The county also has the second highest number of restaurants in the state, behind Dade.

TOURISM:
The tourism season runs from Dec. 15 to April 15. The greatest influx of visitors is during the spring. About 5.2 million visitors came to the area in 1993.

HOUSING PRICES
Median sales price of a single-family existing home in the Fort Lauderdale metropolitan statistical area was $111,000 in June 1994.

Number of vacant residential lots: 33,152; number of single-family residences: 253,146; mobile homes: 4,392; condominiums: 194,594

EDUCATION:
Number of schools: 186
Number of students enrolled: 189,862
Percentage of students continuing education after high school: 70.70
Teacher-to-pupil ratio: 1:19.3
Average teacher's salary: $34,672

Colleges, universities, and junior or community colleges serving the area:
Broward Community College (has four campuses); Fort Lauderdale College; University of Miami branch campus in Fort Lauderdale; Florida Atlantic University in Boca Raton; Palm Beach Community College's branch in Boca Raton; Nova-Southeastern University in Davie; Florida International University's Broward Center.

Trade and technical schools serving the area:
William T. McFatter Vocational-Technical Center in Davie, Sheridan Vo-Tech in Hollywood, Atlantic Vocation Center in Coconut Creek

HEALTH CARE:
Number of general hospitals: 29
Number of hospital beds: 6,738
Number of physicians: 3,028

TAXES: Total county ad-valorem millage rate (1993): 18.6004

STANDARD CRIME RATE: 8,971.5 offenses per 100,000 population (6th out of 67 counties)

LARGEST PRIVATE EMPLOYERS:

Name	Employees	Product/Service
Publix Supermarkets	7,000	Grocery
Winn-Dixie Supermarkets	5,500	Grocery
Eckerd Drug Co.	4,800	Retail drug chain
Southern Bell Telephone	4,057	Telecommunications
American Express	4,000	Financial Services
United Parcel Service	3,000	Package Deliveries
Waste Management North America	3,000	Sanitation Disposal
AT & T	2,200	Telecommunications
Motorola	2,200	Portable radios
Florida Power & Light	1,845	Utility
Sun-Sentinel	1,700	News publishing
Racal-Datacom	1,650	Electronics/communication

COMPANIES PROVIDING LOCAL UTILITIES:
Telephone: Southern Bell
Electricity: Florida Power & Light
Natural Gas: Peoples Gas
Water: Municipalities
Major Water Source: Wells
Sanitary Landfill? Yes

POINTS OF INTEREST:
Everglades Holiday Park, 30 minutes west of Fort Lauderdale, has airboat rides in the Everglades and a stop at a Seminole Indian Village that has arts and crafts; **Billy's Swamp Safari** has a guided tour in all-terrain vehicles through the Seminole Indian wildlife preserve. Overnight camping available.

Coconut Creek:
Butterfly World, a museum, laboratory, tropical rain forest and display that shows butterflies in all stages of life.

Cooper City:
Velodrome at Brian Piccolo Park is a tri-level facility and home to world-class cycling competitions.

Dania:
John U. Lloyd Beach State Recreation Area has picnicking, swimming, saltwater fishing, hik-

ing, canoe rentals, boat ramp, concessions. Area has 244 acres of barrier island that protects Dania from storm waves; **Dania Jai-Alai,** pari-mutuel betting; **Grand Prix Race-O-Rama** features go-kart racing, miniature golf and bumper cars.

Davie/Cooper City area:
Buehler Planetarium at Broward Community College campus has shows for the public and school groups; **Flamingo Gardens** offers botanical gardens, groves, Everglades museum, a Bird of Prey center, a 23,000-square-foot aviary, flamingos and tram rides; **Bar B Ranch** has horseback riding, hayrides and pony rides; **Strawberry picking** at Batten's Farm; **Bob Roth's New River Groves,** a walking tour of an orange grove; **Spyke's Grove and Tropical Gardens,** a walking tour of an orange grove.

Deerfield Beach:
Deerfield Island Park (take boat trip to the island for nature walks); the **Butler House,** a historical attraction that shows life in Deerfield in the 1920s.

Fort Lauderdale:
Port Everglades, second largest cruise port in the world; **Greater Fort Lauderdale/Broward County Convention Center** in Port Everglades contains exhibition halls, meeting rooms and a ballroom; **New York Yankees** spring training camp at Fort Lauderdale Stadium (the team is scheduled to move its camp to the Tampa area in 1996); **Jungle Queen Cruises,** a riverboat offering entertainment and dinner cruises and sightseeing around Fort Lauderdale, including waterfront homes and a stop at the Seminole Indian Village Island; **Museum of Discovery & Science** has a theater, hands-on exhibits for children, live coral reef, exhibits on space travel, the human body; **Bonnet House,** built in 1931, is an oceanfront estate in the heart of the Fort Lauderdale beach area and offers guided tours; **Stranahan House,** dating back to 1901, is the city's oldest meeting place and trading post; **International Swimming Hall of Fame Aquatic Exhibit** is home to a museum that displays gold medals of great swimmers, memorabilia ranging from Johnny "Tarzan" Weissmuller to Mark Spitz. Also has two Olympic-size swimming pools; **water taxis** transport people along the New River or the Intracoastal Waterway and offer historical tours; **Hugh Taylor Birch State Recreation Area** has youth tent camping, picnicking, swimming, saltwater fishing, hiking, canoe rentals and concessions; **Carrie B. Sightseeing Cruises** offer tours of the New River and the Intracoastal Waterway in a riverboat; **Fort Lauderdale Swap Shop** claims to be the second largest flea market in the United States complete with circus shows, a mini-amusement park, an outdoor produce and plant market, a drive-in movie theatre, weekend concerts, restaurants, arcade and acres of vendors; **South Florida Trolley Tours; Discovery I Cruises,** offering one-day cruises to the Bahamas and other cruises; **Las Olas Horse and Carriage Tours; King-Cromartie House,** built in 1907, has unusual antiques; **Riverwalk** is a park along the banks of New River with brick walkways and links downtown arts and science district.

Hallandale:
Gulfstream Park, thoroughbred horse-racing; **Hollywood Greyhound Track,** a dog-racing track; **indoor flea market** on weekends at U.S. 1 and Pembroke Road.

Hollywood:
Seminole Native Village has Indian arts and crafts, alligator wrestling; **Oceanwalk at Hollywood Beach Resort** has beachside shopping, restaurants, amusement center; Broadwalk along Hollywood's public beach has 3 ½-mile-long pathway with souvenir shops, bike path, small hotels, restaurants; **Fred Hunter's Funeral Museum** has collection of antique funeral equipment such as an all-glass casket, antique clothing and early-20th-century hearses; **Seminole Tribe and Bingo Emporium** has bingo and large jackpots.

Pembroke Pines:
C.B. Smith Park is mainly a water-oriented park with waterslides, tube ride, paddleboat rentals.

Pompano Beach:
Pompano Harness Track, open November to April; **Lighthouse Point Ice Arena** offers public skating, figure skating and hockey lessons; **Hillsboro Lighthouse** at Hillsboro Inlet is one of the strongest lights in the area and marks the northern limit of the Florida Reef; **Goodyear Blimps** — the Pompano Beach Air Park is home to two of the blimps during the winter. Area also has a visitors' center; **Ski Rixen,** a water-ski cableway in Quiet Waters Park (you water-ski by cable on a half-mile course at adjustable speeds); charter fishing and diving boats also are available for excursions.

Sawgrass:
Sawgrass Recreation Area is a tropical park with fishing, boat rentals, Everglades airboat tours, guided fishing trips.

Sunrise:
Sunrise Ice Skating Center; Sawgrass Mills outlet shopping.

THE ARTS:
Fort Lauderdale:
Broward Center for the Performing Arts has 2,700-seat **Au-Rene Theater** and 595-seat **Amaturo Theater; Parker Playhouse; Vinnette Carroll Repertory Theater; Story Theatre Productions** stages performances for young people and family audiences; **Fort Lauderdale Children's Theatre; Brian C. Smith's Off Broadway on 26th Street; War Memorial Auditorium; Museum of Art** houses collection of CoBrA art and has collections of primal and pre-Columbian and North American Indian art; **Art Institute of Fort Lauderdale Wheeler Gallery; Broward Art Guild, Gallery and School** features exhibits of local artists; **Young at Art** is a hands-on children's art museum; **Las Olas Boulevard** has a number of private art galleries; **Broward County Historical Commission** has changing exhibits with emphasis on Tequesta Indians; **Fort Lauderdale Historical Museum** has permanent collection and changing exhibits on the growth of Fort Lauderdale; **Museum of Discovery and Science** has interactive exhibits, **IMAX** theater; **Fort Lauderdale Opera; Gold Coast Opera** is affiliated with Broward Community College; **Miami City Ballet** is Broward County's first resident ballet company; **Sinfonia Virtuosi & Chorus of Florida; Broward Friends of Chamber Music; Public Theatre of Fort Lauderdale; Fort Lauderdale Players.**

Hollywood:
The Hollywood Art & Cultural Center has traditional and contemporary art exhibits, lectures, workshops, seminars, children's art classes; **Hollywood Playhouse** has productions ranging from comedies and musicals to dramas; **Young Circle Bandshell** is an outdoor theater that seats 2,400 people; **The Beach Theatre Under the Stars** seats 750 people.

Other cities:
Dania: Museum of Archaeology has permanent displays of natural history featuring pre-Columbian artifacts and exhibits on marine archaeology, evolution and the Tequesta Indians.
Plantation: Ann White Theatre; Deicke Auditorium.
Pompano Beach: Historical Museum houses memorabilia of the area's past; **Pompano Players Community Theatre.**
Sunrise: Sunrise Musical Theater, theatrical productions and pop concerts.
Coral Springs: Coral Springs City Centre.
Deerfield Beach: Drama Center.

ANNUAL EVENTS:
January: Riverwalk Winter Art Show, downtown Fort Lauderdale; Las Olas Art Fair in Fort Lauderdale; Deerfield Beach Art Show; **February:** Florida Renaissance Festival in Fort Lauderdale; Plantation Art Festival; Seminole Tribal Fair in Hollywood with native Americans, Indian dancers, arts and crafts; Annual Greek Festival; Irish Festival, downtown Fort Lauderdale; CanadaFest in Hollywood; Hollywood Festival of the Arts; Taste of Fort Lauderdale; Las Olas Art Fair in Fort Lauderdale; **March:** Florida Derby Stakes; Downtown Festival of the Arts in Fort Lauderdale; Museum of Art Las Olas Art Festival, Fort Lauderdale; **April:** Davie/Cooper City Orange Blossom Festival and Rodeo in Davie features a parade, horse exhibits, car show, arts and crafts show, rodeo, a carnival, citrus showcase, entertainment; Pompano Beach Seafood Festival & Fishing Rodeo where area restaurants show off their best seafood dishes, also has powerboat race, arts and crafts, music, food; Fort Lauderdale Seafood Festival; **July:** Sandblast sand-sculpture contest, road race and fireworks in Fort Lauderdale area; **September:** Las Olas Labor Day Art Fair in Fort Lauderdale; **October:** Hollywood Jazz Festival at Young Circle Park in Hollywood; Fort Lauderdale Oktoberfest; South Florida Senior Games in Fort Lauderdale; Riverwalk Fall Arts Show, Riverwalk and Viva Broward, downtown Fort Lauderdale; Art in the Park in Plantation; **November:** Deerfest, featuring a carnival, arts and crafts, entertainment and food at Deerfield Beach; State Pro Rodeo in the Davie Rodeo Arena (held Thanksgiving holiday weekend) with country music, food, dancing; Broward County Fair in Hallandale; Riverwalk Blues Festival in Fort Lauderdale; Promenade in the Park in Fort Lauderdale with entertainment, art show, bazaar and food; Greater Fort Lauderdale Film Festival; **December:** Winterfest, a tribute to winter fun in

Fort Lauderdale, various events held throughout the month; Holiday Boat Parade in Pompano Beach; Hollywood Beach Candy Cane Parade; Arts & Heritage Holiday Celebration in downtown Fort Lauderdale with a boat parade; Carnival in the Snow at Tradewinds Park; Winterfest Boat Parade with decorated boats along the Intracoastal from Port Everglades; Winterfest Light Up Lauderdale in downtown Fort Lauderdale with food, fireworks, entertainment.

SPORTS AND LEISURE ACTIVITIES:
Most popular local fishing areas: Atlantic Ocean; Intracoastal Waterway; Deerfield Beach Fishing Pier, 720 feet long. About 200 species of fish are also found in the county's freshwater creeks, bayous, streams and lakes.
Number of local golf courses: About 76 in the area
Public beaches? Yes
Tennis courts available to the public? Yes
Boating? Yes
Number of pleasure boats registered in the county (1993): 42,000

SERVICES FOR RETIREES:
Area Council on Aging in Fort Lauderdale and a number of senior citizen meeting places such as the Multi-Purpose Center in Hollywood and the Northeast Focal Point Senior Center and Senior Resource Center in Deerfield Beach.

FINANCIAL SERVICES:
Number of local banks: 251
Number of local savings and loan associations: 191

THE MEDIA:
Largest local newspaper: Sun-Sentinel
Cable television? Yes

MAJOR LOCAL RETAILERS:
Macy's, Saks Fifth Avenue, Neiman-Marcus, Lord & Taylor, Cartier, Burdines, Sears, Mervyn's, Marshalls, JCPenney, K mart, Sears, Byrons, Brooks Brothers. Distinct shopping districts include Las Olas Boulevard shopping area in downtown Fort Lauderdale, which has upscale shops, restaurants and galleries; Fort Lauderdale Swap Shop flea market on Sunrise Boulevard in Fort Lauderdale with indoor and outdoor shopping; Sawgrass Mills outlets in Sunrise include more than 225 specialty stores, such as Sak's Fifth Avenue Clearinghouse; Dania's Antique Row; Schmatta Row in Hallandale (a discount fashion center along First and Second Avenues Northeast); an indoor flea market in Hallandale; and Festival Flea Market in Pompano Beach with hundreds of vendors, games, food, movie theater.

FOOD ESTABLISHMENTS: 4,230

OTHER SERVICES:
Number of local libraries: 25
Number of local hotels/motels: 534
Number of churches: Protestant: 207; Jewish: 22; Catholic: 50; Other: 80

TOURISM INQUIRIES:
Davie/Cooper City Chamber of Commerce, 4185 S.W. 64th Ave., Davie, 33314. Telephone: 305-581-0790; Greater **Deerfield Beach** Chamber of Commerce, 1601 E. Hillsboro Blvd., Deerfield Beach, 33441. Telephone: 305-427-1050; Greater **Fort Lauderdale** Convention & Visitors Bureau, 200 E. Las Olas Blvd., Suite 1500, Fort Lauderdale, 33301. Telephone: 305-765-4466; Greater Fort Lauderdale Chamber of Commerce, 512 N.E. 3rd Ave., P.O. Box 14516, Ft. Lauderdale, 33301. Telephone: 305-462-6000. Fort Lauderdale Welcome Center, A1A, south of Las Olas Boulevard. Telephone: 305-467-8044; Hallandale Chamber of Commerce, 307 E. Hallandale Bch. Blvd., P.O. Box 249, **Hallandale,** 33008-0249. Telephone: 305-454-0541; Greater **Plantation** Chamber of Commerce, 7401 N.W. 4th St., Plantation, 33317. Telephone: 305-587-1410; Greater **Pompano Beach** Chamber of Commerce, 2200 E. Atlantic Blvd., Pompano Beach, 33062-5284. Telephone: 305-941-2940.

DADE County
Southeast
County seat: Miami

POPULATION: 1990: 1,937,194
1993: 1,951,116
Increase: 0.7 percent

AGE DISTRIBUTION (1992) IN PERCENTAGES:
0-14 : 20.9
15-44: 44.6
45-64: 20.5
65+ : 14.0

MUNICIPAL POPULATION:
BAL HARBOUR: 1990: 3,045; 1993: 3,053
BAY HARBOR ISLANDS: 1990: 4,703; 1993: 4,738
BISCAYNE PARK: 1990: 3,068; 1993: 3,062
CORAL GABLES: 1990: 40,091; 1993: 41,055
EL PORTAL: 1990: 2,457; 1993: 2,453
FLORIDA CITY: 1990: 5,978; 1993: 4,089
GOLDEN BEACH: 1990: 774; 1993: 806
HIALEAH: 1990: 188,008; 1993: 199,923
HIALEAH GARDENS: 1990: 7,727; 1993: 9,828
HOMESTEAD: 1990: 26,694; 1993: 18,732
INDIAN CREEK VILLAGE: 1990: 44; 1993: 44
ISLANDIA: 1990: 13; 1993: 13
KEY BISCAYNE: 1990: 0; 1993: 8,881
MEDLEY: 1990: 663; 1993: 862
MIAMI: 1990: 358,648; 1993: 364,679
MIAMI BEACH: 1990: 92,639; 1993: 95,160
MIAMI SHORES: 1990: 10,084; 1993: 10,125
MIAMI SPRINGS: 1990: 13,268; 1993: 13,299
NORTH BAY: 1990: 5,383; 1993: 5,650
NORTH MIAMI: 1990: 50,001; 1993: 50,243
NORTH MIAMI BEACH: 1990: 35,361; 1993: 35,689
OPA-LOCKA: 1990: 15,283; 1993: 15,216
SOUTH MIAMI: 1990: 10,404; 1993: 10,407
SURFSIDE: 1990: 4,108; 1993: 4,263
SWEETWATER: 1990: 13,909; 1993: 14,081
VIRGINIA GARDENS: 1990: 2,212; 1993: 2,206
WEST MIAMI: 1990: 5,727; 1993: 5,743
UNINCORPORATED: 1990: 1,036,902; 1993: 1,026,816

LAND AREA: 1,945 square miles
POPULATION DENSITY: 1,003 people per square mile (4th in the state)

Even before Hurricane Andrew demolished parts of this county in 1992, many people saw the Miami area as years past its heyday; that other, faster-developing metropolitan areas in Florida, notably Orlando and the Tampa Bay area, had siphoned business and tourists from Dade County with more popular attractions, good hotels, similarly modern facilities and, at least to an extent, less-crowded roadways; that Dade's overdevelopment and its influx of refugees had choked the schools, the health care system, and social-service agencies.

Others, however, have viewed Miami as the city of the future. It has a cultural vitality and diversity that is unmatched in Florida. It is the state's second largest city in population, behind Jacksonville. It is an international finance center. It has chic hotels, modern skyscrapers, major-league attractions, arts facilities and sports, and is across the Intracoastal Waterway from manicured beaches and first-class oceanfront condominiums.

To a degree, both groups are right. On the negative side, the traffic problems are legend. The county's reputation was tarnished by nationally publicized racial incidents and, in the early 1990s, by the murders of foreign tourists. Dade has the highest standard crime rate in the state that has the nation's highest crime rate (some criminal justice officials blame the rate locally on crack cocaine). Armed police have been posted at some schools in recent years; the Miami Herald reported in August 1993 that weapons violence was "marring campuses in every corner of the county" and that 60 percent of the county's elementary and secondary schools had reported weapons offenses in 1992-93 (the offenses had been most prevalent in the middle schools).

The percentage of residents 65 and older, in a state known as a retirement mecca, dropped from 15.7 in 1986 to 14 in 1992. Of the county's 26 incorporated municipalities, 10 of them — including Coral Gables, Miami Beach and North Miami Beach — lost population from 1980 to 1993. Homestead and Florida City, which were hit hardest by Andrew, lost significant portions of their population between 1990 and 1993, roughly a quarter and a third, respectively.

Rebuilding from Andrew will take years, especially in those two cities. The numbers behind the devastation are mind-boggling. Thousands upon thousands of homes were destroyed (estimates ranged from 25,000 on up); thousands more were damaged (estimates ranged from 50,000 to 100,000); dozens of deaths were blamed on the hurricane; and the damage overall made Andrew by far the costliest hurricane in U.S. history. Besides ruining many peoples' livelihoods and most of their worldly possessions, the effects of the hurricane — emotional as well as economic — will be felt for some time.

Some people moved away from the area, vowing never to return. But many stayed, determined to rebuild and start over. Within months, many of the area's attractions were up and running again, even if only at reduced levels. A few, though, never reopened.

The storm came at a time when a lot of things were going right in the county. Miami's downtown area was being revitalized and now includes the Miami Convention Center as well as the Bayside Marketplace (a $93 million retail, entertainment and restaurant facility). There also are myriad cultural attractions, the $53 million Miami Arena (home of the Miami Heat, an NBA expansion team; the Florida Panthers, a National Hockey League team; and it is the focal point for a renaissance of the city's Overtown area, once a thriving social center for the black community); and the arrival in 1993 of the Florida Marlins, a major league baseball team.

Many things still are going right. Despite problems in the school system, Dade has the seventh highest rate of students continuing education after high school (79 percent after the 1992-93 school year, according to the state). Culturally, just about any type of art, museum or performance is offered here, and compared with other Florida cities, the nightlife here is what New York's is to Buffalo's.

And just about any other thing, short of snow, is available here. There were 6,808 food-service establishments in the county in 1992 (that was the highest number in the state; Broward was second with 4,230). There are more condominiums — 220,406 — than in any other Florida county except Palm Beach (yet there are only 387 mobile homes). Lifestyles of local residents range from abject poverty to retirement befitting a mega-lottery winner.

There is a variety of land use around Miami — to the west, the Everglades; to the south, the farms in the Homestead and Florida City areas (the two Turkey Point nuclear power plants also are in Florida City); and offshore, the country-club ambience of Key Biscayne and the pricey condominiums of Bal Harbour, with its Fifth Avenue shops. Dade is also the gateway to the Florida Keys.

The county is multi-ethnic. Many residents here have fled Cuba, Nicaragua and Haiti, or have immigrated from other Central and South American areas. No one group of people has a clear majority — Latins made up 46 percent of the population, Anglos 34 percent and blacks about 20 percent, as of 1990.

In 1991, the largest industries in Dade County were services (356,429 workers); wholesale and retail trade (261,653); government (135,675); finance, insurance and real estate (103,383); manufacturing (87,218); transportation and public utilities (80,361); and construction (44,429).

Another local economic factor is the Port of Miami, which is Number One in the world in the number of cruise-ship passengers — three to four million a year.

The **city of Miami** has several other neighborhoods, including: **Little Havana,** a 3.5-square-mile Latin haven for Cuban and Nicaraguan exiles and other immigrants. Here you will find Cuban-style fruit stands, boutiques and food. The area has been built up in the style of pre-Castro Cuba; **Little Haiti,** an enclave for the city's Haitian community; **Coconut Grove,** a waterfront village that is a cultural center and home for professionals, artists, and wealthy residents that has antique jewelry stores, fashions, art galleries, and lots of boats.

Other major communities:

Miami Beach: A city of beaches and famous hotels and clubs, it sits on a 12-square-mile island. Outside of the glitzy nightlife, Miami Beach has a variety of outdoor recreational activities — from miles of beaches to a $12 million marina. Among the city's top employers are Mount Sinai Medical Center (3,000 employees), the City of Miami Beach and the Fontainebleau Hilton.

Coral Gables: This was the first planned community in the United States. It is made up mostly of single-family homes, and is considered one of the prime residential areas of the county. Parts of the Intracoastal Waterway wind through many areas of the city. Spanish Mediterranean architecture is popular here, as are entrance gates, plazas and fountains. The city, three miles from Miami International Airport, has scores of multinational companies as well as foreign trade offices. The University of Miami, also located here, is the largest private educational and research facility in the Southeast and employs 7,000 people. The city also calls itself "the dining capital of South Florida," with dozens of award-winning restaurants and three four-star hotels.

Opa-locka: The inspiration for this community's architecture was the story of the One Thousand and One Tales From the Arabian Nights. Starting around 1925, developers and architects put up Moorish-style buildings graced with domes, spires, arches, minarets, parapets, tiles and arched windows on what was then largely a desert. Major streets were named for characters in the book. Over the years, many buildings became dilapidated, but in recent years the City Hall, one of the most impressive examples of this type of architecture, has been restored and the city was rebuilding or planning to rebuild other structures.

Hialeah: With 199,923 residents, this is Florida's fifth-largest city. It is a largely middle-class residential and industrial community that also has a lot of small businesses. Hundreds of manufacturing firms are located here. The vast majority of local residents were born in Cuba. Many buildings here are in the Spanish Mission style of architecture.

Kendall: This is part of Greater Miami South and is a huge unincorporated area. It is largely a suburban and shopping center and has many lakes and canals.

TOURISM:
Estimates are the county had about 8.4 million visitors in 1991 and 1992.

HOUSING PRICES:
Median sales price of an existing home in the Miami metropolitan area was $99,700 in June 1994.
Number of vacant residential lots: 35,312; number of single-family residences: 283,955; mobile homes: 387; condominiums: 220,406

EDUCATION:
Number of schools: 328
Number of students enrolled: 308,465 (highest number in the state)
Percentage of students continuing education after high school: 79.04
Teacher-to-pupil ratio: 1:21.1 (highest in the state)
Average teacher's salary: $37,980 (highest in the state)

Colleges, universities, and junior or community colleges serving the area:
Florida International University in Miami; University of Miami; Miami-Dade Community College; Broward Community College; Barry University in Miami Shores; Saint Thomas University in Miami; Florida Memorial College in Miami.

Trade and technical schools serving the area:
Robert Morgan; Lindsey Hopkins; Miami Lakes Technical Center.

HEALTH CARE:
Number of general hospitals: 44
Number of hospital beds: 10,732
Number of physicians: 6,742

TAXES: Total county ad-valorem millage rate (1993): 19.4560

STANDARD CRIME RATE:
13,268 offenses per 100,000 population (highest rate among the 67 counties)

LARGEST PRIVATE EMPLOYERS:

Name	Employees	Product/service
Publix	8,000	Grocery
University of Miami	7,000	Education
American Airlines	6,800	Airline
Florida Power & Light	5,800	Utility
Southern Bell	4,925	Communications
Burdines Department Stores	3,400	Retail sales

Columbia Hospital	3,080	Health care
Baptist Hospital of Miami	3,000	Health care
Mount Sinai Hospital	3,000	Health care
Coulter Corp.	2,800	Medical instruments

COMPANIES PROVIDING LOCAL UTILITIES:
Telephone: Southern Bell
Electricity: Florida Power & Light
Natural Gas: Peoples Gas Co./City Gas
Water: Miami-Dade Water & Sewer Authority
Major Water Source: Wells
Sanitary Landfill? Yes

POINTS OF INTEREST:
MIAMI:
Miami Dolphins football at **Joe Robbie Stadium; Florida Marlins** baseball at **Joe Robbie Stadium; Miami Heat** basketball at the **Miami Arena; Florida Panthers** hockey at the **Miami Arena; Vizcaya Museum and Gardens,** tours, gondola rides and a 70-room Italian Renaissance-style palace, built in 1916 and housing European antiques. Grounds include 10 acres of formal gardens and fountains; **Miami Metrozoo,** a cageless 290-acre zoo that was severely damaged by Hurricane Andrew but reopened in early 1993, has 1,000 animals and 240 species, exhibits, shows; **Miami Seaquarium,** shows with a killer whale, sea lions, sharks, dolphins, sea turtles, manatees, new ocean reef presentation, and television's *Flipper;* **Monkey Jungle** has monkeys, apes, gorillas and babboons running freely in a 20-acre reserve; **Bayside Marketplace** has restaurants, shops, cafes, entertainment, a market square focused on a marina, trolley tours; **American Police Hall of Fame and Museum** has more than 10,000 law enforcement-related items; **Miami International Merchandise Mart and Expo Center; Malibu Grand Prix** has mini-race-car tracks, miniature golf, batting cages, video games; Tours of the city and surrounding areas are available by bus, van, airplane, helicopter, boat, trolley and even rickshaw; also available are sailboat charters and deep-sea-fishing trips; other ways of getting around Miami are on the **Metrorail** (elevated rail system serving the downtown and running west to Hialeah and south to Kendall) and the **Metromover** (individual motorized cars run on a 1.9-mile elevated track around the downtown area).

MIAMI BEACH:
Art Deco District, a historic district with more than 800 buildings in ten square blocks designed in tropical pastel color architecture of the 1930s; Ocean Drive, the "main street" of the Art Deco District; **Miami Beach Convention Center** hosts such events as the Miami International Boat Show, the World's Largest Indoor Flea Market and numerous trade and special-interest shows; **Holocaust Memorial** contains a monument, a mural and a "Memorial Wall" listing names of Holocaust victims; **Lincoln Road,** a retail district with restaurants, clubs, boutiques, art galleries, pedestrian mall (through large windows opening onto the mall you can watch Miami City Ballet dancers in training). Also in the area is the **New World Symphony,** a training symphony.

CORAL GABLES:
University of Miami (intercollegiate sports are very popular here, in addition to the cultural offerings); **Fairchild Tropical Gardens,** on 83 acres, has tropical plants from around the world, rain forest, sunken garden, rare-plant house, tram tours; **Coral Gables Merrick House,** boyhood home of George Merrick, founder of the city, is constructed of locally quarried coral rock; the famed **Biltmore Hotel; the Venetian Pool,** a huge swimming pool that has caves, bridges, waterfalls, and a floating barge in the middle of it, built as a tropical lagoon in a Venetian setting.

KENDALL:
Parrot Jungle and Gardens has flowering trees and plants, macaws, flamingos, parrots, cockatoos, peacocks, alligators, tortoises, iguanas, petting zoo and playground (they say the parrots sing, the macaws play cards and the cockatoos roller skate); **Gold Coast Railroad Museum** has historic railroad cars and memorabilia; **Hot Wheels Roller Skating Center** has light show, 90s music, entertainment, video arcade.

HOMESTEAD:
Biscayne National Underwater Park, nine miles east of Homestead, is principally a marine preserve. Headquarters is at Convoy Point. About 95 percent of the 181,500-acre park is water. Activities include boating, fishing, snorkeling, scuba diving, canoeing. Glass-bottom-boat tours are

available through Biscayne Bay and mangrove creeks to 20-foot-high tropical coral reefs. **Coral Castle** is a house built with 1,000 tons of coral, has outdoor coral furniture, nine-ton swinging gate; **Fruit and Spice Park** has more than 500 varieties of fruits, herbs, nuts and spices from around the world; **Everglades Alligator Farm** has 3,000 gators, airboat tours, reptile shows and exhibits.

OTHER AREAS:
Florida City: State Farmer's Market.
Miami Beach: North Shore State Recreation Area has swimming, bicycling and picnicking.
North Miami Beach: Ancient Spanish Monastery, oldest bulding in the western hemisphere, erected in Spain in 1141, dismantled and shipped here in 1954 and now houses art works and antiques; **Oleta River State Recreation Area** has picnicking, swimming, saltwater fishing, biking, canoeing, boating.
Opa-locka/Hialeah: Flea Market, one of the largest flea markets in South Florida, has goods from 1,200 vendors, parking for 10,000 cars, 13 restaurants.
Key Biscayne: Biscayne Nature Center, has hands-on exhibits, information about South Florida flora and fauna, hikes, biking and canoe trips, lectures, beach walks; **Bill Baggs Cape Florida State Recreation Area** was extensively damaged by Hurricane Andrew but has since reopened, has beaches, bike path, fishing.
West Dade County: Miccosukee Indian Village, 30 miles west of Miami, a tribal campsite with a culture center and museum where Indians sell crafts, wrestle alligators and offer airboat tours through the Everglades; **Miccosukee Indian Bingo & Gaming** has bingo, poker, table and video games; **Billie Swamp Safari & Camping Village, Everglades,** has swamp buggy rides.

THE ARTS:
MIAMI:
Gusman Center for the Performing Arts, downtown, hosts special events in addition to a ballet company and two major symphonies. Center has a 1,700-seat Baroque-style theater that is on the National Register of Historic Places; **Miami Museum of Science & Space Transit Planetarium** has demonstrations on electricity and chemistry and laser and astronomy shows; **Miami City Ballet,** at the **Dade County Auditorium,** is a professional company under the direction of the famed Edward Villella. It presents works by contemporary and classical choreographers; **Miami Ballet Company; New World Symphony, Gusman Center,** an advanced-training orchestra that also hosts major guest conductors; **Florida Philharmonic Orchestra,** at the **Dade County Auditorium,** offers classical and pop concerts and children's programs; **Coconut Grove Playhouse,** which includes the Mainstage theatre and the smaller Encore Room Theatre; **Greater Miami Opera** at the **Dade County Auditorium,** west of downtown, features well-known artists and performances; **Center for the Fine Arts,** downtown, is part of the **Metro-Dade Cultural Center** and offers exhibits from art and museum collections from around the world. The cultural center covers a full city block and also includes a public library and the **Historical Museum of Southern Florida** (which has hands-on displays and special exhibits and offers walking tours); **James L. Knight Center,** downtown Miami, is a 5,000-seat theatre; **Cuban Museum of Arts & Culture,** Little Havana, has paintings and drawings from Cuban artists; **Frances Wolfson Art Gallery,** Miami-Dade Community College, has contemporary works by local artists; **Gallery North,** Miami-Dade Community College North campus in Opa-Locka, has traditional, contemporary art; **Inter-American Art Gallery,** Little Havana, has art by Latin American and other artists; **Art Museum at Florida International University** houses permanent collection of works by North and South American artists; **African Heritage Cultural Arts Center; Miami Chamber Symphony; Freddick Bratcher and Company** (a dance company); **Momentum Dance Company; M Ensemble Company** presents contemporary African-American theater.

MIAMI BEACH:
Jackie Gleason Theatre of the Performing Arts hosts Broadway shows (including national touring productions of hit shows, from November through May), ballets, operas and concerts; **Bass Museum of Art** has collections of medieval art, 17th-century Dutch and Flemish paintings, 18th-century portraits, modern European and American art. Permanent collection includes works by Rubens, Van Haarlem and Bol; **Colony Theatre** on Lincoln Road hosts smaller productions and dance presentations; **South Florida Art Center,** a three-block center, is home to visual artists' studios and galleries featuring such media as paint, clay and prints; **Hirschfeld Theatre,** a year-round theater that hosts musical productions from Broadway; **Ballet Flamenco La Rosa,** a Spanish dance company; **Ballet Theatre of Miami** is a professional company; **Concert Asso-**

ciation of Florida, based in Miami Beach, offers concerts by world-famous performers throughout the region and sponsors Prestige Series, Great Artists Series and other concerts; **Wolfsonian Foundation,** a museum and study center with 50,000 art objects and rare books, focuses on decorative, design and architectural arts.

CORAL GABLES:
Lowe Art Museum at the University of Miami carries collection of Renaissance and Baroque art and Spanish masterpieces; **Ring Theatre,** operated by the University of Miami's Department of Theatre Arts, presents musicals, dramas and comedies featuring guest actors as well as students and faculty members; **Coral Gables Playhouse,** home of the Florida Shakespeare Theatre, also hosts dance and other theater productions; **Elite Fine Art Gallery** has a Latin American fine art exhibit; **Coral Gables Gallery Association** has monthly exhibits on the first Friday of every month; **Meza Fine Art** gallery features Latin American contemporary artists.

OTHER CITIES:
Miami Shores: Pelican Theatre and Broad Center for the Performing Arts, Barry University, hosts regional productions.
North Miami: Miamiway Theatre, a 435-seat performing-arts complex that includes recording studio and offers live performances, audio recordings, video productions.
North Miami Center of Contemporary Art has works by Florida artists, sponsors lectures, studio tours and films.
South Miami: Miami Youth Museum, a hands-on children's museum featuring cultural exhibits.
South Miami Beach: Lincoln Theatre, home to the New World Symphony.
Kendall: Actors' Playhouse has off-Broadway productions, children's theater.

PARI-MUTUELS:
Calder Race Course, a thoroughbred track that is home to the Florida Stallion Stakes; Greyhound racing at **Flagler Greyhound Track** and **Biscayne Greyhound Track; Miami Jai-Alai,** pari-mutuel wagering at the oldest U.S. fronton; **Hialeah Park,** Hialeah, referred to — at least locally — as "the world's most beautiful race track," hosts thoroughbred racing and has large colony of American flamingos.

ANNUAL EVENTS:
December to January: Orange Bowl Festival, one of Miami's biggest celebrations, includes international tennis tournament, sailing regatta, golf championship, King Orange Jamboree Parade, road races, fashion shows, and, on Jan. 1, the Orange Bowl Football Classic (the game is scheduled to move to Joe Robbie Stadium starting in 1997); **January:** Ringling Brothers and Barnum & Bailey Circus, Miami Arena; Metropolitan South Florida Fishing Tournament (countywide, through May); International Kwanzaa Festival, throughout the county; Santa's Enchanted Forest, Tropical Park, west of Coral Gables; Carquest Bowl, Joe Robbie Stadium; Art Miami, Miami Beach Convention Center; Art Deco Weekend, Miami Beach, a seven-block street fair that has music, arts and food; Taste of the Grove, Coconut Grove; Martin Luther King Jr. celebrations throughout the area; South Florida Wine and Food Festival, Miami Beach; Hialeah Spring Festival; Beaux Arts Festival of the Arts at the University of Miami campus in Coral Gables; Redlands Natural Arts Festival, Homestead; **February:** Miami Film Festival, Gusman Center for the Performing Arts, 10 days of premiere screenings, lectures, special events; Miami Home Show, Coconut Grove Convention Center; Miami International Boat Show, Miami Beach; Miami Beach Festival of the Arts, Collins Avenue, a family arts fest that features hundreds of artists as well as food and music; Coconut Grove Arts Festival (attracts about 750,000 people each year); Grand Prix of Miami, downtown; **March:** Carnaval Miami/Calle Ocho Festival, an 8-day Rio-style Hispanic celebration culminating in the Calle Ocho Festival, a 23-street block party that includes music, dance, food, parade and art; Florida Derby Festival at Gulfstream Park has music, arts and crafts and food; Florida Derby thoroughbred race at Gulfstream Park; Dade County Youth Fair & Exposition at Tamiami Park with exhibits, food, rides and entertainment; St. Patrick's Day Parade along Ocean Drive; Fine Arts and Crafts Festival in Miami Lakes; South Miami Craft Fest; **April:** River Cities Festival in Miami Springs has bed races, chili cook-off, arts and music; Coconut Grove Seafood Festival has food, nautical crafts, entertainment; **April-May:** Dade Heritage Days, held throughout the county, offers ethnic and family events that include lectures, walking tours, canoe trips, documentaries; Arabian Nights Festival, Opa-locka historic district, celebrates founding of city and its Moorish architecture and features historic tours, family events and a street festival; **May:** Great Sunrise Balloon Race during Memorial Day weekend with balloon races, music, kite-flying contests, food; Miami Home Show in Miami Beach; Miami/Bahamas

Goombay Festival, Coconut Grove, is a black heritage festival with food, entertainment, arts and crafts; **July:** July 4th celebrations at various locations throughout the county; Miami Summer Boat Show, Miami Beach; gun & knife show, Miami Beach; Tropical Agricultural Fiesta, Homestead; Everglades International Music and Crafts Festival, Miccosukee Indian Village (30 miles west of Miami), celebrates Indian heritage and has food, dance, music, arts and crafts; **July-September:** Friday Night Live, South Pointe Park, South Miami Beach, a summer series that includes entertainment, music, amusement rides, small petting zoo, street performances, carriage rides, food; **August:** Miami Reggae Festival; Original Plays Festival; Coconut Grove Cares Antique Show; Home & Garden Show, Miami Beach; **September:** Avmed Cyclefest, throughout Key Biscayne; Coconut Grove Cares Antique Show; Taste of Jazz at Miami Lakes; **October:** South Florida International Auto Show, Miami Beach; Jewish Book Fair, Greater Miami South; Caribbean American Carnival, a 10-day festival throughout downtown Miami that includes costume dance and show, parade; Country Folk Art Show and Sale, Coconut Grove; Columbus Day Regatta; Johnnie Walker Hispanic Heritage Golf Classic, Miami Lakes; International Women's Show, Miami Beach; Caribbean Arts and Crafts Festival; Coconut Grove Cares Antique Show; Miami Fall Boat Show, Miami Beach; Saturday and Sunday in the Park With Art, Miami Metrozoo; Festival of the Americas, Tropical park, west of Coral Gables; M-Car Mini Grand Prix at Miami Lakes; **November:** Junior Orange Bowl Festival, held at various locations throughout the county, goes until January; South Miami Art Festival; November Home Show, Coconut Grove; Key Biscayne Lighthouse Run; Miami Jazz and heritage Festival; Coral Gables International Festival of Craft Arts; Sunstreet Festival, throughout the county; Taste of the Beach, South Miami Beach; Miami Book Fair International; Baron Antique Show, Miami Beach; Holiday Kick-off - Lighted Boat Parade, Bayside marketplace, downtown; Banyan Arts & Crafts Festival, Coconut Grove; Harvest Festival, Tamiami Park Youth Fairgrounds; Miami Lakes Festival of Lights; Home for the Holidays, held along Ocean Drive in Miami Beach's art-deco district; Coconut Grove Cares Antique Show; Bayside's Holiday Celebration, Bayside Marketplace, downtown; Miami Lakes Holiday and Country Crafts Show; **December:** Metropolitan South Florida Fishing Tournament, throughout the county; Sunstreet Festival, throughout the county; Bayside's Holiday Celebration, Bayside Marketplace, downtown; Santa's Enchanted Forest, Tropical Park, west of Coral Gables; Santa's Arrival and Holiday Stroll, Coral Gables; Ramble agricultural festival, Coral Gables; World's Largest Indoor Flea Market, Miami Beach Convention Center; Indian Arts Festival, Miccosukee Indian Village, 30 miles west of Miami; International Golf Championship Invitational, Coral Gables; New Year's Eve Spectacular, Bayside Marketplace; Big Orange New Year's Eve Celebration, Bayfront Park.

SPORTS AND LEISURE ACTIVITIES:
Most popular local fishing areas: Crandon Park in Key Biscayne; Homestead Bayfront Park in Homestead; Larry and Penny Thompson Memorial Park in Kendall; Matheson Hammock County Park in Old Cutler; Tropical Park in Kendall; Atlantic Ocean; Biscayne Bay.
Number of local golf courses: 34 public courses are listed by the convention & visitors bureau (but one must be a member of the bureau to be listed)
Public beaches? Yes
Tennis courts available to the public? Yes
Boating? Yes
Number of pleasure boats registered in the county (1991-92): 46,291

SERVICES FOR RETIREES:
Many services, including transportation, Homemakers Service, Retired Senior Volunteer Program.

FINANCIAL SERVICES:
Number of local banks: 401 domestic and 66 foreign bank agencies
Number of local savings and loan associations: 149

THE MEDIA:
Largest local newspaper: *The Miami Herald*
Cable television? Yes

MAJOR LOCAL RETAILERS:
Macy's, Burdines, JCPenney, Saks Fifth Avenue, Lord & Taylor, Sears, Bloomingdale's, Marshalls, Mervyn's. Other centers: Miracle Mile is the main shopping district in Coral Gables and contains small shops, boutiques and department stores; Bayside Marketplace in Miami; Mayfair

Shops in Coconut Grove; CocoWalk in Coconut Grove, an open-air retail center with shops and cafes in a European motif; Caribbean Marketplace in Little Haiti; Bal Harbour has exclusive shops, such as Gucci, Cartier.

FOOD ESTABLISHMENTS: 6,808

OTHER SERVICES:
Number of local libraries: 30
Number of local hotels/motels: 540
Number of churches: Protestant: 600; Jewish: 65; Catholic: 85; Other: 50

TOURISM INQUIRIES:
Coral Gables Chamber of Commerce, 50 Aragon Avenue, Coral Gables, 33134. Telephone: 305-446-1657; **Hialeah/Miami Springs** Area Chamber of Commerce, 59 West Fifth Street, Hialeah, 33010. Telephone: 305-887-1515; Greater **Homestead/Florida City** Chamber of Commerce, 160 U.S. Highway 1, Florida City, 33034. Telephone: 305-245-9180; **Latin** Chamber of Commerce, 1470 W. Flagler, Miami, 33135. Telephone: 305-642-3870; **Miami** Chamber of Commerce, 1601 Biscayne Blvd., Omni Complex, Miami, 33132. Telephone: 305-350-7700; Greater **Miami** Convention & Visitors Bureau, 701 Brickell Ave., Suite 2700, Miami, 33131. Telephone: 1-800-283-2707 or 305-539-3063; **Miami Beach** Chamber of Commerce, 1920 Meridian Ave., Miami Beach, 33139. Telephone 305-672-1270; **Miami Shores** Chamber of Commerce, 9523 Northeast Second Avenue, Miami Shores, 33138. Telephone: 305-754-5466; **North Miami** Chamber of Commerce, 13100 West Dixie Highway, North Miami, 33161. Telephone: 305-891-7811; **North Miami Beach** Chamber of Commerce, 39 Northeast 167th Street, North Miami Beach, 33162. Telephone: 305-653-1200; **South Miami-Kendall** Area Chamber of Commerce, 6410 S.W. 80th St., South Miami, 33143. Telephone: 305-661-1621.

GLADES County
Southeast
County seat: Moore Haven

POPULATION: 1990: 7,591
1993: 8,269
Increase: 8.9 percent

AGE DISTRIBUTION (1992) IN PERCENTAGES:
0-14 : 20.4
15-44: 35.6
45-64: 24.5
65+ : 19.6

MUNICIPAL POPULATION:
MOORE HAVEN: 1990: 1,432; 1993: 1,538
UNINCORPORATED: 1990: 6,159; 1993: 6,731

LAND AREA: 774 square miles
POPULATION DENSITY: 11 people per square mile (65th in the state)

While there are no hospitals here, just three physicians and two banks, the county does border Lake Okeechobee, and that translates into tourism dollars. Fishing is popular, both commercially and recreationally. Located in the southern middle portion of the state, the county's major business pursuits are cattle and sugar cane. There are about 30,000 head of beef cattle, 3,000 dairy cows that produce about 8,500 gallons of milk, and 3,000 acres of sugar cane. Other major industries are citrus, which has about 1,500 acres in the county, along with vegetables and alligator hides/meat from the three gator farms. The county's labor force of about 3,100 as of the early 1990s earned an average hourly wage of about $6.25. Moore Haven is the county's only incorporated city, but there are a number of unincorporated areas, including Palmdale, which has about 200 residents and is located at the north end of the county on U.S. 27. The community is also on the Fisheating Creek and houses two county tourist attractions: the Cypress Knee Museum (a collection of cypress wood) and Gatorama (a collection of alligators). Palmdale also is in the middle of a 360,000-acre ranch owned by a Tampa company. Among other unincorporated areas are Muse, which is the leading citrus producer for the county and recently led the area in new home construction; and Lakeport, which has fishing resorts.

TOURISM:
Because of Lake Okeechobee, the population about doubles at the peak of the winter tourist season.

HOUSING PRICES:
Realtors say mobile homes typically average about $15,000 and site-built homes about $55,000. Number of vacant residential lots: 3,902; number of single-family residences: 1,384; mobile homes: 2,294; condominiums: 32

EDUCATION:
Number of schools: 5
Number of students enrolled: 1,009
Percentage of students continuing education after high school: 84.78
Teacher-to-pupil ratio: 1:15.9
Average teacher's salary: $26,903

Colleges, universities, and junior or community colleges serving the area:
University of South Florida in Fort Myers; Edison Community College in Fort Myers; Palm Beach Community College in Lake Worth and Belle Glade; Florida Atlantic University in Boca Raton.

Trade and technical schools serving the area:
West Tech and Lee Vo-Tech.

HEALTH CARE:
Number of general hospitals: 0 (nearest one is Hendry General in Hendry County)
Number of physicians: 3

TAXES: Total county ad-valorem millage rate (1993): 19.3100

STANDARD CRIME RATE: 5,526.7 offenses per 100,000 population (28th out of 67 counties)

LARGEST EMPLOYERS:

Name	Employees	Product/Service
Lykes Brothers	100	Agriculture/sugar/cattle
Glades Electric Cooperative	78	Utilities
Graham Dairy Co.	62	Dairy
Second Seasons Motel	26	Restaurant/motel
Barnett Bank	8	Banking
Clewiston National Bank	3	Banking

COMPANIES PROVIDING LOCAL UTILITIES:
Telephone: United Telephone Co.
Electricity: Florida Power & Light and Glades Electric Cooperative
Natural Gas: None
Water: Lakeport Water Association, South Shore Water Association
Major Water Source: Lake
Sanitary Landfill? Yes

POINTS OF INTEREST:
Cypress Knee Museum, one mile south of Palmdale on U.S. 27, has a collection of cypress wood; **Gatorama,** south of Palmdale, has display of alligators; **Lake Okeechobee** for fishing and boating; **Fisheating Creek** for fishing and small boats, especially canoes; **Brighton Indian Reservation,** one of five reservations in the state, houses Seminole Indians on 35,805 acres and has a population of 361; and **Ortona Indian Mound Park** in Ortona has prehistoric Indian mounds with picnic area and walking trails.

ANNUAL EVENTS:
First full week in February: Ortona Cane Grinding Festival, a neighborhood-type fair in the unincorporated town of Ortona in which people grind cane, boil it and make cane syrup; **Second Weekend in February:** Lakeport Sour Orange Festival in Lakeport; **Third Weekend in February:** Brighton Field Day and Rodeo on the Brighton Indian Reservation, includes crafts, Indian dress and food; **Late February:** Glades County Youth Livestock Show and Sale; **First Weekend in March:** Chalo Nitka (translation from the Seminole language: Day of the Bass) Festival and

Youth Livestock Rodeo, a countywide celebration in Moore Haven includes parade, carnival, children's pet parade, fishing contest and arts and crafts. Sunday is La Primavera, an Hispanic heritage celebration with music and food; **May:** Cinco De Mayo (Mexican Independence Day, May 5) in Moore Haven with Mexican bands and food; **July:** Fourth of July activities in Moore Haven City Park; **Early October:** Cracker Day Rodeo in Moore Haven with local counties competing.

SPORTS AND LEISURE ACTIVITIES:
Most popular local fishing areas: Lake Okeechobee (bass, catfish, speckled perch and shellcracker); Fisheating Creek (bluegill, bream, catfish, bass, speckled perch); Caloosahatchee and Kissimmee rivers. The major local commercial catch consists of catfish.
Number of local golf courses: 1 public
Public beaches: No
Tennis courts available to the public? Yes
Boating? Yes
Number of pleasure boats registered in the county (1991-92): 862

SERVICES FOR RETIREES? No

FINANCIAL SERVICES:
Number of local banks: 2
Number of local savings and loan associations: 0

THE MEDIA:
Largest local newspaper: *Glades County Democrat*
Cable television? Yes

MAJOR LOCAL RETAILERS:
No large chain stores; major one here is Lundy's, a department store that also sells feed and ranch supplies.

FOOD ESTABLISHMENTS: 22

OTHER SERVICES:
Number of local libraries: 1
Number of local motels: 10
Number of churches: Protestant: 6; Jewish: 0; Catholic: 1

TOURISM INQUIRIES:
Glades County Chamber of Commerce, P.O. Box 490, Moore Haven, 33471. Telephone: 813-946-0440.

MONROE County
Southeast
County seat: Key West

POPULATION: 1990: 78,024
1993: 81,766
Increase: 4.8 percent

AGE DISTRIBUTION (1992) IN PERCENTAGES:
0-14 : 15.4
15-44: 44.1
45-64: 24.5
65+ : 16.1

MUNICIPAL POPULATION:
KEY COLONY BEACH: 1990: 977; 1993: 1,017
KEY WEST: 1990: 24,832; 1993: 26,122
LAYTON: 1990: 183; 1993: 189
UNINCORPORATED: 1990: 52,032; 1993: 54,438

LAND AREA: 997 square miles
POPULATION DENSITY: 82 people per square mile (36th in the state)

Ravaged in the past by hurricanes and having faced some recent environmental challenges, notably overdevelopment and the possibility of offshore oil drilling, the Florida Keys have survived many threats. The Keys, which stretch for more than 100 miles from Key Largo south to Key West, have been called many names — from beautiful to eccentric. Sunsets here are said to be among the most picturesque anywhere, and some of the sights are unique. The home of North America's only living coral reef system (the third largest in the world), of one of the world's largest charter fishing fleets, and of miles of beaches, the Keys are a natural haven for shell collectors, bird watchers, scuba divers and snorkelers. Perhaps that's why in Key Largo, the entrance to the Keys from Miami and home of the John Pennekamp Coral Reef State Park and the Key Largo National Marine Sanctuary, you won't find any golf courses. Visitors here are too busy underwater. Key Largo is called the "sport diving capital of the world," and attracts about a million divers a year.

The Keys are made up of hundreds of islands stretching from south of Miami to 89 miles north of Havana. It's not hard deciding which road to take when coming here — there's only one, U.S. Highway 1. Traveling the length of this road to Key West, you will go over 42 bridges and see both the Gulf of Mexico and the Atlantic Ocean.

The largest city on the islands is Key West, about 160 miles southwest of Miami, once the home of Spanish conquistadors, pirates, New England mariners and European royalty. American novelist and short-story writer Ernest Hemingway made his home here and other visitors to the area included Thomas Edison, Lou Gehrig, Harry Truman and Tennessee Williams. Cigar-making and turtle canning once were major industries. Today, tourism is No. 1, followed by commercial fishing. About 1.5 million people visit Key West each year, which is an alarming figure to some Key West natives who have seen prices soar, especially for housing, and have been forced to leave. Among the major employers of Key West are the Marriott Casa Marina Resort, the Pier House Inn & Resort and Key West Fragrance, a fragrance distributor.

Going east from Key West, you find yourself in the Lower Keys, which consist of scores of uninhabited islands and which are home to the small key deer. The Looe Key National Marine Sanctuary is also here. It houses coral formations and canyons and tropical fish and is another noted diving and snorkeling spot. Fishing for sailfish, tuna, bonefish, snook, dolphin, tarpon and snapper is also popular. Marathon, a central point in the Keys, is the home of Crane Point Hammock (where there is a museum of natural history). Charter fishing, marinas, dive shops and water sport rentals abound. Commercial fishing is important to the local economy here, too, as is recreational fishing: The area has 12 miles of former bridges that have been permanently closed to automobile traffic and today function as fishing piers. Farther east is Islamorada, home of the Keys' largest charter fishing fleet, which has a reputation as the sportfishing capital of the world. Located 75 miles south of Miami, this area is known as the "Purple Isles" (made up of Plantation Key, Windley Key, Upper Matecumbe Key, Lower Matecumbe Key and Long Key). Among the catches are sailfish, blackfin tuna, cobia, dolphin, blue marlin, bonefish, tarpon, king mackerel, white marlin, swordfish, grouper, mutton, snapper and yellowtail. The Long Key State Park is also located here, as is the Lignumvitae Key State Botanical Site (with a tropical hardwood forest of West Indian origin) and Indian Key (the county seat of Dade County until it was destroyed during a Seminole Indian raid in 1840).

TOURISM:
It is estimated that about 1 million people visit the underwater sights near Key Largo and about 1.5 million people visit the Key West area annually.

HOUSING PRICES:
For all of the Florida Keys, prices have averaged around $120,000 in recent years. Generally are lower in the Key Largo area, where more land is available, and higher in the Lower Keys. The average price for Key West, for example, has been around $200,000; in the city of Marathon, around $190,000; in the Lower Keys, excluding Key West, around $150,000. Prices in the Key Largo area typically bring the overall average price down.

Number of vacant residential lots: 27,721; number of single-family residences: 20,308; mobile homes: 6,033; condominiums: 6,560

EDUCATION:
Number of schools: 17
Number of students enrolled: 8,942
Percentage of students continuing education after high school: 64.25
Teacher-to-pupil ratio: 1:18.5
Average teacher's salary: $32,819 in 1992-93

Colleges, universities, and junior or community colleges serving the area:
Florida Keys Community College in Key West; St. Leo College Center in Key West

Trade and technical schools serving the area:
Florida Keys Community College and Key West High School

HEALTH CARE:
Number of general hospitals: 4
Number of hospital beds: 269
Number of physicians: 150

TAXES: Total county ad-valorem millage rate (1993): 12.1878

STANDARD CRIME RATE: 8,866.8 offenses per 100,000 population (7th out of 67 counties)

LARGEST PRIVATE EMPLOYERS:

Name	Employees	Product/Service
Winn Dixie	600	Grocery
Nation's Bank	69	Banking
Key West Citizen	62	Newspaper
Key West Fragrance	40	Fragrance distributor
Tarmac/Toppino	33	Heavy construction

COMPANIES PROVIDING LOCAL UTILITIES:
Telephone: Southern Bell
Electricity: City Electric; Florida Power & Light, Florida Keys Electric Cooperative
Natural Gas: None
Water: Florida Keys Aquaduct Authority
Major Water Source: Wells
Sanitary Landfill? No, transported outside the county

POINTS OF INTEREST:
The Everglades National Park is 1.4 million acres and contains a variety of bird life and animal life, ranger-guided activities, hiking, saltwater and freshwater fishing, boating, camping, canoeing, boat rentals, boat ramps, picnicking, marina, lodging and meals and gasoline within the park boundaries. Park contains a number of rare and endangered species including the Florida panther, Everglades mink, green sea turtle and manatee; **Dry Tortugas** islands, located 69 nautical miles from Key West, house a large 19th-century fortress called **Fort Jefferson National Monument,** which has 8-foot-thick walls and during the Civil War served as a Union prison. Area has snorkeling, sea turtles, sport fishing, docking facility, tours of fort.

Key West:
Ernest Hemingway Home and Museum is where author resided from 1931 to 1961 and wrote 75 percent of his works. The furnishings are original; **Key West Aquarium** has shark feedings, guided tours; **Key West Seaplane** has trips to **Fort Jefferson National Monument.** Trips include swimming, snorkeling, bird watching, picnicking in the **Dry Tortugas;** Glass-bottom-boat rides over coral reefs; **Old Town Trolley** has 90-minute tour of Key West; **Mallory Market** is along waterfront and contains a number of shops; **Audubon House and Gardens** is a 19th-century home containing original Audubon engravings, furnishings from the 18th and 19th centuries and a gallery of porcelain bird sculptures; **Fort Zachary Taylor State Historic Site** has interpretive center and museum, picnicking, swimming, snorkeling, saltwater fishing, guided tours of fort built in 1866. A number of cannons (the largest collection of Civil War cannons in the United States) and ammunition from the Civil War era have been uncovered here; **West Martello Fort and Gardens; East Martello Fort** is now home to the **Key West Art and Historical Society** and has artifacts from the Keys and art exhibits; **North American Racing Greyhound Track** in Key West; **Conch Tour Train** takes visitors to about 90 points of interest in Key West; **Curry Mansion** is an 1899 Victorian structure. Visitors tour 22 rooms in house; **Harry S Truman Little White House Museum; Ripley's Believe it or Not! Odditorium; Turtle Kraals** is marine turtle exhibit that is home to loggerhead turtles. There's also a touch tank and a bird aviary; **Sunsets on Mallory Dock** (complete with jugglers, mimes, musicians and street artists).

Key Largo:
John Pennekamp Coral Reef State Park has interpretive center, camping, picnicking, swimming, saltwater fishing, hiking, guided tours, including a glass-bottom-boat tour, snorkeling tour

and scuba diving tours, snorkeling, diving, boat and canoe rentals, boat ramp and concessions. Park contains only living coral reef in the continental United States and is the first underwater state park in the country; **Key Largo National Marine Sanctuary** is located three miles offshore and is a protected area of coral reef, seagrass and sand beds and is where the best diving in the area is found. Area also has the **Carysfort Lighthouse**, built in 1852 and the oldest functioning lighthouse of its kind in the country. Other features: Site of shipwrecks and a 9-foot, 4,000-pound bronze statue called "Christ of the Deep," located in 25 feet of water in the Atlantic Ocean within the sanctuary boundaries; Original **African Queen** boat is on display at the MM 100 Marina; Key Largo Holiday Inn; **Maritime Museum of the Florida Keys** has sunken-treasure displays and rare maritime artifacts from around the world.

Lower Keys:
Looe Key National Marine Sanctuary, south of Big Pine Key, contains a number of coral formations and is a good spot for snorkeling and diving; **Bahia Honda State Park,** 6 miles northeast of Big Pine Key, has camping, vacation cabins, picnicking, swimming in Atlantic Ocean and Florida Bay, saltwater fishing, hiking, boat ramp, concessions. Tarpon fishing here is rated among the best in the state. A number of rare species of birdlife can be seen, such as the great white heron, reddish egret and the osprey; **Key Deer National Wildlife Refuge** in Lower Keys was formed to protect the diminutive Florida Key white-tailed deer; **Great White Heron National Refuge** encompasses all the Lower Keys and protects North America's largest wading bird; Boca Chica Key has a **U.S. Naval Air Station** that is a training base for carrier aircraft; **Blue Hole** on Big Pine Key is a fresh water alligator habitat with self-guided walking trail.

Middle Keys:
Marathon: Museum of Natural History of the Florida Keys at Crane Point Hammock in Marathon has a recreated coral reef cave and other exhibits on the Key's Indians, pirates, 17th-century shipwreck items and a collection of turn-of-the-century Bahamian housewares; **Dolphin Research Center** at Marathon Shores has educational tours to inform the public about the dolphin and allows the public to swim with the dolphins.

Upper Keys:
Indian Key State Historic Site near Islamorada is only accessible by boat and has hiking, observation tower, boat dock, shelter area. Site of 1830s-era busy port. Area once housed a store, hotel, warehouses and wharves. Guided three-hour boat tours to Indian Key depart from Indian Key Fill on U.S. 1; **Lignumvitae Key State Botanical Site,** a half mile off Lower Matecumbe, is accessible only by boat. Site has interpretive center, a 1919 house, virgin tropical forest, hiking and guided tours, including boat tour departing from Indian Key Fill; **Long Key State Recreation Area** has camping, picnicking, swimming, saltwater fishing, hiking, canoeing, campfire programs, guided walks and observation tower; swimming with the dolphins at the **Theater of the Sea** in Islamorada. Visitors also see other marine life and interact with it; **San Pedro Underwater Archaeological Park,** south of Indian Key, is site of a 1733 Spanish shipwreck.

THE ARTS:
Key West: Wrecker's Museum is the oldest house in Key West and displays ship models, miniature Conch houses, antiques; **Key West Lighthouse Museum** is Florida's third oldest brick lighthouse, built in 1847, and museum contains historical displays of Key West and the Florida Keys. A climb of 88 steps takes visitors to the top for a view of the city; **Mel Fisher Maritime Heritage Society's Treasure Museum** has artifacts and treasures from the sunken ships "Atocha" and "Margarita" valued at $250 million; **Red Barn Theatre; Tennessee Williams Fine Arts Center; Waterfront Playhouse at Mallory Square; Key Largo: Key Players** give performances during the year ranging from musicals and comedies to dramas; **Purple Isles Art Group** is an artists' organization that sponsors shows during the year.

ANNUAL EVENTS:
January: New Year's Day fireworks, Key West Harbor; Fort Lauderdale to Key West Yacht Race; Key West Literary Seminar; Upper Keys Seafood Festival, Plantation Yacht Harbor; Key West Craft Show; Florida Keys Renaissance Faire with jousting knights, entertainment, food, Marathon; Grace Jones Day Festival, Marathon; **February:** Monroe County Fair; Old Island Days Arts Festival, a fine-arts street fair in Key West; Civil War Days, a re-enactment of battles at Fort Zachary Taylor: **March:** Conch Shell Blowing Contest, Key West; Conch Republic Independence celebration celebrates mock succession of the Keys from U.S. in 1982 over border dispute; Rain Barrel Arts Festival, Islamorada; **April:** Seven-Mile Bridge Run in Marathon; Island

Fest, Longboat Key; **May:** Truman birthday party, Little White House in Key West, a poker party; Pirates in Paradise, Marathon; Sandcastle Sculpture Contest, Islamorada; Caribbean Pirates Festival, Marathon; Buskerfest, a street performers festival, Key West; **June:** Key West International Gay Arts Festival; **July:** Fourth of July fireworks, Key West; Super Picnic benefitting Hospital of Florida Keys; Women in Paradise, a week of activities for women, Key West; Hemingway Days Festival has street fairs, writing seminars, look-alike and short-story contests, Key West; Underwater Music Festival, where divers listen to an underwater symphony, Looe Key Marine Sanctuary; **September:** Key West Theater Festival; **October:** Gatorade Springman Triathlon in Key West; Goombay Festival celebrates Bahamian heritage of Key West with food and music; Fantasy Fest in Key West is a lavish masking and costume festival; Indian Key Festival, Islamorada; **November:** SBR Super Boat Racing, offshore powerboat race season finale, has parade, boat displays, Key West; **December:** Big Pine Key Island Art Fair.

SPORTS AND LEISURE ACTIVITIES:
Most popular local fishing areas: Atlantic Ocean, Florida Bay, Gulf of Mexico
Number of local golf courses: 1 public (in Key West) and 3 private
Public beaches? Yes
Tennis courts available to the public? Yes
Boating? Yes
Number of pleasure boats registered in the county (1991-92): 16,341

SERVICES FOR RETIREES:
Key Largo has a civic club and a senior citizens group; some services are available at the Armory in Key West; Big Pine Key Senior Citizens Center.

FINANCIAL SERVICES:
Number of local banks: 38
Number of local savings and loan associations: 0

THE MEDIA:
Largest local newspaper: Key West Citizen
Cable television? Yes

MAJOR LOCAL RETAILERS:
Sears, JCPenney, K mart and a number of boutiques, including diving boutiques in the Key Largo and Lower Keys areas.

FOOD ESTABLISHMENTS: 656

OTHER SERVICES:
Number of local libraries: 5
Number of local hotels/motels: 176
Number of churches: Protestant: 61; Jewish: 2; Catholic: 12

TOURISM INQUIRIES:
Key Largo Chamber of Commerce, 105950 Overseas Highway, Key Largo, 33037. Telephone: 305-451-1414; **Lower Keys** Area Chamber of Commerce, P.O. Box 430511, Big Pine Key, 33043-0511. Telephone: 305-872-2411; **Key West** Chamber of Commerce, 402 Wall St., P.O. Box 984, Key West, 33040. Telephone: 305-294-5988.

PALM BEACH County
Southeast
County seat: West Palm Beach

POPULATION: 1990: 863,503
1993: 918,223
Increase: 6.3 percent

AGE DISTRIBUTION (1992) IN PERCENTAGES:
0-14 : 17.3
15-44: 38.7
45-64: 19.8
65+ : 24.1

MUNICIPAL POPULATION:
ATLANTIS: 1990: 1,653; 1993: 1,674
BELLE GLADE: 1990: 16,177; 1993: 17,249
BOCA RATON: 1990: 61,486; 1993: 64,818
BOYNTON BEACH: 1990: 46,284; 1993: 48,428
BRINY BREEZE: 1990: 400; 1993: 394
CLOUD LAKE: 1990: 121; 1993: 121
DELRAY BEACH: 1990: 47,184; 1993: 48,644
GLEN RIDGE: 1990: 207; 1993: 215
GOLF VILLAGE: 1990: 184; 1993: 192
GOLFVIEW: 1990: 153; 1993: 150
GREENACRES CITY: 1990: 18,683; 1993: 22,385
GULF STREAM: 1990: 690; 1993: 705
HAVERHILL: 1990: 1,058; 1993: 1,170
HIGHLAND BEACH: 1990: 3,209; 1993: 3,245
HYPOLUXO: 1990: 807; 1993: 1,106
JUNO BEACH: 1990: 2,172; 1993: 2,173
JUPITER: 1990: 24,907; 1993: 27,291
JUPITER INLET COLONY: 1990: 405; 1993: 404
LAKE CLARKE SHORES: 1990: 3,364; 1993: 3,607
LAKE PARK: 1990: 6,704; 1993: 6,695
LAKE WORTH: 1990: 28,564; 1993: 28,327
LANTANA: 1990: 8,392; 1993: 8,316
MANALAPAN: 1990: 312; 1993: 318
MANGONIA PARK: 1990: 1,453; 1993: 1,407
NORTH PALM BEACH: 1990: 11,343; 1993: 11,782
OCEAN RIDGE: 1990: 1,570; 1993: 1,600
PAHOKEE: 1990: 6,822; 1993: 6,856
PALM BEACH: 1990: 9,814; 1993: 9,814
PALM BEACH GARDENS: 1990: 22,990; 1993: 28,635
PALM BEACH SHORES: 1990: 1,035; 1993: 1,034
PALM SPRINGS: 1990: 9,763; 1993: 9,729
RIVIERA BEACH: 1990: 27,644; 1993: 27,308
ROYAL PALM BEACH: 1990: 15,532; 1993: 16,546
SOUTH BAY: 1990: 3,558; 1993: 4,064
SOUTH PALM BEACH: 1990: 1,480; 1993: 1,482
TEQUESTA VILLAGE: 1990: 4,499; 1993: 4,543
WEST PALM BEACH: 1990: 67,764; 1993: 68,006
UNINCORPORATED: 1990: 405,120; 1993: 437,790

LAND AREA: 1,974 square miles
POPULATION DENSITY: 465 people per square mile (9th in the state)

Its crown jewel is Palm Beach, a 14-mile-long island enclave where mansions abound, where the glitterati — such names as Trump and Kennedy — have maintained winter homes, where the wealthy have been known to donate collectively as much as $1 billion during a winter season of charity balls, and where residents can shop at world-famous stores for stocking stuffers that most people would have to pay for with second mortgages. You can be in a 35-foot sailboat, pull up to a marina and feel as if you were paddling a canoe with a stick on it. One-hundred-foot yachts are not uncommon here.

But that's not all there is to Palm Beach County, which is bordered on the east by 47 miles of beaches and, 45 miles to the west and a world apart, by Lake Okeechobee. There are big pockets of poverty here, too. A 1990 census study found that nearly 16,000 families had incomes of less than $10,000.

In absolute population numbers, Palm Beach was the second-fastest-growing county in the state between 1980 and 1990, behind Dade. And between 1990 and 1993, again it was second — this time behind Broward.

Palm Beach County is a center for business, industry, and finance. High-tech companies include United Technologies, IBM and Motorola.

United Technologies' Pratt & Whitney jet-engine group has been the county's largest private employer for years. But, with cutbacks in engine orders, the company has trimmed its local work force — from 8,000 employees in 1989 to 6,000. Similarly, IBM reduced its work force locally from 5,500 to 2,500 in 1994.

Tourism remains the top industry — about $1.5 billion a year. In 1991, the services industry was the largest employer with 166,606 employees, followed by trade, 113,477; finance, insurance and real estate, 53,647; government, 49,638; manufacturing, 33,467; and construction, 29,483.

Palm Beach is the closest county in South Florida to the Gulf Stream, which is roughly a mile offshore and is a sort of warm "river in the ocean" that keeps temperatures mild throughout the year. It also helps make the area popular among scuba divers.

Away from the coast the county contains the Loxahatchee National Wildlife Refuge and quite a bit of agricultural land. Most of the residential and commercial development is along the coast, which is very crowded, particularly during the winter. Traffic will prove frustrating in some areas, as will the waiting lines at many restaurants.

The largest city, and the county seat, is **West Palm Beach,** which lies on Lake Worth (the Intracoastal Waterway) to the west of Palm Beach and which is a cultural and financial center as well as a residential city. Like some other Florida cities, it lost population during the recent recession — more than 6,000 residents between 1989 and 1993.

But overall, since the 1970s, West Palm and environs have seen a massive increase in the number of professional companies (brokers, accountants, lawyers) and light industry, including computer and electronics manufacturing. One of the largest urban renewal projects currently in the country has begun in the city, consisting of 26 city blocks containing 500 run-down buildings. The project is expected to take 20 years. Part of it has involved the construction of the Kravis Center for the Performing Arts, which was completed in November 1992.

Along with the population boom came a phenomenal boom in the construction of office space. What happened is that major urban centers in South Florida became overbuilt; office vacancy rates skyrocketed. The vacancy rate in West Palm Beach's central business district and the surrounding area has been 25 percent and even as high as 33.5 percent in recent years — among the highest rates in the nation.

The other major cities:

Boca Raton, midway between West Palm Beach and Fort Lauderdale, is on the Atlantic Ocean, has expensive homes, wealthy retirees and huge yachts, and is a site for many high-tech industries. The city has claimed to have more corporate headquarters per capita than any city in the Southeast. A few of the companies with regional and national headquarters here are IBM and Siemens (a communications products company). Homes are mainly single-family residences and condominiums. Most residents live here year-round. Average housing prices in recent years have been $200,000-plus, much higher than the countywide median. Tri-Rail, the commuter train serving Palm Beach, Broward and Dade counties, has a station in the city. Cultural and sports amenities, including at least 22 golf courses, abound. Office space construction boomed from 1985 on, creating huge vacancy rates — 32.2 percent at the end of 1989, the highest of 50 metropolitan areas in the United States surveyed by Cushman & Wakefield, a real estate and market-research firm. Of Boca Raton's 5.5 million square feet of office space, 64 percent had been completed since 1985. Boca Raton, the home of Florida Atlantic University, has five miles of ocean frontage.

Boynton Beach also has had a population boom — from 18,115 residents in 1970 to 48,428 in 1993. Because of this growth, which has included many retirees, a number of service, professional and retail businesses have sprung up. One of the largest employers is Motorola (2,300 employees), which has a paging division plant here. There is some agriculture (green peppers and other vegetables) and a number of nurseries and indoor-foliage companies; and more than 50 light industries, including metal and wood products, paper processing machines, radio equipment and plastic. The city is also a stop on the Tri-Rail system. There is a mixture of condos, townhouses and single-family homes.

Delray Beach, unlike many cities on the East Coast, has a shopping district in a downtown area, which was recently revitalized along Atlantic Avenue and which offers frequent festivals. Delray Beach won All-America City status in 1993-94 — one of ten in the nation. President Clinton lauded the city for community activism. There is still some agriculture here (vegetables, citrus, plants and flowers) and light industry. But the largest industry in the city is the selling and servicing of automobiles.

Jupiter, the oldest settlement in the county (founded in 1838) has led the county in growth rates in recent years. The view along A1A — of beautiful residences and lush vegetation — is quite a contrast from miles and miles of waterfront condominium buildings lining most other such areas in South Florida. The city also is a center for theater activities. Nearby **Tequesta** is a residential community between the Intracoastal Waterway and the Loxahatchee River. It houses the Burt Reynolds Institute of Theatre Training, the Lighthouse Gallery and School of Art, the South Florida Youth Ballet and other cultural attractions.

Lake Worth, near Palm Beach, is largely a retirement and tourist city that has related services. Its population roughly triples from November to April. One of its attractions is its city pier, which extends 1,000 feet into the Atlantic. The city transportation system includes "Lolly the Trolley," San Francisco-type trolleys that provide daytime transit to the beach and other tourist attractions. The city is best-known for its fishing.

To the west of Lake Worth are **Greenacres City** and **Palm Springs,** communities of single-family homes, condo complexes, townhouses and shopping centers. In the early 1900s, developers in the Greenacres City area sold five-acre tracts for $250 — and gave away a free lot on the shore of Lake Worth with each.

Lantana is primarily a residential and business community near Lake Worth and is on the Intracoastal Waterway. Ocean Avenue leads to the city's beach on A1A via a drawbridge. The city is the home of the National Enquirer.

In **Riviera Beach** is the Port of Palm Beach, where cement and agricultural products are exported (about half the state's sugar crop goes through the port) and where such items as petroleum are imported. In fiscal 1991-92, the port was Florida's sixth largest, importing and exporting a total of 3.79 million tons of material.

Away from the glitz of Palm Beach and the commercial and tourist centers of the Gold Coast is an agricultural area in the western part of the county along the east and south shores of Lake Okeechobee. This is the Glades area and is referred to as the sugar cane and winter vegetable capital of the world. Net farm income in Palm Beach County totaled $407.6 million in 1990 — the highest in the state. **Pahokee,** on Lake Okeechobee, is a major sugar-producing city that's about 45 miles west of West Palm Beach. It is located at one of the access points to the lake. Fishing is popular here, but there's only one campground, operated by the city. There are very few housing rentals and no boat rentals or repairs (boat rentals are available in Belle Glade). Some of the Glades area — particularly around **Belle Glade** — is known for "black gold," the black muck that the soil is made of. The top crops of Belle Glade, located a few miles south of Pahokee, are sugar and vegetables. Among the 22 varieties of vegetables are celery, corn, pepper, tomatoes, cucumbers, eggplant, lettuce and radishes. Also in the area are sod farms and ranches. To the west of Belle Glade is **South Bay,** the home of South Bay Growers, which operates farms throughout the south Okeechobee area.

TOURISM:
About 3.6 million people visited the county in fiscal 1992-93.

HOUSING PRICES:
Prices generally range from about $40,000 to upwards of $4 million for beachfront property. The median resale price in the West Palm Beach-Boca Raton metropolitan area was $127,900 in June 1994.
Number of vacant residential lots: 41,952; number of single-family residences: 171,006; mobile homes: 3,786; condominiums: 221,891. The county is Number One in Florida in the number of condominiums.

EDUCATION:
Number of schools: 153
Number of students enrolled: 122,145
Percentage of students continuing education after high school: Insufficient data reported to the state for 1992-93.
Teacher-to-pupil ratio: 1:18.2
Average teacher's salary: $35,888

Colleges, universities, and junior or community colleges serving the area:
Florida Atlantic University in Boca Raton; Palm Beach Community College, which has branches throughout the county, from the coast to Belle Glade; College of Boca Raton; Northwood University-Florida Education Center, West Palm Beach; Lynn University, Boca Raton; Nova University, Fort Lauderdale

Trade and technical schools serving the area:
South Technical Education Center in Boynton Beach; North Technical Education Center in Riviera Beach; and West Technical Education Center in Belle Glade.

HEALTH CARE:
Number of general hospitals: 15
Number of hospital beds: 3,831
Number of physicians: 2,264

TAXES: Total county ad-valorem millage rate (1993): 16.4176

STANDARD CRIME RATE: 8,765.8 offenses per 100,000 population (9th out of 67 counties)

LARGEST PRIVATE EMPLOYERS:

Name	Employees	Product/Service
Pratt & Whitney Aircraft	6,000	Jet engines
IBM	2,500	Computers
Motorola	2,300	Electronic pagers
St. Mary's Hospital	2,200	Health care
Flo-Sun Inc.	2,000	Agriculture
Florida Power & Light	2,000	Utilities
Siemens Communications	2,000	Communications products
Boca Raton Resort & Club	2,000	Hospitality
Southern Bell	1,600	Telecommunications
Boca Raton Hospital	1,600	Health care

COMPANIES PROVIDING LOCAL UTILITIES:
Telephone: Southern Bell
Electricity: Florida Power & Light
Water: County and municipalities
Major Water Source: Lakes
Natural Gas: Florida Public Utilities, Peoples Gas
Sanitary Landfill? Yes

POINTS OF INTEREST:
The Breakers, a famous oceanfront resort in Palm Beach that describes itself as "a very Palm Beach tradition." It has a staff in the hundreds, is filled with bronze-and-crystal chandeliers, and was built in 1926, inspired by the Italian Renaissance, by the Henry Morrison Flagler family. It has ceilings hand-painted by 75 European artists and tapestries on walls. **Henry Morrison Flagler Museum** is a mansion, called Whitehall, that was built in 1901 by the Standard Oil millionaire and stands much as it was during Flagler's lifetime; **West Palm Beach Auditorium,** site of major concerts, circus performances, sports, dancing, home shows; **Jupiter Lighthouse and Museum.** Lighthouse was built in 1860 and is still operating; small museum contains photos and artifacts of early Jupiter life. Open to the public on Sundays; **Burt Reynolds Ranch & Film Studios Tour,** Jupiter, has mini-petting farm, gift shop, feed store, tours; **Joseph Verner Reed Wilderness Sanctuary,** Jupiter Island, has 120 oceanfront acres maintained as a bird preserve and Indian shell mounds; **Lion Country Safari,** West Palm Beach, where rhinos, elephants and lions and hundreds of other animals roam over 500-acre African-style preserve, also is a theme amusement park and has a petting zoo; 22-acre **Dreher Park Zoo** and tropical gardens in West Palm Beach has exotic animals and nature trails; **Loxahatchee National Wildlife Refuge** encompasses 221 square miles of the Everglades with activities that include hiking, fishing, boating, canoeing, airboat rides, wildlife observation; **Gumbo Limbo Nature Center,** Boca Raton, provides environmental classes, workships, field trips; **Marinelife Center** in Juno Beach houses aquariums, exhibits, displays on sea turtles and other marine life, also has nature trail, underground tunnel to sea turtle nesting beach; **John D. MacArthur Beach State Park,** North Palm Beach on Singer Island, has swimming, saltwater fishing, popular snorkeling area, shell collecting, hiking and one of the prime nesting beaches for sea turtles in the state; **Belle Glade Marina and Campground,** on Torry Island at Lake Okeechobee, has fish camps, boat ramps, and about 400 camp sites; **Cruises on Lake Worth** and other local waters offered on several riverboats and other craft; **Auctions** of estates are put on by several area companies (see local newspapers for schedules); **Royal Palm Audubon Society** sponsors bird-watching and nature trips; **Flea markets** are popular; **Everglades tours; farm tours** are available, some offering pick-your-own opportunities (tomatoes, strawberries, eggplant, cucumbers, black-eyed peas) in the Boynton Beach area; Orchid nursery tours, **Albert's & Merkel Bros.,** Boynton Beach, has exotic orchids; **Hallpatee Seminole Village** at Knollwood Groves, Lake Worth, a village housing dis-

plays of Seminole Indian culture; **Mounts Botanical Garden,** West Palm beach, features tropical plants; **Okeeheelee Nature Center,** West Palm Beach, has five miles of nature trails, some paved, through 90 acres of pine flatwoods and wetlands; **Pine Jog Environmental Education Center,** West Palm Beach, has nature walks, environmental lectures, displays; **The Rapids Golf and Slide,** West Palm Beach, has four waterslides, mini-golf, children's and adult pools, waterfalls.

SPORTS:
Boca Raton's Royal Palm Polo Sports Club, where players compete for tournament prize money and awards, including the International Gold Cup; **Palm Beach Polo and Country Club,** Wellington; **Gulfstream Polo Grounds,** Lake Worth; **Montreal Expos** and **Atlanta Braves** share the facilities during spring training at West Palm Beach Municipal Stadium; **Moroso Motorsports Park,** in the northwest part of the county, has a quarter-mile drag strip and a 2.25-mile, ten-turn road course and hosts auto, motorcycle races; **International Sports Complex at Mission Bay,** Boca Raton, is a swimming and diving center where Olympic champions, including Greg Louganis, have trained; the **Professional Golfers Association (PGA)** of America and the **U.S. Croquet Association** both have headquarters in Palm Beach Gardens; **Bicycle trails** throughout the county, notably in Palm Beach; **Sailfish Marina** on Singer Island has million-dollar yachts, famed charter fleet, Thursday night exhibits of marine art by local craftsmen; **horseback riding** is popular in the county and the **Palm Beach Polo Equestrian Club,** Wellington, attracts Olympic riders; **Palm Beach Kennel Club** has dog racing and pari-mutuel betting; West Palm Beach Jai-Alai.

THE ARTS:
Belle Glade:
Dolly Hand Cultural Arts Center.

Boca Raton:
Caldwell Theatre Company performs dramas, musicals, comedies; **Boca Ballet Theatre Company; Florida Atlantic University's Griswold Theatre,** a university cultural center; **Florida Atlantic University Auditorium** has shows, concerts, films, ballet; **Royal Palm Dinner Theatre** has dramatic and musical productions; **Little Palm Theatre** performs children's programs; **Boca Raton Museum of Art** has exhibits, arts and crafts classes and field trips; **Florida Atlantic University's Ritter Art Gallery** has fine-art exhibits, community programs and competitions; **Florida Philharmonic Orchestra,** which resulted from a merger of the Boca Raton and Fort Lauderdale symphonies, performs at Florida Atlantic University's Auditorium, which also hosts the **Boca Raton Symphonic Pops; Children's Museum of Boca Raton** at Singing Pines has exhibits, workshops; **Children's Science Explorium** has hands-on science exhibits.

Boynton Beach:
Civic Center has 500-seat auditorium; **Boynton Beach Gold Coast Community Band** holds concerts at the Boynton Beach Civic Center.

Delray Beach:
Morikami Park/Museum/Gardens, Delray Beach, has Japanese gardens, museum of Japanese culture and folk art, and bonsai exhibit; **Cason Cottage and Museum,** Delray Beach, built around 1915 by pioneering minister, has art exhibits, oral histories, Florida memorabilia; **Delray Beach Playhouse** seats 250 and has monthly productions from October through May; **Delray Art League** sponsors shows in the winter; **Old School Square,** a multi-use cultural art center with art exhibitions, children's theater, dance classes, films.

Juno Beach:
Shakespeare-by-the-Sea.

Jupiter and Tequesta:
Burt Reynolds Theatre, a 150-seat professional Equity theatre in Tequesta, produces dramas, comedies and musicals. The theatre is also the home of the **Burt Reynolds Institute for Theatre Training,** a professional training program; **Jupiter Theatre,** also established by Burt Reynolds, is a dinner theatre that presents comedies and musicals featuring well-known stars and also offers Children's Theatre on Saturday mornings; **Loxahatchee Historical Society and Museum,** Jupiter, has historical artifacts, quilt shows, changing exhibits; **Jupiter Civic Theatre** is home of the Coastal Players; **Choral Society of the Palm Beaches** offers concerts; The **Chamber Theatre of the Palm Beaches** is a professional touring repertory company based in

Jupiter and during the winter season is the resident theater company of **The Lighthouse Gallery,** a cultural center and school of art in Tequesta; offshoots of the Chamber Theatre include **The Chamber Telltales,** which presents theater for children using mime, live music and story-telling, **The Chamber Forum,** which presents new work by local and national playwrights, and **The Chamber Potpourri,** providing entertainment from opera to Shakespeare for large and small groups.

Lake Worth:
Lake Worth Playhouse, a community theater featuring amateur actors; **Lannan Museum** has exhibits of sculpture, paintings, ceramic art and glass; **Bryant Park Outdoor Concerts** from mid-April to late September; **Duncan Theater** features chamber music, children's series, local and student productions and ballets; **Chamber Music Society of the Palm Beaches; Demetrius A. Klein & Dancers** holds non-mainstream dance and performance events.

The Palm Beaches:
Kravis Center for the Performing Arts, West Palm Beach, has a 2,200-seat main concert hall, 1,100-seat amphitheater, hosts variety of performances, from country to classical, including some by by the **Florida Philharmonic Orchestra;** Other performing groups: **Greater Palm Beach Symphony; Miami City Ballet,** West Palm Beach, a professional classical dance company; **Palm Beach Opera,** Palm Beach; **Musicana Dinner Theatre,** West Palm Beach; **Royal Palm Gallery of Worth Avenue,** Palm Beach, has an international collection of art works and an international purchasing network for art works. **Norton Gallery of Art,** West Palm Beach, features permanent collection of French Impressionist and post-Impressionist paintings and jade and sculpture collections; **Ann Norton Sculpture Gardens,** West Palm Beach, has brick sculptures and more than 300 palms and rare plants; **Society of the Four Arts,** Palm Beach, hosts art exhibitions, musical events, lectures, films and programs for young people. There is also a **Society of the Four Arts Gardens** and **Society of the Four Arts Library; South Florida Science Museum & Planetarium,** West Palm Beach, features exhibits of different sciences, planetarium programs, aquariums, computer learning center, lectures, tours; **Royal Poinciana Playhouse,** Palm Beach, has limited and national tours of Broadway and off-Broadway hits; **Hibel Museum of Art,** Palm Beach, a tribute to artist Edna Hibel, has lithographs, drawings, sculptures; **Palm Beach Round Table,** the state's oldest cultural, educational, entertainment, lecture and special events forum; **Ballet Florida,** West Palm Beach; **Quest Theatre,** West Palm Beach, an African-American-owned multi-cultural professional theatre; **Palm Beach Community College Museum of Art,** has paintings, sculptures, glass and ceramic art; **Armory Art Center,** West Palm Beach, rotating exhibits of Florida artists' works.

Pahokee:
Pahokee Museum has exhibits on local pioneers and on country-western singer Mel Tillis and pro football player Ricky Jackson, both Pahokee natives.

ANNUAL EVENTS:
January: South Florida Fair & Palm Beach County Exposition has carnival midway, educational exhibits, livestock, entertainment; Downtown Festival of the Arts, Delray Beach; Boca Fest, Boca Raton, features 300 artists and contemporary craftsmen, entertainment, food and dessert fests; Art and Jazz on the Avenue, Delray Beach; **February:** Open House Anniversary, Henry M. Flagler Museum, Palm Beach, has classic cars, guides in period costume, music, clowns, films, stage shows; Palm Beach Seafood Festival, Currie Park, West Palm Beach; Chelsea America Flower Show, Morikami Museum & Japanese Gardens; Teddy Bear Affair, Dreher Park Zoo, has teddy bear contests, games, prizes, stories, music; Audemars Piguet International Open, Palm Beach Polo & Country Club, West Palm Beach; Boca Museum Outdoor Art Festival, Crocker Center, Boca Raton, features 250 artists; Virginia Slims of Florida, Delray Beach Tennis Center, women's professional tennis tournament; **March:** Art and Jazz on the Avenue, Atlantic Avenue, Delray Beach; "Meet Me Downtown" Youth Festival, Boca Raton, a juried art and craft show; Pepsi Drag Racing Championship, Moroso Motorsports Park; USPA Rolex Gold Cup/Final, Palm Beach Polo & Country Club; West Palm Beach Italian Fest; Artfest by the Sea, Jupiter, arts and crafts line a mile of A1A overlooking the beaches; Spring Egg-citement, Dreher Park Zoo, West Palm Beach, egg hunts, games; Findlandia Days, ethnic Finnish festival in Lake Worth; $100,000 World Cup, Palm Beach Polo & Country Club, the Super Bowl of polo; **April:** Palm Beach Invitational Piano Competition, Flagler Museum, Palm Beach, features a dozen of the world's greatest young pianists; The Delray Affair, a street fair with arts and crafts, plants, collectibles, food, entertainment; Bookfest of the Palm Beaches, West Palm Beach; Sunfest, downtown West Palm Beach, has

music, crafts, art show, food, fireworks; Top Gun Invitational Tournament, Palm Beach Polo & Country Club, features radio-controlled B-17 bombers and jet fighters; **May;** Seafare, Jupiter Lighthouse Park, Jupiter, festival celebrating the lighthouse, has seafood, arts and crafts, entertainment; **June:** Art and Jazz on the Avenue, Delray Beach, July 4th kickoff event; **July:** Independence Day Celebration, Moroso Motorsports Park, features jet dragster and funny cars; fireworks celebration on the beach, Delray Beach; **August:** Boca Festival Days, around Boca Raton, has luxury car show, fishing festival, trade show, wine tasting, arts and crafts, contests, concerts; **September:** Palm Beach Home & Garden Show, West Palm Beach Auditorium; Pepsi Jet Car Nationals, Moroso Motorsports Park; **October:** Heritage Month, a month-long celebration of the cultural diversity of Delray Beach; American-German Club Oktoberfest, Lantana; Kidsfest of Delray, Old School Square; Hot Rod Super Show, Moroso Motorsports Park; Art and Jazz on the Avenue, Delray Beach; **November:** Fiesta on Flagler, West Palm Beach, celebration of Hispanic culture, art and heritage; Heritage Festival, South Florida Fairgrounds, West Palm Beach, a music festival with exhibits, food, carnival, entertainment; Harvest Fest, Delray Beach; Budweiser 5-Day Bracket Championship, Moroso Motorsports Park; Pepsi Citrus Nationals, Moroso Motorsports Park, has races in many classes; **December:** Holiday Boat Parade, Intracoastal Waterway, Delray Beach; Holiday Pageant Parade, Delray Beach; Art & Jazz on the Avenue, Delray Beach; Holiday Boat Parade of Lights, Intracoastal Waterway from the Boynton Inlet to the Hillsboro Canal, a family boat parade; Boca Raton Holiday Boat Parade, decorated boats go from the Intracoastal C-15 Canal to the Hillsboro Bridge, Boca Raton.

SPORTS AND LEISURE ACTIVITIES:

Most popular local fishing areas: north fork of the Loxahatchee River; J.W. Corbett Wildlife Management area; the Atlantic Ocean for tarpon, snook, snapper, trout, porgy, flounder, redfish and bluefish from the beach and grouper, snapper, muttonfish, yellowtail, triggerfish, amberjack and mackerel in the reefs; sailfish, marlin and barracuda in the Gulf Stream; the Everglades; Boynton Inlet Jetty; the Lake Worth Pier; the bridges over the Intracoastal waterways; Lake Okeechobee; Lake Ida.

Number of local golf courses: 145 in the county
Public beaches: Yes
Tennis courts available to the public? Yes
Boating? Yes
Number of pleasure boats registered in the county (1991-92): 30,417

SERVICES FOR RETIREES:

Information and referral through the Senior Service Division of Palm Beach County.

FINANCIAL SERVICES:

Number of local banks: 236
Number of local savings and loan associations: 172

THE MEDIA:

Largest local newspaper: Palm Beach Post
Cable television? Yes

MAJOR LOCAL SHOPPING AREAS AND RETAILERS:

Worth Avenue: Legendary shopping district in Palm Beach with more than 200 shops, boutiques, galleries and salons (Van Cleef & Arpels, Gucci, Chanel, Louis Vuitton, Valentino, Ferragamo, Cartier, FAO Schwarz). There are a number of malls in the county. Major retailers include: Sears, Bloomingdale's, Saks Fifth Avenue, Lord & Taylor, Burdines, Macy's, JCPenney, K mart, Marshalls, Byrons, Mervyn's, Jacobson's. Those who like antiques can find shops on Lake Avenue in Lake Worth, South Dixie Highway in West Palm Beach, and, for rare and expensive pieces, Worth Avenue. Also factory outlet stores, flea markets and a farmers' market.

FOOD ESTABLISHMENTS: 3,064

OTHER SERVICES:

Number of local libraries: 18
Number of local hotels/motels: 230
Number of churches: Protestant: 356; Jewish: 19; Catholic: 23; Other: 10

TOURISM INQUIRIES:

Palm Beach County Convention and Visitors Bureau, 1555 Palm Beach Lakes Blvd, Suite 204, West Palm Beach 33401. Telephone: 407-471-3995; **Palm Beach** Chamber of Commerce, 45

Coconut Row, Palm Beach, 33480. Telephone: 407-655-3282; **Jupiter/Tequesta/Juno Beach** Chamber of Commerce, 800 N. U.S. Highway 1, Jupiter, 33477. Telephone: 407-746-7111; Greater **Boca Raton** Chamber of Commerce, 1800 N. Dixie Highway, Boca Raton, 33432-1892. Telephone: 407-395-4433; Greater **Boynton Beach** Chamber of Commerce, First Financial Plaza, Suite 108, 639 E. Ocean Ave., Boynton Beach, 33435. Telephone: 407-732-9501. Greater **Delray Beach** Chamber of Commerce, 64 Southeast Fifth Avenue, Delray Beach, 33483. Telephone: 407-278-0424; Greater **Lake Worth** Chamber of Commerce, 1702 Lake Worth Road, Lake Worth, 33460. Telephone: 407-582-4401; Greater **Lantana** Chamber of Commerce, 212 Iris Street, Lantana, 33462. Telephone: 407-585-8664; **Belle Glade** Chamber of Commerce, 540 South Main Street, Belle Glade, 33430. Telephone: 407-996-2745; **Pahokee** Chamber of Commerce, 115 East Main Street, Pahokee, 33476. Telephone: 407-924-5579.

SOUTHWEST FLORIDA

THE COUNTIES: Charlotte, Collier, De Soto, Hardee, Hendry, Lee and Sarasota

MAJOR CITIES: Cape Coral, Sarasota, Fort Myers, Naples, Venice

TOP INDUSTRIES: Tourism, services and retail trade, agriculture (citrus, vegetables, and watermelons), construction, cattle ranching, sugar cane

MAJOR NEWSPAPERS: *Sarasota Herald-Tribune* and *News-Press* in Fort Myers

WEATHER: On the first line is the average maximum temperature for each month; the second line, the average minimum temperature; the third line, the amount of precipitation, in inches, for 1991, from the national weather station.

Fort Myers	Jan.	Feb.	Mar.	Apr.	May	June	July	Aug.	Sep.	Oct.	Nov.	Dec.
Max.	79.4	77.9	81.5	87.7	90.4	92.1	91.8	92.9	92.1	86.8	79.1	79.2
Min.	61.2	57.7	61.2	67.7	71.3	73.4	74.2	75.1	73.5	69.2	59.2	58.4
Precp.	8.0	0.7	1.1	5.0	8.5	11.2	14.5	5.9	8.0	4.0	0.3	0.3

CHARLOTTE County
Southwest
County seat: Punta Gorda

POPULATION: 1990: 110,975
1993: 121,695
Increase: 9.7 percent

AGE DISTRIBUTION (1992) IN PERCENTAGES:
0-14 : 13.3
15-44: 28.3
45-64: 24.0
65+ : 34.5

MUNICIPAL POPULATION:
PUNTA GORDA: 1990: 10,637; 1993: 11,769
UNINCORPORATED: 1990: 100,338; 1993: 109,926

LAND AREA: 694 square miles
POPULATION DENSITY: 175 people per square mile (25th in the state)

Located 100 miles south of Tampa and 24 miles north of Fort Myers, the county has the highest percentage of residents 65 and older (34.5 percent) in Florida. And nearly 60 percent of the

Sanibel Island is one of the state's premier shell-collecting sites.

A pelican takes a breather at the Naples Pier. Many coastal communities have long piers frequented by tourists. Some allow fishing.

Retirees often fill the stands during spring training games, such as this one at Ed Smith Stadium in Sarasota.

residents are at least 45 years old. The main industries here are services; trade; government; finance, insurance and real estate; and construction.

Farming is also prominent here — 395 farms on 441,600 acres, in addition to about 12,250 acres of oranges producing nearly 3.6 million boxes; and 1,196 acres of vegetables, more than 2,600 acres of grapefruit and 29,047 head of cattle. Mobile homes are popular; high-rise structures are not. Residences are primarily single-family, with some low-rise condominiuims, townhouses and villas. **Punta Gorda** (which claims 157 significant historical residential and commercial structures) is the only incorporated area in the county. **Port Charlotte** is the largest community, with about 90,000 residents. There also are a large number of other unincorporated areas and developments, including Murdock (a shopping-business center), Charlotte Harbor, Charlotte Park, Burnt Store Isles, Burnt Store Meadows, Tropical Gulf Acres, South Punta Gorda Heights, El Jobean, Gulf Cove, Rotonda, South Englewood, Grove City, Cape Haze, Placida, Gasparilla Island, Deep Creek, Harbour Heights, Solona, Cleveland, Tee & Green Estates, Pelican Harbor, Green Ridge Colony, Sans Souci, Charlotte Ranchettes, Ridge Harbor, Peace River Shores and Prairie Creek Park. Most residents here come from the Northeast (14 percent) and from the North Central states (14 percent).

From 1980 to 1992, Charlotte County's growth rate was 104 percent — the 14th highest county growth rate in the country.

TOURISM:
Snowbirds stay in the area one to four months in the winter and add about 30 percent to the local population.

HOUSING PRICES:
The median sales price for a single-family existing home in the Punta Gorda metropolitan statistical area was $72,300 in June 1994.
Number of vacant residential lots: 133,013; number of single-family residences: 44,657; mobile homes: 5,466; condominiums: 9,659

EDUCATION:
Number of schools: 21
Number of students enrolled: 14,650
Percentage of students continuing education after high school: 60.08
Teacher-to-pupil ratio: 1:18.9
Average teacher's salary: $30,536

Colleges, universities, and junior or community colleges serving the area:
Port Charlotte Center of Edison Community College; Florida Southern College at Port Charlotte; Port Charlotte Center of Manatee Community College.

Trade and technical schools serving the area:
Charlotte Vocational-Technical Center

HEALTH CARE:
Number of general hospitals: 3
Number of hospital beds: 674
Number of physicians: 207

TAXES: Total county ad-valorem millage rate (1993): 12.8923

STANDARD CRIME RATE: 3,054.4 offenses per 100,000 population (50th out of 67 counties)

LARGEST PRIVATE EMPLOYERS:
Name	Employees	Product/Service
Medical Center Hospital	979	Health care
Bon Secour St. Joseph Hospital	897	Health care
Fawcett Memorial Hospital	825	Health care
South Port Square	230	Retirement center
Palm Automotive	190	Automobiles
Sprint/United Telephone	177	Communications
Sun Bank	171	Banking
Florida Power & Light	150	Utilities
Inter-Medic Health Care	150	Health care
Life Care Center	135	Nursing home

COMPANIES PROVIDING LOCAL UTILITIES:
Telephone: United Telephone Co.
Electricity: Florida Power & Light Co.
Natural Gas: None
Water: Charlotte County Utilities; City of Punta Gorda
Major Water Source: Rivers
Sanitary Landfill? Yes

POINTS OF INTEREST:
Charlotte County Stadium in Port Charlotte, spring training home of the Texas Rangers; **Gasparilla Island State Recreation Area,** south of Placida, site of wooden lighthouse that was put into use in 1890 as a mariner's guide to the entrance to Port Boca Grande and Charlotte Harbor. Area also has picnicking, swimming, saltwater fishing; **Cayo Costa State Park,** south of Placida, accessible by boat, has primitive cabins, picnicking, saltwater fishing, swimming and hiking, is the site of one of the largest undeveloped barrier islands, and has numerous Indian mounds; **Don Pedro Island State Recreation Area,** located on a barrier island between Knight Island and Little Gasparilla Island and is accessible only by private boat or ferry, has picnicking, fishing, shelling, swimming and nature study.

THE ARTS:
Port Charlotte Cultural Center has cultural, recreational and educational activities year-round; **Charlotte County Memorial Auditorium,** the county's home for the performing arts, has seating capacity for 2,300 people and is equipped to handle events from antique and trade shows to professional and non-professional theater; **Liberty Singers; Charlotte Symphony Orchestra; Charlotte County Pops Orchestra; The Charlotte Players** stage comedy, drama and musical performances; **Visual Art Center** in Punta Gorda houses an exhibit hall, gift shop, library and photographic darkroom; **Museum of Charlotte County** in Punta Gorda has permanent exhibits on African animals, birds, dolls and local history, art and science workshops, films, presentations, field trips and displays; **Charlotte County Concert Band; Charlotte Chorale; Charlotte County Country Music Club; Charlotte County Jazz Society; Charlotte Harbor Area Historical Society; Sunshine Strummers; Harborside Performers** and **Old Punta Gorda Inc.** (stages plays); **Pride of Charlotte** singing group; **YRI Inc.** poetry group; and **Seagrape Artist Gallery.**

ANNUAL EVENTS:
January: Charlotte County Fair at Charlotte County Stadium in Port Charlotte; Senior Expo at Charlotte County Memorial Auditorium; **February:** Peace River Folk Festival at Laishley Park, Punta Gorda; Art Fest at Charlotte County Art Guild; Annual Barbershop Concert at Memorial Auditorium; **March:** Senior Olympics of Charlotte County; Home Show at the auditorium; Seafood Festival at Placida; **April:** La Fiesta de Ponce de Leon where Ponce de Leon's Landing is reenacted. There also is a sailboat regatta, antique car show, and a festival at Laishley Park; Annual Block Party in downtown Punta Gorda; **Spring:** Florida International Air Show at the Charlotte County Airport in Punta Gorda; **May:** Southwest Chili Challenge at Fishermen's Village; **July:** Fourth of July Celebration at Laishley Park, Punta Gorda, with food booths, games and entertainment during the day, and ends with fireworks above the harbor at night; Christmas in July at the cultural center; **Early September:** Labor Day Fish Fry at Gilchrist Park, Punta Gorda; **October:** Octoberfest at Fishermen's Village; Waterfront Festival at Laishley Park; **November:** Fall Festival and Yankee Peddler Fair on the Bon Secour St. Joseph Hospital grounds in Port Charlotte; **December:** (first Saturday in December) Christmas Parade in Punta Gorda; Lighting of the Christmas Tree at Gilchrist Park; Punta Gorda Christmas Light Canal Tours; Annual Peace River Lighted Boat Parade.

SPORTS AND LEISURE ACTIVITIES:
Most popular local fishing areas: Peace River, Myakka River, Charlotte Harbor and the Gulf of Mexico.
Number of local golf courses: 2 public; 3 private; 9 semi-private
Public beaches? Yes
Tennis courts available to the public? Yes
Boating? Yes
Number of pleasure boats registered in the county (1991-92): 13,876

SERVICES FOR RETIREES:
The Senior Lounge, a headquarters for personal services for senior adults, has recreational activities, dances, sing-alongs, games and meals, and is located at the Cultural Center in Port Charlotte.

FINANCIAL SERVICES:
Number of local banks: 36
Number of local savings and loan associations: 20

THE MEDIA:
Largest local newspaper: *Charlotte Sun Herald*
Cable television? Yes

MAJOR LOCAL RETAILERS: Sears, JCPenney, Wal-Mart, Dillards, Burdines, K mart, Montgomery Ward, Bealls, Byrons.

FOOD ESTABLISHMENTS: 351

OTHER SERVICES:
Number of local libraries: 4
Number of local motels: 37
Number of churches: Protestant: 55; Jewish: 1; Catholic: 5; Other: 7

TOURISM INQUIRIES:
Charlotte County Chamber of Commerce, 2702 Tamiami Trail, Port Charlotte, 33952. Telephone: 813-627-2222.

COLLIER County
Southwest
County seat: Naples

POPULATION: 1990: 152,099
1993: 174,664
Increase: 14.8 percent

AGE DISTRIBUTION (1992) IN PERCENTAGES:
0-14 : 17.6
15-44: 37.0
45-64: 22.2
65+ : 23.3

MUNICIPAL POPULATION:
EVERGLADES CITY: 1990: 321; 1993: 342
NAPLES: 1990: 19,505; 1993: 19,811
UNINCORPORATED: 1990: 132,273; 1993: 154,441

LAND AREA: 2,026 square miles
POPULATION DENSITY: 86 people per square mile (34th in the state)

You can drive through some Florida counties and see enough of the same type of scenery that you'd never know when you've left one community and entered another. You won't find that here. Collier County includes **Naples,** which in the late 1980s was listed by the federal government as the fastest-growing metropolitan area of the country in terms of percentage. Between 1980 and 1992, the Census Bureau reported, the growth rate of the county — 91.6 percent — was the 24th highest in the United States.

The county also includes the resorts of **Marco Island** and the **Isle of Capri,** on the Gulf; the agricultural community of **Immokalee,** 45 miles northeast of Naples in a huge farming area; and **Everglades City,** a fishing village in the southeastern part of the county that is near the beginning point of the Ten Thousand Islands of Everglades National Park.

Despite the phenomenal growth of the Naples area, agriculture, in the eastern part of the county, remains one of the top industries, behind services and retail trade related to Naples tourism. In the Immokalee area, where the population of about 15,000 doubles with immigrant farm laborers during the fall and spring harvests, there are about 25 vegetable packing and processing plants and a big State Farmers' Market. The major crops are tomatoes, citrus, cattle, bell peppers, cucumbers, watermelons, squash, potatoes, gladiolus, avocados, seed corn, ornamental flowers and pineapples.

Naples itself is a financial and service center and a mecca for retirees — including thousands of Snowbirds — primarily from the Midwest but also increasingly from the Northeast. There are opulent waterfront estates along parts of the beach and many waterfront condominiums, some selling for more than $1 million. Olde Naples is a wealthy enclave of ritzy shops and expensive homes (one, advertised "just steps to the beach," was on the market for $675,000). The city also is known for its scores of art galleries and arts festivals, and is reputed to have more golf courses per capita than any other place in the United States. And a ride through town will give you the impression that there's at least one mall, mini-mall, strip mall or other type of shopping center per capita. Residential construction is big business, too; the number of single-family homes increased by about 4,500 between 1989 and 1991 and the number of condominium units by 6,000.

Aside from the incorporated city of Naples, there are tens of thousands of residents in the communities of North, Central, East and South Naples, and about 20,000 in Golden Gate, which is at the entrance to the 79-mile Alligator Alley, a cross-Florida highway that extends to the Fort Lauderdale area.

South of the city along the Gulf is Marco Island, a community of about 11,000 where condominiums abound. Marco also has historic buildings in Old Marco and a fishing village called Goodland.

To the east, Everglades City is known for two things — fishing and tour boats. Airboat tours are available through private companies, and the National Park Service also conducts tours.

Also of note is that average teachers' salaries have been among the highest in the state in recent years.

TOURISM:
The tourism season runs from January through March. Chamber of Commerce employees say that the population as much as triples during this season. Roads, particularly U.S. 41, can get very congested.

HOUSING PRICES:
Housing ranges from mobile homes to oceanfront estates. Many homes are advertised in the $65,000 range, many in the $100,000 to $300,000 range, and one condominium building on Gulfshore Boulevard has advertised units "from $1,535,000." Median sales price for a single-family existing home in the Naples metropolitan statistical area was $158,600 in June 1994. Number of vacant residential lots: 50,435; number of single-family residences: 37,247; mobile homes: 2,889; condominiums: 51,455

EDUCATION:
Number of schools: 29
Number of students enrolled: 23,924
Percentage of students continuing education after high school: 71.57
Teacher-to-pupil ratio: 1:17.7
Average teacher's salary: $36,417

Colleges, universities, and junior or community colleges serving the area:
Edison Community College's branch in Naples; International College of Naples; Walden University: Florida Center in Naples

Trade and technical schools serving the area:
J.W. Lorenzo Walker Vo-Tech

HEALTH CARE:
Number of general hospitals: 2
Number of hospital beds: 498
Number of physicians: 319

TAXES: Total county ad-valorem millage rate (1993): 12.3366

STANDARD CRIME RATE: 5,369.2 offenses per 100,000 population (31st out of 67 counties)

LARGEST PRIVATE EMPLOYERS:

Name	Employees	Product/Service
Naples Community Hospital	2,400	Health care
Publix	1,580	Grocery

Ritz-Carlton Hotel	812	Lodging
Marriott Corp.	800	Hotel/resort
Winn-Dixie	700	Grocery
BancFlorida Financial Corp.	613	Banking
Registry Resort	470	Hotel/resort

COMPANIES PROVIDING LOCAL UTILITIES:
Telephone: United Telephone Co. of Florida
Electricity: Florida Power & Light and the Lee County Cooperative
Natural Gas: None
Water: Collier County and areas of Naples, Marco Island, Everglades and Immokalee
Major Water Source: Wells
Sanitary Landfill? Yes

POINTS OF INTEREST:
Jungle Larry's Zoological Park at Caribbean Gardens, Naples, 52 acres of tropical gardens, jungle animals (such as lions, leopards and alligators), petting zoo, tropical birds, animal training center; **Collier-Seminole State Park,** 17 miles southeast of Naples, has camping, picnicking, saltwater fishing, hiking trails, canoe rentals, tropical hardwood forest hammock, mangrove swamp; **Collier Automotive Museum,** Naples, displays 75 racing cars; **Collier County Museum,** Naples, has local artifacts; **Naples Nature Center,** 13-acre facility housing the Conservancy, the **Natural Science Museum** with serpentarium, **Wildlife Rehabilitation Center** with garden riverboat tours and nature store, and self-guided nature trails; **Corkscrew Swamp Sanctuary,** located off Route 846 and 21 miles east of U.S. 41, has one of the largest strands of mature bald cypress trees in the nation (many are nearly 500 years old), a boardwalk trail, visitor's center, picnicking; **Fakahatchee Strand State Preserve,** near Copeland, is major drainage slough of southwestern **Big Cypress Swamp** and contains the largest stand of native royal palms and the largest concentration and variety of orchids in North America; **Delnor-Wiggins Pass State Recreation Area,** six miles south of Bonita Springs, has picnicking, swimming, surf fishing, boating, shell collecting; **Lovers Key State Recreation Area,** comprises part of Black Island, Lovers Key and all of Inner Key, has fishing, swimming, picnicking; **Naples Depot,** an historic civic cultural center that hosts civic functions, some in a restored club car; **Naples Trolley Tours,** tours of Naples on trolleys that stop at shopping areas, attractions, hotels; **Palm Cottage,** tours of a 19th-century house that is home of the Collier County Historical Society; **Thalheimer's Auction Gallery,** Naples, auctions of goods from Africa, Europe, China, Asia; **Rosie Paddleboat,** Mississippi River paddlewheeler that offers sightseeing and dinner cruises; In Everglades City, narrated boat tours of **Everglades National Park** — mangroves, wilderness and Florida's Ten Thousand Islands; **Greyhound racing** at Naples-Fort Myers Greyhound Track; **Teddy Bear Museum** of Naples.

THE ARTS:
Philharmonic Center for the Arts, Naples, home of the **Naples/Marco Philharmonic** (which has a four-month season that starts in December). It is also a center for opera, ballet, jazz, big-band performances and musicals; **Pelican Players Community Theatre; Naples Players** (drama and comedy performances, musicals); **Naples Dinner Theatre; Fine Arts Society of Collier County;** and **Naples Concert Band** (free outdoor concerts, Sundays, October through March, Cambier Park).

ANNUAL EVENTS:
January: Collier County Fair in Naples; **February:** Naples Spring Arts Festival, Cambier Park; Marco Island Fine Arts Show; **First weekend in February:** Seafood Festival, Everglades City, seafood and country and western entertainment; **March:** Swamp Buggy races in mud pits, Florida Sports Park; Juried Crafts Fair, Marco Island; Naples Antiques Show and Sale; Naples Fifth Avenue Festival of the Arts; March or **April:** Harvest Festival, Immokalee, has parade, barbecue and dance; Naples Kiwanis Seafood Festival, Naples Airport; **May:** Naples Tropicool Fest has concerts, art exhibits, a Taste of Collier food sampling, canoe race, Tarzan yell contest, dancing; **October:** October Fest, Fifth Avenue in Naples; Swamp Buggy races with crowning of queen and parade; **November:** Creative Arts Festival at Pelican Bay; **November/December:** Christmas Walk with carolers, Santa visit, Fifth Avenue (one week) and Third Street South (another week), Naples; **December:** Festival of Trees at Philharmonic Center.

SPORTS AND LEISURE ACTIVITIES:
Most popular local fishing areas: There are about 30 marinas in the Naples area, and some charter companies. The Naples Pier also is popular, as is surf-casting; bays around Marco Island and the Isle of Capri; near Everglades City are the Ten Thousand Islands, several rivers, bays and passes; Lake Trafford in Immokalee is also good for large-mouth Florida black bass, crappie, bluegill and shellcracker.
Number of local golf courses: 7 public, 23 private, 5 semi-private
Public beaches: At least seven miles of public beaches
Tennis courts available to the public? Yes
Boating? Yes
Number of pleasure boats registered in the county (1991-92): 13,788

SERVICES FOR RETIREES: Meals on Wheels, transportation services.

FINANCIAL SERVICES:
Number of local banks: 57
Number of local savings and loan associations: 25

THE MEDIA:
Largest local newspaper: *Naples Daily News*
Cable television? Yes

MAJOR LOCAL RETAILERS:
Bealls, Byrons, JCPenney, K mart, Burdines, Dillard's, Jacobson Stores, Saks Fifth Avenue, Sears and Wal-Mart. Among the major shopping areas are **Third Street South** shopping area in Olde Naples (several shops — antiques, art galleries, boutiques — in buildings that were among the first structures in Naples); **Fifth Avenue South** (financial and shopping center) also within walking distance of the Gulf; **Old Marine Market Place at Tin City** (40 stores, set in nautical theme on the Gordon River) and the nearby **Dockside Boardwalk** (specialty shops); **The Village on Venetian Bay** (waterfront complex of small shops); **Coastland Mall; Coral Isle Factory Outlet,** and **Coconut Grove.**

FOOD ESTABLISHMENTS: 757

OTHER SERVICES:
Number of local libraries: 6
Number of local hotels/motels: 70
Number of churches: Protestant: 78; Jewish: 2; Catholic: 9

TOURISM INQUIRIES:
Naples Area Chamber of Commerce, 3620 Tamiami Trail North, Naples, 33940-3724. Telephone: 813-262-6141; **Everglades Area** Chamber of Commerce, P.O. Box E, Everglades City, 33929. Telephone: 813-695-3941; **Immokalee** Chamber of Commerce, P.O. Drawer C, Immokalee, 33934. Telephone: 813-657-3237.

DE SOTO County
Southwest
County seat: Arcadia

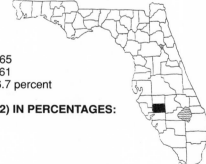

POPULATION: 1990: 23,865
1993: 25,461
Increase: 6.7 percent

AGE DISTRIBUTION (1992) IN PERCENTAGES:
0-14 : 20.0
15-44: 40.6
45-64: 20.1
65+ : 19.3

MUNICIPAL POPULATION:
ARCADIA: 1990: 6,488; 1993: 6,543
UNINCORPORATED: 1990: 17,377; 1993: 18,918

LAND AREA: 637 square miles
POPULATION DENSITY: 40 people per square mile (47th in the state)

Located 50 miles from the Gulf of Mexico and about 49 miles east of Sarasota, the county has one incorporated city, Arcadia, which houses all of the county's government buildings and most of the area's commercial activity. About half the county's residents are native Floridians.

Because of the area's rural atmosphere and natural resources, its lower cost of living and a slower pace, the area attracts some retirees, including a number of Snowbirds. To accommodate them, there are several major recreational vehicle parks or campgrounds that have more than 1,300 spaces.

The Peace River is the county's major tourist attraction, and is especially popular with canoeists who can experience everything from rapids to shallow pools.

While government-related employment is an important contributor to the area's economy, agriculture has been the primary economic base throughout its history. Citrus is the largest agricultural commodity, with around 52,000 acres of groves here, ranking the county sixth in production statewide. During the 1992-93 season, more than 21 million boxes of citrus were produced. Cattle ranching also is big business, with cattle sales amounting to $70 million annually. There are an estimated 50,000-55,000 head of cattle occupying 247,000 acres of pastureland. Other major agriculture pursuits include the production of hay, poultry, show and other horses, swine, sod, timber, nursery and greenhouse products, vegetables and watermelons. Other employers range from grocers and retailers to fast food companies.

Arcadia has a 58-block historic district. More than 370 historic homes and businesses are on the National Register of Historic Places. They include many examples of the early 1900s and "boomtown" architecture.

TOURISM:
There is an increase in population during the winter when some Snowbirds come to the area.

HOUSING PRICES:
A typical 3-bedroom, 2-bath home generally can range from $40,000 to $70,000, but most often goes for $50,000-$60,000. Riverfront homes generally $85,000 and up. Mobile homes are popular with Snowbirds.
Number of vacant residential lots: 4,179; number of single-family residences: 4,656; mobile homes: 2,472; condominiums: 272

EDUCATION:
Number of schools: 13
Number of students enrolled: 4,136
Percentage of students continuing education after high school: 50.27
Teacher-to-pupil ratio: 1:16.4
Average teacher's salary: $29,866

Colleges, universities, and junior or community colleges serving the area:
South Florida Community College branch in Arcadia; University of South Florida branches in Fort Myers and Sarasota; Manatee Community College in Bradenton and its branch in Venice; and Edison Community College in Fort Myers.

Trade and technical schools serving the area:
Charlotte Vo-Tech; Manatee Vo-Tech; and Sarasota Vo-Tech

HEALTH CARE:
Number of general hospitals: 2
Number of hospital beds: 82
Number of physicians: 38

TAXES: Total county ad-valorem millage rate (1993): 17.4550

STANDARD CRIME RATE: 4,516.7 offenses per 100,000 population (39th out of 67 counties)

LARGEST PRIVATE-SECTOR EMPLOYERS:

Name	Employees	Product/Service
Winn-Dixie	160	Grocery
Orange-Co. of Fla.	128	Citrus
Wal-Mart	125	Retail sales
Sorrels Brothers Packing Co.	80	Citrus

Food Lion	65	Grocery
George's Enterprises Inc.	50	Irrigation
McDonalds	39	Fast food
Hardees	34	Fast food
Burger King	30	Fast food

COMPANIES PROVIDING LOCAL UTILITIES:
Telephone: United Telephone Co. of Florida
Electricity: Florida Power & Light and the Peace River Electric Cooperative
Natural Gas: None
Water: City of Arcadia, Lake Suzy Utilities; Peace River; Manasota Water Authority
Major Water Source: Rivers and Wells
Sanitary Landfill? Yes

POINTS OF INTEREST:
The Peace River, a wilderness river, flows about 47 miles in a north-south pattern through the county. Activities include fishing, camping, sightseeing and canoeing; **Arcadia Livestock Market** holds weekly sales. In 1988, 47,333 cattle were sold here; **The Depot** in downtown Arcadia, a restoration of a railroad depot that has a mini-museum and professional offices; **Main Street Historical Walking Tour** in Arcadia gives visitors sampling of area's historic homes, businesses, public buildings and churches.

ANNUAL EVENTS:
March: De Soto County Fair with livestock and swine shows and sales in Arcadia; Arcadia All-Florida Championship Rodeo at the Fenton Arena; **May:** De Soto County Watermelon Festival at De Soto Park, with a horse show, beauty pageants, arts and crafts, antique auto display and games, including a "Wiver Waft Wace" and a watermelon golf scramble, and food, including, of course, watermelon slices; **July** (around the 4th of July) Arcadia All-Florida Championship Rodeo; **December:** Christmas Card Lane, De Soto Park, a display of more than 70 oversized cards with holiday messages in a lighted drive-through setting; Community Christmas Parade and Historic Home Tours; Community Christmas Tree Lighting and Historic Home Tours.

SPORTS AND LEISURE ACTIVITIES:
Most popular local fishing area: Peace River
Number of local golf courses: 2 public
Public beaches? No
Tennis courts available to the public? Yes
Boating? Yes
Number of pleasure boats registered in the county (1991-92): 1,620

SERVICES FOR RETIREES:
The Margaret Way Senior Citizen Center in Arcadia and the Arcadia Tourist Club offer a large number of activities for senior citizens.

FINANCIAL SERVICES:
Number of local banks: 4
Number of local savings and loan associations: 2

THE MEDIA:
Largest local newspaper: *The De Soto Sun Herald*
Cable television? Yes

MAJOR LOCAL RETAILERS: Wal-Mart, Sears Catalog Sales

FOOD ESTABLISHMENTS: 59

OTHER SERVICES:
Number of local libraries: 1
Number of local motels: 6
Number of churches: Protestant: 62; Jewish: 0; Catholic: 1; Other: 5

TOURISM INQUIRIES:
De Soto County Chamber of Commerce, P.O. Box 149, Arcadia, 33821. Telephone: 813-494-4033.

HARDEE County
Southwest
County seat: Wauchula

POPULATION: 1990: 19,499
1993: 22,035
Increase: 13 percent

AGE DISTRIBUTION (1992) IN PERCENTAGES:
0-14 : 24.3
15-44: 42.0
45-64: 18.5
65+ : 15.2

MUNICIPAL POPULATION:
BOWLING GREEN: 1990: 1,836; 1993: 1,861
WAUCHULA: 1990: 3,243; 1993: 3,496
ZOLFO SPRINGS: 1990: 1,219; 1993: 1,249
UNINCORPORATED: 1990: 13,201; 1993: 15,429

LAND AREA: 637 square miles
POPULATION DENSITY: 35 people per square mile (48th in the state)

Hardee joined Gadsden County in having the dubious distinction of being the only Florida counties to lose population between 1980 and 1990. Hardee's population dropped by 4.2 percent.

Hardee is primarily agricultural and citrus is the top crop, with more than 51,000 acres of orange groves. State figures show that the total net farm income dropped from $54 million in 1988 to $46 million in 1989 and $36.6 million in 1990; likewise, the average monthly agricultural employment dropped from 926 to 790 to 732. The county also had one of the highest unemployment rates in Florida in the early 1990s.

Yet by 1993, the county was on the rebound. The population rose by 13 percent between 1990 and 1993 — the sixth highest rate in the state.

Farming is still big business. Other crops are cucumbers, tomatoes, peppers, squash, and watermelon. In addition, the cattle industry consists of about 65,000 head and milk production more than doubled between 1989 and 1991, to 150 million pounds.

Wauchula, the county seat, has three shopping centers, a civic center complex, and medical facilities. Bowling Green, where the national Paso Fino Horse Owners and Breeders Association is headquartered, also has a state historical site. Zolfo Springs, a small rural city, is a magnet for recreational vehicles.

The county is known for Pioneer Park Days, a major festival in Zolfo Springs that attracts about 250,000 people in late February and early March.

TOURISM:
Pioneer Park Days attracts hundreds of thousands. In addition, there are about 3,000 spaces for recreational vehicles in the county.

HOUSING PRICES:
Sales prices range from about $20,000, including mobile homes, to about $150,000. Local Realtors estimate typical prices at about $45,000.
Number of vacant residential lots: 1,267; number of single-family residences: 3,836; mobile homes: 1,482; condominiums: 258

EDUCATION:
Number of schools: 9
Number of students enrolled: 4,978
Percentage of students continuing education after high school: 68.40
Teacher-to-pupil ratio: 1:16.8
Average teacher's salary: $28,597

Colleges, universities, and junior or community colleges serving the area:
University of South Florida campuses in Tampa and Sarasota; Florida Southern College in Lake-

land; Warner Southern College in Lake Wales; South Florida Community College in Avon Park; Polk Community College in Winter Haven

Trade and technical schools serving the area:
Hardee County High School and South Florida Community College in Avon Park

HEALTH CARE:
Number of general hospitals: 1
Number of hospital beds: 50
Number of physicians: 13

TAXES: Total county ad-valorem millage rate (1993): 19.7190

STANDARD CRIME RATE: 5,382.2 offenses per 100,000 population (30th out of 67 counties)

MAJOR PRIVATE EMPLOYERS:

Name	Employees	Product/Service
Florida Inst. for Neurologic Rehab	200	Medical Rehabilitation
Wauchula State Bank	115	Banking
Mancini Packing	115	Packing
Winn-Dixie	100	Grocery
Wal-Mart	95	Retail sales
Peace River Electric Coop.	76	Electricity
C.F. Mining	68	Phosphate
Hardee County Manor	66	Nursing home
Kash-N-Karry	65	Grocery
First National Bank	32	Banking

COMPANIES PROVIDING LOCAL UTILITIES:
Telephone: United Telephone Co. of Florida
Electricity: Peace River Electric Cooperative; Florida Power Corp. and Wauchula City Electric
Natural Gas: None
Water: Cities of Wauchula, Zolfo Springs, and Bowling Green
Major Water Source: Wells
Sanitary Landfill? Yes

POINTS OF INTEREST:
Paynes Creek State Historic Site, one-half mile east of Bowling Green, has interpretive center, picnicking, freshwater fishing, nature study. Site of former trading post, frontier fort, and block-house that guarded a bridge over the Peace River in the mid 1800s; **Peace River,** popular with canoeists who can experience everything from rapids to shallow pools; **Solomon's Castle,** southwest of Zolfo Springs, was designed by a metal sculptor, contains more than 60 stained glass windows, and is popular with artists and nature lovers; **Agri-Civic Center** complex in Wauchula has auditorium, fairgrounds, rodeo arena and athletic facilities; **Hart Cabin,** a restored log cabin of the late 1800s, located in Pioneer Park in Zolfo Springs; **Call of the Wild Wildlife Museum** near Ona (northwest of Solomon's Castle) has mounted animals, birds and fish; **Cracker Trail Museum,** Pioneer Park.

ANNUAL EVENTS:
Late February and Early March: Pioneer Park Days at Pioneer Park, Zolfo Springs, an "old-time country fair" that includes a parade, food, entertainment, flea market, re-enactment of a Civil War skirmish, the Southeast's largest display of antique steam engines, gas engines and cars, auction of antique tractors and stationary engines; **February:** Winter Resident Fun Day, Agri-Civic Center, Wauchula; **March:** Hardee County Fair, Agri-Civic Center. In addition, on the first Saturday of each month from September through May are the Hardee County Jamborees at Pioneer Park from 5:30 to 8:30 p.m.

SPORTS AND LEISURE ACTIVITIES:
Most popular local fishing area: Peace River
Number of local golf courses: 2
Public beaches? No
Tennis courts available to the public? Yes
Boating? Yes
Number of pleasure boats registered in the county (1991-92): 1,302

SERVICES FOR RETIREES:
Through the Department of Health and Rehabilitative Services.

FINANCIAL SERVICES:
Number of local banks: 4
Number of local savings and loan associations: 1

THE MEDIA:
Largest local newspaper: *The Herald-Advocate*
Cable television? Yes

MAJOR LOCAL RETAILERS: Bealls, Wal-Mart

FOOD ESTABLISHMENTS: 56

OTHER SERVICES:
Number of local libraries: 1
Number of local hotels/motels: 3
Number of churches: Protestant: 80; Jewish: 0; Catholic: 1; Other: 4

TOURISM INQUIRIES:
Hardee County Chamber of Commerce, P.O. Box 683, Wauchula, 33873. Telephone: 813-773-6967.

HENDRY County
Southwest
County seat: LaBelle

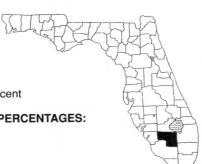

POPULATION: 1990: 25,773
1993: 28,061
Increase: 8.9 percent

AGE DISTRIBUTION (1992) IN PERCENTAGES:
0-14 : 26.9
15-44: 43.8
45-64: 18.4
65+: 10.9

MUNICIPAL POPULATION:
CLEWISTON: 1990: 6,085; 1993: 6,144
LaBELLE: 1990: 2,703; 1993: 2,897
UNINCORPORATED: 1990: 16,985; 1993: 19,020

LAND AREA: 1,153 square miles
POPULATION DENSITY: 24 people per square mile (57th in the state)

The geographical designation for this county is something of a misnomer — it actually is more in the middle of South Florida, between Palm Beach to the east and Fort Myers to the west. **La-Belle,** the county seat, is in the western part of the county, about 30 miles from Fort Myers and 92 miles from Palm Beach. **Clewiston,** the largest city in Hendry, is in the eastern part of the county, and has frontage along a small part of southwest Lake Okeechobee. It is a freshwater sport-fishing center.

LaBelle is largely an oak hammock on the Caloosahatchee River, which is part of the Intracoastal Waterway that crosses the state through Lake Okeechobee to Fort Myers. The local economy is primarily agricultural — citrus (about 100,000 acres in the LaBelle area for oranges and grapefruit, most of which is grown for juice concentrate. During the 1992-93 season, the county produced 28.5 million boxes of citrus, making it the third largest county producer of citrus, according to Florida Agricultural Statistics Service figures), cattle (this is one of Florida's top five counties for cattle production) and sugar cane (U.S. Sugar Corp., in the Clewiston area, is the county's largest private employer, with 2,000 employees, and operates the largest raw sugar cane factory in the United States. Hendry County produces about 20 percent of the sugar consumed in the United States).

Winter vegetable sales (tomatoes, peppers, cucumbers, squash, celery and watermelons) are also substantial, amounting to $55 million a year, according to recent figures. Other industries include honey processing, vegetable packing, oil production, timber production, seasoning manufacturing, cement and bait farms and truss manufacturing.

TOURISM:
The county's population increases by a couple of thousand from November to March. Some Snowbirds stay in RV parks, others in mobile home parks and some in site-built homes.

HOUSING PRICES:
Average prices around $65,000. Recent listings show many homes in the $42,000 to $60,000 range. Prices are much higher for homes on the Caloosahatchee River, which is part of the Intracoastal Waterway ($140,000 and up).
Number of vacant residential lots: 20,728; number of single-family residences: 4,382; mobile homes: 3,162; condominiums: 138

EDUCATION:
Number of schools: 13
Number of students enrolled: 6,498
Percentage of students continuing education after high school: 63.24
Teacher-to-pupil ratio: 1:19.7
Average teacher's salary: $28,795

Colleges, universities, and junior or community colleges serving the area:
Nova-Southeastern University of Fort Lauderdale regularly conducts classes in LaBelle; University of South Florida at Fort Myers; Edison Community College at Fort Myers; Florida Atlantic University in Boca Raton; and Palm Beach Community College at Lake Worth.

Trade and technical schools serving the area:
Lee County Vo-Tech and Palm Beach Vo-Tech

HEALTH CARE:
Number of general hospitals: 1
Number of hospital beds: 66
Number of physicians: 20

TAXES: Total county ad-valorem millage rate (1993): 20.3040

STANDARD CRIME RATE: 4,108.9 offenses per 100,000 population (43rd out of 67 counties)

LARGEST PRIVATE EMPLOYERS:
Name	Employees	Product/Service
U.S. Sugar Corp	2,000	Sugar processing
Berry's Citrus Products	350	Citrus processing
A. Duda & Sons	180	Citrus processing
Winn-Dixie	136	Grocery
U-Save Markets	125	Grocery
A&B Harvesting	75	Citrus processing
Alico Inc.	55	Citrus/Cattle
Bob Paul Groves	55	Citrus products
LaBelle Plant World	54	Plant starts
Hancock Fidelity	30	Citrus products

COMPANIES PROVIDING LOCAL UTILITIES:
Telephone: United Telephone of Florida
Electricity: Florida Power & Light Co.; Glades Electric Cooperative, Lee Electric Cooperative, City of Clewiston Utilities
Natural Gas: None
Water: City of LaBelle; City of Clewiston
Major Water Source: Wells, lakes
Sanitary Landfill? Yes

POINTS OF INTEREST:
Lake Okeechobee; Bird-watching is popular in the county. About 115 species can be found here, including two species that have been considered endangered — the bald eagle and the wood stork; **Clewiston Museum; John B. Boy Auditorium** in Clewiston seats 750 people.

THE ARTS:
Actors Community Theater; Tri-County Community Theater.

ANNUAL EVENTS:
February: (held last full weekend), Swamp Cabbage Festival in LaBelle, includes parade, country music, dancing, rodeos, armadillo races, quilt shows, art and craft displays, food; **March:** Hendry County Fair and Livestock Show; **Early April:** Clewiston Sugar Festival, which includes an arts and crafts show; **April/May:** Harlem-Clewiston's Brown Sugar Festival; **December:** Christmas Parade in LaBelle (first weekend of the month), includes community oak tree along the river, decoration contest, lighted boat flotilla on the river, concerts and pageants; Christmas bazaar in Clewiston. For other events, please see listings for nearby Glades County.

SPORTS AND LEISURE ACTIVITIES:
Water sports popular on the Caloosahatchee River. Popular fishing spots include Lake Okeechobee and Fisheating Creek. Popular freshwater fish catches include bass, crappie, bream, speckled perch, catfish.
Hunting game in the county includes deer, turkey, wild hog, quail and dove.
Number of local golf courses: 2 public
Public beaches? No
Tennis courts available to the public? Yes
Boating? Yes
Number of pleasure boats registered in the county (1991-92): 2,491

SERVICES FOR RETIREES:
State health department services, plus Meals on Wheels and a program in which residents drive elderly people on shopping and other errands; Tri-County Senior Citizen.

FINANCIAL SERVICES:
Number of local banks: 7
Number of local savings and loan associations: 2

THE MEDIA:
Largest local newspapers: *Clewiston News*
Cable television? Yes

MAJOR LOCAL RETAILERS: K mart, Sears catalog store.

FOOD ESTABLISHMENTS: 76

OTHER SERVICES:
Number of local libraries: 2
Number of local hotels/motels: 14
Number of churches: Protestant: 53; Jewish: 0; Catholic: 2; Other: 2

TOURISM INQUIRIES:
Greater **LaBelle** Chamber of Commerce, P.O. Box 456, LaBelle, 33935. Telephone: 813-675-0125; **Clewiston** Chamber of Commerce, P.O. Box 275, 544 West Sugarland Highway, Clewiston, 33440. Telephone: 813-983-7979.

LEE County
Southwest
County seat: Fort Myers

POPULATION: 1990: 335,113
1993: 357,550
Increase: 6.7 percent

AGE DISTRIBUTION (1992) IN PERCENTAGES:
0-14 : 17.1
15-44: 36.2
45-64: 21.8
65+ : 24.9

MUNICIPAL POPULATION:
CAPE CORAL: 1990: 74,991; 1993: 81,339
FORT MYERS: 1990: 45,206; 1993: 45,069
SANIBEL: 1990: 5,468; 1993: 5,616
UNINCORPORATED: 1990: 209,448; 1993: 225,526

LAND AREA: 804 square miles
POPULATION DENSITY: 445 people per square mile (10th in the state)

Agriculture and tourism are the two staples of this county, and the population has grown proportionately — by 68 percent from 1980 to 1991. Agriculture has about a $159 million impact on the local economy. The major crops include cucumbers, green peppers, squash, tomatoes, watermelons, citrus and ornamental plants. Seafood harvesting also is a major component.

The county's two major cities are **Fort Myers,** also known as the "City of Palms," and **Cape Coral.** Both are separated by the Caloosahatchee River, which is part of the cross-Florida waterway and which flows into the Gulf of Mexico. Fort Myers, 15 miles inland from the Gulf, is the center of activity in the county and is the primary destination for shopping and higher education. The city, which celebrated its centennial in 1986, has been revitalizing its downtown area and restoring its historic district. Fort Myers was once the winter home of Thomas Edison and today contains large malls, several specialized retail centers, two colleges, a soon-to-be open state university, a performing arts center and several medical facilities. Cape Coral, although Lee County's largest city, is primarily a residential community of single-family homes and apartments. It has 11 miles of river frontage, a number of city parks, an historical museum, country clubs, recreation fields and more than 125 clubs and organizations. Among the county's other major towns are **North Fort Myers,** a residential community; **Lehigh Acres,** an area of new families, retirees and young first-home buyers; and **Fort Myers Beach,** a city catering to tourists and containing seven miles of beaches, including two public beaches — one with a free public fishing pier and the other with a tram ride.

The state's 10th university is being located in the Fort Myers area. Named Florida Gulf Coast University, the opening is planned for the fall of 1997.

TOURISM:
As with many Florida counties, there are two types of winter visitors: Snowbirds from the north (here November until April) and tourists who spend just a few days or weeks here (mainly from January through March). At the height of the season, January through March, with both tourists and Snowbirds, the population about doubles. On Sanibel and Captiva, the population increases by 200 percent from Christmas to Easter. Lee County Economic Development Office figures show that more than 1.5 million visitors came to the area in 1992.

HOUSING PRICES:
Median sales price of a single-family existing home in the Fort Myers-Cape Coral metropolitan area was $88,600 in June 1994.
Number of vacant residential lots: 237,119; number of single-family residences: 92,617; mobile homes: 11,635; condominiums: 45,908

EDUCATION:
Number of schools: 63
Number of students enrolled: 47,390
Percentage of students continuing education after high school: 58.25
Teacher-to-pupil ratio: 1:19.6
Average teacher's salary: $32,124

Colleges, universities, and junior or community colleges serving the area:
Fort Myers: Edison Community College and a University of South Florida branch; International College's Fort Myers branch

Trade and technical schools serving the area:
Lee County Area Vocational-Technical School, Fort Myers

HEALTH CARE:
Number of hospitals: 6
Number of general hospital beds: 1,544
Number of physicians: 617

TAXES: Total county ad-valorem millage rate (1993): 15.0590

STANDARD CRIME RATE: 6,084.7 offenses per 100,000 population (23rd out of 67 counties)

LARGEST PRIVATE EMPLOYERS:

Name	Employees	Product/Service
Publix	2,493	Grocery
The Mariner Group	2,000	Real estate/resorts
Southwest Fla. Regional Medical Center	1,600	Health care
Cape Coral Hospital	1,439	Health care
Winn-Dixie	1,250	Grocery
Nations Bank	1,100	Banking
United Telephone Co. of Florida	945	Telecommunications
Yoder Brothers	698	Florist/wholesale
News-Press	626	Publishing
Nations Bank	600	Banking

COMPANIES PROVIDING LOCAL UTILITIES:
Telephone: United Telephone Co. of Florida
Electricity: Florida Power & Light Co.; Lee County Electric Cooperative
Natural Gas: Balgas; Petrolane Gas Service
Water: City of Fort Myers Utilities Department, Florida Cities Water Co., City of Cape Coral, Lee County Utilities and Island Water Association (for Sanibel and Captiva)
Major Water Source: Wells
Sanitary Landfill? Yes

POINTS OF INTEREST:
Fort Myers: Edison Winter Home and Laboratory; Henry Ford Winter Home; Boston Red Sox spring training site at The City of Palms Park; **Minnesota Twins** spring training site at the Lee County Sports Complex; **Fort Myers Historical Museum; Nature Center and Planetarium; Lee Civic Center** in North Fort Myers hosts entertainment and sporting events; **Eden Vineyards Winery and Park** with winery tours, wine tasting and tram rides; the **Shell Factory** has shell and coral collection, jewelry, leather goods, shell novelties; **Estero: Koreshan State Historic Site** has camping, picnicking, saltwater fishing, hiking, guided tours through historical area (that was settled in the late 1800s and was planned to be a utopian community); **Bonita Springs: Greyhound racing** at Naples-Fort Myers Greyhound Track; **Centennial Park and Riverwalk** along downtown riverfront in Fort Myers; **Everglades Wonder Gardens,** a showcase of mammals, reptiles and birds of the Everglades; **Cayo Costa State Park,** south of Placida, accessible by boat, primitive cabins, picnicking, saltwater fishing, swimming and hiking and is site of one of the largest undeveloped barrier islands with numerous Indian mounds; **Sanibel and Captiva: Sanibel Lighthouse,** built in 1884; **J.N. "Ding" Darling National Wildlife Refuge; Island historical museum;** beach and shelling activities (Sanibel is rated as one of the best shelling beaches in the world); sailing, powerboating, fishing for both salt and freshwater species, biking (there are more than 22 miles of bike paths on Sanibel and Captiva), birding, nature tours.

THE ARTS:
Barbara B. Mann Performing Arts Hall at Edison Community College is site of Broadway musicals, dance performances and popular and classical music concerts; **Arcade Theater** in Fort Myers; **Lee County Alliance of the Arts** has public art gallery; **Sanibel and Captiva:** located here are two theaters including the **Pirate Playhouse** and the **Olde Schoolhouse Theater,** art galleries, a local artists colony and the **Barrier Island Group (BIG) for the Arts,** which offers a season of art shows and performances.

ANNUAL EVENTS:
January: Lee Sidewalk Arts and Crafts Show in Fort Myers; Riverview Art Festival in Cape Coral; Seniors Festival in Fort Myers; Mid-Florida Golf Festival, Lehigh Acres; **February:** Edison Festival of Lights, Fort Myers; Southwest Florida Fair in Fort Myers; Sanibel-Captiva Rotary Club Arts and Crafts Fair, Sanibel; Antique Collectibles Show and Sale, Estero; **March:** Cape Coral Winter Festival; Fort Myers Beach Shrimp Festival, Fort Myers Beach; Festival of India, Fort Myers; Sanibel Shell Fair on Sanibel Island; the Tomato Snook Festival in Bonita Springs; Lehigh Acres Spring Festival; Cracker Festival, re-enactment of the Battle of Fort Myers, North Fort Myers; Caloosahatchee River Basin Festival, Fort Myers; **April:** Best of Southwest Florida Festival,

Cape Coral; Koreshan Unity Lunar Festival, Estero; **May:** Sounds of Jazz, Cape Coral; **July:** Riverfest, Fort Myers; Cape Coral Red, White and Boom, Cape Coral; Boca Grande Club's Tarpon Tournament; Pine Island Parade and Fireworks, Matlacha; **August:** New Arts Festival at various locations in Lee County; **September:** Annual Taste of the Cape, Cape Coral; **October:** Koreshan Unity Solar Festival, Estero; Jazz on the Green in Sanibel; Hispanic Heritage Festival in Fort Myers; **November:** Tween Waters Inn Oktoberfest in Captiva; Cape Coral Hospital Turkey Trot, Cape Coral; **December:** Edison/Ford Homes Holiday House, Fort Myers; Sea Kayak Classic Race in Captiva; and Kris Kringles' Kloset Arts and Crafts Show, Fort Myers.

SPORTS AND LEISURE ACTIVITIES:
Most popular local fishing areas: Boca Grande and Pine Island Sound area for tarpon.
Number of local golf courses: Around 40
Public beaches: At Fort Myers Beach and Sanibel and Captiva islands
Tennis courts available to the public? Yes
Boating? Yes
Number of pleasure boats registered in the county (1991-92): 29,623

SERVICES FOR RETIREES:
Meals on Wheels and senior citizen centers; Social Security Administration in Fort Myers.

FINANCIAL SERVICES:
Number of local banks: 112
Number of local savings and loan associations: 45

THE MEDIA:
Largest local newspaper: *Fort Myers News-Press*
Cable television? Yes

MAJOR LOCAL RETAILERS:
Burdines, Byrons, K mart, Dillard's, JCPenney, Sears, Wal-Mart. Among the major shopping areas are: around Fort Myers: Centennial Park area shops; Edison Mall, with more than 100 stores; Metro Mall; Royal Palm Square and the Bell Tower Mall. Also, island shops on Fort Myers Beach; department stores, shopping centers and specialty stores in Cape Coral; and shopping centers at Bonita Beach Road and Route 41 in Bonita Springs. On Sanibel: Shopping centers are scattered throughout the islands, as well as small shops and boutiques. There are no anchor stores on the islands.

FOOD ESTABLISHMENTS: 1,244

OTHER SERVICES:
Number of local libraries: 12
Number of local hotels/motels: 164
Number of churches: Protestant: 212; Jewish: 5; Catholic: 17; Other: 111

TOURISM INQUIRIES:
The Chamber of Southwest Florida, 1520 Royal Palm Square Blvd., Suite 210, Fort Myers, 33919. Telephone: 813-278-1231.

Sanibel and Captiva
Sanibel and Captiva are resort-oriented islands with the basic support services. They are a mecca for shell collectors; a haven for conservationists (the sanctuary encompasses some 5,000 acres of wetlands given over to a wildlife refuge); and a fisherman's dream with both bay and Gulf fishing. The arts are also popular here, as the islands have two theaters, year-round performances, art galleries and gallery shows. Single-family residences and condominiums are home to around 6,600 year-round residents. The islands are 15 miles southwest of Fort Myers and are connected to the mainland by a three-mile causeway.

OTHER FACTS:
HOUSING PRICES:
Gulf-front homes have been priced at nearly $1 million in recent years; Bayfront, around $700,000; canal-front, $400,000-plus; inland, $200,000-plus; condominiums, $250,000-plus.

EDUCATION:
Number of public schools: 1 — Sanibel Elementary, Grades K-5. High school students are bused to Cypress Lake High School in Fort Myers. Number of students enrolled: Around 225.

HEALTH CARE:
Nearest hospitals are in Fort Myers and Cape Coral. There are physicians and dentists on the islands, and technical and medical personnel are on call 24 hours a day. A helicopter is available to transport patients from the islands to Fort Myers. The emergency number for paramedics is 911.

LARGEST PRIVATE SECTOR EMPLOYER:
South Seas Plantation, a Captiva resort, which has 700-800 employees.

SPORTS AND LEISURE ACTIVITIES:
Most popular local fishing areas: Gulf of Mexico; San Carlos Bay, including a fishing pier at the Sanibel Lighthouse; Pine Island Sound.
Number of local golf courses: Public: 2 Private: 1
Public beaches: The entire 20 miles of Gulf beach is open to the public with five public access points.

SERVICES FOR RETIREES:
FISH (Friends in Service Here) has 150 volunteers who provide special services, such as Meals on Wheels, companionship, shopping assistance and transportation to needy island residents.

OTHER SERVICES:
Number of local libraries: 2
Number of local hotels/motels: 45
Number of churches: Protestant: 3; Catholic: 1; Other: Christian Science

TOURISM INQUIRIES:
Sanibel/Captiva Islands Chamber of Commerce, P.O. Box 166, Sanibel Island, 33957. Telephone: (813)-472-1080

SARASOTA County
Southwest
County seat: Sarasota

POPULATION: 1990: 277,776
1993: 290,612
Increase: 4.6 percent

AGE DISTRIBUTION (1992) IN PERCENTAGES:
0-14 : 13.5
15-44: 32.1
45-64: 22.4
65+ : 32.0

LONGBOAT KEY (part): 1990: 3,393; 1993: 3,716
NORTH PORT: 1990: 11,973; 1993: 13,591
SARASOTA: 1990: 50,897; 1993: 50,820
VENICE: 1990: 17,052; 1993: 17,768
UNINCORPORATED: 1990: 194,461; 1993: 204,717

LAND AREA: 572 square miles
POPULATION DENSITY: 508 people per square mile (8th in the state)

Mention the word "arts" to a Floridian who's been around, and he or she is likely to tell you about Sarasota. The county, on the Gulf of Mexico about 65 miles south of Tampa, is home to the state's oldest symphony orchestra, the Ringling Museum of Art, drama, dance and opera companies, and art galleries. The arts are so popular that there is even a 24-hour hotline (359-ARTS) for events in the county.

Sarasota is a haven for artists and writers as well as retirees.

High-rise condominiums ring Sarasota Bay, a popular sailing spot, and Siesta Key. Mammoth waterfront estates also dot parts of the city of **Sarasota,** as do Mediterranean-style homes and Old-Florida cottages. East of the city some subdivisions have private airstrips and small ranches with horses. Across Sarasota Bay is **Longboat Key**, a resort and retirement community. The southern part of it, in Sarasota County, consists largely of condominiums (and a few private residences) for wealthy retirees. The northern part of the key, in Manatee County, is mainly a resort.

Not everyone will have to mortgage everything, including his soul, for a piece of the Sarosata County real-estate market. The median price is around $97,100.

About 18 miles south of the city of Sarasota is **Venice,** which has miles of public beaches that contain shells and fossilized sharks' teeth, and is the home, between Thanksgiving and early January, of the Ringling Brothers and Barnum & Bailey Circus. Venice, known as the sharks' tooth capital of the world, also is home to the Clown College, which trains professional clowns.

Between Sarasota and Venice are the unincorporated communities of **Osprey** (which is made up largely of waterfront condominiums), **Laurel** (named for the laurel trees that once abundantly grew here) and **Nokomis** (a beach community that includes Casey Key and its impressive homes). At the far southern end of the county is the large unincorporated community of **Englewood,** which is surrounded by Charlotte Harbor, Lemon Bay and the Gulf, and which is near three islands — Palm, Don Pedro and Little Gasparilla — where beaches abound and access is by ferry or private boat. Other beach areas are Lido and Manasota keys. As in most of the waterfront communities in the county, there is a mix of single-family residences, condominiums and mobile homes.

Tourism is a major trade, as are services; retail trade; construction; finance, insurance and real estate; wholesale trade; and manufacturing (printing and publishing, machinery, electronic and electrical equipment, rubber and plastics, stone, clay and glass products and fabricated metal products).

The largest employer in the county is the county school system. Others include hospitals, groceries and county government.

TOURISM:
The number of people living in the area decreases by about 35 percent during the summer, according to a recent study by tourism officials. The winter Snowbird season begins Oct. 1, peaks in March, and ends around April 1. During fiscal 1990, nearly 880,000 people visited the county.

HOUSING PRICES:
Median sales price of a single-family existing home in the Sarasota-Bradenton metropolitan area was $97,100 in June 1994.
Number of vacant residential lots: 80,529; number of single-family residences: 84,176; mobile homes: 7,442; condominiums: 39,939

EDUCATION:
Number of schools: 39
Number of students enrolled: 30,205
Percentage of students continuing education after high school: 66.22
Teacher-to-pupil ratio: 1:18.1
Average teacher's salary: $34,831

Colleges, universities, and junior or community colleges serving the area:
University of South Florida at Sarasota/New College; University of Sarasota; Manatee Community College campus in Venice; Ringling School of Art and Design.

Trade and technical schools serving the area:
Sarasota County Technical Institute; Manatee Community College (South Campus in Venice).

HEALTH CARE:
Number of general hospitals: 6
Number of hospital beds: 1,294
Number of physicians: 752

TAXES: Total county ad-valorem millage rate (1993): 13.6264

STANDARD CRIME RATE: 6,082.0 offenses per 100,000 population (24th out of 67 counties)

LARGEST EMPLOYERS:

Name	Employees	Product/Service
Sarasota County School Board	3,440	Education
Sarasota Memorial Hospital	2,700	Health care
Publix Supermarkets	2,400	Grocery
Sarasota County Government	1,630	Government

Venice Hospital	1,600	Hospital
City of Sarasota	950	City government
GTE Florida	827	Telephone communications
Winn-Dixie Stores	750	Grocery
Sarasota Herald-Tribune	635	Newspaper
Loral Data Systems Division	600	Aviation recorders, telemetry

COMPANIES PROVIDING LOCAL UTILITIES:
Telephone: GTE Florida
Electricity: Florida Power & Light
Natural Gas: Peoples Gas Systems
Water: Several franchises
Major Water Source: Wells
Sanitary Landfill? Yes

POINTS OF INTEREST:
Myakka River State Park (14 miles east of Sarasota on SR 72, its 28,875 acres make this one of the state's largest parks, offers camping, picknicking, freshwater fishing, hiking, guided tours, boat and canoe rentals, horse trails, vistas of lakes, the river, marshes, hammocks and prairies, flora and fauna); **Oscar Scherer State Park,** two miles south of Osprey on U.S. 41, offers camping, picknicking, swimming, saltwater fishing, hiking, canoe rentals, exotic species of animals and birds; **Sarasota Kennel Club** (pari-mutuel greyhound racing); **Chicago White Sox** spring training at Ed Smith Statium; **Marie Selby Botanical Gardens** (specializes in bromeliads and orchids and offers horticultural courses); **Bellm's Cars & Music of Yesterday** in Sarasota (1,200 music pieces, including a 30-foot Belgian dance organ, and 200 antique and classic cars, including five used by John Ringling); **Sarasota Jungle Gardens** (botanical gardens, tropical jungle, butterfly museum, petting zoo, bird and reptile shows); **Lionel Train & Seashell Museum** in Sarasota (train exhibits, collection of seashells and coral and sea life); **Spanish Point** in Osprey has prehistoric Indian shell mounds, pioneer homes, gardens, archaeological exhibits; **Mote Marine Aquarium** in Sarasota has a 135,000-gallon shark tank and other marine exhibits.

THE ARTS:
Ringling Museum Complex includes the **John and Mable Ringling Museum of Art** (more than 10,000 pieces, including Baroque and Italian works), the **Ca'd'Zan** (Ringling's former winter mansion from the 1920s era) and **Circus Gallery** (which contains memorabilia including parade wagons, photographs, costumes and posters); **Van Wezel Performing Arts Hall** (touring Broadway shows, touring celebrities, dance companies, orchestras); **Asolo Theater Company,** Florida's state theatrical troupe (off-Broadway shows, musicals and dinner theater); **Asolo Performing Arts Center** (houses conservatory of professional actor training and a conservatory of motion picture, television and recording arts); **Florida Studio Theatre; Sarasota Ballet of Florida; Players of Sarasota; Sarasota Opera House; Jazz Club; Sarasota Blues Society; A.B. Edwards Theater** (home of the Sarasota Opera Association); **Florida West Coast Symphony** (the oldest orchestra in the state); **Gloria Musicae, Sarasota/Manatee Community Orchestra; Florida Symphonic Band; Eddy Toussant Ballet USA; Venice Little Theatre** (plays and musicals, a Children's Summer Camp and an Actor's Workshop); **Venice Opera Guild; Venice Symphony** (seasonal concerts); **Venice Art Center** (holds exhibits and gives classes); **Venice Community Center** (site of flower and art shows, exhibits); **Golden Apple Dinner Theatre** in Venice at the Venice Resort Inn; **Englewood Artisans' Guild; Lemon Bay Playhouse** (year-round local productions in Englewood).

ANNUAL EVENTS:
Throughout the winter: Englewood Performing Arts Series (concerts); **January:** Artists of Florida Art Competition, Sarasota Visual Art Center; Venice Area Art Festival; Sarasota Arts Day, downtown; **February:** Sarasota Festival of the Arts; Snow Bird Art Festival; **March:** Medieval Fair with jousting and medieval court parade on grounds surrounding Ringling Museum of Art and Ca'd'Zan, former home of the Ringlings (14th-century European theme); Sarasota Quay Craft Festival; parade in downtown Venice on the Saturday closest to St. Patrick's Day; Sarasota County Fair, fairgrounds; **April:** Sarasota Jazz Festival; **May/June:** Sarasota Music Festival; **June:** Downtown Venice Street Craft Festival; **Fourth of July weekend:** Suncoast Offshore Grand Prix, a national powerboat race (race follows Grand Prix Festival, which benefits handi-

capped children); on the same weekend are the downtown Venice festival and Venice Chamber Business Fair at the Venice Community Center (food booths, sandcastle contests, fireworks display); **August:** Sharks Tooth and Seafood Festival at the Venice Fishing Pier; **Labor Day weekend:** Pioneer Days in Englewood, a celebration of early settlement days that includes parades, pageants, arts and crafts, and street dancing; **October:** Taste of Sarasota at the fairgrounds; St. Armands Art Festival; Venice Sun Fiesta, a week-long festival that features a parade, music, community information exhibits and fair, Miss Venice pageant; Siesta Fiesta Halloween Arts and Crafts Festival in Sarasota; **November:** French Film Festival in Sarasota, with screenings of new films, industry seminars, French film star appearances; Discover the Past Festival, on Spanish Point in Osprey (reenactment of early settlement, music, crafts, canoeing); Downtown Art Fest in Venice; **December:** Venice Christmas Boat Parade; Christmas Parade in Siesta Key and Christmas Boat Parade of Lights in Sarasota Bay; International Circus Parade and Festival, Sarasota Fairgrounds.

SPORTS AND LEISURE ACTIVITIES:
Fishing is popular throughout the county. Saltwater catches include Spanish mackerel, flounder, snook, redfish, shrimp and crabs.

Number of local golf courses: 30+

Public beaches: 35 miles of beaches, including Lido, Casey, Manasota and Siesta Keys, Venice Public Beach

Tennis courts available to the public? Yes

Boating is a big sport here, both in bays and on the Gulf as well as on the Myakka River (for canoeists, and RV enthusiasts camp here); also on canals and lakes in Venice.

Number of pleasure boats registered in the county (1991-92): 16,802

Horseback riding is also a favorite pastime, on bridle trails and ranches. Competitions and shows are held at the Fox Lea Farm in Venice.

SERVICES FOR RETIREES:
Meals on Wheels and many other services offered by the major communities.

FINANCIAL SERVICES:
Number of local banks: 95

Number of local savings and loan associations: 45

THE MEDIA:
Largest local newspaper: *Sarasota Herald-Tribune*

Cable television? Yes

MAJOR LOCAL RETAILERS:
Bealls, Belk Lindsey, Parisian, Jacobson's, J Byron, Burdines, JCPenney, K mart, Dillard's, Marshalls, Sears, Wal-Mart, Woolworth. Among the major shopping centers are the Sarasota Square Mall, Southgate Plaza and Gulfgate Mall. There's also St. Armands Circle near the southern portion of Longboat Key, which has restaurants and ritzy shops.

FOOD ESTABLISHMENTS: 908

OTHER SERVICES:
Number of local libraries: 6

Number of local hotels/motels: 88

Number of churches: Protestant: 213; Jewish: 7; Catholic: 16; Other: 108

TOURISM INQUIRIES:
Greater **Sarasota** Chamber of Commerce, 1819 Main St., Suite 240, Sarasota, 34236. Telephone: 813-955-8187; **Venice** Area Chamber of Commerce, 257 Tamiami Trail N., Venice, 34285-1908. Telephone: 813-488-2236; **Englewood** Area Chamber of Commerce, 601 S. Indiana Ave., Englewood, 34223. Telephone: 813-474-5511.

CENTRAL EAST FLORIDA

THE COUNTIES: Brevard, Indian River, Martin, Okeechobee, St. Lucie, and Volusia

MAJOR CITIES: Daytona Beach, Melbourne, Palm Bay, Port St. Lucie, Titusville, and Fort Pierce

TOP INDUSTRIES: Tourism, services, high-tech, citrus, wholesale and retail trade, aircraft, dairy farming

MAJOR NEWSPAPERS: *Daytona Beach News-Journal* and *Florida TODAY* in Melbourne

WEATHER:
On the first line is the average maximum temperature for each month; the second line, the average minimum temperature; the third line, the amount of precipitation, in inches, for 1990, from the national weather station.

Daytona Beach	Jan.	Feb.	Mar.	Apr.	May	June	July	Aug.	Sep.	Oct.	Nov.	Dec.
Max.	74.0	76.5	77.4	79.6	86.3	90.4	90.6	91.4	88.9	84.0	77.8	77.0
Min.	51.4	58.4	55.3	59.6	68.2	70.9	73.1	72.3	72.0	67.9	56.9	53.2
Precp.	1.4	5.6	1.9	1.5	1.5	2.7	5.9	7.0	1.6	5.9	0.8	0.3

BREVARD County
Central East
County seat: Titusville

POPULATION: 1990: 398,978
1993: 427,035
Increase: 7.0 percent

AGE DISTRIBUTION (1992) IN PERCENTAGES:
0-14 : 18.8
15-44: 42.2
45-64: 21.9
65+ : 17.1

MUNICIPAL POPULATION:
CAPE CANAVERAL: 1990: 8,014; 1993: 8,177
COCOA: 1990: 17,722; 1993: 17,795
COCOA BEACH: 1990: 12,123; 1993: 12,533
INDIALANTIC: 1990: 2,844; 1993: 2,863
INDIAN HARBOR BEACH: 1990: 6,933; 1993: 7,325
MALABAR: 1990: 1,977; 1993: 2,187
MELBOURNE: 1990: 60,034; 1993: 64,191

Daytona is known as "The world's most famous beach." You simply drive right onto it. The beach has been one of the most popular sites for college students during spring break.

Visitors to the NASA Kennedy Space Center's Spaceport USA go past a number of launch pads. The Spaceport is near Titusville.

One of the access points leading to Lake Okeechobee.

MELBOURNE BEACH: 1990: 3,078; 1993: 3,105
MELBOURNE VILLAGE: 1990: 591; 1993: 600
PALM BAY: 1990: 62,543; 1993: 69,197
PALM SHORES: 1990: 210; 1993: 504
ROCKLEDGE: 1990: 16,023; 1993: 17,182
SATELLITE BEACH: 1990: 9,889; 1993: 9,954
TITUSVILLE: 1990: 39,394; 1993: 40,679
WEST MELBOURNE: 1990: 8,399; 1993: 8,635
UNINCORPORATED: 1990: 149,204; 1993: 162,108

LAND AREA: 1,019 square miles
POPULATION DENSITY: 419 people per square mile (11th in the state)

Brevard County, on the central East Coast, is one of the biggest high-tech areas of the southeastern United States. Its major attraction is the NASA Kennedy Space Center's Spaceport USA, which had 2.8 million visitors in 1992 (see Attractions chapter for more information).

The largest employers by far are connected with the John F. Kennedy Space Center and the National Aeronautics and Space Administration. The number of employees working for high-tech and aerospace employers is about 38,550; this includes 10,000 employees of Harris Corp.; 5,900 for Lockheed Space Operations Co.; 3,060 for McDonnell Douglas; 2,800 for EG&G; 2,630 NASA employees; 2,550 for Rockwell International; 2,000 for Johnson Controls World Services; 1,865 for Northrop Grumman Inc.; 1,115 for Martin Marietta; and 1,100 for BAMSI Inc.

Another large employer is Patrick Air Force Base, which employs about 12,000.

The area is made up of many communities, including **Melbourne,** the county's largest city; **Palm Bay,** with about 65 square miles of territory, the largest incorporated area in Brevard and the eleventh-fastest-growing city in the state in the 1980s. Its population rose 237.54 percent between 1980 and 1990. Harris Corp. has employed about 10,000 people in this city in recent years; **Titusville,** the county seat, which is on the Indian River and is adjacent to the Kennedy Space Center; **Satellite Beach,** which has beach-side condominiums, apartment complexes and canal homes; **Indian Harbor Beach,** which also has canal-front homes and is popular among boaters because it is located between the Atlantic Ocean and Indian River; **West Melbourne,** which has more wide open spaces and more of a country atmosphere; **Melbourne Beach,** which is a residential town with homes that run the gamut from small cottages to luxurious oceanfront residences; **Indialantic,** which is popular among Snowbirds and also has many waterfront homes; and a number of unincorporated areas that include small ranch homes and citrus groves.

Many Fortune 500 companies are represented here, including EG&G, Gannett, Northrop Grumman, Harris Corp., Lockheed, McDonnell Douglas, Rockwell International, StorageTek, Engineering & Technical Services, and Scientific Atlanta.

The Melbourne/Palm Bay/Titusville area had the third highest average annual pay ($20,621) of metropolitan statistical areas surveyed by the Florida Department of Labor and Employment Security for 1990. Miami topped the list at $20,988, followed by West Palm Beach at $20,662. According to the U.S. Department of Commerce, Melbourne was ranked No. 6 in terms of income growth during the 1980s with a rate of 36.9 percent. Raleigh, N.C., was No. 1 with a 38.8 percent growth rate.

Growth is one word that is synonymous with this region. For example, during the 1980s, 7,137 new jobs were created by the 40 largest high-tech manufacturing employers in South Brevard alone; the area's high-tech manufacturing employment increased 63 percent during the decade. Countywide, 68,496 new jobs were created during the 1980s.

Port Canaveral is a deep-water port of entry with passenger and cargo facilities. It is the second largest multi-day cruise port in North America, with more than 1 million passengers sailing annually from this port. There are 11 cargo berths, four full-service passenger terminals and a turning basin with space for eight cruise ship terminals. More than 2.9 million short tons of cargo moved through the port in 1991-92.

Recreation includes beach and boating activities, surfing and sea turtle watching. The area from Spessard Holland County Park south to Sebastian Inlet is the largest sea turtle nesting area in the United States. The turtles — greens, leatherbacks and loggerheads — are on shore from May to August.

HOUSING PRICES:
Median sales price for a single-family existing home in the Melbourne-Titusville-Palm Bay area was $74,400 for June 1994.
Number of vacant residential lots: 93,657; number of single-family residences: 119,368; mobile homes: 10,689; condominiums: 22,041

EDUCATION:
Number of schools: 77
Number of students enrolled: 62,556
Percentage of students continuing education after high school: 77.75
Teacher-to-pupil ratio: 1:17.9
Average teacher's salary: $29,507

Colleges, universities, and junior or community colleges serving the area:
Brevard Community College, Cocoa, with Titusville and Melbourne campuses; University of Central Florida campus in Cocoa; Florida Institute of Technology, Melbourne; Rollins College/Brevard campus at Rockledge; Barry University/branch at Merritt Island; Phillips Junior College of Business, Melbourne

Trade and technical schools serving the area:
Brevard Community College's Florida Advanced Technology Center, Palm Bay; Keiser College of Technology, Melbourne; County Trade School.

HEALTH CARE:
Number of general hospitals: 9
Number of hospital beds: 1,503
Number of physicians: 694

TAXES: Total county ad-valorem millage rate (1993): 15.1584

STANDARD CRIME RATE: 6,132.1 offenses per 100,000 population (22nd out of 67 counties)

LARGEST EMPLOYERS:

Name	Employees	Product/Service
Patrick Air Force Base	12,000	Military
Harris Corp.	10,000	Aerospace
Brevard County School District	7,800	Education
Lockheed Space Operations Co.	5,900	Aerospace
McDonnell Douglas	3,060	Aerospace
EG&G	2,800	Aerospace
Holmes Regional Medical Center	2,800	Health care
National Aeronautics & Space Administration	2,630	Aerospace
Rockwell International	2,550	Aerospace
Brevard Board of County Commissioners	2,450	Government
Publix Supermarket	2,249	Grocery
Wuesthoff Hospital	2,057	Health care
Johnson Controls World Services	2,000	High tech
Northrop Grumman Inc.	1,865	Aerospace
Winn-Dixie Supermarkets	1,835	Grocery

COMPANIES PROVIDING LOCAL UTILITIES:
Telephone: Southern Bell
Electricity: Florida Power & Light
Natural Gas: City Gas Co. of Florida
Water: Cities of Cocoa, Melbourne and Titusville
Major Water Source: Rivers
Sanitary Landfill? Yes

POINTS OF INTEREST:
Spaceport USA at the Kennedy Space Center, tours of launch areas, museum and exhibits (see more details in the Attractions chapter); **Merritt Island National Wildlife Refuge,** shows how man co-exists with wildlife on Merritt Island. Sea turtles, armadillos, porpoises, manatees, alligators, eagles, pelicans, wading birds and vultures (there are around 310 species of birdlife here) are some of the sights. Among the endangered and threatened wildlife species are the southern bald eagle, peregrine falcon, eastern indigo snake, manatee, Atlantic loggerhead sea turtle and the Atlantic salt marsh snake. Tours and nature trails are available; **Carnival Cruises** offers three-day and four-day cruises to the Bahamas, leaving from Port Canaveral; **Premier Cruise Lines,** cruises to the Bahamas, leaving from Port Canaveral; **Space Coast Stadium** at Melbourne, spring training site for the **Florida Marlins** baseball team; **Historic Cocoa Village,** a refurbished area near Cocoa with antique and jewelry shops, craft displays, a village playhouse,

restaurants and shopping along cobblestone streets and early-1900-era street lamps and landscaping; **The Porcher House** in Cocoa, a restored 1916 home and an example of 20th-century classic revival architecture, is one of the stops during the Brevard Museum of History and Natural Science's walking tours of the historic district; **Brevard Community College Planetarium and Observatory** in the Astronaut Memorial Space Science Center at the Cocoa campus of Brevard Community College has 360-degree movies and an international hall of space explorers. Florida's largest public telescope is housed here; **United States Astronaut Hall of Fame** in Titusville has spacecraft, personal items from astronauts; **Space Coast Science Center** in Melbourne has exhibits, classes, workshops, lectures, films and field trips; **The Cocoa Beach Pier** stretches 840 feet over the ocean and has 2 ½ miles of boardwalk planks, restaurants, gift and surf shops; **Ron Jon Surf Shop** in Cocoa Beach; **Lone Cabbage Fish Camp's airboat tours** on St. Johns River; **Patrick Air Force Base Missile Display,** Cocoa Beach, in front of the Eastern Test Range Laboratory, has outdoor missile and rocket exhibit including a Titan and Atlas; **Sebastian Inlet State Recreation Area,** Melbourne Beach, has camping, picnicking, swimming, surfing, skin and scuba diving, saltwater fishing and shrimping; **Turkey Creek Sanctuary** has 4,000-foot boardwalk where people can view plant communities and endangered animals, such as the manatee; **Liberty Bell Museum** in Melbourne is home to a Liberty Bell replica; **Brevard Zoological Park,** South Brevard; **Air Force Space Museum** at Cape Canaveral Air Force Station has more than 700 missiles and space-launch vehicles on display; **Merritt Island Dragon,** sitting on the southern tip of Merritt Island north of the Eau Gallie Causeway, this 100-foot-long dragon was constructed with more than 20 tons of concrete and steel and is the work of Tampa sculptor Lewis Vandercar. Four hatchling dragons were later added; **Indian River Lagoon,** half of which is in Brevard County, extends 160 miles and contains more than 3,000 species of animals including birds and 700 species of fish; **Canaveral National Seashore,** protected beach area north of the Kennedy Space Center is open to the public for day use only with picnicking, swimming, boat ramps, hiking, surfing, fishing, crabbing, clamming, shrimping, canoeing, restricted hunting; **Playalinda,** a beach in North Brevard at Canaveral National Seashore with no commerical development, popular for sunning, surfing, swimming and fishing. Accessible only by foot; **greyhound racing** in Melbourne.

THE ARTS:
The Brevard Museum of History and Natural Science in Cocoa has exhibits showing how native Americans and pioneers once lived in Brevard County and Florida; **The Brevard Symphony Orchestra** gives concerts in the area; **Brevard Art Center and Museum** in Melbourne has exhibits from ancient sculptures to modern art and classes; **Valiant Air Command Museum** in Titusville is an historical flying museum and operations center for the Valiant Air Command; **South Brevard Historical Museum; The Florida Space Coast Philharmonic,** a 55-piece group; **Melbourne Chamber Music Society; Melbourne Municipal Band; Melbourne Civic Theatre** performs modern plays to classics; **Ensemble Theatre** of Melbourne performs classic and contemporary musicals and dramas; **Cocoa Village Playhouse** features live, film and multimedia presentations and is home to the Children's Community Theater; **Fine Arts Auditorium** at Brevard Community College has professional entertainment and cultural events; **The Surfside Players,** a community theater group in Cocoa Beach; **Surfside Playhouse** in Cocoa Beach; **Titusville Playhouse** produces dramas, comedies and musicals. One of its subsidiaries is the RisingStars Children's Theatre; **Art Center of Titusville** hosts shows and sales throughout the year and has classes for both beginners and those more advanced; **Emma Parrish Theatre,** a community effort in Titusville; **Brevard Community College Art Gallery,** Melbourne; **Phoenix Production Company,** a professional theater; **East Coast Dance Theatre; Maxwell C. King Center for the Performing Arts** (has 2,000-seat theater) in Melbourne; **Melbourne Auditorium** (seats 1,580).

ANNUAL EVENTS:
January: Titusville Area Chamber of Commerce Country Hoedown; **February:** Cocoa Village Art Show; **March:** Great Chowder Cook-off in Cocoa Beach; Port Canaveral Seafood Festival and Carnival with entertainment and navy ship tours; Valiant Air Command Warbird Airshow at the Space Center Executive Airport in Titusville; **March or April:** Easter Surfing Festival at Cocoa Beach Pier; **April:** Indian River Festival in Titusville, with carnival, live entertainment, boat show, frog-jumping contests, craft displays, food; Melbourne Art Festival, Melbourne; **May:** Jewish Festival at the Melbourne Auditorium; Rib Fest and Hot Air Balloon Rally, Melbourne; Melbourne Beach Art and Craft Show; Memorial Day Rock Fest and Ocean Regatta at Cocoa Beach Pier; **June:** International Food and Music Festival and June Craft Fair at Cocoa Village; **July:** The July

4th Firecracker Festival at Palm Bay Campus of Brevard Community College's Technical Center; July Fourth Concert and Fireworks display at Melbourne; **September:** Labor Day Surfing Contest, Cocoa Beach; **October:** Port Weekend at Port Canaveral with a 5-K race, regatta, trade show, art show, fishing tournaments, touring of military vessels; Cocoa Village Autumn Art Festival; Main Street Harvest Festival in Titusville; Melbourne Arts and Crafts Festival in historic downtown Melbourne; **November:** Space Coast Art Festival in downtown Cocoa Beach; Brevard County Fair at Cocoa Expo; **December:** Cocoa Village Christmas Craft Fair; Festival of Lights and Christmas Parade, Titusville.

SPORTS AND LEISURE ACTIVITIES:
Most popular local fishing areas: Fishing charters leave from Port Canaveral; For saltwater fishing: Indian River, Banana River, Atlantic Ocean, Canaveral Pier (surf casting), Mosquito Lagoon; For freshwater fishing: St. Johns River, Lake Washington, Lake Hellen Blazes.
Number of local golf courses: 15
Public beaches: Yes, including Sidney Fischer Park, Lori Wilson Park and Shepard Park.
Tennis courts available to the public? Yes
Boating? Yes
Number of pleasure boats registered in the county (1991-92): 25,868

SERVICES FOR RETIREES:
Space Coast Area Transit provides transporation for the elderly; Meals on Wheels; adult day care including program called Creative Care for the Aging; Adult Club of Melbourne; American Association of Retired Persons chapters throughout county; Brevard Single Adult Club (for those age 50 and up); New York City Transit Retirees of Florida in Palm Bay; Palm Bay Area Senior Citizens Association; Retired Senior Volunteer Program R.S.V.P. in Cocoa; Satellite Beach Senior Citizens Club; Senior Corps of Retired Executives at Brevard Community College; and South Brevard Senior Association in Melbourne.

FINANCIAL SERVICES:
Number of local banks: 103
Number of local savings and loan associations: 24

THE MEDIA:
Largest local newspaper: *Florida TODAY*
Cable television? Yes

MAJOR LOCAL RETAILERS:
Burdines, Belk Lindsey, JCPenney, K mart, Dollar General Store, Sears, Dillard's, Wal-Mart, Woolworth, Ben Franklin, Bealls, Mervyn's; specialty shops at Peddler's Village in Rockledge and at Cocoa Village. Melbourne Square Mall has more than a million square feet of space. Two other major malls are the Miracle City Mall in Titusville and the Merritt Square Mall on Merritt Island. There also are a number of smaller malls throughout the county.

FOOD ESTABLISHMENTS: 1,216

OTHER SERVICES:
Number of local libraries: 12
Number of local hotels/motels: 114
Number of churches: Protestant: 206; Jewish: 7; Catholic: 9; Other: 14

TOURISM INQUIRIES:
Cocoa Beach Area Chamber of Commerce, 400 Fortenberry Road, Merritt Island, 32952. Telephone: 407-459-2200; The Greater **South Brevard** Area Chamber of Commerce, 1005 E. Strawbridge Ave., Melbourne, 32901-4782. Telephone: 407-724-5400; **Titusville** Area Chamber of Commerce, P.O. Drawer 2767, Titusville, 32781. Telephone: 407-267-3036.

INDIAN RIVER County
Central East
County seat: Vero Beach

POPULATION: 1990: 90,208
1993: 95,641
Increase: 6 percent

AGE DISTRIBUTION (1992) IN PERCENTAGES:
  0-14 : 16.2
  15-44: 34.7
  45-64: 21.7
  65+ : 27.3

MUNICIPAL POPULATION:
FELLSMERE: 1990: 2,179; 1993: 2,260
INDIAN RIVER SHORES: 1990: 2,278; 1993: 2,468
ORCHID: 1990: 10; 1993: 21
SEBASTIAN: 1990: 10,248; 1993: 12,154
VERO BEACH: 1990: 17,350; 1993: 17,404
UNINCORPORATED: 1990: 58,143; 1993: 61,334

LAND AREA: 503 square miles
POPULATION DENSITY:190 people per square mile (23rd in the state)

Located midway down Florida's east coast, the county is famous nationwide as part of the Indian River citrus belt and is noted for its Atlantic beaches and the picturesque Indian River, part of the Intracoastal Waterway. As development has progressed up the coast, the county has become home to a sizeable proportion of retirees: The percentage of those over 65 rose between 1989 and 1993 from 23.6 percent to 27.3. The area has a warm climate, of course, and lacks the congestion of retiree havens in some points south.

Local citrus production was Florida's fourth highest in 1992-93 at 22.5 million boxes (after Polk, St. Lucie and Hendry counties). That number included 7.6 million boxes of oranges and 14.5 million of grapefruit, plus tangerines and tangelos.

Agricultural land includes pastures and ranges, too, and the county's economy also is based on tourism and light industry. Among the major private employers are citrus producers, hospitals, grocery and retail stores, and Dodgertown, the spring training home of the Los Angeles Dodgers.

Among popular recreational activities are boating, water-skiing, scuba diving, swimming, windsurfing, jet-skiing and nature watching. But the activity that has gained nationwide attention is surfing — the area has been called the East Coast Surfing Capital. Surfing contests are held at Sebastian Inlet each year, and Conn Beach on Ocean Drive is a noted surfing area.

Pay attention when you're walking around the beaches here. Gold doubloons have occasionally been found from sunken Spanish galleons.

TOURISM:
The season runs from November to April. As many as half a million tourists visit the area in a year.

HOUSING PRICES:
Generally $80,000 to $90,000 for a three-bedroom, two-bath home.
Number of vacant residential lots: 22,037; number of single-family residences: 27,445; mobile homes: 1,051; condominiums: 10,726

EDUCATION:
Number of schools: 21
Number of students enrolled: 12,597
Percentage of students continuing education after high school: 79.28
Teacher-to-pupil ratio: 1:17.7
Average teacher's salary: $32,542

Colleges, universities, and junior or community colleges serving the area:
Indian River Community College in Fort Pierce, which also offers courses at the Mueller Center in Vero Beach and elsewhere in the county; Webster College Center branch in Fort Pierce; Barry University and Florida Atlantic University have satellite campuses at Indian River Community College; Florida Institute of Technology in Melbourne

Trade and technical schools serving the area:
Indian River Community College; Treasure Coast PIC

HEALTH CARE:
Number of general hospitals: 3
Number of hospital beds: 550
Number of physicians: 242

TAXES: Total county ad-valorem millage rate (1993): 16.5407

STANDARD CRIME RATE: 5,634.6 offenses per 100,000 population (27th out of 67 counties)

LARGEST PRIVATE EMPLOYERS:

Name	Employees	Product/Service
Indian River Memorial Hospital	1,300	Health care
Sun Ag, Inc.	800	Citrus
Publix	750	Grocery
Gracewood Fruit Co.	465	Citrus
Graves Brothers	450	Citrus
Hale Indian River Groves	450	Citrus
Dodgertown Complex	400	Convention center
Sebastian Hospital	375	Health care
Piper Aircraft Corp.	375	Manufacturing
Wal-Mart	330	Retail sales

COMPANIES PROVIDING LOCAL UTILITIES:
Telephone: Southern Bell
Electricity: City of Vero Beach, Florida Power & Light
Natural Gas: None
Water: City of Vero Beach, Indian River County
Major Water Source: Wells
Sanitary Landfill? Yes

POINTS OF INTEREST:
Sebastian Inlet State Recreation Area has the **McClarty Museum,** which houses Indian artifacts and treasure recovered from the wreckage of a Spanish fleet in 1715; also, camping, picnicking, swimming, surfing, skin- and scuba diving, saltwater fishing and shrimping, boat ramp and concessions; **Wabasso Beach Park** has 400 feet of oceanfront beaches, picnic pavilions with grills, showers; **Los Angeles Dodgers** spring training camp at Holman Stadium (Dodgertown) in Vero Beach; **Pelican Island,** the nation's first wildlife refuge, offshore from Sebastian, has thousands of pelicans and other water fowl; **Little Orchid Island,** includes the **Environmental Learning Center.**

THE ARTS:
Riverside Theater in Vero Beach has seating capacity of 600; **Center for the Arts Auditorium** in Vero Beach has seating capacity of 250; **Vero Beach Theatre Guild** has seating capacity of 315.

ANNUAL EVENTS:
March: Under the Oaks at the Vero Beach Art Center Grounds with arts and crafts; Indian River County Fair in Vero Beach; **Memorial Day:** Surfing contests at Sebastian Inlet (national and regional surfing events are also held at various times during the year here); **July 4:** Independence Day celebration in Sebastian with parade, music, food and fireworks; **August:** Chamber of Commerce-sponsored Summerfest with arts and crafts, entertainment, food, antique car show, concert; **October:** Autumn in the Park in Vero Beach with arts and crafts; **November:** Children's Art Festival, sponsored by the Center for the Arts, has hands-on art activities, food, entertainment; **December:** Christmas Lights contest in Sebastian.

SPORTS AND LEISURE ACTIVITIES:
Most popular local fishing area: North jetty protruding from Sebastian Inlet
Number of local golf courses: 15
Public beaches: Yes
Tennis courts available to the public? Yes
Boating? Yes
Number of pleasure boats registered in the county (1991-92): 7,748

SERVICES FOR RETIREES: Council on Aging in Vero Beach

FINANCIAL SERVICES:
Number of local banks: 31
Number of local savings and loan associations: 9

THE MEDIA:
Largest local newspaper: *Vero Beach Press-Journal*
Cable television? Yes

MAJOR LOCAL RETAILERS: JCPenney, Bealls, Byrons, Wal-Mart, K mart

FOOD ESTABLISHMENTS: 289

OTHER SERVICES:
Number of local libraries: 3
Number of local motels: 31
Number of churches: Protestant: 117; Jewish: 1; Catholic: 5

TOURISM INQUIRIES:
Vero Beach-Indian River County Chamber of Commerce, P.O. Box 2947, Vero Beach 32961.
Telephone: 407-567-3491; **Sebastian** River Area Chamber of Commerce, 1302 U.S. Highway 1, Sebastian, 32958. Telephone: 407-589-5969.

MARTIN County
Central East
County seat: Stuart

POPULATION: 1990: 100,900
1993: 106,780
Increase: 5.8 percent

AGE DISTRIBUTION (1992) IN PERCENTAGES:
0-14 : 15.4
15-44: 35.7
45-64: 21.5
65+ : 27.4

MUNICIPAL POPULATION:
JUPITER ISLAND: 1990: 549;1993: 562
OCEAN BREEZE PARK: 1990: 519; 1993: 519
SEWALLS POINT: 1990: 1,588; 1993: 1,651
STUART: 1990: 11,936; 1993: 12,479
UNINCORPORATED: 1990: 86,308; 1993: 91,569

LAND AREA: 556 square miles
POPULATION DENSITY: 192 people per square mile (21st in the state)

Situated 100 miles north of Miami and 250 miles south of Jacksonville on Florida's East Coast, Martin County is a water-oriented area providing easy access to the Atlantic Ocean, Indian River, St. Lucie River and Lake Okeechobee. The St. Lucie Inlet is the starting point for boaters who want to cross the state, from the St. Lucie Canal through Lake Okeechobee, to the Gulf of Mexico near Fort Myers on Florida's west coast. This part of the East Coast is known as the Treasure Coast because many treasure-laden ships lie sunken offshore.

The county's principal city is Stuart, which is the shopping hub and the center for business, finance and medical services. The western portion of the county has more than 54,000 acres of agricultural land (crops include oranges and grapefruit, sugar cane, ornamental plants, beef cattle, dairies, cabbage, potatoes, tomatoes, peppers, squash, melons and greens).

Stuart/Martin County is called the sailfish capital of the world and many tournaments are sponsored each year for fishing enthusiasts. Blue marlin, dolphin, snook, mackerel, bluefish and grouper also are popular catches. The county contains many unincorporated areas, among them Jensen Beach, which is nicknamed the sea turtle capital of the world because large loggerhead and green sea turtles come ashore between mid-May and August to lay their eggs. There are organized turtle watches along the beaches. A small part of Hutchinson Island is located in the county.

Among the state's counties, Martin has the tenth highest percentage of residents 65 and older. And it is an increasingly popular Snowbird haven, offering the amenities of nearby southeastern Florida without the population density.

TOURISM: The population increases by a third between Jan. 1 and April 15.

HOUSING PRICES:
Prices range from $50,000 to $1.2 million and vary widely depending on location, amenities and

density. Generally add $10,000 to $20,000 for canal, lake, or golf course homes. Oceanfront homes are $500,000 and up.

Number of vacant residential lots: 11,082; number of single-family residences: 26,010; mobile homes: 2,906; condominiums: 13,344

EDUCATION:
Number of schools: 27
Number of students enrolled: 13,023
Percentage of students continuing education after high school: 54.78
Teacher-to-pupil ratio: 1:16.5
Average teacher's salary: $29,739

Colleges, universities, and junior or community colleges serving the area: Barry University branch at Indian River Community College, based in Fort Pierce; Indian River Community College; Florida Institute of Technology in Melbourne; Hobe Sound Bible College in Hobe Sound; Florida Atlantic University in Boca Raton; Palm Beach Community College; Palm Beach Atlantic College, West Palm Beach.

Trade and technical schools serving the area:
Martin County High School Vo-Tech; Indian River Community College; Chapman School of Seamanship in Stuart.

HEALTH CARE:
Number of general hospitals: 2
Number of hospital beds: 396
Number of physicians: 231

TAXES: Total county ad-valorem millage rate (1993): 15.8400

STANDARD CRIME RATE: 5,188.2 offenses per 100,000 population (32nd out of 67 counties)

LARGEST EMPLOYERS:

Name	Employees	Product
Martin Memorial Medical Center	2,100	Health care
Martin County School District	1,751	Government
Publix Supermarkets	700	Grocery
Via Tropical Fruits	610	Fruit
Winn-Dixie Supermarkets	550	Grocery
Armellini Express Lines	483	Trucking
Grumman Aircraft Systems	478	Aircraft/flight
Martin County government	450	
Martin Correctional Institute	424	
First National Bank & Trust	308	Banking
Indian River Plantation	285	
Florida Power & Light	240	Utilities
Turbocombuster Technology	225	Aircraft parts

COMPANIES PROVIDING LOCAL UTILITIES:
Telephone: Southern Bell, Indiantown Telephone System
Electricity: Florida Power & Light
Natural Gas: Indiantown Gas Co.
Water: City of Stuart, Martin County Utilities and some private
Major Water Source: Wells
Sanitary Landfill? Yes

POINTS OF INTEREST:
Beaches; **Hobe Sound National Wildlife Refuge; Jonathan Dickinson State Park,** 13 miles south of Stuart, has camping, picnicking, swimming, freshwater fishing, hiking; **Elliott Museum** on Hutchinson Island (antique automobiles and cycles, 12 Early American shops brought from Salem, Mass., and contemporary art); **House of Refuge** on Hutchinson Island (museum displaying articles of shipwrecks, some dating to the 16th century, such as compasses and furniture); **St. Lucie Inlet State Preserve,** Port Salerno, accessible by boat, three quarters of a mile south of the inlet, is a nesting area every summer for loggerhead, green and leatherback turtles and has picnicking, swimming, saltwater fishing and hiking (has a 3,300-foot boardwalk); **Jensen**

Beach, in northeastern Martin County, is the highest point on the East Coast of Florida — 85 feet above sea level — and is nicknamed the sea turtle capital of the world. There also is an environmental studies center here.

THE ARTS:
Downtown Stuart houses a courthouse cultural complex with exhibits and art shows; **Barn Theater** is an amateur theatrical group; **Performing Arts Society of Stuart.** Many cultural activities are in nearby Palm Beach County.

ANNUAL EVENTS:
February: Black Heritage Festival; **March:** Blessing of the Fleet, Stuart; Martin County Fair; Sunshine State Art and Craft Show, Jensen Beach; **July:** July Fourth fireworks display, Jensen Beach; **Early October:** Leif Erikson Day (a re-enactment of Erikson's landing, in traditional Norwegian garb and 100-year-old boats), Jensen Beach; **November:** Pineapple Festival, Jensen Beach; Early **December:** Christmas Parade, Stuart; Christmas Boat Parade, Stuart; Arts Fest in Stuart.

SPORTS AND LEISURE ACTIVITIES:
Most popular local fishing areas: A half dozen offshore reefs in the Atlantic Ocean; along a half dozen bridges and piers; surf casting on Hutchinson Island; Indian and St. Lucie rivers; Lake Okeechobee.
Number of local golf courses: 23
Public beaches: 13 beachfront parks/access areas, covering more than 139 acres
Tennis courts available to the public? Yes
Boating? Yes
Number of pleasure boats registered in the county (1991-92): 12,080

SERVICES FOR RETIREES:
Council for Aging, Meals on Wheels, seniors recreation centers. Nearest Social Security office is in Fort Pierce (a representative is in Stuart one day a week).

FINANCIAL SERVICES:
Number of local banks: 42
Number of local savings and loan associations: 18

THE MEDIA:
Largest local newspaper: *Stuart News*
Cable television? Yes

MAJOR LOCAL RETAILERS:
Burdines, Sears, JCPenney, Byrons, K mart, Wal-Mart, Mervyn's, Dillards, Target.

FOOD ESTABLISHMENTS: 384

OTHER SERVICES:
Number of local libraries: 4
Number of local hotels/motels: 26
Number of churches: Protestant: 24; Jewish: 2; Catholic: 4; Other: 22

TOURISM INQUIRIES:
Stuart-Martin County Chamber of Commerce, 1650 S. Kanner Highway, Stuart, 34994. Telephone: 407-287-1088.

OKEECHOBEE County
Central East
County seat: Okeechobee

POPULATION: 1990: 29,627
1993: 31,758
Increase: 7.2 percent

AGE DISTRIBUTION (1992) IN PERCENTAGES:
0-14 : 23.1
15-44: 40.3
45-64: 20.1
65+ : 16.5

MUNICIPAL POPULATION:
OKEECHOBEE: 1990: 4,943; 1993: 4,979
UNINCORPORATED: 1990: 24,684; 1993: 26,779

LAND AREA: 774 square miles
POPULATION DENSITY: 41 people per square mile (46th in the state)

As the county's name would suggest, Lake Okeechobee is important to this county. The lake is the region's biggest attraction, luring fishermen and some sightseers. The area is known as the "Speckled Perch Capital of the World" and hosts a festival in the fish's honor, with a parade, fish fry and armadillo races.

Agriculture is by far the largest industry, with dairy farming and cattle topping the list. For years, Okeechobee County has been the top milk-producing county in the state. It also is a citrus producer — more than 2.9 million boxes in 1992-93, according to the Florida Agricultural Statistics Service.

The largest private non-agricultural employer in the county, a bank, employs 91 people. Light industry plays a relatively minor role.

Manufactured housing is a popular option here, and there are about two dozen recreational vehicle parks in the area.

TOURISM:
About 15,000 tourists come to the area every year; the highest influx is in the winter and spring.

HOUSING PRICES:
Average price is about $60,000. Many government-subsidized starter homes are available for about $50,000.
Number of vacant residential lots: 14,398; number of single-family residences: 5,235; mobile homes: 5,213; condominiums: 157

EDUCATION:
Number of schools: 12
Number of students enrolled: 6,230
Percentage of students continuing education after high school: 67.07
Teacher-to-pupil ratio: 1:18.3
Average teacher's salary: $30,701

Colleges, universities, and junior or community colleges serving the area:
Indian River Community College's Okeechobee branch; Florida Atlantic University branch at Indian River Community College

Trade and technical schools serving the area:
West Technical Education Center; Okeechobee High School

HEALTH CARE:
Number of general hospitals: 1
Number of hospital beds: 101
Number of physicians: 26

TAXES: Total county ad-valorem millage rate (1993): 19.1650

STANDARD CRIME RATE: 4,597.3 offenses per 100,000 population (37th out of 67 counties)

LARGEST PRIVATE EMPLOYERS:

Name	Employees	Product/Service
Barnett Bank	91	Banking
K mart	60	Retail sales
Wal-Mart	55	Retail sales
Life Services	42	Animal products
Walpole Feed	36	Cattle feed
McArthur Dairy	35	Dairy products
Big Lake National Bank	26	Banking
Rock-A-Way Industries	22	Construction
Sun Bank	16	Banking

COMPANIES PROVIDING LOCAL UTILITIES:
Telephone: United Telephone
Electricity: Florida Power & Light

Natural Gas: None
Water: Big Cypress Water Management District-South Florida
Major Water Source: Lake
Sanitary Landfill? Yes

POINTS OF INTEREST:
Lake Okeechobee, the largest freshwater lake in the United States south of the Great Lakes, is popular for fishing, boating; **Narrated Swampland Tours,** on Kissimmee River; **Okeechobee County Historical Park** has museum and old schoolhouse; **Okeechobee County Civic Center; Okee-Tantie Park,** located at the mouth of the Kissimmee River about 10 miles southwest of Okeechobee, has fishing, camping, picnicking, boating, concessions, boat rentals, guide service, fish cleaning stations, playground.

THE ARTS:
Okeechobee Community Theatre offers drama and comedy performances during the winter.

ANNUAL EVENTS:
Second weekend in March: Speckled Perch Festival, with a parade, fish fry, live music, craft booths, auction, armadillo races. Event is held in conjunction with the Okeechobee Cattlemen's Rodeo; **Second Saturday in March and Labor Day:** Okeechobee Cattlemen's Rodeo — bronc riding, calf roping, steer wrestling, barrel racing and bull riding events; **Memorial Day:** Memorial Day Services in Flagler Park; **July 4:** Fourth of July celebration with fireworks display; **Labor Day:** Rodeo, festival and parade; **December:** (second Saturday) Lighted Christmas parade and festival in downtown Okeechobee.

SPORTS AND LEISURE ACTIVITIES:
Most popular local fishing areas: Lake Okeechobee (speckled perch, largemouth bass, bream, catfish and bluegill)
Number of local golf courses: 4
Public beaches? Yes
Tennis courts available to the public? Yes
Boating? Yes
Number of pleasure boats registered in the county (1991-92): 4,529

SERVICES FOR RETIREES:
Okeechobee Council on Aging; Lottie Raulerson Senior Citizen Center

FINANCIAL SERVICES:
Number of local banks: 5
Number of local savings and loan associations: 1

THE MEDIA:
Largest local newspaper: *Okeechobee News/Buyers Guide*
Cable television? Yes

MAJOR LOCAL RETAILERS: Wal-Mart, K mart, Bealls, Bugle Boy, Cato

FOOD ESTABLISHMENTS: 116

OTHER SERVICES:
Number of local libraries: 1
Number of local motels: 10
Number of churches: Protestant: 44; Jewish: 0; Catholic: 1

TOURISM INQUIRIES:
Okeechobee County Chamber of Commerce, 55 South Parrott Ave., Okeechobee, 34974. Telephone: 813-763-6464 or 1-800-871-4403.

ST. LUCIE County
Central East
County seat: Fort Pierce

POPULATION: 1990: 150,171
1993: 163,192
Increase: 8.7 percent

AGE DISTRIBUTION (1992) IN PERCENTAGES:
0-14 : 19.9
15-44: 38.7
45-64: 20.4
65+ : 21.1

MUNICIPAL POPULATION:
FORT PIERCE: 1990: 36,830; 1993: 36,909
PORT ST. LUCIE: 1990: 55,761; 1993: 65,722
ST. LUCIE VILLAGE: 1990: 584; 1993: 627
UNINCORPORATED: 1990: 56,996; 1993: 59,934

LAND AREA: 573 square miles
POPULATION DENSITY: 285 people per square mile (17th in the state)

Located on the Treasure Coast, St. Lucie County has become a getaway spot for Floridians living in Orlando and other interior cities and for a number of Snowbirds. Between 1980 and 1990, Port St. Lucie had the eighth-highest rate of population growth among Florida cities — 280.3 percent.

Citrus is big business here — the county is in the center of the Indian River citrus district. During the early 1990s, the county has been both No. 1 and No. 2 in citrus production. During the 1992-93 season, St. Lucie was barely edged out of the No. 1 spot by Polk County. St. Lucie County produced nearly 29 million boxes of citrus; Polk County, just more than 30 million boxes. More than 105,000 acres of grapefruit and orange trees are grown here.

Other major employers are the county school system, two hospitals, a utility, county government, a community college and two groceries.

The county also is the site of two nuclear operating units, St. Lucie Plant Unit 1 and St. Lucie Plant Unit 2, both in Fort Pierce, operated by Florida Power & Light Co. And the Port of Fort Pierce has cruise and commercial facilities and handled a total of 127,659 short tons of export and import merchandise in 1992. The major export is citrus.

Pastimes here include fishing, both freshwater and saltwater, and boating. The area has a number of canals; the Savannas (a chain of lakes extending from Jensen Beach to Fort Pierce, known for bass fishing); and, of course, the Atlantic Ocean. Scuba diving is also popular. There are several shipwrecks in the area and coral reefs, some in only 15 feet of water and others at 55-to-90-foot depths.

The county has been the site of U.S. Olympic sailboard trials and has very picturesque beaches.

TOURISM:
The season is from November through Easter and many Snowbirds and people from other parts of Florida visit the area during this time.

HOUSING PRICES:
The median sales price of a single-family existing home in the Fort Pierce-Port St. Lucie area was $81,700 in June 1994.
Number of vacant residential lots: 60,227; number of single-family residences: 48,136; mobile homes: 3,399; condominiums: 11,088

EDUCATION:
Number of schools: 32
Number of students enrolled: 25,250
Percentage of students continuing education after high school: 25.21
Teacher-to-pupil ratio: 1:16.1
Average teacher's salary: $31,589

Colleges, universities, and junior or community colleges serving the area:
Indian River Community College in Fort Pierce; Florida Atlantic University in Boca Raton and branch in Fort Pierce; Barry University branch at Indian River Community College

Trade and technical schools serving the area:
Indian River Community College

HEALTH CARE:
Number of general hospitals: 3
Number of hospital beds: 555
Number of physicians: 218

TAXES: Total county ad-valorem millage rate (1993): 20.3055

STANDARD CRIME RATE: 6,488.1 offenses per 100,000 population (19th out of 67 counties)

LARGEST PRIVATE EMPLOYERS:

Name	Employees	Product/Service
Florida Power & Light	1,173	Utilities
HCA Lawnwood Regional Medical Center	1,045	Health care
Winn-Dixie	821	Grocery
Publix	742	Grocery
HCA Medical Center of Port St. Lucie	540	Health care
Club Med/Village Hotels of Sandpiper	425	Hotel/club
Southern Bell	395	Communications
Wal-Mart	370	Retail
Ft. Pierce Utilities Authority	360	Utilities
Tropicana	360	Citrus

COMPANIES PROVIDING LOCAL UTILITIES:
Telephone: Southern Bell
Electricity: Fort Pierce Utilities Authority; Florida Power & Light
Natural Gas: Fort Pierce Utilities Authority
Water: Fort Pierce Utilities, St. Lucie County Utilities and St. Lucie West Utilities
Major Water Source: Wells
Sanitary Landfill? Yes

POINTS OF INTEREST:
New York Mets spring training at the St. Lucie County Sports Complex in Port St. Lucie; **Fort Pierce Jai Alai; Fort Pierce Inlet State Recreation Area,** four miles east of Fort Pierce, has youth tent camping, picnicking, swimming, surfing, saltwater fishing, hiking, observation tower; **St. Lucie County Historical Museum** in Fort Pierce has exhibits, including artifacts from old Fort Pierce, which was built in 1838, a display of some of the treasure salvaged from wrecks off Fort Pierce and Key West, and pioneer tools; **St. Lucie County Civic Center** hosts such events as operas, recreational vehicle shows and antique shows; **Savannas Preserve,** located in mid-St. Lucie County and Jensen Beach, has a county park and is made up of ecologically fragile marsh and uplands; **Underwater Demolition Team SEAL (Frogman) Museum** in Fort Pierce has displays of the equipment used by U.S. Navy divers, training videos; **Florida Power & Light Energy Encounter** at the nuclear site; **Harbor Branch** Oceanographic Institution between Fort Pierce and Vero Beach has artifacts on marine science subjects; Heathcote Botanical Gardens in Ft. Pierce.

THE ARTS:
A.E. Bean Backus Art Gallery in Fort Pierce; **Ira M. McAlpin Fine Arts Center** at Indian River Community College's main campus has 600-seat theater; **St. Lucie Community Theater,** Fort Pierce, has seasonal performances; **Indian River Community College's Planetarium.**

ANNUAL EVENTS:
January: Annual Rainbow Festival at Mets' stadium; **February:** Cattleman's Parade in Fort Pierce with floats and horses; **Late February and Early March:** St. Lucie County Fair at the Fort Pierce Fairgrounds; **March:** Pow Wow at Indian River Community College with Indian food and artifacts; Spring Craft Fair at the St. Lucie Civic Center; **May:** Black Arts Festival at the St. Lucie County Civic Center; **July:** Fireworks; Chili Cook-off at the civic center; Christmas in July, Buckler Craft Show at the civic center; **October:** Rib Cook-off at the St. Lucie County Fairgrounds; St. Lucie County Rodeo at the fairgrounds; Big Orange Festival at Port St. Lucie; **December:** Christmas parade at Port St. Lucie.

SPORTS AND LEISURE ACTIVITIES:
Most popular local fishing areas: Atlantic Ocean; St. Lucie River, Indian River, the Savannas.
Number of local golf courses: 6 public
Public beaches? Yes
Tennis courts available to the public? Yes
Boating? Yes
Number of pleasure boats registered in the county (1991-92): 9,093

SERVICES FOR RETIREES:
Senior Community Center and Council on Aging, both in Fort Pierce.

FINANCIAL SERVICES:
Number of local banks: 29
Number of local savings and loan associations: 12

THE MEDIA:
Largest local newspaper: *Fort Pierce News Tribune*
Cable television? Yes

MAJOR LOCAL RETAILERS:
Sears, Belk-Lindsey, Byrons, Bealls, Wal-Mart, Woolworth, K mart. There is also a major outlet mall here.

FOOD ESTABLISHMENTS: 503

OTHER SERVICES:
Number of local libraries: 4
Number of local hotels/motels: 39
Number of churches: Protestant: 110; Jewish: 2; Catholic: 5; Other: 29

TOURISM INQUIRIES:
Fort Pierce/St. Lucie County Chamber of Commerce, 2200 Virginia Ave., Fort Pierce, 34982. Telephone: 407-461-2700

VOLUSIA County
Central East
County seat: DeLand

POPULATION: 1990: 370,737
1993: 390,066
Increase: 5.2 percent

AGE DISTRIBUTION (1992) IN PERCENTAGES:
0-14 : 16.9
15-44: 39.5
45-64: 20.6
65+ : 23.0

MUNICIPAL POPULATION:
DAYTONA BEACH: 1990: 61,991; 1993: 62,435
DAYTONA BEACH SHORES: 1990: 2,197; 1993: 2,532
DELAND: 1990: 16,622; 1993: 17,377
EDGEWATER: 1990: 15,351; 1993: 16,745
HOLLY HILL: 1990: 11,141; 1993: 11,258
LAKE HELEN: 1990: 2,344; 1993: 2,381
NEW SMYRNA BEACH: 1990: 16,549; 1993: 17,481
OAK HILL: 1990: 917; 1993: 1,015
ORANGE CITY: 1990: 5,347; 1993: 5,813
ORMOND BEACH: 1990: 29,721; 1993: 30,963
PIERSON: 1990: 2,988; 1993: 1,222
PONCE INLET: 1990: 1,704; 1993: 1,994
PORT ORANGE: 1990: 35,307; 1993: 38,144
SOUTH DAYTONA: 1990: 12,488; 1993: 12,689
UNINCORPORATED: 1990: 156,070; 1993: 167,999

LAND AREA: 1,106 square miles
POPULATION DENSITY: 353 people per square mile (14th in the state)

You don't have to be inside the county limits to figure out that this area depends a lot on tourism. If you're driving south from the northern part of the country, you may even have a hard time finding a hotel room in North Carolina during the major Daytona races and when college students are on their spring breaks.

Hundreds of thousands of people head south each winter and spring for these events and to sun themselves on what the county describes as "the world's most famous beach" — Daytona

Beach, a 23-mile stretch of sand on the Atlantic Ocean that at low tide is as wide as 500 feet. You can't miss the beach — you just drive right onto it, unless you're in a bus, a truck or an RV longer than 33 feet, and you can park along 18 miles of it. The beach has become one of the most popular destinations for college students on their spring breaks, since Fort Lauderdale got tired of being Florida's dean of spring parties. While Daytona Beach businesses have welcomed the $100 million or so that the hundreds of thousands of students pumped into the local economy each spring break season, times might be changing again. Today, local business officials say their area is much more than students and that out of the 8 million visitors who come here each year, there are just three "peak" weeks that bring the students, albeit 200,000 to 400,000 of them. Other Florida localities — notably Panama City — seem to be beckoning more and more spring breakers to their regions. In 1992, for example, Panama City officials estimated that about 525,000 young people came to their area during spring break, or double the number from 1991. The number coming to Panama City rose to 600,000 in 1994.

If you're driving the 10 m.p.h. speed limit on the beach, you may well be going faster than you will on some roads leading to the beach at this time of year, a far cry from the nearby Daytona International Speedway, where speeds are limited only by machine and mechanic. For more than a week in February, the speedway is the site of high-powered races that culminate in the famous Daytona 500. The speedway holds major racing events several months of each year and has given the city the nickname of the "world center of racing."

But Volusia County has other attractions as well, including state parks, museums, theaters, and other cultural organizations.

Of the local workforce, the services industry, as of 1992, employed nearly 38,000 people; Others were trade, 35,400; manufacturing, 11,400; government, nearly 23,000; and finance, insurance and real estate, 5,600.

And although Daytona Beach is a major business and educational center for the county and also the headquarters for the Ladies Professional Golf Association and NASCAR, it's not the only municipality. Among the communities are **DeLand,** the county seat, which is on the St. Johns River (popular for bass fishing), in western Volusia. It is the home of Stetson University and is a commercial and industrial center. **New Smyrna Beach** has 8 miles of beaches and is primarily a tourism city. Other industries here are light manufacturing and agriculture. **Orange City** is mainly a rural area. There are no heavy industrial or manufacturing areas and the city's largest employers are fast-food chains and other service-related businesses. The water here is bottled and shipped to other parts of the country. It is also a winter home to the manatee from November to March; **Ormond Beach,** which borders both the Atlantic and the Halifax River, was the winter home in the early 1900s of Rockefellers, Flaglers, Vanderbilts and Astors. Today it has some manufacturing companies, and includes a community known as Ormond-by-the-Sea, made up mostly of retirees, with a population of about 10,000. **Pierson,** which has been nickhamed the fern capital of the world, exports ferns worldwide for floral decorations. It is the northernmost incorporated municipality in Volusia. **Port Orange** and the **South Daytona** area are made up mainly of small individually owned businesses and are not tourist-oriented except for a site called Sugar Mill Gardens (see points of interest below). **Deltona** was established as a planned unit development in 1962. In recent years, estimates were that about 24,000 single-family homes had been built on its 15,000 acres and that about 60 families were moving into the area every month.

Among the other communities are **Edgewater** (it has a large paint factory, and the building, boat-building and garment industries. One of its employers is Boston Whaler, a fiberglass boat maker); **Holly Hill** (on the Halifax River north of Daytona Beach, made up largely of small industries); **Daytona Beach Shores** (a 5.5-mile strip of hotels, motels and high-rise condominiums); **Ponce Inlet** (home of the Ponce de Leon Inlet Lighthouse at the entrance to the inland waterways); **Lake Helen** (a service-industry community that is popular among bass fishermen and is the town where Nautilus exercise equipment was developed); **Oak Hill** (it has a citrus-growing and packing industry, commercial fishing, and 19th-century homes); **DeBary** (one of Florida's newest incorporated cities); **DeLeon Springs** (primarily a service-industry community); and **Cassadaga** (home of the Southern Cassadaga Spiritualist Camp, a large contingent of mediums, clairvoyants and mind readers).

TOURISM:
About 8 million people are believed to visit the area annually.

HOUSING PRICES:
Median sales price of a single-family existing home in the Daytona Beach metropolitan area was $73,000 in June 1994.

Number of vacant residential lots: 70,805; number of single-family residences: 109,272; mobile homes: 6,793; condominiums: 18,369

EDUCATION:
Number of schools: 69
Number of students enrolled: 53,972
Percentage of students continuing education after high school: 78.05
Teacher-to-pupil ratio: 1:17.9
Average teacher's salary: $28,893

Colleges, universities, and junior or community colleges serving the area:
Stetson University in DeLand; Embry-Riddle Aeronautical University in Daytona Beach; Bethune-Cookman College in Daytona Beach; Daytona Beach Community College; Phillips Junior College of Florida branch in Daytona Beach; Seminole Community College in Sanford; University of Central Florida branch at Daytona Beach; Phoenix College of Aeronautics, Daytona Beach.

Trade and technical schools serving the area:
Daytona Beach Community College

HEALTH CARE:
Number of general hospitals: 8
Number of hospital beds: 1,502
Number of physicians: 591

TAXES: Total county ad-valorem millage rate (1993): 14.1620

STANDARD CRIME RATE: 6,055.4 offenses per 100,000 population (25th out of 67 counties)

LARGEST EMPLOYERS:

Name	Employees	Product/Service
Halifax Medical Center	1,800	Health care
Martin Marietta	1,000	Simulation systems
West Volusia/Fish Memorial Hospital	960	Health care
Sherwood Medical Company	850	Medical devices
The News-Journal Corp.	813	Publishing
Memorial Hospital	578	Health care
Sparton Electronics	500	Sonobuoys
Poe & Brown	450	Insurance
Humana Hospital	365	Health care
Homac Manufacturing Company	350	Electrical connectors
Boston Whaler	325	Fiberglass boats
Brunswick Technical Group/Defense Division	300	Camouflage, electronics

COMPANIES PROVIDING LOCAL UTILITIES:
Telephone: United Telephone Co. and Southern Bell
Electricity: Florida Power Corp., Florida Power & Light Co.; New Smyrna Utilities
Natural Gas: Peoples Gas System, Florida Public Utilities Co., South Florida Natural Gas Co.
Water: NSB Utilities, West Volusia Utilities, cities of Daytona Beach, Holly Hill, DeLand and Edgewater
Major Water Source: Wells
Sanitary Landfill? Yes

POINTS OF INTEREST:
Daytona International Speedway has racing events throughout the year, such as the Daytona 500 in February, supercross, vintage road racing and motorcycle road races in March and the Pepsi 400 NASCAR Winston Cup Series stock car race in July; **Boardwalk on Daytona Beach,** which includes **Ocean Front Park and Bandshell** (a popular concert site), the **Main Street Pier** (where gondola rides are offered over the ocean), and **Boardwalk Amusements** (carnival rides and games); **Daytona Beach Kennel Club** has pari-mutuel wagering and greyhound racing; **Blue Spring State Park** near Orange City is a winter gathering place for manatees, which can be seen from an observation platform from November through April. Area also has an interpretive center, camping, vacation cabins, picnicking, swimming, freshwater fishing, hiking, a ranger-guided canoe tour of the St. Johns River, canoe rentals, boat ramp and concessions; **De Leon**

Springs State Recreation Area near De Leon Springs has picnicking, swimming, freshwater fishing, hiking, canoe rentals, concessions, scuba diving. Area has a spring, once labeled as a fountain of youth; **Bulow Creek State Park,** north of Ormond Beach, has freshwater fishing, hiking and 5,000 acres of coastal hardwood forests and hammock and salt marsh; **Tomoka State Park,** north of Ormond Beach, is site where Indians once lived and today has interpretive center, camping, picnicking, saltwater fishing, hiking, boat ramp, canoe rentals, concessions; **Hontoon Island State Park,** 6 miles west of DeLand, has 80-foot observation tower, camping, picnicking and hiking. It is accessible only by ferry or private boat. Island also has replica of large Indian owl totem and has large Indian mound; **Ponce de Leon Inlet Lighthouse and Museum** has artifacts in three cottages once occupied by lighthouse keepers. Lighthouse, built in 1887, has 213 steps to the top; **Lighthouse Point Park** at Ponce Inlet near the lighthouse has picnicking, swimming, saltwater fishing, hiking; **Klassix Auto Museum,** Daytona Beach, is a collection of Corvettes from each year since 1953; **Sugar Mill Ruins,** New Smyrna Beach, are ruins of a sugar mill that was active in the early 1800s; **Sugar Mill Gardens,** Port Orange, has plantation ruins of an old mill and 12 acres of botanical gardens; **Canaveral National Seashore** stretches from the New Smyrna Beach area to the Kennedy Space Center; **Lake Woodruff National Wildlife Refuge** near DeLand has hiking, fishing, hiking, boating; **Peabody Auditorium** in Daytona Beach (seats more than 2,500); **Ocean Center,** a sports, entertainment and convention center in Daytona Beach (seats 8,400-10,000); **Daytona Flea Market** covers more than 40 acres; **Farmer's Market** at downtown Daytona Beach; **Turtle Mound,** near New Smyrna Beach, has Indian mounds dating back to 2000 B.C.; **Turnbull Ruins,** New Smyrna Beach, the foundation (made of coquina) of a home built by Dr. Andrew Turnbull, founder of the city, in the late 1700s; **Smyrna Dunes Park** at Ponce Inlet has 1.5-mile boardwalk loop, picnicking, beach access ramps; **New Smyrna Speedway** has stock car racing on Saturday nights; **DeBary Hall,** a mansion built in 1871 that is listed on the National Register of Historic Places; **Henry DeLand House** in DeLand is a restored turn-of-the-century home and is headquarters of the DeLand Historical Society; **Spring Garden Ranch,** east of DeLeon Springs, is a winter training center for sulky racing and has trackside restaurant, daily from November through April.

THE ARTS:
Museum of Arts and Sciences in Daytona Beach has a Cuban section, sculpture garden, fossils, planetarium; **The Seaside Music Theater** at Daytona Beach Community College; **Daytona Playhouse** features amateur actors and musicians; **Ormond Beach Performing Arts Center; DeLand Museum of Art; Daytona Beach Community College Gallery of Fine Arts; The Casements,** former mansion of John D. Rockefeller, now operated as a cultural center and museum in Ormond Beach. Among the permanent displays are a Hungarian Folklore Room and a Boy Scout exhibit; **Ormond Beach Memorial Art Museum & Gardens** has art exhibits and three acres of gardens; **Birthplace of Speed Museum** in Ormond Beach traces history of automobile racing; **Gillespie Museum of Minerals** at Stetson University features display of more than 25,000 minerals from around the world; **Halifax Historical Society Museum** in Daytona Beach has artifacts and memorabilia from Volusia County; **Pioneer Settlement** near Barberville is a folk museum with exhibits on lifestyles of early Volusia County settlers; **Sampson Gallery** at Stetson University has artist exhibits that rotate monthly during the school year; **DeLand Historic District; Pope Duncan Gallery** at Stetson University, DeLand, has rotating and permanent collections; **Atlantic Center Dance Company** in the New Smyrna Beach area; **Daytona Beach Civic Ballet; International Folk Dancers; Casement Ballet Company; Bel Canto Singers,** county choral group; **DeLand Little Symphony; Daytona Beach Symphony Society** performs at the Peabody Auditorium; **Daytona Beach Choral Society; Shoe String Theater** in Lake Helen; **Little Theatre** of New Smyrna Beach; **Theater Center Inc.** sponsors the **St. Johns River Players** and the **Storybook Childrens Theater,** both of which are based at the Cultural Arts Center in DeLand. The DeLand Museum of Art and the DeLand Little Symphony are also based here; **Atlantic Center for the Arts** in New Smyrna Beach includes 200-seat amphitheater, art gallery; **Civic Music Inc. of Daytona Beach** gives classical concerts at the Peabody Auditorium; **Gamble Place** and **Spruce Creek Preserve** in Port Orange museum has a turn-of-the-century house; **Mary McLeod Bethune Foundation** museum and national historic landmark in Daytona Beach.

ANNUAL EVENTS:
Last weekend in January: Native American Fesitval, fairgrounds, DeLand; Indian River Native American Festival, New Smyrna Beach; **February:** Daytona 500 race; Art Fiesta at Old Fort Park in New Smyrna Beach; **March:** Frontier Day in Orange City with parade, dance, games, con-

tests, food; **Spring:** Images art festival at Riverside Park in New Smyrna Beach; DeLand Outdoor Art Festival with arts and crafts from around the country; Ormond Art Show at the Casements in Ormond Beach with artists, food; **April:** Magnolia Avenue Celebration, Daytona Beach, is a downtown festival that has food fair, parade and street dances; New Smyrna Beach Jazz Festival; **May:** DeLand's hot air balloon rally at the DeLand Airport; Heritage Day Festival in downtown DeLand celebrates DeLand's early years; **Memorial Day Weekend:** Greater Daytona Beach Striking Fish Tournament, where fishermen on 200 boats compete for prizes; **July:** Pepsi 400 NASCAR Winston Cup Series at the Daytona International Speedway; Daytona Racefest Celebration with NASCAR drivers signing autographs, live entertainment, souvenirs, original race cars; **Around July 4:** Jazz Matazz Celebration at the Casements in Ormond Beach with jazz entertainers, food, exhibits, remote-control car races, fireworks; Port Orange celebration, including fireworks; Edgewater Arts and Craft Show and Bar-b-q, fireworks, Edgewater; **September or October:** King Neptune's Seafood Harvest in downtown Daytona Beach and Riverfront Park has arts and crafts, seafood from local restaurants, boat show; Deland-St. Johns River Firemen's Raft Race; Mullet Festival in Oak Hill; **October:** Biketoberfest/Fall Cycle Scene Championship Cup Series at Daytona International Speedway includes a family festival; Oak Hill Seafood Festival has food, arts and crafts, music; Octoberfest in Orange City; Ormond Senior Games at Ormond Beach Senior Center; **Late October/Early November:** Volusia County Fair and Youth Show near DeLand; **October or November:** Daytona Beach International Air Show, at Daytona Beach International Airport; **November:** Daytona Beach Greek Festival; Birthplace of Speed Antique Car Show and Swap Meet in Ormond Beach features gaslight parade of horseless carriages, flea market; Halifax Art Festival at the Daytona Beach Community College; Barberville Fall Country Jamboree at the Pioneer Settlement grounds; Fall Festival of the Arts, DeLand; Edgewater Folk Art Festival in Edgewater; Daytona Beach Fall Speedway Spectacular Car Show and Swap meet, Thanksgiving weekend; **December:** Enduro World Championship Karting Road races at Daytona International Speedway; Festival of Trees at Ocean Center in Daytona Beach; Port Orange Christmas parade; DeLand Jaycees Christmas Parade (first Saturday in December); DeLand Christmas Boat Parade; Candlelight Tour of Historic Homes in Deland; New Smyrna Beach Christmas Parade; City of Edgewater Christmas Parade; Orange City Christmas Parade

SPORTS AND LEISURE ACTIVITIES:
Most popular local fishing areas: Lake Monroe, Halifax River, Atlantic Ocean, Tomoka River, St. Johns River
Number of local golf courses: 28
Public beaches: Yes
Tennis courts available to the public? Yes
Boating? Yes
Number of pleasure boats registered in the county (1991-92): 18,417

SERVICES FOR RETIREES:
Volusia County Council on Aging with offices in Daytona Beach, New Smyrna and DeLand, Community Care for the Elderly (provides services such as personal care, homemaker, adult day care), Meals on Wheels, Senior Nutrition and Activity Program and Retired Senior Volunteer Program; mini-vans used by hospitals for pickup and return trips for outpatients.

FINANCIAL SERVICES:
Number of local banks: 109
Number of local savings and loan associations: 22

THE MEDIA:
Largest local newspaper: *Daytona Beach News-Journal*
Cable television? Yes

MAJOR LOCAL RETAILERS:
Burdines, Bealls, Belk-Lindsey, K mart, Wal-Mart, JCPenney, Sears, Byrons, Dillard's.

FOOD ESTABLISHMENTS: 1,513

OTHER SERVICES:
Number of local libraries: 13
Number of local hotels/motels: 337
Number of churches: Protestant: 146; Jewish: 4; Catholic: 11; Other: 18

TOURISM INQUIRIES:
Convention and Visitor's Bureau for the **Daytona Beach** Area, 126 E. Orange Ave., Daytona Beach, 32114. Telephone: 904-255-0415; The Chamber of **Daytona Beach** and **Halifax Area**, P.O. Box 2475, Daytona Beach, 32115-2475. Telephone: 904-255-0981; **DeLand** Area Chamber of Commerce, P.O. Box 629, DeLand, 32721-0629. Telephone: 904-734-4331; **Deltona** Area Chamber of Commerce, 682 Deltona Blvd., Deltona, 32725. Telephone: 407-574-5522; **Holly Hill** Chamber of Commerce, P.O. Box 615, Holly Hill, 32017. Telephone: 904-255-7311; **New Smyrna Beach-Edgewater-Oak Hill** Chamber of Commerce, 115 Canal St., New Smyrna Beach, 32168. Telephone: 904-428-2449; Greater **Orange City** Area Chamber of Commerce, 520 N. Volusia Ave., Orange City, 32763. Telephone: 904-775-2793; **Ormond Beach** Chamber of Commerce, 165 W. Granada Blvd., P.O. Box 874, Ormond Beach, 32174. Telephone: 904-677-3454; **Port Orange/South Daytona** Chamber of Commerce, 3431 Ridgewood Ave., Port Orange, 32119. Telephone: 904-761-1601

Central Florida revolves around the tourism industry. Among the attractions are Disney World, which includes the Magic Kingdom; and Cypress Gardens, with Southern Belles in handmade gowns and more than 8,000 varieties of plants and flowers.

CENTRAL FLORIDA

THE COUNTIES: Highlands, Lake, Marion, Orange, Osceola, Polk, Seminole and Sumter

MAJOR CITIES: Orlando, Lakeland and Ocala

TOP INDUSTRIES: Tourism, retail sales, services, defense, agriculture (mainly citrus), horse farming, high-tech manufacturing, phosphate mining

MAJOR NEWSPAPER: *The Orlando Sentinel*

WEATHER:
On the first line is the average maximum temperature for each month; the second line, the average minimum temperature; the third line, the amount of precipitation, in inches, for 1990, from national weather stations.

Orlando	Jan.	Feb.	Mar.	Apr.	May	June	July	Aug.	Sep.	Oct.	Nov.	Dec.
Max.	76.9	79.3	80.6	81.9	89.9	91.6	92.0	93.1	91.6	85.9	79.2	77.5
Min.	54.6	58.9	58.0	61.1	68.8	72.2	73.6	73.9	72.4	68.3	59.3	55.1
Precp.	0.2	4.1	1.9	1.7	0.6	6.2	6.7	3.8	2.5	2.1	1.1	0.8

Lakeland	Jan.	Feb.	Mar.	Apr.	May	June	July	Aug.	Sep.	Oct.	Nov.	Dec.
Max.	78.9	81.4	82.3	84.9	91.6	93.9	94.0	94.4	93.1	87.6	80.2	77.2
Min.	55.4	58.7	57.5	60.7	69.4	72.1	73.2	73.1	72.3	67.5	59.4	54.9
Precp.	0.4	4.3	1.2	1.2	4.4	7.2	7.7	6.4	3.3	2.2	0.9	0.4

HIGHLANDS County
Central
County seat: Sebring

POPULATION: 1990: 68,432
 1993: 73,203
 Increase: 7 percent

AGE DISTRIBUTION (1992) IN PERCENTAGES:
 0-14 : 16.1
 15-44: 29.1
 45-64: 21.4
 65+ : 33.4

MUNICIPAL POPULATION:
AVON PARK: 1990: 8,078; 1993: 8,169
LAKE PLACID: 1990: 1,158; 1993: 1,282
SEBRING: 1990: 8,841; 1993: 8,959
UNINCORPORATED: 1990: 50,355; 1993: 54,793

LAND AREA: 1,029 square miles
POPULATION DENSITY: 71 people per square mile (39th in the state)

Highlands County sits in the middle of the state between Sarasota on the Gulf coast and Fort Pierce on the east coast. Agriculture and tourism are the important staples in the county, where agribusiness has grown by 475 percent in the past 25 years. The county ranks fifth in the state in citrus production. Consequently, much of the acreage is taken up with groves, ranches and farm-lands. Sebring is also home to a number of cultural activities, from a cultural center that includes a civic center and an art league to the Lakeside Playhouse of Highlands Little Theatre, which has dinner theatre shows.

But the city is perhaps best-known for another reason — racing. Every March, the 12-hour endurance auto race is held at the Sebring Race Track and draws thousands of spectators.

Hospitals are a leading employer in the county. Along with citrus, other major products include mowers and fertilizers, fiberglass boats, corrugated boxes and packaging materials. Outdoor recreational activities are popular at the 3,020-acre Lake Jackson and Highlands Hammock State Park, a 3,800-acre wildlife sanctuary. Fish catches include perch, speck, bream, catfish and largemouth bass. For hunters, quail, dove, rabbit, wild boar, squirrel and deer are found at the Avon Park Wildlife Management Area. The county ranks second behind Charlotte County in having the largest percentage of residents age 65 and over.

POPULATION DURING THE TOURIST SEASON: Doubles during the winter.

HOUSING PRICES:
Homes: Typically around $60,000; condominiums: around $45,000; mobile homes: about $25,000; lots, around $7,000
Number of vacant residential lots: 70,399; number of single-family residences: 23,045; mobile homes: 5,135; condominiums: 1,431

EDUCATION:
Number of schools: 15
Number of students enrolled: 9,999
Percentage of students continuing education after high school: 71.36
Teacher-to-pupil ratio: 1:19.6
Average teacher's salary: $29,796

Colleges, universities, and junior or community colleges serving the area:
South Florida Community College, Avon Park

Trade and technical schools serving the area:
South Florida Community College

HEALTH CARE:
Number of general hospitals: 2
Number of hospital beds: 277
Number of physicians: 117

TAXES: Total county ad-valorem millage rate (1993): 17.6280

STANDARD CRIME RATE: 6,289.4 offenses per 100,000 population (20th out of 67 counties)

LARGEST PRIVATE EMPLOYERS:

Name	Employees	Product/Service
Walker Memorial Medical Center	784	Health care
Highlands Regional Medical Center	400	Health care
LESCO	225	Mowers/fertilizer
United Telephone Co.	166	Communications
Consolidated-Tomoka	165	Citrus packing
Wellcraft Marine	161	Fiberglass boats
Barnett Bank	152	Banking
Ben Hill Griffin	150	Citrus
Georgia Pacific	136	Corrugated boxes
Lin Pac Plastics	100	Packaging

COMPANIES PROVIDING LOCAL UTILITIES:
Telephone: United Telephone Co.

Electricity: Florida Power Corp.; Sebring Utilities Commission; Peace River Co-op; Glades Rural Electric
Natural Gas: Peoples Gas System
Water: City of Sebring and other municipalities; Water Management District-South Florida
Major Water Source: Wells
Sanitary Landfill? Yes

POINTS OF INTEREST:
Highlands Hammock State Park, a 3,800-acre wildlife sanctuary; **Avon Park Wildlife Management Area,** 150,000-acre tract east of Avon Park, for boating, camping and hunting in season.

THE ARTS:
Cultural Center Complex on Lake Jackson includes the public library and historical society archives, a civic center, the **Highlands Art League,** which offers art courses and has frequent exhibitions in its **Museum of the Arts,** and the **Lakeside Playhouse of Highlands Little Theatre,** which has dinner theatre shows in the spring and summer; South Florida Community College presents a series of concerts, musicals and dance programs and a 10-week "Enrichment for Seniors" afternoon series; **Highlands County Concert Band, Delta Chorale, Sweet Adelines** and the **Highlands Concert Orchestra** all have programs during the fall and winter seasons; **pavilion** at Firemens' Field has 5,000-seat capacity; and **Highlands County Agri-Civic Center** hosts civic and social functions.

ANNUAL EVENTS:
January: Lake Placid Art League Annual Art Show; **February:** Highlands County Fair, county fairgrounds; Lake Placid Arts & Crafts Show; **March:** 12 Hours of Sebring Endurance Race at Sebring Race Track; **May:** Roaring Twenties Day, a Sebring festival where merchants line the streets, dressed in early 1900s styles, to sell goods at reduced prices; **July:** Annual Fourth of July celebrations at Avon Park, Lake Placid and Sebring; **October:** Lake Placid Caladium Festival; **November:** Annual Highlands Art Festival in Sebring; Christmas Parade, Avon Park; **December:** Annual Christmas parade at Sebring; Carousel of Lights, Sebring on the circle; Christmas Parade in Lake Placid; Christmas on Main Street in Avon Park.

SPORTS AND LEISURE ACTIVITIES:
Most popular local fishing area: Lake Jackson
Golf courses? Yes
Public beaches: Yes
Tennis courts available to the public? Yes
Boating? Yes
Number of pleasure boats registered in the county (1991-92): 7,577

SERVICES FOR RETIREES:
Nu Hope of Highlands County

FINANCIAL SERVICES:
Number of local banks: 15
Number of local savings and loan associations: 15

THE MEDIA:
Largest local newspaper: *News-Sun*
Cable television? Yes

MAJOR LOCAL RETAILERS:
Wal-Mart, Byrons, JCPenney, K mart, Belk-Lindsey

FOOD ESTABLISHMENTS: 208

OTHER SERVICES:
Number of local libraries: 4
Number of local hotels/motels: 25
Number of churches: Protestant: 111; Jewish: 1; Catholic: 3; Other: 12

TOURISM INQUIRIES:
Greater Sebring Chamber of Commerce, 309 S. Circle, Sebring, 33870. Telephone: 813-385-8448

LAKE County
Central
County seat: Tavares

POPULATION: 1990: 152,104
1993: 167,167
Increase: 9.0 percent

AGE DISTRIBUTION (1992) IN PERCENTAGES:
0-14 : 17.0
15-44: 33.1
45-64: 21.9
65+ : 28.0

MUNICIPAL POPULATION:
ASTATULA: 1990: 981; 1993: 1,056
CLERMONT: 1990: 6,910; 1993: 7,013
EUSTIS: 1990: 12,856; 1993: 13,711
FRUITLAND PARK: 1990: 2,715; 1993: 2,810
GROVELAND: 1990: 2,300; 1993: 2,373
HOWEY-IN-THE-HILLS: 1990: 724; 1993: 735
LADY LAKE: 1990: 8,071; 1993: 11,117
LEESBURG: 1990: 14,783; 1993: 14,963
MASCOTTE: 1990: 1,761; 1993: 1,997
MINNEOLA: 1990: 1,515; 1993: 1,783
MONTVERDE: 1990: 890; 1993: 1,051
MOUNT DORA: 1990: 7,316; 1993: 7,606
TAVARES: 1990: 7,383; 1993: 7,766
UMATILLA: 1990: 2,350; 1993: 2,376
UNINCORPORATED: 1990: 81,549; 1993: 90,810

LAND AREA: 953 square miles
POPULATION DENSITY: 175 people per square mile (26th in the state)

There is a good reason why this county, which is just west of Orange County, was named Lake — it has hundreds of lakes. Water-skiers come here to train and scuba divers choose the area as a favorite spot. Citrus is a major contributor to the economy, although freezes in the 1980s forced some farmers to look for hardier crops such as watermelon, corn, tomatoes and strawberries. The county also has some light industry and horticulture developments. Among the major employers are five citrus companies. Other major local firms are a golf and tennis resort; a metal fabricator; and a building supplier.

Among the prominent cities are **Leesburg:** Situated between Lake Griffin and Lake Harris, the city is a finance and business hub. It also devotes a lot of its resources to recreation. About 15 percent of its land area, or 155 acres, is reserved for parks and recreation — from tennis to horseshoe pits, golf, nature trails and lakes. One of its noted spots is Venetian Gardens, which is operated by the city and sits on 80 acres on Lake Harris. Future plans call for a marina, a hotel, restaurants, shops and a boardwalk to be added to the area. One of its most popular annual events is the Megabucks B.A.S.S. Tournament, which lures bass anglers to compete for hundreds of thousands of dollars in prize money; **Mount Dora:** A retirement community that also is becoming more of a bedroom town for Orlando-area commuters, is a New England-style community where one of the mottos is "Escape to Yesterday." It is also known as the antique capital of central Florida. Most of the housing consists of single-family homes, some condominiums and, on the outskirts, several mobile-home parks. The city is on a bluff overlooking the six-mile-long, 3,600-acre Lake Dora. This is also the home of the Lakeside Inn, a turn-of-the-century resort that's listed on the National Register of Historic Places, and Sandybrook Center of Rebound, a 36-bed head-injury rehabilitation center. Among Mount Dora's largest employers is Sundor Brands; **Eustis:** Once mostly reliant on citrus production, the city today also has a number of industries in other fields, including Mercer Products (vinyl flooring and stair treads) and Shasta Beverages (carbonated beverages). Among those who have lived here in recent years are Nobel Prize-winning physicist Robert Shrieffer and astronaut David M. Walker. There also is a farmers and flea market at the Lake County Fairgrounds; **Tavares:** Starting here, connecting waterways enable boaters to get to the Atlantic Coast. Going from the Dora Canal and continuing on Lake Eustis, Haines Creek, Lake Griffin and the Oklawaha River, boaters can reach Silver Springs, Lake George and the St. Johns River to Jacksonville and then the Atlantic. The mile-long Dora Canal is very scenic; **Lady Lake:** The second-fastest-growing city in the state from 1980-90 in population percentage (the increase was 576.5 percent); **Umatilla:** home of the Harry-Anna Crippled Children's Hospital, owned and operated by the Elks.

TOURISM:
The season generally runs from October to April, with population increases estimated at any-where from 15 percent to 30 percent.

HOUSING PRICES:
Average countywide price in the high 60s in recent years, ranging roughly from the mid-50s for a two-bedroom home to about $100,000 for a four-bedroom. In Mount Dora, prices range generally from $50,000 to $300,000 and up. Lake access lots start around $85,000 and lakefront homes typically are $150,000-plus.
Number of vacant residential lots: 18,602; number of single-family residences: 38,454; mobile homes: 16,812; condominiums: 2,450

EDUCATION:
Number of schools: 44
Number of students enrolled: 22,669
Percentage of students continuing education after high school: 39.59
Teacher-to-pupil ratio: 1:18.5
Average teacher's salary: $29,770

Colleges, universities, and junior or community colleges serving the area:
University of Central Florida, Orlando; University of Florida, Gainesville; University of South Florida, Tampa; Florida Southern College, Lakeland; Bethune Cookman College, Daytona Beach; Rollins College, Winter Park; Stetson University, DeLand; Lake-Sumter Community College, Leesburg; Valencia Community College, Orlando; Seminole Community College, Sanford.

Trade and technical schools serving the area:
Lake-Sumter Community College, Leesburg; Seminole Community College, Sanford; Valencia Community College, Orlando; Lake County Area Vocational-Technical Center, Eustis; Orlando Vo-Tech Center; Winter Park Vo-Tech.

HEALTH CARE:
Number of general hospitals: 5
Number of hospital beds: 584
Number of physicians: 214

TAXES: Total county ad-valorem millage rate (1993): 14.5900

STANDARD CRIME RATE: 4,347.7 offenses per 100,000 population (41st out of 67 counties)

LARGEST PRIVATE EMPLOYERS:

Name	Employees	Product/Service
Golden Gem Growers	700	Citrus
Coca-Cola Food Division (Minute Maid)	455	Citrus juice
Mission Inn Golf/Tennis Resort	230	Resort
Sundor Brands	210	Citrus
Growers Container Co-op	190	Citrus
Silver Springs Citrus	158	Citrus
White Aluminum Products	155	Metal fabricators
Clermont Builders Supply	95	Construction
Wolverine Gasket Company	65	Auto parts manufacturing
Exceletech Inc.	46	Steel manufacture/ fabrication

COMPANIES PROVIDING LOCAL UTILITIES:
Telephone: United Telephone Co.
Electricity: Florida Power, Sumter Electric Co-op, City of Leesburg

Natural Gas: Florida Gas, Peoples Gas, Lake Apopka, City of Leesburg
Water: Municipalities
Major Water Source: Rivers
Sanitary Landfill? Yes

POINTS OF INTEREST:
Lake Griffin State Recreation Area in Fruitland Park has camping, picnicking, freshwater fishing, hiking, boat ramp; **Lake Louisa State Park,** seven miles southwest of Clermont, has picnicking, swimming, freshwater fishing in Lake Louisa, canoeing; **Ocala National Forest** has swimming, canoeing, nature trails, camping; **226-foot Citrus Tower** near Clermont offers view of area hills and lakes; **Venetian Gardens** on Lake Harris has public beach, boat ramps, shuffleboard and tennis courts, baseball fields; **Lake Dora; Lake County Fairground's expo building** near Eustis is used for weekly flea market, concerts and dances; **Mount Dora**: three-mile, self-guided historic tour of the city (map available from local Chamber of Commerce); a dozen antique shops scattered throughout the downtown area; **Renninger's Antique Center** in Mount Dora (a sizeable antiques and collectibles market and flea market open weekends year-round); **Palm Island nature preserve,** which has the longest boardwalk on a lake in Florida; **Evans Park,** which is noted for its lawn bowling; and **Gilbert Park,** which has a lighthouse; **Tavares: Magnolia Tree** in Magnolia Park (believed to be one of the largest of its kind in the state); tours along the **Dora Canal,** which is between Lake Dora and Lake Eustis (seen along the mile-long trip are birds, jungle-like vegetation and cypress trees; tours are conducted seasonally); **Civic Center** at Ridge Park.

THE ARTS:
Leesburg: Arts and Cultural Center at Venetian Gardens; **Melon Patch Players** present plays from September through May; **Mount Dora: Mount Dora Center for the Arts; Royellou Museum,** a local historical museum located in a former jail (open Wednesday through Saturday in the winter); **IceHouse Players,** a community theater with scheduled performances throughout the year; and a local series of classical and/or popular-music concerts in the winter; **Tavares: Lake County Historical Society** has collections of historical papers and other artifacts relating to the area; **Fruitland Park: Lake County Dinner Theater; Eustis: Bay Street Players** stage productions each year and a young persons theater; **Clermont: House of Presidents** wax museum.

ANNUAL EVENTS:
February: Washington Birthday Festival in Eustis has floats, marching bands, drill teams, fireworks, arts and crafts show, sailing regatta, pie-eating contest, food booths, street dance. The event is the oldest continually running festival in the state; Megabucks B.A.S.S. Tournament in Leesburg, with a $100,000 first prize for bass anglers; Art Festival in downtown Mount Dora draws 240,000 people the first full weekend of the month to see works of 280 U.S. artists; **March:** Antique Boat Festival on the shore of Lake Dora the fourth weekend of the month. Features around 100 wooden-hull boats from the U.S. and Canada; Leesburg Fine Arts and Craft Festival at Venetian Gardens; **April:** Lake Agriculture & Youth Fair, Eustis; Sailing Regatta, where about 150 boats race on Lake Dora, last weekend of the month; Antique Auto Show and Tour in Mount Dora, displaying antique and classic cars, first weekend of the month; **May:** Art in the Park, Mount Dora, first weekend of the month; **July:** Fourth of July fireworks in Leesburg; All-American Celebration in Tavares including fireworks and a Firecracker Sprint Triathlon; **October:** Dora Invitational Golf Tournament, second weekend of the month (156 amateur players); three-day Bicycle Festival in Mount Dora for 1,500 cyclists, third weekend of the month; Craft Fair, downtown Mount Dora, fourth weekend of the month, with 200 craftspersons; **November:** International Folk Festival in Eustis; Christmas by the Lake arts and crafts show in Tavares; Great Floridian Triathlon in Clermont; Fall Festival Arts and Crafts Show in Umatilla; **December:** Light Up Ceremony in Clermont; Light up Tavares; Christmas Lighting of Mount Dora, a month-long festival of more than 100,000 tiny white lights in the village square area. Lights are turned on at dusk each day until New Year's Day; first Friday, Christmas parade in Leesburg.

SPORTS AND LEISURE ACTIVITIES:
Most popular local fishing areas: "Chain-of-Lakes" through which boaters can get to the St. Johns River and the Atlantic Ocean, including Lake Beauclaire, Lake Dora, Lake Eustis, Lake Griffin, Lake Harris, Little Lake Harris, Lake Apopka, Lake Carlton. Also, Haines Creek and the Dora Canal. Among the most popular catches are bass, blue bream, speckled perch, shellcracker, catfish.
Number of local golf courses: At least 8

Public beaches: Yes
Tennis courts available to the public? Yes
Boating? Yes
Number of pleasure boats registered in the county (1991-92): 15,554

SERVICES FOR RETIREES:
Lake County Council on Aging in Leesburg; Senior Service Center in Eustis; Meals on Wheels.

FINANCIAL SERVICES:
Number of local banks: 49
Number of local savings and loan associations: 12

THE MEDIA:
Largest local newspaper: *Daily Commercial* (Leesburg)
Cable television? Yes

MAJOR LOCAL RETAILERS:
K mart, Bealls, Wal-Mart, Belk Lindsey, JCPenney and Sears.

FOOD ESTABLISHMENTS: 466

OTHER SERVICES:
Number of local libraries: 7
Number of local hotels/motels: 51
Number of churches: Protestant: 220; Jewish: 1; Catholic: 5; Other: 9

TOURISM INQUIRIES:
Greater **Eustis** Area Chamber of Commerce, One Orange Ave., P.O. Box 1210, Eustis, 32726-1210. Telephone: 904-357-3434; **Leesburg** Area Chamber of Commerce, P.O. Box 490309, Leesburg, 34749-0309. Telephone: 904-787-2131; **Mount Dora** Chamber of Commerce, P.O. Box 196, Mount Dora, 32757-0196. Telephone 904-383-2165; **Tavares** Chamber of Commerce, P.O. Box 697, Tavares, 32778. Telephone: 904-343-2531.

MARION County
Central
County seat: Ocala

POPULATION: 1990: 194,835
1993: 212,025
Increase: 8.8 percent

AGE DISTRIBUTION (1992) IN PERCENTAGES:
0-14 : 18.9
15-44: 36.7
45-64: 21.9
65+ : 22.5

MUNICIPAL POPULATION:
BELLEVIEW:1990: 2,678; 1993: 3,106
DUNNELLON: 1990: 1,639; 1993: 1,705
McINTOSH: 1990: 411; 1993: 410
OCALA: 1990: 42,045; 1993: 42,400
REDDICK: 1990: 554; 1993: 570
UNINCORPORATED: 1990: 147,508; 1993: 163,834

LAND AREA: 1,579 square miles
POPULATION DENSITY: 134 people per square mile (30th in the state)

An area known for its horse farms and Florida's Silver Springs attraction, Marion County is located in the middle of the state, south of Gainesville. The county, with tall oaks and more hills than many other Florida areas, has about 600 horse farms and training centers, some offering tours of their facilities. Thoroughbreds are raised on most of these farms and a number of race winners have been produced here, including Needles, the 1956 winner of the Kentucky Derby, and Unbridled, the 1990 winner. This industry here employs more than 21,750 workers, and the annual economic impact from the thoroughbred industry alone is estimated at nearly $1 billion. Silver Springs, one of the state's major tourist attractions, has become famous for its glass-bottom-boat rides over clear-water springs and was the site of the filming of some "Sea Hunt" television episodes. The park also offers jungle cruises and reptile shows and is home to a host of animals, from alligators to llamas.

The largest manufacturer in Marion County is Mark III Industries, a van-conversion firm. Among the county's other major firms are Emergency One Inc., which produces firefighting and rescue equipment; a steel rod producer, two hospitals, several grocers and Martin Marietta, which not long ago was the largest employer in the county but, like other aerospace industries, has experienced recent employee cutbacks.

The area is also one of Florida's largest cattle-producing counties; also, cantelope, peanuts, tomatoes, watermelons, wheat, corn, soybeans and hay are grown on the more than 1,200 farms here.

The county attracts a lot of retirees; as of 1992, 22.5 percent of its year-round population was age 65 and older, up from 19.5 percent in 1988.

TOURISM:
There are two tourist seasons here, from January to April and from June to August. The county population increases about 5 percent during these periods.

HOUSING PRICES:
Median sales price of a single-family existing home in the Ocala metropolitan area was $59,400 in June 1994.
Number of vacant residential lots: 123,978; number of single-family residences: 50,791; mobile homes: 18,033; condominiums: 5,299

EDUCATION:
Number of schools: 43
Number of students enrolled: 32,702
Percentage of students continuing education after high school: 32.52
Teacher-to-pupil ratio: 1:17.6
Average teacher's salary: $27,979

Colleges, universities, and junior or community colleges serving the area:
Central Florida Community College in Ocala; University of Florida in Gainesville

Trade and technical schools serving the area:
Central Florida Community College

HEALTH CARE:
Number of general hospitals: 3
Number of hospital beds: 645
Number of physicians: 289

TAXES: Total county ad-valorem millage rate (1993): 15.6810

STANDARD CRIME RATE: 6,157.3 offenses per 100,000 population (21st out of 67 counties)

LARGEST PRIVATE EMPLOYERS:

Name	Employees	Product/Service
Mark III Industries	1,860	Van conversions
Munroe Regional Medical Center	1,500	Health care
Emergency One Inc.	1,150	Firefighting/rescue equipment
HCA Marion Community Hospital	850	Health care
Publix	843	Grocery
Winn-Dixie	782	Grocery
Clairson International	710	Steel rod products
K mart Distribution Center	600	Retail sales
Martin Marietta	600	Electronics
Certified Grocers-Eli Witt Division	530	Distribution

COMPANIES PROVIDING LOCAL UTILITIES:
Telephone: United Telephone Co.
Electricity: Clay Electric Co-op, Florida Power, City of Ocala and Sumter Electric Corp.
Natural Gas: West Florida Natural Gas
Water: City of Ocala

Major Water Source: Wells
Sanitary Landfill? Yes

POINTS OF INTEREST:
Florida's Silver Springs in Silver Springs has glass-bottom-boat rides over clear-water springs; a Jeep Safari ride among more than 60 species of animals; a Jungle Cruise ride that gives visitors a glimpse of animals in their natural settings; and a petting zoo, where llamas, goats and deer eat from visitors' hands; **Silver Springs Wild Waters** has a wave pool with 4-foot-high surf, volleyball, miniature golf, game room; horse farms, some with tours of the facilities and training shows; **Ocala National Forest** in eastern Marion County with camping, fishing, hiking and swimming; **Don Garlits Museum of Drag Racing** in Belleview has collection of cars on display; **Ocala Jai Alai; Ocala Miniature Harness Racing.**

THE ARTS:
Appleton Museum of Art in Ocala, with collections from the Orient, Central and South America; **Ocala Civic Theatre** is the site of a regular season of plays and musicals; **Marion Performing Ballet; Ocala Dance Theatre; Marion Chamber Music Society; Marion Civic Chorale; Ocala Festival Orchestra.**

ANNUAL EVENTS:
March: Brick City Day with arts and crafts, food, parade in Ocala; St. Patrick's Day Parade in Ocala; **April:** Boom Town Days in Dunnellon; Ma Barker Day in Oklawaha; **May:** Founders Day in Belleview; Horse and Buggy Days, Reddick; **June:** Florida Blueberry Festival in Ocala; **July 4:** God and Country Day in Ocala; **August:** Ocalifest in Ocala; **September:** Shriner's Rodeo and Parade in Ocala; **October:** Marion County Fair; McIntosh Festival; Florida Horse and Agriculture Festival; Dunnellon Fall Festival; **November:** Light Up Ocala; Festival of Trees at the Appleton Museum; **December:** Chamber of Commerce Sunshine Christmas Parade.

SPORTS AND LEISURE ACTIVITIES:
Most popular local fishing areas: Withlacoochee River, Oklawaha River, Lake Weir, Lake Oklawaha and Lake Bryant
Number of local golf courses: 16
Public beaches? No
Tennis courts available to the public? Yes
Boating? Yes
Number of pleasure boats registered in the county (1991-92): 13,676

SERVICES FOR RETIREES:
Meals on Wheels; Marion County Senior Services (helps with special transportation needs)

FINANCIAL SERVICES:
Number of local banks: 48
Number of local savings and loan associations: 17

THE MEDIA:
Largest local newspaper: *Ocala Star-Banner*
Cable television? Yes

MAJOR LOCAL RETAILERS:
Burdines, Belk-Lindsey, Bealls, Kmart, JCPenney and Sears, Wal-Mart, Montgomery Ward.

FOOD ESTABLISHMENTS: 625

OTHER SERVICES:
Number of local libraries: 4
Number of local hotels/motels: 78
Number of churches: Protestant: 258; Jewish: 2; Catholic: 10

TOURISM INQUIRIES:
Ocala/Marion County Chamber of Commerce, 110 East Silver Springs Blvd, P.O. Box 1210, Ocala, 34478. Telephone: 904-629-8051.

ORANGE County
Central
County seat: Orlando

POPULATION: 1990: 677,491
1993: 727,780
Increase: 7.4 percent

AGE DISTRIBUTION (1992) IN PERCENTAGES:
0-14 : 21.0
15-44: 49.7
45-64: 18.2
65+ : 11.1

MUNICIPAL POPULATION:
APOPKA: 1990: 13,611; 1993: 16,307
BAY LAKE: 1990: 19; 1993: 24
BELLE ISLE: 1990: 5,272; 1993: 5,575
EATONVILLE: 1990: 2,505; 1993: 2,470
EDGEWOOD: 1990: 1,062; 1993: 1,111
LAKE BUENA VISTA: 1990: 1,776; 1993: 23
MAITLAND: 1990: 8,932; 1993: 9,096
OAKLAND: 1990: 700; 1993: 746
OCOEE: 1990: 12,778; 1993: 16,418
ORLANDO: 1990: 164,674; 1993: 172,019
WINDERMERE: 1990: 1,371; 1993: 1,667
WINTER GARDEN: 1990: 9,863; 1993: 11,685
WINTER PARK: 1990: 22,623; 1993: 24,197
UNINCORPORATED: 1990: 432,305; 1993: 466,442

LAND AREA: 908 square miles
POPULATION DENSITY: 802 people per square mile (7th in state)

There are few who will argue that without Disney, Orlando would be nothing like it is today. The presence of Disney World 20 miles from the city has made the area the No. 1 tourist destination in the United States. Estimates on the number of visitors each year range from 12 million to more than 20 million.

But there is another side to Disney's presence — some people unaffectionately call Mickey Mouse the "mouse that ate Orlando." The surge of tourists has brought Orlando an array of problems, not the least of which is crowded roadways. Try getting from your downtown Orlando hotel to Disney World and you'll fast discover that you're spending a good deal of your vacation time creeping along in stop-and-go traffic. Some might view it as biting the hand that feeds them, but a growing number of residents are expressing their unhappiness with Disney. When the company approached the state legislature years ago on its plan to build an amusement park in Florida, legislators were quick to please and even allowed Disney to create its own government. Today, some Orlando area officials question the wisdom of that, as Disney to them has become an overbearing neighbor at times. Disney, these Orlando officials say, is growing too fast, causing Orlando more growth headaches. Disney, which employs more than 39,000 area residents, replies that it has always been "a good neighbor to Florida."

Overall, Orange County, centrally located in the state, offers a variety of lifestyles, from Orlando to smaller-size areas such as Windermere. Besides Disney, the county is home to a number of other attractions, from Universal Studios to Sea World, both popular tourist stops. The area also has become one of the fastest-growing business areas in the country. From 1980 to 1987, 38 percent of the $4.3 billion worth of new industry that came to Florida was invested in Orlando. This led to a 66 percent rise in employment during that period. Today, the Metro Orlando Economic Development Commission of Mid-Florida says that labor force growth in the metro Orlando area continues on the upswing and more than 130,000 new jobs between 1992 and 1995 are expected. Nearly half of Orlando's work force is employed at white-collar jobs and more than one third of metro Orlando's residents earn a living in the service industry.

This business growth has not gone unnoticed. For example, Fortune magazine has named Orlando as one of the top 10 U.S. cities best able to meet the challenges of global competition in the 21st century, citing the area's tourism, high-technology, quality of life and transportation mix. High-tech manufacturing, especially, has been a growing field in recent years, namely in the areas of laser technology, computer simulation and silicon chip manufacturing. So much, in fact, that Business Week magazine has labeled the area's laser industry as one of the fastest growing high-tech areas in the country.

Among the Fortune 500 companies that have corporate or regional headquarters here are: American Automobile Association, Tupperware Home Parties, Westinghouse's Steam Turbine Division, General Mills Restaurant Group, Harcourt Brace Jovanovich, Dixon Ticonderoga (a pencil manufacturer), and AT&T.

Still, the service industry is No. 1 as Disney World continues to be king of the state's attractions and has helped foster phenomenal growth in the hotel industry. As of 1994, the metropolitan Orlando area, which also takes in surrounding counties, had more hotel rooms (about 85,000) than any other place in the country, including New York City and the Los Angeles region. It is estimated that tourists and delegates visiting Orlando pump more than $5 billion into the region's economy each year.

Orlando area officials estimate that each week, 1,194 new residents move in, 197,731 visitors arrive, 213 people are married, 271 births are recorded and retail sales total $126 million.

Also booming in recent years has been the housing industry. In 1992, for example, the value of building permits and new housing units in Orange County was more than $1 billion, fourth in the state behind Dade, Palm Beach and Broward counties.

Citrus traditionally has been the top industry in western Orange County, which has many packing houses and processing installations and is mostly an agricultural area. Thousands of people here are employed in this industry.

Other cities in the county include: **Apopka:** Big business here is the foliage industry — Apopka is known as "the indoor foliage capital of the world," producing about 60 percent of all the foliage grown in the world. The name "Apopka" is Indian for "Big Potato" or "Potato Eating Place." Settled in the 1840s, the city built a Masonic Lodge in 1859 that remains on the original site and has the distinction of having the oldest lodge room in Florida. Because of the area's agricultural ties, a number of migrant workers earn their living here; **Windermere:** Known for its upscale housing, the area has been called the "Beverly Hills of Florida;" **Winter Park** has no mobile home parks within the city limits. But it does have Park Avenue, a mile-long area of chic and expensive shops, boutiques, art galleries, restaurants and stores that sell antiques, jewelry and perfume; **Maitland,** in northern Orange, is primarily a residential city made up almost entirely of single-family residences. It has an art center and a holocaust memorial center; **Winter Garden** in western Orange County lies in citrus country and encompasses 3.5 square miles.

TOURISM:
The tourist season is year-round. About 14 million tourists visited metropolitan Orlando in 1993, according to Orlando estimates, making the area the top tourist destination in the United States.

HOUSING PRICES:
Median sales price of a single-family existing home was $91,100 in the metropolitan Orlando area in June 1994.

Vacant residential lots: 34,061; single-family residences: 173,977; mobile homes: 3,850; condominiums: 23,260

EDUCATION:
Number of local schools: 152
Number of students enrolled: 113,638
Percentage of students continuing education after high school: 73.99
Teacher-to-pupil ratio: 1:17.3
Average teacher's salary: $29,740

Colleges, universities, and junior or community colleges serving the area:
University of Central Florida, Orlando; Florida Tech branch campus, Orlando; Florida Southern College branch campus at Orlando; Florida Technical College, Orlando; Orlando College, Orlando; Rollins College, Winter Park; Southern College, Orlando; and Valencia Community College, with five campuses in Orange County.

Trade and technical schools serving the area:
Mid-Florida Tech; Orlando Vo-Tech Center; and Westside Vocational-Technical Center in Winter Garden

HEALTH CARE:
Number of hospitals: 17
Number of hospital beds: 3,289
Number of physicians: 1,664

TAXES: Total county ad valorem millage rate (1993): 14.2189

STANDARD CRIME RATE: 8,819.8 offenses per 100,000 population (8th out of 67 counties)

LARGEST EMPLOYERS:

Name	Employees	Product/Service
Walt Disney World	35,000	Attraction
Orange County Public Schools	20,139	Education
Florida Hospital	6,277	Hospital
AT&T Information Systems	6,000	Communications
Martin Marietta/Electronics/Missile	5,700	Aerospace
Orange County Government	5,348	Government
Orlando Regional Health Care System	4,300	Health Care
Universal Studios	4,250	Attraction
Winn-Dixie Stores	3,177	Grocery
City of Orlando	3,100	Government
University of Central Florida	3,100	Education

COMPANIES PROVIDING LOCAL UTILITIES:
Telephone: Southern Bell and United Telephone Co. of Florida
Electricity: Florida Power; Orlando Utilities
Natural Gas: Peoples Gas
Water: Orlando utilities; Florida Power Corp.
Major Water Source: Wells
Sanitary Landfill? Yes

POINTS OF INTEREST:
ORLANDO area: Walt Disney World, Lake Buena Vista, currently has three theme parks including the Magic Kingdom, EPCOT Center and Disney/MGM Studios (see Attractions chapter); **Sea World** of Florida, Orlando, home of Shamu and other killer whales, penguin, shark and aquarium exhibits, water ski show (see Attractions chapter); **Universal Studios,** opened in mid 1990, has movie-themed ride attractions, production studios tour (see Attractions chapter); **Wet 'N Wild,** a 25-acre water park with such attractions as a kamikaze slide and a corkscrew flume; **hot-air balloon tours** offered by a number of area companies, some with champagne flights and sightseeing over area attractions; **Church Street Station** is a dining, shopping and entertainment complex in downtown Orlando including Rosie O'Grady's Good Time Emporium, Cheyenne Saloon & Opera House and Orchid Garden Ballroom; **Orlando Magic** professional basketball; **Orlando Predators** Arena Football League team; **Fun 'N Wheels,** a family park with rides and games; **Gatorland** has about 5,000 alligators and crocodiles and a jumping alligator show; **King Henry's Feast** features a five-course English banquet with specialty acts and comedy; **Mardi Gras Dinner Attraction** has variety show and four-course Southern hospitality dinner; **Mark II Dinner Theatre** has Broadway shows and buffet; **Mystery Fun House** is a 15-chamber fun house with mazes, game rooms, mini-golf; **Harry P. Leu Botanical Gardens** has collections of orchids, palms, camellias; **Medieval Life** is a village showing craftsmen in their workshops, torture chambers; **Centroplex** in Orlando (a sports-entertainment complex that houses the **Orlando Arena,** home of the Orlando Magic professional basketball team and the site of concerts, plays and other sporting events, the **Bob Carr Performing Arts Centre,** which hosts Broadway shows and concerts, the **Expo Centre,** a convention hall, the **Florida Citrus Bowl Stadium** and **Tinker Field,** home of the **Orlando Twins** minor league baseball team); the **Ben White Raceway,** a harness racing training facility; **Flea World** has more than 1,200 booths, entertainment; **Pirate's Cove Adventure Golf** has three 18-hole mini-golf courses; **WINTER GARDEN area: Central Florida Railroad Museum** has more than 3,000 pieces of railroad history; **WINTER PARK area:** 12-mile **Winter Park scenic boat tours** of Chain of Lakes in area; **Winter Park Civic Center; Beal-Maltbie Shell Museum** on the Rollins College campus displays half of a giant clam shell that is reputed to have weighed 700 pounds and thousands of species of other shells; **Polasek Foundation,** an estate that was once home to the late artist Albin Polasek; **Mead Botanical Gardens** has trails where visitors can see native birds and plants from around

the world; **Kraft Azalea Gardens,** overlooking Lake Maitland, has thousands of azaleas, shrubs, trees and a Grecian sitting temple; **MAITLAND area: Florida Audubon Society's Madalyn Baldwin Center for Birds of Prey** in Maitland is dedicated to rehabilitating injured birds of prey and has tours for visitors. Also sponsors the Save the Manatee Club; **APOPKA area: Wekiwa Springs State Park** has camping, picnicking, swimming, freshwater fishing, hiking, canoe rentals, concessions, horse trail.

THE ARTS:
Music Orlando and **Raintree Players** present symphonic and chamber music performances; **Orlando Opera Company; Southern Ballet Theatre,** Orlando; **Florida Symphony Youth Orchestra;** Loch Haven Park houses the **Civic Theatre of Central Florida,** the **Anne Giles Densch Theatre for Young People,** the **Edyth Bush Theatre,** the **Orlando Museum of Art,** the **Orange County Historical Museum** and the **Orlando Science Center** (includes a planetarium); **Orlando/Orange County Convention/Civic Center** has concerts and other special events; **Bach Festival Society of Winter Park** at Rollins College has concerts; **Central Florida Jazz Society; Mel Fisher's World of Treasure** museum near Lake Buena Vista has artifacts and treasures collected from sunken ships; **Charles Hosmer Morse Museum of American Art** in Winter Park contains large collection of Tiffany leaded and art glass; **Pine Castle Folk Art Center; Central Florida Railroad Museum** in Winter Garden; **Cornell Fine Arts Center Museum** at Rollins College in Winter Park has paintings, photos and prints; **Annie Russell Theatre** at Rollins College in Winter Park; **Maitland Art Center** has changing exhibits of contemporary arts and art classes, gardens, studios; **Holocaust Memorial Center** in Maitland is a museum and library focusing on the Holocaust; **Maitland Civic Center; Maitland Historical Museum; Fort Christmas Museum** in Christmas houses artifacts of the Seminole Indian era; **Zora Neale Hurston National Museum of Fine Arts** in Eatonville has African arts.

MAJOR SPORTING EVENT:
Jan. 1: Florida Citrus Bowl in Orlando

ANNUAL EVENTS:
Jan. 1: Florida Citrus Bowl; **January:** Scottish Highland Games at Central Florida Fairgrounds, with Scottish games, food and music; **Late February/Early March:** Annual Bach Festival at the Knowles Chapel on the Rollins College campus focuses on work of Johann Sebastian Bach; **March:** Central Florida Fair at the Central Florida Fairgrounds in Orlando; Winter Park Sidewalk Art Festival attracts 300,000 people, features exhibits by artists, entertainment, children's workshops, food; Downtown Orlando Art Festival; And All that Jazz, Maitland Art Center, with parade and festivities; **April:** Orlando Shakespeare Festival at Lake Eola Amphitheater; Foutainview Fine Crafts Festival at Lake Eola; Orlando International Fringe Festival with the world's shortest parade; Maitland Spring Festival with an arts and crafts show on Lake Lily; **Memorial Day Weekend:** Zellwood Corn Festival; **July:** Downtown Orlando-Church Street Craft Festival; **October:** Maitland Arts Festival, with more than 200 artist exhibits, on Lake Lily. Festival draws about 250,000 people; Winter Park Autumn Art Festival at Rollins College; Halloween Street Party, Church Street Station, Orlando; **November:** Light up Orlando festivities in Orlando; Fiesta in the Park at Lake Eola Park in Orlando (attracts about 250,000 people); Thanksgiving Day Parade in Orlando; International Drive Winter Festival with parades, live music, lighting displays, carolers, Santa's house; **December:** Lighting of the Great American Christmas Tree at Church Street Station.

SPORTS AND LEISURE ACTIVITIES:
Number of local golf courses: At least 9 public, 13 private, 17 semi-private
Beaches? No
Tennis courts available to the public? Yes
Boating? Yes
Number of pleasure boats registered in the county (1991-92): 28,684

SERVICES FOR RETIREES:
Better Living for Seniors Helpline gives referrals to multiple services, including home-care placement, in-home medical services, transportation and emergency relief, phone 407-648-4357; Area Agency on Aging offers information on health care, phone 407-623-1330.

FINANCIAL SERVICES:
Number of local banks: 147
Number of local savings and loan associations: 32

THE MEDIA:
Largest local newspaper: *The Orlando Sentinel*
Cable television? Yes

MAJOR LOCAL RETAILERS:
JCPenney, F.W. Woolworth, Sears, Belk Lindsey, Dillard's, Marshalls, Burdines, Montgomery Ward, J Byrons, Parisians (coming in 1995). Park Avenue in Winter Park has such stores as Crabtree & Evelyn and Benetton. Also, there are the Church Street Station shops in downtown Orlando.

FOOD ESTABLISHMENTS: 2,911

OTHER SERVICES:
Number of local libraries: 10
Number of local hotels/motels: more than 200
Number of churches: Protestant: 600; Jewish: 6; Catholic: 30; Other: 10

TOURISM INQUIRIES:
Apopka Area Chamber of Commerce, 180 E. Main St., Apopka, 32703. Telephone 407-886-1441; **Maitland/South Seminole** Chamber of Commerce, 110 N. Maitland Ave., Maitland, 32751. Telephone: 407-644-0741; Greater **Orlando** Chamber of Commerce, P.O. Box 1234, Orlando, 32802. Telephone: 407-425-1234; **Orlando/Orange County** Convention & Visitors Bureau, 7208 Sand Lake Road, Suite 300, Orlando, 32819. Telephone: 407-363-5800; **West Orange** Chamber of Commerce, P.O. Box 522, Winter Garden, 32787. Telephone: 407-656-1304; **Winter Park** Area Chamber of Commerce, P.O. Box 1420, 401 Ave. B., Northwest, Winter Park, 33882. Telephone: 407-644-8281.

OSCEOLA County
Central
County seat: Kissimmee

POPULATION: 1990: 107,728
1993: 125,675
Increase: 16.7 percent

AGE DISTRIBUTION (1992) IN PERCENTAGES:
0-14 : 21.5
15-44: 43.7
45-64: 20.2
65+ : 14.6

MUNICIPAL POPULATION:
KISSIMMEE: 1990: 30,337; 1993: 32,759
ST. CLOUD: 1990: 12,652; 1993: 14,779
UNINCORPORATED: 1990: 64,739; 1993: 78,137

LAND AREA: 1,322 square miles
POPULATION DENSITY: 95 people per square mile (31st in the state)

Located 57 miles from the Atlantic Coast and 75 miles from the Gulf Coast, the county lies south of Orlando and had the third-highest percentage increase in population in Florida between 1980 and 1991 behind Flagler (180 percent) and Hernando (135 percent). It counts on tourism as one of its major industries. In trying to lure visitors — and there has been an intense marketing effort to do that — the county touts its proximity to Orlando and has a number of unusual attractions of its own. These include an Arabian Nights dinner show that includes chariot races; a Medieval Times dinner show in a European castle, with knights competing in jousting matches and tournament games; and Alligator and Safari Zoo, which has more than 1,500 alligators.

Local business officials say that as many as 5-plus-million visitors come each year and tourism dollars make up about 40 percent of the total sales taxes collected in the county. In addition, about the same percentage of the county's work force is employed in the tourism industry, but cattle ranching and agriculture have been and still are major forces. Osceola ranks among the top counties in cattle sales and produced 5.3 million boxes of citrus in 1992-93 (13th in the state).

The county has a variety of industrial firms — from Tupperware to Mercury Marine. Tupperware Home Parties' Worldwide headquarters, which employs 620 workers, is located here, and is the area's second largest private employer, behind the Orange/Lake Country Club.

Osceola County also ranks as the sixth fastest growing county in the country — the population increased 141.9 percent from 1980 to 1992. Some of this growth is due to Walt Disney World — about 15 percent of the attraction's 35,000 employees live in Osceola.

TOURISM:
Aside from the tourists, upwards of 6,000 Snowbirds spend the winter in the area.

HOUSING PRICES:
Average about $70,000 in recent years. Median sales price of a single-family existing home for June 1994 was $91,100.

Number of vacant residential lots: 31,621; number of single-family residences: 29,443; mobile homes: 3,800; condominiums: 5,585

EDUCATION:
Number of schools: 29
Number of students enrolled: 23,122
Percentage of students continuing education after high school: 62.89
Teacher-to-pupil ratio: 1:19.6
Average teacher's salary: $27,561

Colleges, universities, and junior or community colleges serving the area:
Florida Bible College and Florida Christian College, both in Kissimmee; Rollins College in Winter Park; Florida Southern College in Lakeland; the University of Central Florida in Orlando; Orlando College; Valencia Community College, based in Orlando, and Polk Community College in the Winter Haven-Lakeland area; Seminole Community College, based in the Sanford area.

Trade and technical schools serving the area:
Technical Education Center of Osceola County; Mid-Florida Technical Institute; Southeastern Academy in Kissimmee; Orlando Vo-Tech Center

HEALTH CARE:
Number of general hospitals: 4
Number of hospital beds: 433
Number of physicians: 143

TAXES: Total county ad-valorem millage rate (1993): 15.4345

STANDARD CRIME RATE: 7,786.8 offenses per 100,000 population (12th out of 67 counties)

LARGEST PRIVATE EMPLOYERS:

Name	Employees	Product/Service
Orange/Lake Country Club	700	Entertainment
Tupperware Worldwide	620	Corporate headquarters
Days Suites Complex	510	Motel/Hotel
Humana Hospital Kissimmee	500	Health care
Hyatt Orlando	475	Hotel
Ramada Resort Maingate	305	Motel
Kissimmee Good Samaritan Village	300	Retirement
Mercury Marine Brunswick Corp.	294	Marine dealer
St. Cloud Hospital	280	Health care
Sheraton Lakeside Inn	267	Motel

COMPANIES PROVIDING LOCAL UTILITIES:
Telephone: United Telephone Co. of Florida
Electricity: Florida Power Corp.; City of St. Cloud; Kissimmee Utility Authority
Natural Gas: Peoples Gas
Water: Cities of St. Cloud and Kissimmee
Major Water Source: Wells
Sanitary Landfill? Yes

POINTS OF INTEREST:

Spring training camp of the **Houston Astros** at the Osceola County Stadium Complex in Klssimmee, with a 5,100-seat stadium; **Alligatorland Safari Zoo** in Kissimmee, has more than 1,500 alligators; **Arabian Nights Dinner Attraction** in Kissimmee, a 1,000-seat theater with nightly shows featuring Arabian dancing horses and chariot races; **Splendid China,** a Chinese-themed attraction with 60 miniaturized replicas of Chinese landmarks with entertainment, shopping, food; **Fort Liberty** in Kissimmee, a Western-style fort with specialty shops and a Wild West dinner show; **Green Meadows Farm** in Kissimmee, a farm where visitors can pet animals; **Peddler's Village Flea Market** between Kissimmee and St. Cloud, has about 300 vendors; **Poinciana Horse World** in Poinciana has horseback riding, petting zoo, fishing pond and hay rides; **Reptile World Serpentarium,** east of St. Cloud, has reptiles in educational exhibits; **Kissimmee Livestock Market,** holds live cattle auctions; **Medieval Times** in Kissimmee, where diners can have dinner in a European-style castle and watch knights competing in jousting matches and tournament games; **Medieval Life,** Kissimmee, a museum showing life in the Middle Ages; **Old Town** on U.S. 192 is a replica of turn-of-the-century Florida, including brick-lined streets and 70 restaurants and specialty shops, horse and carriage rides, a carousel and a ferris wheel; **Water Mania** in Kissimmee is a 38-acre water park with water slides, wave pool; **Xanadu - The Home of the Future** in Kissimmee has techological and electronic prototypes of 21st-century life; **St. Cloud Historic Downtown Antique District** with shops and historical sites.

THE ARTS:

Osceola Center for the Arts houses the Creative Arts League and has facilities for drama and musical concerts; **Osceola Players** do five productions a year at the arts center; **Flying Tigers Warbird Air Museum** at Kissimmee Airport; **Museum of Early History** in St. Cloud.

ANNUAL EVENTS:

February: Kissimmee Valley Livestock Show and Osceola County Fair; Silver Spurs Rodeo; **March:** Kissimmee Bluegrass Festival; St. Cloud Spring Fling (art show and boat race); **April:** Kissimmee JazzFest; **June:** Kissimmee Boat-A-Cade; **July:** Silver Spurs Rodeo; Fourth of July Lakefest in St. Cloud, fireworks; **September:** Osceola Art Festival; **October:** Kissimmee Boating Jamboree; Florida State Air Fair; **November:** Fanfare Extravaganza; **December:** St. Cloud Art Festival; Christmas Parade in St. Cloud; Christmas Boat Parade.

SPORTS AND LEISURE ACTIVITIES:

Most popular local fishing areas: Lake Tohopekaliga (for bass, perch and catfish)
Number of local golf courses: At least 3
Public beaches: Yes
Tennis courts available to the public? Yes
Boating? Yes
Number of pleasure boats registered in the county (1991-92): 5,765

SERVICES FOR RETIREES:

Osceola County Council on Aging in Kissimmee offers a number of services including home emergency response, legal counseling, Meals on Wheels, daily activities and meals at sites in Kissimmee and St. Cloud, transportation and a Senior Help Line for information and referrals (407-846-8532); St. Cloud Senior Citizens Center has large meeting, dining and dancing area and shuffleboard courts.

FINANCIAL SERVICES:

Number of local banks: 23
Number of local savings and loan associations: 7

THE MEDIA:

Largest local newspaper: *News-Gazette* in Kissimmee
Cable television? Yes

MAJOR LOCAL RETAILERS:

Wal-Mart, K mart, Sears, Bealls; Osceola Square Mall on U.S. 192 has 3 department stores, a food court and theaters; and Florida Mall, outside Osceola County on U.S. 441, has 6 department stores, scores of retail stores and about 1.6 million square feet of indoor shopping.

FOOD ESTABLISHMENTS: 532

OTHER SERVICES:
Number of local libraries: 4
Number of local hotels/motels: 129
Number of churches: Protestant: 53; Jewish: 1; Catholic: 2

TOURISM INQUIRIES:
Kissimmee/Osceola County Chamber of Commerce, 1425 East Vine St., Kissimmee, 34744. Telephone: 407-847-3174; The Greater **Osceola County/St. Cloud** Chamber of Commerce, 1200 New York Ave., St. Cloud, 34769. Telephone: 407-892-3671; **Kissimmee/St. Cloud** Tourism and Convention Bureau, 1925 E. Irlo Bronson Memorial Highway, Kissimmee, 34744. Telephone: 407-847-5000.

POLK County
Central
County seat: Bartow

POPULATION: 1990: 405,382
1993: 429,943
Increase: 6.1 percent

AGE DISTRIBUTION (1992) IN PERCENTAGES:
0-14 : 20.6
15-44: 40.7
45-64: 20.3
65+ : 18.4

MUNICIPAL POPULATION:
AUBURNDALE: 1990: 8,858; 1993: 9,063
BARTOW: 1990: 14,716; 1993: 14,902
DAVENPORT: 1990: 1,529; 1993: 1,688
DUNDEE: 1990: 2,335; 1993: 2,447
EAGLE LAKE: 1990: 1,758; 1993: 1,934
FORT MEADE: 1990: 4,993; 1993: 5,247
FROSTPROOF: 1990: 2,875; 1993: 2,907
HAINES CITY: 1990: 11,683; 1993: 12,103
HIGHLAND PARK: 1990: 155; 1993: 153
HILLCREST HEIGHTS: 1990: 221; 1993: 220
LAKE ALFRED: 1990: 3,622; 1993: 3,622
LAKE HAMILTON: 1990: 1,128; 1993: 1,113
LAKE WALES: 1990: 9,670; 1993: 9,759
LAKELAND: 1990: 70,576; 1993: 73,121
MULBERRY: 1990: 2,988; 1993: 3,095
POLK CITY: 1990: 1,439; 1993: 1,613
WINTER HAVEN: 1990: 24,725; 1993: 25,006
UNINCORPORATED: 1990: 242,111; 1993: 261,950

LAND AREA: 1,875 square miles
POPULATION DENSITY: 229 people per square mile (19th in the state)

This county is famous for having one of the most popular attractions in the state — Cypress Gardens, a 223-acre entertainment park that has attracted 35-plus million people in its more than 50 years. Besides showing off more than 8,000 varieties of plants and flowers from 75 countries, the attraction has a world-famous water-skiing show and a number of other shows (See Attractions chapter for more information about Cypress Gardens).

There are many types of industry in the county. To start with, there's citrus — the county is number one in the state, producing roughly 12 percent of Florida's crop. About 65 percent of the land is used for agriculture. In 1991-92, the county became the second-largest citrus-producing county in the state, behind St. Lucie County. It became the top producer in 1992-93, with production of 30.15 million boxes. This industry has a more than billion-dollar impact on the local economy.

The services industry has more non-agricultural workers than any other sector — 50,234 in

1991. Not far behind was trade, with 47,344. Other large sectors were government, 24,943, and manufacturing, 21,444. Mining — primarily of phosphate — accounted for nearly 4,000 jobs. In recent years eight phosphate companies have operated 16 mines and controlled 20 percent of the county's land. One-fifth of the world's fertilizer and 80 percent of the U.S. needs are supplied by central Florida.

Polk ranks second only to Pasco County in the number of mobile homes — there were 24,335 here in 1993 (as opposed to 28,000 in Pasco), according to the state.

All told, there are 17 incorporated municipalities in the 2,003-square-mile county. Among them:

Auburndale: Citrus is still a major industry, but the economy has diversified in recent years. Among the major employers are Comcar, a trucking firm, and Coca-Cola, which has a citrus concentrate plant.

Bartow: The county seat, its major industries are cattle, citrus and phosphate. The city, though not large in population, does have an art guild, a performing arts council and a historical museum. Among its largest employers are several phosphate firms including IMC Fertilizer Inc., which has 2,800 employees.

Fort Meade: Believed to be the oldest community in Polk County, with its history dating back to 1843, the area was the site of the last battle between settlers and the Seminole Indians in 1856. The town today has homes that were built in the late 1800s and early 1900s and that are occupied by descendants of the original builders.

Frostproof: Originally named Keystone City and later Lakemont, the city's name was changed again after a mass of cold air swept the state in late 1896 and early 1897 and killed most of the state's citrus trees — but this city was spared major damage. After a local resident traveled to other parts of the state to view the destruction, he returned home saying, "We've got the name for this place now. It's Frostproof." And the name has stuck ever since.

Haines City: A winter destination point for as many as 25,000 Snowbirds. Manufactured housing is very popular here and citrus is one of the principal industries.

Lakeland: The city is the home of Southern College, which claims to have the largest collection of buildings designed by architect Frank Lloyd Wright. The city also has a number of lakes, including Lake Parker, which is not far from Joker Marchant Stadium, the spring-training home of the Detroit Tigers; Lake Morton, which is a bird sanctuary and is near the Polk Museum of Art and the city's public library; Lake Hollingsworth, which borders Florida Southern College; and Lake Hunter, near the Lakeland Civic Center. The city also has an Antique District, which has one of the largest collection of antique stores in Florida — about 60 of them.

Lake Wales: It is home to a number of tourist attractions such as Bok Tower Gardens, the Black Hills Passion Play and Spook Hill. As in the rest of the county, the production of oranges and grapefruit is critical to the economy. Thousands of residents here work in some aspect of this industry — grove maintenance, citrus packing and processing, shipping, citrus management and related maintenance equipment production.

Winter Haven: The city is nicknamed the City of Lakes because it is bordered by 29 named lakes, including 14 that are connected by canals forming what is called the "Chain of Lakes." Water sports abound here, along with the city's recognition as the water-skiing capital of the world. Cypress Gardens, one of the state's most popular attractions, is located just east of the city on Cypress Gardens Boulevard.

TOURISM:
The county is very popular with tourists. The season runs roughly from November until April.

HOUSING PRICES:
Median sales price of an existing home in the Lakeland-Winter Haven metropolitan area was $73,100 in June 1994.
Number of vacant residential lots: 58,275; number of single-family residences: 98,460; mobile homes: 24,335; condominiums: 6,502

EDUCATION:
Number of local schools: 102
Number of students enrolled: 69,718
Percentage of students continuing education after high school: 63.51
Teacher-to-pupil ratio: 1:17.1
Average teacher's salary: $27,873

Colleges, universities, and junior or community colleges serving the area:
Florida Southern College in Lakeland; Polk Community College in Winter Haven; Warner Southern College in Lake Wales; Webber College in Babson Park; University of South Florida in Tampa; University of Central Florida in Orlando.

Trade and technical schools serving the area:
Traviss Vo-Tech; Ridge Vocational Technical Center

HEALTH CARE:
Number of hospitals: 8
Number of hospital beds: 2,023
Number of physicians: 639

TAXES: Total county ad valorem millage rate (1993): 16.3790

STANDARD CRIME RATE: 8,410.4 offenses per 100,000 population (11th out of 67 counties)

LARGEST PRIVATE EMPLOYERS:

Name	Employees	Product/Service
Publix	6,262	Grocery distribution
IMC Fertilizer	2,800	Phosphate
Lakeland Regional Medical Center	2,700	Health care
State Farm Insurance	2,700	Insurance
Winter Haven Hospital	2,000	Health care
Scotty's	1,200	Hardware
Winn-Dixie	1,076	Grocery
Watson Clinic	950	Health care
Agrico Chemical Co.	900	Phosphate
Comcar Industries	874	Trucking

COMPANIES PROVIDING LOCAL UTILITIES:
Telephone: GTE Florida
Electricity: Lakeland Electric & Water, Tampa Electric, Florida Power
Natural Gas: Central Florida Gas, Peoples Gas
Water: Municipalities, Polk County
Major Water Source: Wells
Sanitary Landfill? Yes

POINTS OF INTEREST:
Cypress Gardens, just outside Winter Haven (see Attractions chapter for details); spring training camps of the **Kansas City Royals** at Baseball City Stadium, Haines City, the **Detroit Tigers** at Joker Marchant Stadium in Lakeland and the **Cleveland Indians** at Chain O' Lakes Park in Winter Haven; **Water Ski Museum/Hall of Fame,** 5 miles east of Winter Haven; **Bok Tower Gardens,** a carillon tower (made up of 57 bronze bells and a mechanical keyboard) in Lake Wales, recitals heard daily. The gardens are 128 acres with azaleas, camellias and magnolias; **Spook Hill** ("stop your car at the foot of the hill and put it into neutral and discover, to your astonishment, that your car will back slowly UP the hill"), near Bok Tower Gardens; **Museum of Fishing,** Winter Haven, the southeast's largest historical and educational facility on fishing, has fishing memorabilia, lure collection, antique and modern motors; **Lake Kissimmee State Park,** 15 miles east of Lake Wales, has camping, picnicking, freshwater fishing, hiking, guided tours, boat ramp, observation platform, re-enactments of life in a cow camp; **Lake Arbuckle State Park,** east of Avon Park, a state open land area; **Catfish Creek State Preserve,** 9 miles east of Dundee, an open land area; **Audubon Center and Nature Trail** in Babson Park, with trail going past Crooked Lake, noted for its bass and bream fishing; **Tiger Creek Nature Preserve,** a 4,500-acre site housing the rarely seen scrub jays and swallow-tailed kites, plus rattle snakes, alligators, located 12 miles southeast of Lake Wales; **Fantasy of Flight,** scheduled to open near Polk City in the winter of 1994/95, planned as an aviation attraction with historical aircraft, interactive exhibits; **Sun 'n Fun Air Museum,** Lakeland, has aircraft exhibits; **Outdoor Resorts River Ranch** has farm animals, petting zoo, hayrides, pony rides, rodeos; **Mulberry Phosphate Museum** has collection of fossilized remains, industry exhibits.

THE ARTS:
Lake Wales Amphitheater/Black Hills Passion Play — play depicts the last seven days in Christ's life, runs from mid-February until Easter, also has Nativity Play in December; **Lakeland**

Civic Center hosts sporting events, ice shows, pageants and other shows. Its arena has seating for more than 10,000 and also includes the 2,282-seat Robert V. Youkey Theater and a conference center; **Polk Community College Fine Arts Theatre; Theatre Winter Haven; Haines City Community Theatre; Polk Museum of Art** in Lakeland, art exhibits and educational programs; **Lake Wales Museum and Cultural Center** at the Depot has exhibits on the history of the city and railroad memorabilia, including a 1916 Pullman train car; **Lake Wales Little Theatre,** hosts productions from October to April; **Explorations V — Polk County's Children's Museum,** offers hands-on education exhibits, including information on banking, medicine, science, as well as **Sense of Wonder Medieval Castle,** miniature firetruck, brain teasers; **Imperial Symphony Orchestra** offers fall, Christmas, winter, pops and young artists concerts; **Fort Meade Historical Museum; Lake Wales Arts Council** sponsors cultural and educational activities.

ANNUAL EVENTS:

January: National Corvette Restorers Society Show, Cypress Gardens; Florida Citrus Festival, Winter Haven, has concerts, rides, entertainment; Polk County Fair; Carillon Festival, Bok Tower Gardens; Ninety Days of Big Band Sounds (through May), Cypress Gardens; **February:** Lake Wales Mardi Gras festival with masquerade parade, gala balls, art exhibits, Dixieland jazz bands, food; **March:** Florida State Bluegrass Championship, Auburndale; River Ranch Chili Cook-off, River Ranch; Child of the Sun Jazz Festival, Florida Southern College; Haines City Heritage Days, Haines City; **April:** Bartow Bloomin' Arts Festival, Bartow; Lake Wales Art Show; American Waterski Hall of Fame induction and tournament; **May:** Mayfaire-by-the-Lake, Lake Morton, Lakeland; **July:** Fourth of July celebrations; **September:** Fall Festival, Lakeland; Fort Meade Arts and Crafts Festival; **October:** Fall Fest — Pioneer Days, Lake Wales, with crafts, concessions, music; Fall Festival — Arts on the Park, Lakeland; **November:** Festival of Fine Arts (through January), Florida Southern College; Native American Pow Wow, Lakeland; Mum Festival, Cypress Gardens; **December:** Winter Fest in Winter Haven features festival of trees, Christmas boat parade, caroling; Poinsettia Festival, Cypress Gardens; Snowfest, Lakeland; Christmas parades in various cities.

SPORTS AND LEISURE ACTIVITIES:

Fishing is very popular in these lakes: Lowery, Hamilton, Marion, Pierce, Hatchineha, Hammock, Haines, Eva, Tracy, Kissimmee, Cypress, Tiger, Rosalie, Ariana, Blue, Juliana, Lena, Mattie, Tennessee, Mariana, Jesse, Crago, Parker, Weohyakapka and Echo and Crooked Lake. Also on the Peace River and Saddle Creek. The county has very good bass fishing, particularly black bass, and other popular catches are bluegill, crappie, shellcracker, gar, channel catfish, chain pickerel, bream, perch and redfinned pike.

Number of local golf courses: 11 public; 10 semi-private; 7 private
Tennis courts available to the public? Yes
Boating? Yes
Number of pleasure boats registered in the county (1991-92): 23,846

SERVICES FOR RETIREES:

In many communities, such as Meals on Wheels and fellowship dining.

FINANCIAL SERVICES:

Number of local banks: 107
Number of local savings and loan associations: 23

THE MEDIA:

Largest local newspaper: *The Ledger* in Lakeland
Is cable television available? Yes

MAJOR LOCAL RETAILERS:

In the county there are 55 shopping centers and several regional malls with such stores as Sears, Bealls, Wal-Mart, Byrons, Belk-Lindsey, Burdines and Dillard's.

FOOD ESTABLISHMENTS: 1,062

OTHER SERVICES:

Number of public libraries: 25
Number of local hotels/motels: 117
Number of churches: Protestant: 378; Jewish: 2; Catholic: 10; Other: 199

Central Florida Convention and Visitors Bureau, P.O. Box 1839, Bartow, 33830. Telephone: 1-800-828-7655. **Auburndale** Chamber of Commerce, 111 East Park St., Auburndale, 33823. Telephone: 813-967-3400; **Bartow** Chamber of Commerce, 510 N. Broadway, P.O. Box 956, Bartow, 33831. Telephone: 813-533-7125; **Fort Meade** Chamber of Commerce, P.O. Box 91, Fort Meade, 33841; 813-285-8253; **Haines City** Chamber of Commerce, P.O. Box 986, Haines City, 33845. Telephone: 813-422-3751; **Lakeland** Area Chamber of Commerce, P.O. Box 3607, Lakeland, 33802-3607. Telephone: 813-688-8551; **Lake Wales** Area Chamber of Commerce, P.O. Box 191, Lake Wales, 33859-0191. Telephone: 813-676-3445; **Winter Haven** Area Chamber of Commerce, P.O. Drawer 1420, Winter Haven, 33882-1420. Telephone: 813-293-2138.

SEMINOLE County

Central
County seat: Sanford

POPULATION: 1990: 287,521
1993: 310,890
Increase: 8.1 percent

AGE DISTRIBUTION (1992) IN PERCENTAGES:
0-14 : 21.2
15-44: 48.0
45-64: 20.3
65+ : 10.6

MUNICIPAL POPULATION:
ALTAMONTE SPRINGS: 1990: 35,167; 1993: 36,770
CASSELBERRY: 1990: 18,849; 1993: 22,816
LAKE MARY: 1990: 5,929; 1993: 6,673
LONGWOOD: 1990: 13,316; 1993: 13,418
OVIEDO: 1990: 11,114; 1993: 15,722
SANFORD: 1990: 32,387; 1993: 34,096
WINTER SPRINGS: 1990: 22,151; 1993: 24,008
UNINCORPORATED: 1990: 148,608; 1993: 157,387

LAND AREA: 308 square miles
POPULATION DENSITY: 1,009 people per square mile (3rd in the state)

Primarily a residential area and known for years simply as a bedroom community of Orlando, Seminole County today is attracting many businesses, industries and tourists. More than 10,000 small businesses are located here along with several major industries, including Siemens Stromberg, a telephone equipment company, in Lake Mary, and the corporate offices of the American Automobile Association (AAA), which moved to the Heathrow International Business Center near Lake Mary.

The county is also noted for its recreational opportunities — it has about 185 lakes. It was mainly an agricultural community until the 1960s. Today the service industry is the largest, with more than 36,000 employees, followed by trade at 33,000; finance, insurance and real estate, 13,300; and, with roughly equal workforces of 10,000-plus employees, manufacturing and construction.

Among cities here are **Altamonte Springs,** the county's largest city in population and home of the 170-store Altamonte Mall; **Casselberry,** reputed to be one of the world's largest suppliers of fernery; **Lake Mary,** the newest city in the county; **Longwood,** the oldest city in the county; **Oviedo,** which has agricultural and horse farms mixed with residential development; **Sanford,** the county seat, which is situated on the south shore of Lake Monroe at the head of navigation on the St. Johns River; and **Winter Springs,** the largest city in land area.

The county is home to the U.S. Soccer Federation's National Teams Training Center. Athletes trained here for the 1994 World Cup and others will train here for the 1996 Summer Olympics, which will be held in Atlanta. In addition, the Amateur Softball Association holds numerous national softball touraments here.

TOURISM:
Some snowbirds spend their winters here, though not high percentages. Tourists come here for canoeing, boating on the St. John's and Wekiva rivers and to visit the Central Florida Zoological Park.

HOUSING PRICES:
Median resale price for the Orlando metropolitan area was $91,100 in the June 1994. While not broken out separately, Seminole County prices in recent years have been estimated at an average of about $95,000, according to local Realtors.

Number of vacant residential lots: 15,105; number of single-family residences: 85,608; mobile homes: 2,065; condominiums: 7,768

EDUCATION:
Number of schools: 50
Number of students enrolled: 52,998
Percentage of students continuing education after high school: 73.73
Teacher-to-pupil ratio: 1:19.6
Average teacher's salary: $31,988

Colleges, universities, and junior or community colleges serving the area:
University of Central Florida in Orlando; Rollins College in Winter Park; Stetson University in DeLand; Seminole Community College in Sanford; Valencia Community College in Orlando

Trade and technical schools serving the area:
Mid-Florida Tech; Orlando Vo-Tech Center; Winter Park Adult Education

HEALTH CARE:
Number of general hospitals: 4
Number of hospital beds: 774
Number of physicians: 479

TAXES: Total county ad-valorem millage rate (1993): 15.8971

STANDARD CRIME RATE: 5,756.4 offenses per 100,000 population (26th out of 67 counties)

LARGEST PRIVATE EMPLOYERS:

Name	Employees	Product/Service
K mart	2,000	Retail sales
Siemens Stromberg	1,934	Telephone equipment
American Automobile Association	1,131	Corporate headquarters
Tri-City Electrical Contractors	654	Contractors
United Telephone	649	Telecommunications
Sears	378	Retail
IBAX Healthcare Systems	300	Software
Goodings of Florida	300	Grocery
ABB Power Distributors	298	Switch gears
Florida Polymers	280	Contract Mfg.

COMPANIES PROVIDING LOCAL UTILITIES:
Telephone: United Telephone Co. and Southern Bell
Electricity: Florida Power, Florida Power and Light
Natural Gas: Peoples Gas and Florida Public Utilities Co.
Water: City of Sanford
Major Water Source: River
Sanitary Landfill? Yes

POINTS OF INTEREST:
Central Florida Zoological Park in Sanford has more than 500 animals; **Flea World/Fun World** near Sanford has 1,500 dealer booths, bingo, fun park with miniature golf, bumper cars, kiddie rides; **Katie's Wekiva River Landing and Campground** in Sanford offers canoe trips on the Wekiva River, camping, fishing, picnicking; **Orlando Jai Alai** in Fern Park; **Seminole Greyhound Park** in Sanford; **Sanford-Orlando Kennel Club** for dog racing in Longwood; **Sanford Civic Center** has seating for 1,300; **Big Tree Park** in Longwood is the site of the world's oldest and largest cypress tree, which is more than 3,500 years old; **St. Johns Riverboat Cruises.**

THE ARTS:

Ballet Guild of Sanford-Seminole; Altamonte Springs Jazz Ensemble; Central Florida Puppet Guild, Longwood; **Central Florida Quilters Guild,** Casselberry; **Sanford/Seminole Art Association; Society for Creative Anachronism,** studies the Middle Ages; **Seminole County Historical Museum** near Sanford has exhibits on the citrus industry, cattle ranching and vegetable farming and railroad and steamboat memorabilia; **Artistic Hand Gallery** in downtown Oviedo exhibits work by local artists; **Cultural Arts Center,** Sanford, is used for meeting space, small concerts and recitals; **Sanford Museum** collects and exhibits materials about the city from 1820 to the present; **Old Lake Mary City Hall,** a site for concerts and plays and art exhibits; **Seminole Community College Fine Arts Concert Hall, Gallery and Theatre; The Stage,** an 85-seat community theater, has year-round season, also has children's performing group known as the Stagestuck Players; **Student Museum and Center for Social Studies,** Sanford, has exhibits on Native Americans and pioneers as well as on geography, climatology and space travel; **Central Florida Society for Historic Preservation; Cultural Society of Central Florida,** makes cultural expressions available to socially and economically disadvantaged people and to the physically challenged; **Triangle Productions,** based in Sanford, performs participative murder mysteries in Winter Park; planned are amphitheatres in Lake Mary and in Altamonte Springs.

ANNUAL EVENTS:

March: St. Johns River Festival in Sanford has arts and crafts, food, entertainment; **October:** Lake Mary-Heathrow Festival of the Arts in Heathrow has arts and crafts; Pioneer Days 'N Ways (first Saturday/Sunday of the month), sponsored by the Seminole County Historical Society; **November (second Saturday):** Great Day in the Country, Lawton Grove Park; Golden Age Games in Sanford (second week); Longwood Arts and Crafts Show (Saturday/Sunday before Thanksgiving); **December:** Florida Citrus Sailfest, held on Lake Monroe, is believed to be the largest inland sailing regatta in the nation; Holiday Tour of Homes in Sanford; St. Lucia Festival in Sanford has Christmas parade, puppet shows, Swedish foods and costumes, musicians, bell ringers, Swedish crafts, lighted boat parade and a folk opera; Winter Springs Art Festival, Winter Springs Park.

SPORTS AND LEISURE ACTIVITIES:

Most popular local fishing areas: Lake Monroe, St. Johns River, Wekiva River, Blackwater Creek
Number of local golf courses: 8
Public beaches? Yes
Tennis courts available to the public? Yes
Boating? Yes
Number of pleasure boats registered in the county (1991-92): 14,015

SERVICES FOR RETIREES:

Council on Aging in Seminole County. Senior centers are located in Casselberry, Lake Mary, Sanford and Winter Springs.

FINANCIAL SERVICES:

Number of local banks: 68
Number of local savings and loan associations: 17

THE MEDIA:

Largest local newspaper: *Sanford Herald*
Cable television? Yes

MAJOR LOCAL RETAILERS:

Burdines, Gayfers, Dillard's, Sears, Montgomery Ward, JCPenney, K mart, Wal-Mart.

FOOD ESTABLISHMENTS: 824

OTHER SERVICES:

Number of local libraries: 3
Number of local hotels/motels: 30
Number of churches: Protestant: 215; Jewish: 2; Catholic: 4; Other: 2

TOURISM INQUIRIES:

Greater **Seminole County** Chamber of Commerce, 4590 South Highway 17-92, Casselberry, 32707; Telephone: 407-834-4404; The Greater **Sanford** Chamber of Commerce, 400 East First St., Sanford, 32771. Telephone: 407-322-2212.

SUMTER County

Central
County seat: Bushnell

POPULATION: 1990: 31,577
1993: 33,814
Increase 32 percent

AGE DISTRIBUTION (1992) IN PERCENTAGES:
0-14 : 18.5
15-44: 35.8
45-64: 22.5
65+ : 23.2

MUNICIPAL POPULATION:
BUSHNELL: 1990: 1,998; 1993: 2,212
CENTER HILL: 1990: 735; 1993: 762
COLEMAN: 1990: 857; 1993: 854
WEBSTER: 1990: 746; 1993: 807
WILDWOOD: 1990: 3,560; 1993: 3,767
UNINCORPORATED: 1990: 23,681; 1993: 25,412

LAND AREA: 546 square miles
POPULATION DENSITY: 62 people per square mile (41st in the state)

It's mainly an agricultural county, but it calls itself the "Transportation Hub of Florida" because the Florida Turnpike originates and converges with Interstate 75 here. Tampa, St. Petersburg, Lakeland and Orlando are all within an hour's drive. The primary source of income is agriculture — cattle, dairy, swine, poultry, horses, citrus, cantaloupes, egg plants, cucumbers, peppers, salad greens, squash, strawberries and watermelons. Recreational activities include freshwater fishing, boating, swimming, canoeing, camping, hiking and hunting. The county bills itself as being close enough to major metropolitan areas while offering residents "the serenity of country living."

TOURISM:
No figures are available,but the population swells from November through April ("All I know is that my church population triples, and we go from one service to two," said one local official).

HOUSING PRICES:
Average prices in recent years typically $45,000 to $55,000 for a 2- or 3-bedroom resale; $55,000 to $65,000 for a new home. Lakefront homes range from $95,000 for a very small house to as much as $300,000. Average lakefront and riverfront prices in the $110,000 to $125,000 range. Number of vacant residential lots: 4,433; number of single-family residences: 6,317; mobile homes: 4,529; condominiums: 106

EDUCATION:
Number of schools: 12
Number of students enrolled: 5,505
Percentage of students continuing education after high school: 73.58
Teacher-to-pupil ratio: 1:18.4
Average teacher's salary: $30,155

Colleges, universities, and junior or community colleges serving the area:
University of South Florida in Tampa; University of Central Florida in Orlando; Lake-Sumter Community College in Leesburg; Central Florida Community College in Ocala; Pasco-Hernando Community College in Dade City.

Trade and technical schools serving the area:
Withlacoochee Vo-Tech (Inverness) and Lake County Vo-Tech (Eustis).

HEALTH CARE:
Number of general hospitals: None in the county; 3 within a 30-mile radius.
Number of Physicians: 9

TAXES: Total county ad-valorem millage rate (1993): 19.7000

STANDARD CRIME RATE: 3,584.3 offenses per 100,000 population (47th out of 67 counties)

LARGEST PRIVATE EMPLOYERS:

Name	Employees	Product/Service
Metal Industries	275	Air dist. products
Winn-Dixie	196	Grocery
WeCare	186	Nursing home
Sumter Electric Cooperative	115	Utilities
CSX Railroad	100	Transportation
Central Packing	100	Meat products
Container Corp.	100	Shipping containers
Florida Power Corp	97	Utilities
Wal-Mart	93	Retail sales
Avesta Sandvik Tubing	87	Pipe and tubing

COMPANIES PROVIDING LOCAL UTILITIES:
Telephone: United Telephone
Electricity: Florida Power, Sumter Electric Cooperative
Natural Gas: None
Water: Municipalities
Major Water Source: Wells
Sanitary Landfill? Yes

POINTS OF INTEREST:
National Veterans' Cemetery for the state of Florida, south of Bushnell; **Dade Battlefield State Historic Site,** Bushnell; **Sumter County Farmers Market** (a large flea market open only on Mondays).

ANNUAL EVENTS:
March: Sumter County Fair at Bevelle's Corner; **May:** Webster Pepper Festival; **October:** Fall Festival; **December:** Second Seminole War battle re-enactment, Dade Battlefield State Historic Site.

SPORTS AND LEISURE ACTIVITIES:
Most popular local fishing areas: Four lakes (Panasoffkee, Okahumpka, Deaton and Miona) and the Withlacoochee River
Number of local golf courses: 2 private
Public beaches? No
Tennis courts available to the public? Yes
Boating? Yes
Number of pleasure boats registered in the county (1991-92): 2,828

SERVICES FOR RETIREES:
Sumter County Senior Services

FINANCIAL SERVICES:
Number of local banks: 5
Number of local savings and loan associations: 2

THE MEDIA:
Largest local newspaper: *Sumter County Times*
Cable television? Yes

LOCAL SHOPPING:
No regional mall; two shopping centers. Wal-Mart in Bushnell. Larger shopping centers nearby in Lake, Marion and Hernando counties.

FOOD ESTABLISHMENTS: 122

OTHER SERVICES:
Number of local libraries: 5
Number of local motels: 9
Number of churches: Protestant: 59; Jewish: 0; Catholic: 2

TOURISM INQUIRIES:
Sumter County Chamber of Commerce, P.O. Box 550, Bushnell, 33513. Telephone: 904-793-3099.

One of the most popular tourist spots in this area is The Pier in St. Petersburg, an upside-down-pyramid complex of shops and restaurants.

The Pinellas Suncoast beaches draw millions of visitors a year.

Boats line the harbor area of the Crystal River in Citrus County.

CENTRAL WEST FLORIDA

THE COUNTIES: Citrus, Hernando, Hillsborough, Manatee, Pasco, Pinellas

MAJOR CITIES: Tampa, St. Petersburg, Clearwater, Bradenton

TOP INDUSTRIES: Tourism, services, retail trade, government, exports/imports, agriculture, manufacturing, health care

MAJOR NEWSPAPERS: St. Petersburg Times, Tampa Tribune

WEATHER: On the first line is the average maximum temperature for each month; the second line, the average minimum temperature; the third line, the amount of precipitation, in inches, for 1990, from the national weather station.

Tampa	Jan.	Feb.	Mar.	Apr.	May	June	July	Aug.	Sep.	Oct.	Nov.	Dec.
Max.	76.6	78.8	80.8	82.7	90.0	91.7	91.3	92.7	92.4	87.2	81.5	78.1
Min.	55.5	59.5	58.5	61.4	71.0	73.7	73.7	75.0	73.1	68.0	58.9	55.6
Precp.	0.5	4.6	1.7	1.5	1.8	5.2	10.0	3.3	2.4	2.6	0.7	0.2

CITRUS County
Central West
County seat: Inverness

POPULATION: 1990: 93,513
1993: 100,829
Increase: 7.8 percent

AGE DISTRIBUTION (1992) IN PERCENTAGES:
0-14 : 14.7
15-44: 29.1
45-64: 24.6
65+ : 31.6

MUNICIPAL POPULATION:
CRYSTAL RIVER: 1990: 4,050; 1993: 4,076
INVERNESS: 1990: 5,797; 1993: 6,462
UNINCORPORATED: 1990: 83,666; 1993: 90,291

LAND AREA: 584 square miles
POPULATION DENSITY: 173 people per square mile (27th in the state)

     Located above Hernando County, the Gulf of Mexico forms this county's western border and the Withlacoochee River its northern and eastern borders. In addition, there is the Tsala Apopka chain of lakes, which is 22 miles long and covers 24,000 acres, and six other rivers. It's no wonder that a number of parks are found here, including Homosassa Springs State Wildlife Park (which has a floating underwater observatory), Fort Cooper State Park, a state historic site, an archaeological site and city-owned park facilities. Popular outdoor activities include fishing, boating, sailing, water skiing, snorkeling and scuba diving. Tourism comes into play here because the manatees hover around Kings Bay, and in the winter they travel inland to escape the chilly Gulf waters. Diving trips, snorkeling excursions and boat trips are conducted from this area to view the mammals. Citrus County has only two incorporated cities — Crystal River and Inverness — but more than a dozen unincorporated communities, including Beverly Hills, Chassahowitzka, Citronelle, Citrus Springs, Floral City, Hernando, Holder, Homosassa, Homosassa Springs, Lecanto, Ozello, and Red Level. Among the principal industries are agriculture, construction, retailing and services, tourism and mining. Florida Power is the largest private employer and operates the Crystal River nuclear power plant in Red Level; several food stores and a discount store are also among the major employers. Other industries include commercial boat building and marinas.

TOURISM:
While no figures are available, the Citrus County Chamber of Commerce estimates that the population rises by about 30 percent, including Snowbirds and tourists, in the winter.

HOUSING PRICES:
Average prices in the mid-60s; lakefront properties generally run $20,000 higher and Gulf-front properties generally run from $100,000 to $300,000-plus.
Number of vacant residential lots: 81,736; number of single-family residences: 32,760; mobile homes: 13,286; condominiums: 1,486

EDUCATION:
Number of schools: 17
Number of students enrolled: 13,106
Percentage of students continuing education after high school: 56.08
Teacher-to-pupil ratio: 1:16.3
Average teacher's salary: $29,141

Colleges, universities, and junior or community colleges serving the area:
Central Florida Community College campus at Lecanto; University of Florida in Gainesville; Pasco-Hernando Community College at Dade City; University of South Florida in Tampa.

Trade and technical schools serving the area:
Withlacoochee Technical Institute

HEALTH CARE:
Number of general hospitals: 3
Number of hospital beds: 387
Number of physicians: 135

TAXES: Total county ad-valorem millage rate (1993): 17.9373

STANDARD CRIME RATE: 2,888.1 offenses per 100,000 population (52nd out of 67 counties)

LARGEST PRIVATE EMPLOYERS:

Name	Employees	Product/Service
Florida Power Corp.	1,342	Electric Utilities
Citrus Memorial Hospital	885	Health care
Seven Rivers Hospital	520	Health care
Winn-Dixie	519	Grocery
Sunshine Material Corp.	350	Contractor
Wal-Mart	295	Retail sales
Publix	283	Grocery
Pro-Line Boats	250	Boat Manufacturing
Kash-N-Karry	201	Grocery
K mart	197	Retail sales

COMPANIES PROVIDING LOCAL UTILITIES:
Telephone: United Telephone Co. and Southern Bell
Electricity: Florida Power Corp., Sumter Electric Cooperative and the Withlacoochee River Electric
Natural Gas: Florida Gas

Water: Citrus County and Crystal River, Inverness, Rolling Oaks, Ozello, Homasassa and Southern States
Major Water Source: Wells
Sanitary Landfill? Yes

POINTS OF INTEREST:
Fort Cooper State Park in Inverness has camping, picnicking, swimming, freshwater fishing, hiking, canoeing. Lake Holathlikaha is within the boundaries of this park, which is the site of an 1800s frontier fort; **Homosassa Springs State Wildlife Park** in Homosassa Springs has a floating underwater observatory where visitors can view freshwater and saltwater fish and manatees. Also offers jungle cruises, alligator and hippopotamus feeding programs, nature museum, nature trail, boat ramp, concessions; **Tillis Hill Recreation Area,** camping, horseback riding, picnicking; **Yulee Sugar Mill Ruins State Historic Site,** Old Homosassa, is a partially restored sugar mill. Area has picnicking facilities; **Crystal River State Archaeological Site,** northwest of Crystal River, is an Indian mound preservation complex. Area has nature trail and visitor center; **Chassahowitzka National Wildlife Refuge,** near Homosassa Springs, accessible only by boat; **Whispering Pines Park** in Inverness, a large city-owned park, has shuffleboard, tennis and racquetball courts, a junior-sized Olympic pool, jogging and nature trail, baseball fields, softball field, activity field and picnic area; **Citrus County Historical Society Museum** in Inverness has an Indian Exhibit Hall with another location in Old City hall in Crystal River; **The Crown Hotel** in Inverness, a duplication of a British hotel and restaurant with Victorian decor, has a European-trained staff, reproduction of the Crown Jewels; **Old Town Inverness,** with historic sites, restaurants, shopping and entertainment; **Curtis Peterson Auditorium** in Lecanto seats 1,200 and hosts concerts, forums, plays and other cultural and civic activities.

ANNUAL EVENTS:
January: Withlacoochee River Chili Cookoff; **February:** The Florida Manatee Festival in Crystal River (food, wine and cheese tasting, arts and crafts); **March:** (first weekend) Floral City Strawberry Festival; Citrus County Fair, Inverness; **April:** Fort Cooper Days at Fort Cooper State Park; **June:** Red, White & Blueberry Day in Crystal River; **August:** Ramblin River Raft Race on Crystal River; **September:** Citrus County Crafts Festival at Crystal River; **October:** Citrus Sertoma Octoberfest, Crystal River; Beverly Hills Octoberfest; Fort Cooper Fall Festival in the park; Lions Art in the Park, Crystal River; **November:** Festival of the Arts in Inverness (about 400 artists and craftspeople display their works); Arts, Crafts and Seafood Festival, Old Homosassa; Under the Pines arts and crafts show at the Plantation Inn & Golf Resort, Crystal River; **December:** Chamber of Commerce Christmas Parade, Crystal River; Citrus County Christmas Parade, Inverness; Christmas tree lighting ceremony, Crystal River; Homosassa Christmas Boat Parade, Homosassa; Christmas Tree Trimming, Inverness.

SPORTS AND LEISURE ACTIVITIES:
Most popular local fishing areas: Gulf of Mexico and Lake Tsala Apopka (fishing from boats and piers). Popular catches are black bass, speckled perch, blue gill, shellcracker, grouper, spotted sea trout, catfish and tarpon. The Homosassa, Chassahowitzka and Crystal rivers are spring fed and also are good fishing areas, as is the Withlacoochee River, which has freshwater and saltwater fishing.
Number of local golf courses: 14
Public beaches? Yes
Tennis courts available to the public? Yes
Boating? Yes
Number of pleasure boats registered in the county (1991-92): 11,818

SERVICES FOR RETIREES:
Senior Center in Lecanto is a clearinghouse for senior services.

FINANCIAL SERVICES:
Number of local banks: 27
Number of local savings and loan associations: 14

THE MEDIA:
Largest local newspaper: *Citrus County Chronicle*
Cable television? Yes

MAJOR LOCAL RETAILERS:
Sears, JCPenney, Belk-Lindsey, Bealls, K mart, Wal-Mart.

FOOD ESTABLISHMENTS: 295

OTHER SERVICES:
Number of local libraries: 8
Number of local hotels/motels: 26
Number of churches: Protestant: 57; Jewish: 1; Catholic: 5; Other: 10

TOURISM INQUIRIES:
Citrus County Chamber of Commerce, 208 W. Main St., Inverness, 34450. Telephone: 904-726-2801; **Crystal River** Chamber of Commerce, 28 Northwest Highway 19, Crystal River, 34428. Telephone: 904-795-3149; **Homosassa Springs** Area Chamber of Commerce, P.O. Box 709, Homosassa Springs, 34447, Telephone: 904-628-2666.

HERNANDO COUNTY
Central West
County seat: Brooksville

POPULATION: 1990: 101,115
1993: 111,695
Increase: 10.5 percent

AGE DISTRIBUTION (1992) IN PERCENTAGES:
0-14 : 14.9
15-44: 29.7
45-64: 23.5
65+ : 32.0

MUNICIPAL POPULATION:
BROOKSVILLE: 1990: 7,589; 1993: 7,659
WEEKI WACHEE: 1990: 11; 1993: 11
UNINCORPORATED: 1990: 93,515; 1993: 104,025

LAND AREA: 478 square miles
POPULATION DENSITY: 234 people per square mile (18th in the state)

   The-second-fastest growing county in the state (135 percent growth from 1980 to 1991) behind Flagler (180 percent), Hernando County also has the fifth highest percentage of residents 65 and older (behind Charlotte, Highlands, Pasco and Sarasota). As Pinellas County (the St. Petersburg are) became the most densely popoulated county in the state, development exploded to the north along the Gulf of Mexico into Pasco County and, more recently, into Hernando. Nearly 4,000 single-family homes were built here between 1989 and 1991.
   Its major tourist attraction, Weeki Wachee Spring, with its underwater mermaid show, attracts about 500,000 visitors a year. Another popular stop is Rogers' Christmas House Gift Shop, which lures about 250,000 yearly. Consequently, tourism is an important industry here along with limestone mining and cement production, dairy products, citrus, forest resources and construction. The county is dotted with small freshwater lakes and natural parks. Housing choices range from apartment complexes to waterfront resort homes.

POPULATION DURING THE TOURIST SEASON:
Winter population increases by about 6,000 Snowbirds.

HOUSING PRICES:
Average prices in the $50,000 to $70,000 range.
Number of vacant residential lots: 41,668; number of single-family residences: 35,710; mobile homes: 8,637; condominiums: 639

EDUCATION:
Number of schools: 19
Number of students enrolled: 14,336
Percentage of students continuing education after high school: 80.12

Teacher-to-pupil ratio: 1:18.5
Average teacher's salary: $27,289

Colleges, universities, and junior or community colleges serving the area:
Pasco-Hernando Community College (main branch in Dade City, a campus in Brooksville and an office in Spring Hill); Central Florida Community College, Ocala; University of South Florida, Tampa; University of Tampa, Tampa; St. Leo College in St. Leo.

Trade and technical schools serving the area:
Withlacoochee Vo-Tech; Marchman Vocational Center; Hernando County Education Center

HEALTH CARE:
Number of general hospitals: 3
Number of hospital beds: 366
Number of physicians: 124

TAXES: Total county ad-valorem millage rate (1993): 18.9898

STANDARD CRIME RATE: 4,688.7 offenses per 100,000 population (36th out of 67 counties)

LARGEST PRIVATE EMPLOYERS:

Name	Employees	Product/Service
Wal-Mart Distribution Center	800	Distribution
HCA Oak Hill Community Hospital	750	Health care
Publix	734	Grocery
Winn-Dixie Stores	500	Grocery
Hernando Health Care	500	Health care
Sparton Electronics	400	Electronics Mfg.
Wal-Mart Stores	300	Department stores
Florida Crushed Stone	285	Aggregate mining
SunBank & Trust Company	260	Banking
Kash-N-Karry	224	Grocery
Barnett Bank of The Suncoast	185	Banking

COMPANIES PROVIDING LOCAL UTILITIES:
Telephone: Southern Bell
Electricity: Florida Power Corp., Withlacoochee River Electric Co-op.
Natural Gas: None
Water: Hernando County, City of Brooksville, Spring Hill Utilities
Major Water Source: Wells
Sanitary Landfill? Yes

POINTS OF INTEREST:
Weeki Wachee Spring, 12 miles west of Brooksville in Weeki Wachee, a nature theme park with an underwater mermaid show (it bills itself as having the world's only underwater spring theater), bird shows including a Birds of Prey show featuring hawks and eagles, a wilderness river cruise, children's petting zoo and pelican orphanage; **Buccanneer Bay** at Weeki Wachee, a water recreation site operated by Weeki Wachee with swimming in the Weeki Wachee River, river flumes, rope swings and children's water play area; **Rogers' Christmas House** in Brooksville, displays of limited edition collectibles and gifts for purchase; **Foxbower Wildlife Museum** in Spring Hill; **Gulf of Mexico** public beach at Pine Island and freshwater beaches at Silver Lake and Rogers Park; Boyette's Grove Petting Zoo and Museum.

THE ARTS:
Heritage House Museum in Brooksville; **Hernando Symphony Orchestra; Stage West Community Playhouse; New Nostalgics** singing group; and **Sneaker Theatre** for children.

ANNUAL EVENTS:
January: Sleepy Hollow Blue Grass Music Featival at the county fairgrounds; Brooksville Raid Festival (held the weekend before the Super Bowl), a Civil War battle re-enactment; **February:** Hernando Historical Museum Heritage Days Festival with museum tours, entertainment, dance groups and exhibits; **March:** Downtown Springtime Festival & Craft Show in Brooksville; **April:** Hernando County Fair and Youth Livestock Show (first week in April); Hernando Beach Tarpon Festival with music, boat parade, reef sinking; **May:** Hernando County Annual Arts and Crafts Festival, Brooksville; Masaryktown Arts and Crafts Show; **October:**

World Champion Chicken Pluckin Contest festival with arts and crafts; Fall Festival at the Heritage Museum in Brooksville; Octoberfest Music Festival at the county fairgrounds; Hernando Beach Seafood Festival; **November:** Under the Spreading Oaks Fine Art Show in Brooksville; Country Craft Show in Brooksville; **December:** Christmas Tree Fantasy at the county fairgrounds; Annual Christmas Parade in Brooksville; Candlelight Tour at the Heritage Museum in Brooksville.

SPORTS AND LEISURE ACTIVITIES:
Most popular local fishing areas: Gulf fishing at Aripeka, Bayport, Pine Island and Minnow Creek. Freshwater fishing at Nobleton, Istachatta, Lake Lindsey, McKethan Lake, Silver Lake, Weeki Wachee River, Jenkins Creek and Withlacoochee River.
Number of local golf courses: 4 public and a number of semi-private and private
Public beaches? Yes
Tennis courts available to the public? Yes
Boating? Yes
Number of pleasure boats registered in the county (1991-92): 5,312

SERVICES FOR RETIREES:
Social Security and Medicare information: 1-800-521-9277; American Association of Retired Persons chapter; senior citizens group.

FINANCIAL SERVICES:
Number of local banks: 30
Number of local savings and loan associations: 14

THE MEDIA:
Largest local newspaper: *Hernando Today*
Cable television? Yes

MAJOR LOCAL RETAILERS:
Bealls, K mart, Wal-Mart, and Target. Also flea markets, including one at Airport Mart in Brooksville.

FOOD ESTABLISHMENTS: 286

OTHER SERVICES:
Number of local libraries: 4
Number of local motels: 14
Number of churches: Protestant: 100; Jewish: 1; Catholic: 9; Other: 4

TOURISM INQUIRIES:
Greater **Hernando** County Chamber of Commerce, 31178 Cortez Blvd. East, Brooksville, Fla. 34602. Telephone: 904-796-4580.

HILLSBOROUGH County
Central West
County seat: Tampa

POPULATION: 1990: 834,054
1993: 866,134
Increase: 3.8 percent

AGE DISTRIBUTION (1992) IN PERCENTAGES:
    0-14 : 21.0
    15-44: 47.3
    45-64: 19.3
    65+ : 12.4

MUNICIPAL POPULATION:
PLANT CITY: 1990: 22,754; 1993: 24,283
TAMPA: 1990: 280,015; 1993: 282,848
TEMPLE TERRACE: 1990: 16,444; 1993: 17,167
UNINCORPORATED: 1990: 514,841; 1993: 541,836

LAND AREA: 1,051 square miles
POPULATION DENSITY: 824 people per square mile (6th in the state)

One of the fastest-growing areas in the nation in the 1980s, the Tampa region is the largest Metropolitan Statistical Area in Florida, having surpassed Dade County in the late 1980s. The region, consisting of Hillsborough, Pinellas, Pasco and Hernando counties, had a population of 2.13 million residents in 1993, compared with the Miami area's nearly 1.95 million.

Tampa has become major-league. It has a National Football League team and in December 1990 was awarded a National Hockey League franchise. It also is becoming more of an art and cultural center year by year.

Tampa is expected to lead Florida in the formation of new jobs through the turn of the century. It has been ranked third nationally by chief executive officers as a place to locate a business. Nationally it ranks 16th in department store sales; 20th in furniture and home furnishing store sales; and 15th in automotive dealer sales and building materials and hardware store sales, according to the Greater Tampa Chamber of Commerce.

The leading non-agricultural industry is services, with 171,082 employees as of 1991, followed by trade at 122,316; government at 73,149; finance, insurance and real estate, 52,276; manufacturing, 39,432; and transportation/public utilities, 29,108.

No one industry dominates the county. Among key services and products are health care, electronics, computer services and retailing.

Tampa also has the state's largest port: It handled more than 49 million tons of exports, imports, and domestic merchandise in fiscal 1991-92, nearly three times the tonnage at the state's second largest port, Port Everglades near Fort Lauderdale. Hillsborough has more than 1,000 import/export companies. Key products are phosphate fertilizer, citrus, machinery parts, orange juice, lumber/building products and agricultural chemicals. Finally, the port is growing in the cruise-ship boom.

Hundreds of manufacturing firms have located here in recent years. And some have chosen Tampa as a base, including GTE Florida Inc. (using Tampa as a headquarters); First Florida Bank (an operations center); and GTE Data Services Inc. (data processing). Other well-known companies with offices here include Continental Airlines, IBM, Dun & Bradstreet Plan Services, CIGNA, Salomon Brothers, Chase Home Mortgage Corp. and Delta Airlines.

Another economic force in the county is MacDill Air Force Base, which has about 6,092 employees. The base's mission is to train F16 fighter pilots and maintenance crews and is also the U.S. Central Command and Special Operations Command headquarters. Its long-term fate remained uncertain in 1994.

If you're younger than 45, Tampa may be the place in the area for you. In neighboring Pasco County, 53.7 percent of the residents are 45 and older; in Pinellas, the figure is 46.8 percent. In Hillsborough, the percentage is 31.7. Put another way, the median age in Hillsborough is 33 years, in Pinellas 44, in Pasco 53.

Tampa is also known for its nightlife and has a number of nightclubs. And the city is home to one of the state's most popular attractions, Busch Gardens, which attracts about 3 million visitors a year.

Because the city is such a commercial and financial center, traffic on Interstate 275 through Tampa and along the Howard Frankland Bridge into Pinellas County can be brutal, especially during rush hours. Contributing to the traffic are people heading to the Suncoast beaches in Pinellas (Hillsborough County is on Tampa Bay, but not on the Gulf of Mexico). There has been some improvement, however, since the bridge was widened in the early 1990s.

Other recent projects also have included a $3.54 billion construction along the I-75 corridor as well as several major downtown Tampa projects, including the Florida Aquarium (housing reefs, caves and 4,300 plants and animals) the Garrison Seaport Center and an outdoor waterfront music dome, all of which were under construction in 1994.

Agriculture's impact is still keenly felt in Hillsborough — to the tune of about $400 million a year, most of it from the eastern end of the county. Among major sources of agricultural production on the county's 2,600 farms are vegetable crops (the county ranked 6th in the state in 1991 with total net farm income estimated at $123.3 million), ornamental horticulture (has ranked in the top 10 in recent years), citrus (9th in the state in 1992-93 with production at 10.7 million boxes), dairy (seventh in 1992), beef cattle forage (has ranked in the top 10), and poultry (one of the top counties).

Plant City: Known as the Winter Strawberry Capital of the World, it produces more than 3 million flats of berries each year. The Florida Strawberry Festival, held during 11 days in late February and early March, attracts an estimated 800,000 visitors to hear country-western and folk singers, to view the arts and crafts of the region, Robinson's racing pigs, amateur talent, exhibits on agriculture, commerce, education, industry, livestock, and horticulture, and to ride the midway. Not to mention to eat the strawberries. The city is 24 miles east of Tampa. While the area has relied on agriculture for years, this is beginning to shift as more manufacturers move into the area. Major products include processed meats and fertilizer.

Temple Terrace: Northeast of downtown Tampa, the area is residential and is popular among faculty at the University of South Florida.

The unincorporated communities:

Brandon: About 12 miles east of Tampa, the area, which includes the communities of Seffner, Valrico, Dover, Durant, Lithia, Mango, Bloomingdale and Riverview, has around 100,000 people. It is popular among younger residents. **Sun City Center:** In southern Hillsborough County, this is a retirement community with single-family homes and condominiums. The community has about 10,000 residents. **Apollo Beach:** In southwestern Hillsborough County, this is a waterfront community that has miles of canals.

Finally, the county is noted for something else — it supplies 95 percent of all tropical fish raised in America.

TOURISM:
The Tampa Chamber says a 1992 study showed that 4.46 million people visited the county. Busch Gardens alone attracts around 3 million visitors a year. The largest influx of tourists is in the winter.

HOUSING PRICES:
Median sales price of existing homes in the Tampa-St. Pete-Clearwater area was $76,700 in June 1994. Average price in Hillsborough was $95,000 through the early 1990s.
Number of vacant residential lots: 32,383; number of single-family residences: 209,945; mobile homes: 11,778; condominiums: 20,090

EDUCATION:
Number of schools: 186
Number of students enrolled: 135,204
Percentage of students continuing education after high school: 70.75
Teacher-to-pupil ratio: 1:17.2
Average teacher's salary: $31,517

Colleges, universities, and junior or community colleges serving the area:
University of South Florida in Tampa; University of Tampa; Tampa College; Florida College in Temple Terrace; Hillsborough Community College in Tampa; Hillsborough Community College branch in Plant City; Eckerd College in St. Petersburg; St. Petersburg Junior College; and St. Leo College in St. Leo

Trade and technical schools serving the area:
Erwin Area Vocational Technical Center, Tampa; ITT Technical Institute, Tampa; Brewster Technical.

HEALTH CARE:
Number of general hospitals: 21
Number of hospital beds: 4,015
Number of physicians: 2,332

TAXES: Total county ad-valorem millage rate (1993): 19.1091

STANDARD CRIME RATE: 10,117 offenses per 100,000 population (4th out of 67 counties)

LARGEST EMPLOYERS:
Name	Employees	Product/Service
Hillsborough County School Board	22,000	Public education
Hillsborough County Government	9,169	Government
University of South Florida	7,349	Education services
MacDill Air Force Base	6,092	Military base
Tampa International Airport	4,497	Airport
GTE Florida	4,435	Corporate Headquarters
St. Joseph's Hospital	4,400	Medical facility

City of Tampa	4,000	Government services
U.S. Postal Service	3,600	Government services
Tampa General Hospital	3,500	Health Care
Tribune Company	3,500	Publishing
Kash 'N Karry	3,162	Supermarket
Tampa Electric Company	3,157	Utilities
Busch Entertainment Corp.	2,500	Entertainment

COMPANIES PROVIDING LOCAL UTILITIES:
Telephone: GTE Florida
Electricity: Tampa Electric Co.
Natural Gas: Peoples Gas System and Central Florida Gas
Water: Cities of Tampa, Temple Terrace and Plant City; Hillsborough County
Major Water Source: Rivers, lakes, wells
Sanitary Landfill? Yes

POINTS OF INTEREST:
Tampa: Busch Gardens, a 300-acre theme park with wild animals and amusement rides (see Attractions chapter for details); **University of South Florida,** which is on an 1,800-acre campus in north Tampa; **Adventure Island,** a 13-acre outdoor water theme park; **Lowry Park Zoo,** exhibits of animals in natural-habitat settings; **Ybor City,** a revitalized Cuban cultural area where cigars are made by hand, has Cuban architectural motifs, shops, museums, renovated cigar worker's cottage, restaurants; **Tampa Bay Buccaneers** professional football at **Tampa Stadium** (the stadium seats 74,000 people and has other events during the year, including concerts, tractor pulls, horse show, other games); **Tampa Bay Lightning** NHL team; **Cincinnati Reds** spring training camp in Plant City (in 1996 the New York Yankees are scheduled to move their spring training camp to the Tampa area); **Florida State Fairgrounds,** new home of the Lightning and the **Premier Equestrian Center,** which hosts weekend horse shows (arena for Lightning on the grounds was expected to be completed in 1995); **Tampa Bay Storm** arena football; **Tampa Greyhound Dog Track; Tampa Jai Alai** (year-round); **Tampa Bay Polo Club** at the Walden Lake Polo Field in Plant City has matches from January through April; **Hyde Park** and **Bayshore Boulevard** in Tampa, areas of exclusive homes; **Tampa Convention Center,** which has 200,000 square feet of exhibit space; **Seminole Bingo of Tampa,** big-stakes bingo with frequent prizes of $100,000; **Port of Tampa,** where huge cruise ships often dock and where phosphate loading facilities can be seen (good vantage point is from Channel Drive, on Davis Islands).
Others: Gator Jungle, near Plant City, where visitors view alligators, crocodiles, and South American caiman living in their natural habitat; **Little Manatee River State Recreation Area,** in southern Hillsborough County, has camping, picnicking, freshwater fishing, horseback riding trails, nature trail, boat ramp; **Hillsborough River State Park,** in northern Hillsborough County, has camping, picnicking, swimming, freshwater fishing, hiking, guided tours of 1830s-era fort, boat and canoe rentals, concessions, suspension bridge.

THE ARTS:
Tampa: Museum of Science and Industry features more than 100 permanent displays, including a Gulf Coast hurricane exhibit and a fossil collection; **Tampa Museum of Art** has rotating art shows in six galleries; **Tampa Bay Performing Arts Center** hosts drama, comedy, music and dance performances and is the largest performing arts center south of the Kennedy Center; **Henry B. Plant Museum** at the University of Tampa displays art works, furnishings and fashions from about 100 years ago; **Children's Museum of Tampa** has hands-on exhibits, such as giant bubbles; **Ybor City State Museum** has exhibits focusing on Tampa's Latin Quarter; **Tampa Theatre,** restored 1926 movie palace featuring films, special events, and concerts; **The Florida Opera; The Florida Orchestra; Tampa Ballet; Tampa Players; Playmakers Theatre Company;** the new **Museum of African-American Art; Florida Center for Contemporary Art,** Ybor City, primarily exhibits works of emerging artists; **Seminole Cultural Center,** an authentic Seminole Indian village, features a museum, live alligator wrestling, snake demonstrations, Florida wildlife; the three **University of South Florida Art Galleries,** which specialize in contemporary and graphic art and student works.
Others: Plant City Community Theatre; Arts Council of Plant City presents variety of cultural events including concerts in the park and the Children's Fun Festival; **East Hillsborough Historical Society** maintains a historical museum and model railroad museum.

ANNUAL EVENTS:

January: First Night Tampa Bay, a New Year's Eve celebration of the arts, includes jugglers, mask-painting, petting zoo, theater troupes, mimes, ballet dances, choruses, through 10 downtown blocks; New Year's Day Hall of Fame Bowl, which pits top college football teams from the Atlantic Coast Conference and the Big Ten for a post-season game (preceded by the Hall of Fame Bowl New Year's Eve Festival, featuring a waterfront pep rally, concert, fireworks at Harbour Island); **February:** Florida State Fair at the Florida State Fairgrounds; Gasparilla Festival, an ongoing celebration featuring parades, concerts, Pirate Fest street festival, running events, Ybor City Fiesta Day, Illuminated Night Parade, music, dancing, ethnic foods, and arts and crafts; GTE Suncoast Classic attracts Senior PGA Tour players to the Tournament Players Club of Tampa Bay at Cheval; **Late February-Early March:** Florida Strawberry Festival in Plant City each year attracts about 800,000 visitors over 11 days, includes big-star country music shows, cookoffs, diaper-decorating and strawberry-eating contests; **March:** Gasparilla Sidewalk Art Festival in Tampa features artists competing for cash prizes; Winter Equestrian Festival, Florida State Fairgrounds, a rich hunter-jumper horse show offering $1 million in prize money, culminates in the American Invitational at Tampa Stadium; **July:** Fourth of July Celebration, Harbour Island; Summer Arts and Crafts Fiesta, Ybor Square; **September:** Brandon League of Fine Arts Artfest at Regency Square in Brandon; **October:** Plant City Arts and Crafts Festival; Fall Arts and Crafts Fiesta, Ybor Square; **November:** Florida Classic, a Thanksgiving tradition in Tampa — a football game between Florida A&M University and Bethune-Cookman College, both predominantly African-American schools (weekend also includes jazz, black-tie ball); **December:** Christmas parade in Plant City; Brandon Balloon Festival in Sabal Park has races and target contests involving hot-air balloons, also arts and crafts and the Brandon Marathon and 5K Fun Run; Santa Fest in downtown Tampa, includes entertainment at the Franklin Street Mall, floats, marching bands, parade and a shipment of snow.

SPORTS AND LEISURE ACTIVITIES:

Most popular local fishing areas: Tampa Bay, Alafia River, Hillsborough River, Little Manatee River, Thonotosassa River, Lake Thonotosassa, Lettuce Lake, Lake Starvation, Lake Weeks, and nearby lakes in Polk County.
Number of local golf courses: 30 in the region.
Public beaches: Yes
Tennis courts available to the public? Yes
Boating? Yes
Number of pleasure boats registered in the county (1991-92): 36,399

SERVICES FOR RETIREES:

For general information in the county, consult your phone book for local offices of the state Department of Health and Rehabilitative Services.

FINANCIAL SERVICES:

Number of local banks: 189
Number of local savings and loan associations: 31

THE MEDIA:

Largest local newspaper: *Tampa Tribune*
Cable television? Yes

MAJOR LOCAL RETAILERS:

Burdines, JCPenney, Sears, Montgomery Ward, Dillards and Belk-Lindsey. Distinctive shopping areas include Ybor Square in Tampa's Latin Quarter; Old Hyde Park Village, just off the exclusive Bayshore Boulevard (shops include Polo/Ralph Lauren, Laura Ashley and Godiva Chocolatier); Harbour Island, near downtown, accessible by two bridges and a skyway people mover; seven major area malls.

FOOD ESTABLISHMENTS: 2,658

OTHER SERVICES:

Number of local libraries: 15
Number of local hotels/motels: 158
Number of churches: Protestant: 444; Jewish: 8; Catholic: 52; Other: 36

TOURISM INQUIRIES:

Greater **Tampa** Chamber of Commerce, P.O. Box 420, Tampa, 33601. Telephone: 813-228-

7777; Greater **Plant City** Chamber of Commerce, P.O. Drawer CC, Plant City, 33564. Telephone: 813-754-3707.

MANATEE County
Central West
County seat: Bradenton

POPULATION: 1990: 211,707
1993: 223,508
Increase: 5.6 percent

AGE DISTRIBUTION (1992) IN PERCENTAGES:
0-14 : 16.8
15-44: 35.1
45-64: 20.2
65+ : 27.9

MUNICIPAL POPULATION:
ANNA MARIA: 1990: 1,744; 1993: 1,808
BRADENTON: 1990: 43,769; 1993: 46,626
BRADENTON BEACH: 1990: 1,657; 1993: 1,650
HOLMES BEACH: 1990: 4,810; 1993: 4,925
LONGBOAT KEY (part): 1990: 2,544; 1993: 2,621
PALMETTO: 1990: 9,268; 1993: 9,385
UNINCORPORATED: 1990: 147,915; 1993: 156,493

LAND AREA: 741 square miles
POPULATION DENSITY: 302 people per square mile (16th in the state)

Manatee County probably is most famous for two things: Tropicana juice products and the Pittsburgh Pirates. The county, and more specifically its largest city, Bradenton, are home to the main plant of the nation's largest orange juice marketer and to the Pirates during spring training. The county, which traditionally has been a haven for Midwestern and Northeastern retirees, is also luring a lot of tourists to its miles of shoreline and to what its cities and beach communities have to offer — from a growing list of cultural and recreational activities to historical sites. In recent years, more than 10,000 people have worked in tourism-related businesses and the annual tourism payroll is estimated at $106 million. Tourist tax collections in 1994 were projected at nearly $1.8 million. More than 1 million tourists come to the county each year.

Agriculture is still a major force here, adding at least $213 million to the area's economy. The county is the leading producer of cabbage in the state, while it ranks No. 2 in its production of tomatoes and watermelon. About 10,000 acres of tomatoes are grown each year and the annual production of livestock and poultry exceeds $23 million. Commercial fishing is also big.

There are six incorporated communities: **Bradenton,** the county seat and the county's hub for shopping, finance, business and industry, medical care and culture; **Palmetto,** center of the county's agricultural industry and eighth in the state in recent years in agricultural income (tomatoes are the No. 1 crop). Area also has some of the largest condominium developments in the county; **Anna Maria,** on Anna Maria Island (a stretch of beaches, dunes and beach communities that lies between the Gulf of Mexico and the Intracoastal Waterway), which prohibits high rises; **Holmes Beach,** on Anna Maria Island, is the largest of the three cities on the island; **Bradenton Beach,** on Anna Maria Island, a popular vacation spot; and **Longboat Key,** an island (a portion of which is in Manatee County and a portion in Sarasota County) that is largely a resort and retirement community. There also are a number of small, unincorporated communities: **Terra Ceia,** near the Sunshine Skyway Bridge (see points of interest below); **Cortez,** a fishing village on Sarasota Bay; and **Parrish** and **Ellenton,** agricultural areas. Manufactured housing is very popular in the southern part of the county.

Port Manatee is the state's third largest port, handling 5.4 million tons of exports and imports and domestic goods in fiscal 1991-92.

TOURISM:
Local tourism officials say that 1.2 million people visit the county each year. Other officials estimate the number of Snowbirds peaks in March at 45,000.

HOUSING PRICES:
Median sales price of a single-family existing home in the Sarasota-Bradenton area in June 1994 was $97,100. The average price for a two-bedroom was $81,665; for a three-bedroom, $109,969; and for a four-bedroom, $149,101. Apartment rentals ranged from $437 a month for a one-bedroom, one-bath to $683 a month for a three-bedroom, two-bath. On Anna Maria Island, typical two-bedroom, two-bath homes sell for $150,000 to $160,000 for canal-front properties, and $85,000 to $120,000 for non-waterfront properties. Gulf-front and bay-front properties can go for $350,000 on up.
Number of vacant residential lots: 11,548; single-family residences: 45,910; mobile homes: 8,652; condominiums: 22,207

EDUCATION:
Number of schools: 56
Number of students enrolled: 29,685
Percentage of students continuing education after high school: 64.85
Teacher-to-pupil ratio: 1:17.9
Average teacher's salary: $30,831

Colleges, universities, and junior or community colleges serving the area:
University of South Florida/New College, Sarasota; University of Sarasota; Ringling School of Art and Design; Manatee Community College

Trade and technical schools serving the area:
Manatee Area Vocational Technical Center; Sarasota County Technical Institute

HEALTH CARE:
Number of general hospitals: 2
Number of hospital beds: 895
Number of physicians: 320

TAXES: Total county ad-valorem millage rate (1993): 16.3783

STANDARD CRIME RATE: 7,358.8 offenses per 100,000 population (14th out of 67 counties)

LARGEST PRIVATE EMPLOYERS:
Name	Employees	Product/Service
Tropicana Products	3,515	Orange juice/ beverages
Staff Leasing Inc.	3,350	Employee leasing
Staff Management	1,500	Employee leasing
Manatee Memorial Hospital	1,246	Health care
HCA L.W. Blake Memorial Hospital	1,200	Health care
Wellcraft Marine Corp.	850	Pleasure boats
Freedom Village Group	750	Care facility
Bealls Department Stores	605	Retail sales
Bausch & Lomb Inc.	600	Contact lenses
Hi-Stat Manufacturing	507	Speed sensors
Albertson's	500	Grocery chain

COMPANIES PROVIDING LOCAL UTILITIES:
Telephone: GTE
Electricity: Florida Power & Light; Peace River Cooperative
Natural Gas: Peoples Gas Co.
Water: Manatee County Public Works; Bradenton Public Works; Palmetto Public Works
Major Water Source: Lake
Sanitary Landfill? Yes

POINTS OF INTEREST:
South Florida Museum & Bishop Planetarium, depicts life in Florida from prehistoric times to the space age. Planetarium has multimedia productions including laser lightshows. There is also an observatory for nighttime sky gazing; **Lake Manatee State Recreation Area** for camping, picnicking, swimming, freshwater fishing and boating; **Myakka River State Park** (14 miles east of Sarasota on SR 72) is on 28,875 acres. It is one of the state's largest parks and offers camping, picknicking, freshwater fishing, hiking, guided tours, boat and canoe rentals, horse trails, vistas

of lakes, the river, marshes, hammocks and prairies, flora and fauna; **Gamble Plantation State Historic Site** in Ellenton is the only antebellum plantation house surviving in this part of the state and the only Confederate museum in the state; **De Soto National Monument,** north of Bradenton, marks the spot where De Soto landed in 1539; **Manatee Village Historical Park,** a restoration of the first courthouse and church in Manatee County; **Braden Castle,** former home of J.A. Braden, a sugar plantation operator during the Civil War; **The Sunshine Skyway Bridge,** 4.1 miles long, connecting St. Petersburg and Manatee County over the mouth of Tampa Bay; Bradenton is spring training site for the **Pittsburgh Pirates**; and **Anna Maria Island Historical Museum** in Anna Maria City.

THE ARTS:

Neel Auditorium, on campus of Manatee Community College, setting for performances by the **Florida West Coast Symphony** and the concert series of the **Manatee Community Concert Association; Manatee Players and Island Players** of Anna Maria Island, theatrical groups; **Art League of Manatee County** in Bradenton offers art exhibits, classes in painting, pottery and basketry and children's art programs; **Manatee Civic Center** has a 4,000-seat auditorium where sporting and special events are held; **Bradenton Municipal Auditorium,** site of exhibits and shows; **Longboat Key Art Center** has exhibits, classes in painting, sculpture, ceramics and jewelry; **Manatee County Council for the Arts** promotes the arts by sponsoring performances and shows; **Manatee Poetry Group** gives working poets a sounding board for current poems; **Artists Guild Gallery** on Anna Maria Island at Holmes Beach and **Gallery of the Anna Maria Island Art League,** Holmes Beach.

ANNUAL EVENTS:

January: Manatee County Fair; Winter Craft Fair in Bradenton; **February:** Singing River Rendevous & Festival in Bradenton; **March:** Springfest Festival of Fine Arts & Crafts at Holmes Beach; Manatee Heritage Week; De Soto Celebration in Bradenton, a week-long event that salutes De Soto's landing on the Florida coast with music, sports, seafood fests, parades and special shows; **April:** Manatee Craft Fair in Bradenton; **July:** Fourth of July Parade and picnic for children on Anna Maria Island; **September:** Christmas in September Craft Fair in Bradenton; **October:** Octoberfest at Island Community Center on Anna Maria Island; **November:** A Taste of Manatee in Bradenton; Heritage Arts Week festival at Anna Maria's Community Center; **December:** Twas the Week Before Christmas festival in Bradenton; Anna Maria Island Festival of Fine Arts behind Holmes Beach City Hall; and Christmas Parade and giveaway of gifts by Santa Claus on Anna Maria Island.

SPORTS AND LEISURE ACTIVITIES:

Most popular local fishing areas: Gulf of Mexico; Manatee River (for largemouth bass, bluegill, shellcracker, freshwater catfish); Lake Manatee (bluegill, sunshine bass, channel catfish, speckled fish); Jiggs Landing, four miles east of Oneco (speckled perch, crappies); offshore reefs (grouper); freshwater fishing piers at 59th St. Park in Bradenton, Fort Hamer in Parrish, Lake Manatee off SR 64, and 24th St. Park in Bradenton; saltwater piers at Anna Maria City Pier on north end of Anna Maria Island, Bradenton Beach City Pier on south end of Anna Maria Island, Sharky's Rod and Reel Pier and Anna Maria Pier where Tampa Bay, the Manatee River and Intracoastal Waterway converge (snook, flounder, redfish, speckled trout), Rod and Reel Pier, north end of Anna Maria Island, and Green Bridge Fishing Pier, located halfway across the Manatee River (snook, speckled trout, flounder, redfish); Intracoastal Waterway from Holmes Beach through Longboat Key (trout, sheepshead, snook, flounder, mangrove snapper, redfish); Palma Sola Causeway at Palma Sola Bay.
Number of local golf courses: 20, including 9 private
Public beaches? Yes
Tennis courts available to the public? Yes
Boating? Yes
Number of pleasure boats registered in the county (1991-92): 12,975

SERVICES FOR RETIREES:

Manatee Council on Aging has information on such retirement support measures such as the Retired Senior Volunteer Program of Manatee County. Also Meals on Wheels.

FINANCIAL SERVICES:

Number of local banks: 51
Number of local savings and loan associations: 34

THE MEDIA:
Largest local newspaper: *The Bradenton Herald*
Cable television? Yes

MAJOR LOCAL RETAILERS:
There are 85 shopping centers in the county with stores such as Bealls, Belk Lindsey, K mart, Burdines, JCPenney, Sears and Wal-Mart.

FOOD ESTABLISHMENTS: 643

OTHER SERVICES:
Number of local libraries: 5
Number of local hotels/motels: 73
Number of churches: Protestant: 165; Jewish: 4; Catholic: 7; Other: 62

TOURISM INQUIRIES:
Manatee Chamber of Commerce, P.O. Box 321, 222-10th St. West, Bradenton, 34206-0321. Telephone: 813-748-3411; **Anna Maria Island** Chamber of Commerce, P.O. Box 1892, Holmes Beach, 34218. Telephone: 813-778-1541.

PASCO County
Central West
County seat: Dade City

POPULATION: 1990: 281,131
1993: 293,966
Increase: 4.6 percent

AGE DISTRIBUTION (1992) IN PERCENTAGES:
0-14 : 15.1
15-44: 31.2
45-64: 21.4
65+ : 32.3

MUNICIPAL POPULATION:
DADE CITY: 1990: 5,633; 1993: 5,688
NEW PORT RICHEY: 1990: 14,044; 1993: 14,352
PORT RICHEY: 1990: 2,521; 1993: 2,601
SAINT LEO: 1990: 1,009; 1993: 912
SAN ANTONIO: 1990: 776; 1993: 786
ZEPHYRHILLS: 1990: 8,220; 1993: 8,467
UNINCORPORATED: 1990: 248,928; 1993: 261,160

LAND AREA: 745 square miles
POPULATION DENSITY: 395 people per square mile (13th in the state)

Once primarily an agricultural area, the county's economic base has moved into light manufacturing and professional and business services. Citrus and livestock remain the primary agricultural products; wholesale nurseries and Christmas tree farms also play a role. The county is heavily influenced by the retailing industry. Of the 10 major private sector employers in Pasco, five are either retailers or supermarkets. This is not surprising, given that the county's percentage of residents 65 or older is the third-highest in the state.

The county has several major cities, including **New Port Richey**. Located in western Pasco, the city is a commercial center with U.S. Highway 19 running through it. Along this highway, which is three lanes in each direction, you can find just about any items you'd want — there are fast food places, shopping centers, and other restaurants and stores. The highway, as in Pinellas County to the south, has countless traffic lights and lots of slow-moving traffic during peak times.

Dade City, the county seat, has been designated a Florida Mainstreet City by the National Trust for Historic Preservation. The city has a number of historic churches and homes along with antique and other small shops. It is also home to Lykes Pasco, a large citrus manufacturer; Pasco-Hernando Community College; and the Pioneer Florida Museum. In **Zephyrhills,** the winter tourist season is also big business. Estimates are that about a third of the city's residents are retirees, many of them from New York and Michigan. Mobile home living is popular, with around 150 mobile home and recreational vehicle parks in the area. Among the major employers are the Lykes-Pasco juice dispenser manufacturing plant and Saddlebrook Resort. Another major business is the sale of the town's drinking water — one of the city's claims to fame — to areas outside the city. Another unusual feature of this city is its appetite for the sport of parachuting. The city's airport is home to the Phoenix Parachute Center and plays host to several parachute meets.

Throughout Pasco County, mobile home living is popular — the county leads the state in the number of mobile homes within its boundaries.

TOURISM:
No figures are available, but snowbirds flock to this county.

HOUSING PRICES:
Average prices typically $48,000 for a two-bedroom home; $80,000 for a three-bedroom; $112,000 for four bedrooms or more.
Number of vacant residential lots: 21,133; number of single-family residences: 86,642; mobile homes: 28,041; condominiums: 11,115

EDUCATION:
Number of schools: 46
Number of students enrolled: 38,265
Percentage of students continuing education after high school: 72.90
Teacher-to-pupil ratio: 1:17.3
Average teacher's salary: $27,516

Colleges, universities, and junior or community colleges serving the area:
Pasco-Hernando Community College, Dade City; St. Leo College in St. Leo; University of South Florida, Tampa; Trinity College of Florida in New Port Richey; University of Tampa; Hillsborough Community College in Tampa; Tampa College in Tampa

Trade and technical schools serving the area:
Marchman Vocational Center; Tampa Technical Institute

HEALTH CARE:
Number of general hospitals: 6
Number of hospital beds: 1,013
Number of physicians: 373

TAXES: Total county ad-valorem millage rate (1993): 18.4050

STANDARD CRIME RATE: 3,954.2 offenses per 100,000 population (45th out of 67 counties)

LARGEST EMPLOYERS:

Name	Employees	Product/Service
Lykes Pasco Packing Co.	1,350	Citrus products
HCA New Port Richey Hospital	1,100	Hospital
Winn-Dixie	1,000	Grocery
Kash-N-Karry	970	Grocery
Saddlebrook Resort	930	Resort
Wal-Mart	845	Retailer
HCA Bayonet Point	800	Health care
Publix	750	Grocery
K mart	500	Retail sales
Barnett Bank of Pasco County	470	Banking

COMPANIES PROVIDING LOCAL UTILITIES:
Telephone: GTE/Florida, United Telephone Co.
Electricity: Florida Power, Tampa Electric, Withlacoochee River Electric Coop.
Natural Gas: Peoples Gas
Water: Pasco County Utilities; Dade County Utilities; City of Zephyrhills
Major Water Source: Wells
Sanitary Landfill? No. Resource recovery facility.

POINTS OF INTEREST:
Pioneer Florida Museum in Dade City has seven main buildings including the Trilby Depot, the Lacoochee one-room schoolhouse, the Overstreet House (built in the mid-1860s) and the Enterprise Methodist Church. Among the exhibits is a collection of Florida's first ladies in miniature from 1821-1976, dressed in inaugural gowns; the **Gulf of Mexico** beaches in western Pasco County; **Hudson Beach Park** for sunbathing; **St. Leo Abbey Church** and historic **Church Avenue** in Dade City.

THE ARTS:
Richey Suncoast Theatre in New Port Richey stages musicals, dramas, comedies, recitals; **West Pasco Art Guild;** art presentations through St. Leo College and Pasco-Hernando Community College.

ANNUAL EVENTS:
January: Senior Citizens Day Parade in Zephyrhills; **February:** New Port Richey Fair; Auto & Antique Winter Festival in Zephyrhills; Pasco County Fair in Dade City; Florida Pioneer Museum Quilt Show and Sale; **March:** Chasco Fiesta in New Port Richey has a parade, fashion show, art exhibit, Indian pageant, carnival rides; Zephyrhills Founders Day; March on Art in New Port Richey; **May:** Annual Mother's Day Pow Wow in Dade City; **July:** Sparklebration in Dade City, with games, competitions, fireworks; **Labor Day:** Pioneer Florida Day Festival at the Pioneer Florida Museum in Dade City commemorates the state's early settlement days with a parade, arts and crafts, music; Labor Day Bluegrass Festival at Sertoma Youth Ranch in Dade City; **October:** Richey Region Antique Car Show & Arts and Crafts in New Port Richey; Livestock Concert at Festival Park south of Zephyrhills; **Third Saturday in October:** Rattlesnake Festival in San Antonio has arts and crafts, snake show; **November:** Golden Harvest Art and Crafts Festival in New Port Richey; Annual Holiday Festival, Zephyrhills, arts and crafts, entertainment, food; Auto & Antique Fall Festival, south of Zephyrhills; Fall Flapjack Festival, Land O'Lakes; Annual Thanksgiving Bluegrass Festival at Sertoma Youth Ranch in Dade City; **December:** Christmas Lighting Contest in Zephyrhills; Lighting of the Trees at East Pasco Center, Zephyrhills; Christmas parade in Dade City (first Friday in December); Downtown Christmas stroll in Dade City (first Saturday in December); tour of homes in Dade City (first Sunday in December); Pioneer Florida Museum Christmas Open House in Dade City; Church Street Christmas in Dade City.

SPORTS AND LEISURE ACTIVITIES:
Most popular local fishing area: Gulf of Mexico
Number of local golf courses: At least 15
Public beaches: Yes
Tennis courts available to the public? Yes
Boating? Yes
Number of pleasure boats registered in the county (1991-92): 14,257

SERVICES FOR RETIREES:
Cares, Inc. with locations in New Port Richey, Hudson, Land O'Lakes, Elfers and Zephyrhills; Meals on Wheels; and Elderly Nutrition Program.

FINANCIAL SERVICES:
Number of local banks: 81
Number of local savings and loan associations: 36

THE MEDIA:
Largest local newspaper: *Zephyrhills News*
Cable television? Yes

MAJOR LOCAL RETAILERS:
Montgomery Ward, JCPenney, Wal-Mart, J Byrons, Bealls, Sears, Belk-Lindsey, K mart

FOOD ESTABLISHMENTS: 739

OTHER SERVICES:
Number of local libraries: 12
Number of local motels: 42
Number of churches: Protestant: 200; Jewish: 1; Catholic: 13; Other: 16

TOURISM INQUIRIES:
Greater **Dade City** Chamber of Commerce, Meridian at 7th St., Dade City, 33525. Telephone: 904-567-3769; **Land O'Lakes** Chamber of Commerce, 6221 Land O'Lakes Blvd., P.O. Box 98,

Land O'Lakes, 34639. Telephone: 813-996-5522. **West Paso Chamber of Commerce** Office, 5443 W. Main St., New Port Richey, 34652. Telephone: 813-842-7651; **Zephyrhills** Chamber of Commerce, 38415 Fifth Ave., Zephyrhills, 33540. Telephone: 813-782-1913.

PINELLAS County

Central West
County seat: Clearwater

POPULATION: 1990: 851,659
　　　　　　　1993: 864,953
　　　　　　　Increase: 1.6 percent

AGE DISTRIBUTION (1992) IN PERCENTAGES:
　0-14 : 15.2
　15-44: 37.9
　45-64: 21.0
　65+　: 25.8

MUNICIPAL POPULATION:
BELLEAIR: 1990: 3,963; 1993: 3,976
CLEARWATER: 1990: 98,784; 1993: 100,768
DUNEDIN: 1990: 33,997; 1993: 34,765
GULFPORT: 1990: 11,709; 1993: 11,812
KENNETH CITY: 1990: 4,351; 1993: 4,360
LARGO: 1990: 65,910; 1993: 66,369
OLDSMAR: 1990: 8,361; 1993: 8,498
PINELLAS PARK: 1990: 43,571; 1993: 43,762
SAFETY HARBOR: 1990: 15,120; 1993: 15,708
ST. PETERSBURG:; 1990: 240,318; 1993: 239,701
SEMINOLE: 1990: 9,251; 1993: 9,430
SOUTH PASADENA: 1990: 5,644; 1993: 5,837
TARPON SPRINGS: 1990: 17,874; 1993: 18,488
UNINCORPORATED: 1990: 257,256; 1993: 265,437

LAND AREA: 280 square mile
POPULATION DENSITY: 3,087 people per square mile (1st in the state)

　　This county, home to St. Petersburg and Clearwater — the fourth and tenth largest cities in Florida — is the most densely populated one in Florida. Year-round, it has 3,087 people per square mile — almost triple the density of Broward (the Fort Lauderdale area), the second county on the list. That doesn't count the thousands of winter Snowbirds and the tourists who frequent the Pinellas Suncoast beaches, a narrow strip on the Gulf of Mexico that offers some of the state's most popular beaches.

　　This is an eclectic area, from mobile homes to million-dollar oceanfront estates, and it has just about everything in between. Developments with $300,000 to $500,000 homes have been built throughout the county in recent years. But you can buy a single-family home for as little as $40,000, though most go for $70,000 to $150,000. And there are as many other price ranges as there are neighborhood developments. In addition, scores of high-rise condominium buildings line the water.

　　In Pinellas, the city lines are blurred. It's not like some areas up north, where you'll find modest $100,000 homes in one community, and historically significant 18th-century houses for $500,000 in the next. Take a drive down some of the major thoroughfares in this county and you'll never know that you've just entered another community. For example, you'll notice little difference driving past the strip malls and residential areas of Largo and Seminole into St. Petersburg. But that is not to say that you won't find many different kinds of unusual sights in this county. There are, just to name a few, the beaches; The Pier in downtown St. Petersburg, a five-story inverted pyramid of shops and restaurants jutting into Tampa Bay; nearby downtown marinas that you wouldn't expect to find in a metropolitan downtown setting; and Tarpon Springs, with turn-of-the-century Spring Bayou estates, Greek sponge divers, shrimp trawlers and antique shops.

　　Traffic is horrendous in parts of Pinellas. U.S. 19, for example, runs north and south and delays can be expected routinely. And, east to west, is Ulmerton Road (Route 688), which extends through the county almost to the beaches. Some residents have an unusual hobby — figuring out circuitous routes down residential streets to avoid this road, especially during rush hour. Traffic lights are not synchronized, and you may have to wait for a light to change several times before proceeding to wait at the next intersection. Parallel thoroughfares pose similar challenges. There's no superhighway passing through, except for Interstate 275 in the eastern part of the county. This means that once you're here, you might want to stay a while (one couple paid more than a quarter of a million dollars for a house in western Largo but, despite thousands of dollars worth of improvements, put it on the market less than a year later because they couldn't stand the commute into St. Petersburg). Waits in line at restaurants are another bane (there are more than 23 pages of restaurant advertisements in the local phone book and during the busy winter season, many places do not, or, more to the point, do not have to, take reservations).

But there are good reasons why the county is so populated. You can expect as much as 360 days of at least partial sunshine a year. You can swim at some of the state's most popular beaches. And there are plenty of cultural activities. If your style is to be around lots of people and to have lots of opportunities to do things, this may be your Shangri-La.

There are miles of beaches (accessible from drawbridges across the Intracoastal Waterway), and relatively small parking lots. You may have to drive around for 15 minutes waiting for someone to vacate a parking space. The main reason for the paucity of parking areas is that the land along the beach is almost exclusively owned by hotels, motels, high-rise condominiums and, in between, a few private residences.

The population varies greatly. The St. Petersburg Times ran a special report in March 1990 about widespread hunger in the Tampa Bay area. In the middle of the scale are thousands of middle-class workers and elderly people who have chosen to retire here. And at the other end are wealthy people (the county has a reputation for having thousands of unpretentious million-aires, in addition to those who live in million-dollar waterfront homes).

Aside from the incorporated cities, there are some unincorporated areas, notably Palm Harbor (1992 population, 65,000), just north of Dunedin, which includes the seaside communities of Crystal Beach and Ozona; Indian Bluff Island and its waterfront homes; and Highland Lakes, which is popular with retirees.

Tourism is the big industry here (there is a combined total of about 20,000 hotel and motel rooms, not to mention condominium rental units). Among the other major industries are retail services, government, defense, health care, finance, real estate and construction. According to the Greater Clearwater Chamber of Commerce, retirees are such a factor here that nearly a third of all personal income in the county comes from dividends, interest, rent and Social Security payments.

TOURISM:
This is one of the most popular areas for Snowbirds and for tourists. The population skyrockets from November through March, but estimates vary greatly. Many people believe that the population at least doubles during the tourist season.

HOUSING PRICES:
Median sales price of an existing home in the Tampa-St. Petersburg-Clearwater metropolitan area was $76,700 in June 1994. In Pinellas, average prices in recent years have been in the high 50s for two-bedroom homes, mid-80s for three-bedrooms, and 150s-plus for four-bedrooms.
Number of vacant residential lots: 19,778; number of single-family residences: 224,381; mobile homes: 3,202; condominiums: 88,501

EDUCATION:
Number of schools: 142
Number of students enrolled: 100,135
Percentage of students continuing education after high school: 62.51
Teacher-to-pupil ratio: 1:17.2
Average teacher's salary: $32,545

Colleges, universities, and junior or community colleges serving the area:
St. Petersburg Junior College (which also has a campus in Clearwater, a center in Tarpon Springs and a Health Education Center in Pinellas Park); Eckerd College, St. Petersburg; Florida Institute of Technology Graduate Center, St. Petersburg; Stetson College of Law, St. Petersburg; University of South Florida, Tampa (has a St. Petersburg campus); University of Tampa; Tampa College branch in Clearwater.

Trade and technical schools serving the area:
Pinellas Technical; Erwin Technical Center; Florida Technical Center.

HEALTH CARE:
Number of general hospitals: 23
Number of hospital beds: 5,151
Number of physicians: 1,942

TAXES: Total county ad-valorem millage rate (1993): 16.1181

STANDARD CRIME RATE: 6,690.5 offenses per 100,000 population (18th out of 67 counties)

LARGEST PRIVATE EMPLOYERS:

Name	Employees	Product/service
Home Shopping Network	4,000	Merchandising
Times Publishing	3,836	Newspaper, magazines
Eckerds	3,373	Drug stores
Honeywell	3,000	Aerospace/avionics
Florida Power	2,645	Utilities
Morton Plant Hospital	2,078	Health care
Mease Hospital	2,000	Health care
Nielsen Media Research	2,119	Market research
E-Systems	1,800	Defense equipment
AT&T Paradyne	1,800	Data communications

COMPANIES PROVIDING LOCAL UTILITIES:
Telephone: General Telephone Company
Electricity: Florida Power Corp.; Tampa Electric
Natural Gas: Peoples Gas, City of Clearwater Gas System
Water: Southwest Coast Water Supply Agency
Major Water Source: Wells
Solid waste disposal: Resource recovery

POINTS OF INTEREST:
St. Petersburg:
The 43,000-seat **ThunderDome,** formerly the Florida Suncoast Dome, downtown, was built in hopes of getting a Major League baseball team, but so far no team has moved here. The dome also was envisioned as the home of a National Hockey League expansion team, but the city lost a bid in 1990; nevertheless, the **Tampa Bay Lightning NHL team** played here (its new home in Tampa was scheduled to be completed in 1995). The dome also is the site of major concerts and festivals; **Sunken Gardens,** five acres of exotic flowers, trees and fruits, 500 tropical animals and birds, bird shows, biblical wax museum; the 4.1-mile **Sunshine Skyway Bridge,** a 183-foot-high suspension bridge (the largest cable suspension bridge in the Western Hemisphere), connects Pinellas and Manatee counties; the **Coliseum Ballroom,** a huge historic ballroom with a wooden floor and seating for 2,000; **Fort DeSoto Park,** encompassing five islands connected by road, contains remains of a late-19th-century fort, has picnicking, camping, swimming, nature sanctuaries; **Planetarium and Observatory,** St. Petersburg Junior College; **Boyd Hill Nature Trail,** 216 acres of trails and boardwalks through hardwood hammocks and lakeshores; **The Pier,** an inverted-pyramid waterfront complex of shops, restaurants and an aquarium; the 610-slip **St. Petersburg Marina,** near the Pier downtown, is home to hundreds of sailboats (and is part of the seven-mile preserved downtown waterfront); **Demens Landing,** a waterfront park and playground where Shakespeare in the Park is performed each spring; **Egmont Key State Park** located at the mouth of Tampa Bay, southwest of Fort DeSoto Beach, access by private boat only, has swimming and fishing and is the home of the only manned lighthouse in the United States. Also is a wildlife refuge; **Stouffer Vinoy Resort,** a luxury hotel built in 1925 that's a historic landmark, was refurbished and reopened in 1992; **Gizella Kopsick Palm Arboretum** has a large collection of rare and exotic palm trees.

Clearwater area:
Clearwater Beach, lined with hotels, condominiums and restaurants, connected with the downtown area by the Memorial Causeway; **Clearwater Marina** has a big sport-fishing fleet; **Big Pier 60,** a Gulf pier popular with fishermen; **Boatyard Village,** 1890s-type fishing village offering arts, shops, restaurants; **Clearwater Marine Science Center,** the only facility on the west coast of

Florida that has government permits to rescue and rehabilitate marine mammals, also has recreational and educational facilities, dolphin and sea-turtle exhibits; **Coachman Park,** downtown, concert site; **Moccasin Lake Nature Park,** an energy and environmental education center, offers information about wildlife, plants, animal exhibits, nature trails, solar and wind energy exhibits; **Belleview Mido Resort Hotel,** reputed to be the world's largest occupied wooden structure, listed on National Register of Historic Places; **Air Museum,** Clearwater, military aircraft.

Largo:
Sturgeon Memorial Rose Gardens, Serenity Gardens Memorial Park, more than 100 varieties of roses; **Heritage Park & Museum,** 21-acre re-creation of a turn-of-the-century Florida village. Museum offers exhibits on county and state history.

Tarpon Springs:
Frog Prince Puppetry Arts Center & Theatre, Tarpon Springs Arcade; **Historic Walking Tour of Tarpon Springs' Golden Crescent,** guided and self-guided tours of turn-of-the-century Victorian mansions built by rich northerners; **Noell's Ark Chimp Farm,** a sanctuary for exotic pets, also displays gorillas, orangutans, chimps, monkeys, birds; **Sponge diving exhibitions,** educational half-hour cruises leaving from Sponge Docks; **Spongeorama,** museum on history of Tarpon Springs sponge diving industry; **St. Nicholas Cathedral,** decorated with icons, including one of a weeping St. Nicholas; **Coral Sea Aquarium** has a living reef, coral, sponges, sharks and other fish; sightseeing cruises and a casino cruise leave from the Sponge Docks.

Dunedin:
Honeymoon Island State Recreation Area, accessible by boat or the Dunedin Causeway, offers picnicking, swimming, saltwater fishing, hiking. Has one of the area's few remaining virgin slash pine stands, important nesting sites for ospreys. Island has more than 208 species of plants; **Caladesi Island State Park,** a barrier island with two miles of beaches, accessible by public ferry from Honeymoon Island or by private boat, also offers picnicking, saltwater fishing, hiking and excellent shelling; **Dunedin Municipal Marina,** filled with private yachts and charter boats; **Railroad Historical Museum; Schiller International University** Dunedin campus has students from around the world who study international business relations, liberal arts and languages.

Other cities:
Sea Adventure of Madeira Beach, marine environment exhibits; **Silas Bayside Market,** St. Petersburg Beach, includes Silas' Funhouse; **John's Pass Village and boardwalk,** Madeira Beach, a replica of a turn-of-the-century fishing village (more grouper is brought into John's Pass than any place in the world, according to local officials); **Redington Long Pier,** North Redington Beach; **Suncoast Seabird Sanctuary,** Indian Shores, a wild-bird hospital, rescues injured and sick birds; **Don CeSar resort hotel,** St. Petersburg Beach, a huge pink historic building on the Gulf.

THE ARTS:
St. Petersburg Bayfront Center and Mahaffey Theater, which has a 2,112-seat auditorium for concerts and shows, and an 8,335-seat arena for circus and ice performances, also features touring Broadway plays and nationally known entertainers; **Florida International Museum,** St. Petersburg, was scheduled to have a six-month exhibit, from Jan. 11 to June 11, 1995, titled "Treasures of the Czars," a collection of royal and state treasurers from the Moscow Kremlin Museums; **Ruth Eckerd Hall at the Richard B. Baumgardner Center for the Performing Arts,** Clearwater, a 2,100-seat performing-arts theater, features concerts, stage productions, educational workshops and festivals, and is the winter home of the **Clearwater Orchestra; Salvador Dali Museum,** St. Petersburg, contains large private collection of Dali's work, including 94 original oils, 100 watercolors and drawings, 1,300 graphics, and sculptures, photographs, documents and archives; **Great Explorations,** a museum with six major exhibit areas and "hands-on" discovery for children; **St. Petersburg Museum of Fine Arts** has European, American, Far Eastern and pre-Columbian art in nine galleries; **St. Petersburg Historical and Flight One Museum** has exhibits on Florida history and a display on a 1914 flight across Tampa Bay that's believed to have given birth to commercial aviation; **Science Center of Pinellas County,** St. Petersburg, has laboratories for school children, laser animation, planetarium, hands-on studies of science, math and technology; **P. Buckley Moss Gallery,** St. Petersburg, displays collection of works by namesake artist; **Cultural Center,** Tarpon Springs, has historical artifacts, art classes; **Fine Arts and Cultural Center,** Dunedin, has art education, local art and culture; **Florida Gulf Coast Art**

Center, Belleair, offers instruction in painting, ceramics, drawing, sculpture; **Glass Canvas Gallery,** St. Petersburg, has collection of contemporary glass art from around the world.

SPORTS:
Al Lang Field, downtown St. Petersburg, spring-training home of the St. Louis Cardinals and Baltimore Orioles; **Jack Russell Stadium,** Clearwater, spring-training home of the Philadelphia Phillies; **Dunedin Stadium,** Dunedin, spring-training home of the Toronto Blue Jays; **Derby Lane,** St. Petersburg, dog-racing track; **Tampa Bay Downs,** Oldsmar, pari-mutuel horse racing; **The Pinellas Trail,** a 47-mile hiking/biking trail — described as the longest urban linear trail in the eastern United States; **Tampa Bay Storm,** an arena football team, plays at the Thunder-Dome.

ANNUAL EVENTS:
January (6th): Epiphany festival in Tarpon Springs, begins at Greek Orthodox Church of St. Nicholas, proceeds to Spring Bayou, features colorful religious garb, dancing, food; Ringling Brothers and Barnum & Bailey Circus, St. Petersburg; Martin Luther King celebrations, St. Petersburg; Antique Show and Sale, Bayfront Center; **February:** Suncoast Travel Show, Bayfront Center; Home and Garden Show, ThunderDome; Garage Sale & Flea Market, ThunderDome; **March:** International Folk Fair, ThunderDome, features exhibits and costumes from 40 countries, food, entertainment, arts and crafts; Renaissance Festival, Largo, runs over six weekends, includes entertainment, artisans' re-creation of old European village, contests, waffle-eating contest, games, costumes, competitions, children's Easter weekend, Old World clowns, "Theatre of Fools"; Snowbird No Snow Fest, St. Pete Pier; Pinellas County Fair; **April:** Festival of States, St. Petersburg, includes food, regattas, other athletic contests, concerts, exhibits, pageants, arts and crafts, fireworks, shows for children; Fun and Sun Festival, Clearwater, a 16-day festival that includes an art festival, beauty pageant, golf tournament, dances, regattas, night parade; **May:** Taste of Treasure Island, Memorial Day weekend, has food, arts and crafts; Madeira Beach Triathlon; Artworks! citywide festival in St. Pete; **June:** Taste of Pinellas, St. Pete; Juneteenth, African-American freedom day celebration; **July:** July 4th celebrations in Clearwater and St. Pete; "Pirate Days" July 4th celebration on Treasure Island; pro volleyball tournament, Treasure Island; Bluegrass Festival, Treasure Island; **September:** Tarpon Springs SeaFest has seafood festival, boat show, fishing tournament; Suncoast Home and Garden Show, ThunderDome; **October:** Johns Pass Seafood Festival, Madeira Beach; Halloween Carnival, St. Petersburg; **November:** Scottish Games and Gathering of the Clans, Treasure Island; late in the month, and into December, is the JCPenney Classic golf tournament, Tarpon Springs, which draws PGA and LPGA pro teams and offers $1.2 million in prize money. It benefits 14 Tampa Bay area charities; Holiday Show of Fine Arts & Fine Crafts, St. Pete; St. Pete Boat Show, Bayfront Center; St. Pete Snowfest; **December:** Christmas parade and concert, Clearwater; lighted Christmas boat parades in Treasure Island, Redington Beach, Madeira Beach and St. Pete Beach; Santa Parade (first Saturday), downtown St. Pete; First Night New Year's Eve celebration and art performance, downtown St. Pete.

SPORTS AND LEISURE ACTIVITIES:
Most popular local fishing areas: Gulf of Mexico; private and charter boats abound in this county and catches include sea bass, porgies, grouper, grunts, and, in the summer, tarpon; surfcasting is also popular, as is fishing from piers up and down the beaches.

Number of local golf courses: About 40.

Public beaches: 23 miles of beaches in the county.

Tennis courts available to the public? Yes

Boating? Yes, this is one of the most popular boating areas in the state.

Number of pleasure boats registered in the county (1991-92): 42,427 (second in the state, behind Dade County).

SERVICES FOR RETIREES:
County and city governments have a broad range of services for elderly residents, including Meals on Wheels, adult day care, transportation and community care. There are also scores of senior citizen clubs.

FINANCIAL SERVICES:
Number of local banks: 251

Number of local savings and loan associations: 99

THE MEDIA:
Largest local newspaper: *St. Petersburg Times*

Cable television? Yes

MAJOR LOCAL RETAILERS:
There are 8 regional malls and 123 shopping centers. Major retailers: Bealls, Belk-Lindsey, Burdines, Dillard's, Dollar General, K mart, Byrons, JCPenney, Marshalls, Montgomery Ward, Sears, Gayfer's, Jacobson's.

FOOD ESTABLISHMENTS: 2,755

OTHER SERVICES:
Number of local libraries: 21
Number of local hotels/motels: 436
Number of churches: Protestant: 230; Jewish: 11; Catholic: 25

TOURISM INQUIRIES:
Greater **Clearwater** Chamber of Commerce, 128 North Osceola Ave., P.O. Box 2457, Clearwater, 34617. Telephone: 813-461-0011; Greater **Dunedin** Chamber of Commerce, 301 Main St., Dunedin, 34698-5764. Telephone: 813-733-3197; Greater **Largo** Chamber of Commerce, 395 1st Ave. S.W., Largo, 34640. Telephone: 813-584-2321; **Pinellas Park** Chamber of Commerce, 5851 Park Blvd., Pinellas Park, 34665. Telephone: 813-544-4777; Greater **Palm Harbor** Area Chamber of Commerce, 33451 U.S. 19 North, Suite 300, Palm Harbor, 34684. Telephone: 813-784-4287; **St. Petersburg** Area Chamber of Commerce, 100 2nd Ave. N., Suite 150, P.O. Box 1371, St. Petersburg, 33731. Telephone: 813-821-4069; Greater **Seminole** Area Chamber of Commerce, P.O. Box 3337, Seminole, 34642-0337. Telephone: 813-392-3245; Greater **Tarpon Springs** Chamber of Commerce, 210 South Pinellas Ave., Tarpon Springs, 34689. Telephone: 813-937-6109.

The Pinellas Suncoast Beaches
MUNICIPAL POPULATION:
BELLEAIR BEACH: 1990: 2,070; 1993: 2,090
BELLEAIR BLUFFS: 1990: 2,234; 1993: 2,213
BELLEAIR SHORE: 1990: 60;1993: 60
INDIAN ROCKS BEACH: 1990: 3,963; 1993: 4,019
INDIAN SHORES: 1990: 1,405; 1993: 1,449
MADEIRA BEACH: 1990: 4,225; 1993: 4,222
NORTH REDINGTON BEACH: 1990: 1,135; 1993: 1,141
REDINGTON BEACH: 1990: 1,626; 1993: 1,630
REDINGTON SHORES: 1990: 2,366; 1993: 2,404
ST. PETERSBURG BEACH: 1990: 9,200; 1993: 9,487
TREASURE ISLAND: 1990: 7,266; 1993: 7,327

In the westernmost part of Pinellas County are the Gulf beaches, which lie on a narrow strip of land between the Gulf of Mexico and the Intracoastal Waterway. This beach area is accessible by drawbridges spanning the Intracoastal. Of the 11 cities listed above, 10 are on the Gulf of Mexico and one, Belleair Bluffs, is strictly on the Intracoastal. This strip is primarily a residential area (a mixture of one- and two-family homes and condominiums, and one mobile home park, in North Redington Beach) and also a popular tourist area. It has miles of wide beaches and is a mecca for those who love watersports. Hotels and condos line the better part of the strip on the Gulf side, and restaurants and homes on the Intracoastal side. The recent recession took a toll in this area — all but Belleair Beach lost population between 1989 and 1991, most by small single-digit percentages but a few by as much as 10 percent.

Other facts about the beaches:
The population of these cities doubles during the tourist season, which runs generally from Christmas to Easter.

Real Estate: Two-bedroom homes range roughly from $80,000 to $175,000 (depending on whether they are on the water). Three-bedroom homes range from $125,000 to $200,000. Gulf-front homes $200,000 to $450,000, some higher. Gulf-front condos go for $75,000 and up. Homes on the Intracoastal are slightly lower than those on the Gulf (not dramatically lower, though, as many Intracoastal residents can walk out into their back yards and hop onto their boats.

Further Information: Gulf Beaches on Sand Key Chamber of Commerce, 501-150th Ave.,

Madeira Beach, 33708. Telephone: 813-391-7373; also, 105-5th Ave., Indian Rocks Beach, 34635. Telephone: 813-595-4575 and toll-free, 800-944-1847; **Treasure Island** Chamber of Commerce, 152 108th Ave., Treasure Island, 33706-4799. Telephone: 813-367-4529 (for Treasure Island only); **St. Petersburg Beach** Area Chamber of Commerce, 6990 Gulf Blvd., St. Petersburg Beach, 33706. Telephone: 813-360-6957 (for St. Petersburg Beach only).

St. Augustine, the oldest permanent European settlement in the continental United States, is known for its Spanish architecture.

The Oldest Schoolhouse, more than 200 years old, is a popular tourist spot in St. Augustine.

Northeast Florida residents enjoy boating on the St. Johns River, on lakes and on the Intracoastal Waterway.

NORTHEAST FLORIDA

THE COUNTIES: Alachua, Baker, Bradford, Clay, Columbia, Duval, Flagler, Hamilton, Nassau, Putnam, St. Johns, Suwannee, and Union

MAJOR CITIES: Jacksonville, Gainesville, St. Augustine

TOP INDUSTRIES: Wholesale and retail trade, manufacturing (including paper, chemicals, and furniture), services, government, tourism, the military, education, forestry, construction, mining, agriculture

MAJOR NEWSPAPERS: *The Florida Times-Union* (Jacksonville), *Gainesville Sun*

WEATHER: On the first line is the average maximum temperature for each month; the second line, the average minimum temperature; the third line, the amount of precipitation, in inches, for 1990, from the national weather station.

Jacksonville	Jan.	Feb.	Mar.	Apr.	May	June	July	Aug.	Sep.	Oct.	Nov.	Dec.
Max.	71.2	73.9	77.7	79.2	87.5	92.3	93.4	93.6	91.0	83.5	76.7	72.8
Min.	45.4	52.2	52.5	54.3	63.1	69.4	73.5	71.9	67.9	61.8	50.1	48.7
Precp.	1.8	4.1	1.6	1.3	0.2	1.6	6.5	3.8	2.6	4.5	1.2	1.9

ALACHUA County
Northeast
County seat: Gainesville

POPULATION: 1990: 181,596
1993: 190,655
Increase: 5 percent

AGE DISTRIBUTION (1992) IN PERCENTAGES:
0-14 : 19.0
15-44: 56.3
45-64: 15.1
65+ : 9.5

MUNICIPAL POPULATION
ALACHUA:1990: 4,547; 1993: 5,030
ARCHER: 1990: 1,372 1993: 1,406
GAINESVILLE: 1990: 85,075; 1993: 93,091
HAWTHORNE: 1990: 1,305; 1993: 1,387
HIGH SPRINGS: 1990: 3,144; 1993: 3,398
LA CROSSE: 1990: 122; 1993: 117
MICANOPY: 1990: 626; 1993: 634

NEWBERRY: 1990: 1,644; 1993: 1,920
WALDO: 1990: 1,017; 1993: 1,021
UNINCORPORATED: 1990: 82,744; 1993: 82,651

LAND AREA: 874 square miles
POPULATION DENSITY: 218 people per square mile (20th in the state)

Strongly influenced by the University of Florida since its establishment in 1906, Gainesville today remains synonymous with the Gators. The university, with a student enrollment of more than 38,000, is the area's largest employer (with more than 11,300 full-time employees). It is Florida's oldest and largest university and offers 114 majors and 52 undergraduate, 123 master's and 76 doctoral programs.

The county has two state preserves, a state historical site and a state geological site. Largely because of the presence of the University of Florida and Sante Fe Community College in Gainesville, the county has a number of cultural offerings, including a state theater and art galleries.

Government and health care are also major employers in Alachua County. Three general hospitals are located in the Gainesville area — Alachua General Hospital, North Florida Regional Medical Center and Shands Teaching Hospital at the university. Energizer Power Systems is the largest manufacturing employer, with 1,350 workers. Also located here is the archery products firm, Bear Archery.

Timber is also big business as there are more than 297,000 acres of forest land in the county. The annual income from forest products has been more than $124 million.

There are about 1,100 farms here. Beef cattle, hogs, dairy products, poultry, ornamental plants, peanuts, watermelons, tobacco, corn, soybeans and blueberries are the major revenue-producing crops.

Alachua County's crime rate ranked third highest in the state.

TOURISM:
Not a major factor here.

HOUSING PRICES:
The median sales price of a single-family existing home in the Gainesville metropolitan statistical area was $87,800 for June 1994.
Number of vacant residential lots: 12,536; number of single-family residences: 40,102; mobile homes: 4,303; condominiums: 3,041

EDUCATION:
Number of schools: 41
Number of students enrolled: 28,426
Percentage of students continuing education after high school: 84.65
Teacher-to-pupil ratio: 1:17.7
Average teacher's salary: $28,542

Colleges, universities, and junior or community colleges serving the area:
University of Florida; Santa Fe Community College; Central Florida Community College in Ocala; Lake City Community College in Lake City

Trade and technical schools serving the area:
Santa Fe Community College; Webster College branch in Gainesville; Career City College in Gainesville

HEALTH CARE:
Number of general hospitals: 6
Number of hospital beds: 1,369
Number of physicians: 1,319

TAXES: Total county ad-valorem millage rate (1993): 22.7308

STANDARD CRIME RATE: 10,174.9 offenses per 100,000 population (3rd out of 67 counties)

LARGEST PRIVATE EMPLOYERS:

Name	Employees	Product/Service
University of Florida	11,326	Education
Shands Teaching Hospital	3,800	Health care
Sante Fe Community College	2,100	Education

Veterans Affairs Medical Center	1,650	Health care
Energizer Power Systems	1,350	
North Florida Regional Medical Center	1,319	Health care
Alachua General Hospital	950	Health care
Publix	927	Grocery
Nationwide Insurance Co.	630	Insurance
AvMed-Santa Fe	524	Health care
Wal-Mart	513	Retail sales
Environmental Science & Engineering	470	Consulting engineer

COMPANIES PROVIDING LOCAL UTILITIES:
Telephone: Southern Bell
Electricity: Gainesville Regional Utilities, Florida Power, Clay Electric Cooperative
Natural Gas: Gainesville Regional Utilities
Water: Gainesville Regional Utilities
Major Water Source: Wells
Sanitary Landfill? Yes

POINTS OF INTEREST:
Devil's Millhopper State Geological Site, northwest of Gainesville, is the site of a huge sink-hole that formed when a cavern roof collapsed. Area also has waterfalls, a 221-foot walkway and an interpretive center; **Fred Bear Museum** in Gainesville has lion, elephant, cape buffalo, brown bear and wolf specimens, Indian artifacts; **Marjorie Kinnan Rawlings State Historic Site,** 21 miles southeast of Gainesville, has interpretive center, hiking, guided tours of a Florida cracker house where this American writer, who authored "The Yearling," lived during her most productive years; **Paynes Prairie State Preserve,** one mile north of Micanopy, has interpretive center, camping, picnicking, swimming, hiking, freshwater fishing, horse trail, observation tower, boat ramp and guided tours of the basin, which is covered by a marsh and wet prairie vegetation. Area is a winter home for many migratory birds such as the sandhill crane; **San Felasco Hammock State Preserve,** northwest of Gainesville, offers seasonal guided hikes and is characterized by its extremes in topography, from pine forests to steep sinkholes and brooks; **Lake Alice,** located near the University of Florida campus, a nature site that has a large population of alligators; **Miracle on 34th Street** cultural complex including the Samuel P. Harn Museum of Art and an 1,800-seat Performing Arts Center; **Morningside Nature Center** in Gainesville has 7 miles of trails and boardwalks and a 278-acre living history farm with an 1840 cabin, a turn-of-the-century kitchen and barnyard animals; **Kanapaha Botanical Gardens** in Gainesville has 62 acres of woodlands and meadows with butterflies, herbs, hummingbirds, rock and sunken gardens and claims to have the largest collection of bamboo in the state; **Bivens Arm Nature Park** in Gainesville is located on 57 acres and is a wildlife sanctuary. Site also has picnic tables and a pavilion; **Gainesville Historical District** encompasses 63 blocks and has 290 buildings and reflects architectural styles of the 1880-1920 era. Area has Victorian homes and the Thomas Center that contains art exhibits and gardens. Guided tours are available; **University of Florida** campus; **University of Florida Gators** football at Florida Field (stadium seats 83,000); **Gatornationals** drag racing in March at the **Gainesville Raceway; Matheson Historical Center** houses post cards, prints, maps and the restored Matheson House built in 1857 and botanical garden; **Sante Fe Community College's Teaching Zoo; City of Micanopy,** 13 miles south of Gainesville, site of former Indian village, today has antique, art and curio shops.

THE ARTS:
Hippodrome State Theatre (one of four state-supported performing arts theaters in the state); **Florida Museum of Natural History** at the University of Florida with a limestone cave and fossil study center; **Florida Players; Across-town Repertory Theatre; Santa Fe Players** at Santa Fe Community College; **Gainesville Community Playhouse Little Theatre; Gainesville Civic Ballet; Gainesville Ballet Theatre; Danscompany; Dance Alive!; Chamber Orchestra; Gainesville Friends of Jazz; University Gallery** on the University of Florida campus and **Santa Fe Gallery** at the Santa Fe Community College campus have art exhibits year-round; **Center for Modern Art; Performing Arts Center, Samuel Harn Museum of Art.**

ANNUAL EVENTS:
February: Hoggetowne Medieval Faire in Gainesville has people dressed in medieval costumes and offers medieval-style dinner at the fairgrounds; **March:** Alachua County Youth Fair in Gainesville; Gatornationals in Gainesville; **April:** Pioneer Days in High Springs; Railroad Days in

Waldo; Spring Arts Festival in Gainesville; **May:** Zucchini Festival in Windsor; **June:** Watermelon Festival in Newberry has a watermelon-eating contest, watermelon crafts; **October:** Melrose Arts and Crafts Festival; Good Life Jubilee in Alachua; **November:** Alachua County Fair in Gainesville; Downtown Fall Arts Festival in Gainesville; Micanopy Fall Festival; **December:** Hawthorne Annual Arts and Crafts Festival; O'Connell Center Arts and Crafts Show in Gainesville.

SPORTS AND LEISURE ACTIVITIES:
Most popular local fishing areas: Orange Lake (bass); Cross Creek and Paynes Prairie State Preserve
Number of local golf courses: 6
Public beaches? No
Tennis courts available to the public? Yes
Boating? Yes
Number of pleasure boats registered in the county (1991-92): 8,670

SERVICES FOR RETIREES:
Santa Fe Community Care

FINANCIAL SERVICES:
Number of local banks: 43
Number of local savings and loan associations: 4

THE MEDIA:
Largest local newspaper: *Gainesville Sun*
Cable television? Yes

MAJOR LOCAL RETAILERS:
Belk-Lindsey, Burdines, Dillards, JCPenney, Sears, Wal-Mart.

FOOD ESTABLISHMENTS: 477

OTHER SERVICES:
Number of local libraries: 20
Number of local hotels/motels: 48
Number of churches: Protestant: 235; Jewish: 3; Catholic: 6; Other: 6

TOURISM INQUIRIES:
Gainesville Area Chamber of Commerce, P.O. Box 1187, 300 E. University Ave., Gainesville, 32602-1187. Telephone: 904-334-7100.

BAKER County
Northeast
County seat: Macclenny

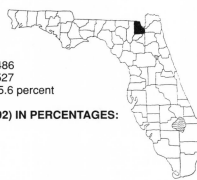

POPULATION: 1990: 18,486
1993: 19,527
Increase: 5.6 percent

AGE DISTRIBUTION (1992) IN PERCENTAGES:
0-14 : 24.7
15-44: 49.0
45-64: 18.0
65+ : 8.2

MUNICIPAL POPULATION:
GLEN SAINT MARY: 1990: 480; 1993: 479
MACCLENNY: 1990: 3,966; 1993: 4,050
UNINCORPORATED: 1990: 14,040; 1993: 14,998

LAND AREA: 585 square miles
POPULATION DENSITY: 33 people per square mile (50th in the state)

Baker County is largely a rural, agricultural area — mainly forestry and ornamental horticulture — and has some manufacturing. Wholesale nurseries have played a large role in the local economy, as have timber-related products (poles, lumber, paper and turpentine). Two major state institutions also are located here — Northeast Florida State Hospital (a state mental facility) in Macclenny and the Baker Correctional Institution in Olustee, which together employ about 1,500 people. According to the county Chamber of Commerce, however, about 45 percent of employed residents, including many skilled workers, commute outside the county, which is located just west of the major city of Jacksonville. The chamber says, "The Baker County labor force (is) willing to stay in the county if employment is available." The county also borders Georgia and is 25 miles east of Lake City and 45 miles north of Gainesville. Part of the county is the Osceola National Forest, which offers swimming, water-skiing, boating, canoeing and fishing on the 800-acre Ocean Pond, and which also is a popular hunting area.

TOURISM:
Not a major factor here. There are three local motels with 107 rooms.

HOUSING PRICES:
An 1,800-square-foot house on about an acre is likely to run in the high $70s or $80s. Acre lots outside Macclenny run $5,000 in the more rural areas, $8,000 closer to town, and more in the city (lots in one recent subdivision went for $11,000 for half an acre).
Number of vacant residential lots: 1,659; number of single-family residences: 2,572; mobile homes: 1,240; condominiums: 0

EDUCATION:
Number of schools: 8
Number of students enrolled: 4,587
Percentage of students continuing education after high school: 74.63
Teacher-to-pupil ratio: 1:19.3
Average teacher's salary: $27,780

Colleges, universities, and junior or community colleges serving the area:
University of North Florida, Jacksonville; University of Florida, Gainesville; Florida State University, Tallahassee; Jacksonville University; Edward Waters College, Jacksonville; Lake City Community College; Florida Community College, Jacksonville; Santa Fe Community College, Gainesville.

Trade and technical schools serving the area:
Bradford Vo-Tech; Westside Skills Center.

HEALTH CARE:
Number of general hospitals: 2
Number of hospital beds: 25
Number of physicians: 19

TAXES: Total county ad-valorem millage rate (1993): 22.8244

STANDARD CRIME RATE: 2,826.9 offenses per 100,000 population (53rd out of 67 counties)

LARGEST PRIVATE EMPLOYERS:
Name	Employees	Product/Service
Ray's Nursery	275	Wholesale plants
Macclenny Products	169	Clothing
Wiremil, Inc.	92	Prestress concrete

COMPANIES PROVIDING LOCAL UTILITIES:
Telephone: Northeast Florida Telephone Company
Electricity: Florida Power & Light, Clay Electric, Okeefenokee Rural Electric
Natural Gas: None
Water: City of Macclenny
Major Water Source: Wells
Sanitary Landfill? Yes

POINTS OF INTEREST:
Osceola National Forest; Olustee Battlefield State Historic Site, two miles east of Olustee on U.S. 90, has interpretive center, nature and hiking trails. It commemorates an 1864 Civil War battle won by the Confederates; **Lake Butler Wildlife Management Area.**

ANNUAL EVENTS:
February: Re-enactment of the Battle of Olustee at the Olustee Battlefield State Historical Site;
November: Baker County Fair in Macclenny.

SPORTS AND LEISURE ACTIVITIES:
Most popular local fishing areas: Ocean Pond; St. Mary's River
Number of local golf courses: 1 semi-private
Public beaches? No
Tennis courts available to the public? Yes
Boating? Yes
Number of pleasure boats registered in the county (1991-92): 1,381

SERVICES FOR RETIREES:
Better Living for Seniors coordinates meals, activities and services. Meal sites in Macclenny and
in Sanderson.

FINANCIAL SERVICES:
Number of local banks: 1
Number of local savings and loan associations: 1

THE MEDIA:
Largest local newspaper: *Baker County Press*
Cable television? Yes

MAJOR LOCAL RETAILER:
Wal-Mart

FOOD ESTABLISHMENTS: 37

OTHER SERVICES:
Number of local libraries: 1
Number of local hotels/motels: 3
Number of churches: Protestant: 36; Jewish: 0; Catholic: 1

TOURISM INQUIRIES:
Baker County Chamber of Commerce, Commerce Center, 20 East Macclenny Ave., Macclenny,
32063. Telephone: 904-259-6433.

BRADFORD County
Northeast
County seat: Starke

POPULATION: 1990: 22,515
1993: 23,312
Increase: 3.5 percent

AGE DISTRIBUTION (1992) IN PERCENTAGES:
0-14 : 20.0
15-44: 48.0
45-64: 19.6
65+ : 12.4

MUNICIPAL POPULATION:
BROOKER: 1990: 312; 1993: 312
HAMPTON: 1990: 296; 1993: 303
LAWTEY: 1990: 676; 1993: 679
STARKE: 1990: 5,226; 1993: 5,097
UNINCORPORATED: 1990: 16,005; 1993: 16,921

LAND AREA: 293 square miles
POPULATION DENSITY: 80 people per square mile (37th in the state)

   Located 42 miles southwest of Jacksonville and 25 miles northeast of Gainesville, the county
contains a number of lakes, and the Santa Fe River forms part of its western boundary. Brad-

ford's economic base is a combination of agriculture, mining, furniture manufacturing, clothing, feed supplies and masonry products. The poultry industry, including broilers, eggs and breeder farms, is the largest of the county's agricultural pursuits. Others are cattle breeding, along with crops ranging from strawberries to greens, squash, peas and beans. Another primary industry is timber and forest products, generating about $19 million annually.

TOURISM:
Not a big factor here.

HOUSING PRICES:
Typical average price is about $45,000; lakefront properties are roughly $80,000-$100,000. Number of vacant residential lots: 2,682; number of single-family residences: 4,617; mobile homes: 1,317; condominiums: 18

EDUCATION:
Number of schools: 9
Number of students enrolled: 4,105
Percentage of students continuing education after high school: 64.17
Teacher-to-pupil ratio: 1:16.1
Average teacher's salary: $27,759

Colleges, universities, and junior or community colleges serving the area:
Santa Fe Community College, based in Gainesville, operates the Andrews Center in Starke; Lake City Community College, Lake City; St. Johns River Community College, Palatka; University of Florida, Gainesville; University of North Florida, Jacksonville; Jacksonville University; Flagler College in St. Augustine.

Trade and technical schools serving the area:
Bradford-Union Vocational-Technical Center; Santa Fe Community College; Florida Community College at Jacksonville

HEALTH CARE:
Number of general hospitals: 1
Number of hospital beds: 54
Number of physicians: 15

TAXES: Total county ad-valorem millage rate (1993): 16.2130

STANDARD CRIME RATE: 7,215.2 offenses per 100,000 population (15th out of 67 counties)

LARGEST EMPLOYERS:

Name	Employees	Product/Service
Bradford County School System	497	
E.I. Dupont	290	Mineral sand
Florida National Guard	234	
Starke Uniform Manufacturing Co.	210	Work clothing
Whispering Pines Care Center	128	Nursing care
Windsor Manor	120	Nursing care
Sunshine Industries	90	Wood products
Vogue Manufacturing Co.	72	Women's apparel
Griffin Industries	60	Animal by-products
Riverside Uniform Rentals	41	Uniform rentals

COMPANIES PROVIDING LOCAL UTILITIES:
Telephone: Central Telephone Co. of Florida
Electricity: City of Starke, Florida Power & Light, Clay Electric, City of Starke
Natural Gas: Florida Gas
Water: City of Starke
Major Water Source: Wells
Sanitary Landfill? Yes

POINTS OF INTEREST:
Lakes Crosby, Rowell, Sampson, Hampton and Santa Fe; wildlife management areas:
Camp Blanding, Santa Fe Swamp and Alligator Creek, which are home to deer, wild turkey, doves and wild boar and which also are popular hunting spots.

THE ARTS:
Bradford Repertory Arts Theater and **Bradford Players,** offering musical and dramatic performances; **Jones-Rosenburg Auditorium.**

ANNUAL EVENTS:
April: Bradford County Fair (livestock exhibits, midway, food, games); **July:** Freedomfest; **September through November:** Santa Fe Community College's Fall Festival of the Performing Arts (dance, music, theater events); **October:** Fall Art Festival (about 100 arts and crafts displays on West Call Street, entertainment, food); **December:** Christmas Parade.

SPORTS AND LEISURE ACTIVITIES:
Most popular local fishing areas: 5 lakes in the county
Golf courses? Yes
Public beaches: No
Tennis courts available to the public? Yes
Boating? Yes
Number of pleasure boats registered in the county (1991-92): 1,757

SERVICES FOR RETIREES:
Bradford County Senior Citizens of Starke.

FINANCIAL SERVICES:
Number of local banks: 3
Number of local savings and loan associations: 0

THE MEDIA:
Largest local newspaper: *Bradford County Telegraph*
Cable television? Yes

MAJOR LOCAL RETAILERS:
Wal-Mart, Stump's Department Store

FOOD ESTABLISHMENTS: 50

OTHER SERVICES:
Number of local libraries: 1
Number of local hotels/motels: 15
Number of churches: Protestant: 45; Jewish: 0; Catholic: 1

TOURISM INQUIRIES:
Starke-Bradford County Chamber of Commerce, P.O. Box 576, Starke 32091. Telephone: 904-964-5278.

CLAY County
Northeast
County seat: Green Cove Springs

POPULATION: 1990: 105,986
1993: 114,918
Increase: 8.4 percent

AGE DISTRIBUTION (1992) IN PERCENTAGES:
0-14 : 23.8
15-44: 47.4
45-64: 19.9
65+ : 8.9

MUNICIPAL POPULATION:
GREEN COVE SPRINGS: 1990: 4,497; 1993: 4,688
KEYSTONE HEIGHTS: 1990: 1,315; 1993: 1,320
ORANGE PARK: 1990: 9,488; 1993: 9,456
PENNEY FARMS: 1990: 609; 1993: 651
UNINCORPORATED: 1990: 90,077; 1993: 98,803

LAND AREA: 601 square miles
POPULATION DENSITY: 191 people per square mile (22nd in the state)

Clay County is bordered on the north by the City of Jacksonville and on the east by the St. Johns River, which is nicknamed the bass fishing capital of the world. The county also is about 25 miles from St. Augustine and its beaches. Manufacturing is the major industry here — products include concrete, asphalt, lumber and wood chips, PVC pipes and sewer equipment. Orange Park Medical Center is the county's top private-sector employer. Water sports are popular on the St. Johns River and on several lakes, and activities include fishing, boating, crabbing, and water skiing. The county also is home to a state park and several major festivals each year.

TOURISM:
Not a major tourist county.

HOUSING PRICES:
Average prices in recent years typically in the $79,000 to $82,000 range. Houses along the St. Johns River start at about $180,000.
Number of vacant residential lots: 17,305; number of single-family residences: 27,538; mobile homes: 6,246; condominiums: 1,072

EDUCATION:
Number of schools: 27
Number of students enrolled: 23,142
Percentage of students continuing education after high school: 48.87
Teacher-to-pupil ratio: 1:18.1
Average teacher's salary: $27,207

Colleges, universities, and junior or community colleges serving the area:
University of Florida, Gainesville; Jacksonville University; Edward Waters College, Jacksonville; Jones College, Jacksonville; University of North Florida, Jacksonville; Florida Community College at Jacksonville; St. Johns River Community College, Palatka, and a branch in Orange Park.

Trade and technical schools serving the area:
Clay High School; Westside Skills Center; St. Augustine Technical Center.

HEALTH CARE:
Number of general hospitals: 2
Number of hospital beds: 284
Number of physicians: 186

TAXES: Total county ad-valorem millage rate (1993): 17.9165

STANDARD CRIME RATE: 4,583.3 offenses per 100,000 population (38th out of 67 counties)

LARGEST PRIVATE EMPLOYERS:

Name	Employees	Product/Service
Orange Park Medical Center	950	Health Care
Kustom Karr Inc.	350	Rail car repair
Gustafson's Dairy	350	Dairy
Food Lion	210	Grocery
Taylor Concrete & Supply Inc.	146	Ready-mix Concrete
Fla. Asphalt Contracting Inc.	142	Asphalt
Gilman Paper Co.	135	Lumber/wood chips
RGC Mineral Sands	130	Mining/mining equipment
JM Manufacturing	112	PVC pipe
Vac-con International	111	Sewer equipment

COMPANIES PROVIDING LOCAL UTILITIES:
Telephone: Southern Bell
Electricity: Clay Electric Cooperative; Jacksonville Electric Authority; City of Green Cove Springs, Florida Power & Light
Natural Gas: Peoples Gas
Water: Green Cove Springs; Keystone Heights; Kingsley Service; Mid-Clay; Clay Utilities; Orange Park

Major Water Source: Rivers, lakes and wells
Sanitary Landfill? Yes

POINTS OF INTEREST:
St. Johns River, for boating and fishing; **Mike Roess Gold Head Branch State Park,** six miles north of Keystone Heights on State Road 21, offers camping, picnicking, swimming, freshwater fishing, hiking, canoe rentals, seasonal campfire programs, guided walks. Park also contains four lakes; **Orange Park Kennel Club,** greyhound racing; **Camp Blanding Museum and Memorial Park of the Second World War; Clay County Historical Museum; Middleburg Museum.**

THE ARTS:
Mission Grove Playhouse, a cultural center for exhibits and home of the **Orange Park Community Theatre,** which offers programs year-round.

ANNUAL EVENTS:
March/April: Clay County Agricultural Fair; **May:** Rodeo at Clay County Fairgrounds; Art Festival in Spring Park; **July:** Orange Park Mall Parade and Fireworks; Middleburg Celebration, fireworks; **September:** Keystone Heights Festival of Lakes; Fall Family Fun Day and Benefit Craft Show, Orange Park; **October:** Orange Park Fall Festival; **Early November:** Clay County Ham Jam, Florida's official pork barbecue cooking contest; **December:** Last Chance Benefit Craft Show in Orange Park; Christmas in the Park, Green Cove Springs.

SPORTS AND LEISURE ACTIVITIES:
Most popular local fishing areas: St. Johns River, Kingsley Lake, Strickland Lake, Lowry Lake, Lake Johnson
Number of local golf courses: 4
Public beaches: No
Tennis courts available to the public? Yes
Boating? Yes
Number of pleasure boats registered in the county (1991-92): 7,169

SERVICES FOR RETIREES:
Clay County Council on Aging

FINANCIAL SERVICES:
Number of local banks: 21
Number of local savings and loan associations: 1

THE MEDIA:
Largest local newspaper: *Clay Today*
Cable television? Yes

MAJOR LOCAL RETAILERS:
Dillard's, Gayfers, JCPenney and Sears at the Orange Park Mall. Also, K mart, Wal-Mart.

FOOD ESTABLISHMENTS: 252

OTHER SERVICES:
Number of local libraries: 4
Number of local motels: 9
Number of churches: Protestant: 100; Jewish: 0; Catholic: 3; Other: 4

TOURISM INQUIRIES:
Clay County Chamber of Commerce, P.O. Box 1441, 1734 Kingsley Ave., Orange Park, 32067-1441. Telephone: 904-264-2651.

COLUMBIA County
Northeast
County seat: Lake City

POPULATION: 1990: 42,613
1993: 46,430
Increase: 9 percent

AGE DISTRIBUTION (1992) IN PERCENTAGES:
 0-14 : 23.5
 15-44: 43.2
 45-64: 20.4
 65+ : 13.0

MUNICIPAL POPULATION:
FORT WHITE: 1990: 468; 1993: 502
LAKE CITY: 1990: 9,626; 1993: 9,764
UNINCORPORATED: 1990: 32,519; 1993: 36,164

LAND AREA: 797 square miles
POPULATION DENSITY: 58 people per square mile (42nd in the state)

 This county is known for recreation — swimming, boating, fishing, snorkeling and tubing. It is home to two state parks, a culture center honoring the work and life of Stephen Foster, two country clubs, each with an 18-hole golf course, swimming pools and tennis courts. Interstate 10 and 75 run through the county and two railroads, Norfolk Southern and Seaboard, have main lines through it. The economy in recent years has shifted from agricultural to manufacturing, government and services. Products include mobile homes, garments, finished lumber and asphalt. Tourism also plays a large role, as more than half the auto visitors to Florida pass through the county. The county seat, Lake City, is 45 miles northwest of Gainesville and 65 miles southwest of Jacksonville, where Interstates 75 and 10 intersect. The area calls itself the "Florida of the South," where it says the history of the old South blends with the new, such as at Lake City's Olustee Festival. The festival, commemorating the Battle of Olustee, is held in February.

HOUSING PRICES:
Real estate agents report average prices around $50,000.
Number of vacant residential lots: 6,146; number of single-family residences: 8,681; mobile homes: 2,788; condominiums: 44

EDUCATION:
Number of local schools: 12
Number of students enrolled: 8,710
Percentage of students continuing education after high school: 33.83
Teacher-to-pupil ratio: 1:19.1
Average teacher's salary: $28,924

Colleges, universities, and junior or community colleges serving the area:
Lake City Community College; University of Florida in Gainesville (45 miles away); and Jacksonville University (65 miles away)

Trade and technical schools serving the area:
Lake City Community College

HEALTH CARE:
Number of hospitals: 2
Number of hospital beds: 203
Number of physicians: 80

TAXES: Total county ad-valorem millage rate (1993): 20.0994

STANDARD CRIME RATE: 7,641.6 offenses per 100,000 population (13th out of 67 counties)

LARGEST EMPLOYERS:

Name	Employees	Product/Service
Columbia County School System	1,022	School system
VA Medical Center	908	Health care
Department of Transportation	603	Transportation
Aero Corporation	400	Aircraft maintenance
Homes of Merit	370	Manufactured housing
Occidental Chemical Corp.	336	Phosphate mining
Columbia County	325	Government services
Lake Shore Hospital	248	Health care

| Lake City Medical Center | 240 | Health care |
| S&S Food Stores | 232 | Convenience stores |

COMPANIES PROVIDING LOCAL UTILITIES:
Telephone: Southern Bell
Electricity: Florida Power & Light, Clay Electric Cooperative
Natural Gas: City of Lake City
Water: City of Lake City
Major Water Source: Wells
Sanitary Landfill? Yes

POINTS OF INTEREST:
Olustee Battlefield State Historic Site, 13 miles east of Lake City, has Civil War museum; **O'Leno State Park,** 20 miles south of Lake City, has camping, picnicking, swimming, freshwater fishing, canoeing, horseback riding, hiking, alligators and turtles; **Ichetucknee Springs State Park,** south of Columbia City, has picnicking, swimming, hiking, tubing/snorkeling, springs; **Stephen Foster State Folk Culture Center,** 12 miles north of Lake City in White Springs, has museum; **Osceola National Forest; Columbia County Historical Museum,** Lake City, has Civil War artifacts; **Columbia Motorsports,** auto racing, seasonal; **Florida Sports Hall of Fame,** covers all aspects of sports in the state; **Suwannee Valley Zoo.**

THE ARTS:
Columbia Art Guild; Community Concert series; Lake City Community College Performing Arts Center hosts plays, operas, musicals.

ANNUAL EVENTS:
February: Olustee Battle Festival and Re-enactment, Lake City, has re-enactment of battle at Olustee Battlefield, arts and crafts, food, antique show; **March or April:** Florida Sports Hall of Fame induction ceremony; **October:** Alligator Fest, Lake City, with crafts and food; **October/November:** Columbia County Fair, fairgrounds; Antique Auto Show; **November/December:** Christmas Crafts Show and Festival of Lights at Olustee Park; **December:** Christmas parade, Lake City.

SPORTS AND LEISURE ACTIVITIES:
Most popular local fishing areas: Suwannee and Santa Fe rivers
Number of local golf courses: 2
Public beaches? No
Tennis courts available to the public? Yes
Boating? Yes
Number of pleasure boats registered in the county (1991-92): 3,352

SERVICES FOR RETIREES:
Columbia County Senior Citizen Center

FINANCIAL SERVICES:
Number of local banks: 6
Number of local savings and loan associations: 3

THE MEDIA:
Largest local newspaper: *The Lake City Reporter*
Cable television? Yes

MAJOR SHOPPING CENTERS:
Area is served by one regional mall and seven shopping centers. Major retailers are K mart and Wal-Mart.

FOOD ESTABLISHMENTS: 134

OTHER SERVICES:
Number of local libraries: 3
Number of local motels: 34
Number of churches: Protestant: 80; Jewish: 0; Catholic: 1

TOURISM INQUIRIES:
Columbia County Chamber of Commerce, 15 E. Orange St., Lake City, 32055. Telephone: 904-752-3690.

DUVAL County
Northeast
County seat: Jacksonville

POPULATION: 1990: 672,971
1991: 701,608
Increase: 4.3 percent

AGE DISTRIBUTION (1992) IN PERCENTAGES:
0-14 : 22.7
15-44: 48.3
45-64: 18.1
65+ : 10.9

MUNICIPAL POPULATION:
ATLANTIC BEACH: 1990: 11,636; 1993: 12,383
BALDWIN: 1990: 1,450; 1993: 1,513
JACKSONVILLE: 1990: 635,230; 1993: 661,243
JACKSONVILLE BEACH: 1990: 17,839; 1993: 19,234
NEPTUNE BEACH: 1990: 6,816; 1993: 7,235

LAND AREA: 774 square miles
POPULATION DENSITY: 907 people per square mile (5th in the state)

Jacksonville, the city with the largest land mass in the continental United States, encompasses most of Duval County. It is known for its port, for the military and for its beaches. In 1994 it also gained attention when it beat Baltimore, St. Louis and Memphis for a National Football League expansion team. The Jacksonville Jaguars were to begin play in September 1995 in a newly renovated Gator Bowl, thanks in large part to a group of business and civic leaders who organized a $121 million renovation of the bowl. The stadium will contain 73,000 seats.

Even besides the awarding of the franchise to the local area, economic activity in Jacksonville had rebounded from the recession, up in every category — including business investment and construction — and grew overall at a rate of 8.1 percent during 1993.

What has been uncertain in recent years has been the fate of the massive military bases in the area. The Naval Air Station Cecil Field, as of 1994, was on a list of bases to be closed, scheduled to shut down by September 1999. It employed 9,300 people in 1993. The military, which also includes the Mayport Naval Station (14,000 employees) and the Jacksonville Naval Air Station (15,000 employees) accounts for a huge chunk of the local economy — nearly $2 billion a year. The Navy, the Coast Guard and the Florida National Guard all are represented here. Nearly 10,000 civilians are employed by the military, and in recent years 17,500 military retirees and their families were making the area their home. The county in 1992 had the sixth highest rate in the state in the number of residents age 44 and younger — 71 percent.

The services industry, with 115,188 employees in 1991, topped trade (98,295) as the biggest employer in the county. Other major ones: government (85,912); finance, insurance and real estate (52,896); transportation and public utilities (30,682); manufacturing — shipping, publishing, paper products, chemicals, beer — (29,449), and construction (24,018).

Downtown Jacksonville is the center for government, commerce, retail and hotel trade, and entertainment. Housing for the elderly and low-income housing are available. Also here is the Prime Osborn Convention Center, the Civic Auditorium, the Gator Bowl and the Florida Theatre. The St. Johns River flows through the downtown.

Among the other areas in the county are Mandarin, in the southeastern part of the city, one of the fastest-growing areas here in recent years. Average house price is about $125,000, with some on the river going for $1 million or more. Among the three beach cities, Jacksonville Beach is the largest and includes commercial, retail, residential and industrial areas. According to Jacksonville Business Journal's Discover Jacksonville, "It also has a downtown area that has yet to reach its potential, and still has a discouraging amount of vacant property and run-down buildings." Atlantic Beach's Atlantic Boulevard has a concentration of nightlife and restaurant spots and the Mayport Naval Station is at the north end of Mayport Road, Atlantic Beach's other main thoroughfare. Neptune Beach is mainly residential. The village of Mayport, on the northern tip of the island, has a fishing fleet, ferry and casino cruise ship. Homes typically sell for $90,000 to $100,000 in the beach areas, and small oceanfront condos go for $75,000 and up.

Northside includes industrial complexes and the Jacksonville International Airport and is just across the border from the Kings Bay Submarine Base in Georgia. Westside includes many Navy retirees and the economy depends largely on the Jacksonville Naval Air Depot and the Cecil Field Naval Air Station. Southside runs almost to the beaches and to the St. Johns County line. Commercial and retail activity — and housing construction — have increased here in recent years.

Other areas: Riverside, on the west side of the St. Johns River, has a lot of hospitals and medical-related businesses. Avondale/Ortega, farther south on the west side of the St. Johns, are upscale neighborhoods with a view of downtown Jacksonville. Also there are pricey specialty shops and homes. Arlington is a bedroom community between the downtown and the beaches. It includes the Regency Square mall and Jacksonville University. Housing ranges from apartment complexes to gated communities. West Beaches is the home of Mayo Clinic Jacksonville, a famous medical institution, and the new American Heritage Life headquarters. It's largely an executive community. San Jose, north of Mandarin toward the downtown, has lots of Spanish-style architecture. It is one of the city's older neighborhoods. House prices start at $100,000 and some on the river top $1 million.

Jacksonville calls itself "Florida's Business City" because a number of companies opened offices here in recent years, including Merrill Lynch, American Express Travel-Related Services Co., AT&T American Transtech and the Mayo Clinic.

Jacksonville is home to the largest deepwater port facility in the South Atlantic, which has about a $2 billion direct economic impact on the city each year and is responsible for about 18,000 jobs. It also is the leading port in the United States for automobile imports and a hub for petroleum, liquid bulk, phosphate rock and coffee. Five million tons of merchandise passed through facilities owned by the Jacksonville Port Authority in fiscal 1991-92, the fourth highest in the state behind Tampa, Port Everglades and Manatee. The city is also served by three airports, including Jacksonville International Airport. Three railroads — CSX Corp., Norfolk Southern Railway and Florida East Coast Railway Co. — plus Amtrak also serve the area.

Another thing the city has been famous for in recent years has been an air pollution problem. The state compares concentrations of "particulate matter," and the level here — reported in "annual arithmetic means" — was the state's highest in 1991. The level was 34, still below the state standard of 50. The level had dropped to 28 in 1992, the sixth highest in the state. Nevertheless, foul odors for years have been evident in parts of the city, in large part from pulp and paper mills, but local officials say the complaint rates have dropped dramatically.

TOURISM:

As a north Florida county, Duval does not have the Snowbird influx that other more southern counties have. Beaches are popular in the summer, though.

HOUSING PRICES:

Median sales price of an existing home in the Jacksonville metropolitan area was $86,000 in June 1994. The average price of a new 2,200-square-foot house with four bedrooms, 2.5 baths, a family room and a two-car garage is about $116,000.

Number of vacant residential lots: 24,816; number of single-family residences: 182,505; mobile homes: 8,255; condominiums: 7,575

EDUCATION:

Number of schools: 152
Number of students enrolled: 119,785
Percentage of students continuing education after high school: 66.56
Teacher-to-pupil ratio: 1:20.2
Average teacher's salary: $30,782

Colleges, universities, and junior or community colleges serving the area:
Jacksonville University; University of North Florida; Jones College; Edward Waters College; Florida Community College; University of Florida in Gainesville; and Flagler College in St. Augustine.

Trade and technical schools serving the area:
Florida Community College; A. Phillip Randolph school; North/South/Westside schools

HEALTH CARE:
Number of general hospitals: 13
Number of hospital beds: 3,265
Number of physicians: 1,842

TAXES: Total county ad-valorem millage rate (1993): 21.2088

STANDARD CRIME RATE: 9,956.3 offenses per 100,000 population (5th out of 67 counties)

LARGEST PRIVATE EMPLOYERS:

Name	Employees	Product/Service
Winn-Dixie	8,000	Grocery
AT&T American Transtech	5,300	Telemarketing
Publix Supermarkets	5,018	Grocery
Blue Cross/Blue Shield Fla.	4,890	Insurance
CSX Technology	4,100	Computer services
St. Vincent's Medical Center	4,050	Hospital
Barnett Bank of Jacksonville	4,000	Banking
Prudential Insurance	3,850	Insurance
First Union Nat'l Bank Fla.	3,281	Banking
Southern Bell	3,196	Telephone services

COMPANIES PROVIDING LOCAL UTILITIES:
Telephone: Southern Bell
Electricity: Jacksonville Electric Authority
Natural Gas: Peoples Gas
Water: City of Jacksonville
Major Water Source: Wells
Sanitary Landfill? Yes

POINTS OF INTEREST:
The beaches (Seminole, Atlantic, Neptune and Jacksonville) are 12 miles from downtown across the Intracoastal Waterway and accessible by three bridges; **Seawalk Plaza** at Jacksonville Beach, which includes a concert and festival pavilion; **Jacksonville Beach Flag Pavilion,** which has a 2,000-seat auditorium; the 983-foot **Jacksonville Beach Fishing Pier; Jacksonville Zoological Park,** a 61-acre zoo with 700 animals; **Fort Caroline National Memorial** in Arlington, a 130-acre memorial on the site of America's first Protestant colony (founded in 1564); **Anheuser-Busch brewery tours;** the **Riverwalk,** a 1.2-mile boardwalk on the city's Southbank riverfront; the 120-foot **Friendship Park fountain,** which is lit at night; five companies offer **river cruises** on the St. Johns River; **Automated Skyway Express,** an elevated rail system connecting the Omni Jacksonville Hotel downtown and the Prime Osborn Convention Center; **Jacksonville Landing,** a marketplace of 40 shops and 25 restaurants on the Northbank of the St. Johns River; **Metropolitan Park,** on the river; the 450-acre **Kathryn Abbey Hanna Park** south of Mayport, which has a 1.5-mile beach; **Tree Hill,** Jacksonville's Nature Center, a 42-acre center with walking trails, exhibits, hardwood forest; **Mayport,** a fishing village that is home to a large commercial shrimp boat fleet; **Mayport ferry,** which connects Mayport with Fort George Island; **Mayport Naval Station,** an aircraft carrier basin; **Little Talbot Island State Park,** 17 miles northeast of Jacksonville, has camping, picnicking, swimming, surfing, saltwater fishing, observation deck, sand dunes, seasonal campfire programs and guided walks; **Big Talbot Island State Park,** 20 miles east of downtown Jacksonville and just north of Little Talbot park, has canoeing, fishing, swimming, hiking trails, bird-watching; 119 municipal parks; **Fort George Island State Cultural Site,** Fort George, at 65 feet, is the highest point along the Atlantic south of Sandy Hook, N.J., offers bicycling, hiking; **Prime Osborn Convention Center,** used for business and trade conventions; **Civic Auditorium,** a 3,000-seat complex that offers Jacksonville Symphony Orchestra concerts, touring Broadway shows, conventions and trade shows; the **Gator Bowl Stadium,** which seats 82,000 and is used for sporting events and concerts; **Veterans Memorial Coliseum,** across the street from the Gator Bowl, which seats 10,168 people and is used for concerts and sporting events such as basketball, wrestling, hockey and gymnastics; **Jacksonville Suns,** a Double-A Southern League pro baseball team, plays from April to August at **Wolfson Park,** which seats 8,000 people; **Jacksonville University Dolphins** play basketball at the Veterans Memorial Coliseum; **Greyhound pari-mutuel racing** takes place at the **Orange Park Kennel Club, St. Johns Greyhound Park** in Bayard and **Jacksonville Kennel Club.** Rac-

ing is year-round, but at a different park each month; **Pablo Historical Park** has restored steam engine and tender, 1880s exhibits; **Jacksonville Raceways,** a dirt track for auto racing.

THE ARTS:

Florida Theatre, a 1,700-seat downtown facility, which hosts concerts, plays and other events; **Jacksonville Symphony; St. Johns River City Band; Florida First Coast Pops Orchestra;** the **Florida Ballet; Jacksonville Art Museum; Cummer Gallery of Art** (2,000 works of art from the fifth century B.C. to the present); **Museum of Science and History; Florida East Coast Railway House Museum** (railroad memorabilia); **Karpeles Manuscript Library Museum** houses one of the world's largest private holdings of historical documents on literature, music, science, politics; **Jacksonville Maritime Museum** has scale model ships, paintings, photos; **Jacksonville Historical Center** traces the city's history; **Alexander Brest Museum,** Jacksonville University, has permanent collection of Steuben glass, ivory, pre-Columbian art.

ANNUAL EVENTS:

January: Ringling Brothers and Barnum & Bailey Circus; **February:** Jacksonville Boat Show; Home & Patio Show; **March:** Jacksonville Lifestyle Show; Spring St. Augustine Arts & Crafts Fair; Blessing of the Fleet; **April:** St. Johns River Riverfest; St. Augustine Easter Parade; Jacksonville Landing Annual Folk Festival; Feast & Fest, a Taste of Jacksonville; Beaches Opening Weekend Festival has sand-castle contests, parade; River City Kids Day, a fair benefitting the Wolfson Children's Hospital; Jacksonville Beach Annual Art Festival; African American Heritage Festival, University of North Florida; Wave Masters Surf Contest, Jacksonville Beach; Jacksonville Pro Rodeo; **May:** Mug Race (29 classes of sailboats race on the St. Johns River from Palatka to Jacksonville); World of Nations, Metropolitan Park, has food, music and showcases the city's ethnic cultures; Kuumba Festival has traditional African entertainment, food, clothing; Memorial Day Festival, Jacksonville Landing; **June:** Marine Fest Boat Show, Metropolitan Park; Shell Show, Jacksonville Beach; **July:** Independence Day celebrations at Jacksonville Landing, Metropolitan Park, Jacksonville Beach Seawalk; **August:** Jacksonville Summer Symphonette Concerts; **September:** Beaches Labor Day Festival; International Festival by the Sea, Jacksonville Beach; Labor Day Celebration, Jacksonville Landing; Springfield Jazz and Heritage Festival; Greek Festival; Antique Show for Charity, Civic Auditorium; Fall Home & Patio Show; **October:** Arts Mania, Jacksonville Landing; Jacksonville Jazz Festival; Southern Women's Show, Osborn Convention Center; Greater Jacksonville Agricultural Fair; Octoberfest, Metropolitan Park; Spooktacular, Halloween activity at the Jacksonville Zoo; **November:** Caribe Carnival, a Caribbean cultural festival; Jacksonville International Auto Show; Light Up Jacksonville, the lighting of a 50-foot Christmas tree at Jacksonville Landing; Jacksonville Light Parade, a boat parade on the St. Johns River; **December:** Holiday Table Settings at the Jacksonville Art Museum; Festival of Trees, Cummer Gallery of Art, has decorated trees from all parts of the world; Historic Riverside Luminaria, Riverside and Avondale neighborhoods, has 30,000 candles in white sand-filled bags lining neighborhood streets; Outback Steakhouse Gator Bowl, a matchup of two top college football teams (in 1994 was held in Gainesville while the Gator Bowl was undergoing renovations); New Year's Eve Celebration, Jacksonville Landing.

SPORTS AND LEISURE ACTIVITIES:

Most popular local fishing areas: St. Johns River, Atlantic Ocean, Intracoastal Waterway, several tributaries.
Number of local golf courses: 14 public
Tennis courts available to the public? Yes
Boating? Yes
Number of pleasure boats registered in the county (1991-92): 27,432

SERVICES FOR RETIREES:

Volunteer Jacksonville is a clearinghouse for about 300 local agencies, some of which serve the elderly.

FINANCIAL SERVICES:

Number of local banks: 122
Number of local savings and loan associations: 19

THE MEDIA:

Largest local newspaper: *The Florida Times-Union*
Cable television? Yes

MAJOR LOCAL RETAILERS:
Beall's, Byron's, Dillard's, Gayfer's, K mart, JCPenney, Sears, Montgomery Ward, Stein Mark, Wal-Mart. There are 4 regional malls and 187 shopping centers.

FOOD ESTABLISHMENTS: 2,015

OTHER SERVICES:
Number of local libraries: 17
Number of local hotels/motels: 120
Number of churches: Protestant: 294; Jewish: 6; Catholic: 26; Other: 38

TOURISM INQUIRIES:
Jacksonville Convention and Visitors Bureau, 6 E. Bay St., Suite 200, Jacksonville, 32202. Telephone: 904-353-9736; Jacksonville Chamber of Commerce, 3 Independent Drive, Jacksonville, 32201. Telephone: 904-366-6600.

FLAGLER County
Northeast
County seat: Bunnell

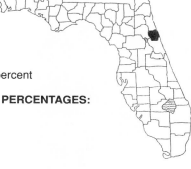

POPULATION: 1990: 28,701
1993: 33,544
Increase: 16.9 percent

AGE DISTRIBUTION (1992) IN PERCENTAGES:
0-14 : 16.0
15-44: 31.8
45-64: 24.6
65+ : 27.6

MUNICIPAL POPULATION:
BEVERLY BEACH: 1990: 314; 1993: 322
BUNNELL: 1990: 1,873; 1993: 1,977
FLAGLER BEACH: 1990: 3,818; 1993: 4,031
MARINELAND (part): 1990: 21; 1993: 12
UNINCORPORATED: 1990: 22,675; 1993: 27,202

LAND AREA: 485 square miles
POPULATION DENSITY: 69 people per square mile (40th in the state)

Flagler County, 23 miles south of St. Augustine and 23 miles north of Daytona Beach, has been the fastest-growing county in the United States — its population rose 207.7 percent between 1980 and 1992, according to a 1994 Census Bureau study. The percentage of residents age 65 and over — 27.6 in 1992 — was the 9th highest among Florida's counties.

Eighty percent of the growth during the 12 years was in unincorporated Palm Coast, a retirement community begun in the 1970s by ITT Development Corp. Palm Coast's population rose from 4,560 to 14,000 during the period. One of the draws has been the county's relatively low tax rate.

Despite the boom, the total population is 42nd among the 67 counties, and almost 47,000 vacant residential lots remain. Local Chamber of Commerce publications tout the area as "the Quiet Side of Florida."

The largest employer is the county school board. ITT Development is the largest private employer. The economy is diverse, from construction, industrial operations and educational and recreational services to administrative facilities. The service industry accounts for about a third of the employment, followed by retail trade at 22 percent and manufacturing at 15.

The county has 26 miles of beaches and part of the Intracoastal Waterway. There are three state park facilities here — Washington Oaks State Ornamental Gardens, Bulow Plantation Ruins State Historic Site and Gamble Rogers Memorial State Recreation Area at Flagler Beach.

TOURISM:
The seasons run from February to April and from June to September.

HOUSING PRICES:
Average prices in recent years have been in the 90s for 1- and 2-bedroom homes: $120s for 3-bedrooms; and around $175,000 for 4-bedrooms.
Number of vacant residential lots: 46,790; number of single-family residences: 12,339; mobile homes: 1,104; condominiums: 1,569

EDUCATION:
Number of local schools: 7
Number of students enrolled: 4,757
Percentage of students continuing education after high school: 82.28
Teacher-to-pupil ratio: 1:15.9
Average teacher's salary: $28,694

Colleges, universities, and junior or community colleges serving the area:
Daytona Beach Community College, Palm Coast branch; St. Johns River Community College; Flagler College in St. Augustine; Embry-Riddle Aeronautical University in Daytona Beach; Stetson University in DeLand; University of North Florida in Jacksonville; University of Central Florida, near Orlando.

Trade and technical schools serving the area:
St. Augustine Technical Center, St. Augustine; Daytona Beach Community College; and Flagler Adult Education

HEALTH CARE:
Number of hospitals: 1
Number of hospital beds: 81
Number of physicians: 28

TAXES: Total county ad-valorem millage rate (1993): 14.0079

STANDARD CRIME RATE: 3,064.6 offenses per 100,000 population (49th out of 67 counties)

LARGEST PRIVATE EMPLOYERS:
Name	Employees	Product/Service
ITT Community Development Corp.	536	Developer
Palm Coast Data	320	Subscription service
Winn-Dixie stores	300	Grocery
American Radionic Co. Inc.	290	Capacitors service
Sea Ray Boats Inc.	280	Luxury yachts
Publix	185	Grocery
Marineland of Florida	175	Tourist attraction
Sheraton Palm Coast Resort	156	Hotel
Memorial Hospital - Flagler	125	Hospital

COMPANIES PROVIDING LOCAL UTILITIES:
Telephone: Southern Bell
Electricity: Florida Power and Light
Natural Gas: None
Water: Palm Coast Utility Corp.
Major Water Source: Wells
Sanitary Landfill? Yes

POINTS OF INTEREST:
Little Theater of Palm Coast, Palm Coast; **Marineland of Florida,** Marineland, the state's original marine life attraction, has dolphin shows and oceanariums; **Washington Oaks State Gardens,** south of Marineland, has picnicking, saltwater fishing, hiking. Formal gardens include azaleas, camellias, roses and exotic species; **Bulow Plantation Ruins State Historic Site,** west of Flagler Beach, houses ruins of a sugar mill and offers picnicking, freshwater and saltwater fishing, hiking and canoe rentals; **Gamble Rogers Memorial State Recreation Area at Flagler Beach** has camping, picnicking, swimming, fishing and nature study; **Flagler County auditorium,** which seats 1,000, hosts theatrical performances.

ANNUAL EVENTS:
January: Tree City USA, Bunnell, a street festival with entertainment, parade, children's fishing contest, 5K run, arts/crafts, rides, antique car show; **February:** Home show/service fair, including

arts/crafts, at Flagler/Palm Coast High School; **March:** Cracker Day and Rodeo; **April:** Flagler County Fair in Bunnell; **May:** Kidsfest; Bluegrass Jamboree Art and Craft Festival; **July:** Fourth of July Celebration, includes parade, arts/crafts, children's games, fireworks; **October:** International Festival, includes Parade of Nations from Palm Coast Marina to Daytona Beach Community College; **December:** Holiday at the Beach.

SPORTS AND LEISURE ACTIVITIES:
Most popular local fishing areas: Flagler Beach pier, Intracoastal Waterway
Number of local golf courses: 1 public, 2 private, 4 semi-private
Beaches? Yes
Tennis courts available to the public? Yes
Boating? Yes
Number of pleasure boats registered in the county (1991-92): 2,675

SERVICES FOR RETIREES:
Flagler County Council on Aging, Palm Coast, links medical, social and community services, support services such as shopping assistance, telephone reassurance companionship and legal services, nutrition services and transportation to doctor's offices, medical facilities, shopping centers and to meal sites. Telephone: 904-437-2446.

FINANCIAL SERVICES:
Number of local banks: 9
Number of local savings and loan associations: 2

THE MEDIA:
Largest local newspaper: *The Trade Winds Paper*
Is cable television available? Yes

MAJOR LOCAL RETAILER:
Wal-Mart, major grocery stores

FOOD ESTABLISHMENTS: 118

OTHER SERVICES:
Number of local libraries: 2
Number of local hotels/motels: 14
Number of churches: Protestant: 28; Jewish: 1; Catholic: 4

TOURISM INQUIRIES:
Flagler County Chamber of Commerce, Star Route, Box 18-N, Bunnell, 32110. Telephone: 904-437-0106.

HAMILTON County
Northeast
County seat: Jasper

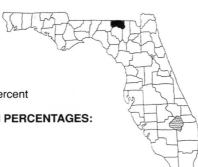

POPULATION: 1990: 10,930
1993: 11,604
Increase: 6.2 percent

AGE DISTRIBUTION (1992) IN PERCENTAGES:
0-14 : 23.1
15-44: 47.8
45-64: 17.4
65+ : 11.7

MUNICIPAL POPULATION:
JASPER: 1990: 2,099; 1993: 2,084
JENNINGS: 1990: 712; 1993: 721
WHITE SPRINGS: 1990: 704; 1993: 726
UNINCORPORATED: 1990: 7,415; 1993: 8,073

LAND AREA: 515 square miles
POPULATION DENSITY: 23 people per square mile (58th in the state)

Hamilton, the first county you enter when driving to Florida on Interstate 75, is mainly an agricultural area. Bordered on three sides by rivers and to the north by Georgia, Hamilton is the only Florida county that touches no part of the state by land. Farming, including forestry production and livestock, is a big industry here. Tobacco, corn and soybeans are the major crops.

Phosphate mining is also a main source of income; the Occidental Chemical Co. employs 900 people. Other products include clothing, windows and doors. Among the top 10 private employers are two grocery stores and a hardware supply company.

The Suwannee River, along with wilderness areas near the Alapaha and Withlacoochee rivers, offers a number of recreational activities, including fishing, hunting, boating, hiking, swimming and camping. Jasper, the county seat, has some turn-of-the-century homes along its Central Avenue. Of note here is that the standard crime rate decreased at a significant rate from 1989 to 1993 — from 3,760.1 offenses per 100,000 population (45th out of 67 counties) to 198.2 (66th among the counties).

TOURISM:
Does not affect this area.

HOUSING PRICES:
Average price about $50,000; roughly $40,000 for a typical two-bedroom and $60,000 for a 3-bedroom.
Number of vacant residential lots: 5,259; number of single-family residences: 1,803; mobile homes: 591; condominiums: 0

EDUCATION:
Number of schools: 7
Number of students enrolled: 2,332
Percentage of students continuing education after high school: 59.84
Teacher-to-pupil ratio: 1:15.9
Average teacher's salary: $27,267

Colleges, universities, and junior or community colleges serving the area:
North Florida Junior College, Madison; Lake City Community College, Lake City; Valdosta State College, Valdosta, Ga.; University of Florida, Gainesville; Florida State University, Tallahassee; Florida A&M University, Tallahassee

Trade and technical schools serving the area:
Valdosta Vocational-Technical School, Valdosta, Ga.; Suwannee-Hamilton Vo-Tech School, Live Oak; North Florida Junior College, Madison

HEALTH CARE:
Number of general hospitals: 1
Number of hospital beds: 42
Number of physicians: 6

TAXES: Total county ad-valorem millage rate (1993): 18.6964

STANDARD CRIME RATE: 198.2 offenses per 100,000 population (66th out of 67 counties)

LARGEST PRIVATE EMPLOYERS:

Name	Employees	Product/Service
Occidental Chemical Corp.	900	Phosphate
Jasper Textiles	275	Clothing
Suwannee Valley Nursing Center	65	Health care
Hamilton Turpentine	65	Timber/vegetables
Energy Saving Products	60	Windows/doors
Holiday Inn of Jennings	56	Food, lodging
Jasper Foodway	40	Grocery
Piggly Wiggly	30	Grocery
Florida Rock & Tank	29	Common carrier
Jasper Hardware & Supply	18	Hardware

COMPANIES PROVIDING LOCAL UTILITIES:
Telephone: ALLTEL
Electricity: Florida Power Corp. and Suwannee Valley Electric Co-Op.
Natural Gas: South Georgia Natural Gas

Water: Cities have their own wells
Major Water Source: Wells
Sanitary Landfill? Yes

POINTS OF INTEREST:
Stephen Foster State Folk Culture Center, White Springs, honors memory of composer Stephen Foster and displays a piano that he played along with a desk at which he arranged his composition, "Old Folks at Home."

ANNUAL EVENTS:
May: Rodeo (first weekend) at the county arena in Jasper, a sanctioned rodeo sponsored by the Hamilton County Riding Club; Annual Folk Festival (last weekend) at Stephen Foster State Folk Culture Center; **July:** July 4th all-day celebration at the Stephen Foster center; **October:** Hamilton County Fair Week offers activities for young people and county farmers including a 5K road race, fishing tournament and golf tournament; Jeanie Audition & Ball, at the Stephen Foster Folk Culture Center, is open to young women vocalists 19 to 21; **December:** Christmas Parade (first Saturday) in Jasper, sponsored by the Hamilton County Chamber of Commerce.

SPORTS AND LEISURE ACTIVITIES:
Most popular local fishing areas: Suwannee River and Occidental lakes
Number of local golf courses: 1 public
Public beaches: No
Tennis courts available to the public? Yes, 2
Boating? Yes
Number of pleasure boats registered in the county (1991-92): 618

SERVICES FOR RETIREES:
Council on Aging has Meals on Wheels program

FINANCIAL SERVICES:
Number of local banks: 1
Number of local savings and loan associations: 2

THE MEDIA:
Largest local newspaper: *Jasper News*
Cable television? In the cities

MAJOR LOCAL RETAILERS:
No large malls, but two large grocery stores. Shopping in downtown Jasper.

FOOD ESTABLISHMENTS: 31

OTHER SERVICES:
Number of local libraries: 1
Number of local motels: 10
Number of churches: Protestant: 57; Jewish: 0; Catholic: 1

TOURISM INQUIRIES:
Hamilton County Chamber of Commerce, P.O. Drawer P, Jasper, 32052. Telephone: 904-792-1300.

NASSAU County
Northeast
County seat: Fernandina Beach

POPULATION: 1990: 43,941
1993: 46,450
Increase: 5.7 percent

AGE DISTRIBUTION (1992) IN PERCENTAGES:
0-14 : 22.8
15-44: 45.6
45-64: 21.4
65+ : 10.2

MUNICIPAL POPULATION:
CALLAHAN: 1990: 946; 1993: 950
FERNANDINA BEACH: 1990: 8,765; 1993: 9,177
HILLIARD: 1990: 1,751; 1993: 1,911
UNINCORPORATED: 1990: 32,479; 1993: 34,412

LAND AREA: 652 square miles
POPULATION DENSITY: 71 people per square mile (38th in the state)

Located in the northeastern-most corner of Florida, Nassau is the first county you enter after leaving Georgia on Interstate 95. Like St. Augustine, the county has a colorful history, and it has 13 miles of beaches and sand dunes along its most frequently visited area, Amelia Island. Bordered by the Atlantic Ocean and named for the unmarried daughter of King George II, the island is the only U.S. location to have been under eight different flags, including England, Spain, France and Mexico.

For years, the county depended in part on the shrimping industry and two paper mills. The mills are still a major economic force and the shrimping industry is still having an impact, though a relatively small one. Today the largest employer is the county school board and the largest private employer is Amelia Island Plantation, a resort on 1,250 acres that is instrumental in luring tourists to the area. Among the other large employers are another resort, the Ritz-Carlton, on Amelia Island; the Federal Aviation Administration (operating an air traffic control center in Hilliard, in northwestern Nassau); a producer of corrogated cardboard; a producer of chemical cellulose; a maker of bullet-proof armor; a department store, a paper bag and paper producer; and two grocers.

Tourism efforts have focused on Amelia Island and the county's largest city, Fernandina Beach, which has a 50-block historic district, a museum of history, the oldest saloon in Florida, and Fort Clinch State Park, which offers re-enactments of Civil War events.

TOURISM:
Number of tourists estimated at 650,000 a year.

HOUSING PRICES:
Average prices in recent years in the mid-50s for a two-bedroom home and high 90s for a three-bedroom. Beach condominium prices $120,000-plus for two or fewer bedrooms and $150,000 for three or more.
Number of vacant residential lots: 8,690; number of single-family residences: 9,760; mobile homes: 3,880; condominiums: 2,222

EDUCATION:
Number of schools: 18
Number of students enrolled: 9,128
Percentage of students continuing education after high school: 41.93
Teacher-to-pupil ratio: 1:20.9
Average teacher's salary: $30,817

Colleges, universities, and junior or community colleges serving the area:
All in Jacksonville: University of North Florida; Jacksonville University; Edward Waters College; Florida Community College at Jacksonville; Jones College

Trade and technical schools serving the area:
Florida Community College at Jacksonville

HEALTH CARE:
Number of general hospitals: 1
Number of hospital beds: 54
Number of physicians: 39

TAXES: Total county ad-valorem millage rate (1993): 16.3531

STANDARD CRIME RATE: 4,092.6 offenses per 100,000 population (44th out of 67 counties)

LARGEST PRIVATE EMPLOYERS:

Name	Employees	Product/Service
Amelia Island Plantation	900	Resort
Container Corporation of America	720	Cardboard and paper products

Ritz-Carlton	600	Resort hotel
Winn Dixie	431	Grocery
ITT-Rayonier, Inc.	380	Chemical cellulose
Stone Container Corp.	185	Paper bags, paper products
Wal-Mart	175	Retail sales
Publix	150	Grocery
Amelia Island Care Center	148	Health care
American Body Armor	81	Bullet-proof protection

COMPANIES PROVIDING LOCAL UTILITIES:
Telephone: Southern Bell, ALLTEL Florida
Electricity: Florida Public Utilities and Florida Power & Light
Natural Gas: None
Water: Florida Public Utilities, Southern States Utilities, Sun Ray Utilities
Major Water Source: Wells
Sanitary Landfill? Yes

POINTS OF INTEREST:
Fort Clinch State Park at Fernandina Beach has Civil War-era re-enactments with role-playing soldiers, bugle calls and drills, interpretive center, camping, picnicking, swimming, saltwater fishing, hiking and tours of the restored fort (guides are dressed as Union soldiers); **Amelia Island State Recreation Area** on A1A, eight miles south of Fernandina Beach, has swimming, horseback riding and fishing; **Historic Fernandina Beach** has 50 blocks of homes labeled as a historic district, mainly because of the preservation of Victorian architecture, and contains **Centre Street,** which has a number of shops where everything from fudge to jewelry is sold. Renovated shops are in a 19th-century setting; **Old Town** area near Fort Clinch State Park was Amelia Island's original settlement, and traces of Spanish heritage still exist; **Amelia Island Lighthouse** near the state park has a beacon that can be seen for 19 miles; **Amelia Island Museum of History** in Fernandina Beach tells the story of the island's progression under eight flags — France, Spain, England, the Patriots of Amelia Island, the Green Cross of Florida, Mexico, the Confederacy and the United States; **carriage rides** in Fernandina Beach; **Palace Saloon** in Fernandina Beach is Florida's oldest (opened in 1903) and has a hand-carved back bar; **horseback riding** on Amelia Island beaches; ferry service from St. Mary's, Ga. (just over the Florida line), to **Cumberland Island National Seashore** in Georgia.

THE ARTS:
Amelia Community Theatre presents several productions each year; **Peppermint Players** produce plays for schoolchildren; **Amelia Island Chorale; Amelia Island Handbell Choir; Island Art Association Gallery** on Centre Street; **Fernandina Little Theater.**

ANNUAL EVENTS:
April: Bausch & Lomb Tennis Championship at Amelia Island Plantation; Timberfest at the Northeast Florida Fairgrounds, Callahan, has arts and crafts festival, music, food; **May:** Annual Isle of Eight Flags Shrimp Festival in Fernandina Beach has arts and crafts, contests, entertainment, food; **June:** Annual Fernandina Beach Invitational Golf Tourney; **October:** Ameliafest arts festival on Centre Street in Fernandina Beach; Northeast Florida Fair in Callahan; **September:** DuPont All-American Tennis Championship, Amelia Island Plantation; **November:** Heritage Festival; **December:** Tour of Homes in historic district of Fernandina Beach is a guided tour through 10 homes; Victorian Seaside Christmas in Fernandina Beach; and Christmas parades in Callahan, Hilliard and Fernandina Beach.

SPORTS AND LEISURE ACTIVITIES:
Most popular local fishing areas: Nassau Sound, St. Mary's River, 1,500-foot Municipal Fishing Pier in Fort Clinch State Park, Atlantic Ocean.
Number of local golf courses: 2 public and 2 private
Public beaches? Yes
Tennis courts available to the public? Yes
Boating? Yes
Number of pleasure boats registered in the county (1991-92): 2,940

SERVICES FOR RETIREES:
Nassau County Council on Aging in Hilliard and Fernandina Beach; AARP

FINANCIAL SERVICES:
Number of local banks: 10
Number of local savings and loan associations: 3

THE MEDIA:
Largest local newspaper: *Fernandina Beach News-Leader*
Cable television? Yes

MAJOR LOCAL RETAILERS:
Sears, Wal-Mart, K mart, shops on Centre Street

FOOD ESTABLISHMENTS: 148

OTHER SERVICES:
Number of local libraries: 2
Number of local hotels/motels: 29
Number of churches: Protestant: 61; Jewish: 0; Catholic: 1; Other: 2

TOURISM INQUIRIES:
Amelia Island-Fernandina Beach-Yulee Chamber of Commerce, P.O. Box 472, Fernandina Beach, 32034. Telephone: 904-261-3248.

PUTNAM County
Northeast
County seat: Palatka

POPULATION: 1990: 65,070
1993: 67,625
Increase: 3.9 percent

AGE DISTRIBUTION (1992) IN PERCENTAGES:
0-14 : 21.4
15-44: 38.1
45-64: 22.0
65+ : 18.6

MUNICIPAL POPULATION:
CRESCENT CITY: 1990: 1,859; 1993: 1,846
INTERLACHEN: 1990: 1,160; 1993: 1,254
PALATKA: 1990: 10,444; 1993: 10,447
POMONA PARK: 1990: 726; 1993: 749
WELAKA: 1990: 533; 1993: 555
UNINCORPORATED: 1990: 50,348; 1993: 52,774

LAND AREA: 722 square miles
POPULATION DENSITY: 94 people per square mile (32nd in the state)

Putnam County is bisected by the St. Johns River, which is nicknamed the bass fishing capital of the world. Ten-to-12-pound trophy catches are not infrequent each spring as the largemouth bass move to shallow water. The county, which includes 24 fishing resorts, charges an extra dollar on all fishing licenses for conservation purposes. There are more than 70 square miles of recreational lakes and rivers in the county, which is about 22 miles inland from the Atlantic.

Two-thirds of the county's labor force is broken down into four major components — services, trade, government and manufacturing. The local economy also includes agriculture — potatoes, cabbage, citrus, ferns and livestock. The county seat, Palatka, is 53 miles south of Jacksonville, 45 miles east of Gainesville and about 25 miles southwest of St. Augustine. Palatka is 17 miles west of I-95. The nearest major airports are in Gainesville and 45 miles away in Daytona Beach.

TOURISM:
No figures are available, but bass fishing draws American and Canadian tourists, peaking in March and April with the Azalea and Catfish festivals (see events listings below).

HOUSING PRICES:
Average resale pricein recent years around $60,000. Mobile homes available at varying prices, building lots for as little as $3,500 per acre.
Number of vacant residential lots: 57,674; number of single-family residences: 14,651; mobile homes: 12,250; condominiums: 143

EDUCATION:
Number of schools: 20
Number of students enrolled: 12,649
Percentage of students continuing education after high school: 72.27
Teacher-to-pupil ratio: 1:18.3
Average teacher's salary: $29,105

Colleges, universities, and junior or community colleges serving the area:
Within about a 50-mile radius are the University of Florida in Gainesville; the University of North Florida in Jacksonville; Stetson University in DeLand; Flagler College in St. Augustine; Jacksonville University; St. Johns River Community College in Palatka; Santa Fe Community College in Gainesville; and Central Florida Community College, Ocala.

Trade and technical schools serving the area:
St. Augustine Vo-Tech.

HEALTH CARE:
Number of general hospitals: 1
Number of hospital beds: 161
Number of physicians: 66

TAXES: Total county ad-valorem millage rate (1993): 16.8910

STANDARD CRIME RATE: 8,739.4 offenses per 100,000 population (10th out of 67 counties)

MAJOR PRIVATE EMPLOYERS

Name	Employees	Product/Service
Georgia-Pacific	1,300	Pulp, paper
Florida Furniture Industries	500	Furniture
Georgia-Pacific	360	Plywood
Seminole Electric Cooperative	289	Utilitiy
Central States Diversified	220	Bags
Offshore Shipbuilding	150	Boats
Max-E Corp.	135	Garments
Sheffield Steel	85	Steel bridges
Georgia-Pacific Sawmill	72	Lumber
Best Packers	72	Meat packing

COMPANIES PROVIDING LOCAL UTILITIES:
Telephone: Southern Bell, ALLTEL
Electricity: Florida Power & Light, Clay Electric Cooperative
Natural Gas: Palatka Gas Authority, Crescent City Gas Authority
Water: Palatka, Interlachen, Crescent City
Major Water Source: Wells
Sanitary Landfill? Yes

POINTS OF INTEREST:
Ravine State Gardens, Palatka; **Bronson-Mulholland House** (an ante-bellum Greek Revival mansion built in 1854 by Judge Isaac Bronson, a congressman who proposed the act under which Florida became a state), Palatka; **Putnam Historic Museum,** Palatka; **Larimer Arts Center**, Palatka, is home of the Arts Council of Greater Palatka and the River City Repertory Company theater, and has a gallery operated by the Arts Council with changing monthly exhibits; **Welaka Aquarium and Fish Hatchery,** Welaka; **Florida School of the Arts Galleries,** Palatka.

ANNUAL EVENTS:
January: Putnam County African American Cultural Arts Festival, Palatka Waterfront Park; **First weekend in March:** Azalea Festival, Palatka; Palatka Horseman's Club Rodeo; **Last full week in March:** Putnam County Fair, Palatka; **April (first Saturday):** Catfish Festival, Crescent City,

also has arts and crafts; Fifth District Rodeo (same weekend as Catfish Festival); **First Sunday in May:** Mug Race (29 classes of sailboats race on the St. Johns River from Palatka to Jacksonville); **July:** Independence Day Celebration, Palatka riverfront; **October:** Melrose Arts and Crafts Festival; Rod Run Car Show, Palatka Amphitheater; Antique Show and Sale, Palatka Armory; Fall Riverfest Arts Festival; **November:** Fun Fest carnival, downtown Palatka; **Day After Thanksgiving:** Christmas Parade, Palatka.

SPORTS AND LEISURE ACTIVITIES:
Most popular local fishing areas: St. Johns River (largemouth bass, speckled perch, bream, striped bass and catfish). In season, the river also yields blue crabs and shrimp. In addition, there are several lakes and the Rodman Reservoir.
Hunting is popular in the county and in the nearby Ocala National Forest. The Florida Trail, a hiking spot, runs through the county.
Golf courses: 2 public
Public beaches? Yes
Tennis courts available to the public? Yes
Boating? Yes
Number of pleasure boats registered in the county (1991-92): 6,702

SERVICES FOR RETIREES:
An Over-50 club and an AARP office.

FINANCIAL SERVICES:
Number of local banks: 12
Number of local savings and loan associations: 4

THE MEDIA:
Largest local newspaper: *Palatka Daily News*
Cable television? Yes

MAJOR LOCAL RETAILERS:
JCPenney, K mart, Wal-Mart, Goody's.

FOOD ESTABLISHMENTS: 153

OTHER SERVICES:
Number of local libraries: 6
Number of local motels: 20
Number of churches: Protestant: 102; Jewish: 0; Catholic: 3; Other: 5

TOURISM INQUIRIES:
Putnam County Chamber of Commerce, P.O. Box 550, Palatka, 32178-0550. Telephone: 904-328-1503.

ST. JOHNS County
Northeast
County seat: St. Augustine

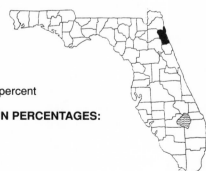

POPULATION: 1990: 83,829
1993: 91,197
Increase: 8.8 percent

AGE DISTRIBUTION (1992) IN PERCENTAGES:
0-14 : 19.0
15-44: 42.6
45-64: 21.5
65+ : 16.9

MUNICIPAL POPULATION:
HASTINGS: 1990: 595; 1993: 632
ST. AUGUSTINE: 1990: 11,695; 1993: 11,747
ST. AUGUSTINE BEACH: 1990: 3,657; 1993: 3,814
UNINCORPORATED: 1990: 67,882; 1993: 75,004

LAND AREA: 609 square miles
POPULATION DENSITY: 138 people per square mile (29th in the state)

St. Augustine, founded more than 425 years ago and the oldest permanent European settlement in the continental United States, is a city that prides itself on its Spanish heritage. Tourism is the county's leading industry and has lured as many as 1.7 million visitors in recent years. About 13,000 people are employed in service industry jobs.

The county is 45 miles south of Jacksonville and 50 miles north of Daytona. There are several geographic areas here including **St. Augustine; Anastasia Island,** a barrier island that contains most of the county's 43 miles of oceanfront and encompasses St. Augustine Beach, Crescent Beach and part of Marineland; the **Northwest** area, bordered by the St. Johns River; the **Northeast** area, including Ponte Vedra; and **Palm Valley**. Ponte Vedra is home of the Association of Tennis Professionals and the PGA Tour Headquarters and is a wealthy community. According to the 1990 census, its average household income was $62,756, roughly $10,000 higher than the next highest community in the five-county First Coast area. **Hastings,** an agricultural community in southwestern St. Johns County, is the potato and cabbage capital of Florida. More than 20,000 acres of potatoes were harvested here in 1990.

Because of its distinction as the oldest permanent European settlement, St. Augustine has many points of interest and attractions, including an old fort, old homes of Spanish architecture, churches and museums. The city also hosts a large number of events around the year, from parades to a blessing of the fleet.

More than 25 new industries have located in the area in recent years, with Grumman and the Luhrs Corp. ranking among the county's largest private employers. The county is also home of the general offices of Florida East Coast Railway and the Florida School for the Deaf and the Blind.

TOURISM:
The tourist season runs from June to Labor Day and the population doubles during that time.

HOUSING PRICES:
Average prices in recent years have ranged roughly from the high 50s to near $90,000.
Number of vacant residential lots: 22,144; number of single-family residences: 24,373; mobile homes: 4,040; condominiums: 6,813

EDUCATION:
Number of schools: 22
Number of students enrolled: 13,747
Percentage of students continuing education after high school: 77.21
Teacher-to-pupil ratio: 1:17.1
Average teacher's salary: $29,403

Colleges, universities, and junior or community colleges serving the area:
Flagler College in St. Augustine; St. Johns River Community College in Palatka; University of North Florida in Jacksonville; Jacksonville University in Jacksonville; Jones College in Jacksonville; Edward Waters College in Jacksonville.

Trade and technical schools serving the area:
St. Augustine Technical Center

HEALTH CARE:
Number of general hospitals: 2
Number of hospital beds: 280
Number of physicians: 177

TAXES: Total county ad-valorem millage rate (1993): 15.7020

STANDARD CRIME RATE: 5,513.3 offenses per 100,000 population (29th out of 67 counties)

LARGEST PRIVATE EMPLOYERS:

Name	Employees	Product/Service
Grumman St. Augustine Corp.	850	Aircraft modification
Flagler Hospital	786	Health care
V.A.W. of America	530	Aluminum products
Luhrs Corp.	350	Pleasure boats

Tree of Life Inc.	300	Health foods
Florida East Coast Railroad	190	Transportation
Ideal Division Stant Corp.	160	Auto parts manufacturer
Tensolite	155	High-tech wire
Holloway Sportswear Inc.	105	Clothing
St. Augustine Record	86	Newspaper

COMPANIES PROVIDING LOCAL UTILITIES:
Telephone: Southern Bell
Electricity: Florida Power & Light, Jacksonville Electric Authority, Ponte Vedra Utilities
Natural Gas: None
Water: St. Johns County Mainland Water System, St. Augustine Water Department
Major Water Source: Wells
Sanitary Landfill? Yes

POINTS OF INTEREST:
(All in St. Augustine unless otherwise noted): **Castillo de San Marcos,** a fort built in 1672-95 that by the mid-1700s was a primary fortification preserving Spanish rule in Florida. Today the fort is a national monument and visitors can roam through the structure; **Anastasia State Recreation Area,** 2 miles east of downtown St. Augustine, has beach flanked by sand dunes and also has camping, picnicking, swimming, saltwater fishing, hiking, sailboard and paddle cruiser rentals, and summer concessions; **Faver-Dykes State Park,** 15 miles south of St. Augustine, has camping, picnicking, fishing, hiking, boat ramp and 752 acres of pine and hardwood forests; **Guana River State Park,** north of St. Augustine, has swimming, saltwater fishing, boat ramp; **Fort Matanzas National Monument,** 14 miles south of St. Augustine, is a stone tower that was used as a fortification in the defense of the St. Augustine area; **Fountain of Youth** is site where Ponce de Leon landed in his search for the fountain of youth. Area also has planetarium and Indian burial ground; **Lighthouse Museum of St. Augustine** has exhibits and a video theater presentation about a lightkeeper's life; **Lightner Museum** has displays of cut crystal and Tiffany glass and natural history, American, European and Oriental art exhibits; **Marineland of Florida** has a porpoise show, two oceanariums including sharks, barracuda, stingrays and sea turtles; **Oldest House (The Gonzalez-Alvarez House)** sits on a site believed to have been occupied since the early 1600s and includes the **Museum of Florida's Army,** the **Albert Manucy Museum of St. Augustine History** and the **Historical Society Research Library; Oldest Schoolhouse** was built more than 200 years ago; **Oldest Store Museum** has collection of high-wheeled bicycles, animal-powered treadmills and thousands of other items from yesteryear; **Old Jail** was built in 1890-91; **Potters Wax Museum** has more than 170 wax figures; **Ripley's Believe It or Not Museum** houses 750 exhibits collected by Robert Ripley; **St. Augustine Alligator Farm** was established in 1893 and has monkeys, deer, goats, ducks and, of course, alligators; **Spanish Quarter in Old St. Augustine** includes tour of restored, furnished buildings and a museum; **Tragedy in U.S. History Museum** depicts tragedies such as the assassination of John F. Kennedy and has such items as the car Lee Harvey Oswald used to get to the Texas Book Depository; **Zorayda Castle** is a reproduction of a wing of the Alhambra, a famous Spanish castle; **Basilica-Cathedral; Dr. Peck House** is a furnished antebellum home; **Memorial Presbyterian Church** was built in 1889 by tycoon Henry Flagler; **Mission of Nombre de Dios** is America's oldest Marian Shrine and the site of the first Mass said in the New World; **St. Photios Chapel** is a national Greek Orthodox shrine; **Sanchez House** is furnished with 19th-century antiques; and **Ximenez-Fatio House** was constructed around 1797.

THE ARTS:
The **Little Theater** produces several shows each year; the **Emil Maestre Music Association** sponsors annual concert series

ANNUAL EVENTS:
Easter: St. Augustine Easter Festival, a two-week event celebrating the city's Spanish heritage, includes the St. Augustine Passion Play (performances mid-March to April at Cross & Sword Amphitheatre on Anastasia Island); Arts and Crafts Spring Festival, held on Palm Sunday weekend in the downtown Plaza; Blessing of the Fleet on Palm Sunday, where commerical and pleasure craft pass by the City Yacht Pier to receive a blessing from the bishop of the Diocese of St. Augustine; and the St. Augustine Easter Parade, held on Easter Sunday downtown, features

city's carriage horses wearing hats, also has marching bands and floats; **Memorial Day Weekend:** Race of the Century and Regatta at Camachee Cove, features offshore sailing races; **June:** Beach Spring Festival at St. Johns County Pier at St. Augustine Beach, has seafood, surf contests, volleyball tournament; **Summer:** Northeast Florida Marlin Tournament; **Early June:** Bluewater Fishing Tournament at the Camachee Cove Yacht Harbor; **Third Saturday in June:** Spanish Night Watch Ceremony is a torchlight procession through the Spanish Quarter with people in 18th-century period dress; **Mid-July to Late August:** Cross & Sword play performances, which depict the settlement of St. Augustine by Spanish colonists; **Late June:** Greek Landing Day Festival has folk dancing, music, Greek food and crafts celebrating the arrival of the first colony of Greeks in North America in the late 18th century; **Fourth of July:** Barbecue, games, swimwear and surfing contests, fireworks; **Sept. 8:** Founding of St. Augustine, held on the grounds of the Mission of Nombre de Dios at the site where Don Pedro Menendez de Aviles landed in 1565. There is a re-enactment of landing; **October:** St. Augustine Folk Festival at the St. Augustine Amphitheatre; Maritime Festival with seafood, dinghy races, costume balls, marine exhibits; Cracker Day with barbecue, rodeo, entertainment at the St. Johns County Fairgrounds; **November:** Lincolnville Festival, celebrates the city's black heritage; Great Chowder Debate, where restaurants compete for title of best-tasting chowder; Fall Arts and Crafts Festival, held on Thanksgiving weekend; **December:** Grand Illumination (held on the first Saturday) is a torchlight procession through the Spanish Quarter re-enacting British colonial customs; Christmas parade with bands, holiday floats and the arrival of Santa Claus; Christmas Tour of Homes.

SPORTS AND LEISURE ACTIVITIES:
Most popular local fishing areas: St. Johns River (bass); Matanzas River; Atlantic Ocean
Number of local golf courses: 3 public
Public beaches? Yes
Tennis courts available to the public? Yes
Boating? Yes
Number of pleasure boats registered in the county (1991-92): 5,369

SERVICES FOR RETIREES:
Council on Aging in St. Augustine.

FINANCIAL SERVICES:
Number of local banks: 25
Number of local savings and loan associations: 2

THE MEDIA:
Largest local newspaper: *St. Augustine Record*
Cable television? Yes

MAJOR LOCAL RETAILERS:
Belk-Hudson, JCPenney, Wal-Mart, K mart.

FOOD ESTABLISHMENTS: 398

OTHER SERVICES:
Number of local libraries: 4
Number of local hotels/motels: 77
Number of churches: Protestant: 50; Jewish: 1; Catholic: 7; Other: 18

TOURISM INQUIRIES:
St. Augustine and St. Johns County Chamber of Commerce, One Riberia St., St. Augustine, 32084. Telephone: 904-829-5681.

SUWANNEE County
Northeast
County seat: Live Oak

POPULATION: 1990: 26,780
1993: 28,598
Increase: 6.8 percent

AGE DISTRIBUTION (1992) IN PERCENTAGES:
  0-14 : 21.6
  15-44: 39.9
  45-64: 21.7
  65+ : 16.8

MUNICIPAL POPULATION:
BRANFORD: 1990: 670; 1993: 682
LIVE OAK: 1990: 6,332; 1993: 6,479
UNINCORPORATED: 1990: 19,778; 1993: 21,437

LAND AREA: 688 square miles
POPULATION DENSITY: 42 people per square mile (45th in the state)

Named for the Suwannee River, which borders this county on three sides, the area is a rural, agricultural community in north central Florida, between Jacksonville and Tallahassee. The farming economy is based on such crops as tobacco, soybeans, corn, peanuts, livestock and poultry. The oldest and largest flue-cured tobacco market in the state is found in Live Oak. Manufacturing is also playing a role in the county's economy, and a chicken processing plant is the major private employer. Housing in the area is mostly made up of single-family and mobile homes. Because of the river and a number of lakes, recreational activities are not scarce here. Fishing for largemouth bass, Suwannee bass, bream and bluegill and hunting for dove, quail, boar and deer are popular. An unusual activity here is cave-diving in the springs feeding the Suwannee River. Other outdoor sports include scuba diving, swimming, tubing, canoeing, boating and camping.

TOURISM:
Tourism does not cause a significant increase in population. But the Suwannee Springs and the Suwannee River bring some tourists in the summer.

HOUSING PRICES:
Average price of a home in recent years: $50,000; price of a typical 2-bedroom, 2-bath home: $40,000; price of a typical 3-bedroom, 2-bath home: $60,000; riverfront homes: $60,000; lakefront homes: $80,000.
Number of vacant residential lots: 11,216; number of single-family residences: 4,437; mobile homes: 2,819; condominiums: 0

EDUCATION:
Number of schools: 7
Number of students enrolled: 5,525
Percentage of students continuing education after high school: 66.98
Teacher-to-pupil ratio: 1:18.8
Average teacher's salary: $30,604

Colleges, universities, and junior or community colleges serving the area:
North Florida Junior College, Madison; Lake City Community College, Lake City; Santa Fe Community College, Gainesville; University of Florida, Gainesville; Tallahassee Community College, Tallahassee; Florida State University, Tallahassee; Jacksonville University, Jacksonville; Florida A&M University, Tallahassee; Edward Waters College, Jacksonville; University of North Florida, Jacksonville.

Trade and technical schools serving the area:
Suwannee-Hamilton Vocational-Technical School

HEALTH CARE:
Number of general hospitals: 1
Number of hospital beds: 30
Number of physicians: 10

TAXES: Total county ad-valorem millage rate (1993): 18.8424

STANDARD CRIME RATE: 3,000.3 offenses per 100,000 population (51st out of 67 counties)

LARGEST PRIVATE EMPLOYERS:

Name	Employees	Product/Service
Gold Kist Inc.	1,200	Chicken processing

Advent Christian Village	365	Nursing home
ALLTEL Florida Inc.	230	Communications
Suwannee Healthcare Center	171	Health care
Florida Sheriff's Youth Ranch	140	Social services
W.S. Badcock Corp.	125	Furniture distributor
Winn Dixie	105	Grocery
Olsen Health Care	100	Health care
Weeks/Musgrove Construction	96	Utility construction
Publix	85	Grocery

COMPANIES PROVIDING LOCAL UTILITIES:
Telephone: ALLTEL Florida
Electricity: Florida Power & Light, Suwannee Valley Electric Co-op
Natural Gas: City of Live Oak; South Georgia Natural Gas
Water: City of Live Oak
Major Water Source: Wells
Sanitary Landfill? Yes

POINTS OF INTEREST:
Suwannee River State Park, 13 miles west of Live Oak, offers camping, picnicking, freshwater fishing, hiking and overlook view of Withlacoochee and Suwannee rivers; **Peacock Springs State Recreation Area** near Luraville has scuba diving for certified divers only, swimming, picnicking; **Suwannee Springs** has a boat ramp and springs; **Florida Sheriff's Boys Ranch** covers 3,300 acres and is located nine miles north of Live Oak on the Suwannee River. This child-care program has about 100 boys in residence at any given time; **Advent Christian Village** in Dowling Park is a community with a village square consisting of a cafe, apothecary, post office, a rustic shop, country store, hospitality center, beauty shop, a "Twice Nice Shop," barber shop, bank and village lodge and conference center, a fire department and churches and serves as a haven for orphaned, neglected and abused children, offers living arrangements for retirees, nursing care for elderly residents and has a summer youth camp and weekend retreat center; **The Spirit of the Suwannee** park in Live Oak is the site of bluegrass music festivals, canoeing, swimming, camping, fishing and picnicking on the Suwannee River; **Suwannee County Museum.**

ANNUAL EVENTS:
January: Live Oak Garden Show; **February:** A Horsey Happening at Valahalla Farms, an events/competition in dressage, stadium jumping and cross country; **Spring:** Live Oak Woman's Club Arts Festival, with artists, craftsmen, dancers and live music and is held every spring for one week at the Suwannee County Coliseum; **April:** Blue Grass Festival at the Spirit of the Suwannee park; Live Oak's Birthday Celebration; **July:** Branford River Reunion, a July Fourth event with arts and crafts in downtown Branford in Hatch Park where all former residents of the city are invited to return for a homecoming; **Fall:** Suwannee County Agricultural Fair, held one week during the fall with exhibits, animal show and carnival rides; **October:** Blue Grass Festival at the Spirit of the Suwannee park; **December:** Christmas on the Square Festival in Live Oak, held the first Saturday of the month, has arts and crafts displays.

SPORTS AND LEISURE ACTIVITIES:
Most popular local fishing areas: Suwannee River, White Lake, Peacock Lake and Suwannee Lake
Number of local golf courses: 2 private
Public beaches: No
Tennis courts available to the public? Yes
Boating? Yes
Number of pleasure boats registered in the county (1991-92): 2,003

SERVICES FOR RETIREES:
Meals on Wheels

FINANCIAL SERVICES:
Number of local banks: 5
Number of local savings and loan associations: 4

THE MEDIA:
Largest local newspaper: *Suwannee Democrat*
Cable television? Yes

MAJOR LOCAL RETAILER:
K mart

FOOD ESTABLISHMENTS: 62

OTHER SERVICES:
Number of local libraries: 2
Number of local hotels/motels: 10
Number of churches: Protestant: 55; Jewish: 0; Catholic: 1

TOURISM INQUIRIES:
The Suwannee County Chamber of Commerce, P.O. Drawer C, Live Oak, 32060. Telephone: 904-362-3071.

UNION County
Northeast
County seat: Lake Butler

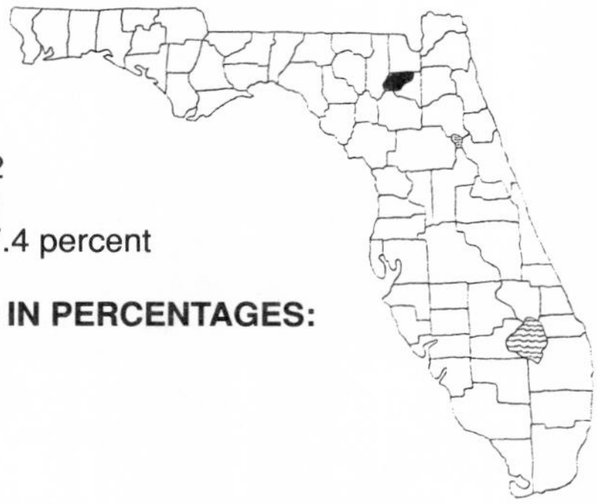

POPULATION: 1990: 10,252
1993: 12,031
Increase : 17.4 percent

AGE DISTRIBUTION (1992) IN PERCENTAGES:
0-14 : 20.3
15-44: 55.4
45-64: 16.7
65+ : 7.5

MUNICIPAL POPULATION:
LAKE BUTLER: 1990: 2,116; 1993: 2,126
RAIFORD: 1990: 198; 1993: 232
WORTHINGTON SPRINGS: 1990: 178; 1993: 228
UNINCORPORATED: 1990: 7,760; 1993: 9,445

LAND AREA: 240 square miles
POPULATION DENSITY: 50 people per square mile (43rd in the state)

Located southwest of Jacksonville, Union County is about 60 miles from the Atlantic Ocean. It is close to several major highway arteries — about 25 miles from Interstate 10, about 15 miles from Interstate 75 and 15 miles from Highway 301. State Roads 100 and 121 run through the county. The county is mostly rural, consisting largely of agriculture and forestry. Poultry and poultry products account for the largest source of agricultural sales; cattle ranks second. There are more than 31,000 acres of woodland in the county and the forestry industry provides more than 600 jobs. The prison system, with two state prison complexes here, is the largest employer. Hunting is plentiful in the Lake Butler Wildlife Management Area and fishing in three lakes and two small rivers.

The county has the lowest percentage of residents age 65 and up (7.5 percent) in Florida and the highest percentage of residents age 44 and under (75.7 percent).

TOURISM:
Not a tourism area.

HOUSING PRICES:
Average price typically $40,000-$50,000.
Number of vacant residential lots: 574; number of single-family residences: 869; mobile homes: 622; condominiums: 0

EDUCATION:
Number of schools: 5
Number of students enrolled: 2,044
Percentage of students continuing education after high school: 65.28
Teacher-to-pupil ratio: 1:17.9
Average teacher's salary: $25,519

Colleges, universities, and junior or community colleges serving the area:
University of Florida in Gainesville, Lake City Community College in Lake City and Sante Fe Community College in Gainesville, all about 25 miles from the county.

Trade and technical schools serving the area:
Bradford-Union Vocational-Technical Center, Santa Fe Community College in Gainesville and Lake City Community College.

HEALTH CARE:
Number of general hospitals: 2
Number of hospital beds: 180
Number of physicians: 17

TAXES: Total county ad-valorem millage rate (1993): 19.7934

STANDARD CRIME RATE: 565.2 offenses per 100,000 population (64th out of 67 counties)

LARGEST EMPLOYERS:

Name	Employees	Product/Service
Florida Department of Corrections	1,600	Prison
Pritchett Trucking	340	Trucking
Lake Butler Apparel	240	Clothing manufacturer
Union County Schools	238	Education
Gilman Building	120	Lumber
Ramadan Hand Institute	90	Health care
Mid-Florida Hauling	80	Trucking
Shadd's Trucking	80	Trucking
Pride of Florida	70	Manufacturing
Spires IGA	40	Grocery

COMPANIES PROVIDING LOCAL UTILITIES:
Telephone: ALLTEL Florida
Electricity: Florida Power & Light and Clay Electric Cooperative
Natural Gas: Sawyer Gas
Water: City of Lake Butler
Major Water Source: Wells
Sanitary Landfill? Yes

ANNUAL EVENT:
July Fourth Celebration.

SPORTS AND LEISURE ACTIVITIES:
Most popular local fishing areas: Lake Butler, Palestine Lake, New River and Sante Fe River.
Number of local golf courses: None
Public beaches? No
Tennis courts available to the public? Yes
Boating? Yes
Number of pleasure boats registered in the county (1991-92): 533

SERVICES FOR RETIREES:
Meals on Wheels and other services at the Outreach Center.

FINANCIAL SERVICES:
Number of local banks: 1
Number of local savings and loan associations: 0

THE MEDIA:
Largest local newspaper: *Union County Times*
Cable television? Yes

MAJOR LOCAL RETAILERS:
No shopping centers

FOOD ESTABLISHMENTS: 7

OTHER SERVICES:
Number of local libraries: 1

Number of local hotels/motels: 0 (county does have one bed and breakfast with four rooms)
Number of churches: Protestant: 32; Jewish: 0; Catholic: 0; Other: 1 Mormon

TOURISM INQUIRIES:
Union County Chamber of Commerce, P.O. Box 797, 175 W. Main St., Lake Butler, 32054. Telephone: 904-496-3624.

NORTHWEST FLORIDA

THE COUNTIES: Bay, Calhoun, Dixie, Escambia, Franklin, Gadsden, Gilchrist, Gulf, Holmes, Jackson, Jefferson, Lafayette, Leon, Levy, Liberty, Madison, Okaloosa, Santa Rosa, Taylor, Wakulla, Walton, and Washington

MAJOR CITIES: Tallahassee, Pensacola, Panama City, Fort Walton Beach

TOP INDUSTRIES: The military, timber, agriculture, tourism, pulp and paper products, seafood, dairy farming, apparel, retailing, chemicals, poultry

MAJOR NEWSPAPERS: *Pensacola News Journal, Tallahassee Democrat, The News-Herald* in Panama City, and *Northwest Florida Daily News* in Fort Walton Beach

WEATHER: On the first line is the average maximum temperature for each month; the second line, the average minimum temperature; the third line, the amount of precipitation, in inches, for 1990, from the national weather stations.

Apalachicola	Jan.	Feb.	Mar.	Apr.	May	June	July	Aug.	Sep.	Oct.	Nov.	Dec.
Max.	67.3	69.6	72.3	76.8	84.1	90.1	90.5	91.8	88.2	81.2	74.0	69.6
Min.	48.1	53.5	53.7	57.7	65.4	72.2	74.3	74.7	69.9	62.3	51.5	51.0
Precp.	2.4	3.9	4.2	2.2	0.5	2.8	9.3	2.3	5.2	2.0	1.6	1.6

Pensacola	Jan.	Feb.	Mar.	Apr.	May	June	July	Aug.	Sep.	Oct.	Nov.	Dec.
Max.	65.0	68.5	73.2	76.3	83.4	90.9	92.0	94.5	90.1	80.5	73.8	67.3
Min.	45.3	50.9	52.6	56.0	65.0	72.5	74.1	73.5	69.6	58.7	50.2	48.1
Precp.	4.7	5.0	9.2	4.9	4.6	5.5	2.1	2.5	1.5	8.5	1.1	2.0

Tallahassee	Jan.	Feb.	Mar.	Apr.	May	June	July	Aug.	Sep.	Oct.	Nov.	Dec.
Max.	70.6	72.7	78.0	80.8	87.9	93.8	93.6	95.2	92.1	83.8	76.8	71.1
Min.	40.9	49.5	48.7	51.4	61.6	68.9	71.1	71.1	66.1	58.2	45.1	46.2
Precp.	3.1	7.3	3.4	3.4	1.9	4.0	3.4	6.8	4.9	2.5	0.6	4.5

BAY County
Northwest
County seat: Panama City

POPULATION: 1990: 126,994
1993: 134,059
Increase: 5.6 percent

AGE DISTRIBUTION (1992) IN PERCENTAGES:
0-14 : 21.7
15-44: 45.3

Tourists walk along Panama City Beach on a blustery day.

A man wades into the Suwannee River at Fanning Springs in Gilchrist County.

The Capitol Complex in Tallahassee.

45-64: 20.6
65+ : 12.4
MUNICIPAL POPULATION:
CALLAWAY: 1990: 12,253; 1993: 13,504
CEDAR GROVE: 1990: 1,479; 1993: 1,501
LYNN HAVEN: 1990: 9,298; 1993: 10,050
MEXICO BEACH: 1990: 992; 1993: 1,013
PANAMA CITY: 1990: 34,396; 1993: 35,914
PANAMA CITY BEACH: 1990: 4,051; 1993: 4,341
PARKER: 1990: 4,598; 1993: 4,834
SPRINGFIELD: 1990: 8,719; 1993: 9,051
UNINCORPORATED: 1990: 51,208; 1993: 53,851

LAND AREA: 764 square miles
POPULATION DENSITY: 176 people per square mile (24th in the state)

Claiming to have "the world's most beautiful beaches," the Panama City area prides itself on its white-sand beaches and emerald-green-colored water, not unlike the water color found in parts of the Caribbean. For this reason, the area lures millions of tourists, including college students on spring break — about 600,000 of them in 1994 alone.

To back up the county's beach claim, the St. Andrews State Recreation Area near Panama City was ranked the fourth best beach in the nation in 1994, according to a Maryland Laboratory for Coastal Research survey of 650 public beaches.

As in Pensacola, the military's presence is strongly felt here. Two military installations have a major impact on the county's economy — Tyndall Air Force Base and the Coastal Systems Station, which are the county's largest employers: nearly 7,000 military and civilian employees at Tyndall and around 3,000 at the coastal station. Major private employers include hospitals and resorts; products manufactured here include linerboard, oil and terpines and line pipe. The county is also home to the ninth largest port in the state, Port Panama City.

One of the state's top attractions is here — the Miracle Strip Amusement Park in Panama City Beach.

Despite some healthy industries, the county is among those that lost population over the course of the early 1990s recession — about 7,000 residents in total between 1989 and 1991. And the crime rate jumped from 26th in the state to 16th.

The county includes a number of incorporated communities, including Panama City, the county seat and the county's largest city; Panama City Beach, a tourist-oriented city on the Gulf of Mexico with attractions, hotels, motels and condominiums; Springfield, which is home to a medical center; Callaway, which is popular among retired military personnel; Parker, located near Tyndall Air Force Base, which is home to many active-duty military personnel; Lynn Haven, north of Panama City; Cedar Grove, which has about 100 businesses; and Mexico Beach, in eastern Bay County, a vacation area along the Gulf of Mexico.

TOURISM:
Officials say that in 1993, 3 million people visited the Panama City Beach area.

HOUSING PRICES:
The median sales price for a single-family existing home in the Panama City area was $69,000 for June 1994.
Number of vacant residential lots: 18,603; number of single-family residences: 38,286; mobile homes: 5,111; condominiums: 9,026

EDUCATION:
Number of schools: 33
Number of students enrolled: 23,873
Percentage of students continuing education after high school: 69.64
Teacher-to-pupil ratio: 1:16.6
Average teacher's salary: $29,470

Colleges, universities, and junior or community colleges serving the area:
Gulf Coast Community College in Panama City; Florida State University campus in Panama City

Trade and technical schools serving the area:
Haney Technical Center in Panama City

HEALTH CARE:
Number of general hospitals: 4
Number of hospital beds: 558
Number of physicians: 210

TAXES: Total county ad-valorem millage rate (1993): 13.7740

STANDARD CRIME RATE: 7,114 offenses per 100,000 population (16th out of 67 counties)

LARGEST PRIVATE EMPLOYERS:

Name	Employees	Product/Service
Sunshine Food Stores	700	Groceryheadquarters
Stone Container Corp.	685	Kraft linerboard
HCA Gulf Coast Community Hospital	650	Health care
Hilton Inc.	610	Resort
SallieMae	605	Broker/student loans
Marriott Bay Point Resort	457 (summer)	Hotel/resort
	350 (winter)	
Arizona Chemical Co.	410	Oil, terpenes
Edgewater Beach Resort	284	Resort
Allied Signal Automotive	250	Brake Disc Pads
Bay Point Yacht & Country Club	221	Resort

COMPANIES PROVIDING LOCAL UTILITIES:
Telephone: Southern Bell
Electricity: Gulf Power Co.
Natural Gas: West Florida Natural Gas
Water: Municipalities
Major Water Source: Lakes
Sanitary Landfill? Yes

POINTS OF INTEREST:
The beaches; Miracle Strip Amusement Park in Panama City Beach has about 30 rides and attractions including a roller coaster, a Sea Dragon ride that sways back and forth covering a radius of more than 80 feet and reaches a 65-degree angle, concessions, gift shops, midway games, arcade; **Junior Museum of Bay County** in Panama City has pioneer log structures and farming tools and other historical items; **Museum of Man in the Sea** in Panama City Beach features diving and scuba technology exhibits and serves as preservation center for the Institute of Diving; **Shipwreck Island** at Panama City Beach is a water park with a 300-foot slide, flume ride, 500,000-gallon wave pool, tubing areas; **St. Andrews State Recreation Area** west of Panama City has camping, picnicking, swimming, saltwater fishing, interpretive center, seasonal campfire programs and guided walks, hiking, boat ramp, rental boats during the summer, concessions, a reconstructed turpentine still, white-sand beaches and sand dunes; **Gulf World** in Panama City Beach has dolphin shows, a Tropical Garden filled with parrots, flamingos and peacocks, shark tank, scuba diving demonstration, parrot show, sea lions; **Zoo World** in Panama City Beach is a zoo and reptile park with snakes, alligators, monkeys and birds; a number of **cruises** including the Capt. Anderson excursions; **Port Panama City** handled 565,302 tons of exports and imports and domestic cargo in 1992; **Marina Civic Center** in Panama City, a municipal auditorium.

THE ARTS:
Bay County Arts Alliance sponsors plays and other art events; **Gulf Coast Community College's Fine Arts Auditorium; Visual Arts Center of Northwest Florida** houses three galleries of contemporary art; **Panama City Chamber Players; Ballet Theatre of Northwest Florida; Kaleidoscope Theatre; Gulf Coast College Symphony Orchestra.**

ANNUAL EVENTS:
February: John A. Centrone Memorial Biathlon, a 4-mile run and 20-mile bike race; **March:** Scottish Festival in Panama City; **April:** Spring Heritage Day at the Junior Museum offers look into pioneer life; national triple crown slow-pitch softball series at Frank Brown Park; **May:** Spring Festival of the Arts at McKenzie Park in Panama City has arts and crafts, concessions; **July:** Fourth of July fireworks in Panama City, Panama City Beach, Tyndall Air Force Base and Lynn Haven; Bay Point Marina Invitational Billfish Tournament; **August:** Bay Art Show at the Visual Arts Center; **September:** Bay Culinary Classic, a food festival; **October:** Indian Summer

Seafood Festival at Panama City Beach with arts and crafts, seafood, entertainment; Oktoberest, with music, dancing, German food, beer at Grace Avenue and the Mini Mall; Bay County Fair at the Bay County Fairgrounds; **November:** Miracle Strip Bowl on Thanksgiving weekend features Gulf Coast Midget League Football; **December:** Panama City Christmas parade; Holly Fair at the fairgrounds.

SPORTS AND LEISURE ACTIVITIES:
Most popular local fishing areas: Gulf of Mexico (snapper, grouper, sailfish, marlin, tuna); Dan Russell Pier in the Gulf (Spanish and king mackerel); Deer Point Lake and the Choctawhatchee River for freshwater fishing (largemouth bass, bluegill, shellcracker).
Number of local golf courses: 10
Public beaches? Yes
Tennis courts available to the public? Yes
Boating? Yes
Number of pleasure boats registered in the county (1991-92): 13,096

SERVICES FOR RETIREES:
Bay County Council on Aging, Panama City.

FINANCIAL SERVICES:
Number of local banks: 21
Number of local savings and loan associations: 16

THE MEDIA:
Largest local newspaper: *The News-Herald*
Cable television? Yes

MAJOR LOCAL RETAILERS:
Sears, JCPenney, Gayfers, Belk Hudson, Wal-Mart, K mart

FOOD ESTABLISHMENTS: 590

OTHER SERVICES:
Number of local libraries: 5
Number of local hotels/motels: 218
Number of churches: Protestant: 153; Jewish: 1; Catholic: 5

TOURISM INQUIRIES:
Bay County Chamber of Commerce, P.O. Box 1850, Panama City, 32402. Telephone: 904-785-5206.

CALHOUN County
Northwest
County Seat: Blountstown

POPULATION: 1990: 11,011
1993: 11,479
Increase: 4.3 percent

AGE DISTRIBUTION (1992) IN PERCENTAGES:
0-14 : 21.4
15-44: 43.6
45-64: 20.6
65+ : 14.4

MUNICIPAL POPULATION:
ALTHA: 1990: 497; 1993: 536
BLOUNTSTOWN: 1990: 2,404; 1993: 2,388
UNINCORPORATED: 1990: 8,110; 1993: 8,555

LAND AREA: 567 square miles
POPULATION DENSITY: 20 people per square mile (61st in the state)

Located northeast of Panama City in Florida's Panhandle, and 45 miles west of Tallahassee, Calhoun County originally included parts of Bay County and all of Gulf County until the early 1900s.

Named after U.S. Senator John C. Calhoun of South Carolina, the county was formed in 1838. Because of its natural resources, it is known for its recreational opportunities. The Apalachicola River forms the county's eastern border and the Chipola River runs through the the county as well. Fishing, hunting, tubing and canoeing are popular pastimes here. The area also has 10 parks, with a total of 180 acres for local recreation. The county has some catfish farms and is attempting to lure more. It hosts an annual catfish festival to promote the industry. Other products grown and manufactured here include pulpwood, peanuts and cotton, plants and flowers, and elevators.

TOURISM:
Very little.

HOUSING PRICES:
Estimated average price is about $60,000.
Number of vacant residential lots: 1,734; number of single-family residences: 2,316; mobile homes: 545; condominiums: 0

EDUCATION:
Number of schools: 7
Number of students enrolled: 2,259
Percentage of students continuing education after high school: 69.90
Teacher-to-pupil ratio: 1:16.6
Average teacher's salary: $29,973

Colleges, universities, and junior or community colleges serving the area:
Chipola Junior College, Marianna; Tallahassee Community College, Florida State University and Florida A&M University, all in Tallahassee; and Gulf Coast Community College in Panama City.

Trade and technical schools serving the area:
Blountstown High School; Washington-Holmes Vo-Tech Center in Chipley; Haney Vo-Tech Center in Panama City; Lively Vo-Tech Center in Tallahassee.

HEALTH CARE:
Number of general hospitals: 1
Number of hospital beds: 36
Number of physicians: 6

TAXES: Total county ad-valorem millage rate (1993): 16.6750

STANDARD CRIME RATE: 487.8 offenses per 100,000 population (65th out of 67 counties)

LARGEST PRIVATE EMPLOYERS:

Name	Employees	Product/Service
Shelton Trucking	315	Trucking
Forestry Operations	225	Pulpwood
Independent Farmers	225	Peanuts, cotton
Apalachee Nursing Home	160	Nursing home
Hartford Farms	120	Gladiolas
Mowrey Elevator	100	Elevators
Calhoun-Liberty Hospital	85	Hospital
Oglesby Nursery & Lab	75	Plant cloning
Altha Farmers Co-op	50	Agricultural suppliers

COMPANIES PROVIDING LOCAL UTILITIES:
Telephone: St. Joseph Telephone
Electricity: Gulf Coast Co-Op; Florida Public Utilities; City of Blountstown;
    West Florida Electric Co-Op.
Natural Gas: City of Blountstown
Water: City of Blountstown, Town of Altha; Calhoun County
Major Water Source: Wells
Sanitary Landfill? No

POINTS OF INTEREST:
Apalachicola and Chipola rivers, both popular for fishing, and the Chipola is also noted for tubing and canoeing; **W.T. Neal Civic Center** in Blountstown hosts fine arts performances, from puppet shows and concerts to the ballet, and is also a meeting place for clubs and other groups; **Sam Atkins Park,** site of the annual Catfish Festival.

ANNUAL EVENT:
Last Saturday in April: Catfish Festival features arts and crafts, food, games for children, entertainment.

SPORTS AND LEISURE ACTIVITIES:
Most popular local fishing areas: Apalachicola and Chipola rivers.
Number of local golf courses: None
Public beaches? No
Tennis courts available to the public? Yes
Boating? Yes
Number of pleasure boats registered in the county (1991-92): 1,017

SERVICES FOR RETIREES:
Meals on Wheels

FINANCIAL SERVICES:
Number of local banks: 2
Number of local savings and loan associations: 1

THE MEDIA:
Largest local newspaper: *County Record*
Cable television? Yes

MAJOR LOCAL RETAILERS:
No major chain stores. Largest one is Pelt's department store in Blountstown.

FOOD ESTABLISHMENTS: 20

OTHER SERVICES:
Number of local libraries: 4
Number of local motels: 3
Number of churches: Protestant: 42; Jewish: 0; Catholic: 1; Other: 3

TOURISM INQUIRIES:
Calhoun County Chamber of Commerce, 425 E. Central Ave., Courthouse Building, Room 127, Blountstown, 32424. Telephone: 904-674-4519.

DIXIE County
Northwest
County seat: Cross City

POPULATION: 1990: 10,585
1993: 11,810
Increase: 11.6 percent

AGE DISTRIBUTION (1992) IN PERCENTAGES:
0-14 : 21.0
15-44: 40.4
45-64: 23.7
65+ : 14.8

MUNICIPAL POPULATION:
CROSS CITY: 1990: 2,041; 1993: 2,037
HORSESHOE BEACH: 1990: 252; 1993: 245
UNINCORPORATED: 1990: 8,292; 1993: 9,528

LAND AREA: 704 square miles
POPULATION DENSITY: 17 people per square mile (63rd in the state)

Georgia-Pacific Corp. owns most of the land and is also one of the county's largest employers. Consequently, it's no surprise that timber and lumber are the major business in the county, which is on the Gulf of Mexico just across the Suwannee River from Levy County. Along with Georgia-Pacific, another major employer is Suwannee Lumber Co., which makes pine and cypress lumber, mulch and pulpwood chips. Besides being a landowner, Georgia-Pacific has a pine mill, pulpwood chip mill, a fence factory and a mulch plant. Other business pursuits here include textiles (Great Bear Industries has a plant employing 175 people); asphalt paving; and seafood processing (fish, blue crabs, stone crabs, scallops and oysters for markets on the Eastern seaboard).

There are 12,665 acres of farmland; the community of the First District in the northeast section of the county is the hub of agricultural activity. Major crops are tobacco, watermelon, peanuts, corn, cucumbers, okra, tomatoes and bell peppers. Fishing and hunting are popular; the villages of Suwannee, Jena and Steinhatchee offer amenities such as guide services.

A figure of note: the county's standard crime rate has jumped in recent years — from 64th among the 67 counties in 1989 to 34th in 1993.

TOURISM:
Very little. The few tourists that visit the area generally come from November to April.

HOUSING PRICES:
Local Realtors estimate the average in recent years at $45,000; around $37,500 for a two-bedroom, two-bath home; and $45,000-$55,000 for a three-bedroom, two-bath home. Riverfront homes and those on the Gulf of Mexico are about 40 percent higher.
Number of vacant residential lots: 5,594; number of single-family residences: 2,360; mobile homes: 2,935; condominiums: 0

EDUCATION:
Number of schools: 5
Number of students enrolled: 2,163
Percentage of students continuing education after high school: 69.01
Teacher-to-pupil ratio: 1:16.5
Average teacher's salary: $25,883

Colleges, universities, and junior or community colleges serving the area:
University of Florida, Gainesville; Santa Fe Community College, Gainesville; Lake City Community College, Lake City.

Trade and technical schools serving the area:
Dixie County Adult Center; Dixie County Vo-Tech; and Taylor County Technical Institute

HEALTH CARE:
Number of general hospitals: 0
Number of hospital beds: 0
Number of physicians: 2

TAXES: Total county ad-valorem millage rate (1993): 19.3160

STANDARD CRIME RATE: 5,097.4 offenses per 100,000 population (34th out of 67 counties)

LARGEST PRIVATE EMPLOYERS:
Name	Employees	Product/Service
Georgia-Pacific Corp.	210	Timber
Great Bear Industries	175	Textiles
Suwannee Lumber Co.	140	Timber
Rick's Seafood	60	Seafood
Cross City Veneer	40	Timber
Anderson/Columbia	40	Asphalt paving
Gulf Stream Crab Plant	30	Seafood
Knights Sawmill	22	Timber
S & T Service	15	Construction

COMPANIES PROVIDING LOCAL UTILITIES:
Telephone: Southern Bell
Electricity: Central Florida Electric Co-op; Florida Power Corp.; Tri-County Electric Co-op
Natural Gas: None
Water: Town of Cross City; Horseshoe Beach; Suwannee Water Association
Major Water Source: Wells
Sanitary Landfill? Yes

POINTS OF INTEREST:
Suwannee River and its springs for fishing, swimming, snorkeling and scuba diving; **Stein-**

hatchee River for fishing; **underwater archaeological preserve** in western Dixie County houses what remains of the "City of Hawkinsville" steamboat — the last steamboat to be stationed on the Suwannee River that served Branford, Clay's Landing, Old Town and Cedar Keys. Access to the site is by boat only; **Suwannee Belle Riverboat** in Old Town.

ANNUAL EVENTS:
Spring: Dixie County Springfest in Cross City; **May:** Dixie County Chamber of Commerce festival, includes parade, booths.

SPORTS AND LEISURE ACTIVITIES:
Most popular local fishing areas: Suwannee and Steinhatchee rivers for bream and bass; Gulf of Mexico for grouper, red snapper, kingfish, sea trout, redfish, flounder, cobia and Spanish mackerel. Hunting: For deer, turkey, squirrel, ducks and wild hogs. There are five hunting clubs with thousands of acres (including the 200,000-acre Steinhatchee game preserve) of open hunting for gun, bow and black powder enthusiasts.
Number of local golf courses: None
Public beaches: Yes
Tennis courts available to the public? Yes
Boating? Yes
Number of pleasure boats registered in the county (1991-92): 1,496

SERVICES FOR RETIREES:
Tri-County Council for Senior Citizens provides transportation; Meals on Wheels

FINANCIAL SERVICES:
Number of local banks: 2
Number of local savings and loan associations: 1

THE MEDIA:
Largest local newspaper: *Dixie County Advocate*
Cable television? Yes

MAJOR LOCAL RETAILERS:
TG&Y and Dollar. The largest other retail store is Jones' Department Store.

FOOD ESTABLISHMENTS: 32

OTHER SERVICES:
Number of local libraries: 1
Number of local motels: 9
Number of churches: Protestant: 42; Jewish: 0; Catholic: 1; Other: 1

TOURISM INQUIRIES:
Dixie County Chamber of Commerce, P.O. Box 547, Cross City, 32628. Telephone: 904-498-5454.

ESCAMBIA County
Northwest
County Seat: Pensacola

POPULATION: 1990: 262,798
1993: 272,083
Increase: 3.5 percent

AGE DISTRIBUTION (1992) IN PERCENTAGES:
0-14 : 21.7
15-44: 46.6
45-64: 19.7
65+ : 12.0

MUNICIPAL POPULATION:
CENTURY: 1990: 1,989; 1993: 1,994
PENSACOLA: 1990: 59,198; 1993: 59,858
UNINCORPORATED: 1990: 201,611; 1993: 210,231

LAND AREA: 664 square miles
POPULATION DENSITY: 410 people per square mile (12th in the state)

Escambia, the first county you enter coming east on Interstate 10 into Florida, is synonymous with the Navy and has gained the nickname "Cradle of Naval Aviation" — it has the Pensacola Naval Air Station; the Naval Technical Training Center at Corry Field; Whiting Field, and Saufley Field. The bases employ about 9,500 civilians.

Among the largest private employers is Monsanto Co., which makes nylon fiber and industrial organic chemicals (2,100 employees). Other leading private employers are hospitals, a utility and a paper company.

The white-sand beaches here, namely at Perdido Key State Recreation Area, have been ranked among the nation's most picturesque.

Besides its strong military ties, the county has two historic areas — the Seville Historic District (with nearly 30 Creole houses, many predating the Civil War period) and Historic Pensacola Village (museums and historic sites that interpret Pensacola's past). A number of festivals and events are held in the Seville District, including the Great Gulfcoast Arts Festival, which attracts about 150,000 people a year. Also popular among tourists is Pensacola Beach, which sits on the Gulf of Mexico and next to the Gulf Islands National Seashore.

There are two incorporated cities here, Pensacola and Century (located near the Alabama border in northern Escambia).

A port facility — the Port of Pensacola — handled 1,372,879 tons of exports and imports in fiscal 1991-92, about double the tonnage recorded in fiscal 1987-88. The major cargoes included petroleum products, fertilizer, scrap steel, sulphur and agricultural and forest products. Major ocean and land transportation companies serve the facility.

The county is also home to the University of West Florida, which has nearly 8,000 undergraduate and graduate students.

Pensacola has gained notoriety over the past decade as a site of violent confrontation over the abortion issue.

TOURISM:
The Pensacola area is a very popular spot, particularly in the summer, for tourists.

HOUSING PRICES:
Median sales price for a single-family existing home in the Pensacola metropolitan area was $80,400 in June 1994.
Number of vacant residential lots: 19,657; number of single-family residences: 74,023; mobile homes: 4,563; condominiums: 3,652

EDUCATION:
Number of schools: 68
Number of students enrolled: 44,641
Percentage of students continuing education after high school: 81.26
Teacher-to-pupil ratio: 1:17.3
Average teacher's salary: $29,049

Colleges, universities, and junior or community colleges serving the area:
University of West Florida in Pensacola; Troy State University - Florida Region in Pensacola; Pensacola Junior College; Pensacola Christian College

Trade and technical schools serving the area:
George Stone Area Vocational Technical Center in Pensacola

HEALTH CARE:
Number of general hospitals: 6
Number of hospital beds: 1,506
Number of physicians: 635

TAXES: Total county ad-valorem millage rate (1993): 18.2640

STANDARD CRIME RATE: 6,960 offenses per 100,000 population (17th out of 67 counties)

LARGEST PRIVATE EMPLOYERS:

Name	Employees	Product/Service
Baptist Hospital	2,994	Health care
Sacred Heart Hospital	2,490	Health care

Monsanto Company	2,100	Nylon fibers/industrial chemicals
West Florida Regional Medical Center	1,756	Health care
Gulf Power Co.	1,576	Utility
Champion International Corp.	1,210	Paper products
Medical Center Clinic	950	Health care
Lakeview Center	950	Health care
Instrument Control Service	750	Instrumentation
Westinghouse Electric Corp.	618	Nuclear components

COMPANIES PROVIDING LOCAL UTILITIES:
Telephone: Southern Bell
Electricity: Gulf Power Co.
Natural Gas: Energy Services of Pensacola
Water: Escambia County Utilities Authority
Major Water Source: Wells
Sanitary Landfill? Yes

POINTS OF INTEREST:
Gulf Islands National Seashore has white sand and dunes covered with sea oats (visitor center is off the Gulf Breeze Parkway) and **Fort Pickens National Park** near Gulf Breeze, with a three-mile hiking/bike trail; **Big Lagoon State Recreation Area,** 10 miles southwest of Pensacola, has camping, picnicking, swimming, fishing, crabbing, hiking, boat ramp, amphitheatre and observation tower; **Perdido Key State Recreation Area,** 15 miles southwest of Pensacola, has picnicking, swimming, saltwater fishing, nature trails, dunes covered with sea oats; **Blue Angels,** a naval flight demonstration aerobatic team based in Pensacola; **National Museum of Naval Aviation in Pensacola,** visited by nearly 600,000 people in 1991, has exhibits on the history of naval aviation from 1911 to the space age, including a Skylab Command Module and a F6F Hellcat-F4U Corsair; **Seville Historic District** in Pensacola has about 30 Creole homes, many predating the Civil War period, and Seville Square, a park that has been a public gathering place since the Spanish occupied the county; **North Hill Preservation District** in Pensacola is a residential area developed as an upper-class enclave between 1870 and 1930. There are van tours through the area; **Palafox Historic District** includes a hotel built in 1910, a 1925 Vaudeville theatre and a number of late-1800-to-early-1900-era buildings; **Historic Pensacola Village** includes museums and historic sites spanning from the Spanish colonial years to the 20th century; **T.T. Wentworth Junior Florida State Museum** in Pensacola houses artifacts relating to the archaeology and history of west Florida including memorabilia from early Coca-Cola collections; **Pensacola Civic Center** seats more than 10,000 people and hosts such events as circuses and concerts; **Bayfront Auditorium** in Pensacola has seating capacity of 3,000 for concerts and stage events; **Port of Pensacola; Pensacola Greyhound Track.**

THE ARTS:
Pensacola Symphony Orchestra; The Choral Society of Pensacola, an ensemble of 75 voices and orchestra; **Pensacola Opera Company; University of West Florida's Music Hall Artists Series; Pensacola Junior College's Lyceum Series; Saenger Theatre** in Pensacola seats 1,778 people and hosts the **Pensacola Symphony Orchestra,** jazz artists and Broadway touring companies; **Pensacola Museum of Art** has traveling exhibits and promotes area talent; **Quayside Art Gallery** in Pensacola claims to be the largest art co-op in the Southeast; **University of West Florida Art Gallery; Pensacola Junior College Visual Arts Gallery; Pensacola Little Theatre** stages dramatic presentations for the Pensacola community; **First City Dance Theatre; Kaleidoscope Dance Theatre** (youth ballet); **Pensacola Civic Band; Fiesta Chorus,** a local chapter of the **Society for the Preservation and Encouragement of Barbershop Quartet Singing in America.**

ANNUAL EVENTS:
January: Snow Fest at Pensacola Beach; **February and March:** Mardi Gras celebrations; **April:** Pensacola Jazz Fest in Seville Square; **May:** Crawfish Fiesta at Bartrum Park; **June:** Fiesta of Five Flags in Pensacola, celebrating the founding of Pensacola, has parades, festivals, food and entertainment; **September:** Pensacola Seafood Festival on Pensacola Beach; Seafood Festival at Seville Square with arts and crafts, entertainment, seafood; **October:** Greek Festival, Pensacola; Pensacola Interstate Fair; **November:** Great Gulfcoast Arts Festival in Seville Square,

Pensacola; **December:** Christmas parade in downtown Pensacola, a Christmas Walk in Seville Square and a Pensacola Beach Christmas parade and decorated boat procession.

SPORTS AND LEISURE ACTIVITIES:
Most popular local fishing areas: Escambia River, Perdido River, Gulf of Mexico and the bays. Area is well known for billfishing.
Number of local golf courses: At least 6 public and a number of private courses
Public beaches? Yes
Tennis courts available to the public? Yes
Boating? Yes
Number of pleasure boats registered in the county (1991-92): 15,558

SERVICES FOR RETIREES:
Escambia County Council on Aging provides such programs as Alzheimer's respite care, home-maker services, congregate meals, home-delivered meals, adult day health care, transportation and energy assistance.

FINANCIAL SERVICES:
Number of local banks: 66
Number of local savings and loan associations: 1

THE MEDIA:
Largest local newspaper: *Pensacola News-Journal*
Cable television? Yes

MAJOR LOCAL RETAILERS:
Dillard's, Gayfers, JCPenney, McRae's, Montgomery Ward, Sears; several antique areas. There also are a number of shops in Seville.

FOOD ESTABLISHMENTS: 645

OTHER SERVICES:
Number of local libraries: 7
Number of local hotels/motels: 65
Number of churches: Protestant: 286; Jewish: 2; Catholic: 21; Other: 18

TOURISM INQUIRIES:
Pensacola Area Chamber of Commerce, Convention and Visitor Information Center, 1401 E. Gregory St., Pensacola, 32501. Telephone: 904-434-1234.

FRANKLIN County
Northwest
County seat: Apalachicola

POPULATION: 1990: 8,967
1993: 9,775
Increase: 9 percent

AGE DISTRIBUTION (1992) IN PERCENTAGES:
0-14 : 20.0
15-44: 38.1
45-64: 24.5
65+ : 17.5

MUNICIPAL POPULATION:
APALACHICOLA: 1990: 2,602; 1993: 2,701
CARRABELLE: 1990: 1,200; 1993: 1,258
UNINCORPORATED: 1990: 5,165; 1993: 5,816

LAND AREA: 534 square miles
POPULATION DENSITY: 18 people per square mile (62nd in the state)

Franklin County, where only about 3 percent of the acreage is made up of municipalities or residential developments, is located southwest of Tallahassee along the Gulf of Mexico. The major industries are seafood (about 20 percent of the state's seafood is caught in waters off Franklin County; the seafood industry is also the largest employer and generates the most revenue) and forestry products (about 97 percent of the county is public or private forest land).

The major seafood product processed here is the famous Apalachicola Bay oyster (comprising 90 percent of the state's oyster harvest). But this industry has been subject to the whims of nature. For instance, in 1985 a hurricane forced the closure of oyster beds for almost a year. And in 1988, state officials blamed a summer drought for a dramatic reduction in the harvest. Still another setback came in 1994: tropical storms churned up the bay so much that the bay was ordered shut again.

Besides oysters, fishing for crab and shrimp also produces substantial income.

Most of the population is situated in the southern portion. There are four barrier islands — St. George, Little St. George, St. Vincent and Dog Island. St. George Island, one of the state's largest barrier islands — 28 miles long — is the most developed recreational area, containing summer homes, restaurants and motels. Undeveloped areas, though, are much more common and are found even on St. George Island. The state park there has nine miles of undeveloped beaches and dunes. Little St. George Island houses the Cape St. George Lighthouse, built in 1833 and accessible only by boat. St. Vincent Island is a national wildlife refuge that also is accessible only by boat. And Dog Island is accessible by ferry from Carrabelle and is primarily a wildlife preserve.

The environment is a major concern. Residential lots on the Gulf and on Apalachicola Bay have been zoned for one-acre-minimum sizes. The county also has a 35-foot height restriction on buildings to limit high rises and condominiums. A developer's proposal for the county's first major golf course underwent intense scrutiny, largely because the county has a high water table and residents have expressed concern about contamination from chemicals required to maintain the course.

TOURISM:
The season generally runs from March to August, when the population increases by 25 roughly percent.

HOUSING PRICES:
Realtors estimate average prices at $50,000-$55,000. Gulf-front lots (1-acre minimums) go for about $100,000; bayfront lots for $40,000-$75,000; interior lots in Apalachicola for $7,000 and up.

Number of vacant residential lots: 4,974; number of single-family residences: 4,205; mobile homes: 807; condominiums: 0

EDUCATION:
Number of schools: 6
Number of students enrolled: 1,637
Percentage of students continuing education after high school: 45.33
Teacher-to-pupil ratio: 1:15.2
Average teacher's salary: $27,671

Colleges, universities, and junior or community colleges serving the area:
Florida State University and Florida A&M University in Tallahassee; Gulf Coast Community College in Panama City

Trade and technical schools serving the area:
Haney Vo-Tech in Panama City

HEALTH CARE:
Number of general hospitals: 2
Number of hospital beds: 219
Number of physicians: 5

TAXES: Total county ad-valorem millage rate (1993): 16.7620

STANDARD CRIME RATE: 2,189.3 offenses per 100,000 population (55th out of 67 counties)

LARGEST PRIVATE EMPLOYERS:

Name	Employees	Product/Service
Senior Care Properties	350	
Leavins Seafood	100	Oysters, shrimp

D.W. Wilson Seafood	100	Seafood
Annewakee	92	Private school
Bayside Shellfish	90	Seafood
IGA	70	Groceries
Rainbow Inn	50	
Eastpoint Nursing Home	47	Nursing home
Red Rabbit	45	
Florida Power Corp.	35	Utility
Jr. Foods	30	Mini-grocery
Gibson Inn	30	Hotel
Miller Trucking Co.	30	Trucking

COMPANIES PROVIDING LOCAL UTILITIES:
Telephone: St. Joseph Telephone & Telegraph
Electricity: Florida Power Corp.
Natural Gas: Amerigas
Water: City of Apalachicola and private wells
Major Water Source: Wells
Sanitary Landfill? Yes

POINTS OF INTEREST:
John Gorrie State Museum, Apalachicola, honors the inventor of the first artificial ice machine in 1851 that eventually led to air-conditioning and refrigeration. Has reproduction of the machine and displays on history of Apalachicola and exhibits of navigational instruments; **St. George Island State Park,** 10 miles southeast of Eastpoint, offers camping, picnicking, swimming, saltwater fishing, hiking, boat ramp, observation platforms, nine miles of undeveloped beaches and dunes; **Little St. George,** popular among shell collectors; **Cape St. George Lighthouse,** popular among artists and photographers; **Alligator Point,** site for collecting sand dollars; **Crooked River,** popular for canoeing; **Apalachicola National Estuarine Sanctuary** is 184,225 acres and was established to preserve the land basin bordering the Apalachicola River; **National Wildlife Refuge Museum; Apalachicola National Forest,** camping and fishing; historic homes in Apalachicola, tours of old Victorian residences; **Dog Island** beaches, accessible by boat or ferry; five art galleries in the county.

ANNUAL EVENTS:
February: Square Dance Festival, Carrabelle; **March:** St. George Island Volunteer Fire Department Chili Cookoff and Auction; **March or April:** Apalachicola Antique Car Race and Show; **May:** (first Saturday)Tour of Homes; **July:** Franklin Firecracker Festival, Carrabelle; Ole' Fashioned Fourth of July, Apalachicola; **August:** Harry A's Fishing Tournament, St. George Island; **October:** The Newell Fund Concert Series, Lafayette Park, Apalachicola; **First Weekend in November:** Florida Seafood Festival, Battery Park, Apalachicola, has oyster-shucking and oyster-eating contests.

SPORTS AND LEISURE ACTIVITIES:
Most popular local fishing areas: Apalachicola River, Apalachicola Bay, St. George Sound, Gulf of Mexico, several rivers (bream, bass, catfish, perch); surfcasting at Alligator Point, Lanark Beach, Carrabelle Beach and St. George Island.
Local golf courses: None
Public beaches? Yes
Tennis courts available to the public? Yes
Boating? Yes
Number of pleasure boats registered in the county (1991-92): 1,366

SERVICES FOR RETIREES:
Franklin County Senior Citizens Council in Carrabelle; Meals on Wheels and transportation services

FINANCIAL SERVICES:
Number of local banks: 3
Number of local savings and loan associations: 1

THE MEDIA:
Largest local newspaper: *The Apalachicola Times*
Cable television? Yes

MAJOR LOCAL RETAILERS:
2 Dollar stores; downtown Apalachicola has historic area with shops and galleries.

FOOD ESTABLISHMENTS: 57

OTHER SERVICES:
Number of local libraries: 2
Number of local hotels/motels: 18
Number of churches: Protestant: 22; Jewish: 0; Catholic: 2; Other: 3

TOURISM INQUIRIES:
Apalachicola Bay Chamber of Commerce, 57 Market St., Apalachicola, 32320. Telephone: 904-653-9419.

GADSDEN County
Northwest
County seat: Quincy

POPULATION: 1990: 41,116
1993: 43,239
Increase: 5.2 percent

AGE DISTRIBUTION (1992) IN PERCENTAGES:
0-14 : 24.9
15-44: 44.8
45-64: 18.0
65+ : 12.2

MUNICIPAL POPULATION:
CHATTAHOOCHEE: 1990: 4,382; 1993: 4,380
GREENSBORO: 1990: 586; 1993: 599
GRETNA: 1990: 1,981; 1993: 2,064
HAVANA: 1990: 1,717; 1993: 1,784
MIDWAY: 1990: 976; 1993: 1,112
QUINCY: 1990: 7,452; 1993: 7,551
UNINCORPORATED: 1990: 24,022; 1993: 25,749

LAND AREA: 516 square miles
POPULATION DENSITY: 84 people per square mile (35th in the state)

Located 20 minutes from Tallahassee, Gadsden is a rural county, but offers nearby access to the cultural and economic benefits of the state's capital. The county has a diverse economic base; the prominent forces are state government employment, agribusiness and manufacturing. Among the products of the largest private employers are wholesale food, mushrooms, lumber, furniture and fabrics. The county seat, Quincy, has a legacy with the Coca Cola Co.: It is believed that at one time, about 68 percent of Coke's stock was held by local residents.

TOURISM SEASON:
Not a big factor here.

HOUSING PRICES:
Average price of a home about $60,000.
Number of vacant residential lots: 5,633; number of single-family residences: 8,643; mobile homes: 1,719; condominiums: 0

EDUCATION:
Number of local schools: 18
Number of students enrolled: 8,537
Percentage of students continuing education after high school: 58.51
Teacher-to-pupil ratio: 1:19.0
Average teacher's salary: $27,193

Colleges, universities, and junior or community colleges serving the area:
Tallahassee Community College's Gadsden Center in Quincy; Florida State University, Florida

A&M University and the main Tallahassee Community College branch all are located in Tallahassee, 23 miles away.

Trade and technical schools serving the area:
Gadsden Vo-Tech and Lively Vo-Tech

HEALTH CARE:
Number of hospitals: 2
Number of hospital beds: 51
Number of physicians: 45

TAXES: Total county ad-valorem millage rate (1993): 21.1340

STANDARD CRIME RATE: 4,953.9 offenses per 100,000 population (35th out of 67 counties)

LARGEST PRIVATE EMPLOYERS:

Name	Employees	Product/Service
Quincy Farms	575	Mushrooms
SuperValu	460	Wholesale food distributor
Coastal Lumber Co.	250	Lumber
Floridin Company	200	Fuller's earth
The Printing House	185	Web printing
Higdon Furniture Company	180	Wood furniture
Talquin Electric Cooperative	155	Utilities
Mactavish Furniture Company	125	Furniture
Imperial Nursery	100	Ornamentals
Weavexx	100	Forming fabrics

COMPANIES PROVIDING LOCAL UTILITIES:
Telephone: Quincy Telephone Co., Southern Bell, Central Telephone Co., St. Joe Telephone
Electricity: City of Quincy, City of Havana, City of Chattahoochee and Talquin Electric Cooperative
Natural Gas: South Georgia Natural Gas and Florida Gas Transmission
Water: City of Quincy, City of Havana, City of Chattahoochee and Talquin Electric Cooperative
Major Water Source: River and wells
Sanitary Landfill? Yes

ANNUAL EVENTS:
May: Old-Fashioned Days (arts and crafts), held in Havana, which is an antiques shopping center; **October:** Quincyfest, in Quincy (arts and crafts).

SPORTS AND LEISURE ACTIVITIES:
Most popular local fishing areas: Lake Talquin, Lake Seminole, Apalachicola River.
Number of local golf courses: 2 public, 1 private
Public beaches? No
Tennis courts available to the public? Yes
Boating? Yes
Number of pleasure boats registered in the county (1991-92): 2,125

SERVICES FOR RETIREES:
The Gadsden County Senior Citizens Project provides programs and meals on site as well as home-delivered meals.

FINANCIAL SERVICES:
Number of local banks: 10
Number of local savings and loan associations: 0

THE MEDIA:
Largest local newspapers: *The Gadsden County Times*
Cable television? Yes

MAJOR LOCAL RETAILERS:
There are several shopping centers in the area with such stores as Wal-Mart, Dollar, Winn-Dixie and IGA. There also is specialty shopping for antiques in Havana.

FOOD ESTABLISHMENTS: 78

OTHER SERVICES:
Number of local libraries: 3
Number of local motels: 7
Number of churches: Protestant: 77; Jewish: 0; Catholic: 2

TOURISM INQUIRIES:
Gadsden County Chamber of Commerce, P.O. Box 389, Quincy, 32353. Telephone: 904-627-9231.

GILCHRIST County
Northwest
County seat: Trenton

POPULATION: 1990: 9,667
1993: 10,722
Increase: 10.9 percent

AGE DISTRIBUTION (1992) IN PERCENTAGES:
0-14 : 20.1
15-44: 44.0
45-64: 22.0
65+ : 14.0

MUNICIPAL POPULATION:
BELL: 1990: 267; 1993: 282
FANNING SPRINGS (part): 1990: 230; 1993: 246
TRENTON: 1990: 1,287; 1993: 1,310
UNINCORPORATED: 1990: 7,883; 1993: 8,884

LAND AREA: 349 square miles
POPULATION DENSITY: 31 people per square mile (51st in the state)

Gilchrist County, in the north central part of the state 14 miles west of Gainesville and 25 miles from the Gulf of Mexico, was named after Albert H. Gilchrist, who was governor of Florida from 1909 to 1913. Once a part of Alachua County, a group of citizens asked the state to form a new county after Alachua County commissioners refused to build a road to Gainesville so that residents could carry their agricultural products and other items to market. Today, the county has 221,560 acres of land and 9 square miles of water, including a number of freshwater springs. The Santa Fe and Suwannee rivers provide natural borders for the county. In the heart of the county lies the Waccasassa Flats, which are wetland preserves. Once an area where timber was the main source of income, the area's economic sources today are dairy farming, cattle ranching and other agriculture.

HOUSING PRICES:
Average sales price around $50,000.
Number of vacant residential lots: 4,501; number of single-family residences: 1,391; mobile homes: 1,399; condominiums: 0

EDUCATION:
Number of schools: 5
Number of students enrolled: 2,201
Percentage of students continuing education after high school: 75
Teacher-to-pupil ratio: 1:16.2
Average teacher's salary: $28,502

Colleges, universities, and junior or community colleges serving the area:
University of Florida in Gainesville; Santa Fe Community College in Gainesville; Central Florida Community College in Ocala; Lake City Community College.

Trade and technical schools serving the area:
Taylor County Technical Institute; Dixie County Vo-Tech

HEALTH CARE:
Number of general hospitals: 0 (There are home health-care services in Fanning Springs, but the nearest hospitals are in Gainesville.)
Number of hospital beds: 0
Number of physicians: 3

TAXES: Total county ad-valorem millage rate (1993): 19.8734

STANDARD CRIME RATE: 1,296.4 offenses per 100,000 population (61st among the 67 counties)

LARGEST PRIVATE EMPLOYERS:

Name	Employees	Product/Service
Medic-Ayers Nursing Home	113	
White Farms	106	Dairy
North Florida Holsteins	75	Dairy
Tri-County Health Center	60	Health care
Gen-Farm	58	Dairy
Buddha's Inc.	48	Furniture Mfg.
Bell Concrete	28	Concrete
Farmer & Merchants Bank	27	Banking

COMPANIES PROVIDING LOCAL UTILITIES:
Telephone: Southern Bell
Electricity: Florida Power Corp. and Central Florida Electric Co-op
Natural Gas: None
Water: Cities of Trenton and Fanning Springs
Major Water Source: Wells
Sanitary Landfill? Yes

POINTS OF INTEREST:
Hart Springs: a county-owned park along the Suwannee River that has swimming, camping, fishing and covered pavilions (used by Creek Indians as landing stage on hunting expeditions); **Otter Springs,** privately owned resort, offers nature hikes, canoe rides and rentals, camping, fishing, swimming; **Ginnie Springs,** privately owned park that is known for its cave diving. Park also has nature trails, volleyball, swimming, snorkeling, canoe and tube rental, rafting, boat ramp, camping and a dive shop.

ANNUAL EVENTS:
November: Down Home Days in Trenton, an arts and crafts and antique festival with entertainment and more than 100 exhibitors; Suwannee River Shriners Cane Grinding and Festival held during Thanksgiving week; **December:** Christmas Boat Parade in Fanning Springs, with arts and crafts, entertainment and a parade of boats down the Suwannee River decorated in Christmas themes.

SPORTS AND LEISURE ACTIVITIES:
Most popular local fishing areas: Hart Springs, Otter Springs, Suwannee River.
Golf courses? Yes
Public beaches? No
Tennis courts available to the public? Yes
Boating? Yes
Number of pleasure boats registered in the county (1991-92): 981

FINANCIAL SERVICES:
Number of local banks: 4
Number of local savings and loan associations: 1

THE MEDIA:
Largest local newspaper: *Gilchrist County Journal*
Cable television? Yes

FOOD ESTABLISHMENTS: 23

OTHER SERVICES:
Number of local libraries: 1
Number of local motels: 1
Number of churches: Protestant: 27; Jewish: 0; Catholic: 0

GULF County
Northwest
County seat: Port St. Joe

POPULATION: 1990: 11,504
1993: 12,393
Increase: 7.7 percent

AGE DISTRIBUTION (1992) IN PERCENTAGES:
0-14 : 20.3
15-44: 41.9
45-64: 22.5
65+ : 15.3

MUNICIPAL POPULATION:
PORT ST. JOE: 1990: 4,044; 1993: 4,071
WEWAHITCHKA: 1990: 1,779; 1993: 1,806
UNINCORPORATED: 1990: 5,681; 1993: 6,516

LAND AREA: 565 square miles
POPULATION DENSITY: 22 people per square mile (59th in the state)

Gulf County, about 100 miles southwest of Tallahassee and 36 miles southeast of Panama City, is known for having been the site where Florida's constitution was signed. The city of Port St. Joe, which is on St. Joseph's Bay on the Gulf of Mexico, has a deep-water port with facilities for ships and barges. The Intracoastal Waterway passes through the county; the Gulf County Canal connects St. Joseph Bay with the Intracoastal in White City, about seven miles north of Port St. Joe. Fishing is popular, both recreationally and commercially, and includes scalloping and oystering. The county, one of only a handful in the state to have single-digit population increases between 1980 and 1990, is largely an industrial one (paper, oil, magnesite, coal and boxes). Timber also plays a major role here for the forest products industry. Smaller industries are farming (cattle and nurseries) and construction. Miles of beaches, nature preserves and a state park also are here.

TOURISM:
Thousands of people visit St. Joseph Peninsula State Park each year (89,632 in 1992-93). Local officials say that 50 to 100 Snowbirds live here from January through March.

HOUSING PRICES:
Typical 2-bedroom homes go for about $40,000, and 3-bedroom homes for about $55,000. Oceanfront condos generally range from about $80,000 to $150,000, and homes on the Intracoastal Waterway roughly a quarter to a third less.
Number of vacant residential lots: 3,930; number of single-family residences: 4,350; mobile homes: 1,274; condominiums: 36

EDUCATION:
Number of schools: 7
Number of students enrolled: 2,228
Percentage of students continuing education after high school: 70.63
Teacher-to-pupil ratio: 1:16.1
Average teacher's salary: $27,081

Colleges, universities, and junior or community colleges serving the area:
Florida State University, Panama City branch; Gulf Coast Community College, Panama City.

Trade and technical schools serving the area:
Haney Vo-Tech, Panama City.

HEALTH CARE:
Number of general hospitals: 1
Number of hospital beds: 45
Number of physicians: 10

TAXES: Total county ad-valorem millage rate (1993): 15.9410

STANDARD CRIME RATE: 1,533.1 offenses per 100,000 population (60th out of 67 counties)

LARGEST PRIVATE EMPLOYERS

Name	Employees	Product/Service
St. Joe Forest Products	986	Paper
Raffield Fisheries	160	Fishing
Arizona Chemical Corp.	126	Crude oil
Premier Services	106	Magnesite
Whitfield Timber Co.	100	Lumber and millwork
Apalachicola NRR	98	Railroad services
St. Joe Paper Container	87	Boxes
Material Transfer Inc.	15	Coal

COMPANIES PROVIDING LOCAL UTILITIES:
Telephone: St. Joseph Telephone & Telegraph
Electricity: Florida Power Corp.
Natural Gas: St. Joe Natural Gas
Water: City of Port St. Joe
Major Water Source: Wells
Sanitary Landfill? Yes

POINTS OF INTEREST:
The beaches on the Gulf of Mexico and on St. Joseph Bay; **Constitution Convention State Museum** in Port St. Joe, which commemorates Florida's first State Constitutional Convention (the draft of the constitution was finished in 1838) and the one-time boom town of Port St. Joseph. The town died after an outbreak of yellow fever in 1841 and after a hurricane in 1844; the new town of Port St. Joe was founded in 1900. Also in the county is the **St. Joseph Peninsula State Park,** near Port St. Joe off SR 30 on the St. Joseph Peninsula. It's a prime area for bird-watchers, who have reported sightings of 209 species, including migrating hawks in the fall. The park, which is on 2,516 acres, offers camping, picnicking, swimming, saltwater fishing, hiking and guided walks; and the **Dead Lakes State Recreation Area,** north of Wewahitchka, famed for the thousands of dead trees that still stand in the waters of a lake. Area has camping, picnicking, freshwater fishing, hiking and a boat ramp. Also along the peninsula is the **St. Vincent National Wildlife Refuge.** And in St. Joseph Bay is **Black's Island,** known for vegetation, birds and sea life that includes sea urchins, crabs, octopus and sea turtles.

ANNUAL EVENT:
December: Christmas Parade in Downtown Port St. Joe, first weekend in December.

SPORTS AND LEISURE ACTIVITIES:
Most popular local fishing areas: Gulf of Mexico, St. Joseph Bay (also good for scalloping, particularly in July), Dead Lakes in Wewahitchka. Saltwater species include grouper, cobia, Spanish mackerel, king mackerel, redfish, flounder, snapper and bonita. Freshwater species are bass, trout, speckled perch, shellcracker, mullet and catfish.
Hunting is also popular for deer, wild turkey, wild hogs, rabbits and game birds.
Number of local golf courses: 1 private
Public beaches: St. Joe Beach, Cape San Blas. Almost all area beaches are public.
Tennis courts available to the public? Yes
Boating? Yes
Number of pleasure boats registered in the county (1991-92): 1,917

SERVICES FOR RETIREES:
Meals on Wheels, Meals for Seniors, Social Security office in Panama City.

FINANCIAL SERVICES:
Number of local banks: 3
Number of local savings and loan associations: 2

THE MEDIA:
Largest local newspaper: *The Star* in Port St. Joe
Cable television? Yes

MAJOR LOCAL RETAILERS:
In Port St. Joe, Western Auto, Bill's Discount Store, Dollar General, IGA, Piggly Wiggly, Saveway.

FOOD ESTABLISHMENTS: 29

OTHER SERVICES:
Number of local libraries: 1
Number of local hotels/motels: 10
Number of churches: Protestant: 24; Jewish: 0; Catholic: 3; Other: 2

TOURISM INQUIRIES:
Port St. Joe/Gulf County Chamber of Commerce, P.O. Box 964, Port St. Joe, 32456. Telephone: 904-227-1223.

HOLMES County
Northwest
County Seat: Bonifay

POPULATION: 1990: 15,778
1993: 16,331
Increase: 3.5 percent

AGE DISTRIBUTION (1992) IN PERCENTAGES:
0-14 : 19.5
15-44: 43.0
45-64: 21.5
65+ : 16.0

MUNICIPAL POPULATION:
BONIFAY: 1990: 2,612; 1993: 2,677
ESTO: 1990: 253; 1993: 294
NOMA: 1990: 207; 1993: 211
PONCE de LEON: 1990: 406; 1993: 433
WESTVILLE: 1990: 257; 1993: 263
UNINCORPORATED: 1990: 12,043; 1993: 12,453

LAND AREA: 483 square miles
POPULATION DENSITY: 34 people per square mile (49th in the state)

Situated in the middle of the Florida Panhandle, the county is about a 30-minute drive from the Gulf of Mexico and about 35 miles from Dothan, Ala. A mainly rural area, major industries are agriculture (namely poultry), manufacturing, forestry and government. Apparel is the big manufacturing industry, with three factories in the county. Other products include concrete and wood items. There is a state farmers' market in Bonifay for a variety of crops. A number of springs with bathing facilities, picnic areas and camping sites are found here, along with creeks and lakes and a navigable river (the Choctawhatchee) that flows to the Gulf of Mexico. Fishing, swimming and scuba diving in the springs are popular sports; deer, ducks, wild turkey and small game are plentiful for hunters.

TOURISM:
Not a big factor here.

HOUSING PRICES:
Vary considerably, but very few are sold for more than $125,000. A small, FHA-backed 3-bedroom, 1.5-bath home will sell for as little as $35,000.
Number of vacant residential lots: 2,054; number of single-family residences: 2,957; mobile homes: 766; condominiums: 0

EDUCATION:
Number of schools: 8
Number of students enrolled: 3,877
Percentage of students continuing education after high school: 65.83
Teacher-to-pupil ratio: 1:16.3
Average teacher's salary: $28,809

Colleges, universities, and junior or community colleges serving the area:
Chipola Junior College in Marianna; Gulf Coast Community College in Panama City; Troy State University branch campus in Dothan, Ala.; Florida State University has facilities in Panama City; Okaloosa-Walton Community College in Niceville.

Trade and technical schools serving the area:
Washington-Holmes Area Vocational-Technical Center; Walton County Vo-Tech; Haney Vo-Tech in Panama City.

HEALTH CARE:
Number of general hospitals: 1
Number of hospital beds: 34
Number of physicians: 8

TAXES: Total county ad-valorem millage rate (1993): 16.6240

STANDARD CRIME RATE: 1,249.2 offenses per 100,000 population (62nd out of 67 counties)

LARGEST PRIVATE EMPLOYERS:

Name	Employees	Product/Service
Holmes Shirt Co.	200	Clothing
Bonifay Manufacturing	165	Clothing
Bonifay Nursing Home	129	
New Ponce Industries	110	Clothing
Doctors Memorial Hospital	96	
Food Masters	48	Restaurant
Hardees of Bonifay	41	Restaurant products
Jerkins Incorporated	40	Concrete products
Piggly Wiggly	40	Grocery
McDonald's	34	Fast food

COMPANIES PROVIDING LOCAL UTILITIES:
Telephone: Central Telephone Co. of Florida
Electricity: West Florida Electric; Gulf Power Co.
Natural Gas: None
Water: Individual municipalities
Major Water Source: Wells
Sanitary Landfill? Trash hauled out of county

POINTS OF INTEREST:
Ponce de Leon Springs State Recreation Area, a 433-acre facility with a natural spring. Two main boils produce 14 million gallons of water daily at a year-round temperature of 68 degrees. Area also has picnicking, swimming, hiking; **Vortex Spring** diving facility is the largest of its kind in Florida and is also a camping resort with a dive shop, group lodging, a campground store and a restaurant; **Lake Cassidy,** a popular fishing, boating and skiing spot.

ANNUAL EVENTS:
July: The Biggest All-Night Gospel Sing in the World, Memorial Field (first Saturday), has gospel groups from around the country; **September:** Two-Toed Tom Festival in Esto (Saturday before Labor Day), has food, arts and crafts and exhibits; **October:** Northwest Florida Championship Rodeo at Memorial Field (first weekend of the month); Greater Holmes County Fair; Pioneer Day at Merchants Parking Lot, has arts and crafts, old-fashioned soda fountain, food, contests, barn dance; **November:** Collard Festival in Ponce de Leon (late in the month); **December:** Santa Day at Merchants Parking Lot (first week of the month).

SPORTS AND LEISURE ACTIVITIES:
Most popular local fishing areas: Lake Cassidy, Smith Lake, Lake Victor, the Choctawhatchee River. Dogwood Lakes Golf and Country Club has several stocked lakes. In addition, the Gulf of Mexico is about a 30-minute drive from the county.
Number of golf courses: 1 public, 1 private
Public beaches? No
Tennis courts available to the public? Yes
Boating? Yes
Number of pleasure boats registered in the county (1991-92): 1,385

SERVICES FOR RETIREES:
AARP chapter.

FINANCIAL SERVICES:
Number of local banks: 2
Number of local savings and loan associations: 1

THE MEDIA:
Largest local newspaper: *Holmes County Advertiser*
Cable television? Yes

MAJOR LOCAL RETAILERS:
Bill's Dollar Store, IGA, Piggly Wiggly

FOOD ESTABLISHMENTS: 25

OTHER SERVICES:
Number of local libraries: 1
Number of local motels: 6
Number of churches: Protestant: 80; Jewish: 0; Catholic: 1; Other: 3

TOURISM INQUIRIES:
Holmes County Chamber of Commerce, P.O. Box 779, Bonifay, 32425. Telephone: 904-547-4682.

JACKSON County
Northwest
County seat: Marianna

POPULATION: 1990: 41,375
1993: 44,386
Increase: 7.3 percent

AGE DISTRIBUTION (1992) IN PERCENTAGES:
0-14 : 20.1
15-44: 45.5
45-64: 19.5
65+ : 14.9

MUNICIPAL POPULATION:
ALFORD: 1990: 482; 1993: 489
BASCOM: 1990: 90; 1993: 90
CAMPBELLTON: 1990: 202; 1993: 232
COTTONDALE: 1990: 900; 1993: 927
GRACEVILLE: 1990: 2,675; 1993: 2,675
GRAND RIDGE: 1990: 536; 1993: 591
GREENWOOD: 1990: 474; 1993: 507
JACOB CITY: 1990: 261; 1993: 293
MALONE: 1990: 765; 1993: 1,583
MARIANNA: 1990: 6,292; 1993: 6,249
SNEADS: 1990: 1,746; 1993: 1,854
UNINCORPORATED: 1990: 26,952; 1993: 28,896

LAND AREA: 916 square miles
POPULATION DENSITY: 48 people per square mile (44th in the state)

The only county in Florida bordered by two states (Alabama and Georgia), Jackson County is largely an agricultural area: The major cash crop is peanuts, followed by cotton and corn. Beef cattle production is also extensive. Among the area's other industries are government institutions (the county houses a federal prison and three state correctional institutions), retail trade, services and light manufacturing (sportswear, furniture and laundry equipment). The county is home to the Florida Caverns State Park, its most popular attraction, which offers tours of a network of caverns. The area is also known for vast deposits of pure limestone.

A number of parks and lakes provide a variety of recreational opportunities, from fishing and swimming to camping and hiking. The county is 60 miles north of the Gulf of Mexico and 35 miles south of Dothan, Ala., and is bordered on the east by Lake Seminole and the Chattahoochee-Apalachicola River. The river provides barge access between the city of Sneads and the Gulf of Mexico near Apalachicola, 100 miles away. It is used by the Jackson County Port Authority, in Sneads.

TOURISM:
In the summer, the number of vacationers visiting the Florida Caverns State Park increases considerably (the total for 1992-93 was more than 126,000) but there is no Snowbird season to speak of.

HOUSING PRICES:
New homes generally range from $30,000 to $300,000 depending on size and location.
Number of vacant residential lots: 11,899; number of single-family residences: 8,841; mobile homes: 1,539; condominiums: 0

EDUCATION:
Number of schools: 17
Number of students enrolled: 8,042
Percentage of students continuing education after high school: 42.05
Teacher-to-pupil ratio: 1:14.4
Average teacher's salary: $27,170

Colleges, universities, and junior or community colleges serving the area:
Chipola Junior College in Marianna; Florida Baptist Theological College in Graceville; Florida State University in Tallahassee; Florida A&M University in Tallahassee; Troy State in Dothan, Ala.

Trade and technical schools serving the area:
Chipola Vo-Tech; George C. Wallace Community College; Washington-Holmes Vo-Tech

HEALTH CARE:
Number of general hospitals: 2
Number of hospital beds: 157
Number of physicians: 42

TAXES: Total county ad-valorem millage rate (1993): 16.3020

STANDARD CRIME RATE: 1,752.8 offenses per 100,000 population (57th out of 67 counties)

LARGEST PRIVATE EMPLOYERS:

Name	Employees	Product/Service
Russell Corp.	850	Sportswear
Apalachee Correctional Institution	503	Prison
Lehigh Furniture Division	450	Furniture
UniMac Co.	425	Laundry equipment
Federal Correctional Institution	390	Prison
Jackson Hospital	300	Health care
Malone State Prison	298	Prison
WalMart	170	Department store
Fla. Baptist Theological College	120	College
Jackson Co. Convelescent Center	120	Nursing home
Marianna 76 Auto/Truck Stop	105	Restaurant/service center

COMPANIES PROVIDING LOCAL UTILITIES:
Telephone: Central Telephone Co. of Florida and Southern Bell
Electricity: Florida Public Utilities, West Florida Electric Cooperative
Natural Gas: City of Marianna
Water: Individual cities and towns and county wells
Major Water Source: Wells
Sanitary Landfill? Yes

POINTS OF INTEREST:
Florida Caverns State Park, 3 miles north of Marianna, contains a network of caverns and formations including stalactites, stalagmites and columns. The largest caves are lighted and open to the

public for ranger-guided tours. Also has camping, picnicking, swimming, freshwater fishing, hiking; **Three Rivers State Recreation Area,** 2 miles north of Sneads, has camping, picnicking, freshwater fishing, hiking, summer campfire programs, 4 miles of shoreline on Lake Seminole; **Blue Springs Recreation Area,** northeast of Marianna on Highway 164 (open in summer only) has diving boards, slides, picnicking, bath houses, concessions and life guard; **Sneads Park,** off U.S. 90, has swimming, boat ramps and picnicking; Battle of Marianna Monument, dedicated to Confederate soldiers.

ANNUAL EVENTS:
May: Cottondale Crossroads U.S.A. Fun-Day Parade; Memorial Day Parade in Sneads, includes boat and recreational vehicle show and arts and crafts; **October:** Jackson County Fair, including flower exhibit; Sunland Fall Festival; in addition, many cultural events are scheduled periodically at Chipola Junior College.

SPORTS AND LEISURE ACTIVITIES:
Most popular local fishing areas: Freshwater fishing at Florida Caverns State Park in the Chipola River (bass, bream, catfish) and at Three Rivers State Recreation Area on Lake Seminole (largemouth and smallmouth bass, catfish, bluegill, speckled perch and bream).
Number of local golf courses: Two 9-hole courses
Public beaches? No
Tennis courts available to the public? Yes
Boating? Yes
Number of pleasure boats registered in the county (1991-92): 3,411

SERVICES FOR RETIREES:
Through the Senior Citizen Center in Marianna.

FINANCIAL SERVICES:
Number of local banks: 13
Number of local savings and loan associations: 2

THE MEDIA:
Largest local newspaper: *Jackson County Floridan*
Cable television? Yes

MAJOR LOCAL RETAILERS:
K mart, Wal-Mart and Woolworth's

FOOD ESTABLISHMENTS: 119

OTHER SERVICES:
Number of local libraries: 2
Number of local motels: 10
Number of churches: Protestant: 88; Jewish: 0; Catholic: 3; Other: 1.

TOURISM INQUIRIES:
Jackson County Chamber of Commerce, P.O. Box 130, Marianna, 32447. Telephone: 904-482-8061.

JEFFERSON County
Northwest
County seat: Monticello

POPULATION: 1990: 11,296
1993: 12,988
Increase: 15 percent

AGE DISTRIBUTION (1992) IN PERCENTAGES:
0-14 : 23.4
15-44: 42.5
45-64: 18.9
65+ : 15.2

MUNICIPAL POPULATION:
MONTICELLO: 1990: 2,603; 1993: 2,733
UNINCORPORATED: 1990: 8,693; 1993: 10,255

LAND AREA: 598 square miles
POPULATION DENSITY: 22 people per square mile (60th in the state)

Mainly an agricultural area, this county's seat, Monticello, is 23 miles east of Tallahassee. Jefferson County extends from Georgia to the Gulf of Mexico in Florida's Panhandle. The landscape is hilly and contains oak trees draped in Spanish moss and historically significant turn-of-the-century homes and public buildings. Nearly two-thirds of the county's residents are 44 or younger. The dairy industry is prominent; others are nurseries and an apron and smock factory. Among the primary crops are pecans and watermelons. Lake Miccosukee covers more than 6,200 acres in the county and the Aucilla, Wacissa and St. Marks rivers cover hundreds more. Fishing, canoeing, sailing and powerboating are among the outdoor activities found here.

TOURISM:
Not a factor.

HOUSING PRICES:
Average price in recent years roughly $60,000-$65,000 for a three-bedroom, two-bath home. Number of vacant residential lots: 928; number of single-family residences: 1,684; mobile homes: 547; condominiums: 0

EDUCATION:
Number of schools: 6
Number of students enrolled: 2,082
Percentage of students continuing education after high school: 65.48
Teacher-to-pupil ratio: 1:16.1
Average teacher's salary: $28,321

Colleges, universities, and junior or community colleges serving the area:
Florida State University and Florida A&M University, both in Tallahassee; North Florida Junior College in Madison; Tallahassee Community College.

Trade and technical schools serving the area:
Thomasville (Ga.) Vo-Tech; Lively Vo-Tech in Tallahassee

HEALTH CARE:
Number of general hospitals: 0
Number of hospital beds: 0
Number of physicians: 8

TAXES: Total county ad-valorem millage rate (1993): 17.4234

STANDARD CRIME RATE: 3,541.7 offenses per 100,000 population (48th out of 67 counties)

LARGEST PRIVATE EMPLOYERS:

Name	Employees	Product/service
Command Enterprise	145	Aprons and smocks
Simpson Nursery	125	Plants
Brynwood Center	105	Nursing home
Florida Power Corp.	55	Electric services
Bassett's Dairy	50	Dairy/milk
Winn-Dixie	46	Food retailer
Farmers & Merchants Bank	34	Banking
Monticello Foodway	28	Grocery
Kaleidoscope Limited	20	Framed pictures
Jefferson County Kennel Club	19	Dog racing

COMPANIES PROVIDING LOCAL UTILITIES:
Telephone: Central Telephone Co. of Florida
Electricity: Florida Power, Tri-County Electric Cooperative
Natural Gas: None
Water: City of Monticello
Major Water Source: Wells
Sanitary Landfill? Yes

POINTS OF INTEREST:
Wacissa River, a designated state canoe trail; **Jefferson County Kennel Club,** three miles north of Monticello, has year-round pari-mutuel dog racing.

THE ARTS:
Monticello Opera House offers year-round performances of plays and musicals, also has lectures and films.

ANNUAL EVENTS:
March or April: Semi-annual Tour of Homes, sponsored by the Jefferson County Historical Society, has tours of buildings in Monticello on the National Register of Historic Places (also, self-guided tours are available year-round); **June:** Jefferson County Watermelon Festival has food, arts and crafts, parade, beauty pageant.

SPORTS AND LEISURE ACTIVITIES:
Most popular local fishing areas: Wacissa River, Aucilla River and Lake Miccosukee.
Number of local golf courses: 1 private
Public beaches? No
Tennis courts available to the public? Yes
Boating? Yes
Number of pleasure boats registered in the county (1991-92): 659

SERVICES FOR RETIREES:
Through the senior center in Monticello.

FINANCIAL SERVICES:
Number of local banks: 2
Number of local savings and loan associations: 0

THE MEDIA:
Largest local newspaper: *Monticello News*
Cable television? Yes

MAJOR LOCAL RETAILERS:
Winn-Dixie and Monticello Foodway. There are no major chain department stores.

FOOD ESTABLISHMENTS: 40

OTHER SERVICES:
Number of local libraries: 1
Number of local motels: 5, plus 2 hotels
Number of churches: Protestant: 41; Jewish: 0; Catholic: 1

TOURISM INQUIRIES:
Monticello-Jefferson County Chamber of Commerce, 420 West Washington St., Monticello, 32344. Telephone: 904-997-5552.

LAFAYETTE County
Northwest
County seat: Mayo

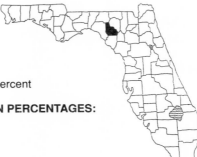

POPULATION: 1990: 5,578
1993: 5,603
Increase: 0.4 percent

AGE DISTRIBUTION (1992) IN PERCENTAGES:
0-14 : 20.1
15-44: 49.5
45-64: 18.7
65+ : 11.7

MUNICIPAL POPULATION:
MAYO: 1990: 917;1993: 925
UNINCORPORATED: 1990: 4,661; 1993: 4,678

LAND AREA: 543 square miles
POPULATION DENSITY: 10 people per square mile (66th in the state)

Lafayette County, created in 1856, is primarily an agricultural area. The major cash crop is tobacco, and there are about 30 dairies. Other crops are peas and soybeans. The county is just north of Dixie County, and is about 40 miles from Gainesville, the home of the University of Florida. Part of the county is the Steinhatchee Wildlife Management Area, a popular hunting and nature-trail area.

In recent years, the county seat, Mayo, has been among the top five areas in the United States in concentration of residents of Irish ancestry. Along the county's eastern and northern borders is the Suwannee River, which is big enough for barges and too treacherous for swimming, but popular among fishermen. One of Lafayette County's distinctions is having the smallest population in the state. Liberty County is next smallest, with 117 more residents.

Aside from agriculture, Lafayette's largest employer overall has been the Mayo Correctional Institute, with about 230 employees. The largest private employer is a boat manufacturer; its employment level dropped from 125 in 1989 to 30 in 1992, and then jumped to 92 in 1994.

TOURISM:
Very little; the county has just 32 motel rooms.

HOUSING PRICES:
No countywide statistics are available, and local real estate agents declined to hazard a guess, but say that many young families live in mobile homes worth about $10,000. The upper end of the scale is about $125,000, and those homes generally are owned by dairy farmers.
Number of vacant residential lots: 1,573; number of single-family residences: 743; mobile homes: 400; condominiums: 0

EDUCATION:
Number of schools: 4
Number of students enrolled: 1,046
Percentage of students continuing education after high school: 58.06
Teacher-to-pupil ratio: 1:15.4
Average teacher's salary: $25,804

Colleges, universities, and junior or community colleges serving the area:
University of Florida, Gainesville; Florida State University, Tallahassee; Lake City Community College, Lake City; North Florida Junior College, Madison; Santa Fe Community College, Gainesville.

Trade and technical schools serving the area:
Suwannee-Hamilton Vocational-Technical School; Taylor County Technical Institute, Perry.

HEALTH CARE:
Number of general hospitals: 0
Number of hospital beds: 0
Number of physicians: 3

TAXES: Total county ad-valorem millage rate (1993): 19.4134

STANDARD CRIME RATE: No figures were available for 1993. In 1992, there were 590 offenses per 100,000 population, an exceptionally low rate.

LARGEST PRIVATE EMPLOYERS:

Name	Employees	Product/Service
F.R.P. Industries	92	Boats
Crofts Thriftway	21	Grocery
Central Florida Lands & Timber	20	Nursery products
Lafayette Forest Products	11	Cypress mulch
Proctor and Gamble Co.	10	Paper production
Gillman Paper Co.	6	Timber
Mayo Fertilizer	6	Fertilizer
L&M Catfish Processors	8	Catfish processors
Mayo Truss Co.	5	Truss builders
J&J Gas Service	4	L.P. gas

COMPANIES PROVIDING LOCAL UTILITIES:
Telephone: ALLTEL Florida
Electricity: Suwannee Valley Electric Co-op, Florida Power
Natural Gas: None
Water: Mayo
Major Water Source: Wells
Sanitary Landfill? Yes

POINTS OF INTEREST:
Blue Springs Park has camping, swimming, picnicking, nature trails; **Jim Hollis River Rendezvous** has scuba diving, camping; also popular among county residents are the cultural activities of Gainesville, Live Oak and Lake City.

ANNUAL EVENTS:
Second Saturday in October: Pioneer Day Festival honors county's heritage with arts and crafts, a rodeo, parade, art show, food, old cars and entertainment.

SPORTS AND LEISURE ACTIVITIES:
Most popular local fishing areas: Suwannee River and a number of small lakes
Number of local golf courses: 0
Public beaches? No
Tennis courts available to the public? Yes
Boating? Yes
Number of pleasure boats registered in the county (1991-92): 463

SERVICES FOR RETIREES:
Meals on Wheels, district community centers

FINANCIAL SERVICES:
Number of local banks: 1
Number of local savings and loan associations: 1

THE MEDIA:
Largest local newspaper: *Mayo Free Press*
Cable television? Yes

MAJOR LOCAL RETAILERS:
No major national chains and no large department stores.

FOOD ESTABLISHMENTS: 5

OTHER SERVICES:
Number of local libraries: 1
Number of local motels: 2
Number of churches: Protestant: 26; Jewish: 0; Catholic: 1

TOURISM INQUIRIES:
Lafayette County Chamber of Commerce, P.O. Box 416, Mayo, 32066. Telephone: 904-294-2705.

LEON County
Northwest
County seat: Tallahassee

POPULATION: 1990: 192,493
1991: 206,302
Increase: 7.2 percent

AGE DISTRIBUTION (1992) IN PERCENTAGES:
0-14 : 19.1
15-44: 56.3
45-64: 16.2
65+ : 8.4

MUNICIPAL POPULATION:
TALLAHASSEE: 1990: 124,773; 1993: 206,302
UNINCORPORATED: 1990: 67,720; 1993: 74,619

LAND AREA: 667 square miles
POPULATION DENSITY: 309 people per square mile (15th in the state)

Leon County is home to Tallahassee, Florida's capital, a government and cultural center with an Old Florida ambience that's 20 miles from the Gulf of Mexico and 14 miles from the Georgia line in a part of the state known as "the Big Bend." The first thing you'll notice about the city, especially if you're coming from the flat territory of south and central Florida, is the hills — there are seven of them here, foothills of the Appalachian Mountains. The second thing you'll notice are the southern accents — there are proportionally more here in this northern part of Florida than you'll likely find anywhere in South Florida.

Tallahassee is far from the center of the state; it was chosen as the state capital in 1824 because it was halfway between St. Augustine and Pensacola, which then were the only major cities in the state. Today, it has a modern government center built around the turn-of-the-century Old Capitol, historic buildings, moss-draped oaks that form "canopy roads," two major universities, and enough government buildings to employ more than 40 percent of the local nonagricultural work force (trade and service industries also employ more than 40 percent). In the 1970s and 1980s, public and private facilities in the city's downtown area were renovated at a cost of at least $220 million. Multi-story white state government buildings dot the area around the State Capitol (if you're planning to visit any of the agencies, pay attention — some building signs are hard to read, buildings look alike, some of the streets are one-way, and it may take you a while to find a metered parking spot). Aside from the government centers, Tallahassee also is home to two major educational institutions:

— Florida State University, which has nearly 29,000 students and 1,500 faculty members in colleges of arts & sciences, education, business, engineering, communication, home economics, law, and social sciences; and schools of nursing, music, social work, theater, criminology, library and information studies, and visual arts. The university houses the Supercomputer Computations Research Institute and has a Cray Supercomputer capable of performing 1.3 billion calculations per second.

— Florida Agricultural & Mechanical University, with an enrollment of nearly 10,000, of whom 92 percent are minorities. It has schools of business and industry, pharmacy, architecture, journalism, arts & sciences, and nursing; and programs in allied health sciences, engineering, education, general studies, engineering sciences, technology, and agriculture.

The crime rate here in 1993 was the second highest in the state. Only Dade County (the Miami area) had a higher rate.

The area also has a number of museums, art galleries, state historical sites, performing arts agencies, and dozens of shops for antiques buffs.

TOURISM:
The city is the first big stop in Florida for travelers coming from the western and midwestern states. In addition, the State Capitol draws tourists.

HOUSING PRICES:
Median sales price for a single-family, existing home in the Tallahassee metropolitan area was $100,800 for June 1994.
Number of vacant residential lots: 16,021; number of single-family residences: 49,451; mobile homes: 5,252; condominiums: 959

EDUCATION:
Number of schools: 44
Number of students enrolled: 29,836
Percentage of students continuing education after high school: 47.23
Teacher-to-pupil ratio: 1:17.7
Average teacher's salary: $30,334

Colleges, universities, and junior or community colleges serving the area:
Florida State University and Florida A&M University, both in Tallahassee; Tallahassee Community College; North Florida Junior College, Madison

Trade and technical schools serving the area:
Lively Area Vocational/Technical Center, Tallahassee

HEALTH CARE:
Number of general hospitals: 5
Number of hospital beds: 758
Number of physicians: 521

TAXES: Total county ad-valorem millage rate (1993): 19.2440

STANDARD CRIME RATE: 11,962.6 offenses per 100,000 population (2nd out of 67 counties)

LARGEST PRIVATE EMPLOYERS:

Name	Employees	Product/service
Tallahassee Memorial Regional Medical Center	2,961	Health care
Publix Super Markets	1,170	Grocery
Sprint/Centel-Florida	918	Communications
Tallahassee Community College	878	Education
Wal-Mart	843	Retail
Tallahassee Community Hospital	701	Health care
McDonalds Hamburgers Restaurants	680	Restaurants
Davgar Restaurants (Burger King)	454	Restaurants
Gayfers	375	Retail

COMPANIES PROVIDING LOCAL UTILITIES:
Telephone: Central Telephone Co. of Florida
Electricity: City of Tallahassee, Talquin Electric Cooperative
Natural Gas: City of Tallahassee
Water: City of Tallahassee
Major Water Source: Wells
Sanitary Landfill? Yes

POINTS OF INTEREST:
Florida Capitol Complex, Apalachee Parkway and S. Monroe Street, includes the Old Capitol, built in 1902, and the newer 22-story New Capitol (both Capitols open daily); **Tallahassee-Leon County Civic Center,** which seats 13,500 people; **Florida Governor's Mansion,** N. Adams Street, modeled after Andrew Jackson's Tennessee mansion, the Hermitage; **Florida State University** and **Florida A&M University; Brokaw-McDougall House,** 329 N. Meridian, an example of classic revival architecture, now a meeting and conference center; **Calhoun Street Historical District,** site of some of the city's oldest homes, which were built between 1830 and 1880; **Claude Pepper Library** at Florida State University houses archives of the late congressman's papers; **The Columns,** 100 N. Duval St., oldest building in Tallahassee that now houses the chamber of commerce; **Canopy Roads,** five protected roads — St. Augustine, Miccosukee, Meridian, Old Bainbridge and Centerville — with moss-draped live oak trees forming natural tunnels; **DeSoto Archaeological and Historic Site,** Goodbody Lane and Lafayette Street, site of DeSoto's 1539 encampment; **Natural Bridge Battlefield State Historical Site,** six miles east of Woodville, offers picnicking, freshwater fishing and a Civil War battle re-enactment in early March; **Lake Talquin State Recreation Area,** located 20 miles west of Tallahassee, has sport fishing, picnicking, boating and nature walks; **First Presbyterian Church,** 110 N. Adams St., built in 1838; **Florida's Vietnam Era Veterans' Memorial,** S. Monroe Street, across from the Capitol, honors the state's veterans; **Lafayette Vineyards and Winery,** east of Tallahassee on U.S. 90, one of four Florida vineyards, this one on land once owned by the French nobleman, open for tours and wine tastings; **Lake Jackson Indian Mounds State Archaeological Site,** 2 miles north of I-10 off U.S. 27 on Crowder Road, offers picnicking, hiking, Indian mounds from 1200 to 1500 A.D.; **Maclay State Gardens,** on U.S. 391 north of I-10, has picnicking, swimming, freshwater fishing, canoeing, hiking, as well as 200 varieties of plants that include azaleas, camellias, magnolias, redbud, amaryllis. Also has house that was winter retreat of New York businessman Alfred B. Maclay; **Old City Cemetery** and **Episcopal Cemetery,** Park Avenue and Bronough Street, have graves of Union and Confederate soldiers and two Florida governors; **Park Avenue Historical District,** a walking area of historic homes and old trees; **San Luis Archaeological and Historic Site,** Mission Road, site of 17th-century Apalachee Indian town and Spanish mission; **Tallahassee Junior Museum,** off Lake Bradford Road, has zoo of native Florida animals, trails, wildlife exhibits, 1880s working Florida farm, plantation home; **Union Bank Building,** Apalachee Parkway, circa-1840

building that contained Florida's first major bank; **Walker Library,** East Park Avenue, earliest public library in the city; **Bradley's Country Store,** 15 miles from Tallahassee, 1927 store known for homemade sausage.

THE ARTS:
Museum of Florida History, 500 S. Bronough St., displays Indian artifacts, items from sunken Spanish galleons and Civil War memorabilia, and has exhibits on the state's lumber and citrus industries; **Black Archives Research Center and Museum,** Florida A&M University, has artifacts and exhibits on black culture; **Florida State University Gallery and Museum,** touring exhibits and permanent collection of American, Dutch, Japanese and pre-Columbian art; **Florida State University Planetarium,** shows for those in third grade or older; **Tallahassee Museum of History and Natural Science; Knott House Museum** is a restored 1840s home; **Foster Tanner Fine Arts Gallery,** Florida A&M University, has works by black artists; **LeMoyne Art Gallery,** 125 N. Gadsden St., has pottery, sculpture, photography and painting exhibits; **Tallahassee Symphony Orchestra** performs in FSU's Ruby Diamond Auditorium; **Tallahasse Little Theatre** stages community productions of well-known plays; **Florida State University Mainstage/ School of Theatre** has student-faculty performances; **Capital City Band,** marching band that plays at major holidays and city festivals; **FSU School of Music** offers concerts and recitals each year; **FSU Flying High Circus,** the nation's only collegiate circus, has clowns, jugglers, and acrobats.

Sports:
Florida State University and Florida A&M University offer major college sports events.

ANNUAL EVENTS:
March: San Luis Archaeological and Historic Site Heritage Festival with re-enactments, traditional foods and music; Natural Bridge Battlefield State Historical Site Re-enactment, recreates the March 6, 1865 battle between Union and Confederate troops. After 12 hours of skirmishes, Union forces had to retreat and evacuate the area; **March/April:** Springtime Tallahassee, a three-week festival celebrating of the city's heritage with parades, arts and crafts displays, food, live performances; Jazz and Blues Festival at the Tallahassee Museum of History and Natural Science; **April:** Flying High Circus, Florida State University; Rose Festival in Thomasville, Ga., with parade, rose show, country fair and Flying High Circus performance; Mini Grand Prix in Tallahassee with a street race, food booths and festival-style activities; **July:** Fourth of July Celebration, Tom Brown Park, Capital Circle, arts and crafts, music, and fireworks; Summer Swamp Stomp, Tallahassee Museum of History and Natural Science, folk music and bluegrass festival; **August:** Caribbean Carnival with food, music, parades and dances in Tallahassee; **September:** Discover Downtown Street Festival in Tallahassee; Native American Heritage Festival with Indian culture demonstrations, food, storytelling, dance, arts and crafts; **October:** Florida Forest Festival at the Forest Capital State Museum with parade, crafts and "world's largest free fish fry"; **October/November:** North Florida Fair, fairgrounds; Bradley's Fun Day at Bradley's Country Store with wagon rides, live entertainment, arts and crafts, free sausage samples, cane grinding and syrup making; Market Days with fine arts and crafts booths, at North Florida Fairgrounds; **December:** Winter Festival and Celebration of Lights, marks beginning of Christmas season with lighting of downtown, twilight parade, outdoor ice skating, entertainment; Holiday Candlelight Tours at Maclay State Gardens and Knott House Museum; DeSoto's 1539 Winter Encampment Re-enactment at DeSoto Historic Site.

In addition: There are rotating art exhibits at the New and Old Capital Galleries; City Hall Gallery and The Gallery at the Florida State Conference Center.

SPORTS AND LEISURE ACTIVITIES:
Most popular local fishing areas: Lake Jackson (largemouth bass, lunker bass, bream, shellcracker and crappie); Lake Talquin (striped bass); Lake Iamonia (panfish); Carr Lake (largemouth bass and panfish); Ochlockonee River; Wakulla River; Lake Miccosukee
Number of local golf courses: 3 public, 3 private
Public beaches? No
Tennis courts available to the public? Yes
Boating? Yes
Number of pleasure boats registered in the county (1991-92): 10,389

SERVICES FOR RETIREES:
Through the Leon County Senior Citizens' Center.

FINANCIAL SERVICES:
Number of local banks: 52
Number of local savings and loan associations: 7

THE MEDIA:
Largest local newspaper: *Tallahassee Democrat*
Cable television? Yes

MAJOR LOCAL RETAILERS:
Dillard's, Parisian, Gayfers, JCPenney, Burdines, Sears, K mart, Montgomery Ward, and Wal-Mart.

FOOD ESTABLISHMENTS: 542

OTHER SERVICES:
Number of local libraries: 41
Number of local hotels/motels: 55
Number of churches: Protestant: 295; Jewish: 3; Catholic: 7; Other: 33

TOURISM INQUIRIES:
Tallahassee Area Chamber of Commerce, 100 North Duval St., P.O. Box 1639, Tallahassee, 32302. Telephone: 904-224-8116; Tallahassee Area Convention and Visitors Bureau, 200 W. College, P.O. Box 1369, Tallahassee, Fla., 32302. Telephone: 1-800-628-2866.

LEVY County
Northwest
County seat: Bronson

POPULATION: 1990: 25,912
1993: 28,236
Increase: 9 percent

AGE DISTRIBUTION (1992) IN PERCENTAGES:
0-14 : 20.0
15-44: 37.8
45-64: 22.9
65+ : 19.3

MUNICIPAL POPULATION:
BRONSON: 1990: 875; 1993: 852
CEDAR KEY: 1990: 668; 1993: 694
CHIEFLAND: 1990: 1,917; 1993: 1,997
FANNING SPRINGS (part): 1990: 263; 1993: 291
INGLIS: 1990: 1,241; 1993: 1,290
OTTER CREEK: 1990: 136; 1993: 119
WILLISTON: 1990: 2,168; 1993: 2,227
YANKEETOWN: 1990: 635; 1993: 631
UNINCORPORATED: 1990: 18,009; 1993: 20,135

LAND AREA: 1,118 square miles
POPULATION DENSITY: 25 people per square mile (55th in the state)

   A county where the largest incorporated city's population is only 2,227 and where there are few people per square mile, this area bills itself as one that gives people "room to live." The major industries include food retailing, logging, cattle, seafood and construction.
   Tourism centers around Cedar Key, a small fishing village on a group of islands in western Levy. Cedar Key is about three miles off Florida's mainland, about 100 miles north of Tampa and 60 miles southwest of Gainesville. The major access highway is State Road 24, which connects to Gainesville. The area is well known for its seafood restaurants, several of them built over the water. Fishing is also a big draw. Because of its remoteness, retirees do not usually enjoy the area unless they are in good health — there are no hospitals or doctors on the islands. The area does attract artists and photographers, especially in the winter. Residences on the island are mostly one-family, with a few condos and some mobile homes.

Cedar Key is one of the earliest settlements in the state; archaeologists say that Indian artifacts found here indicate habitation as early as 500 A.D., if not earlier. The first railroad that crossed Florida ran from Cedar Key to Fernandina Beach, making Cedar Key a major supplier of seafood and timber products to the Northeast. Shipments came down the Mississippi River by steamboat over to Cedar Key, where they were loaded on railroad cars for shipment to Fernandina Beach and then loaded on boats to Europe or the northern United States. The railroad line was abandoned after the Tampa line was constructed, and now there are not even any railroad tracks left to show where the old line ran. Until the 1950s, Cedar Key also housed a fiber factory where brooms and brushes were made from cabbage palm trees.

Today, tourism plays a large role in the economy, along with fishing, crabbing and oystering.

Inland, the major cities are Williston and Chiefland, home of the Watermelon Festival, which is held in June.

TOURISM:
Tourists about double the population in the Cedar Key area during the season, which runs from February to the end of April.

HOUSING PRICES:
In the Cedar Key area: Average price of a home: $85,000; for a typical 2-bedroom, 2-bath home: $120,000 (waterfront), $75,000 (inland); for a 3-bedroom, 2-bath home: $155,000 (waterfront), $100,000 (inland); condos, $65,000 to $125,000.
Inland: A standard 1,800-square-foot home with a garage on a one-acre lot is likely to cost about $65,000 and up. The most popular range is from the high $30s to $60,000.
Number of vacant residential lots: 25,338; number of single-family residences: 5,463; mobile homes: 5,011; condominiums: 125

EDUCATION:
Number of local schools: 15
Number of students enrolled: 5,331
Percentage of students continuing education after high school: 36.21
Teacher-to-pupil ratio: 1:16.7
Average teacher's salary: $27,816

Colleges, universities, and junior or community colleges serving the area:
Central Florida Community College in Ocala has an extension in Bronson and sometimes offers classes on Cedar Key; Santa Fe Community College in Gainesville; University of Florida in Gainesville

Trade and technical schools serving the area:
Central Florida Community College

HEALTH CARE:
Number of general hospitals: 1 (in Williston)
Number of hospital beds: 40
Number of physicians: 20

TAXES: Total county ad-valorem millage rate (1993): 18.5090

STANDARD CRIME RATE: 4,444.7 offenses per 100,000 population (40th out of 67 counties)

LARGEST PRIVATE EMPLOYERS:

Name	Employees	Product/Service
White Industries	241	Construction/ automobiles
Oakview Care Center	159	Health care
Wal-Mart	135	Retail sales
Winn-Dixie	100	Grocery
Central Fla. Electric Cooperative	95	Utilities
Williston Memorial Hospital	76	Health care
V.E. Whitehurst & Sons	75	Construction
Levy County State Bank	66	Banking
J-MAK Inc.	58	Fiberglass components
Perkins State Bank	47	Banking

COMPANIES PROVIDING LOCAL UTILITIES:
Telephone: Southern Bell, United Telephone Co. of Florida
Electricity: Florida Power Corp., Central Florida Electric Cooperative, Clay Electric
Natural Gas: City of Williston
Water: Municipalities
Major Water Source: Wells
Sanitary Landfill? Yes

POINTS OF INTEREST:
Manatee Springs State Park, six miles west of Chiefland, has camping, picnicking, swimming, diving, freshwater fishing, hiking, canoe rentals (summer only), boat ramp, summer concessions. The flow from the springs totals 116.9 million gallons of water daily; **Cedar Keys National Wildlife Refuge,** accessible by boat only, is a group of islands in the Gulf of Mexico with a seabird rookery and an 1850s lighhouse on the state's highest coastal elevation; **Cedar Key Scrub State Reserve** has hiking and birdwatching; **Devil's Den/Blue Grotto** is a natural spring between Williston and Bronson for cave divers; **Suwannee River** for fishing and other water activities; **Lower Suwannee National Wildlife Refuge,** between Cedar Key and Chiefland, has 40,000 acres and hiking trails; **Waccasassa Bay State Preserve,** between Yankeetown and Cedar Kay, offers access to canoeists, fishing, hiking; **Shell Mound Park** outside Cedar Key has a prehistoric Indian mound and nature trail, camping, boat ramp, picnicking; **Blue Springs Park** between Bronson and Chiefland has picnicking, swimming, diving; and **Bird Creek/Vassey Creek Park** in Yankeetown has camping, swimming, fishing, picnicking and boat ramps.

THE ARTS:
Cedar Key Historical Museum has artifacts and old clippings and photos; **Cedar Key State Museum** contains shell collection and exhibits on history of Cedar Key area.

ANNUAL EVENTS:
April: Cedar Key Sidewalk Art Festival; **May:** Art Festival in Williston; **June:** Watermelon Festival in Chiefland with parade, arts and crafts, food, watermelon seed-spitting contest, watermelon auction, climbing-up-a-greased-pole contest; **July:** Independence Day celebration in Williston; Fourth of July celebration in Cedar Key; **October:** Cedar Key Seafood Festival; Manatee Springs Festival in Chiefland with craftsmen making candles, leather goods; **November:** Fall Folks Festival in Bronson; Peanut Festival in Williston with parade, food booths, arts and crafts and sale of products made from peanuts; **December:** Christmas Festival in Chiefland.

SPORTS AND LEISURE ACTIVITIES:
Most popular local fishing areas: Gulf of Mexico, Suwannee River
Number of local golf courses: 1 in Chiefland
Public beaches? Yes
Tennis courts available to the public? Yes
Boating? Yes
Number of pleasure boats registered in the county (1991-92): 2,154

SERVICES FOR RETIREES:
Levy County Health Service Extension (also visits Cedar Key one day a month); Tri-County Council for Senior Citizens

FINANCIAL SERVICES:
Number of local banks: 12
Number of local savings and loan associations: 3

THE MEDIA:
Largest local newspaper: *Chiefland Citizen*
Cable television? Yes

MAJOR LOCAL RETAILERS:
Wal-Mart and Thriftway, Winn-Dixie, all in Chiefland

FOOD ESTABLISHMENTS: 97

OTHER SERVICES:
Number of local libraries: 5
Number of local motels: 20
Number of churches: Protestant: 27; Jewish: 0; Catholic: 3; Other: 6

The **Cedar Key** Area Chamber of Commerce, P.O. Box 610, Cedar Key, 32625. Telephone: 904-543-5600; Greater **Chiefland** Area Chamber of Commerce, P.O. Box 1397, Chiefland, 32626. Telephone: 904-493-1849.

LIBERTY County
Northwest
County seat: Bristol

POPULATION: 1990: 5,569
1993: 5,720
Increase: 2.7 percent

AGE DISTRIBUTION (1992) IN PERCENTAGES:
0-14 : 19.3
15-44: 50.8
45-64: 18.5
65+ : 11.5

MUNICIPAL POPULATION:
BRISTOL: 1990: 937; 1993: 959
UNINCORPORATED: 1990: 4,632; 1993: 4,761

LAND AREA: 836 square miles
POPULATION DENSITY: 7 people per square mile (67th — lowest in the state)

The best way to describe Liberty County is to quote Ida Larkins, who wrote about the area in a chamber of commerce brochure: "Liberty County is the last frontier, a home for those who are willing to challenge raw forces and elemental struggles — a country unto itself."

The area, according to Larkins, has retained its "frontier, primitive and rural sameness," while those who live here are characterized as "slow-speaking, rugged individuals who boast of their rural Southern roots and their robust living." A challenge is issued to the adventurer to see what the area has to offer.

It is a county that has the second-smallest population of any in Florida (behind Lafayette) and has the lowest level of population density. It is a county where farming ranks alongside logging and timber production as primary industries. It is an area where farmers are described as "physically strong, outdoor people who take pride in pitting their strength against the worst that nature can offer." The area's resources include the Apalachicola River — the "county's lifeline," which forms the county's western boundary — as well as the Ochlockonee River, which is the county's eastern boundary, and lots of "untamed wood and swamp lands." The Apalachicola National Forest makes up a good part of the county.

Some of the best resources of the county, which is located about midway between Panama City to the west and Tallahassee to the east, are the natural ones. Hardwoods in the Torreya State Park are said to provide the best display of fall color in Florida. The Apalachicola River is "guarded jealously by the natives who enjoy the fishing, hunting, boating, skiing and hiking privileges it provides." Camping is allowed anywhere in the National Forest except during the general gun season (mid-November through late January). The lowlands of the county are interspersed with fresh-water streams, resulting in "woodlands, swamps and much lush vegetation. This quite literally makes the county a botanist's paradise," writes Larkins.

All in all, there is something here for a lot of people: "adventure laced with danger for the brave and foolhardy, challenge for the scientist and economic security for the ambitious."

TOURISM:
"Liberty remains untouched by the commercial concerns and the economic projects which might destroy the picturesque quaintness and somnolent nature of its makeup." (Liberty County Chamber of Commerce).

HOUSING PRICES:
Unavailable. Chamber of Commerce lists no real estate agencies.
Number of vacant residential lots: 912; number of single-family residences: 1,176; mobile homes: 374; condominiums: 0

EDUCATION:
Number of schools: 5
Number of students enrolled: 1,173
Percentage of students continuing education after high school: 47.76
Teacher-to-pupil ratio: 1:15.8
Average teacher's salary: $29,985

Colleges, universities, and junior or community colleges serving the area:
Chipola Junior College, Marianna (30 miles to the northwest); Florida State University, Tallahassee; Tallahassee Community College; Florida A&M University, Tallahassee; Gulf Coast Community College, Panama City.

Trade and technical schools serving the area:
Chipola Junior College; Lively Voc-Tech Center in Tallahassee; Washington-Holmes Vo-Tech.

HEALTH CARE:
Number of general hospitals: 0 (nearest one is in Blountstown in Calhoun County, four miles from Bristol)
Number of hospital beds: 0
Number of physicians: 3

TAXES: Total county ad-valorem millage rate (1991): 17.5380

STANDARD CRIME RATE: 891.6 offenses per 100,000 population (63rd out of 67 counties)

LARGEST PRIVATE EMPLOYERS:

Name	Employees	Product/Service
Liberty Intermediate Care	110	Health care
North Florida Lumber Co.	75	Sawmill
Shuler Brothers	58	Forestry
C.W. Roberts Construction Co.	56	Road construction
Timber Energy Resources	55	Electricity
Apalachee Pole Company	25	Wood treatment
St. Joe Paper Company	21	Forestry
Apalachee Restaurant	20	Food

COMPANIES PROVIDING LOCAL UTILITIES:
Telephone: St. Joseph Telephone & Telegraph
Electricity: Florida Public Utilities, Talquin Electric Cooperative
Natural Gas: None
Water: City of Bristol, Liberty County
Major Water Source: Wells
Sanitary Landfill? No. Hauled out of the county.

POINTS OF INTEREST:
Apalachicola and Ochlockonee rivers; Torreya State Park (steep bluffs along the Apalachicola River and deep ravines); **Lake Mystic; Shingle Lake; Camel Lake; Hitchcock Lake; Whitehead Lake; Porter Lake;** a 33-mile section of the Florida Trail, a popular hiking spot, runs through the area.

SPORTS AND LEISURE ACTIVITIES:
Most popular local fishing areas: Ochlockonee River, Camel Lake, Sheep Isle Pond, Equaloxic Creek, Kennedy Creek, Owl Creek. Popular catches are bass, catfish, bream.
Number of local golf courses: 0
Public beaches? No
Tennis courts available to the public? Yes
Boating? Yes
Number of pleasure boats registered in the county (1991-92): 782

SERVICES FOR RETIREES:
Through Liberty County Senior Citizens

FINANCIAL SERVICES:
Number of local banks: 1
Number of local savings and loan associations: 0

THE MEDIA:
Largest local newspaper: *Calhoun/Liberty Journal*
Cable television? Yes

MAJOR LOCAL RETAILERS:
No regional malls or shopping centers

FOOD ESTABLISHMENTS: 14

OTHER SERVICES:
Number of local libraries: 1
Number of local motels: 1
Number of churches: Protestant: 25; Jewish: 0; Catholic: 0; Other: 1

TOURISM INQUIRIES:
Liberty County Chamber of Commerce, P.O. Box 523, Bristol 32321. Telephone: 904-643-2359.

MADISON County
Northwest
County seat: Madison

POPULATION: 1990: 16,569
1993: 17,316
Increase: 4.5 percent

AGE DISTRIBUTION (1992) IN PERCENTAGES:
0-14 : 23.4
15-44: 44.7
45-64: 18.3
65+ : 13.6

MUNICIPAL POPULATION:
GREENVILLE: 1990: 950; 1993: 948
LEE: 1990: 306; 1993: 315
MADISON: 1990: 3,345; 1993: 3,417
UNINCORPORATED: 1990: 11,968; 1993: 12,636

LAND AREA: 692 square miles
POPULATION DENSITY: 25 people per square mile (56th in the state)

With ante-bellum mansions, the county has preserved a portion of the Old South. Only a few years ago Madison County had one of the strongest agricultural-based economies in the region; now diversified light industry is the largest employer. Businesses range from food processing, printing and timber products (in recent years 72 firms have been engaged in pulpwood and timber-related activities in the county) to cabinet-making and fuel oil production. By no means has agriculture disappeared, though, as Madison has been the major peach-producing county in the state. Vegetables, corn, soybeans and tobacco are also major crops here. In addition, there are more than 60,000 acres of pastureland. The county has a number of parks, rivers and ponds. Freshwater fishing is popular and bass are a favorite catch — 10- to 15-pounders are not unusual. Besides fishing, hunting is a popular pastime, with such game as dove, deer, quail and small game.

HOUSING PRICES:
Average price about $44,000-$45,000 for a three-bedroom, two-bath home and for a three-bedroom, one-bath home.
Number of vacant residential lots: 2,847; number of single-family residences: 2,824; mobile homes: 794; condominiums: 0

TOURISM:
Not a big factor here

EDUCATION:
Number of schools: 8
Number of students enrolled: 3,306

Percentage of students continuing education after high school: 41.57
Teacher-to-pupil ratio: 1:18.1
Average teacher's salary: $28,006

Colleges, universities, and junior or community colleges serving the area:
North Florida Junior College

Trade and technical schools serving the area:
North Florida Junior College

HEALTH CARE:
Number of general hospitals: 1
Number of hospital beds: 42
Number of physicians: 11

TAXES: Total county ad-valorem millage rate (1993): 16.9344

STANDARD CRIME RATE: 2,783.6 offenses per 100,000 population (54th out of 67 counties)

LARGEST PRIVATE EMPLOYERS:

Name	Employees	Product/Service
Dixie Packers	725	Processed meats
Relief Printing	125	Business cards
Florida Plywood	100	Plywood veneer
Sherrod Lumber	90	Rough lumber
Agri-Products	60	Landscape mulch
Real Wood	45	Cabinet doors
Jimmy Davis Enterprises	35	Fuel oil
Superior Trees	35	Pine seedlings
Johnson & Johnson	35	Fuel oil

COMPANIES PROVIDING LOCAL UTILITIES:
Telephone: Central Telephone Co. of Florida
Electricity: Florida Power Corp., Tri-County Electric Cooperative
Natural Gas: City of Madison
Water: Cities of Madison, Lee and Greenville
Major Water Source: Wells
Sanitary Landfill? Yes

POINTS OF INTEREST:
Suwannee River and **Withlacoochee River** designated canoe trails; **Four Freedoms Park** in Madison containing a Confederate monument, a gazebo and another monument in tribute to Captain Colin P. Kelly Jr., hero of World War II; **nation's tiniest post office,** previously located at Ellaville, now is at the Madison Garden Club overlooking Lake Francis; **Baptist marker** in Confederate Memorial Park commemorates organization of the State Baptist Convention in the county in 1854; **Wardlaw-Smith-Goza Conference Center** in Madison was a confederate hospital during the Civil War and is an example of Greek Revival architecture; **Van H. Priest Auditorium,** with seating for more than 700, hosts plays and other community events; and **Madison Blue Springs** recreation area has nature trails, scuba diving, camping, canoeing, swimming, snorkeling, fishing and picnicking.

ANNUAL EVENT:
Third weekend in April: Down Home Days celebration with arts and crafts, entertainment, parade; **December:** County Christmas celebration in Greenville with arts and crafts, entertainment and a parade.

SPORTS AND LEISURE ACTIVITIES:
Most popular local fishing area: Cherry Lake
Number of local golf courses: 1 private
Public beaches? Yes
Tennis courts available to the public? Yes
Boating? Yes
Number of pleasure boats registered in the county (1991-92): 829

FINANCIAL SERVICES:
Number of local banks: 3
Number of local savings and loan associations: 1

THE MEDIA:
Largest local newspaper: *Madison County Carrier*
Cable television? Yes

MAJOR LOCAL RETAILERS:
County has no major national chain department stores. The largest store is a Pick 'N Save.

FOOD ESTABLISHMENTS: 36

OTHER SERVICES:
Number of local libraries: 1
Number of local motels: 3
Number of churches: Protestant: 86; Jewish: 0; Catholic: 1

TOURISM INQUIRIES:
Madison County Chamber of Commerce, 105 N. Range St., Madison, 32340. Telephone: 904-973-2788.

OKALOOSA County
Northwest
County Seat: Crestview

POPULATION: 1990: 143,777
1993: 154,512
Increase: 7.5 percent

AGE DISTRIBUTION (1992) IN PERCENTAGES:
0-14 : 22.6
15-44: 48.9
45-64: 19.3
65+ : 9.2

MUNICIPAL POPULATION:
CINCO BAYOU:1990: 386; 1993: 388
CRESTVIEW: 1990: 9,886; 1993: 11,567
DESTIN: 1990: 8,090; 1993: 8,644
FORT WALTON BEACH: 1990: 21,407; 1993: 21,921
LAUREL HILL: 1990: 543; 1993: 587
MARY ESTHER: 1990: 4,139; 1993: 4,194
NICEVILLE: 1990: 10,509; 1993: 11,150
SHALIMAR: 1990: 341; 1993: 350
VALPARAISO: 1990: 6,316; 1993: 6,413
UNINCORPORATED: 1990: 82,160; 1993: 89,298

LAND AREA: 936 square miles
POPULATION DENSITY: 165 people per square mile (28th in the state)

Tourism joins the military as the major economic forces here along "the Emerald Coast." Eglin and Hurlburt Air Force bases surround the Twin Cities of Niceville and Valparaiso and bring not only personnel (about 15,700 military and 5,600 civilian personnel here in the early 1990s) but also millions of dollars to the region.

The largest U.S. base in the free world, Eglin covers 724 square miles and controls 86,500 square miles of water test ranges in the Gulf of Mexico. The base is home to the Air Force Development Test Center; its mission is to plan, direct and conduct tests and evaluations of non-nuclear munitions, electronic combat and navigation and guidance systems. The base also houses the McKinley Climatic Laboratory, the world's largest environmental test facility. This lab is capable of producing climates with temperatures ranging from 165 degrees Fahrenheit to minus 65 degrees Fahrenheit. Among the aircraft housed at Eglin are the F15s, F16s, F4s, F111s and T38s.

Hurlburt is the headquarters of the Air Force Special Operations Command, whose mission focuses on unconventional warfare, such as psychological operations during low-intensity conflicts.

Major private employers in the county are associated with the military's presence, either directly or indirectly. These firms produce instruments, radar systems, electronics and jet engines. Among the high-tech firms are Vitro Services Corp., Keltec Florida, Metric Systems, and Aero Component Technology.

Outside of its military connections, the county has a number of recreational opportunities because of its location along the Gulf of Mexico and the Choctawhatchee Bay. Beaches have some of the state's whitest sands and the waters of the Gulf are emerald green. Among the popular activities along the bay or the Gulf are sailing, parasailing, skin diving, snorkeling and fishing. Other outdoor activities include hunting on the Eglin Air Force Base reservation, canoeing along inland waterways, camping and horseback riding (although riding is not permitted on Okaloosa County beaches). A number of festivals also take place here, among them the Boggy Bayou Mullet Festival, which attracts about 200,000 people over three days and which includes entertainment, arts and crafts and food.

The county seat is Crestview, located in the middle of the county at the second highest altitude in the state (235 feet above sea level). Known as the "hub city," Crestview is located near many major highways including U.S. Highway 90 and Interstate 10, which run east and west near the city, and State Road 85, running north and south. The county's other major cities are Fort Walton Beach, Valparaiso and Niceville, and Destin, all of which are either on or near the Gulf of Mexico or Choctawatchee Bay.

Tourism brings about $400 million into the area. Visitors come mainly from the United States and Canada.

TOURISM:
About 1.75 million visitors come to the county each year.

HOUSING PRICES:
Median sales price of an existing single-family home was $87,100 in the Fort Walton Beach area for June 1994.
Number of vacant residential lots: 14,642; number of single-family residences: 41,680; mobile homes: 729; condominiums: 7,097

EDUCATION:
Number of schools: 35
Number of students enrolled: 28,856
Percentage of students continuing education after high school: 69.39
Teacher-to-pupil ratio: 1:18.1
Average teacher's salary: $30,771

Colleges, universities, and junior or community colleges serving the area:
Okaloosa-Walton Community College in Niceville; University of West Florida centers in Fort Walton Beach and Eglin Air Force Base; Saint Leo College's Hurlburt-Eglin Area Center; University of Florida's College of Engineering center at Eglin Air Force Base; Troy State University's centers at Eglin and at Hurlburt Field; Pensacola Junior College

Trade and technical schools serving the area:
Okaloosa-Walton Community College's Vocational Technical School in Fort Walton Beach; Crestview High School; Bay Area Vo-Tech

HEALTH CARE:
Number of general hospitals: 3
Number of hospital beds: 384
Number of physicians: 229

TAXES: Total county ad-valorem millage rate (1993): 13.8650

STANDARD CRIME RATE: 3,742.1 offenses per 100,000 population (46th out of 67 counties)

LARGEST PRIVATE EMPLOYERS:

Name	Employees	Product/Service
Vitro Services Corp.	1,400	Instrumentation
Metric Systems	786	Radar systems

Russell Corporation	430	Athletic Sweats
Sverdrup Technologies	425	Technical Engine Support
Keltec Florida	325	Electronics
Gulf Power Corp.	163	Utilities
Aero Component Technology	150	Jet engine components
Tybrin Corporation	150	Scientific data processing
Northwest Fla. Daily News	145	Newspaper
RMS Technologies	110	Engineering services
Rainbow Koolers	100	Sportswear

COMPANIES PROVIDING LOCAL UTILITIES:
Telephone: Central Telephone Co.
Electricity: Gulf Power Co.; Choctawhatchee Electric Co-op
Natural Gas: Okaloosa County Gas District
Water: Okaloosa Water & Sewer and Auburn Water System
Major Water Source: Wells
Sanitary Landfill? Yes

POINTS OF INTEREST:
Air Force Armament Museum, located outside the main gate of Eglin Air Force Base (the base itself is closed to the public), houses about 5,000 artifacts, including aircraft such as a B-17 Flying Fortress, a P-47 Thunderbolt, a B-52 and an SR-71, and gives an overview of the history of the U.S. Air Force. It is the only facility in the country dedicated to the display of Air Force armament; **Gulfarium** on U.S. 98, Okaloosa Island, has living sea exhibit, porpoise performances, sea lions; **Historical Society Museum** in Valparaiso has exhibits of Northwest Florida area and sponsors classes in quilting, basketry, needlepoint and other crafts; **Fred Gannon Rocky Bayou State Recreation Area,** 5 miles east of Niceville, has camping, picnicking, swimming, saltwater and freshwater fishing, hiking, seasonal ranger-guided walks and campfire programs, boat ramp, alligators; **Henderson Beach State Recreation Area** near Destin has swimming, saltwater fishing; **Eglin Air Force Base tours; Indian Temple Mound Museum** in Fort Walton Beach has Indian relic exhibits from Pre-Columbian cultures; **Destin Fishing Museum; Museum of the Sea and Indian** in Destin has Indian artifacts, exhibits from the ocean, small zoo; fishing pier in Fort Walton Beach extends 1,261 feet into the Gulf; **Blackwater River State Forest** extends to northwestern Okaloosa County and is popular for canoeing; **Fort Walton Civic Auditorium; Camp Walton Schoolhouse** in Fort Walton Beach was built in 1912 and is an example of an early Northwest Florida school.

THE ARTS:
Stage Crafters Community Theater stages four productions a year in the Fort Walton Beach Civic Auditorium; **Northwest Florida Ballet** gives several performances during the year; **Emerald Coast Community Band** provides music for community events; **Northwest Florida Symphony Orchestra** gives performances throughout the county; **Okaloosa Symphony Orchestra; Fort Walton Beach Art Museum** houses collection of American paintings, pottery and sculptures; **Fort Walton Beach Community Chorus** holds concerts; **Okaloosa Community Concert Association** gives performances on a subscription-only basis at the Okaloosa-Walton Community College Auditorium; **Okaloosa-Walton Community College Fine Arts Department** hosts symphony, theater and band performances, recitals and workshops.

ANNUAL EVENTS:
Easter: Destin Underwater Easter Egg Hunt; **April:** Saturday in the Park in Valparaiso, held the last Saturday in April, with arts and crafts booths, food, entertainment and demonstrations of pioneer handiwork; Fort Walton Beach Seafood Festival with arts and crafts; **April and May:** Old Spanish Trail Road Race, Bazaar and Parade in Crestview; **May:** Destin Mayfest with arts and crafts, gourmet food, music; Blessing of the Fleet in Destin; **June:** Billy Bowlegs Festival in Fort Walton Beach honors legendary pirate with torchlight parade, "pirates market," square dance, ballet performances by the Northwest Florida Ballet Association; **July:** All-day Fourth of July celebration in Valparaiso with food, entertainment and fireworks; Liberty Days Celebration in Crestview; Destin Shark Fishing Rodeo; **October:** Destin Fishing Rodeo (held throughout the month); Destin Seafood Festival (first full weekend in October) with arts and crafts; Okaloosa County Fair at the county fairgrounds in Fort Walton Beach; Boggy Bayou Mullet Festival in

Niceville, the third weekend in October, features entertainment, arts, crafts and food; **Fall:** Fiesta Italiana in downtown Fort Walton Beach with Italian food and entertainment; Fort Walton Beach Shrine Fair; **December:** Niceville/Valparaiso Bay Area Christmas Parade; Fort Walton Beach Christmas parade; Christmas parade and bazaar in Crestview with arts and crafts, food; Destin Christmas parade.

SPORTS AND LEISURE ACTIVITIES:
Most popular local fishing areas: Gulf of Mexico (for amberjack, grouper, snapper, king mackerel, cobia, blue and white marlin, sailfish and bluefish); Choctawhatchee Bay (for flounder, speckled trout, redfish, oysters, shrimp); Eglin Air Force Base game preserve (for freshwater fishing).
Number of local golf courses: 11
Public beaches? Yes
Tennis courts available to the public? Yes
Boating? Yes
Number of pleasure boats registered in the county (1991-92): 12,767

SERVICES FOR RETIREES:
Fort Walton Beach Senior Citizen's Center; Council on Aging in Crestview and Twin Cities.

FINANCIAL SERVICES:
Number of local banks: 42
Number of local savings and loan associations: 6

THE MEDIA:
Largest local newspaper: *Northwest Florida Daily News*
Cable television? Yes

MAJOR LOCAL RETAILERS:
Gayfers, Sears, Wal-Mart, K mart, McRae's, JCPenney, also Russell Mills Outlet Mall

FOOD ESTABLISHMENTS: 509

OTHER SERVICES:
Number of local libraries: 6
Number of local hotels/motels: 90
Number of churches: Protestant: 112; Jewish: 1; Catholic: 10; Other: 5

TOURISM INQUIRIES:
Crestview Area Chamber of Commerce, 502 S. Main St., Crestview, 32536. Telephone: 904-682-3212; **Destin** Chamber of Commerce, P.O. Box 8, Destin, 32540. Telephone: 904-837-6241; Greater **Fort Walton Beach** Chamber of Commerce, P.O. Box 640, Fort Walton Beach, 32549. Telephone: 904-244-8191; **Niceville/Valparaiso** Bay Area Chamber of Commerce, 170 N. John Sims Parkway, Valparaiso, 32580. Telephone: 904-678-2323.

SANTA ROSA County
Northwest
County Seat: Milton

POPULATION: 1990: 81,608
1993: 90,259
Increase: 10.6 percent

AGE DISTRIBUTION (1992) IN PERCENTAGES:
0-14 : 22.7
15-44: 46.6
45-64: 20.8
65+ : 9.9

MUNICIPAL POPULATION:
GULF BREEZE: 1990: 5,530; 1993: 5,802
JAY: 1990: 666; 1993: 669
MILTON: 1990: 7,216; 1993: 7,451
UNINCORPORATED: 1990: 68,196; 1993: 76,337

LAND AREA: 1,016 square miles
POPULATION DENSITY: 89 people per square mile (33rd in the state)

Santa Rosa County, located between Pensacola and Fort Walton Beach, was once a lumber and shipbuilding center but today relies on tourism and agriculture. It extends from Georgia to the Gulf of Mexico and attracts thousands of tourists to the Blackwater River State Park and, farther south, to the white beaches at Navarre and to part of the Gulf Islands National Seashore.

The county seat, Milton, has been nicknamed the "canoe capital of Florida." Several canoe rental businesses offer trips along the Blackwater, Sweetwater/Juniper, and Coldwater rivers. Other popular outdoor recreational activities include tubing through the water trails of the Blackwater River State Forest, fishing, hunting and camping.

The naval air station at Whiting Field is the county's largest employer, with around 4,000 military and civilian personnel. About 1,200 students complete their primary flight training each year at the station. Field crops, forestry and livestock also play a big part in the county's economy.

Though the big lumber and ship-building industries are gone, their legacies include some 19th-century homes — many on the National Register of Historic Places.

TOURISM:
County attracts canoe enthusiasts and visitors who like to see old homes in Milton and in Bagdad, an unincorporated community near Milton. Heaviest tourist season is from March through the summer.

HOUSING PRICES:
Countywide prices unavailable, but generally average in the 40s and up.
Number of vacant residential lots: 27,833; number of single-family residences: 24,826; mobile homes: 4,819; condominiums: 863

EDUCATION:
Number of schools: 27
Number of students enrolled: 18,056
Percentage of students continuing education after high school: 43.42
Teacher-to-pupil ratio: 1:17.5
Average teacher's salary: $29,404

Colleges, universities, and junior or community colleges serving the area:
Pensacola Junior College, Milton campus; University of West Florida, Pensacola; Troy State University, Fort Walton Beach; Pensacola Christian College

Trade and technical schools serving the area:
Radford-Locklin Vocational-Technical Center; Coastal Training; George Stone Vo-Tech

HEALTH CARE:
Number of general hospitals: 4
Number of hospital beds: 244
Number of physicians: 92

TAXES: Total county ad-valorem millage rate (1993): 15.4070

STANDARD CRIME RATE: 4,267.7 offenses per 100,000 population (42nd out of 67 counties)

LARGEST PRIVATE EMPLOYERS

Name	Employees	Product/Service
Vanity Fair Mills	750	Retail clothing
Beech Aerospace	321	Aircraft maintenance
Santa Rosa Medical Center	310	Health care
Air Products & Chemicals	309	Chemicals/fertilizer
Cytec Inc.	300	Acrylic fibers
Russell Corporation	265	Sportswear
UNC Support Services	250	Helicopter support svcs
Mold-Ex Rubber Co.	150	Rubber products
Custom Cushions	100	Boat seats
Exxon	92	Oil/gas products

COMPANIES PROVIDING LOCAL UTILITIES:
Telephone: Southern Bell
Electricity: Gulf Power Co., Escambia River Electric Co-op
Natural Gas: City of Milton, Okaloosa Gas Pipeline
Water: City of Milton and five other water systems
Major Water Source: Wells
Sanitary Landfill? Yes

POINT OF INTEREST:
The Zoo and Botanical Gardens in Gulf Breeze has more than 700 animals, bird shows, petting zoo, elephant shows; **Blackwater River State Park** northeast of Milton has campsites, picnicking, swimming, canoeing, freshwater fishing, nature/hiking trails, boat ramp; **Imogene Theater** in Milton, site of concerts, plays, ballroom dancing and other activities.

ANNUAL EVENTS:
February: Mardi Gras, Navarre Beach; **March:** Scratch Ankle Spring Festival, Milton; **April:** Santa Rosa County Fair, Milton; **June:** Navarre Chamber of Commerce Fun Fest with entertainment, food, arts and crafts, fireworks at Navarre Beach; **July:** Independence Day Riverfest in Milton, boat parade, arts and crafts, carnivals, fireworks; **September/October:** Juana's Good-Time Regatta, Navarre Beach, with catamaran racing, beach competitions; **November:** Juana's Chili Cookoff, Navarre Beach; **December:** Blackwater Heritage Tour, Milton; Winter Wildlife Wonderland at The Zoo in Gulf Breeze.

SPORTS AND LEISURE ACTIVITIES:
Most popular local fishing areas: Four lakes in Blackwater River State Forest, Blackwater River, Yellow River, Blackwater Bay, Gulf Breeze Fishing Pier and Navarre Beach on the Gulf of Mexico.
Number of local golf courses: 4
Public beaches? Yes
Tennis courts available to the public? Yes
Boating? Yes
Number of pleasure boats registered in the county (1991-92): 6,927

SERVICES FOR RETIREES:
Santa Rosa Council on Aging.

FINANCIAL SERVICES:
Number of local banks: 19
Number of local savings and loan associations: 0

THE MEDIA:
Largest local newspaper: *Santa Rosa Press-Gazette*
Cable television? Yes

MAJOR LOCAL RETAILERS:
K mart and Wal-Mart. Other major retailers are in Pensacola.

FOOD ESTABLISHMENTS: 165

OTHER SERVICES:
Number of local libraries: 4
Number of local motels: 10
Number of churches: Protestant: 124; Jewish: 0; Catholic: 4; Other: 9

TOURISM INQUIRIES:
Navarre Beach Area Chamber of Commerce, P.O. Box 5336, Navarre, Fla., 32566. Telephone: 904-939-3267.

TAYLOR County
Northwest
County seat: Perry

POPULATION: 1990: 17,111
1993: 17,374
Increase: 1.5 percent

AGE DISTRIBUTION (1992) IN PERCENTAGES:
- 0-14 : 23.2
- 15-44: 42.0
- 45-64: 20.7
- 65+ : 14.1

MUNICIPAL POPULATION:
PERRY: 1990: 7,151; 1993: 7,198
UNINCORPORATED: 1990: 9,960; 1993: 10,176

LAND AREA: 1,042 square miles
POPULATION DENSITY: 17 people per square mile (64th in the state)

Taylor County, on the Gulf of Mexico, has nearly 600,000 acres of forests — about 90 percent of the county land. Perry, the county seat, is 50 miles southeast of Tallahassee. The county is known as the Tree Capital of the South and, not surprisingly, is home to a major forestry industry. The western part of the county has 50 miles of well-preserved coastline, dotted with fishing villages. Among them is Steinhatchee at the mouth of the Steinhatchee River, which is known for its redfish and speckled trout. Here commercial fishing (mainly shrimp and mullet) and sport-fishing are popular, as are fish camps, lodges and boat rentals. The Army Corps of Engineers and the county worked on dredging projects in the late 1980s to clear boat passage in beach canals into the Gulf. Hunting is also a popular pastime here.

TOURISM:
Not a major factor here.

HOUSING PRICES:
Prices range from less than $30,000 to $175,000. Many in the $30,000-to-$80,000 range.
Number of vacant residential lots: 4,181; number of single-family residences: 4,714; mobile homes: 1,906; condominiums: 0

EDUCATION:
Number of schools: 8
Number of students enrolled: 3,612
Percentage of students continuing education after high school: 41.03
Teacher-to-pupil ratio: 1:16.6
Average teacher's salary: $29,843

Colleges, universities, and junior or community colleges serving the area:
Florida State University and Florida A&M University, both in Tallahassee; North Florida Junior College, Madison; and Tallahassee Community College.

Trade and technical schools serving the area:
Taylor County Technical Institute

HEALTH CARE:
Number of general hospitals: 1
Number of hospital beds: 48
Number of physicians: 11

TAXES: Total county ad-valorem millage rate (1993): 17.4954

STANDARD CRIME RATE: 5,174.4 offenses per 100,000 population (33rd out of 67 counties)

LARGEST PRIVATE EMPLOYERS:
Name	Employees	Product/Service
Buckeye Florida	1,007	Cellulose
Watkins Engineering	250	Construction
Martin Electronics	232	Pyrotechnics
Doctors Memorial Hospital	123	Health care
Tom's Snack Foods	98	Food
Perry Lumber Company	83	Lumber
Consolidated Forest Products	54	Fence/mulch

COMPANIES PROVIDING LOCAL UTILITIES:
Telephone: Gulf Telephone

Electricity: Florida Power Corp. and Tri-County Electric Cooperative
Natural Gas: City of Perry
Water: City of Perry
Major Water Source: Wells
Sanitary Landfill? Yes

POINTS OF INTEREST:
Fishing villages along the county coast; Perry parks (71 acres in seven locations); **Hodges Park,** a county facility; the beaches — **Keaton Beach, Dark Island, Cedar Island, Ezell Beach, and Dekle Beach; artificial fishing reef** in the Gulf west of Steinhatchee; **Forest Capital State Museum,** site of a Cracker homestead, picnicking; visitor center.

ANNUAL EVENT:
October: Florida Forest Festival, a month-long family celebration that draws 50,000 people. Includes a 10,000-meter "Great Race" for joggers; a King Tree Parade; "the world's largest free fish fry" (3.5 tons of fried mullet); chainsaw, cross-cut and tobacco-spitting contests; arts and crafts; antique cars.

SPORTS AND LEISURE ACTIVITIES:
Most popular local fishing areas: Gulf of Mexico; freshwater ponds and lakes; five rivers; salt and brackish creeks. Among the saltwater species are Spanish mackerel, flounder, speckled trout, redfish, bluefish, rock bass, sheepshead. Freshwater catches include largemouth bass, catfish, bream, speckled perch, shellcracker.
Hunting: About 450,000 acres are open to public hunting. Game includes deer, wild hog, turkey and rabbit.
Golf courses? Yes
Public beaches? Yes
Tennis courts available to the public? Yes
Boating? Yes
Number of pleasure boats registered in the county (1991-92): 2,391

SERVICES FOR RETIREES:
Taylor Adult Meals Program, Senior Citizens Club.

FINANCIAL SERVICES:
Number of local banks: 4
Number of local savings and loan associations: 1

THE MEDIA:
Largest local newspapers: *Perry News Herald*
Cable television? Yes

MAJOR LOCAL RETAILER:
K mart

FOOD ESTABLISHMENTS: 49

OTHER SERVICES:
Number of local libraries: 1
Number of local motels: 24
Number of churches: Protestant: 50; Jewish: 0; Catholic: 1

TOURISM INQUIRIES:
Perry-Taylor County Chamber of Commerce, 428 North Jefferson St., P.O. Box 892, Perry, 32347. Telephone: 904-584-5366.

WAKULLA County
Northwest
County seat: Crawfordville

POPULATION: 1990: 14,202
1993: 15,401
Increase: 8.4 percent

AGE DISTRIBUTION (1992) IN PERCENTAGES:
    0-14 : 23.2
    15-44: 44.3
    45-64: 20.6
    65+ : 11.9

MUNICIPAL POPULATION:
ST. MARKS: 1990: 307; 1993: 303
SOPCHOPPY: 1990: 367; 1993: 398
UNINCORPORATED: 1990: 13,528; 1993: 14,700

LAND AREA: 607 square miles
POPULATION DENSITY: 25 people per square mile (54th in the state)

Crawfordville, located southwest of Tallahassee, is the only unincorporated county seat in the state. In fact, 95 percent of local residents live in unincorporated areas. The county has two incorporated communities — Sopchoppy and St. Marks, each with a population between 300 and 400. Most of the county is made up of timberland, much of it national forest and wildlife areas. As of 1990, there were 160,472 acres of farmland in the county. Around 90 percent is forest land, 6 percent has been devoted to crops (such as peanuts, sweet potatoes, corn, sugar cane and velvet beans), and 4 percent to pasture and rangeland. Another large industry is seafood. There also is some manufacturing; the largest private employer is the Olin Corp. in St. Marks, which manufactures gun powder. The county government and county school board are among the other major employers. Hunting and camping in the Apalachicola National Forest are popular, and there are two state parks and a state historic site. In addition, Shell Point is a popular windsurfing area on the Gulf.

TOURISM:
Not a major factor here.

HOUSING PRICES:
Real estate agents say the average price range is about $45,000 to $75,000. Gulf-front properties range from $100,000 to $500,000.
Number of vacant residential lots: 9,574; number of single-family residences: 3,397; mobile homes: 2,435; condominiums: 64

EDUCATION:
Number of schools: 7
Number of students enrolled: 3,755 as of April 1994
Percentage of students continuing education after high school: 64.06
Teacher-to-pupil ratio: 1:18.3
Average teacher's salary: $27,027

Colleges, universities, and junior or community colleges serving the area:
Florida State University and Florida A&M University, Tallahassee; Tallahassee Community College; Tallahassee campus of Keiser College of Technology.

Trade and technical schools serving the area:
Lively Vocational Technical Center in Tallahassee

HEALTH CARE:
Number of general hospitals: 0
Number of hospital beds: 0
Number of physicians: 5

TAXES: Total county ad-valorem millage rate (1993): 19.6810

STANDARD CRIME RATE: 1,727.2 offenses per 100,000 population (58th out of 67 counties)

LARGEST PRIVATE EMPLOYERS

Employer	Employees	Product/Service
Olin Corporation	500	Gun powder
Wakulla Manor	150	Nursing home
Wakulla County State Bank	50	Banking

The county's other major employers include the U.S. Forestry Service, Wakulla County Schools and Wakulla County government.

COMPANIES PROVIDING LOCAL UTILITIES:
Telephone: Central Telephone Co. of Florida
Electricity: Florida Power Corp. and Talquin Electric Cooperative
Natural Gas: None
Water: Talquin Electric Cooperative; Sopchoppy
Major Water Source: Wells
Sanitary Landfill? Yes

POINTS OF INTEREST:
Edward Ball Wakulla Springs State Park, off Route 61, has picnicking, swimming, hiking, glass-bottom- and wildlife-observation boat tours, concessions, overnight accommodations. Contains one of the world's largest and deepest freshwater springs. From glass-bottom boats, visitors see entrance of a cavern 120 feet below; **Ochlockonee River State Park,** four miles south of Sopchoppy on U.S. 319, has camping, picnicking, swimming, freshwater and saltwater fishing, hiking, boat ramp, scenic drive; **St. Marks National Wildlife Refuge** has lighthouse, hiking, picnicking, fishing, hunting, boat launch; **San Marcos De Apalache State Historic Site,** near St. Marks, has interpretive center, military cemetery, hiking. Site of building and launching of first ships made by white men in the New World around 1528. A fort was later built here and was occupied at various times by Spaniards and Englishmen until it was turned over to the United States in 1821; **Talla-hassee-St. Marks Historic Railroad State Trail** is a 16-mile trail (the tracks are gone); **Wakulla County Courthouse** in Crawfordville, on the **National Register of Historic Places,** is one of three existing wooden courthouses in the state and houses the Wakulla County Public Library.

ANNUAL EVENTS:
February: Youth Fair Association Swine Show & Sale in Crawfordville includes beauty pageant, parade, pig scramble, swine show and hog sale; **March:** re-enactment of the Civil War Battle of Natural Bridge (which the South won); **April:** Steven C. Smith Memorial Regatta, one of the largest events in the Southeast for sailboarders; **May:** Panacea Blue Crab Festival, parade, arts and crafts, live music, gospel sing, contests and games; HuManatee Festival at San Marcos de Apalache State Historic Site welcomes the manatee herd into the area, also has arts, crafts, music; **July:** Sopchoppy's Fourth of July festival with parade, canoe race, games, food, live music, craft booths, fireworks; July (fourth Saturday), Smokey Bear Run, sponsored by the Forest Service, a 10K race at Wakulla Springs State Park.

SPORTS AND LEISURE ACTIVITIES:
Most popular local fishing areas: Ochlockonee River, St. Marks River, Sopchoppy River
Number of local golf courses: One was under construction in late 1994
Public beaches? Yes
Tennis courts available to the public? Yes
Boating? Yes
Number of pleasure boats registered in the county (1991-92): 2,874

SERVICES FOR RETIREES:
Wakulla Senior Citizens Center in Crawfordville, including Meals on Wheels

FINANCIAL SERVICES:
Number of local banks: 2
Number of local savings and loan associations: 0

THE MEDIA:
Largest local newspaper: *Wakulla News*
Cable television? Yes

MAJOR LOCAL RETAILERS:
There are no major department stores.

FOOD ESTABLISHMENTS: 38

OTHER SERVICES:
Number of local libraries: 1
Number of local hotels/motels: 8
Number of churches: Protestant: 38; Jewish: 0; Catholic: 1; Other: 1

Wakulla County Chamber of Commerce, P.O. Box 598, Crawfordville, 32326. Telephone: 904-926-1848.

WALTON County

Northwest
County Seat: DeFuniak Springs

POPULATION: 1990: 27,759
1993: 30,568
Increase: 10.1 percent

AGE DISTRIBUTION (1992) IN PERCENTAGES:
0-14 : 19.2
15-44: 39.6
45-64: 24.3
65+ : 16.8

MUNICIPAL POPULATION:
DeFUNIAK SPRINGS: 1990: 5,200; 1993: 5,259
FREEPORT: 1990: 843; 1993: 867
PAXTON: 1990: 600; 1993: 582
UNINCORPORATED: 1990: 21,116; 1993: 23,860

LAND AREA: 1,058 square miles
POPULATION DENSITY: 29 people per square mile (53rd in the state)

Situated in Florida's Panhandle, with Alabama touching its northern borders and the Gulf of Mexico its southern borders, the county has three incorporated towns — DeFuniak Springs, Freeport and Paxton. **DeFuniak Springs** is home of the Chautauqua Festival, an annual event that promotes the historical, religious and cultural traditions of the county. The festival's emphasis is on arts and crafts, with efforts to revive the cultural drama and entertainment of the Florida Chautauqua Association, which was formed in 1884 to improve educational opportunities. Early lecture programs featured such speakers as William Jennings Bryan. The town of **Freeport,** on the Choctawhatchee Bay, is a shipbuilding, fishing and commerce area on the Intracoastal Waterway. It also has a winery. **Paxton** lies near the home of Florida's highest point, Britton Bill, 345 feet above sea level. Eglin Air Force Base, home of the largest U.S. base in the free world, stretches from Okaloosa County into Walton County and consequently helps make up part of Walton's economy. Tourism is the big draw in the southern portion of the county, while the poultry industry is the principal economic force in the northern half. Also playing large roles in the county's economy are the dairy and beef cattle industries, timber and wood products, and farming (corn, soybeans, peanuts, wheat, sugar cane and sweet potatoes).

In 1994, Maryland's Laboratory for Coastal Research rated Grayton Beach State Recreational Area as the nation's best beach — long noted for its clean, white sand, extensive dunes and quiet, undeveloped atmosphere.

TOURISM:
Population doubles during the tourist season that runs from May to August.

HOUSING PRICES:
Average price in DeFuniak Springs in the mid-50s. Average prices for beachfront homes around $225,000; for beachfront condos $125,000.
Number of vacant residential lots: 17,161; number of single-family residences: 9,044; mobile homes: 2,325; condominiums: 5,568

EDUCATION:
Number of schools: 10
Number of students enrolled: 4,890
Percentage of students continuing education after high school: 54.31
Teacher-to-pupil ratio: 1:16.4
Average teacher's salary: $28,219

Colleges, universities, and junior or community colleges serving the area:
Okaloosa-Walton Community College; University of West Florida in Pensacola

Trade and technical schools serving the area:
Okaloosa-Walton Community College, Niceville and DeFuniak Springs; Walton Vo-Tech Center, DeFuniak Springs; Washington-Holmes Area Vo-Tech, Chipley

HEALTH CARE:
Number of general hospitals: 1
Number of hospital beds: 50
Number of physicians: 16

TAXES: Total county ad-valorem millage rate (1993): 15.9050

STANDARD CRIME RATE: 2,083.9 offenses per 100,000 population (56th out of 67 counties)

LARGEST PRIVATE EMPLOYERS:

Name	Employees	Product/Service
Showell Farms of Florida	800	Processed chicken
Sandestin Beach Resort	500	Tourist resort
Topsail Beach & Racquet Club	150	Tourist resort
Walton Regional Hospital	140	Health care
Seascape Resort	120	Tourist resort
Walton County Convalescent Center	115	Health care
Wal-Mart	115	Retail sales
Professional Products	110	Orthopedic wear
Continental Apparel	106	Ladies sportswear
Choctawhatchee Electric Cooperative	99	Utitlity

COMPANIES PROVIDING LOCAL UTILITIES:
Telephone: Central Telephone Co. of Florida
Electricity: Gulf Power; Choctawhatchee Electric Cooperative
Natural Gas: City of DeFuniak Springs; Okaloosa Gas District
Water: DeFuniak Springs; South Walton Utilities; Florida Community Services
Major Water Source: Wells
Sanitary Landfill? Yes

POINTS OF INTEREST:
Emerald Coast, a 30-mile stretch of beach running from Okaloosa to Inlet Beach; **Eden State Gardens** in Point Washington; **Grayton Beach State Recreation Area** has sand dunes, sea turtles nesting during the summer, camping, picnicking, swimming, saltwater fishing, hiking; the **Walton-DeFuniak Library,** opened in 1887 (believed to be Florida's oldest public library operating continuously in its original building).

ANNUAL EVENTS:
March and April: Chautauqua Festival (annual county-wide event honoring history and cultural traditions of Walton County. Festival marked by cultural events, arts, crafts, music, drama, children's activities and fireworks); **October:** Walton County Fair.

SPORTS AND LEISURE ACTIVITIES:
Most popular local fishing areas: Lake Holly, King Lake, Campbell Lake (for bream and bass fishing), Choctawhatchee River (for alligator gar, bluegill, shellcracker, largemouth bass, sunshine bass), numerous artificial and natural ponds, natural lakes and creeks at Eglin Field (for bass and bream), and Juniper Lake (for bass and bluegills)
Number of local golf courses: 1 public, 4 private
Public beaches? Yes
Tennis courts available to the public? Yes
Boating? Yes
Number of pleasure boats registered in the county (1991-92): 2,374

SERVICES FOR RETIREES:
Council on Aging, Meals on Wheels, Tri-County Community Council transportation; Social Security representative comes to DeFuniak Springs once a month.

FINANCIAL SERVICES:
Number of local banks: 5
Number of local savings and loan associations: 4

THE MEDIA:
Largest local newspaper: *DeFuniak Springs Herald-Breeze*
Cable television? Yes

MAJOR LOCAL RETAILERS:
Wal-Mart in Walton Plaza; The Market at Sandestin; Per-Spi-Cas-ity and other shops at Seaside; and The Shops of Topsail Beach & Racquet Club.

FOOD ESTABLISHMENTS: 149

OTHER SERVICES:
Number of local libraries: 2
Number of local hotels/motels: 12
Number of churches: Protestant: 101; Jewish: 0; Catholic: 3

TOURISM INQUIRIES:
Walton County Chamber of Commerce, P.O. Box 29, DeFuniak Springs, 32433. Telephone 904-892-3191.

WASHINGTON County
Northwest
County seat: Chipley

POPULATION: 1990: 16,919
1993: 17,554
Increase: 3.8 percent

AGE DISTRIBUTION (1992) IN PERCENTAGES:
0-14 : 20.4
15-44: 39.2
45-64: 22.3
65+ : 18.1

MUNICIPAL POPULATION:
CARYVILLE: 1990: 631; 1993: 615
CHIPLEY: 1990: 3,866; 1993: 3,936
EBRO: 1990: 255; 1993: 264
VERNON: 1990: 778; 1993: 831
WAUSAU: 1990: 313; 1993: 310
UNINCORPORATED: 1990: 11,076; 1993: 11,598

LAND AREA: 580 square miles
POPULATION DENSITY: 30 people per square mile (52nd in the state)

Washington County, bordered on the west by the Choctawhatchee River and the Pine Log State Forest to the south, is about 45 miles north of the Gulf community of Panama City. The leading employment sector here is government. Second is agriculture: forestry (the county is covered with pines), peanuts and watermelons. The third sector is trade, followed by services and then manufacturing (notably WestPoint Stevens, a maker of bed products such as pillows, bedspreads, and comforters; other county products include telephone lines and turbine engine repair). Water sports are popular here, as there are dozens of small lakes. One local attraction is Cypress Springs, which produces nearly 90 million gallons of water a day and is good for canoeing, snorkeling, and diving, with water visibility of more than 300 feet.

TOURISM:
Very little in the county.

HOUSING PRICES:
Most popular price range is $35,000 to $50,000. Very few houses sell for more than $85,000.

Number of vacant residential lots: 15,161; number of single-family residences: 3,688; mobile homes: 836; condominiums: 0

EDUCATION:
Number of schools: 9
Number of students enrolled: 3,101
Percentage of students continuing education after high school: 55.66
Teacher-to-pupil ratio: 1:15
Average teacher's salary: $29,026

Colleges, universities, and junior or community colleges serving the area:
Florida State University, Panama City campus; Chipola Junior College, Marianna; Gulf Coast Community College.

Trade and technical schools serving the area:
Washington-Holmes Area Vocational Technical Center, Chipley; Chipola Junior Colllege, Marianna.

HEALTH CARE:
Number of general hospitals: 1
Number of hospital beds: 81
Number of physicians: 13

TAXES: Total county ad-valorem millage rate (1993): 17.0530

STANDARD CRIME RATE: 1,606.5 offenses per 100,000 population (59th out of 67 counties)

LARGEST EMPLOYERS:

Name	Employees	Product/service
WestPoint Stevens, Inc.	700	Bed products
Washington County Schools	600	Public schools
Fla. Department of Transportation	350	Highways
Wal-Mart Super Center	350	Retail
Washington Correctional Facility	350	State prison
Northwest Florida Community Hospital	220	Health care
Washington County Convalescent Center	125	Nursing home
AT&T	125	Communications
Winn-Dixie	70	Grocery
Trawick Construction Co.	65	Telephone lines

COMPANIES PROVIDING LOCAL UTILITIES:
Telephone: Southern Bell
Electricity: Gulf Power, West Florida Electric Cooperative; Gulf Coast Electrical Co-op
Natural Gas: City of Chipley
Water: Municipal
Major Water Source: Wells
Sanitary Landfill? Yes

POINTS OF INTEREST:
Falling Waters State Recreation Area, 3 miles south of Chipley, has camping, picnicking, swimming, hiking, waterfall; **Washington County Kennel Club,** Ebro, greyhound racing.

ANNUAL EVENTS:
June (last full weekend): Panhandle Watermelon Festival and Parade, Chipley, includes parade, arts and crafts, food, melon auction, seed-spitting contest, melon-rolling contest; **First Saturday in August:** Annual Wausau Possum Fun Day and Parade, Wausau, has foot race, possum auction, arts and crafts, clogging, music, food (such as possum, taters, and hamburgers); **Saturday before Labor Day:** Caryville Worm Fiddling Contest (you put a stake in the ground, take a stick or other implement, use it as if you're fiddling, and the vibrations on the stake are supposed to bring worms out of the ground).

SPORTS AND LEISURE ACTIVITIES:
Most popular local fishing areas: Streams and rivers and dozens of small lakes in the county
Number of local golf courses: 2 private

Public beaches? No
Tennis courts available to the public? Yes
Boating? Yes
Number of pleasure boats registered in the county (1991-92): 1,456

SERVICES FOR RETIREES:
Council on Aging, state Department of Health and Rehabilitative Services, AARP local chapters.

FINANCIAL SERVICES:
Number of local banks: 3

THE MEDIA:
Largest local newspaper: *Washington County News*
Cable television? Yes

MAJOR LOCAL RETAILERS:
Wal-Mart, Winn-Dixie, Piggly Wiggly

FOOD ESTABLISHMENTS: 42

OTHER SERVICES:
Number of local libraries: 1
Number of local motels: 4
Number of churches: Protestant: 70; Jewish: 0; Catholic: 2

TOURISM INQUIRIES:
Washington County Chamber of Commerce, P.O. Box 457, Chipley, 32428. Telephone: 904-638-4157.

INDEX